Chicago Architecture
1872–1922

The Art Institute of Chicago
in collaboration with
the Réunion des musées nationaux and
the Deutsches Architekturmuseum

Chicago Architecture
1872–1922
Birth of a Metropolis

Edited by John Zukowsky

With essays by
Robert Bruegmann, Sally Chappell, Meredith L. Clausen, Joan E. Draper,
Roula M. Geraniotis, Elaine Harrington, Neil Harris,
Heinrich Klotz, Gerald R. Larson, Henri Loyrette, Ross Miller,
Martha Pollak, Thomas J. Schlereth, Stanley Tigerman,
David Van Zanten, Lauren S. Weingarden, C. W. Westfall,
Richard Guy Wilson, and John Zukowsky

Prestel-Verlag, Munich

in association with The Art Institute of Chicago

This book was published in conjunction with the exhibition *Chicago Architecture, 1872–1922: Birth of a Metropolis* held at the Musée d'Orsay, Paris (October 2, 1987–January 4, 1988), the Deutsches Architekturmuseum, Frankfurt am Main (February 5–April 25, 1988), and The Art Institute of Chicago (July 16–September 5, 1988).

Essay by Heinrich Klotz translated from the German by Timothy Watson.
Essay by Henri Loyrette translated from the French by Evelyn Dorin and Gloria Groom.

Front cover: Wrigley Building, 1921–25 (photo 1985)
Back cover: Elevation of the proposed Civic Center, 1908 (cat. no. 235)
Spine: R. Y. Mine, Competitive entry for the Chicago Tribune tower, 1922 (cat. no. 255)
Frontispiece: Aerial view of Chicago, c. 1930

Published by Prestel-Verlag,
Mandlstraße 26, D-8000 München 40,
Federal Republic of Germany

Distribution of the hardcover edition in the USA and Canada by te Neues Publishing Company, 15 East 76 Street, New York, NY 10021

Distribution of the hardcover edition in the United Kingdom, Ireland and the Commonwealth (except Canada) by Lund Humphries Publishers Ltd, London

Design: Dietmar Rautner, Munich

Printed in the Federal Republic of Germany
Paper: Phoeno-Matt
Papierfabrik Scheufelen, Lenningen
Composition: Fertigsatz GmbH, Munich
Color separations: Repro Dörfel GmbH, Munich
Printing and binding: Passavia Druckerei GmbH, Passau

ISBN of the English softcover edition (not available to the trade):
0-86559-077-x
ISBN of the English hardcover edition (trade edition): 3-7913-0837-8

Contents

Foreword

The year 1987 is a landmark one for Chicago. It marks the 150th anniversary of the granting of the city's first charter and the election of its first mayor, William B. Ogden. Mayor Ogden achieved an equal, if not greater, fame as one of Chicago's first real estate developers, and he was also responsible for bringing to Chicago its first architect, John M. Van Osdel (1811-1891). Although our museum and school are not as old as the city of Chicago, they were founded during the city's architectural heyday in 1879 as the Chicago Academy of Fine Arts. By 1882 the institution had assumed its present name, and in 1887 it took up residence on Michigan Avenue in a building designed by one of Chicago's foremost firms, the partnership of Daniel H. Burnham and John Wellborn Root. Six years later, at the close of the 1893 World's Columbian Exposition, the Art Institute moved into a new building by Shepley, Rutan and Coolidge on Michigan Avenue at Adams Street, its present site. Throughout its history, which spans more than a century, our institution has interacted in significant ways with Chicago architects and architecture. In 1912 Daniel H. Burnham bequeathed to the Art Institute funds to establish an architectural library. The Burnham Library of Architecture opened in 1919 and it began then to collect and exhibit architectural drawings. With the Art Institute's Ryerson Library of Art, founded in 1901, it constitutes one of the major research centers for art and architecture in North America. In addition to Burnham and Root, architects such as Frank Lloyd Wright, Howard Van Doren Shaw, Ludwig Mies van der Rohe, and, more recently, Walter A. Netsch and Harry Weese have created installations, spaces, and additional structures for our institution. Renowned architects such as David Adler, John A. Holabird, and, now, Bruce J. Graham have served on our Board of Trustees. Art Institute committees have drawn on the talents of still other architects, from Thomas E. Tallmadge and Edward H. Bennett in the 1930s and 1940s to Stanley Tigerman today.

This year also marked the reinstallation of our permanent collection of European art in the second-floor galleries of our original 1893 building. This fine structure has had its skylights and galleries renovated, and its Beaux-Arts circulation plan reinstated by architects Skidmore, Owings and Merrill and John Vinci. Next year will witness the opening of the Regenstein Temporary Exhibitions Hall and the Field-McCormick Galleries of American Art in a new building, designed by Thomas Beeby of Hammond, Beeby and Babka to be compatible with the original Beaux-Arts building in scale, design detail, and spatial experience. But our continued commitment to the art of architecture goes well beyond bricks and mortar.

Since the creation of the Department of Architecture in 1981, Curator John Zukowsky and Assistant Curator Pauline Saliga have been involved in the design community on all levels — locally, nationally, and internationally. Their activities have ranged from exhibitions of the works of the Chicago Architectural Club and the Chicago Chapter of the American Institute of Architects, to major publications on our architectural collection that include *Chicago Architects Design* (1982) and the forthcoming *Fragments of Chicago's Past*, and traveling exhibitions and their catalogues, such as *Chicago and New York: Architectural Interactions* (1983) and *Mies Reconsidered: His Career, Legacy, and Disciples* (1986). The last represents an international exhibition that traveled to the Deutsches Architekturmuseum in

Frankfurt, the Centre Pompidou in Paris, and the Ministerio des Obras Publicas in Madrid. The book that accompanied the exhibition has been translated into three languages.

"Chicago Architecture, 1872-1922: Birth of a Metropolis" continues in this vein, not only because it will be seen at the Musée d'Orsay in Paris and the Deutsches Architekturmuseum in Frankfurt, as well as in Chicago, but also because it stresses the connections between Chicago's architecture and that of northern Europe. The major publication generated on the occasion of this exhibition is the first trilingual edition of a book on Chicago's architectural history, being published simultaneously in English, French, and German. It accompanies the first international exhibition of more than 250 original drawings and artifacts that document Chicago's contribution to architecture and design, from the rebuilding after the Great Fire of 1871 through the international competition for the Chicago Tribune tower of 1922. As such, it is the largest project undertaken by the Department of Architecture at our museum under the efficient coordination of John Zukowsky, its organizer, and through the generous funding of the National Endowment for the Humanities, with additional support from the National Endowment for the Arts and the Illinois Humanities Council. This major book and exhibition, then, represent our Department of Architecture's close collaborations with similar institutions abroad, and they signify the long-term commitment that the department and museum have both to document and interpret Chicago's architectural environment. *Chicago Architecture, 1872-1922* is an appropriate commemoration of our city's sesquicentennial, and an international tribute to the many architects who molded this city's distinctive urban setting.

James N. Wood
Director
The Art Institute of Chicago

Acknowledgments

This project represents the culmination of eight years of planning that began in 1979 at the first International Confederation of Architectural Museums conference held in Helsinki. It was there that my initial discussions about this exhibition began with Henri Loyrette, Conservateur at the Musée d'Orsay, Paris, and Heinrich Klotz, Director of the Deutsches Architekturmuseum, Frankfurt. We realized that, for all that has been written about the classic period of Chicago architecture, from the Great Fire of 1871 to the Chicago Tribune tower competition of 1922, there has not been enough attention paid to the strong influences from Europe that helped define the character of the renowned schools of architecture and buildings that took shape in this city.

We decided to invite many of the scholars working on various aspects of Chicago architecture to contribute their ideas to an encompassing reassessment of this seminal period of Chicago's architectural history. I am grateful to Henri Loyrette and to Heinrich Klotz for the enthusiasm and commitment they brought to this project, without which it could never have been realized. The European exposure this book and the exhibition it accompanies will receive should generate meaningful discussion about the formation of a new American architecture in this great metropolis.

James N. Wood, Director of The Art Institute of Chicago, and Deputy Director Katharine C. Lee encouraged me to seek funding to make this international project a reality. In order to stimulate discussion among these scholars about the shape this project should take, the National Endowment for the Humanities awarded the Art Institute a planning grant. In April 1985, we were able to host a two-day symposium involving all of the participants. The exhibition and book that have resulted, as well as the installation and interpretive programs in Chicago, were then funded by a second, generous grant from the National Endowment for the Humanities. Marsha Semmel, Acting Assistant Director of the National Endowment's Division of General Programs for Museums and Historical Organizations, and Gabriel P. Weisberg, formerly Assistant Director and now Professor of Art History at the University of Minnesota, were both especially helpful in sharing their advice and expertise in the early stages of the project. In addition to this continued support of the National Endowment for the Humanities, further funds were received from the National Endowment for the Arts, the Illinois Humanities Council, and the Queene Ferry Coonley Foundation, each of whose contributions helped insure the future of the project as it developed through its final stages.

The generosity of our donors and an international group of lenders, both public and private, made the exhibition a reality. Donations to the Art Institute's permanent collection are responsible for most of the core of the exhibition. The private collections deserve special thanks for making their resources available to the public. In addition, other individuals representing various institutions were especially helpful in providing access to works that we have included in the exhibition. These individuals include Irwin J. Askow, representative of the University Club of Chicago; Lisbet Balsler-Jorgensen, Curator of Architectural Drawings Collections of the Royal Academy Library, Copenhagen; John Carswell, Director, and Richard Born, Curator, David and Alfred Smart Gallery of the University of Chicago;

Russell Bowman, Director of the Milwaukee Art Museum, and Terrence Marvel, Curator of that museum's Prairie Archives; Maynard Brichford, Archivist, and William J. Maher, Assistant Archivist, University of Illinois at Urbana-Champaign; Ellsworth Brown, Director of the Chicago Historical Society and his curatorial staff — Wim de Wit, Curator of the Architectural Collections, Larry Viskochil, Curator of the Graphics Collections, and Joseph Zywicki, formerly Curator of Paintings; Yvonne Brunhammer, Conservateur en Chef of the Musée des Arts Décoratifs, Paris; Bruce A. Cerling, Vice-President of the Chicago Tribune Company; Joseph Czestochowski, Executive Director of the Cedar Rapids Museum of Art; Nancy Finlay, Assistant Curator of Printing and Graphic Arts of the Houghton Library, Harvard University, Cambridge, Mass.; Angela Giral, head of the Avery Architectural and Fine Arts Library, Columbia University, New York, and Janet Parks, Curator of its Architectural Archives; Paul A. Karas, Commissioner of Public Works for the City of Chicago; Alan K. Lathrop, Curator of the Northwest Architectural Archives at the University of Minnesota; Nell McClure, Director of the Chicago Architecture Foundation and the Foundation's former curator Elaine Harrington; R. Craig Miller, Associate Curator of Twentieth-Century Decorative Art, The Metropolitan Museum of Art, New York; Richard Murray, Director of the Archives of American Art, Smithsonian Institution, Washington, D.C.; Peter Nisbet, Assistant Curator of the Busch-Reisinger Museum of the Harvard University Art Museums, Cambridge, Mass.; Jane Preger, Curator of Exhibitions, the Drawings Collection of the Royal Institute of British Architects, London; Marie Cimino Spina, Archivist for the architectural firm of Haines Lundberg Waehler; Lila Stillson, Curator of the Architectural Drawings Collection of the University of Texas at Austin; Sirkka Valanto, Head of the Archives Department of the Museum of Finnish Architecture, Helsinki; and George M. Wittkopp, Associate Curator of the Cranbrook Academy of Art Museum, Bloomfield Hills, Michigan.

Beyond the continual exchange of ideas with Henri Loyrette and Heinrich Klotz, a number of people at the participating institutions share in the responsibility of organizing this exhibition and book. At the Réunion des Musées Nationaux in Paris, Irène Bizot was especially helpful in organizing meetings among the three collaborating institutions; and Ute Collinet's coordination of the French catalogue was much appreciated. Françoise Cachin, Director of the Musée d'Orsay, was also a vital participant in the arrangements for the French exhibition. Our colleagues at the Deutsches Architekturmuseum — Hans Peter Schwarz, Volker Fischer, and Lumi Sabau — were particularly attentive to the myriad details of the project.

At the Art Institute, many people should be thanked. In the Department of Architecture, Assistant Curator Pauline Saliga, Technical Assistant Luigi Mumford, and Secretary Angela Licup each shared in the physical and intellectual preparation of this exhibition and book over the last year or more. Paolo Giradelli and John Wright assisted in the framing of the objects on view. In addition, many other Art Institute personnel assisted in the organization, research, interpretive programs, photography, and art handling and crating: Department of Architecture researchers Ines Dresel, Maya Moran, and Gabriella Scanu; Mary Woolever, Architectural Archivist of the Ryerson and Burnham Libraries; in Museum Education, Celia Marriott and Jane Clarke, who advised on the films and developed the interpretive audio-visual and symposium planning for the Chicago venue; Alan Newman, Executive Director of Photographic Services and his staff; George T. Preston, Executive Director of Physical Plant; Ron Pushka, Associate Director of Physical Plant; Darrell Willson, Executive Director of Protection Services; Virginia Mann, Registrar, Mary Solt, Assistant Registrar, and Reynold Bailey, Head of Art Installation. The financial and contractual aspects of the project were capably supervised by Robert E. Mars, Vice-President for Administrative Affairs, and Dorothy Schroeder, Assistant to the Director and Exhibition Coordinator. Finally, the Committee on Architecture of the Art Institute was, as always, supportive of our active fundraising and organization of the project: David C. Hilliard (chairman), James N. Alexander, J. Paul Beitler, Edwin J. DeCosta, Stanley Freehling, Bruce J. Graham, Neil Harris, Carter H. Manny, Jr., Peter Palumbo, Mrs. J. A. Pritzker, and Stanley Tigerman. Mr. Tigerman, as well as John Holbert, Rick Dakich, Melany Thompson, and James Dallman of his architectural firm, deserves special thanks for the very creative design of the Chicago installation of the exhibition.

The monumental publication — appearing simultaneously in English, French, and German — which this exhibition has occasioned represents an effort of such magnitude that its realization required a team of gifted and devoted individuals. The organization of the book and substantive editing of the essays were the work of Fannia Weingartner, whose incisive and informed command of its contents, along with her great enthusiasm for the project, resulted in the addition of significant depth, breadth, and style to the book. She was assisted in every way in this over-whelming task by Sarah C. Mollman, Assistant Editor, Publications Department of the Art Institute, who also contributed much invaluable research and checking. Also in the museum's Publications Department, Associate Editor Robert V. Sharp assumed, jointly with me, the responsibility for picture editing, and he supervised the book's design and production stages with characteristic intelligence and sensitive attention to detail. Associate Editor Elizabeth Pratt and Tom Fredrickson, Publications Intern, assisted us in many ways. Holly Stec Dankert and Cris Ligenza heroically typed much of the manuscript. The publisher Jürgen Tesch of Prestel-Verlag, Munich, was also most helpful, providing substantial advice concerning the illustrative and graphic contents of the book. We are also grateful to editors Michael Foster and Sabine Thiel-Siling at Prestel-Verlag and to the book's designer, Dietmar Rautner. Also to be thanked in connection with the book are the eighteen authors, who met their deadlines and graciously complied with the many demands this publication put on them. Other people to be acknowledged for assistance with translations, research, and various other aspects are Grant Dean, Lydia Wills, Timothy Watson, Carol Presser, Gloria Groom, and Evelyn Dorin. For their help with photographic requests, we wish to thank Michael Houlahan of Hedrich Blessing, Ltd., Raymond S. Waszak of Huey Reprographics, Jerry Kerto of Santa Fe Southern Pacific Corp., and Alice Sinkevitch of Holabird and Root, and, finally, a number of Chicago's wonderful photographers, Bob Thall, Ron Gordon, Kathleen Culbert-Aguilar, Howard Kaplan, Don DuBroff, Harold Allen, John Gronkowski, Chester Brummel, and Judith Bromley.

I would like to thank Pablo Diaz and his son Pablo, as well as Robert Weinberg and his staff at the Chicago Conservation Center, who conserved and matted most of the works on paper in the exhibition. Pam Hayes of Frameway Studios fabricated a number of the vitrines for the smaller three-dimensional objects. Terri Laine Enterprises made many of the frames for the exhibition. Richard Tickner of Chicago and his staff created several exquisite architectural models for the exhibition, and the staff of the Museum of Southern Illinois University, Edwardsville — David C. Huntley, Director; Michael Mason, Curator; and Eric Barnett, Registrar — graciously permitted plaster casts of Louis Sullivan fragments in their collection to be made for all three exhibition locations. Finally, I would like to thank Phyllis Lambert, Director of the Canadian Centre for Architecture in Montreal, and Eve Blau, the Centre's Curator of Exhibitions and Publications, for helping to give this project an afterlife in the form of a smaller exhibition that will travel to Montreal and other sites through 1989.

John Zukowsky
Curator of Architecture
The Art Institute of Chicago

Lenders to the Exhibition

Archives of American Art, Smithsonian Institution, Washington, D.C.

The Art Institute of Chicago

Avery Architectural and Fine Arts Library, Columbia University

Mr. and Mrs. Edward H. Bennett, Jr., Chicago

The British Architectural Library: Drawings Collection,
    Royal Institute of British Architects

Mr. and Mrs. Daniel H. Burnham IV, Del Mar, California

Cedar Rapids Museum of Art

Chicago Architecture Foundation, Glessner House

Chicago Historical Society

Chicago Tribune

City of Chicago, Department of Public Works, Bureau of Engineering

Mr. and Mrs. Dale Cowel, Wilmette, Illinois

Cranbrook Academy of Art Museum, Bloomfield Hills, Michigan

Deutsches Architekturmuseum, Frankfurt

Mr. and Mrs. Joseph A. Guyer, Chicago

Haines Lundberg Waehler, New York

Harvard University Art Museums (Busch-Reisinger Museum)

Alice Ryerson Hayes, Lake Forest, Illinois

The Houghton Library, Harvard University

Deborah and Helmut Jahn, Chicago

Kunstakademiets Bibliothek, Copenhagen

John and Susan Dart McCutcheon, Lake Forest, Illinois

The Metropolitan Museum of Art, New York

Milwaukee Art Museum

More Collection, Evanston, Illinois

Musée des Arts Décoratifs, Paris

Museum of Finnish Architecture, Helsinki

Rapp and Rapp Architectural Collection, Evanston, Illinois

Seymour H. Persky, Highland Park, Illinois

Robert H. Reinhold, Chicago

Rubloff, Inc., Chicago

Timothy Samuelson, Chicago

Patrick Shaw, Chicago

The David and Alfred Smart Gallery, The University of Chicago

The University Club of Chicago

The University of Illinois at Urbana-Champaign, University Archives

The University of Minnesota, Northwest Architectural Archives, St. Paul

The University of Texas at Austin, Architectural Drawings Collection

Chicago Architecture,
1872–1922

Essays

Introduction to Internationalism in Chicago Architecture

John Zukowsky

Chicago, in the eyes of much of the world, has long been considered the capital of American architecture. Its role in the development of the tall office building of the Chicago School and the single-family house of the Prairie style have both been considered, internationally, the epitome of America's contributions to the history of world architecture. Yet Chicago's architecture has too often been viewed within a regional or national context only. The purpose of our exhibition and of this book is to consider some of the city's significant architectural forms and their creation from a broader international perspective.

Many of the essays focus specifically on the interchanges between Chicago and northern Europe and on the impact of that interaction on America's urban development. But before we proceed, a brief survey of the city's history seems appropriate.

It is thought that Chicago derives its name from the river Checagou, so called by the native Indians after the wild onions that grew on the swampy marshland between the great broad prairies and the massive inland sea that was later called Lake Michigan. Some four hundred million years earlier, the area had been covered by a large sea which deposited a layer of limestone known as the Niagara Formation. This would later yield a wealth of building stone and mortar for the nineteenth-century builders of the city.

The first non-native visitors to the site were two Frenchmen who came in 1673. The Jesuit missionary Jacques Marquette and his fellow-explorer Louis Jolliet stopped to meet Potawatomi Indians nearby because Jolliet had been informed that they would be a fine source of furs for the French. Another century passed before Haitian-born Jean Baptiste Point du Sable established his fur trading post in the area in 1772. Although the impact of sporadic French exploration was generally short-lived, some tangible urban and architectural reminders are to be found in such place names as Des Plaines, Joliet, and La Salle, and in such reconstructions as Fort de Chartres from the 1750s and the Cahokia Courthouse of the 1760s (fig. 2), both in southern Illinois.[1]

It was only after the Revolutionary War that the northern part of Illinois began to develop, following the establishment of Fort Dearborn on the Chicago River in 1803. The fort's mission was to guard the western frontier of the new nation of the United States of America, and especially to protect the river routes connecting the Great Lakes with the Mississippi Valley. The favorable location of the fort and the town that grew up around it after the defeat of the British in the War of 1812 would shape Chicago's future importance as a transportation hub.

The Northwest Ordinance of 1785 had organized the relatively flat land of the territories northwest of the Ohio River into an enormous grid of quadrangular plots. In 1830, Chicago's destiny was set when it was designated to serve as the northern terminus of a major canal that would connect the Great Lakes with the Mississippi River. The town was platted, and the federal government began to construct a harbor, which was completed in 1833. That year the grid-planned town was incorporated, its population having grown from 60 to more than 150, the minimum required for legal incorporation. By the time the Illinois and Michigan Canal was completed in 1848, the population had reached 20,000.[2]

Fig. 1 View of Chicago, looking north, showing Michigan Avenue and bridge, c. 1928.

Fig. 2 Cahokia, Illinois, Courthouse, c. 1760/70.

*Fig. 3 Union Stock-
yards, c. 1900
(demolished).*

The rapid physical growth of the city was aided by the development of the balloon frame (fig. 4; cat. no. 2). This technique, by which lightweight milled lumber was quickly nailed together rather than mortised and tenoned, is said to have led one wit to observe that it made housebuilding as easy as blowing up a balloon. Chicagoan George Snow is

credited with devising the method in 1832; before long, warehouses, residences, and institutional and ecclesiastic buildings were being constructed quickly by this efficient system.[3]

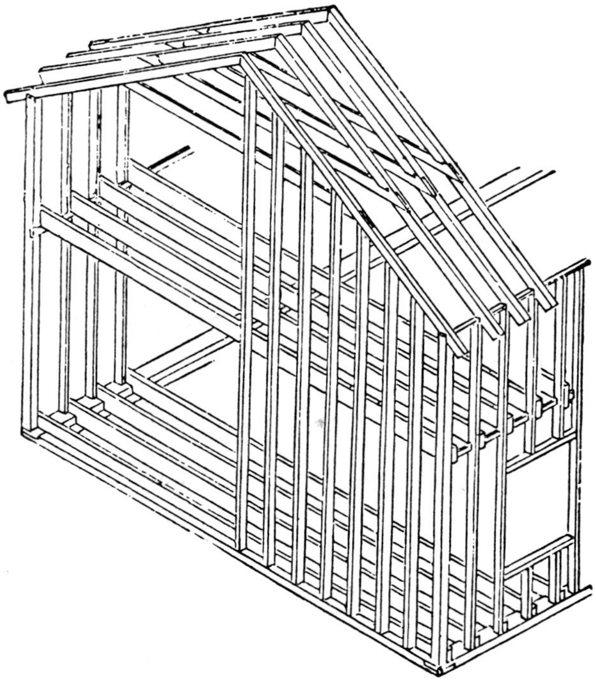

However, the city's early rate of growth was minuscule when compared to the rapidity of its development over the next three decades. By 1870, Chicago had become a commercial and industrial center of some 300,000 people and had earned the appellation "lightning city" from British visitor Sara Jane Lippincott.[4] Chicago's accessibility by water transportation and, after the 1860s, its increasing importance as the center of a national railroad network spurred its economic growth. Lumber milling and the production of agricultural implements (the McCormick Reaper Factory was established in 1847) prospered.

The consolidation of the area's stockyards by nine railroads during the waning days of the Civil War (1861-65) turned Chicago into the livestock and meatpacking capital of the world for more than a century. When the Union Stockyard opened in 1865, it virtually functioned as a city within a city, providing housing, hotels, restaurants, and an exchange. Its pens could hold 20,000 cattle, 75,000 hogs, and 20,000 sheep. In 1871 the meatpackers processed more than 500,000 cattle and some 2,400,000 hogs, and the introduction of refrigerated railroad cars in 1869 facilitated the transporta-

Fig. 4 Isometric perspective view of the balloon frame; from George Woodward, Woodward's Country Homes *(1865).*

Fig. 5 John M. Van Osdel, Page Brothers Building, southeast corner of State and Lake streets, 1872; cast-iron facade by Daniel Badger, New York; view before later alterations.

Fig. 6 Bauer and Loebnitz, Illinois Staats Zeitung Building, northeast corner of Washington and Wells streets, 1872-73 (demolished); from Land Owner *(June 1872).*

tion of various meat products throughout the country (fig. 3). At their peak around the turn of the century, the stockyards received 3 million cattle and 6 million hogs! It is no wonder that they became a symbol for the city itself. Chicago was dubbed "Pork'opolis" and "Hog Butcher of the World" by poet Carl Sandburg, and pilloried by novelist Upton Sinclair in *The Jungle* (1906), an exposé of living and working conditions in the stockyards.[5]

In the years after the Civil War, Chicago's growth as a commerce and transportation center was reinforced by the drive to unite the two coasts through the construction of transcontinental railroad routes. The first to be completed was the Union Pacific Railroad in 1869. Chicago's identification with railroading was strengthened when, in 1879, George M. Pullman built a railroad car factory and model town (to which he gave his name) to house his workers south of the city (see Schelereth, figs. 2, 4, 6, 8).[6]

The proliferating railroads not only carried goods and livestock into the city and transported machinery, commodities, and lumber out of the city, but first and foremost they brought people to live and work in Chicago. The early settlers came principally from the East Coast and were of northern European stock. Many Irish immigrated to Chicago to work as laborers on the Illinois and Mi-

Fig. 7 Carter, Drake and Wight, Stewart Bentley Building, 112-14 Dearborn Street, 1872 (demolished).

Fig. 8 Holabird and Roche, Gage Building, 18-22 South Michigan Avenue; facade by Louis H. Sullivan; view during construction, Aug. 11, 1899 (altered).

chigan Canal during the 1830s and, with the onset of potato famine of 1846 in Ireland, thousands more came to work on the railroads, particularly the Illinois Central.⁷ Although some Irish immigrants worked in the building trades, most of Chicago's earliest professional architects came from eastern cities within the United States. John M. Van Osdel, Chicago's first architect, came from Baltimore via New York in 1837. But it took the railroads of the mid-century to transport increasing numbers of professional architects from the East Coast, and later from central Europe, especially Germany.

The unsuccessful revolutions of 1848, subsequent wars, and Bismarck's "blood and iron" tactics to unify the German states in the 1860s brought increasing numbers of Germans to Chicago, including a host of architects and others in related occupations: engineers, technicians, drafting equipment suppliers, engravers, and printers. Augustus Bauer, one of the first German architects to practice in Chicago (fig. 6), arrived as early as 1853; Eugene Dietzgen established his drafting supply factory in Chicago in 1891. German immigrant workers played a central role in the development of the labor movement in Chicago and were also associated with the Haymarket Affair of May 4, 1886. Chicago became, in many ways, the capital of a mid-American "Germania" that stretched from Milwaukee through Indianapolis to Cin-

cinnati and St. Louis from the mid-nineteenth century until World War I. As late as 1914, Germans were the largest ethnic group – close to seventeen percent – of the city's population of some two and a half million.⁸ The railroads also brought another group of building professionals to Chicago from the East Coast, namely real estate speculators. In many ways, they contributed to the astonishing growth of the city as much as architects, engineers, and corporate investors. Although the full story of their input has yet to be told, their financing shaped the cityscape both before and after the Great Fire of 1871.⁹ Thus Chicago owed most of its post-Civil War growth to the railroad rather than the sloop or steamship, as was the case with cities like New York, Boston, and even, perhaps, San Francisco, much of whose prosperity was due to their role as great seaports.¹⁰

Then came the Chicago Fire of October 8-10, 1871. The city had suffered earlier conflagrations, including one on October 27, 1839, which had spread rapidly through the wooden buildings downtown. However, nothing in the past equaled the damage caused by the 1871 fire, which laid waste to nearly 2,000 acres of the city (pl. 3).¹¹ The need to rebuild an entire city offered opportunities to a large number of architects and engineers, attracting them to Chicago and keeping them there during a time of national economic recession.

16358

Essentially, the commercial buildings constructed soon after the fire were much like their predecessors. Many, especially on Lake Street, had cast-iron and masonry facades resembling those from before the fire (fig. 5). Constructed in a variety of styles — High Victorian or Ruskinian Gothic, neo-Grec, or Rundbogenstil Romanesque — they were mostly four stories high. The sunken ground floor and the first floor, which sported equally large windows, were reserved for commercial spaces. The remaining windows in the elevations were usually smaller, denoting office and other spaces (fig. 7; pl. 8). However, the Great Fire did bring about one important innovation in building: fireproofing. This derived from the realization that the Nixon Building, designed by German émigré Otto H. Matz, had survived the fire partly because its structural members were covered with concrete and plaster of paris. George H. Johnson, Peter B. Wight, and Sanford Loring were among those who developed and patented fireproofing systems which protected iron structural members from melting during a fire by covering them with such materials as oak and terracotta. The most successful of the techniques was patented on October 27, 1874, by Sanford Loring (see essay by Larson).

Fireproofing the iron and steel frame was one of the technical innovations that, when combined with others — especially the development by Elisha Otis of the safety passenger elevator, first used in New York in 1857 — helped produce the tall office buildings often called "sky-scrapers" in Chicago during the late 1880s.[12] These buildings, designed by what came to be known as the Chicago School of architects, included the Richardsonian Romanesque structures of John Wellborn Root, Solon Spencer Beman, Henry Ives Cobb, and Otto H. Matz (fig. 9), as well as the skeletal, functional-looking edifices of Holabird and Roche (fig. 8; plate 20; cat. no. 62) and others.

Many of these buildings have been celebrated by twentieth-century architectural writers in books such as Sigfried Giedion's *Space, Time and Architecture* (1941) and Carl W. Condit's *The Rise of the Skyscraper* (1952) and *The Chicago School of Architecture* (1964), as well as in exhibitions such as *100 Years of Architecture in Chicago* (1976), because they were thought to prefigure the modernist works designed by Ludwig Mies van der Rohe, Skidmore, Owings and Merrill, and Harry Weese during the 1950s and 1960s. More recent research, inspired by the revisionist book and exhibition *Chicago Architects* (1976), organized by Stanley Tigerman and Stuart Cohen, has re-examined Chicago architecture in a broader context, analyzing the contributions of the lesser lights in relation to the masters.[13]

Fig. 10 Adler and Sullivan, Schiller Theater, 64 West Randolph Street, 1891-92 (demolished).

Fig. 11 D. H. Burnham and Co., Conway Building, 111 West Washington Street, 1912.

Among architects who made major contributions to the American cityscape, and Chicago in particular, was Louis H. Sullivan. He is probably best known for his elaborate individualistic ornament (pls. 40, 41; cat. nos. 113, 115-16, 157-64), based on a rational underlying geometry that he claimed was to be found within all natural forms. Equally important was his "tripartite" theory. This

asserted that because skyscrapers were essentially vertical in nature they should be designed as if they were a column with an articulated base, an uninterrupted shaft, and a capital on termination.[14] The Schiller Theater on which he collaborated with Dankmar Adler in 1892 is a good example of the actualization of this philosophy (fig. 10; cat. nos. 122-23).

Fig. 12 Frank Lloyd Wright, Robie House, 5757 South Woodlawn Avenue, 1909.

Although Sullivan consciously strove to create a distinctly American architecture, the roots of his design philosophy can be found in Europe, particularly in the rationalism of Viollet-le-Duc; we are reminded that Sullivan was among the earliest of Chicago architects to study at the Ecole des Beaux-Arts in Paris. Perhaps because of his individuality and eccentricities, Sullivan had few followers. Yet his importance was recognized abroad, especially in France and Scandinavia, even during his lifetime.[15] His foremost student, Frank Lloyd Wright, is considered by many to have been America's most important architect.

Wright, as Sullivan did in his later years, concentrated on the design of smaller buildings, particularly residences. He and his followers were responsible for spreading the Prairie School philosophy of residential design across the nation. The style was distinguished by rambling, open, horizontal spaces that were said to relate to the gently rolling landscape of Wright's native Wisconsin. Be that as it may, Wright's works were built in suburban Chicago (fig. 12; pls. 50-53; cat. nos. 173-83) as much as they were in rural areas.

The northern European and oriental influences on the Prairie School are widely known. Well documented, too, is the subsequent impact of the Prairie School on the modern architecture of Holland and Germany, especially following the publication in Berlin of the renowned Wasmuth portfolio of 1910, the *Ausgeführte Bauten und Entwürfe von Frank Lloyd Wright*; of C. R. Ashbee's smaller 1911 edition of Wright's work published by Wasmuth and called *Frank Lloyd Wright: Ausgeführte*

Figs. 13-15 D. H. Burnham and Company, Peoples Gas Company Building, 122 South Michigan Avenue, 1911; view during construction, c. 1910, showing light court; exterior; lobby.

Fig. 16 Waldemar Hansteen, Norwegian Pavilion, World's Columbian Exposition, 1893; dismantled and rebuilt as a part of Little Norway, Blue Monds, Wisconsin.

Fig. 17 Krupp Pavilion, World's Columbian Exposition, 1893 (demolished).

Bauten; and of Dutchman H. T. Wijdeveld's 1925 publication on Wright in the *Wendingen*. The Prairie School was exported to Asia through Wright's work in Japan during the late 1910s and 1920s, and to the Southern Hemisphere by the departure to Australia of two of Wright's followers: Walter Burley Griffin and his wife, Marion Mahony Griffin (cat. nos. 184-85; see essay by Van Zanten).

If one were to say that Wright shaped our concept of Chicago's suburbs, Daniel H. Burnham, even more than Sullivan, shaped the city itself. It was he who attempted to create in Chicago a version of what he believed to be the best of Europe's urban environments. French influences generally dominated American architecture and architectural education after the Civil War, and Burnham was especially interested in what Paris had to offer. Scores of American and Chicago architects studied at the Ecole des Beaux-Arts and carried its design and educational principles back to the architectural school at the Armour Institute of Technology and to the city's architectural offices. Although the first architectural school in Illinois had been established by Nathan Clifford Ricker at Champaign-Urbana in the 1870s, based in good measure on German curricula (see essay by Geraniotis),[16] French influence was the strongest and most pervasive on Chicago architecture, since it cut across ethnic boundaries and affected many architects, regardless of their national origins. An early example of this is the suburban town of Riverside, designed by the firm of Olmsted, Vaux and Co. in 1868. One of its designers, William Le Baron Jenney, was in-

spired by the Parisian commuter suburb of Le Vésinet, developed in the late 1860s. Many of Potter Palmer's improvements on Chicago's State Street during the same period, some in the Second Empire style, were likened to Baron Georges-Eugène Haussmann's rebuilding of Paris a few years earlier.[17] The Chicago architect who would work on a scale comparable to Haussmann's was Daniel Burnham (see essay by Draper).

Daniel Burnham's firms of Burnham and Root and D. H. Burnham and Co. specialized in speculative office buildings (fig. 11; pl. 59; cat. nos. 215, 226), corporate high-rises (figs. 13-15; pl. 54), and large department stores (pl. 55; cat. nos. 219-24) — whose large atriums were based, in part, on Parisian prototypes. Yet he is probably best remembered for his coordination of large-scale planning, which began when he was Chief of Construction for the 1893 World's Columbian Exposition. The Exposition brought international recognition to Chicago, not only because of foreign participation (figs. 16, 17), but, more importantly, because it served as a catalyst for the creation of a number of substantial cultural and public facilities that became permanent additions to Chicago's cityscape. Many of Chicago's important educational and cultural institutions and buildings owe their existence, at least in part, to the World's Columbian Exposition: the University of Chicago, begun in 1891; The Art Institute of Chicago's 1893 building (fig. 18), constructed principally as a meeting hall for the Fair's Congresses; the Exposition's Fine Arts Building, later reconstructed as Chicago's Museum of Science and Industry; and the first part of the

Fig. 18 Shepley, Rutan and Coolidge, The Art Institute of Chicago, Michigan Avenue at Adams Street, 1891-93 (altered).

elevated rail system, constructed in 1891 to connect the South Side fairgrounds with the central business district. These facilities, as well as Orchestra Hall designed in 1904-05 by D. H. Burnham and Co. (cat. nos. 216-17); the Cliff Dwellers Club, constructed on top of that building about 1907 (cat. no. 218); and the nearby University Club, the work of Holabird and Roche in 1905 (pl. 38), established the city as a cultural center for mid-America.[18] Chicago was declaring itself the equal of the older, more established East Coast cities like Boston and New York, and laying claim to being an American Renaissance version of Paris on the Prairie.

Burnham continued to work on increasingly large-scale planning projects, as a participant in the MacMillan Commission Plan for Washington, D. C., in 1902; as a designer of the proposed Civic Center complex for Cleveland in 1905; and as co-author with Edward Bennett of the Plan for San Francisco in the same year. Simultaneously, Burnham developed plans for Manila and Baguio in the Philippines, which exported the precepts of the City Beautiful movement overseas. All of this planning work made use of a classicizing vocabulary with imperial overtones and nationalist connotations.[19] However, the *piece de résistance* of Burnham's career was the Chicago Plan of 1909 (pls. 74-78; cat. nos. 227-36), developed with the assistance of Edward H. Bennett and implemented, in part, under Bennett's direction through the 1920s. This, then, is Burnham's legacy. He, more than Sullivan or Wright, shaped Chicago's cityscape and provided the vocabulary for its architecture of the 1920s. The public associates Chicago of that period

Fig. 19 View of Chicago, looking north, showing Michigan Avenue and bridge, c. 1928.

Fig. 20 Holabird and Root, Palmolive Building (now Playboy Building), 919 North Michigan Avenue, 1928-29.

Fig. 20 Holabird and Root, Palmolive Building (now Playboy Building), 919 North Michigan Avenue, 1928-29.

by Holabird and Root: 333 North Michigan Avenue, 1927-28; the Board of Trade from 1927-30, and the Palmolive (later Playboy) Building of 1928-29 (fig. 20). But the cityscape also bristled with buildings by less well known, yet competent, designers such as Benjamin H. Marshall, Andrew Rebori, and Frank A. McNally and James Edwin Quinn, among others.[20] Emigrants from central Europe continued to come to the city to practice, spurred on, no doubt, by the image of Chicago in publications by European architects.[21] Others, such as Richard Yoshijiro Mine (pl. 92), came from as far away as Japan to study in the region and work in Chicago in recognition of the city's preeminence in architecture.[22]

Although the depression that eventually followed the stock market crash of October 29, 1929, greatly inhibited the practice of architecture in America and elsewhere, European interchange with Chicago continued. It was reflected in the national pavilions designed by Swedish, Italian, and Czechoslovakian architects, and in the fantasy European villages designed mostly by Chicagoans, for the Century of Progress Exposition of 1933-34 (figs. 21, 22), as well as in a host of unexecuted projects. International exchange would reach new levels beginning in the late 1930s with the arrival of German and other middle European architects fleeing from National Socialist Germany, among them Ludwig Mies van der Rohe. But that is another story.[23]

Suffice it to say that, from the mid-nineteenth century through the 1930s, there was a continuous

chiefly with speakeasies and gangsters. Yet this was when limestone and terracotta skyscrapers rose throughout the city, particularly off the newly widened Michigan Boulevard, near the Michigan Avenue Bridge which had been designed by Bennett and constructed between 1918 and 1920 (fig. 19).

The architecture of the boom years after World War I and before the Great Depression of the 1930s included such major monuments as the Wrigley Building of 1921, with its addition of 1924 (see essay by Chappell), and the Merchandise Mart of 1923-30, both by one of Burnham's successor firms, Graham, Anderson, Probst and White, to local landmarks of American modernism designed

Fig. 21 Mario de Renzi and Adelberto Libera, Italian Pavilion, Century of Progress Exposition, 1933 (demolished).

Fig. 22 Schmidt, Garden and Erikson, Italian Village, Century of Progress Exposition, 1933 (demolished); delineated by Vale Faro.

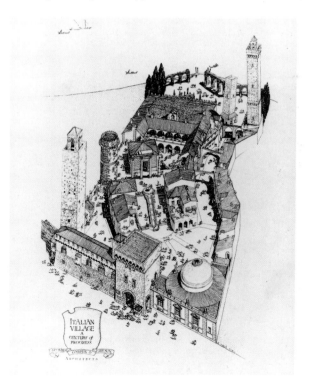

flow of architectural influences between Chicago and much of the rest of the world, particularly northern Europe. Whether immigrant or foreign-trained, Chicago's architects drew freely on the treasure chest of European architecture and, in turn, created a distinctly American architecture that has made its mark in many parts of the world. The exhibition and the related essays presented here explore these international connections, reassessing the contributions of some of Chicago's major architects, as well as calling attention to the achievements of some who are less well known.

The book begins with a discussion of the spirit that animated the spectacular resurgence of the city after the Great Fire. The subsequent essays are clustered into sections that are partially chronolog-ical and partially thematic. The epilogue is by architect Stanley Tigerman, designer of the Chicago installation of the exhibition.

The essays offer divergent approaches to American architecture, providing the insights of current scholarship on Chicago's built environment through a variety of methodologies and disciplines, from traditional structural and stylistic analyses through extensive use of social and cultural history. In the end, we have what we hope is a well-rounded, though by no means comprehensive, study of the work of the architects who shaped this flat lakeside site into the metropolis of mid-America in the fifty-year period between the Great Fire of 1871 and the 1922 international competition for the Chicago Tribune tower.

NOTES

1. Excellent summaries of this very early history of Chicago and French exploration can be found in Lois Wille, *Forever Open, Clear and Free: The Historic Struggle for Chicago's Lakefront* (Chicago, 1972), pp. 1-12; Anna Price, "The French Regime in Illinois, 1718-1740," *Historic Illinois* 5, 3 (Oct. 1982), pp. 1-6; David Keene, "Excavations at Fort de Chartres Answer Some Questions, Pose Others," *Historic Illinois* 9, 2 (Aug. 1986), pp. 5, 10-13; Harold M. Mayer and Richard C. Wade, *Chicago: Growth of a Metropolis* (Chicago, 1969), pp. 3-12; and Molly McKenzie, "Reconstructing the Cahokia Courthouse," *Historic Illinois* 7, 1 (June 1984), pp. 8-10. Some of the information in this introduction was synthesized from the author's previous publications; see John Zukowsky, "The Midwest," in David D. DeLong, Helen Searing, and Robert A. M. Stern, eds., *American Architecture: Innovation and Tradition* (New York, 1986), pp. 246-52; and idem, "The First Chicago School and Chicago Architecture, 1872-1909," *Process Architecture* 35 (1982), pp. 29-36.
2. Wille (note 1), p. 15, and Mayer and Wade (note 1), p. 32, for the 1848 population statistic.
3. Paul Sprague, "Origin of Balloon Framing," *Journal of the Society of Architectural Historians* 40 (Dec. 1981), pp. 311-314.
4. Mayer and Wade (note 1), p. 35.
5. Ibid., p. 50. See also John Brinckerhoff Jackson, *American Space: The Centennial Years 1865-1876* (New York, 1972), pp. 72, 83, 85-86, for railroad-related industries in Chicago, and Sigfried Giedion, *Mechanization Takes Command: A Contribution to Anonymous History* (1948; rpt. New York, 1969), pp. 209-42, especially for the comparisons of the 1860s slaughterhouses at La Villette in Paris with Chicago and the meatpacking inventions of Philip Armour and Gustavus Swift. Carl S. Smith, *Chicago and the American Literary Imagination 1880-1920* (Chicago, 1984), ch. 7.
6. Mayer and Wade (note 1), pp. 432-50, passim. Chicago's role as a national transit hub continued even after World War II with the construction of O'Hare International Airport – the world's busiest – and several interstate highways.
7. Melvin G. Holli and Peter d'A. Jones, eds., *Ethnic Chicago*, rev. ed. (Grand Rapids, Mich., 1984), p. 413.
8. Ibid., p. 462 ff. Also see Philip S. Foner, ed., *Wilhelm Liebknecht, Letters to the Chicago Workingman's Advocate* (New York, 1982). National Register Nomination Form, prepared April 4, 1982, for the Eugene Dietzgen Building, 954-990 W. Fullerton Avenue, Chicago. The building itself was constructed in 1906 by E. Lawrence Hallberg.
9. Gerald Larson is preparing a study of this subject for publication. Until that comprehensive work is published, see David Van Zanten, "The Nineteenth Century: The Projecting of Chicago as a Commercial City and the Rationalization of Design and Construction," in John Zukowsky, David Van Zanten, and Carol Herselle Krinsky, *Chicago and New York: Architectural Interactions* (Chicago, 1984), pp. 30-32.
10. For more on the key position of the railroads in Chicago in relation to port and rail traffic in other American cities, see Jackson (note 5), and Smith (note 5), ch. 5. For comparison, see Carl W. Condit, *The Port of New York* (Chicago, 1980), and idem, *Chicago, 1910-29: Building, Planning and Urban Technology* (Chicago, 1973), ch. 6.
11. Mayer and Wade (note 1), pp. 106-16.
12. For fireproofing, see Sarah Bradford Landau, *P. B. Wight: Architect, Contractor, and Critic, 1838-1925* (Chicago, 1981), pp. 44-50 and Sharon S. Darling, *Chicago Ceramics and Glass: An Illustrated History from 1871-1933* (Chicago, 1979), pp. 170-71. Zukowsky, "The First Chicago School" (note 1), p. 30, for discussion of the first elevator in New York in 1857 and Chicago in 1864, citing Frank Randall, *History of the Development of Building Construction in Chicago* (Urbana, Ill., 1949), pp. 14, 65, 71. Carl W. Condit, *American Building* (Chicago, 1968), p. 115, cites 1889 references for the term "skyscraper" as first applied to Chicago buildings, and p. 121, discusses fireproofing and the Nixon Building.
13. Sigfried Giedion, *Space, Time and Architecture* (Cambridge, Mass., 1941); Carl W. Condit, *The Chicago School of Architecture: A History of Commercial and Public Building in the Chicago Area, 1875-1925* (Chicago, 1964); Oswald Grube, Peter Pran, and Franz Schulze, *100 Years of Architecture in Chicago: Continuity of Structure and Form* (Chicago, 1976). For a discussion of these interpretations in relation to the revisionist approach of the 1976 book and exhibit *Chicago Architects*, organized by Stanley Tigerman and Stuart Cohen, see Zukowsky, "The First Chicago School" (note 1), p. 29, and *New Chicago Architecture*, ed. Maurizio Casari and Vincenzo Pavan (New York, 1981), esp. pp. 41-49, 71-73.
14. Louis H. Sullivan, "The Tall Office Building Artistically Considered," in *Kindergarten Chats and Other Writings*, ed. Isabella Athey (New York, 1947), pp. 202-13.
15. Leonard Eaton, *American Architecture Comes of Age: European Reaction to H. H. Richardson and Louis Sullivan* (Cambridge, Mass., 1972), and Lauren Weingarden, "Louis H. Sullivan: Investigation of a Second French Connection," *Journal of the Society of Architectural Historians* 39, 4 (Dec. 1980), pp. 297-303. See also DeLong, Searing, and Stern (note 1), pp. 69-70, for H. P. Berlage's recognition of Sullivan's importance, yet inability to distinguish the American's personal style.
16. Roula Geraniotis, "The University of Illinois and German Architectural Education," *Journal of Architectural Education* 38 (Summer 1985), pp. 15-21.
17. Theodore Turak, "Riverside, French Roots," *Inland Architect* 25 (Nov.-Dec. 1981), pp. 12-21; and Mayer and Wade (note 1), pp. 54-55.
18. Jean F. Block, *The Uses of Gothic: Planning and Building the Campus of the University of Chicago 1892-1932* (Chicago, 1983); John Zukowsky, "The Art Institute of Chicago: Constructions, Concepts, and Queries," *Threshold* 3 (1985), pp. 60-63, 71; Helen Lefkowitz Horowitz, *Culture and the City: Cultural Philanthrophy in Chicago from the 1880s to 1917* (Lexington, Ky., 1976); Mayer and Wade (note 1), pp. 142, 208-10, for the elevated in Chicago. See also Brian J. Cudahy, "Chicago's Early Elevated Lines and the Construction of the Union Loop," *Chicago History* 8, 4 (Winter 1979-80), pp. 194-205. George Upton, ed., *Theodore Thomas: A Musical Autobiography* (Chicago, 1905). Thomas was the founder of the Chicago Symphony and a close friend of Daniel H. Burnham's.
19. Mario Manieri-Elia, "Toward an 'Imperial City': Daniel H. Burnham and the City Beautiful Movement," in Giorgio Ciucci, et al., *The American City: From the Civil War to the New Deal*, trans. Barbara Luigia La Penta (Cambridge, Mass., 1979), pp. 1-122, passim; and Zukowsky, "The First Chicago School" (note 1), pp. 33-35.
20. Carroll William Westfall, "Benjamin H. Marshall of Chicago," *Chicago Architectural Journal* 2 (1982), pp. 8-28; Joan E. Draper and Raymond. T. Tatum, "The Buildings of Andrew Nicholas Rebori," *Chicago Architectural Journal* 4 (1984), pp. 14-24, and John Zukowsky, "Chicago in the Twenties: More than Speakeasies and Skyscrapers," *Chicago Architectural Journal* 4 (1984), pp. 25-27.
21. See Richard J. Neutra, *Wie baut Amerika?* (Stuttgart, 1927), pp. 24-47, for an extensive discussion of the construction of the Palmer House in Chicago; and Ludwig Hilberseimer, *Großstadt-Architektur* (Stuttgart, 1927), pp. 26-27, 52, 55, 56, 63-68, for the work of Frank Lloyd Wright, Louis Sullivan, and the skyscraper in Chicago and New York. Another such architect is Vladimir Karfik, designer of the Bata Department Store in Brno, Czechoslovakia from 1930, who worked for Holabird and Roche and for Wright in Chicago for four years before. See Vladimir Slapeta, *The Brno Functionalists* (Helsinki, 1983), p. 112.
22. For Richard Yoshijiro Mine's biography, see John Zukowsky, Pauline Saliga, and Rebecca Rubin, *Chicago Architects Design: A Century of Architectural Drawings from The Art Institute of Chicago* (Chicago, 1982), pp. 82-83. Japanese immigration to Chicago in any considerable numbers did not occur until after World War II, when the relocation centers in the Western states closed. See Holli and Jones (note 7), p. 514 ff.
23. For the mixed reaction in Chicago to Germans and Germany from World War I through the 1930s, see Holli and Jones (note 7), pp. 462-511, passim, and Frederik Heller, "German-Americans in Chicago: Conflicting Loyalties and Assimilation in the 1930s," *Humanities* 7, 1 (Winter 1986), pp. 10-14.

Chicago's Secular Apocalypse:
The Great Fire and the Emergence of the Democratic Hero

Ross Miller

Within hours of the Great Chicago Fire of October 8-10, 1871, people were raking the ashes, busy planning new businesses and new lives. For Chicagoans the disaster was an instant coming of age. The flames tested them in a way normally reserved for the triumphs and struggles of the city's pioneer generation. Until the fire, tales of battles with Indians and tenacious wrestlings with the muddy land seemed by definition to dwarf any contemporary accomplishment. But the fire was an event large enough to compete with the city's mythic past. A genuine catastrophe to the nearly 300 who lost their lives and the thousands left homeless, the fire for a brief moment made equals of the vast majority who survived. Memory of a heroic time was no longer a privileged possession of a single class; all Chicagoans could claim the fire as their own mythic origin (fig. 1).

What is astonishing about the myth is, first, the immediacy of its creation, and, second, the universality of its acceptance both by those who lived through it and those who viewed it from afar. The Chicago Fire created a rare convergence of fact and myth. In fact, the city had suffered a terrible calamity. Frederick Law Olmsted, sent by *The Nation* to observe the damage, reported: "It will be seen that a much larger part of the town proper was burned than a stranger would be led to suppose by the published maps."[1] But even Olmsted, a rationalist and acclaimed landscape planner, was not immune to the fire's mythic proportions: "Very sensible men have declared that they were fully impressed at such a time with the conviction that it was the burning of the world."[2] Within days, the fire replaced the Fort Dearborn Massacre (1812) and the frontier trials of the city's founders of the 1830s as Chicago's seminal experience. And whereas few alive in the 1870s had any firsthand memory of the Massacre and only a handful of select families could count themselves founders, the fire included everyone. It was a universal experience in which

simple survival was made to seem heroic. An eyewitness recalled the scene as a "chapter of horrors that can only be written as it was, with a pen of fire."[3]

Chicago was quickly transformed even before any of the rebuilding began. It became the only American city whose myth of founding and development was absolutely contemporaneous with its modern condition. Boston's origins went back to the Puritans, New York's to the Dutch, and Philadelphia's to a large English land grant. As a result, the roots of eastern cities were emotionally remote from most of their nineteenth-century citizenry.[4] This was not true of Chicago. A Chicagoan needed to look no further back than October 8, 1871, for his city's origins.[5] The fire allowed him to think of himself as being both pioneer and modern. It so conflated time — making the heroic past seem present and the present appear immediately part of the mythic past — that a Chicagoan might, if he chose, be released from his own history. History was thus so personalized that the city's resurrection seemed directly to apply to him. As one contemporary, Everett Chamberlin, observed, in an article entitled "Five Months After," *The Lakeside Monthly* (April 1872), "To participate in such scenes made every man feel like a hero among heroes."

What separates Chicago's sense of emerging modernity from that of other nineteenth-century cities[6] is the clarity of its imagery. Where others suffered the modern through a host of neurasthenic symptoms — their bodies if not their minds expressing Marx's sense of the suffocating airlessness of the Victorian era — Chicagoans were restless with possibilities.[7]

The city's postfire view of the modern was decidedly positive. From the omnipresent engravings of phoenix birds rising from the ashes to the apocalyptic talk of preachers and reporters, Chicagoans had images to represent the way they felt. And because these images were not the mere fancy of artists and intellectuals, but ideas supported by the extraordinarily material nature of change to be seen every day as the shells of new buildings rose out of the tons of rubble, all Chicagoans had a way to authenticate their sense of the transformation.

Fig. 1 Ruins of the Lakeside Building, southwest corner of Clark and Adams streets, following the Chicago Fire of October 8-10, 1871.

Nowhere is this more eloquently described than in another passage from Everett Chamberlin's "Five Months After":

Oh, it was an enlivening, inspiring sight, to look out each morning upon a brave wall of solid masonry, which one had not noticed before! – to watch the summits of those already risen, and see, perhaps relieved against the glow of a prairie sunset, the heroic platoons of workingmen building, building, building them still higher, and paying no heed either to approaching night or the benumbing chill of piercing winter winds! – to observe the long files of laborers bearing, in the familiar hods upon their shoulders, the magic elements out of which the most powerful of conjurers, patience and energy, were to bespeak a builded city! – to mind the constant stream of vehicles that went plunging through the streets, like fire engines bent on saving a city from destruction; and, indeed, their errand was of equal moment – the building up of the New, since the Old could no longer be saved!

At the time of the fire, Chicago had just recently consolidated its position as the West's preeminent city, having displaced St. Louis as a transportation hub during the Civil War. The opening of the Illinois and Michigan canal (1848) and the founding of the Galena (1850), Illinois Central (1851), and Michigan Southern and Michigan Central (1852) railroads, all of which helped transform the city from a retailing market to a prominent wholesaling center were not far in the past (fig. 2). In fact, Chicagoans were nearly as close in time to their city's beginnings in 1833 as they were to its more recent renown. But Chicago always seemed to encourage visionaries who were more concerned with future opportunities than immediate realities. Little more than a glorified army outpost when Charles Butler, one of the city's earliest financiers, arrived in 1833, it was still compelling enough to tempt him to invest $100,000 and declare: "The experienced observer saw the germ of a city, destined from its peculiar position near the head of the Lake and its remarkable harbor formed by the river, to become the largest inland commercial Emporium in the United States."[8] Butler was looking back fifty years when he recorded these impressions. His brother-in-law William Ogden, Chicago's first mayor, was another of the city's early prophets who turned a quick profit on land investments.[9]

The infant city's heady promise coexisted with the base realities of a muddy western settlement, for Butler's and Ogden's visionary Emporium was also a spot where "wolves during the night roamed all over . . . the city."[10] Chicago always contained such contradictions. One had to, in effect, look beyond the present condition or back into an idealized past to locate a consistent reality. Had Butler's vision of Chicago materialized, it might well have resembled Thomas Cole's painting "The Architect's Dream" (1840) or the Court of Honor of the 1893 World's Columbian Exposition. Projected back to the time of the fire, the vision of the city's founding was unified through the fortunes of her dynastic families, established by the trader John Kinzie, real estate baron Potter Palmer, and meat packer Gustavus Swift. The desired singleness of purpose always seemed to compete with the gritty actuality at hand.

This duality between vision and reality became, at a very early date, the way Chicagoans saw themselves. As long as positive single identity was denied, they would look to the future or the past to avoid the present; dress rich to forget recent poverty; and build grand facades on firetraps and structurally flawed buildings for show. An ingrained, and finally institutionalized, schizophrenia was, in part, compensation for the strains of the city's meteoric growth. Although a visitor in 1857 could declare, "Truly there is but one Chicago," he could not in all honesty overlook the mixed results of progress: "Miserable hovels are mixed up with the most beautiful and costly stores and edifices, such as I never saw in any other place."[11] The "one Chicago" frustrated singular devotion; the costs of development, both material and human, were too apparent. "The only drawback, perhaps, to the comfort of the money-making inhabitants, and of the stranger within the gates, is to be found in the clouds of dust and in the unpaved streets and thoroughfares, which give anguish to horse and man."[12]

Chicago's spectacular incongruities became a part of any portrait of the city. Praise, tempered by references to the city's less appealing side, began to structure the ways people thought and wrote about Chicago. It was not as though Chicago were the only American city with dark recesses. George W. Cable's New Orleans and Frank Norris's San Francisco were just as bleak. But in Chicago's case there was a certain pride in the city's divided nature because of the abiding faith in an eventual coherence that would vindicate its heroic struggles. Here was a city founded on and developed from a dialectic of forces: as in America itself, unity would emerge from diversity. The mud, foul weather, and visible depravity denounced by countless preachers gave Chicago its special character. Chicagoans always looked past the disadvantages that others might find daunting to a heroic outcome.

The wickedness and the piety of Chicago are, in their way, marvelous. It is a city of church-building, church-going people, and yet contains more people who are not church-going in proportion to the population, than any other place. The Sabbath day in Chicago is, so far as the

eye can discover externally, as quiet and orderly as in any New England city; yet, all laws for Sunday observance have been repealed, and in no other American city are there so many people who devote the day to festivity. Everything undertaken here is done promptly and on a grand scale.[13]

Writing in the September 1875 issue of *Scribner's Monthly*, J. W. Sheahan, a Chicagoan who later published a comprehensive account of the fire, employs the contemporary trope of a divided Chicago. Where others used the contrast between hovels and mansions, Sheahan divides the city between churchgoer and religious truant.

But there is a critical difference. Sheahan notices none of the cultural anxiety expressed in earlier accounts. Something had happened to change the ways in which Chicagoans presented and perceived themselves. Not that the facts were different; only the attitudes toward development had changed. *Chicago had found a way to see itself.* Instead of trying to resolve its divisions, like the cities of the

East Coast and Europe, Chicago used its conflicts as *the basis* of its identity. The differences of tone and attitudes that Sheahan reports would have been little more than the stuff of Sunday supplements were it not for the Chicago Fire of 1871.

The fire instantly provided substance for the inchoate sense of Chicago's uniqueness. Sheahan, for instance, discovered in the events of the fire an objective correlative to the city's four-decade-long claim to "greatness."[14] The fire became the key to understanding the city, so that an event that did nothing to resolve the city's deep divisions along class and ethnic lines did something far more radical. It provided a model for individual initiative and innovation. The fire implied to Chicagoans that their history would not evolve in millennia, like the history of European cities, nor in centuries, like that of established American cities, but in explosive bursts that liberated and inspired individuals to do their best, for they could see the outcome. Divisions that might paralyze other places provided the

Fig. 2 View of Chicago, looking northwest from the dome of the Court House, 1858.

Fig. 3 The Water Tower and Pumping Station (1868-69), designed by W. W. Boyington, on North Michigan Avenue at Chicago Avenue, were two of the few structures to survive the fire.

Fig. 4 Corner of State and Madison streets following the fire.

very condition for Chicago's existence. Change, as demonstrated by the fire on the largest scale, was to be permanent in modern Chicago.

Starting on the Southwest Side's De Koven Street, on the evening of October 8, the fire raged late into the next day and night, ending in the northeast on Fullerton Avenue, frustrated finally by Lake Michigan and persistent rain showers (figs. 3, 4).[15] Contemporary reports estimated that 2,000 acres were lost; 18,000 buildings were destroyed; and 90,000 people were left homeless.[16] City Coroner Stephens and Cook County physician, Dr. Ben C. Miller, estimated deaths at near 300, noting the difficulty of identifying bodies charred beyond recognition.[17] Clearly, the fire was a major disaster, but the city could consider itself lucky because so few lives were lost, in large part because the wind headed consistently in a northeast direction (fig. 5). Although the wind never achieved a velocity of over thirty miles per hour, the blaze was aided by "fire devils," a convection effect that greatly added to its destructive energy.[18]

The eyewitness accounts understandably stress the dramatic and life-threatening aspects of the disaster. Chicago's "sluggish river seemed to boil."[19] The event was immediately made to take on mysterious powers. "The wind blowing a stiff gale had possession of the flames, and the beautiful buildings, Chicago's glory, lay before them . . . and within an incredibly short space of time nearly a mile of brick blocks was consumed as if by magic."[20] Not the act of nature it surely was: the culminating act of a ninety-eight-day drought, beginning on July 4, during which less than two inches of rain had fallen;[21] nor the carelessness of man, who overbuilt the city with flammable materials and protected it with a spectacularly inadequate fire department;[22] the fire took on attributes of a full-blown act of God or the Devil, complete with Biblical overtones.

An account published in the Chicago *Post* of October 17 suggests the tone of the response:

From the roof of a tall stable and warehouse to which the writer clambered, the sight was one of unparalleled sublimity and terror. He was above the whole fire. The crowds directly under him could not be distinguished because of the curling volumes of crimsoned smoke, through which an occasional scarlet rift could be seen. He could feel the heat and smoke and hear the maddened Babel of sounds, and it required but little imagination to believe one's self looking over the adamantine bulwarks of hell into the bottomless pit.[23]

The Chicago Fire was a one-and-a-half-day apocalypse: an enormous event that instantly confirmed the city's importance to both its citizens and to all outsiders who watched or heard about its

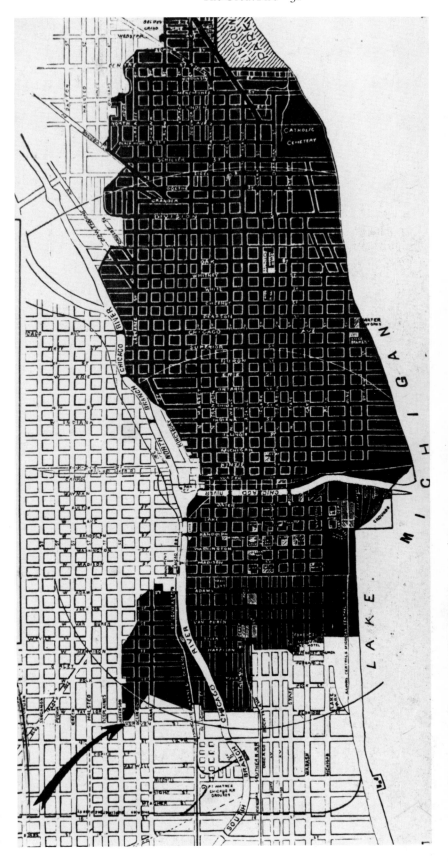

trials. Although some compared the event to the destruction of Rome, Babylon, and Troy,[24] this was a particularly American apocalypse. Instead of leveling the city and destroying forever man's vain-

Fig. 5 Map showing the area destroyed by the fire; arrow indicates the site on De Koven Street where the fire began.

glories, this act of magic, Devil, or God was decidedly latitudinarian. The Kingdom of God to which Chicagoans awoke the next morning was not among the angels in heaven, but back in Chicago.

Twenty years after the fire, the Chicago evangelist David Swing wrote:

When we awoke we were in a new world ... the tens of thousands of sleepers sunk away in weariness and grief, but when they awoke they saw around them a Nation full of kindness, and a great circle of states and empires all colored deeply by an undreamed of civilization.[25]

Swing echoes here an idea of worldly trial and redemption that has its American roots in William Bradford's *Of Plymouth Plantation* (1630), itself a retrospective account of a great human test. For what the Puritans found in the trials of a sea voyage, Chicagoans like Swing discovered in the fire. The New World of the Puritans was simply projected again onto Chicago's cooling ashes: a recurrence of the initial American apocalypse in which all dissonance vanished, however, this time not so that the righteous could claim the next world, but so that all might have a new chance to prosper *materially*. Thus, Chicago after the fire could perhaps finally shed both the ragged image of a western town, and its double identity as a culture of rare highs and frequent lows; it was now free to begin its own urban idyll. Like those who survived the perils that claimed so many lives aboard Bradford's ship, Chicago's survivors were extraordinary individuals who "resisted beastly drunkenness"[26] and overcame the rage of their fellow citizens "maddened by the sight of pillage or arson who fell upon the miscreant and beat him to death."[27] Before long the eyewitness accounts began to read like modern morality plays wherein good was destined to overcome evil. The difference was that this was living theater which threatened to get out of hand.

A sense of that led to the United States Army being called in to insure order. Although General Sheridan denied that there was widespread civil unrest, his presence helped stabilize the situation and assured outsiders that Chicago was going to survive intact.[28] In response, there was almost immediately a tremendous outpouring of aid from national businesses, other states, and foreign countries. Within hours, Chicago began to rebuild, content with its new notoriety, finally confirming to others the greatness it had projected for itself nearly four decades earlier. So it was quite natural to find in the first comprehensive report on the fire, Elias Colbert and Everett Chamberlin's *Chicago and the Great Conflagration,* language linking the city to the nation's beginnings. The authors declared that reconstruction would issue from the "firm foundation rock of her business, the Plymouth Rock of her society."[29] This too was a time to start over like the country's first settlers or as naked as Adam.

Let any man figure to himself what he would endure if he were stripped not only of everything that may make him conventionally "respectable" or eminent, but of the wherewithal to supply the first conditions of physical existence — food and shelter — and all his neighbors stripped of all that could alleviate his sufferings, and he will form a notion, faint and far off indeed, but far truer than description, however ample, could give him, of what has befallen, and for many days to come will befall, myriads of men as capable as himself to suffer and enjoy.[30]

The city's swift recovery lent support to such self-important analogies. Chicago had been tested — her people stripped to essentials — and had been found more than equal to the challenge. Instantly, it became the newest old city of the New World, incarnating in microcosm the country's century-long westward expansion.[31]

The facts of Chicago's initial reconstruction gave further substance to the city's boast. Within days of the disaster, a General Relief Committee was established to provide refuge and create distribution centers to handle the influx of donations and charitable aid. Answering the Chamber of Commerce's October 10 call to rebuild at once, there were by November 18 over 5,000 cottages completed or under construction.[32] And by October 1872 over $34 million worth of new building was to be found on the South Side, almost $4 million on the North, and nearly $2 million on the West Side.[33] Trade quickly increased and real estate values inflated at or above prefire levels (fig. 6). The fire, in fact, allowed land values to catch up with and surpass their true assessments. Chicago's forty years of constant development led to the paradoxical result that land was more valuable without structures than with them. Perversely, elaborate buildings constructed only a few years before the fire turned out to be more valuable as rubble, when the growing city converted debris from the fire into landfill to extend its boundaries. Potter Palmer, the city's most successful and flamboyant real estate speculator, recouped and extended his fortune after losing all his buildings to the fire.[34]

While the city's physical plant was severely affected, its importance as a commercial and industrial hub remained essentially undisturbed.[35] Chicago maintained its unrivaled geographic superiority for railroad, canal, river, and lake traffic. The city's grain, lumber, and stock, according to the Chicago Board of Trade, were left seventy-five to eighty percent intact, as was almost ninety percent of its manufacturing, machinery, and products. Within a year after the fire, Chicagoans began to plan a memorial to their city's escape from destruction (fig. 7). But the memorial was never completed; instead, the city's visionaries managed to organize the Inter-State Industrial Exposition just short of a year following the fire as a celebration of Chicago's material resurrection. Here was factual support for the city's maturing mythology. Even visitors were affected by it and identified Chicago as the archetypal American city. A British traveler (quoted in the *Chicago Tribune*, January 18, 1874) called Chicago the "concentrated essence of Americanism."[36] An outsider had inadvertently confirmed Butler's and his entrepreneurial brethren's prophecy.

Fairs, memorials, and the impressive statistics of reconstruction were only the more palpable manifestations of a phenomenon directly attributable

Fig. 6 Burling and Adler, Marine Building, northeast corner of LaSalle and Lake streets, under reconstruction in 1872.

to the fire. The conflagration was immediately enlisted to validate Chicago's claim to uniqueness. Here was a city that not only could survive adversity, but one that welcomed such powerful events as a cleansing anodyne to the more negative aspects of development. On the Sunday following the fire, Henry Ward Beecher, preaching at Plymouth Church, declared that Chicagoans "could not afford to do without the Chicago Fire."[37] Beecher, like the Reverend Swing, used the fire as a model of

change. This American apocalypse was a scene of great disruption but one that would create both material and moral opportunities.[38] Chicago's experience with disaster secularized the biblical notion of the end of history, and incorporated it into a growing civic mythology.

The facts of Chicago's phenomenal recovery and growth after the fire seemed to confirm the secularized theology that identified determination and enterprise as capable of prevailing even against the

Fig. 7 William Le Baron Jenney, Proposed monument of safes and broken columns to commemorate the Chicago Fire; from Chicago Illustrated: One Year From the Fire *(Chicago, 1872).*

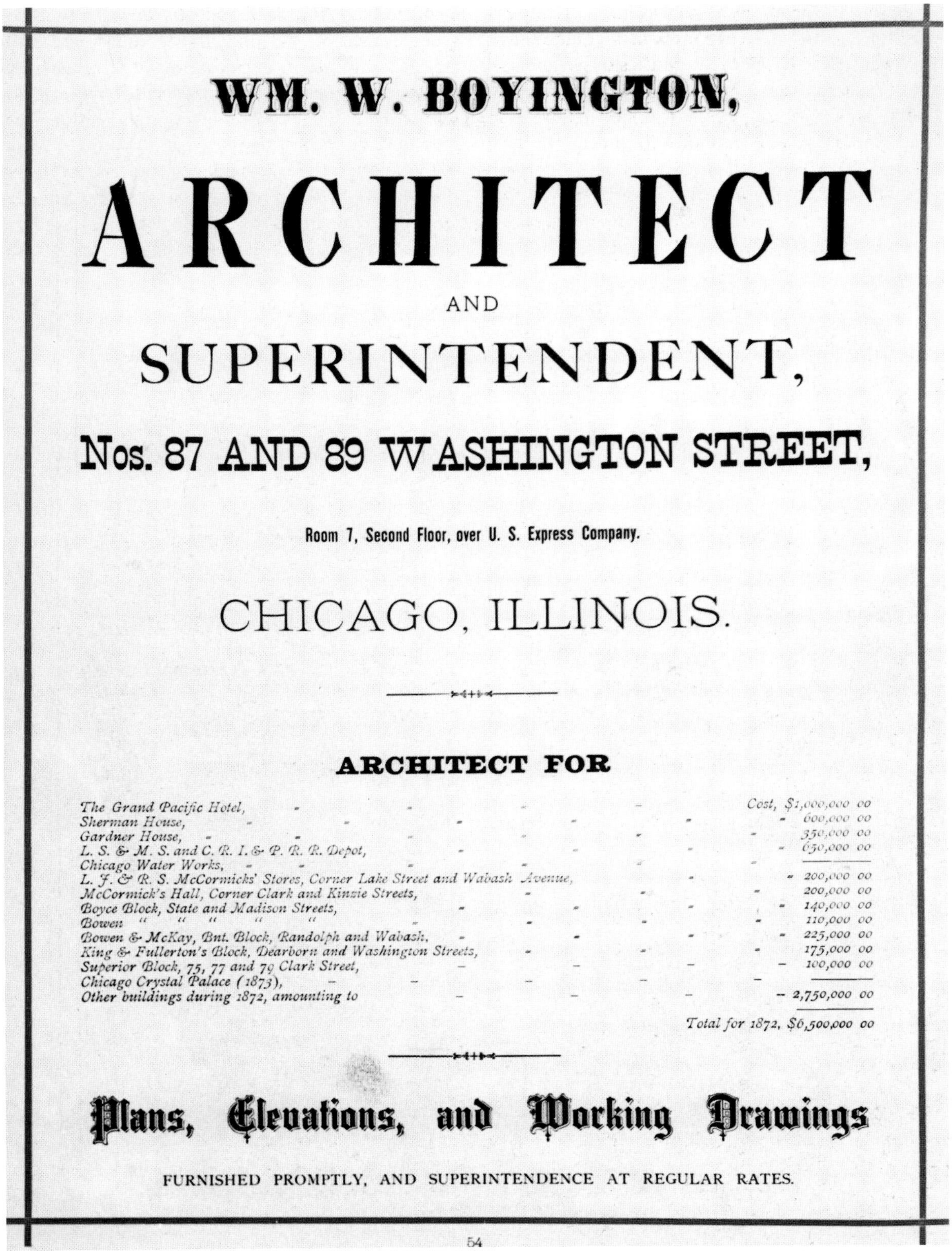

WM. W. BOYINGTON,

ARCHITECT

AND

SUPERINTENDENT,

Nos. 87 AND 89 WASHINGTON STREET,

Room 7, Second Floor, over U. S. Express Company.

CHICAGO, ILLINOIS.

ARCHITECT FOR

The Grand Pacific Hotel,	Cost, $1,000,000 00
Sherman House,	" 600,000 00
Gardner House,	" 350,000 00
L. S. & M. S. and C. R. I. & P. R. R. Depot,	" 650,000 00
Chicago Water Works,	
L. J. & R. S. McCormicks' Stores, Corner Lake Street and Wabash Avenue,	" 200,000 00
McCormick's Hall, Corner Clark and Kinzie Streets,	200,000 00
Boyce Block, State and Madison Streets,	140,000 00
Bowen " " " "	110,000 00
Bowen & McKay, Bnt. Block, Randolph and Wabash,	225,000 00
King & Fullerton's Block, Dearborn and Washington Streets,	175,000 00
Superior Block, 75, 77 and 79 Clark Street,	100,000 00
Chicago Crystal Palace (1873),	
Other buildings during 1872, amounting to	2,750,000 00
	Total for 1872, $6,500,000 00

Plans, Elevations, and Working Drawings

FURNISHED PROMPTLY, AND SUPERINTENDENCE AT REGULAR RATES.

54

Fig. 8 Advertisement by W. W. Boyington recording his architectural achievements in 1872 in the rebuilding of the city; from Rebuilt Chicago (Chicago, 1874).

most severe tests. Thus industry replaced faith as the affirmation of belief. Chicagoans had had proven to them that such chaos and judgment could be survived by a modern city's fortunate fall into the future.

This faith enabled Chicagoans to view positively two decades of cyclical reversals, including financial panics and labor unrest. It inevitably also became the conceptual underpinning of all who would come to think and write about Chicago. Perpetuated around the time of the fire was a myth that proposed to exclude the city from the ravages of history: Chicago was the beneficiary, not the victim, of conflicts. Initially the stuff of sermons, the city began to be seen universally as Fortune's child, the happy survivor of the "day after." It was the American city that was not only free of a long and deadening history, but was also released from its own past mistakes. If they could seize the opportunity, Chicagoans could regain the energy represented by Butler's pioneering generation, but without the attendant problems. The fire then could be viewed as the necessary hygiene of modernization, a cyclical fact of modern life. What men could not correct, nature would. Could anything stand in the path of a city that had successfully resisted a test of biblical severity that was enough to "reverse the Westward current of human migration and unsettle the business of the world?"[39] Swing had the answer: "Twenty years would transform a painful experience into rather a pleasing dream."[40]

The fire's immediate legacy insured that Chicago would not be allowed to become old and decadent. Even staid works of documentary history like *Chicago: Its Past, Present and Future* (1871), *The Lost City: Chicago As It Was and As It Is and Its Glorious Future* (1872), and *Chicago and the Great Conflagration* (1872) adopted the developing apocalyptic tone. Future visitors to the city, wrote the authors of the first of these, "will find her changed from the Chicago of yesterday in such manner as the wild and wanton girl, of luxurious beauty, and generous, free ways, is changed."[41] The earliest speculators and developers had provided the original impetus for change which, left alone, had been on the way to becoming detrimental to the city's moral development:

The people of Chicago were, before the fire, fast lapsing into luxury – not as yet to any degree as the people of New York – but still more than was for their good. The fire roused them from this tendency, and made them the same strong men and women, of the same simple, industrious, self-denying habits, which built up Chicago, and pushed her so powerfully along her unparalleled career. All show and frivolity were abandoned, and democracy became the fashion.[42]

In one great act, the American promised land arrived on the streets of Chicago. Tired men and women were given new energy. Young again like the city, they could now get back to work and abandon their "dawdling lives." The fire viewed in this way became a timely moral correction. And given Chicago's more worldly interests, the fire also aided in the "correction of besetting [physical] faults, which it is fair to assume would not have been corrected if the city had not been burned."[43] Contemporary commentators reinforced the notion that Chicago's physical cleansing had also been a spiritual one.

The "Great Awakening," the American religious revival of the eighteenth century that had taken three long generations to develop after the initial Puritan settlements, seemed to occur almost instantly in Chicago. A day-and-a-half of flames and hot winds were more than equal to Jonathan Edwards's "fire and brimstone": "If God should only withdraw his hand from the flood-gate, it would immediately fly open, and the fiery floods of the fierceness and wrath of God, would rush forth with inconceivable fury."[44] Chicagoans had seen the "fiery floods" and their experiences made Edwards's rhetoric palpable. The city made metaphor literal by the very materiality of its history. Through the fire's urgency, Chicago was compelled to experience in microcosm the eighteenth-century American passage from spiritual degeneration to attempted purification. But what were merely words and images to Edwards's congregation (which he perceived as spiritually lapsed) were now facts. Chicago could see itself not only in terms of its own particular history but as a paradigm for the larger development of America as a nation. In no small measure, the city was the national testing ground for abstractions through which the country was coming to know itself.

All the local commentators took advantage of their city's tragic rush to prominence. The moralists and theologians among them argued the fine points, but all initially appeared to agree that any city that survived such a calamity would in the end, like Edwards's congregation contemplating its nasty fate, be better off. The facts supported such optimism. On a strictly economic and political basis, Chicago in the months and years after the fire could be shown to have made startling corrections for four decades of nearly random, unplanned development (fig. 8). To this end, Colbert and Chamberlin wrote that real estate speculators who suffered severe losses might, in the future, become less reckless; their buildings would be made of better materials. The fire, because it "checked the two [*sic*] rapid spread of the city in all directions,"[45] would lead to a rebuilding of the city's central business district. In addition, by getting rid of failing or marginal businesses,[46] the fire could be seen literally as a "purifying" act.[47] In fact, Mayor Joseph Medill and other politicians who ran on a "Fire-Proof" ticket – arguing for a strict building code which included the elimination of flammable architectural ornament – won by a five-to-one margin.

Colbert and Chamberlin's report, published within months of the fire – on December 1, 1871 – quickly became the document of record. The authors combined authoritative facts and figures, describing the disaster graphically in chapters with such evocative titles as "Good Out of Evil" and

"The New Chicago." As a result, they articulated an instant history, a seemingly objective account that gave Chicagoans a way to view a common experience.

The aftermath of the Chicago Fire was a truly modern phenomenon – a population learned how it felt about the catastrophe by reading about itself. In this way, primary experience was immediately distanced and subordinated until given the authority of interpretation. For instance, by reading about the damage done to "individual fortunes," Chicagoans were encouraged to bemoan their own bad luck and simultaneously to consider their city's greater destiny. And in so doing, they were spared painful personal introspection and encouraged to sublimate their fate to Chicago's. The city's recovery then could be thought of in the same dramatic terms as its narrowly averted destruction, until it became "simply a question of how long it will require for the country to produce the bricks and the stone to lay up her walls."[48] Worldly Chicagoans expected restitution in *this* and not the next world.

After assembling their contributors' eyewitness accounts, the editors of the November 4, 1871, issue of *Harper's Weekly* added their imprimatur to the myths gathering around the rebirth of the city.

It will all come back again in time, if not to every loser, certainly to those who believe in the future of Chicago. It will be made a better city than it ever could have become but for this fire. A better building system, a more shapely development, a spirit of enterprise and determination, literally tried as by fire, will bring all these results.[49]

The fire was seen by Chicagoans as a great generative event. On the most basic level it was a palpable demarcation between Chicago's past and its future, signaling the beginning of modern time. A harrowing, life-threatening experience, the fire defined all Chicagoans. No longer could an elite of founding families lay a monopolistic claim to the memory of the past. In the 1870s a heroic past was as available to all Chicagoans as everyman's memory of yesterday. History was democratized and every citizen of Chicago, by dint of having survived, had become a hero among heroes.

NOTES

1 Frederick Law Olmsted in *The Nation* (Nov. 9, 1871), p. 303.
2 Ibid.
3 Frank Luzerne, *The Lost City: Chicago As It Was and As It Is and Its Glorious Future* (New York, 1872), p. 19.
4 See John Higham, *Strangers in the Land: Patterns of American Nativism 1860-1925* (New Brunswick, 1963) for the effect of nineteenth-century immigration.
5 Interestingly, this was more a feeling than a fact since eighty percent of Chicago's infrastructure was left intact.
6 See Dostoevsky's St. Petersburg and the Goncourts' Paris.
7 There are three suggestive recent works on modernity's effects: Marshall Berman, *All That is Solid Melts into Air* (New York, 1982); T. J. Jackson Lears, *No Place of Grace* (New York, 1981); and Alan Trachtenberg, *The Incorporation of America* (New York, 1982).
8 Charles Butler in *As Others See Chicago*, ed. Bessie L. Pierce (Chicago, 1933), p. 45.
9 Charles Butler, *Autograph Letters* (1881), based on 1833 diaries and letters, vol. 23, Chicago Historical Society.
10 William Bross, *History of Chicago* (Chicago, 1876), p. 64.
11 Edward L. Peckham in *As Others See Chicago* (note 8), p. 167.
12 William Howard Russell in *As Others See Chicago* (note 8), p. 173.

13 J. W. Sheahan, *Scribner's Monthly* 10, 5 (1875), p. 529.
14 Ibid.
15 Bessie L. Pierce, *A History of Chicago* (Chicago, 1957), vol. 3, pp. 3-5.
16 *Report of the Chicago Relief and Aid Society of Disbursements of Contributions for the Sufferers of the Chicago Fire* (Cambridge, Mass., 1874), pp. 9-10.
17 Elias Colbert and Everett Chamberlin, *Chicago and the Great Conflagration* (Chicago, 1872), p. 276.
18 H. A. Musham, quoted in *The Great Chicago Fire of 1871*, ed. Paul M. Angle (Ashland, 1969), p. 10.
19 "Chicago in Ashes," *Harper's Weekly* (Oct. 28, 1871), p. 17.
20 Ibid., p. 17.
21 Joseph Kirkland, "The Chicago Fire," *New England Magazine* 6, 4 (June 1892), p. 726.
22 Ibid., p. 727.
23 Quoted in Kirkland (note 21), p. 737.
24 David Swing, "Historic Moments: A Memory of the Chicago Fire," *Scribner's Magazine* 11 (Jan.-June 1892), p. 693.
25 Ibid., p. 696.
26 "Chicago in Ashes" (note 19), p. 25.
27 Ibid., p. 27.
28 Angle (note 18), p. 11.
29 Colbert and Chamberlin (note 17), p. 451.
30 Eyewitness account in the *World* quoted by Paul M. Angle (note 18), p. 15.
31 John R. Chapin, *Harper's Weekly* (Nov. 4, 1871), reprinted in Angle (note 18), p. 40.

32 Pierce (note 15), vol. 3, p. 9.
33 Ibid., p. 17.
34 Emmett Dedmon, *Fabulous Chicago* (New York, 1953), p. 124.
35 Pierce (note 15), vol. 3, p. 10.
36 Ibid., p. 19.
37 Colbert and Chamberlin (note 17), p. 445.
38 The idea of a "fortunate fall" or *felix culpa* had its most popular expression in Nathaniel Hawthorne's *The Marble Faun* (1860). In this formulation one sins or fails only to succeed later. See particularly pp. 183, 311 and 329 of the Signet Edition (1961). Chicago's use of this idea was especially stunning because the transition from bad to good news was almost instantaneous.
39 Kirkland (note 21), p. 726.
40 Swing (note 24), p. 691.
41 Colbert and Chamberlin (note 17), p. 462.
42 Ibid., p. 450.
43 Ibid., p. 446.
44 "Sinners in the Hands of an Angry God" (July 8, 1741) in *Jonathan Edwards: Basic Writings*, ed. Ola Elizabeth Winslow (New York, 1966), p. 158.
45 Colbert and Chamberlin (note 17), p. 446.
46 Pierce (note 15), p. 12.
47 Colbert and Chamberlin (note 17), p. 448.
48 Ibid., p. 455.
49 Quoted in Angle (note 18), p. 55.

The Iron Skeleton Frame:
Interactions Between Europe and the United States

Gerald R. Larson

The year 1985 marked the centennial of the completion in Chicago of the Home Insurance Building designed by William Le Baron Jenney in early 1884 (fig. 1). Until recently, this building was generally accorded the distinction of being considered the first skyscraper, that is, the first tall office building to be constructed with its floors and walls entirely supported on a rigid skeleton of iron columns and beams. In fact, this does not seem to have been the case; increasingly the evidence suggests that the concept of using iron skeleton framing to support a multistory building predates the Home Insurance Building by at least ninety years and that the technique of iron framing was more advanced in 1884 than Jenney's relatively antiquated structural design of that year.[1]

The earliest known proposal to build a tall, iron-framed structure incorporating an elevator was designed in 1832 by the English engineer Richard Trevithick. To commemorate the reforms enacted by Parliament that year, he proposed to build a 1,000-foot-high tower (fig. 2) to be constructed entirely of iron. In his design Trevithick ingeniously applied the contemporary technology of steam to transport observers to the top of the tower. A hollow cylinder, ten feet in diameter, located in the center of the structure, ran up the tower's entire height. A cab, in the form of a piston large enough to carry twenty-five people, was to be raised or lowered within the cylinder at a safe speed by varying the steam pressure in the core cylinder below the piston. Unfortunately, Trevithick died in April 1833, and so did his idea for the tower.[2]

Actually, multistory iron framing had originated in England in 1792 (twenty-two years after the first use of cast-iron columns in English churches), when William Strutt erected his six-story Calico Mill in Derby.[3] By 1844 iron framing in England had progressed to the point that it could be used at the exterior of buildings to eliminate the need for a heavy masonry wall; this appears to have been the case with the Fire Station built in that year at the Royal Navy's Dockyard in Portsmouth. The iron frame was extended into the exterior and left exposed by placing the enclosing skin and windows at the inside of the structure.[4]

Fig. 1 William Le Baron Jenney, Home Insurance Building, LaSalle and Adams streets, 1884 (demolished).

Fig. 2 Richard Trevithick, Proposed monument to the Reform Act, 1832; from Journal of the Society of Architectural Historians *16, 4 (Dec. 1957).*

Fig. 3 James Bogardus, Proposed 300-foot tower for the 1853 New York Crystal Palace, 1852; from Sigfried Giedion, Space, Time and Architecture *(Cambridge, Mass., 1941).*

Ironically, that same year, the London building code was revised to improve the fire resistance of the city's building stock, which indirectly prevented the use of exposed iron construction.[5] In addition, just as the English were on the verge of solving the technical problems of the iron frame in order to be able to exploit its architectural potential, the movement opposing the consequences of the Industrial Revolution began to gather momentum. Unquestionably, the most influential leader of the anti-iron campaign was John Ruskin, whose opinion of iron in architecture was best presented in his *Seven Lamps of Architecture,* first published in 1849, in which the chapter entitled "The Lamp of Truth" proclaimed "that architecture does not admit iron as a constructive material, and that such works as the cast-iron . . . roofs and pillars of our railway stations, and of some of our churches, are not architecture at all."[6] The combined effects of the 1844 London building code and the prevalent aesthetic theory of critics like Ruskin forced the iron frame back into the corset of the masonry wall, thus preventing it from ever showing itself on the streets of London.

Meanwhile, on July 19, 1845, New York City suffered its second major conflagration in ten years. Although London had just banned exposed cast-iron construction because of its poor resistance to fire, the New York fire apparently served as the impetus for James Bogardus, an innovative manufacturer of milling machines for grain and lead, to propose in the summer of 1847 to build a new four-story factory with an exterior solely of glass and "incombustible" cast iron.[7] Bogardus had

no prior experience in construction but appears to have become familiar with iron construction during a trip to England and the Continent in the period 1836 to 1840, when the English were developing prefabricated iron building systems not unlike those that Bogardus eventually patented in May 1850.[8] Although cast iron had been used in American buildings since at least 1822, Bogardus's design contained an important refinement.[9] He devised a bolted connection, in place of the more typical friction connections of earlier American iron work, that imparted to the beam-column assembly sufficient rigidity so that it could stand by itself without the need of either diagonal crossbracing or masonry walls. This overcame one of the major obstacles to unleashing the potential of the iron frame to support tall buildings.

Another consequence of the 1845 New York fire was the reorganization of the city's fire districts, which necessitated the erection of several additional fire watchtowers. Late in 1850, Bogardus suggested that these could be fabricated of incombustible cast iron. The City Council eventually gave him a contract to build a prototype on 33rd Street near Ninth Avenue. Completed by mid-August 1851, the tower consisted of a ten-sided, open, rectilinear framework of iron, erected in six levels to a height of almost 100 feet. The tower appears to have been the predecessor of Bogardus's well-known proposal in 1852 for the New York Crystal Palace (fig. 3), which incorporated a similar 300-foot-high tower of thirteen levels that telescoped out of two shorter, wider towers.[10] While Bogardus's iron towers were by no means the first to be

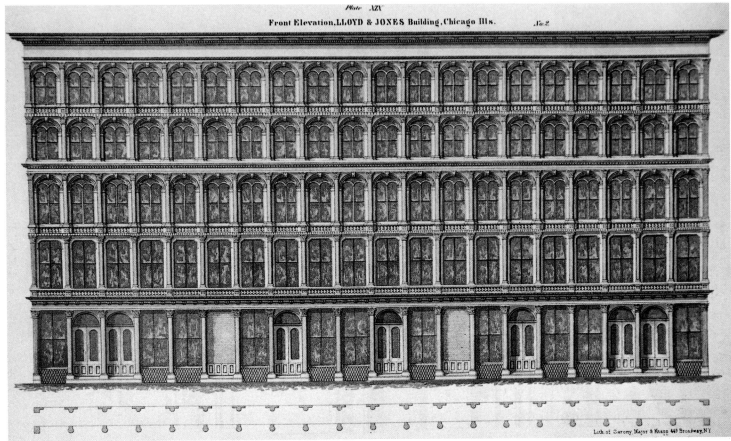

Fig. 4 Daniel Badger and John M. Van Osdel, Lloyd and Jones Building, Lake Street, c. 1860 (demolished); from Daniel Badger, Illustrations of Iron Architecture *(1865) in* The Origins of Cast Iron Architecture in America *(New York, 1970).*

Fig. 5 Daniel Badger and George H. Johnson, U. S. Warehousing Co. Grain Elevator, Brooklyn, 1860; from Badger, Iron Architecture.

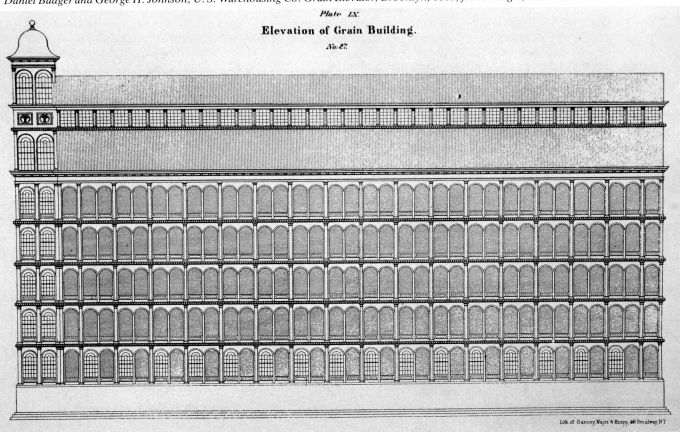

designed or built, they were typically more expressive of their construction than their predecessors, in that the iron framework was not covered by an enclosing membrane. With these structures, Bogardus consciously invented the modern iron skeleton frame, which he described in an 1856 publication: "On these columns rest another series of sills; and so on, continually for any required number of stories . . . to erect a tower or building many times the height of any other ediface [*sic*] in the world."[11]

Bogardus's proposed tower for the New York World's Fair of 1852 bears a striking resemblance to English architect C. Burton's proposed Prospect Tower described in the May 1, 1852, issue of the *Builder.* As dictated by the House of Commons, Joseph Paxton's Crystal Palace in Hyde Park, London, was to be dismantled at the end of the 1851 World's Fair. Burton proposed to reuse the iron and glass pieces to erect a structure of five concentric towers, the tallest to reach a height of 1,000 feet.[12] Meanwhile, 1852 also marked the beginning of the Second Empire in France following the crowning of emperor Napoleon III, whose reign was associated with the construction of many of France's important structures.[13] Determined not to be upstaged by either the English or American world's fairs, France held a design competition that year for a Palais de l'Industrie for an exposition to be held in 1855. The winning project by Viel and Desjardin would have been France's first building that relied on a freestanding iron structure as well as eliminating all exterior masonry in favor of cast-iron and glass panels.[14] In the final design, however, several compromises were made to bring the cost of the building within reason, one being the replacement of the iron and glass exterior with less expensive masonry. France's Palais de l'Industrie was far bolder in structure and construction than Paxton's Crystal Palace. It spanned 157.5 feet with wrought iron, while Paxton's building had a span of only 72 feet in wood. Nonetheless, the Palais de l'Industrie's iron structure was still sheathed with a masonry envelope, although it was not used to support any of the iron.[15]

While the changes to Viel and Desjardin's design were under consideration, Victor Baltard designed in late 1853 France's first truly freestanding iron structure, Paris's Central Markets at Les Halles. Earlier Baltard had developed a masonry scheme for Les Halles, which had actually been under construction since 1851. Apparently bowing to unfavorable public opinion, Napoleon III halted its construction in June 1853, when it was almost completed, telling Baron Georges-Eugène Haussmann, the newly appointed Prefect of the Seine, that he wanted the markets to consist of glass and iron canopies. Haussmann accordingly told Baltard to use "iron, iron, nothing but iron." A competition was held for a new design, and Baltard's iron and glass entry was selected. In this scheme the cast-iron columns at the exterior were left exposed and connected to the iron roof trusses with curved knee braces, freeing the structure of Les Halles from dependency on masonry for stability.[16]

The imperial decree for Les Halles, however, had little immediate effect on the tyranny of France's masonry tradition during the 1850s, even though French commentators, contrary to their English counterparts, began to advocate the use of iron, especially in visionary designs. One of the earliest of these was architect Louis-Auguste Boileau, whose first essay on iron, *Nouvelle architecturale forme,* was published in 1853. Two years later he applied his theory in his design for the Church of Saint-Eugène in Paris. Although its structure was an independent iron frame, the building was still enclosed by a non-load-bearing masonry wall that was built around the perimeter iron columns, a technique that became generally accepted throughout France.[17] Even though Boileau had wrapped the building in traditional masonry, his use of iron still came under attack from many critics, most notably Eugène-Emmanuel Viollet-le-Duc, who at this time, in contrast to Bogardus and Boileau, was opposed to the use of exposed iron in public buildings. Among other reasons of a more philosophical nature, he claimed that temperature variations could produce a "hail of bolt-heads, and during rain, a shower of rust."[18]

While Viollet-le-Duc was challenging Boileau's use of iron, Bogardus was actually taking the final step in divorcing the multistory iron frame from the masonry wall. In 1855 he designed and built a shot tower for the McCullough Shot and Lead Company of New York City, that was the first multistory iron structure to support its masonry enclosure. Bogardus designed a lightweight, eight-sided, iron skeletal framework of eight stories to a height of 175 feet. Twelve-inch-thick brick infill panels were constructed on the beams at each level to enclose the tower's interior. This not only significantly reduced the weight that needed to be supported by the foundations, but also allowed the ground floor to be entirely free of any enclosure, facilitating the movement of the plant's workers. This solution was so successful that within a year another shot company, Tatham & Brothers, contracted Bogardus for a similar but even taller (217 feet) structure.[19] Thus, Bogardus can be credited not only with having built the first two tall, iron skeleton framed structures that also supported their masonry enclosures, but also with understanding and exploiting the potentials of iron and masonry construction prior to Viollet-le-Duc's ultimate conversion to the use of iron in architecture.

Bogardus's shot towers were quickly followed by the first known multistory building to be completely supported by a rigid iron skeleton independent of any masonry or diagonal crossbracing. In 1858, English architect Godfrey Greene designed the boat store at the Sheerness Naval Dockyard, one of the last English contributions to the evolution of the iron frame. Greene's four-story moment-resisting frame was achieved by riveting the wrought-iron beams along their entire depth to the cast-iron columns. To enclose the four-story skeleton, however, Greene used alternating bands of glass and corrugated iron sheets instead of traditional masonry.[20] This left the honor of erecting the first multistory building to be supported by an iron frame upon which was placed a masonry enclosure, for Daniel Badger, Bogardus's chief competitor.

In 1856, Badger incorporated his expanding construction business as the Architectural Iron Works of New York; he appointed George H. Johnson, a young builder who had emigrated from England in 1852, chief designer of the newly created architectural department. The formation of the new company may have been in response to Badger's first large, multistory commission, the storefronts for Chicago's premier shopping district at the time, the block of Lake Street between Wabash and State streets (see Harris, fig. 4). Erected on both sides of the street, the Venetian Renaissance style cast-iron facades had been designed by John M. Van Osdel, Chicago's first architect (fig. 4). Confronted with the scope and complexity of this undertaking, Badger sent Johnson to Chicago to supervise the construction.[21]

In 1859, responding to the growing number of fires in grain elevators, Badger and William S. Simpson patented an iron system for the construction of these buildings. This consisted of cylindrical bins fabricated with riveted cast-iron plates that were supported by a multistory iron skeleton. A year later, Johnson designed the first elevator to incorporate this system for the U. S. Warehousing Company (fig. 5). Located on South Brooklyn's Atlantic Dock, the seven-story elevator was framed completely in iron, both in the interior and the exterior. Much of the iron exterior was enclosed with brick infill panels, a technique similar to that used in Bogardus's shot towers five years earlier.[22]

By the Civil War, five-story, light-colored cast-iron and glass facades glistened in many of America's larger cities. Sometimes, as in A. T. Stewart's new department store in New York City,

designed by John Kellum in 1859,[23] these were backed up by complete skeletons of iron framing, a technique developed in the 1850s through the efforts of Bogardus and Badger. Thus the American iron skeleton frame originated in New York City some thirty years prior to its first use in Chicago. Bogardus and Badger had also shown how to enclose the voids of the exterior framing with curtains of glass and/or masonry. With the addition of another New York invention, Otis's safety elevator, first revealed to the public at the 1853 World's Fair, all the parts necessary for the development of the skyscraper seemingly were in place in New York by the start of the Civil War.

With the suspension of further large-scale experiments with iron framing in the United States during the war, the momentum finally swung to the French, who became the leaders in iron construc-

Fig. 6 Eugène-Emmanuel Viollet-le-Duc, Rendering of Pan de Fer Apartment Building, Paris, 1863; from Entretiens sur l'architecture (Paris, 1864).

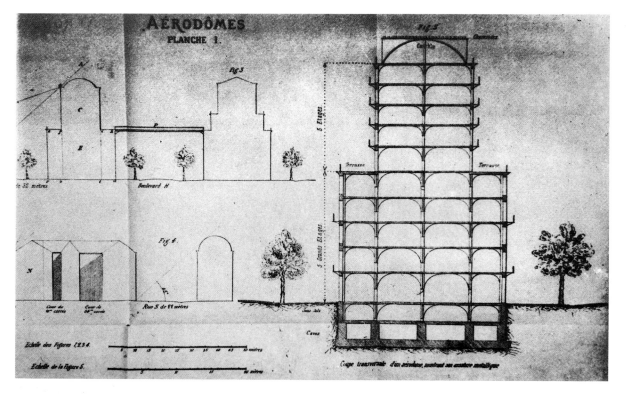

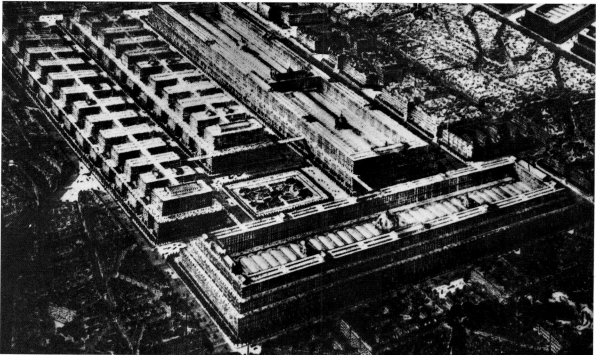

tion for the next thirty years.[24] In the early 1860s, a new generation of French designers in iron emerged who would be intimately involved with pushing the iron frame into a building's exterior, even though the Paris building code not only required street walls to be twenty inches thick, but also prohibited the incorporation of iron members in those walls.[25] The increasing use of iron by this generation was heralded in an illustration published in 1863 by Viollet-le-Duc, who, having re-

cently been converted to the cause of iron, was about to become its major spokesman. In the *Atlas* that accompanied the publication of the first volume of his *Entretiens sur l'architecture,* he included a color rendering (fig. 6) of a proposed apartment building that honestly revealed its diagonally braced iron frame on its exterior at the floors above the ground-floor iron shopfront. The iron framework, reminiscent of traditional European half-timber construction, was enclosed with an infill of polychromed terracotta tiles, using the technique earlier employed in Bogardus's shot towers and Badger's grain elevators.[26]

Napoleon III and Haussmann's plans for the rebuilding of Paris, well under way by the 1860s, created a receptive climate for the exploration of revolutionary techniques and materials. The evolving iron frame, coupled with the elevator, represented a conspicuous potential to extend Paris's urban renaissance and combined to produce one of the earliest visionary proposals for a skyscraper. In 1865 French engineer Henri-Jules Borie published a design for an entire section of the city containing eleven-story, elevatored buildings, which he called *Aérodômes* (fig. 8). These consisted of ten stories of iron framing, enclosed with a stone veneer erected on a masonry ground floor (fig. 7).[27] With exaggerated height, elevators, and a fireproofed iron skeleton frame, Borie's *Aérodômes,* conceived twenty years before the Home Insurance Building, truly merit the appellation of skyscrapers.

The first French building erected with an independent, multistory iron frame came in the same year, when Préfontaine designed a six-story warehouse for the Saint-Ouen Railway and Dock Company. Except for the formal, masonry facade on the south, the entire building was supported by a cast- and wrought-iron skeleton frame that was left exposed on the exterior by erecting its masonry enclosure on the inside of the perimeter framework.[28] Whether or not the wall was self-supporting or infilled on the frame at each floor is unclear; nonetheless, the French had finally succeeded in pushing the iron frame into the exterior of a multistory building only five years after the construction of Badger's first grain elevator.

By 1867, the year in which the world once again came to Paris to celebrate a world exposition, numerous iron and terracotta construction systems, known as *pan de fer,* were being proposed to build Paris's much-in-demand fireproof apartments.[29] A parallel manifestation of the city's vigorous growth was the development of the large, under-one-roof department store, generally recognized as originating in 1867 with the new Les Magasins-Réunis. Most likely in response to this move by its competitors, the Grands Magasins du Bon Marché engaged Louis-Auguste Boileau, architect of Saint-Eugène, to construct a new building, appropriately with iron and glass. Boileau's son, Louis-Charles, suggested in 1869 that the entire store be erected solely on an iron frame. This revolutionary idea was rejected on the grounds that the structure would be unstable, so in the final design the exterior columns were revised to be of stone.[30]

Fig. 9 John M. Van Osdel, Perspective view of the proposed design for the Kendall Building, 40 North Dearborn Street, 1871; the building was under construction when destroyed by the Great Fire of October 8-10, 1871; from Land Owner (Oct. 1871).

By 1869, the independent multistory iron frame was technically feasible, but once again, as at Saint-Ouen, it appeared outside the stranglehold of the Parisian building code. In 1869 architect Jules Saulnier designed a three-story factory building to replace the Menier Chocolate Works' half-timbered building erected in 1840 over the Marne River near the village of Noisiel. Keeping two existing masonry piers that dated from 1157 in the river, Saulnier and the engineer Moisant, designed a three-story iron framework cantilevered off the piers. The skeleton was stabilized with diagonal I-sections, which were left exposed on the exterior by infilling the framework with polychromed terracotta tiles, a technique remarkably similar to Viollet-le-Duc's rendering of 1863.[31]

In fact, Viollet-le-Duc would succeed in leading the French architectural community to focus on the issue of exposed iron framing in 1872 with the publication of the second volume of his *Entretiens sur l'architecture.* Now, nine years after the publication of his enticing but unexplained rendering of *pan de fer* construction in the 1863 *Atlas,* he was

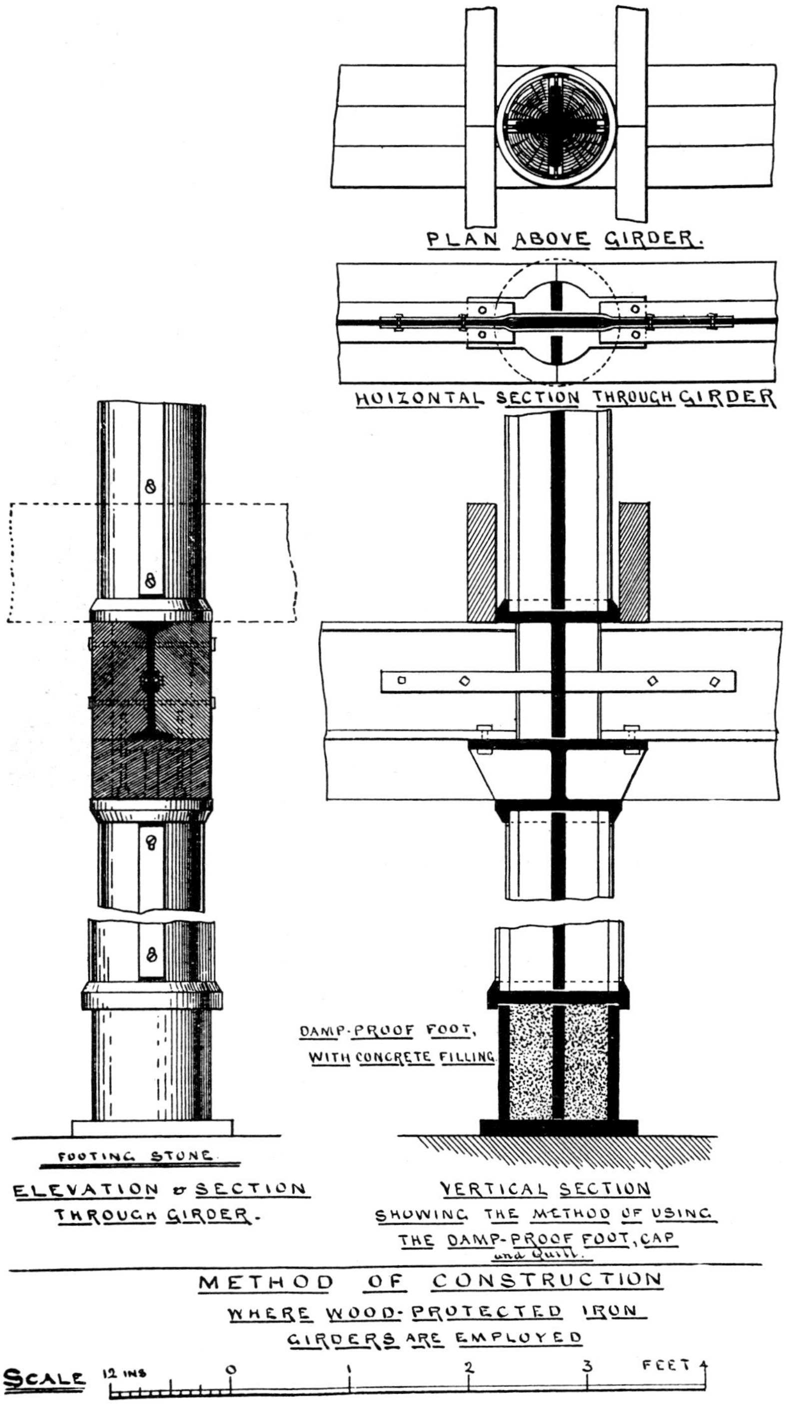

PLAN ABOVE GIRDER.

HOIZONTAL SECTION THROUGH GIRDER

DAMP-PROOF FOOT,
WITH CONCRETE FILLING

FOOTING STONE

ELEVATION & SECTION
THROUGH GIRDER.

YERTICAL SECTION
SHOWING THE METHOD OF USING
THE DAMP-PROOF FOOT, CAP
and Quill.

METHOD   OF   CONSTRUCTION
WHERE WOOD-PROTECTED IRON
GIRDERS ARE EMPLOYED

SCALE 12 INS   0   1   2   3   FEET 4

Figs. 10/11 William H. Drake and Peter B. Wight, Fireproof design of iron columns encased in wood and terracotta, 1874; from Brickbuilder *6 (Aug. 1897).*

cago Fire would confront that city's architects and builders with the problem of fireproofing the iron frame.

The person responsible for transferring the French technique of fireproofed iron construction to Chicago was George H. Johnson, Daniel Badger's former chief designer and architect of the U. S. Warehousing grain elevator of 1860. Following the end of the Civil War, Johnson resumed his earlier efforts to fireproof grain elevators. On March 7, 1869, he patented a system of hollow clay-tile blocks to construct fireproof grain bins. Pursuing his interest in fireproofing systems, he apparently traveled to France early in 1871 to study the latest developments in fireproof floor construction. Johnson coupled this new information with his experience in clay manufacturing, and collaborated with Balthazar Kreischer to patent on March 2, 1871, a hollow clay-tile floor system that consisted of a one-piece floor arch that spanned the space between iron channels.[33]

It is unclear whether Johnson left New York for Chicago just prior to or immediately after the fire of October 8-10, 1871, to promote his system of hollow tile walls and floors. Chicago architect John M. Van Osdel, for whom Johnson had worked fourteen years earlier in the erection of the cast-iron fronts on Lake Street, provided Johnson with his first contract, the fireproofing of the Kendall Building at 40 North Dearborn Street. Van Osdel had actually begun to design this building earlier in 1871, prior to the fire. It was originally planned (fig. 9) to be the best, and at six stories the tallest, building in Chicago, the height and construction undoubtedly due to the building's major tenant, the Equitable Life Assurance Company of New York.[34]

Equitable had moved into a brand new building in New York City in May 1870. Initially designed in 1867 by Arthur D. Gilman and Edward H. Kendall, it had been completed by George B. Post, a young engineer/architect hired by Equitable to revise the design within cost guidelines. This building marked the beginning of the post-Civil War construction boom in the United States, reviving the development of the American skyscraper from where it had left off in 1861. Architectural historians increasingly agree that the Equitable Building was the first American skyscraper, for although it contained only five floors, its total height was 130 feet, more than double that of any comparable structure. This was the result of a decision by Equitable's vice-president, Henry B. Hyde, to exploit the potential of the elevator and make the floor-to-floor height in each story almost double that of traditional walkup buildings.[35]

providing a theoretical and technical basis for the evolving French technique of the encased iron frame:

A practical architect might not unnaturally conceive the idea of erecting a vast edifice whose frame should be entirely of iron, and clothing that frame – preserving it by means of a casing of stone.[32]

His challenge would not find its final resolution in France, however, for the Prussians had marched into Paris on January 28, 1871, bringing the Second Empire to an end. The final peace treaty was signed on May 10, 1871, only five months before the Chi-

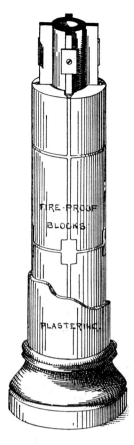

Chicago was also experiencing a postwar building boom, which accounts for the Equitable Company's proposal to erect in Chicago an even taller building with six floors, one more than their New York building. Van Osdel's pre-fire Kendall Building in Chicago was the next logical step in the evolution of the skyscraper that had begun with the Equitable Building, and reveals that, prior to the October fire, Chicago was just as ready and able to build skyscrapers as was New York.[36] Unfortunately, the holocaust of October 8-10, 1871, put an end to Chicago's chance to compete with New York in the next stage of that evolution. The Kendall's foundations had been laid and the lower walls were under construction when the fire broke out. Construction on the building resumed after the fire, but because of the problems plaguing early passenger elevators and the inability of the Chicago Fire Department to fight conflagrations in the upper floors of a tall building, it was decided to build only five of the Kendall's originally proposed six floors.[37] Thus, instead of starting Chicago's development of the skyscraper, as most historians have claimed, the 1871 Fire actually snuffed out Chicago's first planned skyscraper and postponed the city's reentry into the race with New York for nine years. While Chicago struggled to rebuild, New York continued to construct taller buildings like the Western Union Telegraph Building (230 feet) designed in 1872 by George B. Post, and the New York Tribune Building (260 feet) designed in 1873 by Richard Morris Hunt.

Instead of aiming for height, the objective of the Kendall Building now became to erect a completely fireproof building. Its five stories consisted of exterior masonry walls enclosing and supporting a cage of cast-iron columns and wrought-iron beams and joists, which supported Johnson's hollow tile flat arches. As yet, it had not been possible to ascertain where Johnson would have had such a large volume of clay tiles produced. The facts suggest that they were manufactured by architect Sanford Loring's Chicago Terra Cotta Company, which had recently incorporated the latest English innovations in the manufacture of terracotta, and had become the leading producer of this material in the United States.[38]

Unfortunately, the panic of September 1873 and the ensuing depression put a quick stop to Chicago's rebuilding efforts as well as to construction throughout the United States. Johnson's hollow tile floor system, too expensive for the hurried rebuilding of Chicago, never gained acceptance, and the economic collapse forced him to retreat to New York early in 1874. In addition, the insurance companies that had paid out millions on claims

from the Great Fire and had also loaned a substantial sum for the reconstruction of the city, found defaults on these loans increasing at an alarming rate after the 1873 panic. As a result, they came into possession of large amounts of real estate, especially in Chicago's business district. Meanwhile, the dangerous conditions that had contributed to the rapid spread of the Great Fire in the business district and Near North Side still existed on the South Side, which had been left untouched by that fire and awaited a similar fate. On July 14, 1874, forty-seven acres bounded by Clark, Polk, Michigan, and Van Buren burned with an intensity reminiscent of the recent holocaust. Although the fire was stopped when it reached the rebuilt business district, the insurance companies realized that the defaulted property they now held was in potential danger. On the night following the second fire, the National Board of Underwriters met and demanded that Chicago's Common Council immediately enact reforms pertaining both to construction and the fire department, or else face the cancellation of all existing fire insurance policies.[39]

The 1874 outbreak had confirmed the suspicions of many of cast iron's detractors about its ability to withstand fire. One of the new regulations promoted by the insurance companies was the prohibition of the use of cast-iron columns in favor of heavy timber framing. This action threatened the entire structural iron market of N. S. Bouton's Union Foundry in Chicago and forced him to take an active role in developing a fireproofing system for iron framing. In August 1874, only three weeks after the second fire, Bouton offered the use of his plant, as well as iron columns, to test a method of fireproofing iron columns with wood that had been quickly devised by Chicago architects Peter B. Wight and William Drake. Within a month after the second fire they had allowed their design (fig. 10) to be exposed to a controlled test fire, but the results were inconclusive. Nevertheless, Drake and Wight patented their invention on September 8, 1874.[40]

Meanwhile, the Common Council continued to ignore the insurance companies' threats, and on October 1, 1874, the National Board formally requested that its members cancel all current fire insurance policies covering property within Chicago. On October 8, only a week after these policies began to be withdrawn (and symbolically the third anniversary of the 1871 Fire), Wight and Drake ran a successful test at Bouton's foundry. However, the wood-encased column was never used. A portion of the test furnace was constructed with hollow clay tiles from Loring's Chicago Terra Cotta Company. These were similar to Johnson's

Figs. 12/13 James McLaughlin, Shillito's Department Store, 7th and Race streets, Cincinnati, 1877-78, exterior and ground-floor plan with details of interior columns and girders; from American Architect and Building News *2, 94 (Oct. 13, 1877).*

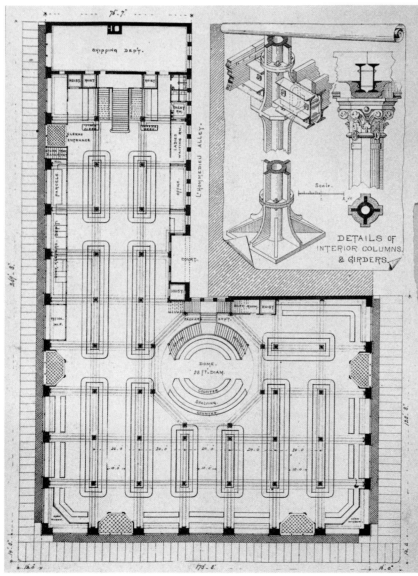

original wall units with one important exception. They were made of porous terracotta, a new material Loring had recently developed as a lightweight substitute for Johnson's fireclay in order to circumvent the latter's patent. Porous terracotta's insulative properties proved to be a distinct advantage over hardwood. Realizing this, Wight quickly revised his system to use the new material (fig. 11). In essence, Wight and Loring had coupled an English material with French theory to solve an American problem.[41]

As noted earlier, Bogardus and Badger had developed the iron skeleton frame in New York during the 1850s. What kept the New York iron frame from gaining universal acceptance was iron's inherent lack of resistance to the heat of fire. It is the solution to this problem, and not the origin of iron skeleton framing, that is Chicago's true claim to fame. The innovation of the Chicago skeleton-framed skyscraper was to support the exterior masonry envelope, especially the fireproof covering of the column, completely on the iron frame, thereby relieving the masonry from any load-bearing function. Since Wight's column was the first successful example of a masonry covering being mechanically attached to an iron column, it is appropriate to state that the Chicago iron skeleton frame was officially born in 1874, the product of Peter B. Wight and Sanford Loring. Over the course of the next six years, Wight and Loring mounted a campaign that eventually convinced American builders of the soundness of their system. Meanwhile, iron construction continued to be refined to the point of being ready to utilize Wight's system when the economy rebounded in 1880. This came about primarily through the efforts of one man, but he was French rather than American.

In 1875 Gustave Eiffel burst on to the international scene, winning two large, important foreign commissions: the new railroad station for Pest, Hungary, and the Maria-Pia Bridge over the Douro River at Oporto, Portugal.[42] The following year Eiffel began to design a series of wrought-iron, multistory, skylighted atriums throughout Paris.[43] The revision of the Paris building code, which allowed the use of exterior iron framing in 1878, unleashed Eiffel's *pièce de résistance*, the addition to the Grands Magasins du Bon Marché. Designed with L. C. Boileau, the freestanding wrought-iron framework soared for five stories at various points throughout the store.[44]

This change in the Paris building code would become a fitting memorial to Viollet-le-Duc, who had led the fight and who lived to see the acceptance of the exterior iron frame just prior to his death on September 17, 1879. The aesthetic potential of this decision, foreseen by his rendering of sixteen years earlier, would be quickly realized by Parisian architects. One of the more exciting structures following the code's revision was Paul Sédille's new Magasins du Printemps, designed in 1881 to replace the building that had burned in March 1881. A sixty-five-foot-high central atrium was surrounded by seven stories of freestanding wrought iron skeleton framing, painted gray-blue on the interior.[45]

In the United States, the department store was also a major vehicle for the development of the iron frame, and although its design was not technically as advanced as the French, the American version was at least equal, if not grander, in size and spatial effect. In 1877, Cincinnati dry goods merchant John Shillito built the country's largest department store (fig. 12) under one roof, designed by architect James McLaughlin. He conceived its seven floors to be as open visually and spatially as possible. There were no interior bearing walls to divide the huge floors into smaller spaces, for the structure consisted of an iron skeleton frame surrounded on the exterior by masonry piers (fig. 13). This effect was further enhanced by the central atrium that was sixty feet in diameter and extended through every floor for the entire height of 120 feet to the underside of the iron and glass domed skylight. It was the exterior of this building, however, that made a direct impact on Chicago's architecture in the coming decade. McLaughlin designed a plain exterior of a rectilinear gridwork of red pressed brick that was orchestrated in a tripartite scheme of a two-story base, a three-story shaft, and a capital that incorporated the top floor and parapet.[46]

Shillito's store opened on September 1, 1878. Within a year, his major midwestern competitors, Marshall Field and Levi Leiter, had hired William Le Baron Jenney to design a small, five-story warehouse (fig. 14) for the northwest corner of Wells and Monroe streets.[47] Jenney's elevations for what is now called the first Leiter Building (usually acknowledged as the first building of the Chicago School) is almost a direct copy of McLaughlin's design.[48] The true significance of Jenney's building, however, is that he took the skeleton structure of Shillito's building one step further by using the French technique of placing an iron pilaster on the inside face of the masonry piers in the Wells Street front to support the timber floor girders. This relieved these masonry piers from carrying any floor loads and allowed them to be reduced in section. This maximized the size of the windows to admit more daylight. Nonetheless, it was far from a true skeleton frame such as the French were construct-

Fig. 14 William Le Baron Jenney, First Leiter Building, 208 West Monroe Street, 1879 (demolished); top two stories were added in 1888.

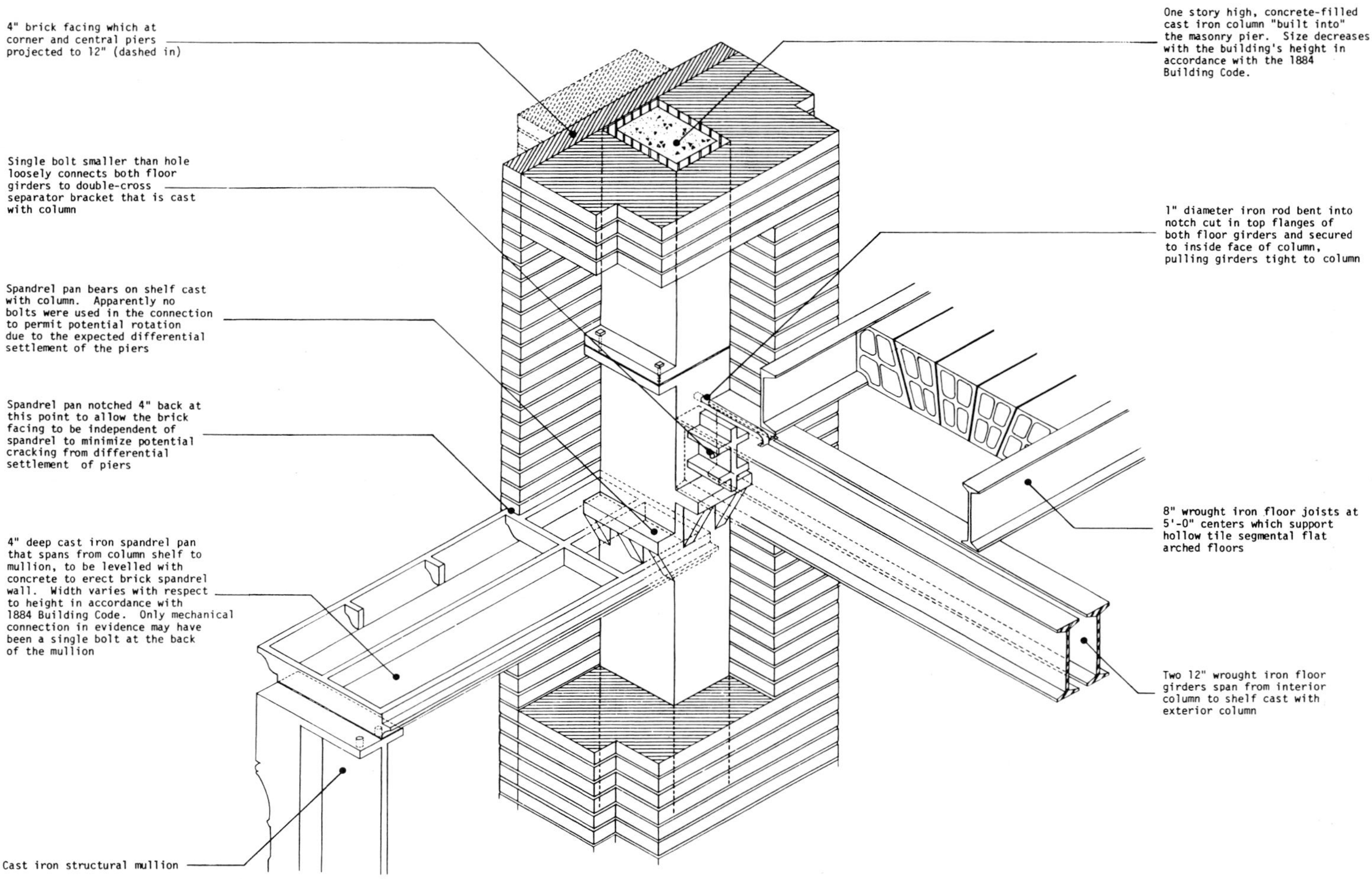

4" brick facing which at corner and central piers projected to 12" (dashed in)

Single bolt smaller than hole loosely connects both floor girders to double-cross separator bracket that is cast with column

Spandrel pan bears on shelf cast with column. Apparently no bolts were used in the connection to permit potential rotation due to the expected differential settlement of the piers

Spandrel pan notched 4" back at this point to allow the brick facing of spandrel to be independent of spandrel to minimize potential cracking from differential settlement of piers

4" deep cast iron spandrel pan that spans from column shelf to mullion, to be levelled with concrete to erect brick spandrel wall. Width varies with respect to height in accordance with 1884 Building Code. Only mechanical connection in evidence may have been a single bolt at the back of the mullion

Cast iron structural mullion

One story high, concrete-filled cast iron column "built into" the masonry pier. Size decreases with the building's height in accordance with the 1884 Building Code.

1" diameter iron rod bent into notch cut in top flanges of both floor girders and secured to inside face of column, pulling girders tight to column

8" wrought iron floor joists at 5'-0" centers which support hollow tile segmental flat arched floors

Two 12" wrought iron floor girders span from interior column to shelf cast with exterior column

Fig. 15 Reconstruction of the structural system of the exterior piers used by Jenney in the Home Insurance Building; drawing by Deborah Cohen and Maxwell Merriman.

Fig. 16 Home Insurance Building during demolition in 1931.

ing at the time, for the masonry piers still carried the iron spandrel beams. Moreover, the Monroe Street masonry piers did not contain the iron pilasters, therefore they still supported the portion of the floor that framed into them.

A comparison between Eiffel's Bon Marché wrought-iron skeletal structure of 1878 and Jenney's comparatively crude attempt at exterior iron framing of 1879 reveals how much more advanced the French were in iron construction than Chicago's builders and enables one to evaluate critically the structural system (fig. 15) that Jenney employed in 1884 in the Home Insurance Building. The only departure from standard early 1880s construction in the Home Insurance Building was in the two street facades. The two rear masonry bearing party walls that ran the entire height of the building and the interior iron cage were typical for the period. In fact, even the first two floors of the street fronts consisted of rock-faced granite piers. Upon these were set story-high, hollow rectangular cast-iron columns, bolted one on top of another to support the upper seven floors and roof. The columns were filled with concrete and surrounded with brick that at times was as thick as twelve inches, creating a solid cross section in the building's exterior piers (fig. 16).[49]

To support the windows and masonry spandrels between the piers, cast-iron lintels in the form of four-inch deep hollow pans, also filled with concrete like the columns, spanned from a column shelf bracket to an intermediate cast-iron mullion. The cast-iron lintels were not one continuous piece but comprised two halves that joined over the mullions. The lintels were evidently not bolted to either the column brackets or the mullions, but simply rested on the bearing surfaces, apparently relying on the supported masonry knee wall that was bonded into the masonry pier to hold the iron armature in place laterally. While the iron lintels carried the weight of the masonry spandrels to the iron mullions and columns, the resulting structure was far from being a rigid, self-supporting iron skeleton that independently carried its masonry envelope at each floor, which the Home Insurance Building was later claimed to have been.[50]

From the evidence on record, we can conclude that the iron frame conceived and used by Jenney was not entirely self-sufficient and independent of the masonry. To begin with, he initially did not refer to the masonry as a covering, but always stated that he embedded the iron column within the masonry pier in order to reduce its size and maximize the amount of daylight.[51] Second, the lintel pans were not bolted to the columns, so rigidity of the mullion/lintel assembly was gained through the masonry spandrel wall. Third, the exterior brick facing of the piers was not supported on the iron column at any point, thus it was continuously bearing from the granite piers. Finally, without the rigidity of the two rear party walls and the masonry piers, the iron frame with its loosely bolted and clamped connections could not have resisted any wind loads.

Therefore, the historical significance of the Home Insurance Building's structure is that it marked the first extensive use in the United States of iron in the exterior of a multistory building to support a portion of its masonry enclosure since Badger's grain elevators of 1860 and 1862.[52] However, when compared to Eiffel's riveted fixed connections or to Sédille's seven-story wrought-iron frame in the Magasins du Printemps, designed three years earlier, Jenney's loosely bolted, eight-story framework of masonry-stiffened cast-iron columns appears somewhat anachronistic. Not surprisingly, following Jenney's description of its structural system at the 1885 A. I. A. convention in October, the Home Insurance Building and the potential of its "revolutionary" system were not discussed for the next two and a half years in American trade magazines and conference proceedings.[53] Why was no one in Chicago apparently

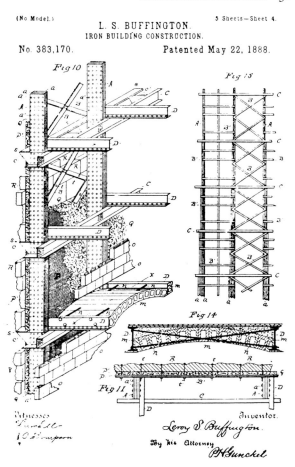

Fig. 17 Leroy S. Buffington, Patent for iron building construction, 1888; from Art Bulletin 26 (Mar. 1944).

Fig. 18 Leroy S. Buffington, Proposed twenty-eight-story "Cloudscraper," 1887; from Inland Architect and News Record 11 (July 1888).

interested in exploiting the potential of the system?[54] This begs the question of what was responsible for the next step in the evolution of the iron
skeleton frame that eventually led to the final resolution of the technique.

On May 22, 1888, three years after the completion of the Home Insurance Building, a patent for a
system of self-supporting wrought-iron framing intended for tall buildings (fig. 17) was granted to
Minneapolis architect Leroy S. Buffington.[55] Two
months earlier he had published an article extolling
the almost unlimited height potential of such a
system in the March 1888 issue of *Northwestern
Architect*.[56] Appropriately, there was no mention
of the Home Insurance Building as a precedent in
any of the early articles pertaining to Buffington's
system, for his design had made an important departure from Jenney's structure. As opposed to the
Home Insurance Building, Buffington's rigid system (with no dependence on masonry) utilized
built-up wrought-iron columns (not cast-iron) that
were riveted (not bolted) to floor girders as well as
iron shelf angles that supported the building's lightweight masonry and glass envelope at each floor.
This revolutionary system allowed him to propose
his "Cloudscraper," a twenty-eight-story office
tower (fig. 18), which was more than twice the
height of any office building then in existence. The

design was published in the July 1888 issue of
Inland Architect.[57]

While Buffington never erected a building based
on this system, his patent and corresponding project were historically significant, marking the true
beginning of the interest in, and development of,
skeleton framing in America. For even though the
proposal was scoffed at, especially on the East
Coast, it set the minds of a number of architects and
engineers to working on the eventual resolution of
the skeleton frame.[58] The Home Insurance Building generated no comparable contemporary exposure or influence.

As was the case with Johnson's earlier solution to
building fireproof floors, Buffington's idea for
wrought-iron framing most likely was inspired by
the more technically advanced iron structures being erected by the French, best represented in the
riveted iron structures of Eiffel. As the Home Insurance Building was being completed in the spring
of 1885, the United States literally imported Eiffel's technology by shipping the Statue of Liberty,
fabricated in France, across the Atlantic Ocean.
The statue arrived on June 17, 1885. Eiffel had
designed the ninety-six-foot-high riveted wrought-
iron framework that supported and was enclosed
by Auguste Bartholdi's copper-plated statue. Erection of the diagonally crossbraced tower began in

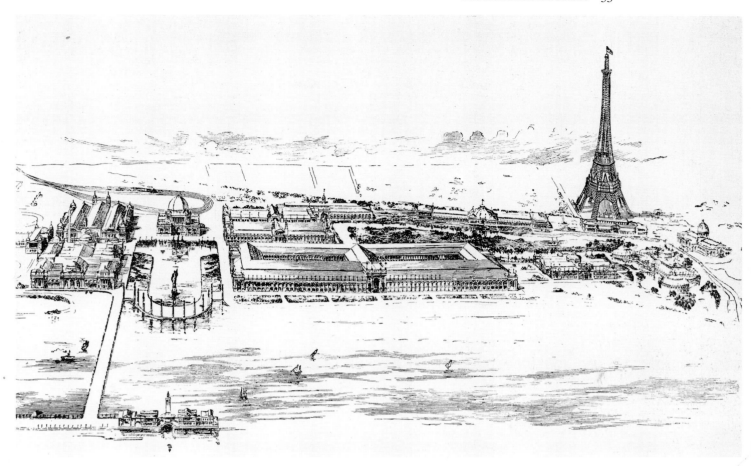

the spring of 1886 and its dedication took place on October 28, 1886.[59] It is thought that Buffington began to work on his iron system early in 1886, having been inspired by an article by Jenney in the December 1885 issue of *Inland Architect* which described the structure of the Home Insurance Building.[60] However, during the period in which Buffington developed and refined his patent application — from winter 1886 until November 14, 1887, when he submitted his application — the Statue of Liberty was under construction and in the news, but, more importantly, the first articles of Eiffel's proposed 300-meter iron tower were published in the United States. (Eiffel's design was officially chosen on June 12, 1886.) Buffington's final design employed riveted wrought-iron plates and diagonal lattice bracing, a technique much more in line with Eiffel's structures than with Jenney's unbraced and loosely bolted cast-iron columns.

Even more indicative of Buffington's apparent awareness of Eiffel's tower design is his entry for the Indiana State Soldiers and Sailors Monument competition (fig. 19), published in the April 1888 issue of *Inland Architect*.[61] The sleek, parabolic profile of Buffington's tower bore a striking resemblance to Eiffel's tower, by then under construction and attracting the attention of the world's building community. Buffington's "Cloudscraper," towering over the tallest ten-story buildings of America's cities and most likely inspired by the image of the Eiffel Tower soaring over Paris, was to ignite the imagination of Chicago's designers and builders and prompt them to solve the problem of the iron-framed skyscraper. Within two years of the publication of Buffington's "Cloudscraper" design, Burnham and Root had realized the potential of the iron frame in the 302-foot-high, twenty-one story Masonic Temple building in Chicago (see Klotz, fig. 7). That city's interest in the Eiffel Tower was so strong that a proposal was made in the summer of 1889 to erect a similar iron tower (figs. 20, 21) even taller than Eiffel's for Chicago's 1893 World's Columbian Exposition.[62] Although the idea was ultimately rejected in 1891 because it did not fit the neoclassical style chosen for the Fair, it is hard to imagine a more fitting tribute by Chicago in recognition of its debt to France's master builders with iron in the development of the skyscraper.

Figs. 20/21 David Proctor, Proposed "Columbian Tower," for the World's Columbian Exposition, 1890; bird's-eye view and elevation; from H. G. Cutler, The World's Fair (Chicago, 1891).

THE COLUMBIAN TOWER.

NOTES

1. Even Chicago's professional press at the time did not consider the Home Insurance Building to be the first skyscraper in Chicago. The August 2, 1884, issue of *Real Estate and Building Journal* listed ten Chicago buildings that it considered to be "skyscrapers." Three of these (S. S. Beman's Pullman Palace Car Building, W. W. Boyington's Royal Insurance Building, and Burnham and Root's Insurance Exchange Building) were already completed and were taller than the final height of the Home Insurance Building, which at the time of this article was only two stories out of the ground. "High Towers and Buildings," *Real Estate and Building Journal* (Aug. 2, 1884), p. 364.
2. The profile of the tower was conical, tapering from a base diameter of 100 feet to a mere 12 feet at the top. Trevithick proposed to build the tower with curved cast-iron plates two inches thick and ten feet square. These were to be formed with a six-foot circular hole in the center in order to reduce both the dead weight of the structure and its resistance to wind. In addition, the panels were to be cast with perimeter flanges that would allow them to be stacked on top of each other and bolted together from the inside. Frank I. Jenkins, "Harbingers of Eiffel's Tower," *Journal of the Society of Architectural Historians* 16 (Dec. 1957), pp. 22-24.
3. For a comprehensive survey of the early history of cast-iron framing, see Turpin C. Bannister, "The First Iron-Framed Buildings," *The Architectural Review* 107 (Apr. 1950), pp. 231-46. Reprinted in *The Garland Library of the History of Art: Volume 11 – Nineteenth and Twentieth Century Architecture* (New York, 1976), pp. 73-88. Also consult R. J. M. Sutherland, "Pioneer British Contributions to Structural Iron and Concrete: 1770-1855," *Building Early America*, ed. Charles E. Peterson (Radnor, Penn., 1976), pp. 96-118.
4. Sutherland (note 3), p. 104. Independent, freestanding iron frames did evolve in the first third of the nineteenth century in England. However, these were all single-story roofing systems that typically employed arched members, thereby avoiding the critical connection of beam to column. The better-known examples of this type of framing include Thomas Rickman and John Cragg's prefabricated cast-iron churches of 1813-16 and John Claudius Loudon's greenhouses of 1817-31.
5. Henry-Russell Hitchcock, "Sullivan and the Skyscraper," *Journal of the Royal Institute of British Architects* 60 (July 1953), p. 354. Reprinted in *Garland* (note 3), p. 118. This was a cruel twist of fate, for the following year (1845) the Glass Tax was repealed, reducing the cost of glass and thus encouraging its greater use in buildings.
6. John Ruskin, *The Seven Lamps of Architecture* (New York, 1961), p. 44.
7. Turpin C. Bannister, "Bogardus Revisited – Part I: The Iron Fronts," *Journal of the Society of Architectural Historians* 15 (Dec. 1956), p. 12.
8. Bannister (note 7), p. 12 and 15. During the 1830s and 1840s entire buildings, from lighthouses to factories, were prefabricated in iron and shipped to the distant outposts of the British Empire. Not only were many of these structures independently rigid, but their exteriors also consisted of exposed cast iron and glass. Much of the credit for their development can be given to William Fairbairn, an engineer committed to the use of iron in ships and bridges, as well as in buildings.
9. For a survey of early American iron structures, see Bannister (note 7) and Carl W. Condit, *American Building* (Chicago, 1982).
10. Turpin C. Bannister, "Bogardus Revisited – Part II: The Iron Towers," *Journal of the Society of Architectural Historians* 16 (Mar. 1957), pp. 11-12. His failure to win the fair commission apparently was not a reflection of a lack of confidence in Bogardus's tower system, for he did build a second bell tower in 1853 near the corner of Macdougal and Spring streets.
11. James Bogardus, *Cast Iron Buildings: Their Construction and Advantages* (New York, 1856), pp. 7-8.
12. Jenkins (note 2), p. 25. Although the contractors of the Crystal Palace stated that such a project was feasible, it is obvious that the original structural members were not capable of sustaining loads of such magnitude.
13. France's earliest known multistory cast-iron structure had been erected in 1838 in the Galeries du Commerce et de l'Industrie in Paris, designed by J. L. V. Grisart and C. M. A. Froehlicher. The masonry building contained a four-story skylighted atrium that used iron columns to support the upper three levels of balconies which surrounded the open court. Frances H. Steiner, *French Iron Architecture* (Ann Arbor, Mich., 1984), p. 57 and pl. 21. Steiner's work contains a comprehensive survey of the development of French iron construction up to 1900.
14. While the English were to address the problem of the rigidity of the iron frame during the period of 1834-45, the French still had to rely on masonry to stabilize their iron structures. In 1833, Charles Rohault de Fleury designed France's first large-scale greenhouse for the Jardin des Plantes, after having traveled to England to observe English methods of construction with iron and glass. Although he was able to duplicate the English cast-iron column and arched beam, the structure still relied on a northern exterior masonry wall for stability. Steiner (note 13), pp. 37-38.

In 1836, France's most noted iron structure of this era, the market hall of the Madelene, designed by M. G. Veugny as early as 1824, was finally erected. Although it used cast-iron columns to support wrought-iron trusses that spanned forty feet, the connections were such that it too had to rely on its masonry exterior for stability. Apparently, even this was somewhat insufficient, for a storm led to the collapse of the structure eight years later. Steiner (note 13), pp. 47-48, 79.

In 1839, architect Henri Labrouste designed the Bibliothèque Ste.-Geneviève. The roof over the second-story reading room is entirely spanned by a series of double iron arches that meet at and are supported by a row of iron columns running down the center of the building; at the perimeter the arches bear on the exterior masonry wall. Without these, Labrouste's weak connections would not have been able to resist the wind loads.
15. Steiner (note 13), pp. 92-93.
16. Ibid., pp. 48-51. David H. Pinckney, *Napoleon III and the Rebuilding of Paris* (Princeton, N. J., 1958), pp. 76-79.
17. Steiner (note 13), pp. 14, 102.
18. Eugène-Emmanuel Viollet-le-Duc's letter to Adolphe Lance, translated in *Eugène-Emmanuel Viollet-le-Duc* (London, 1980), pp. 55.
19. Bannister (note 10), pp. 12-14.
20. Sutherland (note 3), pp. 114-15 and Nikolaus Pevsner, *Pioneers of Modern Design* (Baltimore, 1975), p. 124.
21. Thomas Eddy Tallmadge, *Architecture in Old Chicago* (Chicago, 1941), p. 109; Bannister (note 10), p. 18, n. 110. Johnson (1830-1879) began his apprenticeship at the age of sixteen in the Manchester construction firm of Robert Neil and Sons. Alfred T. Andreas, *History of Chicago* (Chicago, 1885), vol. 3, p. 87. Van Osdel's Venetian fronts may well have been the model for Badger's best known building, the five-story E. V. Haughwout & Co. Building at Broadway and Broome Street. Designed in 1857 by architect John P. Gaynor, also in a Venetian Renaissance mode, it is famous as the site of the first known commercial installation of an Elisha Graves Otis safety elevator in New York.
22. Bannister (note 10), p. 18, n. 107. Daniel D. Badger, *Illustrations of Iron Architecture* (New York, 1856), pp. 7, 23. Peter B. Wight later mentioned that the exterior of the elevator was "constructed of a cast-iron framework filled in with a light wall of brick, the iron showing on the outside. There is also a shot tower in New York, which was built about the same time in the same manner." Peter B. Wight, "Recent Fireproof Buildings in Chicago-Part 2," *Inland Architect and News Record* 19 (Mar. 1892), p. 22. This would tend to confirm the influence that the construction of the McCullough Shot Tower had on Johnson, as it was only a block away from Badger's office. In 1862, Badger was contracted to build a similar elevator for the Pennsylvania Railroad on Washington Street in Philadelphia.
23. The A. T. Stewart Building was gutted by fire on July 14, 1956, revealing that the majority of the building was indeed skeleton-framed with iron in the interior as well as the exterior. Alan Burnham, "Last Look at a Structural Landmark," *Architectural Record* (Sept. 1956), pp. 273-79.
24. With the exception of Les Halles and the 1855 Palais de l'Industrie, however, the French had not yet divorced the iron frame from its masonry wall prior to 1863 as shown by Henri Labrouste's 1859 design for the four-story skylighted stacks for the Bibliothèque Nationale.
25. Steiner (note 13), p. 101. At the same time, France's engineers also began to push the iron-framed tower to greater heights. For example, in 1858, an engineer named Mathieu designed a 279-foot high iron water tower in Lyons, some 62 feet taller than Bogardus's Tatham Shot Tower done two years earlier. The hexagonal plan of the water tower consisted of six hollow cast-iron columns that sloped inwards to the central iron water pipe. As opposed to Bogardus's bolted connections, however, Mathieu had to rely on diagonal crossbracing to make the skeleton rigid. Steiner (note 13), pp. 114-16.
26. Ibid., pp. 14-15 and 107.
27. To reduce the impact of their shadows, the buildings stepped back at the sixth floor, revealing a continuous pedestrian walkway system that linked the various buildings with skybridges. Steiner (note 13), pp. 120-21 cites Peter Wolf, "Urban Redevelopment 19th Century Style: Older, Bolder Ideas for Today," *Design Quarterly* 85 (1972), pp. 10-15. Another scheme for Paris that utilized ten-story buildings was proposed by Jules-Antoine Moilin in 1869.
28. Closely resembling the design of England's first exposed iron-framed building, the Royal Navy's Fire Station at Portsmouth erected over twenty years earlier, Préfontaine's exterior cast-iron columns were connected by beams with an arched bottom chord. The columns were formed with a semicircular exterior face and flat internal back that had a perpendicular rib to allow the masonry enclosure to be built flush with the column, the projecting rib anchoring the wall to the column (or vice versa). Steiner (note 13), pp. 104-5 and pl. 60.
29. Some of the better known fireproof apartment buildings in Paris were designed by architects like Stanislas Ferrand, and builders like Maurice Grand and F. Liger, who, in 1871, succeeded in erecting a five-story apartment building at the corner of rue de Bourgogne and rue de Lillie, supported entirely on an iron skeleton frame, with the legal exception of the masonry street facade. Steiner (note 13), pp. 105-6 and pls. 62-63.
30. Ibid., pp. 59-61.
31. Ibid., pp. 110-11.
32. Eugène-Emmanuel Viollet-le-Duc, *Entretiens sur l'architecture,* trans. Benjamin Bucknall (Boston, 1881), p. 128.
33. Andreas (note 21), p. 87; Peter B. Wight, "Details of Fire-proof Construction with Burned Clay – Part 2," *Brickbuilder* (Sept. 1897), p. 201; Bannister (note 10), pp. 14, 19n. 107, Johnson had actually seen this technique in the Cooper Union, built in New York City in 1854. Designed by architect Frederick A. Peterson, it incorporated one-piece, hollow clay-tile floor arches that had been molded by hand and then fired. These spanned between two three-by-six-inch rolled wrought-iron channels that were spaced on two-foot-six-inch centers. This was an attempt by Peterson to improve the building's resistance to fire, a technique that he later patented on April 3, 1855. The Union's interior cast-iron frame, as well as the first-floor cast-iron storefront, was manufactured by Badger, for whom Johnson was working at the time. Peter B. Wight, "Origin and History of Hollow Tile Fireproof Floor Construction – Part I," *Brickbuilder* (Mar. 1897), p. 54. Johnson and Kreischer's system consisted of a monolithic piece that spanned between joists. The only difference from Peterson's patent was a set of recesses formed in the top of the piece to receive wood sleepers for the flooring. The monolithic nature of the design is curious in that patented French systems that incorporated segmental arches had been in existence for at least five years.
34. "The Kendall Block," *Land Owner* 3 (Oct. 1871), p. 316; Henry Ericsson, *Sixty Years a Builder* (Chicago, 1942), pp. 205-6. The Equitable Company's concern over fireproofing was also manifested in the Kendall's original design. It was to have been entirely fireproof, as even the mansard roof was to have been of iron, instead of the usual wood. In essence, then, the original Kendall design can be viewed as a New York exterior enclosing the latest New York concerns with fireproofing. Peter B. Wight, "The Fire Question – Part III," *American Architect and Building News* 1 (July 1, 1876), p. 209.

35. Winston Weisman, "New York and the Problem of the First Skyscraper," *Society of Architectural Historians Journal* 12 (Mar. 1953), pp. 13-21. The fact that the Equitable's five-story building was designed two years after Borie's eleven-story *Aérodômes,* however, does emphasize the revolutionary nature of the French proposal and the commanding position of Paris's urban design at this time.

36. The quality of Van Osdel's design as well as the fact that it was contemporary with New York developments raises some doubts concerning Henry-Russell Hitchcock's assertion that "if the Chicago architectural scene had any virtues around 1880, they were largely negative ones: no established traditions, no real professional leaders, and ignorance of all architectural styles past or present." Henry-Russell Hichtcock, *Architecture: Nineteenth and Twentieth Centuries* (Harmondsworth, England, and New York, 1977), p. 337. Peter B. Wight's national stature within the A. I. A. and his command of Ruskinian Gothic, as well as William Le Baron Jenney's knowledge of architectural history and first-hand acquaintance with Viollet-le-Duc's works in Paris, call into question the accuracy of Hitchcock's assumptions.

37. Ericsson (note 34), p. 206.

38. The floor tiles were nine inches thick and formed with side angles of eighteen degrees. Also for the first time in commercial building, the wall partitions were of Johnson's hollow tile units. "Johnson's Fireproof Hollow Tile, Flat-Arch Walls and Ceilings," *Land Owner* 4 (July 1872), p. 115. Ericsson also alludes to the possibility that Loring had made the tile for the Kendall. Ericsson (note 34), p. 206. Loring had been a draftsman for Van Osdel and enjoyed a close personal relationship with his former employer.

From the beginning of the Chicago Terra Cotta Company in 1868, Loring had close ties with the business and showed a keen interest in the use of terracotta in building. Loring's junior architectural partner at this time was the young William Le Baron Jenney, who had moved to Chicago in 1867. Concerned about the quality of his product, Loring wrote to the world's largest terracotta company, John M. Stamford of England, and eventually secured the talents of the company's foreman, James Taylor, who arrived in Chicago in August 1870.

Due to its location, Loring's plant had not been harmed by the fire. It may be more than just coincidence that by the summer of 1872, when production of the great amount of clay tile required for the Kendall Building would have begun, Loring had left his architectural practice to become the president of the Chicago Terra Cotta Company. For a history of the Chicago Terra Cotta Company, see: "The Manufacture of Terra-Cotta in Chicago," *The American Architect and Building News* 1 (Dec. 30, 1876), p. 420, and Sharon S. Darling, *Chicago Ceramics and Glass* (Chicago, 1979).

39. Chad Wallin, *The Builder's Story* (Chicago, 1966), p. 3; Wight, "Origin and History..." (note 33), p. 54.

40. Wight encased a cruciform iron section with four pieces of red oak that were attached to the column by recessed plates and screws. Wrought-iron battens covered the joints between the pieces of wood and plaster of paris was poured in from the top of the assembly to fill all of the gaps between the metal and the wood. Wight (note 34), p. 209; idem, "Fireproof Columns," *American Architect and Building News* 1 (Jan. 22, 1876), p. 29; and Sarah Landau, *Peter B. Wight: Architect, Contractor, and Critic, 1838-1925* (Chicago, 1980), p. 45.

41. Wight (note 34), p. 210; "Fireproof Columns" (note 40), p. 30; "Terra-Cotta," (note 38), p. 421; Peter B. Wight, "Details of Fire-Proof Construction with Burned Clay – Part 1," *The Brickbuilder* (Aug. 1897), p. 173; and Peter B. Wight, "Recent Fireproof Building – Part 6," *The Inland Architect and News Record* 19 (July 1892), p. 71.

42. The specifications for the Pest Station were clearly stated by the Austrian State Railroad Company and appear to have been tailored for Eiffel: "The building should consist of a metal framework filled in with ashlar for the base and facing brickwork for the upper walls," which aptly describes Eiffel's design. Henri Loyrette, *Gustave Eiffel* (New York, 1985), p. 57. The better-known Douro Bridge, completed on October 31, 1877, consisted of a wrought iron central arch span of 525 feet, the longest non-suspension bridge to date, and iron open framework piers 140 feet high that had the familiar truncated pyramid profile. Loyrette, p. 60.

43. Together with architect W. O. W. Bouwens van der Boyer, he designed the four-story skylighted courtyard for the stock exchange of the Credit Lyonnais Bank. The following year he collaborated with H. J. B. Dubois in designing the skylighted galleries for the new Louvre Department Store. Steiner (note 13), pp. 61-63.

44. Ibid., pp. 59, 106.

45. Ibid., pp. 61-62, 106 and pl. 24.

46. "John Shillito and Company's Store," *American Architect and Building News* (Oct. 13, 1877), p. 330; "The Present Condition of Cincinnati's Three Large New Buildings," *American Architect and Building News* (Aug. 24, 1878), p. 67; Nancy House, *James W. McLaughlin* (Master's thesis, University of Cincinnati, 1984), pp. 17-18. Even the shelving display units were kept to a uniform height of 4′ 6″, to reinforce the store's interior vastness.

47. Jenney graduated in 1856 from the Ecole centrale des arts et manufactures in Paris, specializing in civil engineering. He started in the fall of 1853, living in Paris from 1853 to 1856, and returned in 1858-59. Therefore, although he witnessed the construction of Les Halles and the 1855 World's Fair, he left prior to the onset of France's development of multistory iron framing. Theodore Turak, "The Ecole Centrale and Modern Architecture: The Education of William Le Baron Jenney," *Journal of the Society of Architectural Historians* 24 (Mar. 1970), pp. 40-47. Much has been made of the fact that Eiffel also attended the Ecole centrale, only one year ahead of Jenney. While it is possible that they knew of each other, as well as receiving the same basic courses in their first two years, it must be remembered that Eiffel specialized not in civil engineering, but in chemistry. Loyrette (note 42), p. 29. Jenney was also intimate with Viollet-le-Duc's writings, so much so that he used them in 1877, prior to their English translation, for the architecture courses he taught at the University of Michigan. Turak, p. 41.

48. Wight, Chicago's leading architectural writer at the time, linked the first Leiter Building to the John Shillito Building in: Peter B. Wight, "On the Present Condition of Architectural Art in the Western States," *American Art Review* (1880), pp. 141-42.

49. The columns were cast with projecting shelf brackets to receive the appropriate horizontal framing members. Two twelve-inch wrought-iron I-beam floor girders sat on the ledge at the interior face of the column. These were loosely bolted to the column by a single bolt that passed through each of the beam webs and a projecting bracket that was also cast with the column. As a good amount of tolerance was needed for site erection, the holes were larger than the bolt, leaving the connection with a considerable amount of play. Therefore, Jenney employed a clamp consisting of a one-inch-diameter wrought-iron rod that was bent at one end and placed into a notch cut in the top flange of both beams. The clamp was screwed to the column by a nut placed inside the column, thereby pulling the beams tight to the column face. The floor girders supported eight-inch wrought-iron I-beams at five-foot centers, within which were placed hollow tile floor arches.

To ascertain the actual detailing of Jenney's structure, I referred to his working drawings for the Home Insurance Building that are on microfilm at The Art Institute of Chicago. I also examined the four-columned bay fragment that is in the collection of Chicago's Museum of Science and Industry.

50. The lack of bolts may have been a technique on Jenney's part to impart some rotational flexibility at the column/spandrel connection to accommodate differential settlement of the piers. This flexible joint was reinforced by notching the front of the lintel back four inches, which allowed the pier's face brick to continue past the lintel without sitting on it, thereby the facing was continuously self-supporting from the granite piers at the third floor and would not crack if a spandrel rotated due to the settlement of an adjacent pier.

On the subject of the flexible joint, Jenney wrote: "As the building must settle... the first settlement must be uneven, therefore every care must be taken to make the construction elastic." William Le Baron Jenney, "The Construction of a Heavy, Fireproof Building on Compressible Soil," *Inland Architect and Builder* 6 (Dec. 1885), p. 100.

51. "As it was important in the Home Insurance Building to obtain a large number of small offices provided with abundance of light, the piers between the windows were reduced to the minimum... a square iron column was *built into* each of the piers in the street fronts." Jenney (note 50).

52. For an analysis of the sequence of events in the development of the iron skeleton frame in Chicago, see Gerald R. Larson and Roula Mouroudellis Geraniotis, "Toward a Better Understanding of the Evolution of the Iron Skeleton Frame in Chicago," *Journal of the Society of Architectural Historians* 46 (Mar. 1987), pp. 39-48.

53. Curiously, the only mention of the Home Insurance Building during this period that I have seen was British: John B. Gass, "Some American Methods," *Royal Institute of Architects, Transactions*, n. s., 2 (1885-86), pp. 145-46, as cited in Theodore Turak, "Remembrances of the Home Insurance Building," *Journal of the Society of Architectural Historians* 44 (March 1985), p. 62.

54. For instance, why didn't Burnham and Root use the skeleton frame in the Rookery? As the Rookery was to be located directly opposite the Home Insurance Building and Root was in the process of designing it in the summer of 1885, when the Home's construction was just being completed, Root must have been aware of Jenney's technique. In fact, the two tallest buildings designed and constructed after the Home Insurance, Cobb and Frost's Owings Building, and Adler and Sullivan's Auditorium Tower, did not utilize Jenney's device in the Home Insurance Building.

55. Although Buffington's work on the skyscraper was legitimate and its publication brought the issue of iron-framing to the attention of the professional community, Buffington's role and importance was later downplayed by his peers in Chicago. After unsuccessfully trying to get royalty payments from Chicago architects for using "his" idea, Buffington eventually made an unfortunate effort to gain historical priority over Jenney's Home Insurance Building by postdating many of his patent sketches. This desperate action has tended to negate Buffington's important contribution to the evolution of the skyscraper. For a documented study of Buffington's actions see: Dimitris Tselos, "The Enigma of Buffington's Skyscraper," and Muriel B. Christison, "How Buffington Staked His Claim," *Art Bulletin* (Mar. 1944), pp. 1-24.

56. *Northwestern Architect* 6 (Mar. 1888), p. 23.

57. "Our Illustrations," *Inland Architect and News Record* 9 (July 1888), p. 89.

58. "We do not know whether the scheme is a serious one, but, if so, we are decidedly inclined to agree with the persons who believe that such inordinately lofty structures are not likely to prove profitable to their owners." *American Architect and Building News* 24 (Nov. 17, 1888), p. 226.

59. Loyrette (note 42), p. 100.

60. Tselos (note 55), pp. 10-11.

61. "Our Illustrations," *Inland Architect and News Record* 9 (Apr. 1888), p. 49.

62. *Inland Architect and News Record* 4 (Sept. 1889), p. 16. The proposed tower was to be 1,500 feet high (Eiffel's is 984 feet) with a diameter of 480 feet at the base. The four main entrance porticoes led to a central dome with a diameter of 237 feet that was 230 high. Within the tower was to be located a 4,000-room hotel. The entire structure was to be lighted with 15,000 colored Edison electric lights. "World's Fair Tower," *Real Estate and Building Journal* (June 21, 1890), p. 497. The location of the proposed tower was officially moved from the exposition site to the Midway Plaisance at the February 24, 1891, meeting of the Committee of Architects. *Inland Architect and News Record* 17 (Mar. 1891), p. 24.

The Chicago Multistory as a Design Problem

Heinrich Klotz

Only seldom does an architectural historian have the opportunity to analyze both a mode of building that is completely novel and all the preconditions that have brought it into being. The American architectural historian Carl W. Condit recognized and seized this opportunity in *The Chicago School of Architecture: A History of Commercial and Public Building in the Chicago Area, 1875-1925*, published in 1964.

In Condit's books, the technical and economic preconditions that led to the development of the multistory building are discussed in detail. What is lacking, however, and has hitherto been neglected, is an attempt to give genuine architectural-historic significance to this subject and to address a specific issue in the history of the multistory, namely, that of architectural design. How, we should ask, did the architects respond when confronted with an entirely new kind of assignment, one for which traditional design, the architectural theory of the past, simply offered no model? For the multistory there was no Vitruvius, Alberti, or Palladio. And in this respect the architects of the first multistories found themselves in a similar position to the engineers of the nineteenth century; somewhat like Joseph Paxton and his Crystal Palace in London, and Alexandre Gustave Eiffel and his tower in Paris, or the bridge-builders and their truss-structures. But even this analogy is rather lame, since in contrast to Paxton's Crystal Palace, the Chicago multistories were not built for an exhibition season, but to last. And unlike Eiffel's tower they were not symbolic, ostentatious, and exceptional constructions, but were meant for everyday use. And while the bridges were special structures to facilitate the movement of traffic, the tall buildings quickly came to be the very substance of the city. Planned to be part of the everyday world of work, they could not be incongruous, but had to establish an affinity with the city.

Fig. 1 William Le Baron Jenney, The Fair store, Adams Street between State and Dearborn streets, 1890-91 (demolished).

Fig. 2 Rand McNally and Co., Map of Chicago central business district, 1898; from Frank A. Randall, History of the Development of Building Construction in Chicago *(Urbana, Ill., 1949).*

Toward the end of the nineteenth century, Chicago differed from European cities in that almost no original town structure housing its permanent institutions survived. Chicago was still virgin territory, all the more so as the Great Fire of 1871 had necessitated almost a completely new beginning. The city lay entirely open to land speculation; the land had been divided into rectangular lots (fig. 2), and each lot was free of traditional restraints, such as hereditary leasehold rights remain-

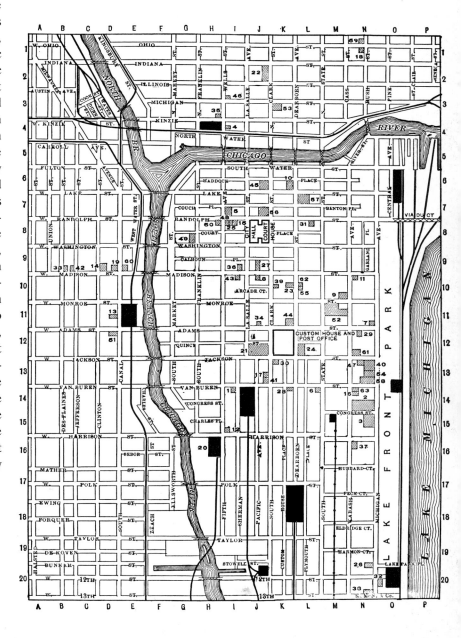

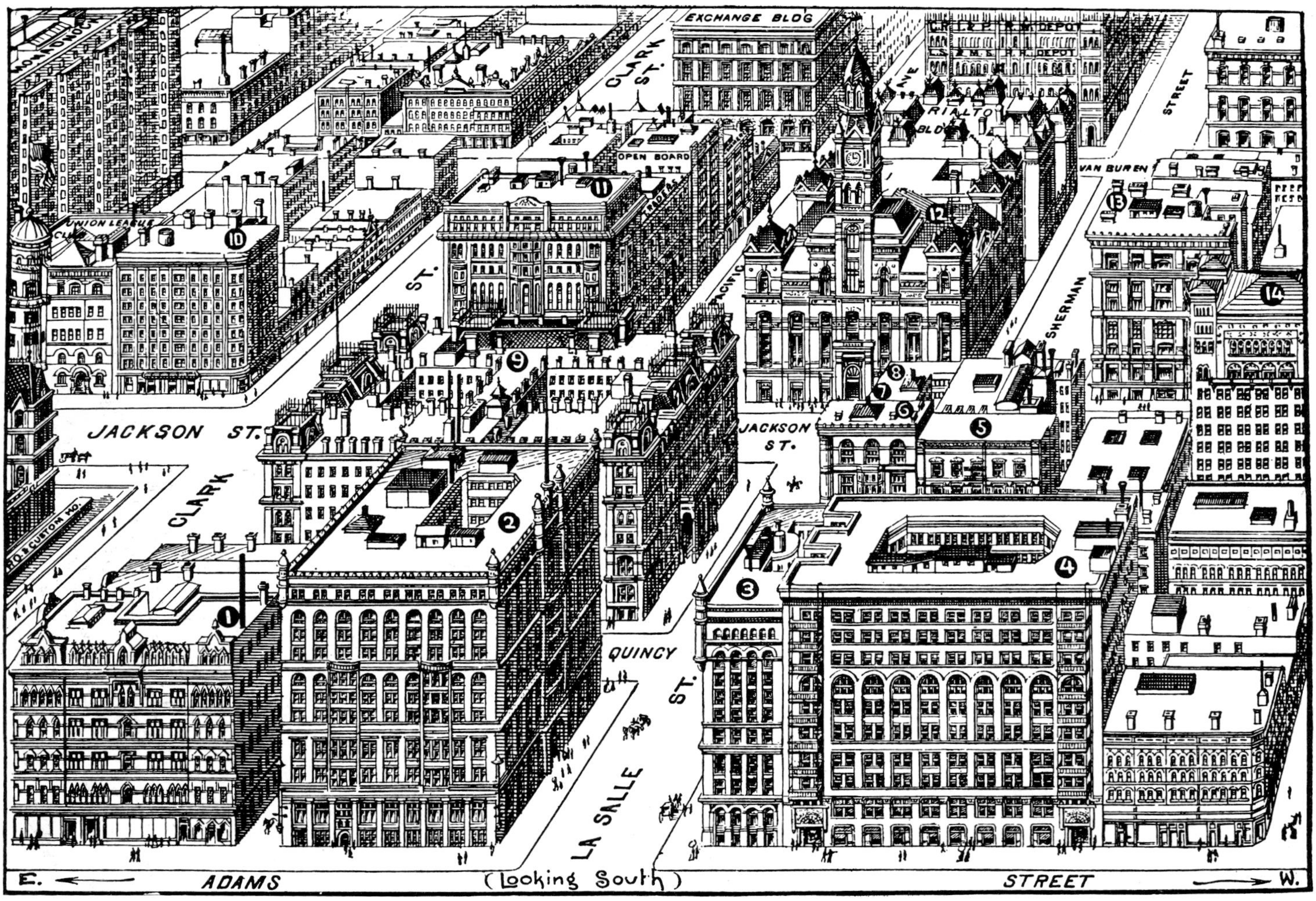

*Fig. 3 Rand McNally and Co.,
Bird's-eye view of Chicago, in the
vicinity of the Board of Trade,
1898; from Randall,* Building
Construction in Chicago.

*Fig. 4 Adler and Sullivan,
Auditorium Building,
Congress Parkway between
Michigan and Wabash avenues,
1887-89.*

ing from the Middle Ages, or lasting institutional land-privileges like those of the church, etc. Every parcel of ground became a piece of merchandise and was completely developed as never before. The buyers sought to exploit their plots to best advantage to the outer limits of their property. The consequences of this exploitation of property all the way to its boundaries have not been clearly recognized. Optimal use of one's property meant occupying the lot to its full extent, that is, developing one's land "flush" (fig. 3).

This demand on the part of the client strongly affected the design process. From the outset, each different program had its basic form: the rectangular construction block, and within it the three-dimensional extention of the ground space identical to the dimensions of the property tract. Areas of floor space materialized, the outer wall abutting the street building line or the equally rectangular boundaries of the adjacent building. The boundaries of the plot of land thus lined up directly with the boundaries of the building's walls, while the facade directly abutted the public space – the streets and the sidewalks. There was no thought of setting the structure back so as to give it some surrounding space. As a result, the architect was denied the possibility of giving each building a distinctive site and therefore an individually designed construction form. The different kinds of buildings – the city hall, stock exchange, law courts, opera, or theater – all disappeared to become identical in the generally prevailing primary form of the rectangle. The Rookery (pls. 10, 11), City Hall, or other buildings like the Stock Exchange (fig. 5) were all, without exception, rectangular blocks. Thus, the architect's particular design problem lay in having little or no flexibility in the drafting of the site: he was obliged to dispense altogether with the traditional variety of building styles, due to the geometric, primary grid of the plots of land determined by the city plan.

Sullivan's Auditorium Building (fig. 4; pl. 25) is an outstanding example of a design conceived chiefly for its functional value, e. g., an especially large auditorium with a stage, a foyer, a hotel, a restaurant, etc., all built within an outwardly uniform, rectangular block. Traditionally, such a project would have taken the form of a rather colorful edifice set in an open space, a plaza, or a park. In these circumstances, the secondary design proposals take on a unique importance. Thus, City Hall (fig. 6) stands out from the other rectangular blocks as a result of its very lavish order of granite columns, intended to lend the municipal "monumental structure" the special nobility of public authority. But it is highly characteristic that the large win-

dows between the columns, the display windows of the businesses that are to be found on the ground level even in a public building, were not dispensed with. Rather than enjoying an exceptional role, City Hall also participated in the fullest exploitation of land.

A wealth of similar examples could be cited in this context. I will restrict myself to a building that is not usually identified as a temple, namely, Burnham and Root's Masonic Temple (1891-92; fig. 7).[1] At the turn of the century such quintessential temples were built in many American cities – Roman or Egyptian in style, with colonnades and entablature, sometimes with a tympanum as well. The Masonic Temple in Chicago is a tall commercial building whose rectangular austerity is made somewhat less severe by a high-set saddle roof with dormer windows and gables.

The 1898 Rand McNally bird's-eye map of Chicago, which shows each block of buildings in a three-dimensional perspective, reveals the pervasiveness of the principle of having a distinct building typology develop in a rectangular space with plots varying in size. This typology had to serve all

Fig. 5 Adler and Sullivan, Chicago Stock Exchange Building, 30 North LaSalle Street, 1893-94 (demolished).

Fig. 6 Holabird and Roche, City Hall and County Building, La-Salle Street between Randolph and Washington streets, 1911.

Fig. 7 Burnham and Root, Masonic Temple, northeast corner of State and Randolph streets, 1891-92 (demolished).

Fig. 8 Bird's-eye view of the Place de l'Opéra, Paris.

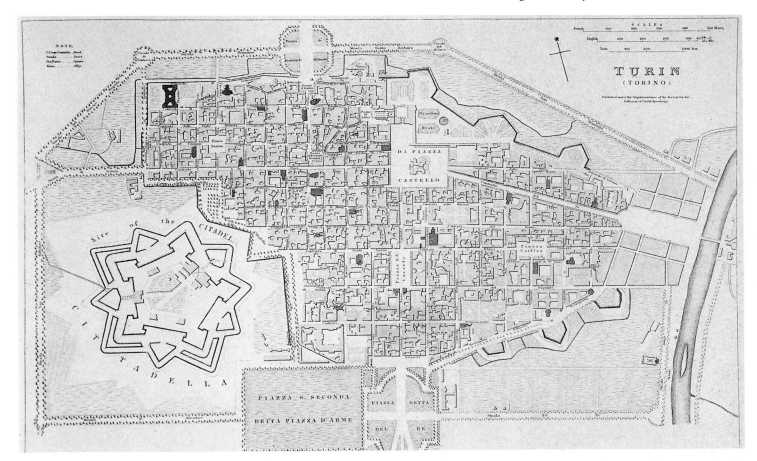

Fig. 9 Map of Turin, 1833; from Melville Campbell Branch, Comparative Urban Design: Rare Engravings, 1830-1843 (New York, 1978).

sorts of purposes and made no distinction between the quality of public and private edifices, or between their different contents and purposes. We have here the prototype of the functionalist city, which, having discarded from its building typology every manner of symbolic significance, endeavors with the aid of secondary forms — details of facade and roof silhouettes — to restore something of the entirely suppressed, illustrative character of a building's content. As a result, the facade acquires an unexpected significance; and it is characteristic that Chicago architects of the late nineteenth century should have attached such particular importance to the fashioning of the facades, a fact that merits close attention.

Yet before we consider the specific characteristics of Chicago's multistory facades, we should first consider the city's block development and its place in the history of eighteenth- and nineteenth-century architecture, for it was frankly the break with this tradition that lent Chicago its novel character after the turning point of 1871. Urban planning in the nineteenth century was marked by the creation of contrasts between the uniform and the spectacular, rather like Baron Georges-Eugène Haussmann's post-1851 designs for Paris, in which streets lined with buildings of relative uniformity, with blocks of apartment houses, led to the distinctly

different park and public building developments (fig. 8). The Paris Opéra, for example, stands as a summit point, a monument of public prestige, at once an axial vista and free in prospect, so that all sides of this wholly individual edifice are shown off to best advantage. As a result, it stands out in striking fashion from the surrounding apartment and commercial buildings and the general cityscape.

In Chicago this ceremonial urban aspect — the contrast between the commonplace and the spectacular — is abandoned for the generally operative block. An urban plan that contrasts the usual (which predominates quantitatively) with the singular and significant (which is qualitatively exceptional) is not to be found in Chicago. Instead of the axial vistas and important urban prospects, there is the grid, which declares every lot of land equal. In short, Haussmann's Paris remains bound to a baroque planning idea that recognizes hierarchies, and though the bourgeoisie no longer accepted the absolutist hierarchical order of Versailles, it shared in this hierarchy to its own advantage. Louis Sullivan's Chicago meanwhile, offers a checkered pattern that has exchanged the hierarchical order for the parceling of land. The emphasis is not on any planned preeminence, but on the greatest possible utilization of land on lots which are, in princi-

*Fig. 10 Guarino Guarini,
Church of San Lorenzo,
Turin, 1668-87.*

ple, of equal status. Prestige is attainable through extending one's lots and through the new possibility of towering upward, of building up into the sky, that is, through quantitative differentiation.

Surprisingly, the urban planning of the city of Turin in the seventeenth and eighteenth centuries is outwardly comparable, although it materialized within a content of wholly different premises (fig. 9). It was the King of Savoy who dictated the marked trend toward rigid block development in the planning of the Piedmontese capital during the seventeenth century.[2] The determining factor was not the marketing of plots of land, but rather the notion of a baroque urban plan that could be imposed upon the existing monuments associated with the royal house. The street-grid pattern of Turin, as decreed by the king, not only had the individual palaces and residential buildings set out in unusually severe, geometric order, but also prescribed a particular building style — a matter over which property owners normally had control.

   Guarino Guarini's church of San Lorenzo (fig. 10), which is the Royal Chapel of the Palazzo Reale, is recognizable by its dome as a dominating edifice, while its actual structure is completely worked into a comprehensive architectural synthesis. San Lorenzo is essentially nothing more than a street corner. In similar fashion, a great

*Fig. 11 Guarino Guarini,
Palazzo Carignano,
Turin, begun 1679.*

number of Turin's parish churches are set uniformly in the stiff block plan of the grid. Even the Palazzo Carignano, which Guarini built for the king, is essentially a grid square in the city's ground plan; the neighboring church of San Filippo and the Royal Academy are merged into the block just described, marked off by the four street building lines. Such fierce control over the design of royal and ecclesiastical edifices is quite unusual in baroque urban planning. The grid remains primarily a gesture of absolutist planning to which even the royal buildings were subjected.

In such a setting, the free design of the chancel in Guarini's Santa Maria Consolatione Church has the effect of a liberating counter-demonstration against the generally prevailing square form, a demonstration that was at least possible. As regards the royal Palazzo Carignano (fig. 11), a degree of respectful distance is indeed encouraged, as the rectangular area in front of its main facade was left open to form a piazza. There was never a plaza in front of City Hall in the business center of Chicago. But in Turin, as in Chicago, the ideas for secondary design became especially important when architects tried to achieve a certain freedom from the rigidity imposed by the grid through the use of architectural detail. The curved facade of the Palazzo Carignano has the effect of a conscious counterstatement to the ever-dominating, ruler-drawn building lines of the streets. And the oval, circular, and star-shaped designs of the entrance halls, which caused a sensation in Turin in the seventeenth and eighteenth centuries, lent the palaces of the aristocracy there, as they did the inner structures of the large apartment blocks in Chicago, that special character not permitted for the exterior. This included the free flow of circles and arcs: great staircases sweeping out to all sides and upward, and domes and vaulted ceilings soaring easily upon columns, as if it were a matter of recovering in the interior that liberality of expression that was denied outside. That, in general terms, is how the architecture of Guarini and his successors appeared, creating out of the restricted nature of rectangular forms high-soaring vaults and arches, and circular and oval outlines — the sole reaction to the contraints of urban planning which held sway outside. Put emphatically, the aesthetic of Turin baroque architecture is an aesthetic of inner space, a mode of liberation from the axis and the severity of the building line imposed by the city plan.

In the course of European architectural history, vocabularies of form had developed to provide a ready arsenal of building styles for the nineteenth century. They constituted a repertory of style with the aid of which a great diversity of construction jobs could be rendered acceptable to the urban public. The structure of building was, to some extent, covered, and thus it assumed a comprehensible and fitting form. The traditional styles were the means of rapprochement that gave some communicative coherence to even such completely unusual constructions as a railway station or a tunnel. These structures became Doric or Romanesque, and thereby entered the representational sphere of architecture. They had shed the "lack of style" label of purely functional architecture.

What was now to be done with that monstrous iron structure (fig. 12), which even in its contruction was so very far removed from what one might call a "building"? How was it possible, first of all, to make of these tall commercial buildings the sort

Fig. 12 Adler and Sullivan, Wainwright Building, 709 Chestnut Street, St. Louis, 1890-91, under construction.

of structure that fitted into the representational, and therefore also into the communicative, sphere of urban architecture? Traditional stylistic devices had hardly been created for a ten- or even twenty-story building. If one wanted to make use of the styles and forms of the Renaissance, one immediately encountered problems. Not only were the proportions of the new multistory buildings an obstacle to this otherwise very flexible canon, but so was the limitation to at most five orders of columns. Palaces of the Renaissance and later centuries were no more than five or, under exceptional circumstances, six stories high. Correspondingly, the five orders of columns could be superimposed one upon the other, provided that in general all the orders went through from one floor to the next. With the advent of the electric elevator this limitation disappeared. The number of stories grew. And the iron skeleton simultaneously made possible a new structural engineering that proved to be the decisive factor in the upward development. But after the unfortunate experiences of the Chicago Fire, the metal framework had to be covered with fireproof material, namely, brick. Thus it was only the outer casing that placed any traditional demands upon the architect.

If the five orders of columns of the Renaissance were inadequate, might not slender Gothic truss-construction prove suitable for the execution of the new vertical design? But Chicago multistories were not comparable to Gothic church steeples. They were not tracery constructions soaring into weightlessness, but were mostly sturdily set blocks which, though considerably taller than usual, were nonetheless more comparable to a Renaissance palace than to a Gothic structure. As a result, in wanting to have their building representative of an established order, and in hoping to see it incorporated into a traditional urban context, Chicago architects were confronted with a difficult choice. For not only did they have to choose between one or another historical vocabulary, they were also in the tricky position of having to convert an existing style to perform a task for which none of the styles had been created. The Renaissance model was not appropriate to the multistory building. This is how the design problem of the facade arose.

The architects of the early Chicago multistories frequently departed from representational standards. The first Leiter Building of 1879 (see Larson, fig. 14), designed by William Le Baron Jenney, exhibited some of the simplicity and directness of the later multistories of the early twentieth

Fig. 13 William Le Baron Jenney, Manhattan Building, 431 South Dearborn Street, 1890.

century. The brick pillars, first left red and later whitewashed, remain almost bare of any ornamental circles to set off the structure. At a glance one recognizes the cage structure of the iron frame, whose wide, horizontally elongated intervals characterize the positioning of the entire outline. The wide gaps between the supports are characteristic of steel construction even today. Later it came to be used for the horizontal Chicago window, which above all had its formulation in Sullivan's architecture. However, Jenney subdivided every interval with two uprights, so that three perpendicular windows materialized in each one. The Leiter Building holds its own in a uniquely changing environment, which suggests to the present-day observer the continued advance of the horizontal ordering of intervals, though this should not be confused with the discarded perpendicular window system of the nineteenth century.

Yet the facade of Sullivan's Auditorium hardly exposes with similar clarity the framework of the steel construction that remains visible on the Leiter Building. The Auditorium is an example of how, following the construction of the first Leiter Building, both the design efforts of architects and the demands of clients must have undergone a fundamental change. William Le Baron Jenney's first tall building may bear witness to a client mentality which, for the moment, placed the purely functional aspect of these new buildings in the foreground, as was the case when Boston businessman Peter Brooks gave instructions to his architect in 1881. The psychic distance of the Boston city-dweller from the inhabitants of the far-off city in the West surfaces through his words. In Boston one was concerned with prestige and self-image, while in Chicago, with purely practical matters: "Tall buildings will pay well in Chicago hereafter, and sooner or later a way will be found to erect them." Brooks then gave instructions for the construction of an eight-story building, the first building in Chicago to exceed seven floors. It was actually built with ten: "I prefer to have a plain structure of face brick, eight stories high and also a basement, with flat roof.... The building throughout is to be for use and not for ornament. Its beauty will be in its all-adaptation to its use."[3]

These formulations, descending to sheer usefulness, betray a functionalist rationale which has rid itself of any representational intention and that leads us to the crux of the matter. Long before Sullivan's claim that "form follows function," Chicagoans had already developed an appoach that began with a strict calculation of capital investment, rather than with a definition of the construction task. The new matter-of-factness of functionalism tried to reduce architecture to a common denominator as early as 1881. In this respect the rosettes on the pillars of the Leiter Building, for which the capital would have to compensate, and, similarly, the brick frieze on the roof cornice are to be regarded as a small concession to the eye. Not much more ornament than was deemed appropriate for a typical factory building could be expected. Later there would be talk of the "truthfulness" of the architecture, which did not gloss anything over. On the one hand it is the architect's moral truth, meaning the undisguised clarity of construction;

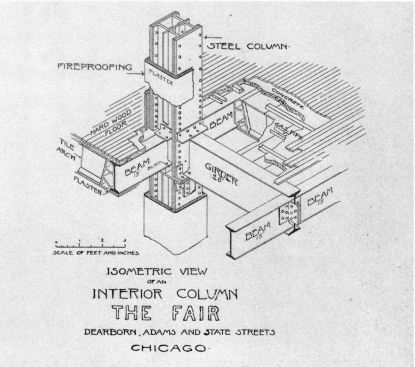

ISOMETRIC VIEW OF AN
INTERIOR COLUMN
THE FAIR
DEARBORN, ADAMS AND STATE STREETS
CHICAGO.

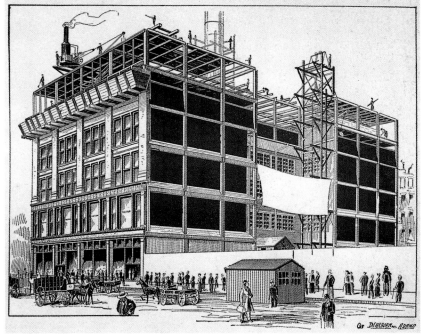

Fig. 14 Jenney, The Fair store under construction, with detail of typical column-and-beam joint; from Inland Architect and News Record 18 (1891).

Fig. 15 San Pedro de Roda, Spain, 1022, nave.

Fig. 16 Reconstruction of nave of Speyer Cathedral; from Kenneth J. Conant, Carolingian and Romanesque Architecture 800 to 1200 (Harmondsworth and New York, 1959).

and on the other hand it is the truth of the client, who has his eye on the greatest possible return for the smallest expenditure. It is the architecture of utilitarianism.

Eleven years later, in 1890, William Le Baron Jenney designed the Manhattan Building (fig. 13). Besides one other tall building that appeared in Chicago in the same year, it was the first to be completely erected on a steel frame. How was Jenney to cope with the facade of this sixteen-story edifice? There is no longer any question of the original simplicity of the first Leiter Building. Jenney and his client wished to make a Renaissance palace out of the superelevated structure. Thus the design presents a simply monstrous creation, all the more so because the typical accoutrements of a palace facade are hung about it. The steel skeleton takes on the substance of carefully chiseled, square stone blocks. And however little the steel skeleton tapers toward the top, the structures taper to the same degree. It remains a block, even though the

external intervals stop abruptly above the ninth floor, in order to have the remaining seven intervals rise to an overhanging cornice.

In accordance with the pattern of a Renaissance palace, Jenney begins with a rusticated plinth which, however, entirely lacks the usual appearance of solidity. The intervals, following the permanently fixed distance of the steel supports, are wide open – set just as widely as in the stories above it. Just as the line of the entire structure is vertical, so the rusticated story is also stretched upward; contrary to one's expectations, it extends up three floors and concludes with a horizontal ledge. Set above that is a great order of pilasters, an order that breaks all the classical rules of proportion and stretches, thin and seemingly fragile, up nine stories. Far above sit the capitals, situated beneath a cornice that sets off the upper third of the building. And there the fragile order ends. But whoever supposed that the building finished here, met with a new surprise. Above the pilaster cornice is set a

row of round arches, which extend up an additional three floors to support the massive weight of the mezzanine story with its overhanging roof cornice. The impression given is as if one building had been set upon another, as if Jenney had placed a round arch structure upon the excessively stretched order of pilasters so as to deal somehow with the problem posed by the height of the building.

To give the facade an additional horizontal support, Jenney drew a third ledge, like a belt, across the surface above the ninth story, so that the three middle oriel towers — which one would not expect to find between pilasters anyway — appeared to be actually strapped to the facade. At the same time, the ledge cut through the pilasters in a manner that suggested that they were not based on the rustic story below. And indeed, on closer scrutiny, it turned out that they were attached to their own plinths only above the belt of the ledge. The lower order, then, was no more than a row of stripes on the wall. No doubt the classical system of

elevation is a bridging maneuver to handle the unending series of floors between ground level and roof cornice. The ambition to transform a steel skeleton structure into a period facade of traditional design transformed the forced facade of a palace into a chimeric one.

Dividing and patching, Jenney continually added more horizontals in the hope of somehow reaching an end. Patching and chopping, he at last completed the facade. In the meantime, he had positively run out of breath when he suddenly thought of an arcade of round arches. The vertical line of the tall building vitiates the form of a pilaster system devised for broad development. When to all the other excesses oriel windows are added to catch some light in the narrow street, the pastiche is perfect. If we evaluate such a facade system according to the traditional standards of a Renaissance facade, it is carried out according to customary tenets. Thus the contradiction between tradition and innovation makes this facade, if not beautiful,

Fig. 17 William Le Baron Jenney, Second Leiter Building (later, Sears, Roebuck and Co.), State Street between Jackson and Van Buren streets, 1889-91.

then certainly interesting, for the design problem remains unsolved. Abandoning this decor altogether would have been the only solution.

In the same year that Jenney erected the Manhattan Building (1890-91), he also built The Fair store (figs. 1, 14) in Chicago. In the design for this department store, to an even greater degree than in the design for the Manhattan, it becomes clear what difficulties were encountered in transposing the well-proportioned lines of a Renaissance palazzo onto a tall block edifice, in this case one that was eleven stories high. Jenney actually divided the facade in the middle — placing a rusticated story between the upper and lower sections — so that in an oddly ambiguous way it may be taken either as a mezzanine sitting on the lower five stories or as a rusticated plinth for the upper order of pilasters. Fundamentally the building is two palazzi, one set on top of the other and fitting into each other in the "mezzanine plinth." Quite as prescribed, the building begins with the entrance hall, above which lies a corresponding mezzanine floor that supports the great row of tremendous pilasters rising up through three stories and finally culminating in the mezzanine. Above the mezzanine, which now becomes the plinth, stands the row of tremendous pilasters in their height, rising up five stories. The architects of the Renaissance managed the superimposition of orders in a similar manner; they sought to convey the towering aspect of the facade through the elongation of the pillars by changing from a stocky to a more slender order. But they never set colossal orders on top of one another, only single orders. Yet in Jenney's design the colossal order sweeping up through several stories would not have balanced the proportions of the entire facade correctly, and so two orders were used.

To handle the parts of classical buildings properly, one needs to adhere to the standard proportions and not to distort the different portions by stretching them. That calls to mind the early Romanesque designs of the first vaulted basilicas. The architect of the nave of San Pedro de Roda in Spain (fig. 15) simply placed one column on top of another to connect the extension of the girder arch with the pillars in front of the nave. When the architect of the nave of Speyer Cathedral in Germany (fig. 16) broke all the rules of classical proportion by having a pillar tower from its base straight up to the vault, thereby converting the pillar into an engaged column, it was a great departure from tradition.

Fig. 18 D. H. Burnham and Co., Fisher Building,
343 South Dearborn Street, 1896.

Fig. 19 Henry Hobson Richardson, Marshall Field Wholesale Store, Adams Street between Wells and Franklin streets, 1885-87 (demolished).

Fig. 19 Henry Hobson Richardson, Marshall Field Wholesale Store, Adams Street between Wells and Franklin streets, 1885-87 (demolished).

Admittedly, Jenney's was an entirely different kind of perpendicular construction. Nevertheless, in his second Leiter Building of 1889-91 (fig. 17) he abandoned any regard for Renaissance proportions of design, and it could well be said that this building became Jenney's Speyer Cathedral. From the first floor to the roof cornice, the department store's gigantic block with its eight-and-a-half stories appears to be united in a single perpendicular line. Massive columns stand at the corners, giving the whole structure a certain solidity. The facade pilasters likewise extend all the way up to the overhanging cornice, although they do not keep to the classical proportions that the corner columns retain. To some degree they have become engaged shafts, or rather, engaged pilasters. The supports between the pilasters are reminiscent to an even greater degree of Gothic columns. Maintaining the same diameter, they are short at the bottom (not exceeding the height of a window), they extend up as high as three stories, and, at the top, they are shortened to the height of two stories. Despite the dominance of the pilasters, this Gothic element also carries some weight in the facade, and so becomes a deviation from the norms of style and classical proportion. Structural engineering made

demands that Jenney no longer made any attempt to suppress.

D. H. Burnham took a very different path with his Reliance Building of 1895 and his Fisher Building of 1896 (fig. 18; pls. 18, 19). Up to now, the possibility of working with the extended, perpendicular elements of Gothic style had not been recognized, although it would have been much more appropriate to associate the perpendicularity of the tall multistory with a Gothic framework than with a Renaissance palace. Slender rods, single and bound together, run up through the entire facade to form the scaffolding frame. They align the polygonal sides of the oriel projections without any difficulty. The window spandrels span the spaces between them in the manner of filagree tracery. Undoubtedly, fine-line form supports and tracery elevations are more appropriate to a multistory facade than are the necessarily substantial forms of classical architecture. The more the multistory building moved toward becoming a skyscraper, the more obvious it became that the Gothic cathedral tower would have to be its legitimate design model.

But even Richardson's Romanesque style did not bypass Chicago. In 1887 the Marshall Field Wholesale Store (fig. 19) was completed. Occupy-

*Figs. 20/21 Adler and
Sullivan, Wainwright
Building, exterior and
detail of facade.*

ing an entire block, it enjoyed the special privilege of standing free on all four sides – the Palazzo Strozzi of Chicago.⁴ Richardson divided the facades with comprehensive arch designs, setting a segment arch in the plinth, and, above it, as on the first floor, a series of arches rising up to dominate three stories. Above these he erected two more narrow, coupled arches that span only two stories. The entire design is completed with a truly massive mezzanine with windows arranged in a staccato

Fig. 22 Adler and Sullivan, Guaranty Building, 28 Church Street, Buffalo, 1894-96.

debted to Richardson's Marshall Field Wholesale Store.

Was any innovation, any further advance toward solving the posed design problem, to be expected from these architects who had proven themselves so strongly inspired by Richardson?

At this point it is appropriate to introduce a methodological consideration. If one is to talk of advances in the solution of a design problem, one would appear to be assuming a development with something of a beginning and an end. Immanence of form development signifies that there are relatively distinct, autonomous processes of form which, as George Kubler puts it, compose a "series" and progress to a logical conclusion.[5] Ways of looking at the problem that lead to a solution by trial and error allow for a certain variation in the outcome, but always in relation to the basic problem that is posed. The process of finding forms with which to fashion the facade of the Chicago multistory building included nearly all the available styles in freely subjective expression. All kinds of possibilities were tried, but an acceptable solution rarely materialized. The specific design problem in Chicago lay in combining the multistory's new building typology — its structure being immediately interwoven with the facade — with the demand for representational merit that had found expression in the stylized architecture of the nineteenth century. It was these curious characteristics of forms in their various styles, such as the system of proportions of a Renaissance palace, that proved to be as much of an encumbrance as a means of creative expression — the encumbrance being that the stylistic devices had not been created for the new structure of the multistory. The solution lay in finding a form through adaptation of these stylistic devices to the multistory that would serve to clarify the multistory's individuality rather than force it into the ready-made corset of a styled exterior.

Frank Lloyd Wright referred to this situation in a 1953 conversation:

When buildings first began to be tall, architects were confused – (no precedents) – didn't know how to make them *tall*. They would put one 2 or 3 story buildings on top of another until they had enough.[6]

Thus Wright quite clearly recognized the design problem being discussed here. He also provided a solution to it by pointing to Sullivan's Wainwright Building (fig. 20) in St. Louis, Missouri.

This radiant red brick building has precisely the properties that Wright credits his teacher with using to solve the former confusion. As he stated in the continuation of the conversation:

style, resembling a Romanesque arcade. As the openings become ever more narrow toward the top of the facade, a powerful movement appears to overtake the edifice. To a greater degree than anyone else, Richardson succeeded in breaking away from traditional notions of design and developed a formulation that was quite unexpected and novel in Chicago.

In the period following, the round-arch motif became the accepted thing. When the Chicago Stock Exchange was built in 1894, Sullivan used Richardson's theme again. The Auditorium Building of 1889 shows his influence still more clearly. The heavy, rusticated wall of the basement was adopted from Richardson, as were the series of great arches, the coupled arches standing above them, and the development of the culminating mezzanine into a miniature ambulatory. In his design for the Auditorium, Sullivan was clearly in-

I remember the master came in and threw something on my table – it was a "stretch" with the Wainwright building in St. Louis designed in outline upon it. He said, "Wright, this thing is *tall*. What's the matter with a tall building?" Well, there it was, *tall*! After that the skyscraper began to flourish – tall.[7]

When one looks at the Wainwright Building today, it is not difficult to share, in retrospect, Sullivan's pleasure of discovery. One sees immediately that the entire structure develops upward in a single continuous movement, with the pink sandstone plinth of the two first floors serving as the pedestal from which the slender elongated brick pilasters rise up. Just as decisively, the perpendicular momentum is brought to a halt by an unusually high cornice with corbels projecting outward. The roofing panel juts out and accentuates the horizontal counterforce with its heavy shadow. As Wright says, Sullivan no longer placed one building on top of another, forcing up the height by adding more layers, but rather united all the ten stories into a completely uniform design. The two first floors form the base, on top of which is set an angular, projecting horizontal ledge that provides a flat surface for the bright red pilasters. These pilasters, like engaged columns, ignore the classical proportions of a roughly one-to-eight ratio of diameter to height and shoot up the seven stories of the edifice. The tenth story is surrounded by the fanciful foliage frieze of the roof entablature. At the same time, the circular windows are the center of each leaf tendril. The perpendicularity is emphasized by the setback of the window spandrels, which lie in a deeper relief-plane without impeding the full development of the pilasters. The spandrels carry a most unusual brick ornamentation, which makes it seem as if decorative images have been hung between the flanks of the pilasters (fig. 21). Instead of giving up ornamentation, Sullivan simply invented his own. Cliché of style is swept aside, and with it, the ties to classical proportions of order.

In 1890, paralleling what Jenney had attempted to achieve in Chicago with the second Leiter Building of that same year, Sullivan broke the norm of pilaster proportions. But unlike Jenney, he did not take into account the broad intervals of the inner iron construction; instead, he arranged his pilasters at narrow, parallel distances on the facade so that the difference between the intervals' real supports and the interposed uprights was no longer apparent. He actually disfigured the construction by making the facade into something other than the form suggested by the inner skeletal frame. He thereby avoided the contrast between pilasters and the spindly supports so characteristic of Jenney's Leiter Building. With a narrow staccato of parallel

pilasters, he disregarded the steel scaffolding's horizontal intervals. By this means he succeeded in expressing perpendicularity where the other architects of Chicago multistories had so far failed. With its aesthetic the design surmounts technology. Sullivan, whom the functionalists like to regard as their progenitor, was anything but a pure functionalist. This is evident not only in his use of rich ornamental decoration on his buildings and in his filling of bare utilitarian surfaces with images, but also in his never being dogmatic about inner and outer congruence, about construction and facade. We see that the aesthetic quality of this edifice, its strongly expressive characterization of perpendicularity together with the unifying harmoniousness of the whole building in its three stages – the plinth, the order of pilasters, and the roof-frieze – was achievable only through a deliberate contradiction of the supposed formulation of the building. Four

Fig. 23 Holabird and Roche, Brooks Building, 223 West Jackson Street, 1909-10.

*Fig. 24 Holabird and Roche, McClurg Building,
218 South Wabash Avenue, 1899-1900.*

The process of finding a representative form for the new task of constructing tall buildings had begun by applying and rearranging the traditional eclecticism of architectural styles, and had found its first formulation by simultaneously overcoming the guarantors of representation and historical styles through Sullivan's achievements. For the time being, ways of viewing the problem had been exhausted. The attempts that followed were to some degree interesting, but they were generally unimportant variations of what had come before.

At the turn of the century, the architects of Chicago's tall buildings began to look back to the beginnings of that form and once again began to give prominence to what they had for twenty years endeavored to overcome with the help of representational ornament, namely, its simple, bare skeleton structure. The Chicago Business College building (1910) by D. H. Burnham and Co.[8] and many other comparable buildings – such as Holabird and Roche's Brooks Building (fig. 23) and McClurg Building (fig. 24; pl. 20) – portray the new sobriety that led the way for and served to inspire the European functionalism of the 1920s. The smooth stone casing of the edifice, free of any ornamental embellishment, reflects the inner construction in all its simplicity. Sullivan himself did a volte-face with the Schlesinger and Mayer Store (now Carson Pirie Scott; fig. 25), built in the years 1899 to 1904, and made the horizontal interval between the supports the chief element in the structuring of the entire facade.

When, twenty years later, European participants in the Chicago Tribune competition like Walter Gropius and Max Taut proposed the Chicago horizontal window facade, imagining it to be the most modern of the avant-garde, the Chicago clients had long since experienced a reawakened desire for representational architecture. The example of New York had already made them blind to sober functionalism – now they visualized Gothic multistories and Renaissance towers. Only with the arrival of Mies van der Rohe did Chicago break with this tradition, and go on to adopt an entirely new model for the multistory, the glazed steel skeleton. This posed a fundamentally new design problem, one which has kept architects well occupied to this day.

years later, in 1894, it seemed an obvious and virtually natural progression for Sullivan to abandon the pilaster order completely and to substitute his own order for the classical in his design for the Guaranty Building (fig. 22) in Buffalo. Here Sullivan keeps the perpendicular design that he introduced in St. Louis, but discards everything that calls to mind the Wainwright Building's architectural vocabulary. The design problem on which so many architects in Chicago had worked found its most complete solution outside of Chicago in St. Louis and in Buffalo.

Fig. 25 Louis H. Sullivan, Schlesinger and Mayer Store (now Carson Pirie Scott), southeast corner of State and Madison streets, 1899-1904.

NOTES

1   The Masonic Temple was located at the northeast corner of State and Randolph streets. It was demolished in 1939.

2   The grid plan was dictated by Charles Emmanuel II of Savoy, who ruled Piedmont from 1648 to 1675. Many of the baroque palaces and churches in the area were built by the architect Guarino Guarini (1624-1683).

3   Carl W. Condit, *The Chicago School of Architecture: A History of Commercial and Public Building in the Chicago Area, 1875-1925* (Chicago, 1964), p. 52.

4   The Palazzo Strozzi was built between 1489 and 1539 in Florence, Italy.

5   George Kubler, *The Shape of Time: Remarks on the History of Things* (New Haven, Conn., 1962).

6   Frank Lloyd Wright, *The Future of Architecture* (New York, 1953), p. 12.

7   Ibid.

8   This building is located at 207 S. Adams Street.

Buildings Serving Commerce

C. W. Westfall

Chicago was the first new city to grow to international prominence after the advent of the commercial age. Chicago grew because through it the world could be fed. Grain was Chicago's first and most dependable source of prosperity. Grain and lake boats made Chicago the hub of the nationwide railroad network. Grain served as collateral for commerce, and as commerce increased, so did the diversity of raw, semi-finished, and finished materials moving through the river port. By the end of the century, the narrow river was the world's busiest port. The banks of the river were lined with grain elevators, freight sheds, and factories, and behind them, stretching away from the commercial center, were the rugged commercial and industrial lofts serving the harbor, the city, and, ultimately, the world.

Elevators and lofts dominated the city's commercial fringe. The grain elevator was developed in Chicago, based in part on an early model designed in Buffalo in 1842, and for decades gave the city's center a distinctive appearance. After new, more efficient systems were found to perform the single function they were built to carry out, examples of the original models gradually disappeared from the land bordering the city's waterways and railroads, although a few survive in lonely outposts on the prairie.

Lofts are as general in distribution, use, and appearance as elevators are specific. When seen today in places as diverse as Seattle and Trieste, or as similar as Chicago and Manchester, England, the loft is instantly recognizable both as a generic type and as an example of local building designs and techniques. The reason for this is that the generic loft gradually gave way to buildings specifically designed to perform particular functions.

The Grain Elevators

Grain made Chicago a port, and its location at the mouth of the Chicago River made Chicago into a city. While nature had favored the city's site, man's industry was required to raise the city to unrivaled status among the world's entrepôts.[1] Over New Orleans, the first of its two competitors as "stacker of wheat," Chicago enjoyed a dual natural advantage. One was climate; the heat and humidity of the city on the Gulf often condemned grain in storage to rot or to be eaten by rodents. In Chicago, in contrast, grain put in storage during the fall and winter remained safely cool during the period when lake navigation was shut down by winter weather. As late as 1880, eighty percent of the grain shipped through Chicago was stored before it was shipped. The second advantage was geography, which linked St. Louis to New Orleans by the Mississippi River, while leaving Chicago as an independent linchpin in a different geographic complex. To reach the rapidly growing cities on the East Coast and in northern Europe, the route from the grain-producing prairie down the Mississippi River to St. Louis, through New Orleans, and around Florida was much longer than the route by rail or along the Illinois and Michigan Canal (opened in 1848) to Chicago. There it could then enter the Great Lakes system and reach New York via Buffalo and the Erie Canal (opened in 1825) or be shipped to Europe directly via the St. Lawrence River. Moreover, unlike the St. Louis waterfront, Chicago's harbor was undisturbed by currents and changing water levels and afforded both ample dockside space for boats and an unbounded prairie in which to marshal the railcars bearing the grain to the waterways.

In addition to enjoying these natural advantages, Chicagoans liked to boast that they could throw themselves into commerce unhindered by traditional ways of doing things, in contrast to St. Louis, where custom dictated that grain be handled in bags, each of which was graded, labeled, and carried by hand. The first consignment of grain from Chicago — seventy-eight bushels shipped to Buffalo in 1838 — was the last to be handled in this way in Chicago. The 3,678 bushels shipped the next year were elevated in buckets with ropes and pulleys to the second story of a frame riverside building for storage; then they were carried by way of bucket brigade to a chute which deposited the grain into four-bushel boxes on the deck of the vessel, which were then weighed and dumped straight into the ship's hold. Over the next decade

Fig. 1 Alfred S. Alschuler, Ilg Electric Ventilating Co. Building, 2850 North Pulaski Road, 1919, detail of entrance and tower; from Alfred S. Alschuler, Commercial and Industrial Buildings (Chicago, 1926).

and a half, Chicagoans perfected this procedure into a system of which the elevator became the most essential and conspicuous physical embodiment.[2]

In the traditional system it had been known which farmer grew the grain that was packed in any particular bag; in the new system developed in Chicago, the bagged grain was poured into bins to commingle with grains grown by many farmers. Central to this new system was a nexus of trust among grain dealers and their clients, a trust that was policed and enforced by the Chicago Board of Trade (founded in 1848 and chartered in 1850), whose members had devised the system and subsequently controlled the grain it handled.[3]

The storage capability of the grain elevator was essential to the system. While stored in Chicago, grain served as the basis for credit for both the businessmen in the expanding city and the farmers in its vast hinterland. In times of economic turmoil when eastern paper lacked gold backing, Chicago paper was supported by grain. Chicago grain secured loans from the East that built railroads and the cities that sprang up along the rail routes. Speculation in grain amassed fortunes for Chicagoans who then invested their winnings in other enterprises. In a city built for commerce, it was not surprising that the grain elevators rose higher than the church steeples or the cupola of the city and county building, as can be seen in views of the city dating from 1857, 1864, and 1879 (see pls. 1, 3; cat. no. 7).

While large, the elevators were otherwise unspectacular. They needed equipment to collect and elevate loose grain, bins to store it, and chutes to deposit it into carriers. Irishmen wielding buckets did the first collecting and elevating, but after many of them moved on to dig the Illinois and Michigan Canal, horses and mules powering bucket chains took over. The opening of both the canal and the first stretch of railroad into Chicago in 1848 produced an increase in transportation capacity that called for a commensurate increase in elevator capacity. This was provided not only by larger buildings but also by new technology, such as the bucket conveyor at the Bristol Elevator driven by a steam engine made at a Chicago iron foundry operated by Elihu Granger. Involved in the development of elevator design and equipment was the city's first architect, John M. Van Osdel, a sometime partner of Granger and a man as interested in mechanics as he was in buildings.[4]

The Bristol Elevator, constructed of brick, held a mere 80,000 bushels, only a small portion of the 2,160,000 bushels of wheat and 615,770 of corn and oats that moved through Chicago in 1848. By 1854, when Chicago shipped thirteen million bushels — outstripping Odessa in the Ukraine to become the world's greatest grain port — steam would drive a screw hoist and the city's two newest elevators would dwarf their predecessors.[5]

These two elevators, built on the basis of recent experience, would serve as models for the next half century. Standing on the north bank of the river opposite the commercial district, the Armour, Dole and Co. Elevator held 300,000 bushels, while the Gibbs, Griffin and Co. Elevator (one of the few early ones identified with an architect — the part-

nership of Burling and Baumann) held 500,000 bushels.[6] The next year they were joined by a larger one located across the river and nearer the lake, the Sturges, Buckingham and Co. "A" Elevator holding 700,000 bushels brought by the Illinois Central Railroad, whose 705 miles of right-of-way led upward from southern Illinois (fig. 2). In a single day, the elevator's four great steam engines could unload 236 carloads of grain, measuring 80,000 to 90,000 bushels, while discharging even more in a day into lake steamers.

The design of the Gibbs and Griffin Elevator is fairly well known. With an L-shaped plan instead of the more usual rectangular one, it could make the best use of its site. Following customary proportions, it was 190 feet deep, 60 feet along the riverfront, 110 feet along the railroad, and 87 feet high (later raised to 155 feet). Its interior was also typical, with a series of vertical bins standing in a row between the river and the rail tracks; each bin was the length of a railcar, allowing several cars to be emptied at once. The elevator used a crib construction in which the walls of each bin rested on wooden piles driven down into the mud. The walls were made of two-by-six-inch lumber in the upper levels and two-by-twelve-inch lumber in the lower levels, laid with one broad side upon another. An uncommon refinement was the brick lining of the bins. The elevator's motive power was provided by stationary steam engines housed in low brick structures along the narrow ends. The grain's outward pressure was contained by wrought iron rods running through the structure and anchored by large iron plates on the exterior. Usually the elevator's

exterior was made resistant to sparks from passing locomotives and the elevator's own engines by the use of slate, brick, or even sheet metal cladding. These materials were also used in the penthouse, which was built of timber and had a gable roof — usually of slate — with small windows to provide light and ventilation. Within the penthouse were the distribution conveyors fed by the screw lifts and driven by steam engines down below.

The only relief from the sheer mass of these structures (fig. 3) was to be found in the giant letters spelling out their names, although the chutes, angled out from the bottom in neat rows pointing toward the dock and rail sidings, provided some means of discerning their scale. Some of the elevators swallowed whole groups of railcars through arches on the narrow ends of their brick lower floors; others lapped the golden freight from sidings alongside, but most did both. A few may have been equipped with a device apparently introduced in Lockport, Illinois (a collection basin on the Illinois and Michigan Canal), which allowed a chained-down farmer's wagon or a railroad car to be rotated on its side to spill its grain into a hopper, from which the grain was elevated into the bins above.

The Great Fire of 1871 consumed seven of the city's seventeen giant elevators, but replacements were quickly rebuilt on their old sites. They were soon joined by others that were even larger than their predecessors, some with a capacity of 2,000,000 bushels each. The amount of grain moving through the city continued to increase, but not as rapidly as it had earlier. During the depression of

Fig. 3 South Chicago grain elevators.

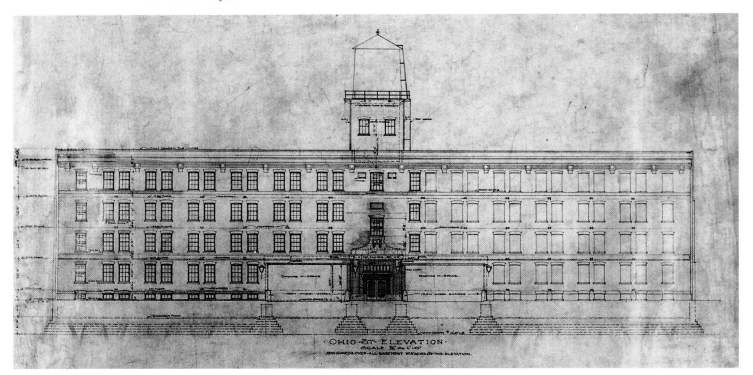

· OHIO ST ELEVATION ·

Fig. 4 Marshall and Fox, Ohio Street elevation of a warehouse for A.C. McClurg and Co., 330-50 East Ohio Street, 1907 (cat. no. 94).

the mid-1890s, traffic in grain and in every other kind of cargo moving through Chicago's harbor declined sharply. A drop followed by a sharper rise formed part of the predictable business cycle, but this time, as the economy rebounded, the harbor remained largely dormant. In 1898 Chicago was equipped with twenty-two giant elevators with the combined capacity of thirty-two million bushels, but new shipping patterns were making Milwaukee and Duluth more important grain ports than Chicago. In Chicago itself the task of moving and storing grain was shifting from the harbor to outlying railyards. Improved direct rail transportation was obviating the need for storage and transshipment to lake boats. At the same time, new construction techniques using the stark, cylindrical, reinforced concrete bins that so impressed a generation of European modernists were providing larger and more efficient structures than outdated building methods and operating equipment going back nearly a half century. Gradually, the elevators disappeared from the central city. With them went the most impressive symbol of Chicago's early role as a port serving commerce.

The Lofts

The new Chicago envisaged in the 1909 Burnham and Bennett *Plan of Chicago* had no place for these towering, bulky behemoths along the central city's river. Where they had stood, the plan showed double-decked boulevards, the upper level for recreational and business traffic, the lower one for moving the masses of small-scale package freight into and out of the street-hugging commercial warehouses and factories that would remain fixtures along the river harbor.[7] These were the legacy of the industrial loft districts that had claimed ever deeper stretches of land along the river as the city's commerce and industry expanded.

By the turn of the century, when commercial activity at the river mouth began to decline, little land was left around the original harbor area for new enterprises except in the far eastern section of the harbor area which was laid out in a new industrial district.[8] Consequently, the fringe of the central area changed little until the 1930s, when, as the national economy sloughed into the Great Depression, the area began to decline. Today one needs a vivid imagination to recover a sense of what it was like a century ago when the area was jammed to capacity with a great variety of activities directed toward the production of wealth rather than the enhancement of the city's appearance.

Like similar buildings elsewhere, the lofts that characterized the area were little more than the product of a standardized building technique embodying the calculus of commercial investment. A standard loft could be built quickly by throwing a wooden floor structure between brick bearing-walls set twenty feet apart and sealing the front and back with non-structural diaphragm walls. The twenty-foot span was undoubtedly arrived at on the basis of the spanning capacity of the wooden members, the convenience of shipping and handling the members, and the length of a clear span that could serve the light and heavy commercial and industrial activities the building was to accommodate.

Most of the industrial buildings predating the boom times of the 1880s were a single, twenty-foot-module wide, although several such modules could be thrown together to accommodate a larger enterprise. Lofts were most commonly built by a capitalist intending to lease them to someone who would use them to manufacture, process, or store some product or other. Lofts were therefore built as flexible structures that could be used for any number of successive functions. Farthest from anyone's mind was the thought that loft buildings would be identified with either their owners or users.

In conjunction with the economic recovery that heralded the new century, a new kind of loft structure appeared. Instead of being built by an investor and leased for use by others, lofts increasingly were built by the companies that would use them. Such buildings tended to be larger, to be designed to serve more specialized functions, and to establish an identity for their owners by displaying the firm's logo or name. The anonymous lofts of the previous century may well be classified as "investment lofts," while these later structures may properly be called "company lofts."

For a generation, the differences between these types of lofts were only skin deep, for internally the structural system remained the same. The timber loft construction system (also called mill construction and loft construction), developed soon after dimension-cut lumber became available in the 1830s, and was employed for these new buildings as well. It was challenged at the turn of the century when reinforced concrete began to be used in special applications, but this alternative to traditional construction did not become the dominant system until after World War I. The lightweight fire-proofed steel structural system used for the tall commercial buildings in the Loop found little application in the construction of the rugged industrial lofts.

An example of the loft construction used in a company loft is the first warehouse Benjamin Marshall designed for A. C. McClurg and Co., the respected Chicago book publisher, in 1907–08 (fig. 4).[9] The building was 240 feet long and 100 feet deep, with a basement and four stories. Its central space included a precocious use of steel framing fireproofed with concrete and with reinforced concrete floors supporting, ultimately, a pair of rooftop water tanks to feed the fire-sprinkler system.[10] Within this central section were the entrances, stairs, offices, elevators, and other specialized spaces required to make use of the extensive loft spaces stretching out on either side. The building

(no longer extant) was on East Ohio Street in the newly developed and newly platted St. Claire Industrial District.

The warehouse was enclosed on all four sides by brick bearing-walls. Inside, the length was divided into sixteen-foot bays and the depth into fourteen-foot bays. In a multicell loft, the alternative to having rows of posts was to have a series of brick bearing-walls with the various bays connected by punching a door through the bearing-wall. This method made sense for an investment loft. If a leaser using several bays was to be replaced by several leasers wanting one each, the connections between the bays could simply be closed. The floor was covered by one-inch-thick tongue-and-groove flooring in maple, the only departure from the universal use of yellow pine elsewhere in this structure.

A loft's front facade was the only place for any architectural pretense. Since the addition of such pretense did not increase the return on the investor's capital, it tended to be absent from investment lofts. This does not mean that investment lofts were not designed; but their appearance was less the result of conscious calculation than an illustration of the practices, traditions, experience, and habits of a city's builders. Thus the distinctive appearance of Chicago's lofts reveals the city's unique local

Fig. 5 Architect unknown, 225 West Illinois Street, 1883.

Fig. 6 Burnham and Root, Montauk Block, 64 West Monroe Street, 1881-82 (demolished).

Fig. 7 Architect unknown, 10-18 West Hubbard Street, 1883.

building history. For example, experience had taught Chicagoans that cast iron survives an intense fire no better than any other material. Thus, relatively few post-fire commercial or industrial buildings were built with cast-iron facades, and when the ground floor of an investment loft was to be opened up with large plate glass windows, cast-iron columns were seldom used as structural members without being enclosed within brick piers. Above that level of the loft's facade there tended to be a nonstructural diaphragm that had to be opened with windows to allow light and air into the building. The way this was done in an investment loft usually revealed aspects of designs being used for more pretentious buildings in the city's commercial center.

A discussion of two utilitarian, industrial investment lofts surviving in the blocks immediately north of the original river harbor will illustrate these points. Both were begun in 1883, both measure 100 by 100 feet, both rise five stories, and both have load-bearing exterior walls of brick and interiors with standard loft (or mill) construction. In neither case is the name of the architect known.

One of the buildings, at 225 West Illinois Street on the southeast corner of Franklin (fig. 5), was built as an investment by the Estate of Walter Newberry for use as a foundry.[11] Its two finished street facades give the impression that the posts of the interior's mill construction have been converted to brick piers. To fill the intervening spaces, the ground floor (recently altered) was originally equipped with a pair of plate-glass windows below a wrought-iron lintel and separated by a cast-iron post, while the floors above originally received a brick diaphragm wall opened up with two six-over-six double-hung windows.[12]

The design is perhaps most easily understood as a union of two different and unremarkable construction techniques, one based on the lintel, the other on the arch. The power of Chicago's architecture from this period resides in the clarity with which a building's actual materials allow a person to see the structural system that actually supports the building. This is true no matter how much elaboration or ornamentation had been added to the basic structural system in order to raise the building's status. In every case, either the arch or the lintel system is dominant, although sometimes the subordinate system is extensively interwoven with the dominant one. As had always been the case in architecture, the less important the building, the less extensive the elaboration. For example, the lintel system, in its ultimate reduction to a cage, could produce a building with the stark simplicity of William Le Baron Jenney's first Leiter

Fig. 8 Hugh M. G. Garden for Richard E. Schmidt, Grommes and Ullrich Co. Building, 114 West Illinois Street, 1901.

Building of 1879, but no important building at this time reduced itself to such a direct expression of post-and-beam construction. In Burnham and Root's bearing-wall commercial structures – the Grannis Block (1880-81), the Montauk Block (1881-82; fig. 6), the Calumet Building (1882-84), and the Counselman Building (1883-84), all designed by the time this loft was begun[13] – the arch system, reduced to a wall opened up with arches, is dominant; but the status of each building was elevated by elaborating the designs with a subordinate lintel system and spare ornament. These buildings partake thoroughly of the art of building as practiced in Chicago. Strip them down to basic construction, in which the lintels do the heavier work, and one can find the foundry's facades. Had the larger labor been given to the arches, the result would have resembled George Edbrooke's Hiram Sibley Warehouse (also from 1883), only a few blocks away along the river,[14] or the other extant loft from 1883 on West Hubbard Street (fig. 7).

Originally a wool warehouse, this essay in arcuation is located at 10-18 West Hubbard,[15] in an area that was well established in the brokering and warehousing of wool and hides and the storing, processing, and packaging of various animal products and foodstuffs. The ground floor resembles that of the foundry at 225 West Illinois, but because its piers do not continue into the upper floor, it is read here as a plinth for the floors above. The upper floors appear as brick walls opened with segmentally arched windows, whose headers remain flush with the wall plane. The design's sophistication becomes clear when one notices the three ma-

Fig. 9 Grommes and Ullrich Co. Building, detail of brickwork.

jor disruptions in the wall plane, each related to structure yet none dictated by constructional imperatives. In other words, each exploits an aspect of structure to produce an architectonic effect in the most economical manner.

One of these departures from a strict planar treatment is the slight projection of the continuous line of thin stone window sills. These give the building the appearance of being constructed as a series of floors piled one atop another, as in fact it was. In this sense the building remains unfinished – the tops of the building's posts project through the roof a foot or so, and could be used to carry a sixth story. A second departure is in the three pairs of slots in the central four bays on every floor, each in line with the brick pier on the ground floor. Unobtrusive as these construction details are, they invest the building with a certain grandeur and relate it to the more sophisticated buildings rising in the Loop. The third departure is in the treatment given the end bays which appear to step forward and which contain a grouping of three windows rather than the pairing found in the central bays.

The foundry and wool warehouses could have been built at any moment up to the hiatus in construction accompanying the depression of the 1890s. More than that: with very few changes in appearance, but none of any consequence in the method of construction, either one could have been built at any time before World War I, although the level of finish would have been higher, and wrought-iron lintels rather than segmental arches would have been used above the window openings. The new century, however, brought a decline in investment loft construction and a growth in the construction of company lofts. In part this stemmed from new patterns of investment, and in part from the decision by local capitalists that in the City Beautiful and the City Efficient, even loft buildings should be attractive. Builders and architects were no longer content with examples of an indigenous "commercial style" or buildings developed as seemingly unselfconscious or unprecedented solutions to the problem of merging utility, cost, construction technique, and architectural character. Instead, they sought historical forms to suggest that the Chicago that had hosted the 1893 World's Columbian Exposition was not merely an entrepôt on the edge of a narrow world of commerce but a world center with a past reaching back into antiquity and touching every part of the globe.

Representative of this new self-consciousness was the four-story, 80-by-100-foot building at 114 West Illinois Street, designed by Hugh M. G. Garden to provide office and warehouse facilities for the Grommes and Ullrich Company, distributors of liquor (figs. 8, 9).[16] The building has been cited as an important point in architectural development that occurred between the construction of William Le Baron Jenney's first Leiter Building of 1879 and the Chicago work of Ludwig Mies van der Rohe,[17] but its fame in that context has not led to a clear understanding of its design.

The building's design is clearly indebted to classicism. Most conspicuous is the tripartite scheme controlling the facade's division into a base, a middle section, and a top – a design device found in almost everything produced during this period. Another aspect of its classicism is as rare in buildings lacking strong connections with classicism during the period as its tripartite division is usual, although this aspect is always present in the best classicism. This is the way the parts, ranging in scale from individual bricks to whole floors, are defined both as discrete components and as integral parts of a coherent whole.

This aspect arises, as is always the case in the best classicism, from using construction materials in a way that calls attention to the character of the building's structural system. In this case the trabeated system was employed. The extent to which the building is classical has been overlooked, probably because Garden did not use the kind of canonic classical components that the architects of the 1893 World's Columbian Exposition had rendered in plaster and horsehair. It is classical nonetheless, because like any knowledgeable essay in this style, it presents a vivid representation of structure.

In addition, the facade's design also presents a clear exposition of the character of the interior structural framework and spatial configuration. The actual facade is only as thick as the outer layer of pressed brick; behind that are brick piers spanned by long steel or wrought-iron lintels, and behind that is timber frame construction. But what one sees suggests much more. The design proportions the openings, manipulates the outer layer of brick, and fills voids with windows to evoke the character of a classical structural system and to signal that within this building one will find regularly disposed slots of unencumbered space.

Although this warehouse is like any other well-designed classical structure based on the orders, because it is a mere warehouse its design did not merit an explicit reference to historical classicism. Therefore, its classicism has been diluted to a level appropriate for a warehouse. Although it evokes classicism in very austere forms, the building could nonetheless take a proper place among the hierarchy of designs for buildings that would have filled in the blocks that Burnham and Bennett would eventually portray in their 1909 *Plan of Chicago*.

In calling it a classical design, one is merely stressing the sources drawn upon, rather than the results achieved by its architect, Hugh M. G. Garden. Studies of Garden and others with similar interests have noted that some among them "accepted the historical styles, desiring only to simplify them and thereby achieve a contemporary freshness," while others sought "consciously to create a new style — by evolving new forms from old, or by applying some theory or system of design."[18] This latter group has been of greater interest to historians who have neglected a number of competent, independent, and prolific architects of unpretentious buildings, among them Samuel Crowen, Andrew Sandegren, and Benjamin Marshall. Marshall was also the designer of some of the city's most pretentious buildings.

Marshall is noted for his skilfull use of historical, particularly classical, forms. But his first McClurg Warehouse of 1906-07 is as independent from precedent as anything Garden did, and is also just as dependent on the underlying character of classicism as Garden's liquor warehouse for Grommes and Ullrich. The seriousness of its design is appropriate for the building of a company that took itself seriously, just as that design's unorthodoxy is proper for what was, after all, a mere warehouse.

The facade of the McClurg Warehouse was separated from the street by a ten-foot strip of lawn. The pedestrian and freight entrances located at the center of the building at street level were faced with stone on the lower level, including the zone with the legend A. C. McClurg & Co. and, above it, the company logo, an open book on a bookstand. The

rest of the facade was face brick over load-bearing walls laid up with a spareness appropriate to a warehouse, but with a rich subtlety in the disposition and proportion of the brick courses and of the windows and doors.

Fig. 10 Alfred S. Alschuler, John Sexton and Co. Building, 500 North Orleans Street, 1916; from Alschuler, Commercial and Industrial Buildings.

Fig. 11 John Sexton and Co. Building, detail of side entrance at 352 West Illinois Street; from Alschuler, Commercial and Industrial Buildings.

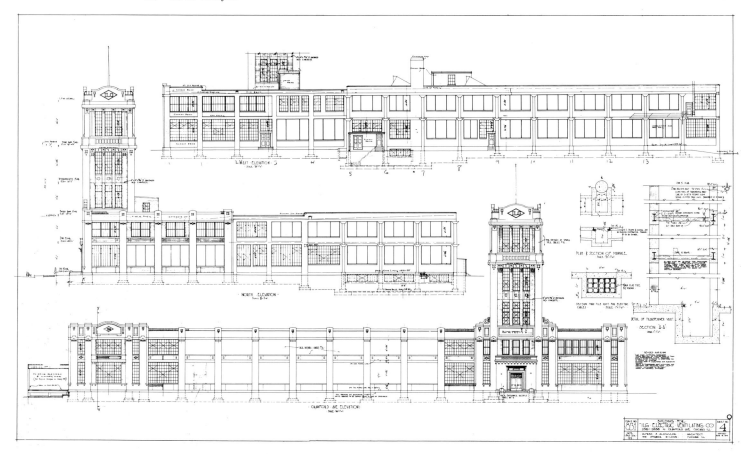

Fig. 12 Alfred S. Al-schuler, Facade elevation of the Ilg Electric Ventilating Co. Building, 1919 (cat. no. 98).

As was the case with Garden's Grommes and Ullrich building and many other buildings used for similar purposes, the architects made good use of Chicago's readily available high quality brick work, which could be laid up in economical, simple, unadorned patterns. These patterns made no direct reference to historical forms, but constituted forceful architectonic expression of traditional structural systems. Such a congruence of structural material, construction technique, and formal representation was characteristic of Chicago's architecture at the moment when these loft buildings were being designed, whether their architects were interested in pursuing historical precedents, new forms, or a formal expression of a personally contrived design theory. But within a decade, these aspects of construction and design had become separated from one another, with a resulting decline in the overall quality of architectonic design. This happened at the very time that companies began to use their lofts as one of the ways to assert their identities.

Characteristic of this later period of Chicago's industrial and commercial architecture is the John Sexton and Company building of 1916 by Alfred S. Alschuler (fig. 10).[19] Built as the office, warehouse, and manufacturing plant for a grocery and food-processing company, the building is extant in the original harbor area, its six stories and 100-foot depth stretching along Illinois Street between Orleans and Kingsbury Streets, east of the North Branch of the Chicago River.

The building's structure is entirely traditional — load-bearing brick walls and a timber loft interior — but its size is not: its street facade is more than 400 feet long. The carefully designed finished facades include departures from absolute regularity that suggest the differing uses of the floors, and indicate the location of interior stairways, shaftways, and elevators, while also evoking the building's structural character, as earlier Chicago lofts had done.

Similarly, the wall itself possesses the same careful differentiation between post-and-lintel and arch systems noticeable on the 1883 foundry building at 225 West Illinois Street. The wall plane holding the window lintels is set well back from the piers. In an intermediary zone between that plane and the face of the piers is a flange that rises to receive the segmental arches above the top floor windows and bears the parapet. The complicated intersection at the piers' tops is articulated with a nicely detailed capital in white glazed terracotta, the material also used for the facing of the segmental arches, the parapet coping, the window sills, various decorative accents on the building, and the frame for the pedestrian entrance (fig. 11).

The pattern traced by this interweaving of lintels and arches described by the careful location of glazed terracotta enrichments is as carefully contrived here as the pattern on Burnham and Root's buildings of the 1880s, except that in the Alschuler building the historical source for the terracotta ornamentation and for the general compositional pattern is less original and can be traced to the period's fascination with English Tudor architecture.

Alschuler was not alone among his contemporaries in using historical sources in such a literal, if piecemeal, manner; others, like Garden and Marshall, were doing the same. This tendency to use ornament to enrich the surface rather than to clarify the structure is most visible in the increasingly extensive use of glazed terracotta in places where architects had formerly used unglazed terracotta, or Lemont or Bedford stone.[20] The glaze's eternal shine stresses the piece's surface rather than its depth.

In 1919, the Sexton building was extended eastward 150 feet to reach Orleans Street. The floor levels matched those in the older building and were devoted to similar functions, so that the exterior design could easily be replicated line for line. But there is a difference — the bays in the addition were larger, a change made possible by the use of rein-

forced concrete for the structural system. The difference in appearance was quite minor, explicable by the fact that in an addition it was more important to fit the new to the old than to fit the skin to the structure. The addition makes it clear, first, that reinforced concrete had become an efficient way to construct loft buildings, and second, that the loft buildings would henceforth be so large as to make that the efficient structural system. What was needed to obtain the same high architectonic expression with the new material was a compositional pattern and a repertoire of formal details appropriate to the building and its purpose. Those elements would not be present in a building faced with a false front, as this addition was.

In the same year that he designed the Sexton addition, Alschuler produced a model of such a design for a two-story factory commissioned by the Ilg Electric Ventilating Company, to be located in a railside industrial district several miles from the constricted river harbor district (figs. 1, 12, 13).[21] It exemplifies the next generation of industrial buildings that would be larger, more specialized, usually of reinforced concrete, and often sited in the industrial districts growing up along the newly opened canals and beltline railroads illustrated in the Burnham and Bennett *Plan of Chicago*.[22] An industrial building, Alschuler wrote in 1924, "is

Fig. 13 Ilg Electric Ventilating Co. Building; from Alschuler, Commercial and Industrial Buildings.

really one large operating machine. ... A handsome building is an asset which should not be ignored. It should not be secured, however, at a disproportionate first cost or at the expense of operating economy."[23] Producing buildings like this, and others that were taller than they were broad, would assure that Alschuler's office remained one of the largest in Chicago during the century's second and third decades.[24] This one stands apart only by making better and more conspicuous use of the trio of materials Alschuler could integrate so well into a design — reinforced concrete, brick (usually wire cut to produce a rough surface), and unglazed terracotta.[25]

To an extent far superior to what he had done in the first part of the Sexton building, Alschuler used the materials in the Ilg building in ways that were appropriate to their character and to their role within the structure. Indeed, illustrated here is what he meant when he later wrote that if one used reinforced concrete, "the exterior piers [may] be made both structural and ornamental in themselves, eliminating the veneer that is ordinarily required to cover the piers of a mill building."[26]

The potential for broad and high structures innate within the structural system that uses reinforced concrete efficiently is played out here with the broad horizontality of the shop floors, broken by a tower marking the location of the company's offices at the northern end (fig. 1). Brick forms the spandrels and jambs. At the base of the tower, glazed terracotta dresses the office entrance in what is the least successful part of the design. In the area where the tower departs from the block, glazed terracotta reappears in a fillet marking the transition from horizontal to vertical. Its role is clearly not structural but ornamental, and its design is abstracted from classical forms. The reticulated structural concrete frame, which still bears the marks of the boards into which it was poured, has a number of planes and carefully designed cast-in-place forms to articulate the joining of horizontal and vertical, with most joints further enriched with let-in geometric panels of unglazed terracotta. The tower's termination receives a similar set of materials which provide a clear setting for the company name and logo.

To find buildings like the one for Ilg one must go to areas that were on the periphery of the city at the time they were built. For some years there had been no room for them in the center; there were a few holes to be filled in the harbor district, but for the most part, the land in that part of the city was occupied. Builders in the city's center now concentrated on improving what had been jerry-built. The Burnham and Bennett Plan, the establishment of the Chicago Plan Commission, the ongoing attempts to reform the city's political system, and the enactment of a comprehensive land use and building height ordinance in 1923 sought to direct the form of the entire city. At the level of individual buildings, the Chicago Tribune Company sought to find a design for "the most beautiful and distinctive office building in the world," through a competition.[27] Alfred Alschuler explored new materials and forms in low-level industrial buildings, and Benjamin Marshall sought a way to make a new architecture from the new materials, or at least to find a new architectonic character for them.

Recognizing that steel frame buildings clad in terracotta would not survive as well across the centuries as more traditional materials had, Marshall wrote in 1929:

Let us build our commercial structures of concrete frames with metal windows placed in openings, with all ornament cast in the concrete structure in color, or otherwise. Let us dress the concrete so that it will give a finished and beautiful surface. This will insure buildings both permanent and beautiful. It will be a true expression of a lasting type of architecture — a type of permanent construction which undoubtedly has to come.[28]

For whatever reason, Alschuler and Marshall's colorful vision of what a new architecture based on reinforced concrete might become, was not to be. That was not the direction in which the architects interested in a new architecture were looking. That call would be as much ignored as Jenney's precocious stripped-down trabeation at the first Leiter Building had been. Instead, architects were subjecting traditional architectural forms to an increasing abstraction, wringing out of them all structural vigor and leaving behind only an ornamental surface. In that approach it made no difference what the interior structure might be — the exterior form was no longer expected to represent anything within. Nor did one expect a congruence between a building's formal properties and its purpose. All buildings were now considered equal and equally deserving of the best design. These two disjunctions, one between skin and structure, the other between form and use, loosened the final bonds tying architecture to past practice and knowledge and assumed dominance in what people understood architecture to be. As a result, it became possible for mere construction to be confused with architectural form and for buildings erected for the meanest uses to be viewed as instructive about the design of important buildings. Emblematically put, the world became a place in which the giant concrete tubes that replaced the crib-construction grain elevators could be looked to as models for buildings.

NOTES

1.   See Guy A. Lee, "The Historical Significance of the Chicago Grain Elevator System," *Agricultural History* 11 (1937), p. 18.

2.   A useful review is in Wyatt Winton Belcher, *The Economic Rivalry Between St. Louis and Chicago, 1850-1880* (New York, 1947).

3.   Useful résumés of the Board of Trade's history are found in Alfred T. Andreas, *History of Chicago*, 3 vols. (Chicago, 1884-86), vol. 2, pp. 376-79; and in Charles H. Taylor, *History of the Board of Trade of the City of Chicago*, 3 vols. (Chicago, 1917).

4.   Granger specialized in grain-carrying lake boats and in equipment for elevators; earlier he had been a contractor on the Illinois and Michigan Canal (Andreas [note 3], vol. 1, p. 567). Between 1843 and 1845, Van Osdel operated the iron foundry with Granger, where in 1841 Van Osdel "built Chicago's first grain elevator," apparently referring to a building specially fitted out for handling loose grains rather than sacks of grain. This may have been H. Norton & Co.'s elevator which was equipped with the bucket conveyor. Henry Ericsson, *Sixty Years a Builder* (Chicago, 1942), pp. 134-35, points out that Van Osdel had also been involved in work on the canal, where he devised wind-driven pumps for which he received a United States patent, the first Chicagoan to do so, and that around 1840 he was in New York in association with D. D. Badger, the pioneer in cast-iron building components. Ericsson also stresses the link between Granger, Van Osdel, and the early Chicago grain elevators.

5.   See Andreas (note 3), vol. 2, pp. 374-76, for the most useful information about the elevators.

6.   See Andreas (note 3), particularly vol. 1, pp. 579-81; and vol. 2, p. 566, for much of the material about construction given below. Additional information, especially for the later period, is found in *Insurance Maps of Chicago Grain Elevators* (New York, 1901).

7.   The opportunity exists, the authors of the Plan stated, "to plan a comprehensive and adequate development of the river banks, so that the commercial facilities shall be extended, while at the same time the aesthetic side of the problem shall be worked out." Daniel H. Burnham and Edward H. Bennett, *Plan of Chicago* (Chicago, 1909), p. 97. See also plate 107, "View looking north on the South Branch of the Chicago River, showing the suggested arrangement of streets and ways for teaming and reception of freight by boat, at different levels." The proposals need to be understood in conjunction with a series of extensive inquiries seeking the cause of decline in traffic in the river harbor and suggestions for adjusting to the changed circumstances uncovered by those inquiries. See, for example, Harbor Commission of the City of Chicago, *Report* (Chicago, 1905); Chicago Harbor Commission, *Digest of Hearings* (Chicago, 1909); The Harbor and Subway Commission of the City of Chicago, *Report on Dock and Pier Development, Harbor District No. 1* (Chicago, 1915); B. P. Brown, *Drainage Canal and Waterway* (Chicago, 1894); and *Report of the Submerged and Shore Lands Legislative Investigating Committee*, 3 vols. (Springfield, Ill., 1911).

8.   See, for example, "New St. Claire Manufacturing District Forging Ahead with Great Strides," *The Real Estate and Building Journal* (June 20, 1908), pp. 5-14; and Burnham and Bennett (note 7), ch. 5, esp. p. 64 and pl. 71.

9.   The information that follows was taken from the plans, dated from late 1907 and early 1908, now in the Architectural Drawings Collection, General Libraries, The University of Texas at Austin. Other McClurg warehouse buildings and additions to earlier ones followed in 1908, 1909, 1914, and 1920. See C. W. Westfall, "Benjamin H. Marshall of Chicago," *Chicago Architectural Journal* 2 (1982), pp. 8-27.

10.   Loft construction was also known as slow-burning construction and was not fireproof. To protect property and assure safety, buildings had to be equipped with a sprinkler system fed by roof-top water tanks.

11.   Walter Newberry was an early settler and an extensive landowner in this area of the city. A City of Chicago Building Permit was issued December 10, 1883, to the Newberry Estate for a five-story factory, 100 by 100 by [illegible] feet. The building's predecessor was also a foundry. Early in the city's history this area became known for its foundries.

12.   Because the brick has been painted extensively in the lower levels, with the result that all the surfaces appear to be of one material, it is easy to misinterpret a photograph showing the ground-floor piers.

13.   See Donald Hoffmann, *The Architecture of John Wellborn Root* (Baltimore, 1973), ch. 2, figs. 8-9, 17, and 20.

14.   Carl W. Condit, *The Chicago School of Architecture: A History of Commercial and Public Building in the Chicago Area, 1875-1925* (Chicago, 1964), p. 58, fig. 16. See also the string of notices given the building in *Inland Architect* 2 (1883) and 3 (1884).

15.   City of Chicago building permit for December 5, 1883, issued to H. T. Thompson for a five-story warehouse, 100 by 99 by 60 feet. The upper floors of the building presently house the offices of Harry Weese and Associates, Architects, who restored it and have been sponsoring a preservation and reinvestment effort in the area. The building was not originally painted.

16.   City of Chicago Building Permit dated April 27, 1901, issued to Grommes and Ullrich with Richard E. Schmidt as architect of record. By that date, Hugh Garden was working for Schmidt but was not yet his partner.

17.   See, for example, Condit (note 14), pp. 186-87; and H. Allen Brooks, *The Prairie School: Frank Lloyd Wright and his Midwest Contemporaries* (Toronto, 1972; reprinted New York, 1976), p. 50.

18.   Brooks (note 17), p. 47.

19.   The building's working drawings, dated November, 1916, are in the collection of the Department of Architecture at The Art Institute of Chicago. The building is illustrated along with four others by Alschuler in George C. Nimmons, "Modern Industrial Plants: II," *Architectural Record* 94, 6 (Dec. 1918), pp. 533-549. A collection of Alschuler's scrapbooks in the possession of the Chicago Architecture Foundation is available in the library of the Spertus Museum of Judaica of Chicago.

20.   Lemont stone, also euphemistically known as Athens Marble, was discovered in the 1840s near Lemont, south of Chicago, while the Illinois and Michigan Canal was being dug. It was a very high quality limestone with a creamy yellow hue but had a tendency to spall, or exfoliate, which made it unsuitable for carved ornamentation. Because of its abundance in quarries next to the canal, it replaced stone imported by boat from New York State as the dominant material for foundations, sills, lintels, and facade revetments on the city's better buildings at the middle of the century. Later in the century, Indiana or Bedford bluestone, a better limestone, replaced it in more expensive buildings. After 1900, concrete replaced limestone in foundations and terracotta predominated in other building details.

21.   Drawings dated July to August, 1919, for the building at 2800-58 North Pulaski Road (formerly Crawford Avenue) are in the collection of the Department of Architecture at The Art Institute of Chicago.

22.   For this dispersal of industry from the center of the city and the preparations made for this shift, see Harold M. Mayer and Richard C. Wade, *Chicago: Growth of a Metropolis* (Chicago, 1969), pp. 234 ff.

23.   Alfred S. Alschuler, "The Design of the Modern Printing Building: II," *The Inland Printer* (Sept. 1923), p. 857.

24.   The building's horizontal configuration exemplifies the industrial buildings that, since the turn of the century, had been developed by using reinforced concrete to enclose broad, open manufacturing spaces on cheap land on the outskirts of the city. Those buildings had their models in broad, low buildings such as train sheds and the factory sheds of Solon Spencer Beman's Pullman Palace Car Company Works in the model city far south of Chicago, rather than the lofts near the city's center.

25.   This trio of materials was perhaps popularized in Chicago in the Montgomery Ward Warehouse, located on the north branch of the Chicago River a few blocks north of the John Sexton site. The plans for the Montgomery Ward Warehouse by Schmidt, Garden and Martin were dated from late 1906 to early 1907.

26.   Alfred S. Alschuler, "The Design of the Modern Printing Building: III," *The Inland Printer* (Oct. 1923), p. 131.

27.   So said the terms of the competition. See *The International Competition for a New Administration Building for the Chicago Tribune* (Chicago, 1923). The text is slightly abridged in Stanley Tigerman, ed., *Late Entries to the Chicago Tribune Tower Competition*, 2 vols. (New York, 1980), vol. 1, p. 10.

28.   "Architecture of an Expanding Metropolis and Some of Its Towers," *Chicago: The World's Youngest Great City* (Chicago, 1929), pp. 53-58.

An Early German Contribution to Chicago's Modernism

Roula Mouroudellis Geraniotis

The Chicago School and the Prairie School were Chicago's most important contributions to the development of modern architecture and the leading architectural phenomena of the period covered by the essays in this volume. Although both have been accurately identified and are properly admired, the process of their emergence and flowering remains partially unexplored and is still awaiting definitive scholarly treatment. Some research now suggests that the Chicago and Prairie schools owed as much to a multitude of international influences and interrelations as to the particular qualities of Chicago's architectural scene. One such influence that has been totally overlooked so far came from Germany and was channeled directly into Chicago by the city's German architects.[1]

Chicago differed from other major American metropolises in the very large number of German-born or German-educated architects who practiced in the city. These architects formed the largest ethnic entity in the profession and, in combination with Chicago's prominent German community, constituted a cultural force that profoundly affected the intellectual atmosphere of the city. German architects started pouring into the Midwest in the early 1850s, following the failure of the 1848-49 democratic revolution in Germany, and continued to arrive until World War I. Many developed prolific careers and achieved great prominence. Moreover, they helped establish a direct connection to the leading architectural mainstreams in Germany, thus introducing a significant international component into Chicago's architecture. This essay explores one particular aspect of this cultural and architectural relationship — the influence of Karl Friedrich Schinkel, the master of

Figs. 1/2 Richard E. Schmidt, Albert Madlener House, 4 West Burton Place, 1902, detail of entrance and exterior.

German neoclassicism, and his followers, the architects of the Berlin School, on Chicago's architectural theory and design as reflected in the work of several of the city's German architects.[2]

The chronological limits of the exhibition that this book accompanies were milestones of the German presence in Chicago. The year 1872 witnessed an intensification of immigration from Germany following the end of the Franco-Prussian War, during which emigration had been restricted severely;[3] at the same time, the feverish rebuilding of the city that followed the Great Fire of 1871 made Chicago very attractive to German builders and architects. In 1922, the year of the Chicago Tribune tower competition, Germans constituted the largest group of competitors from outside the United States.[4] Between these two events, which brought the two architectural traditions together in a more conspicuous way, unfolds the story of German architectural accomplishment in Chicago. It began in 1850, when the young German architect Frederick

Baumann (1826-1921) reached Chicago, becoming the first known German architect to practice in the city (cat. no. 90). Baumann was born in Angermünde, Prussia, and studied architecture and building in various trade schools there, including the *Königliches Gewerbeinstitut* in Berlin, where he also attended classes at the university and at the Royal Academy.[5] In the course of his studies in Berlin, and especially during an early period of employment with his uncle, a royal *Bauinspektor* (building inspector) in Bromberg, Baumann became thoroughly acquainted with the architecture of Karl Friedrich Schinkel and his followers.[6]

Baumann's earliest professional affiliation in Chicago was with John M. Van Osdel, Chicago's first professional architect, for whom he worked in 1851-52. After associating himself with Edward Burling from 1852 to 1854, Baumann returned to work with Van Osdel again until 1856. From 1858 to 1864 Baumann worked as a mason and building contractor. In 1868 he formed a partnership with

his cousin Edward Baumann (1838-1889) that lasted until 1879. He practiced alone for the next decade and then in association with J. K. Cady. Although Baumann had left Germany as a young man, the work of Schinkel had made a lasting impression on him, one that many years of life in Chicago would not diminish. In 1869, for example, Baumann prepared an abridged translation for publication in Chicago of the festival oration delivered by the Berlin architect Friedrich Adler at the 1869 *Schinkelfest,* the annual celebration of Schinkel's birthday.[7] Undoubtedly Baumann believed that this event, celebrated with great pomp in Berlin, was worthy of some commemoration in the prairie city, and he was probably the person best qualified to accomplish this. Further, he may have wanted to promulgate a message that he viewed as particularly significant. This becomes apparent if one compares his translation with the original; Baumann's careful editing emphasized the point that Schinkel was a precursor of modern architecture.[8]

Fig. 6 Burling and Adler, Lunt Building, 69-73 West Washington Street, 1873-74 (demolished); from Land Owner *6 (May 1874).*

tions become necessary to create such a new thing which has in it the power of allowing a real progression in history. This ... is only possible where a complete knowledge of what exists in history is accompanied by a phantasy and divinative power of finding ... the exact *plus* just necessary in art [emphasis in the original].[10]

In other words, architects should abandon the slavish imitation of historic styles and focus instead on the effort to produce a new architecture that would be truly "historic" in stature, although modern in form and function. For this, knowledge of the architecture of the past was important. Yet even more important was the imaginative and creative design process in accordance with the given condition.

The Bauakademie was seen as the realization of Schinkel's philosophy of architecture, particularly of that proposition of architectural progress. To achieve this, Adler explained, Schinkel adopted the "permanent formation laws of the middle ages" and stamped them with the "ever acknowledged form of Hellenic art." In this way the Bauakademie became a "creative structure" of the nineteenth century.[11] This statement was highly significant, as it related to the notion of architectural creativity current in nineteenth-century Chicago: in the design of skyscrapers this was expressed as a synthesis of structural versatility and inventiveness, akin to that of the Gothic style, with the formal regularity and serenity of the classical revival.

Frederick Baumann's own work occasionally emulated the stylistic features of contemporary architecture in Berlin, although not in the creative fashion that Schinkel had asked for, but in the rather dry and academic manner that many of his followers, including Friedrich Adler, occasionally adopted. One such example was the Ashland Block built in 1872 by the firm of F. and E. Baumann (fig. 3).[12]

Born in Marienwerder, Prussia, Edward Baumann attended the trade school at Graudenz, graduating in 1856 and leaving for Chicago the same year. There he worked as a draftsman for the firm of Burling and Baumann, subsequently serving as a draftsman and later partner for Edward Burling. While a partner with his cousin Frederick, he participated actively in the rebuilding of Chicago.[13] The Ashland Block was an office building in the *palazzo* mode, which dominated European and American architecture from the 1850s through the 1870s, although in an unusual version. It was characterized by severity, compactness, regularity, and the predominance of solids over voids. Its facades were in a strict trabeated mode, the only ornamentation being the segmental and triangular pediments of the windows. This design was re-

Friedrich Adler was convinced that, of all Schinkel's works, the Bauakademie in Berlin was the building most prophetic of the architecture of the future:

[W]hich of his works has not only achieved universal admiration, but, as if breaking a new path, thrust toward modern architecture to higher development in conformity with our age? Involuntarily ... our eye is directed beyond over Grecian and arched domes of the roman [*sic*] age, Gothic churches and Florentine palaces; and with growing interest it remains fixed upon one building, the size of which is not imposing, the form of which is not captivating; but which ... attracts ever and ever with silent potency. This building is Schinkel's "Bauschule."[9]

The reasons for such unreserved admiration were its "chaste severity, sober beauty, ... and engaging originality," which made it resemble a "seed which promises further organic development." This emanated directly from Schinkel's ideas on design. As quoted by Adler and translated by Baumann, Schinkel had explained that

the aspiring for the ideal will modify itself in every age, according to newly entering conditions ... new inven-

markably similar to that of contemporary buildings in Berlin, like the residence at Bauhofstrasse 7 by Friedrich Adler from before 1866 (fig. 5), or the residences on the Waterloo-Ufer in Berlin from around 1860 (fig. 4). Like them, the Ashland Block had plain, smooth wall surfaces pierced by flat-linteled windows surrounded by simply articulated classicizing frames; the central part of each front projected slightly and was crowned by a pediment; the building terminated in an ornamental frieze and a classical cornice. Of course, the Chicago building was much taller and had the ground-story facades opened up to continuous glazed surfaces. Yet its basic design principles and overall proportioning were very similar to the Berlin buildings cited here, works with which the German cousins may have been acquainted.

The firm of Burling and Adler also designed commercial buildings that deserve our attention. Edward Burling was a native American architect. Dankmar Adler, one of Chicago's leading architects and a longtime partner of Louis H. Sullivan, was born in Lengsfeld, Saxony, and came to Chicago with his family in 1861. He apprenticed with several architects there, fought in the Civil War, and then entered successively the offices of Augustus Bauer and Ozias S. Kinney. From 1871 to 1879 Adler was associated with Edward Burling. The earliest example of their design was the Lunt Building, erected in 1873-74 (fig. 6).[14] It had a severely trabeated front terminating in a cornice; stringcourses dividing the facades at the level of

each story; and two entrances contained in slightly projecting central bays. In terms of the overall formal organization and the character of the decoration, this design was unusual for Chicago at the

Fig. 7 Martin Gropius, Achenbach residence, Berlin, c. 1870 (demolished); from Börsch-Supan, Berliner Baukunst.

Fig. 8 Burling and Adler, Haddock Block, northeast corner of Wabash Avenue and Monroe Street, 1875 (demolished); from Land Owner 6 (Aug. 1875).

Fig. 9 Residences at Matthaikirchstrasse 13 and 15, Berlin, c. 1845 (demolished); from Börsch-Supan, Berliner Baukunst.

time, but compares plausibly with contemporary works in Germany, like Martin Gropius's Achenbach residence in Berlin from around 1870 (fig. 7). Both buildings had flat facades pierced by the window openings and terminated by a cornice. Moreover, they utilized the same motif: paired windows contained within a frame consisting of a fragment of a cornice supported on small pilasters. Although not altogether visually successful, this was seen as an expedient for organizing the facade and for avoiding monotony. Again, the two entrances were located in slightly projecting vertical bays. The small pediments that topped some of the windows of the Lunt Building were also a common feature of Berlin architecture, as shown on the residence on the Waterloo-Ufer (fig. 4), and so was the use of pediments to crown projecting bays in the middle of the facade. This design had no precedent in Chicago and found no imitators.[15]

Far more successful was the firm's Haddock Block of 1875 (fig. 8).[16] Basically rectangular, similar in shape to the Ashland Block (fig. 3), the Haddock Block was much more advanced in design. All derivative ornament was left out, with the exception of the small triangular bay crowning a slightly projecting vertical bay. All stories were clearly identified with the help of cornices, and the windows were framed by pilasters, with the openings occupying almost the entire window bays. This design was essentially based on the structural frame. Yet even this had precedence in the architecture of Berlin, as shown in the residences at Matthaikirch-

strasse 13 and 15 from about 1845 (fig. 9). In these buildings, too, the individual stories were marked by cornices supported by pilasters, thus creating a formal grid containing the window bays. But the Haddock Block was decidedly more tectonic in character.[17]

The Haddock Block and other Chicago buildings discussed here belong to the *palazzo* type considered appropriate for prominent business buildings. As a result of the particular backgrounds of their designers, they derived much of their formal apparatus from Germany. But the very same vocabulary could lead to academic and conservative results, like Baumann's Ashland Block, or could generate much more novel ones, like the Haddock Block. Although this trabeated mode was in fact the least common one among the available *palazzo* styles, it proved the style most closely associated with the subsequent development of the Chicago School.[18] This becomes apparent if one considers another important commercial work, the Borden Block (fig. 10) built in 1879-80 by D. Adler & Co. with Louis Sullivan as chief draftsman. In this work, the "skeletonization" of the facade went a step further in opening up the wall and restricting the solid surface to the supporting frame. The ornament was subordinated to the basic design and was decidedly non-historical. But its use on the facade (with the exception of the arched lunettes) was not unrelated to the use encountered on the German works discussed here, in which the delicate floral decoration was also placed on the window spandrels, the frieze, and the stringcourses (figs. 7, 9).

All these formal developments led directly to a frequently overlooked masterpiece of the Chicago School, the Chamber of Commerce Building by Baumann and Huehl, 1888-89 (fig. 11). This was the last work by Edward Baumann and the first important building by Harris W. Huehl (1862-1919), a native Chicagoan who had received all his architectural training in the office of Edward Baumann, for whom he worked as a draftsman from 1877 to 1888.[19] Huehl was admitted to partnership when this lucrative commission came to the office; after Baumann's sudden death he carried it to successful completion alone. The Chamber of Commerce was almost completely framed, and only a very small proportion of the total load was supported by the masonry piers in which the peripheral columns were embedded;[20] the structural frame, encased in a smooth covering, was made the basic means of formal expression. The slablike form of the building volume related to earlier Chicago office buildings, including the Haddock Block, down to the use of vestigial pediments crowning the vertical bays containing the entran-

ces. Broad stringcourses divided the facades horizontally, and the extensive glazing suggested the possibility of a total dissolution of the wall.

The use of the trabeated scheme (with the exception of the small arcade at the attic story) and the extensive glazing of the bays had precedence in the local commercial tradition – going back to works like the Haddock Block – and was echoed in other contemporary buildings like William Le Baron Jenney's second Leiter Building of 1889-91. But there was an important German design – Schinkel's famous 1827 project for a department store on Unter den Linden (fig. 12) – which may have inspired Baumann. Both the Chamber of Commerce and the department store project had large glazed bays, set almost flush with the structural frame. It is worth noting that the formal potential of Schinkel's splendid project could have found its first full realization in Chicago, where great structural advances had been made. Indeed, it was in works like the Chamber of Commerce that a synthesis of the honesty and expediency of Gothic construction and the

formality and regularity of the classical order was attained.

Another remarkable example of commercial work by Chicago's German architects related to well-known Schinkel designs was the bakery of the New York Biscuit Company by Treat and Foltz, 1890-91 (fig. 13). One of Chicago's most prolific firms in the nineteenth century, Treat and Foltz specialized in the design of residences, apartment buildings, hospitals, and commercial establishments. Samuel A. Treat was a native American, but Fritz Foltz (cat. nos. 75-77) was born in Darmstadt and educated at the Technical University there and at the Royal Academy in Munich. Foltz came to Chicago in 1868 and was employed by Gurdon P. Randall and by Dankmar Adler. Established in 1872, the firm of Treat and Foltz lasted until 1896, enjoying continuous success.[21] Most frequently its work was a local version of the Victorian Gothic or Richardsonian Romanesque. But in designing the bakery of the New York Biscuit Company the architects adopted a functionalist

Fig. 10 D. Adler and Co., Borden Block, northwest corner of Randolph and Dearborn streets, 1879-80 (demolished); from American Architect and Building News *(Jan. 1897).*

Fig. 11 Baumann and Huehl, Chamber of Commerce Building, southeast corner of LaSalle and Washington streets, 1888-89 (demolished).

attitude, appearing to derive the design elements from the function and construction of the building.[22] Such means could be manipulated to provide excellent results, as in the case of this work: the fronts were composed of a series of pilasters that contained the recessed panels of the windows. The large horizontal expansion of the facades was balanced by the uninterrupted verticality of the pilasters, which continued on to the simply molded cornice. This design resembled another famous work by Schinkel, the Bauakademie of 1831-35 (fig. 14). This is not surprising, as the Bauakademie, which was widely admired in Germany, had become known in Chicago as early as 1869, when Baumann translated Friedrich Adler's festival oration, hailing this building as a masterpiece of modern architecture. But Foltz most likely knew this famous work from his own student years in Germany.

From the early 1870s until the end of the century, architectural education in the Midwest was under strong German influence. The University of Illinois at Champaign-Urbana was the first institution in that part of the country (and the second in the nation after the Massachusetts Institute of Technology) to establish a curriculum in architecture.[23] Nathan Clifford Ricker (1843-1924), the person most responsible for the development and solidification of the architectural program of the University of Illinois, had received his own education in architecture there and at the Bauakademie in Berlin. Ricker (pls. 5, 9) attended this prestigious institution (then under the directorship of the noted German architect Richard Lucae) in 1873 for a period of six months. There he became thoroughly acquainted with German architectural design, theory, and education.[24] Ricker considered this relatively brief period of study in Berlin very valuable as preparation for the organization of the architectural curriculum of the University of Illinois and for the creation of its architectural library.[25]

Ricker went on to translate German books for use by the students, including Rudolf Redtenbacher's *Architektonik* (translated as *The Architectonics of Modern Architecture*), and the volume *Die architektonische Composition* of the monumental series *Handbuch der Architektur* (translated as *Architectural Composition*).[26] More importantly, the educational program that Ricker initiated followed the example of the technical universities in Germany, in which architectural education was part of the polytechnic system and therefore imbued with a scientific spirit. Ricker adopted the rigidly structured curriculum that he had encountered in Germany, characterized by a series of technical and structural studies preceding any courses in design.

This was completely different from the atelier system of the Ecole des Beaux-Arts followed at MIT. As Ricker explained:

[It] has been my aim to send out graduates who were well grounded in the principle of scientific construction and were well fitted for office work, as well as this preparation may be made at a school; and then to improve their tastes as much as possible at the time.[27]

Indeed, Ricker preferred to provide education based on the more solid aspects of architecture, the technical and functional ones, instead of those depending on the passing tastes of the times.

Ricker's educational program was superseded by the growing Beaux-Arts influence after the turn of the century; at the same time, the other schools of architecture enlarged their own programs to include a variety of technical and scientific courses and subjected their instruction to an equally rigid organization. But Ricker's pioneering work found its true fulfillment in the program that Ludwig Mies van der Rohe adopted at the Illinois Institute of Technology. After all, Mies also insisted that the students learn the fundamentals of building before taking up design. As he explained in his inaugural address at IIT, one should start by learning the properties of the materials and the functions of the buildings; this should be followed by an understanding of the spiritual factors of the time, and only then would the student be ready to start learning design.[28]

The residential work of Chicago's German architects after the turn of the century also included some notable works suggesting the influence of Berlin's neoclassical architecture. One of them is the Madlener House (1901-02; figs. 1, 2) in Chicago, designed by Richard E. Schmidt with the assistance of Hugh M. G. Garden.[29] Schmidt (1865-1958) was born in Ebern, Bavaria, and was brought to Chicago at the age of one (cat. nos. 87, 88). He began his architectural training in the office of the German-born and German-educated architect Adolph A. Cudell (pl. 27), attended the two-year architectural course at MIT, and began his Chicago practice in 1887. From 1890 to 1895 he was associated with Theodore O. Fraenkel, then practiced alone, and in 1906 established the firm of Schmidt, Garden and Martin, which after 1926 became Schmidt, Garden and Erikson.

The Madlener House is basically a compact and plain cube resembling closely the severely cubical villas built or projected in great numbers by Schinkel's followers in Berlin in the 1860s and 1870s, like the Villa Schöne by Gropius and Schmieden of 1874 (fig. 15), or August Hermann Spielberg's project for a villa from the early 1860s (fig. 16).[30] Both the Chicago residence and the Berlin works

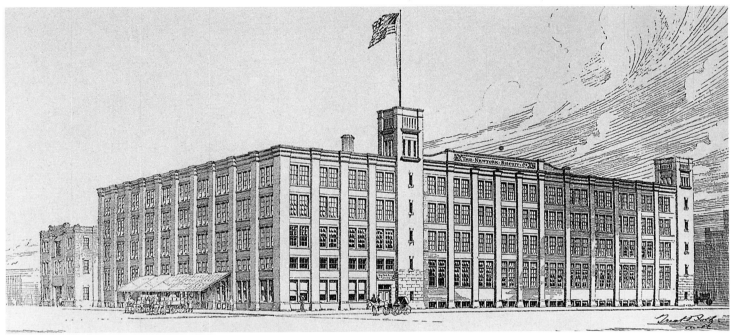

Fig. 12 Karl Friedrich Schinkel, Design for a department store on the Unter den Linden, Berlin, 1827; from Carl Von Lorck, Karl Friedrich Schinkel *(Berlin, 1939).*

Fig. 13 Treat and Foltz, Bakery of the New York Biscuit Company, Randolph Street between Morgan and Carpenter streets, 1890-91; from Inland Architect and News Record *20 (Oct. 1892).*

Fig. 14 Schinkel, Bauakademie, Berlin, 1831-35 (demolished); from Sammlung Architektonischer Entwürfe von Carl Friedrich Schinkel *(Berlin, 1858).*

Fig. 15 Gropius and Schmieden, Villa Schöne, Berlin, 1874 (demolished); from Börsch-Supan, Berliner Baukunst.

Fig. 16 August Hermann Spielberg, Project for a villa, before 1867; from Börsch-Supan, Berliner Baukunst.

have low-hipped roofs rising above projecting cornices, three stories above a raised basement, simply framed windows and doors, and attic stories with a series of small windows contained between two horizontal bands. More bands and stringcourses were used to identify the stories and to articulate the walls. Indeed, the formal similarities are so

close that one must assume that Schmidt was familiar with the Berlin works. It is certain that Schmidt was studying German-language publications on architecture and design and this appears to have started during his apprenticeship with Cudell. According to Thomas E. Tallmadge, in Cudell's office Schmidt would have been exposed to such important German works as *Die Tektonik der Hellenen,* the magnum opus of Karl Bötticher, who was the leading theorist of the neoclassical school of Berlin and an ardent supporter of tectonic design.[31]

The work of Schmidt, Garden and Martin only rarely maintained the functionalist traditions of the Chicago and Prairie schools in the years after World War I. One such instance was the Bunte Brothers Candy Factory built at 3301 West Franklin Boulevard in 1920-21 (fig. 17).[32] The long wings of the factory section were articulated with strongly projecting piers flanking the wall surfaces, into which plain window openings were cut; the building terminated in an attic story with small windows. Although there is little reason to believe that the firm needed any prototypes for this design, it does resemble German industrial buildings of some years earlier, including Peter Behrens's AEG Hochspannungsfabrik of 1910 (fig. 18). Moreover, both buildings pointed to Schinkel's Barracks of the Lehreskadron and Military Detention Center in Berlin from 1818 (fig. 19) as the ultimate source of such design ideas. Although Schmidt may indeed have been familiar with the two German buildings, the design of the Bunte Brothers' Candy Factory could equally well have been rooted in the

functionalist traditions of the Chicago and Prairie schools.[33]

Another Chicago firm, Hill and Woltersdorf, was instrumental in maintaining continuous contact with architectural developments in Germany. Both members of the firm were of German origin. Henry W. Hill (1852-1924), the senior partner, was born in Elmshorn, Holstein, and educated at the Technical University of Hamburg. Hill came to Chicago in 1872, worked for several architects, and in 1875 became the partner of James J. Egan. In 1881 Hill joined forces with Augustus Bauer, one of Chicago's earliest German architects (fig. 20; see cat no. 14), and after the latter's death in 1894

Fig. 17 Schmidt, Garden and Martin, Bunte Brothers Candy Company Factory, 3301 West Franklin Boulevard, 1920-21.

Fig. 18 Peter Behrens, AEG Hochspannungsfabrik, Berlin, 1910; from Julius Posener, Berlin auf dem Wege zu einer neuen Architektur *(Munich, 1979).*

Fig. 19 Schinkel, Barracks of the Lehreskadron and Military Detention Center, Berlin, 1818; from Paul Ortwin Rave, Karl Friedrich Schinkel *(Berlin, 1981).*

took the young Arthur F. Woltersdorf into partnership.[34] Woltersdorf (1870-1948) was born in Chicago to distinguished Prussian parents (cat. no. 97). He began his architectural training in the offices of Bauer and Hill and Burnham and Root and then attended the two-year architectural course at MIT. Subsequently he traveled in Europe and attended lectures at the Technical University of Berlin. For twenty years (1894-1914) Woltersdorf was associated with Hill (fig. 22); he then practiced alone, and from 1919 to 1923 as a member of the firm of Woltersdorf and Bernhard (fig. 21), before becoming independent again.

Woltersdorf considered his firm as one of Chicago's oldest, placing its beginning in 1853, the year that the firm of Carter and Bauer was founded.[35] He was an extremely prolific writer, publishing his articles on architectural subjects in periodicals and the Chicago daily newspapers.[36] Most important in our context are his unmitigated efforts to present the best past and contemporary German work to the American public through his articles,[37] and his translation of two articles by Peter Behrens for publication in the *American Architect*.[38] Wol-

Fig. 20 Bauer and Hill, Foreman and Kohn Building, 305 West Adams Street, 1886 (demolished).

tersdorf was acquainted with Behrens's turn-of-the-century architecture through his frequent and extensive travels in Germany, and he left us descriptions of some of Behrens's buildings both in English and German.[39] He may have known the German master personally; in any case, he believed that Behrens's writings contained much sound advice regarding modern architecture and design and that such advice was sorely needed in this country. But even before the publication of these articles, Hill and Woltersdorf had repeatedly paraphrased Behrens's ideas in their own writings, especially the ideas pertaining to the design of factories and other commercial establishments.[40] The architectural work of the firm of Hill and Woltersdorf, which included many factories, warehouses, and office buildings, was clearly imbued with the same functionalist principles that had inspired the Prairie and Chicago schools and the recent architecture of Germany, to which Behrens's own oeuvre belonged. Even a superficial comparison of the firm's warehouse of the Eastman Kodak Company in Chicago of 1905 (fig. 23)[41] with the factory of the Ludwig Loewe A. G. in Berlin-Moabit by Arnold Vogt of 1898 (fig. 24) suggests this.

The accomplishment of the Chicago School, largely overlooked at home, was not lost on the German leaders of modernism in the 1920s. This is shown in the project submitted to the Chicago Tribune competition by Walter Gropius and Adolf Meyer (pl. 93); this design, like the one submitted

Fig. 21 Woltersdorf and Bernhard, Driscoll's Danceland, Madison Street, 1915.

Fig. 22 Hill and Woltersdorf, Addition to Tree Studios Building (1894), State Street between Ohio and Ontario streets, 1912-13.

by Max Taut (see Bruegmann, fig. 11), was based on the most advanced structuralism of the Chicago School and constituted a premonition of the Internationalism of the 1950s.

Starting in the middle of the nineteenth century and for a hundred years thereafter, Chicago's German architects provided a continuous link to the architecture of Germany, which they studied carefully and frequently emulated in their own work. This essay has focused on the influence that a particular architectural mainstream, the architecture of Karl Friedrich Schinkel and the Berlin School, exercised on the architecture of Chicago, and how this was incorporated in the designs of some of its German architects and firms. The lessons that Chicago could learn from this particular connection were twofold: the formal vocabulary of the Berlin School — with its orderly and rational facade articulation based on the repetition of identical elements and the visual emphasis on the structural grid — provided a useful prototype for Chicago's commercial architecture. Moreover, the plainness and cubical compactness of its residential work could inspire Chicago works of striking modernity, such as the Madlener House (figs. 1, 2). This kind of tectonic design was very useful because it could be remarkably free of historic allusions (like Schinkel's Bauakademie and the department store project) and thus could adapt itself to the structural and functional rationalism of Chicago's commercial architecture.

The neoclassicism of Berlin profoundly influenced the leading masters of the modern movement in Germany such as Peter Behrens and Ludwig Mies van der Rohe, both of whom subjected the architecture of Schinkel to the most careful scrutiny and extracted from it valuable lessons in design. But Chicago's German architects also studied the architecture of Schinkel and his followers. Thus, at a time of limited communications between German and American architectural developments, Chicago's German architects added a powerful "international" component to the city's architecture, preparing the way for the enthusiastic adoption of Internationalism in the middle of the twentieth century.

Fig. 23 Hill and Woltersdorf, Eastman Kodak Company Warehouse, northeast corner of Indiana Avenue and 18th Street, 1905; from Architectural Record 19 (May 1906).

Fig. 24 Arnold Vogt, Factory of the Ludwig Loewe A.G., Berlin-Moabit, 1898; from Posener, Berlin Architektur.

NOTES

1. The work of Chicago's German architects was first examined in Roula M. Geraniotis, "German Architects in Nineteenth-Century Chicago" (Ph. D. diss., University of Illinois, Urbana, 1985).

2. For a thorough study of the Berlin School, see Eva Börsch-Supan, *Berliner Baukunst nach Schinkel 1840-1870*, Studien zur Kunst des 19. Jahrhunderts, vol. 25 (Munich, 1977).

3. See the article "German Immigration," *Land Owner* 4 (July 1872), p. 111.

4. This was pointed out by Gerhard Wohler in his article "Das Hochhaus im Wettbewerb der Chicago Tribune," *Deutsche Bauzeitung* 58 (July 5, 1924), pp. 325-30, and (July 16, 1924), pp. 345-47.

5. The most important account of Baumann's educational and professional experiences is the autobiographical essay "Life, Reminiscences and Notes of Frederick Baumann," written by him and read by Peter B. Wight before the Illinois Chapter of the American Institute of Architects on the occasion of the unveiling of Baumann's portrait donated to the Chapter by the painter Oskar Gross. This essay was published in *Construction News* 41 (Jan. 15, 1916), pp. 5-9. See also Wight's introductory remarks, "Frederick Baumann, America's Oldest Living Architect," in the same issue.

6. Baumann (note 5), pp. 6-7.

7. See Friedrich Adler, "Architectural Academy Building," abridged trans. Frederick Baumann, *American Builder and Journal of Art* 2 (Nov. 1869), pp. 199-200. For the German original, see idem, "Die Bauschule zu Berlin," *Zeitschrift für Bauwesen* 19 (1869), cols. 469-75. Adler attended the Bauakademie in 1848-50; in 1861 he became professor of architectural history there and in 1866 of architectural design as well. It is likely that Baumann knew Adler personally as he was also studying architecture and construction in Berlin in the late 1840s. The fact that Baumann's translation appeared in the same year as the oration itself testifies to the speed with which the German publications were reaching Chicago.

8. The parts of the speech that were left out were also interesting; these included a documentation of Schinkel's interest in the rich *Backsteinbau* tradition of the Mark Brandenburg, the native province of Schinkel and Baumann.

9. Schinkel's Bauakademie (at that time called "Bauschule") was built in 1831-35.

10. Adler (note 7), p. 199.

11. Ibid.

12. See "The Ashland Block," *Land Owner* 4 (Aug. 1872), p. 130.

13. After 1879 Edward Baumann practiced alone, although at times he was associated with the German-born and German-educated engineer William H. Lotz. In 1888 Baumann created a partnership with Harris W. Huehl, who had been trained in his office, but died the following year in Berlin, where he had gone hoping to recover his failing health.

14. On this building, see *Land Owner* 6 (May 1874), p. 74.

15. One may safely assume that Adler was the designer of this "Berlinesque" work. A clue is provided by Adler himself, who complained in his "Autobiography" (manuscript at the Newberry Library, Chicago) that Burling, the senior partner, would eagerly overload him with design responsibilities, a fact that induced strong feelings of resentment in him.

16. See *Land Owner* 6 (Aug. 1875), p. 120.

17. The granite fronts that Alexander Parris was designing in Boston in the 1820s also used a trabeated system; but their overall effect was one of plainness and modesty which disqualified them for use on the prominent commercial establishments of the second half of the nineteenth century. On Parris, see Henry-Russell Hitchcock, *Architecture: Nineteenth and Twentieth Centuries* (Harmondsworth, England, and New York, 1977), p. 328.

18. The commercial *palazzo* became popular in the United States in the 1850s and persisted for two decades. In Chicago it was represented also by the Renaissance- and baroque-inspired mode, the Romanesque-inspired mode, and the Second Empire or mansarded one. Chicago's German architects provided designs in all of the above modes but generally seemed to prefer the plain

round-arched version that was often remarkably similar to the German *Rundbogenstil*. This study focuses on a specific type of design, namely the "tectonic" or trabeated one, which emerged in Chicago in the 1870s and was carried on in the Chicago School.

19. In 1890 Huehl formed a partnership with Richard G. Schmid (1863-1937), the son of Robert Schmid, one of Chicago's earliest German architects. See "Harris William Huehl. Huehl and Schmid, Architects," *Construction News* 19 (Feb. 11, 1905), p. 98; obituary in *Western Architect* 28 (June 1919), p. 57; and *Who's Who in Chicago and Illinois* (Chicago, 1905-50), passim.

20. The Chamber of Commerce was structurally one of the most advanced buildings in Chicago at the time of its completion and in the quality of finish and design it was equaled by few. Its construction, which included the remodeling of the post-Fire Chamber of Commerce and its transformation into a skyscraper on new foundations, was a true engineering feat. On this building, see "The Chamber of Commerce Building: a Noted Structure almost Completed and Ready for Occupancy," *Economist* 3 (Mar. 8, 1890), p. 266; "Chicago Heightening Old Buildings," *American Architect* 29 (Sept. 20, 1890), p. 185; *Building Budget* 6 (June 1890), p. 74; *Industrial Chicago*, vol. 1 (Chicago, 1891), pp. 197-204; Carl W. Condit, *The Chicago School of Architecture: A History of Commercial and Public Building in the Chicago Area, 1875-1925* (Chicago, 1964), p. 87; and idem, *American Building Art: The Nineteenth Century* (New York, 1969), pp. 58-59.

21. Foltz was a Fellow of the A. I. A. See "Fritz Foltz, Architect, Chicago," *Construction News* 22 (July 28, 1906), p. 67, and *Who's Who in Chicago* (note 19), passim.

22. On this building, which is still standing on Randolph Street between Morgan and Carpenter streets, see *Economist* 4 (Dec. 13, 1890), pp. 480 ff. and *Inland Architect* 17 (Apr. 1891), p. 39.

23. See Roula M. Geraniotis, "The University of Illinois and German Architectural Education," *Journal of Architectural Education* 38 (Summer 1985), pp. 15-21.

24. In his typewritten autobiography "The Story of a Life" (Urbana, Ill., 1922), p. 14, Ricker summed up his experience as follows: "The principal object of the young man was to observe German methods of instruction, apparatus employed, especially the library of the academy, which proved to be large and very valuable, affording good acquaintance with the best standard works in architecture and art: ... all spare time was spent in the library and in the city observing German methods of construction and design, also visiting the more important historical monuments, including a trip to Potsdam."

25. As he explained, "The results of the European trip was a good knowledge of the German system of instruction ... with severe examinations and prescribed course of study in architecture.... Further a good knowledge of architectural and art books, of great value later in collecting and establishing the architectural library." See "The Story of a Life" (note 24), p. 23.

26. See Rudolf Redtenbacher, *Die Architektonik der modernen Baukunst* (Berlin, 1884); and Heinrich Wagner, Josef Bühlmann, and August Thiersch, *Die architektonische Composition*, vol. 1 of *Entwerfen, Anlage und Einrichtung der Gebäude*, part 4 of *Handbuch der Architektur*, 2nd ed. (Darmstadt, 1893). Ricker did the full translation, "The Architectonics of Modern Architecture," in 1884. In 1888 he prepared an abridged translation as well, titled "The Esthetics of Modern Architecture" and also intended for use by the students. The translation "Architectural Composition" was done in 1900.

27. Excerpted in Turpin C. Bannister, "Pioneering in Architectural Education; Recalling the First Collegiate Graduate in Architecture in the U. S. A. – Nathan Clifford Ricker," *Journal of the AIA* 20 (Aug. 1953), p. 78.

28. See Peter Blake, *The Master Builders* (New York, 1966), pp. 217-18.

29. On this building, still standing at 4 West Burton Place, see Russell Sturgis, "The Madlener House in Chicago," *Architectural Record* 17 (June 1905), pp. 491-98.

30. Such works realized "tectonic" design in its purest form; see Börsch-Supan (note 2), pp. 101 ff.

31. See Thomas E. Tallmadge, *Architecture in Old Chicago* (Chicago, 1941), p. 118. On Bötticher, see Börsch-Supan (note 2), pp. 556-58.

32. For a description of this building, see Condit, *Chicago School* (note 20), pp. 194-95.

33. The initial flowering of the Prairie School came to an end at about the time of World War I.

34. Hill was a Fellow of the A. I. A. See *Industrial Chicago* (note 20), vol. 1, p. 601; *Who's Who in Chicago* (note 19), passim; and Arthur F. Woltersdorf, "Henry William Hill," *Journal of the AIA* 12 (Apr. 1924), p. 206.

35. Woltersdorf claimed this on numerous occasions. Robert C. McLean repeated it in the article "Some Works of Woltersdorf and Bernhard," *Western Architect* 31 (July 1922), pp. 87-89, that he appears to have written in collaboration with Woltersdorf himself. It is interesting to note that the German architects of Chicago were becoming aware of the existence of a historical continuity in the German presence in the city. Woltersdorf was intensely interested in the German architectural impact on this country and in 1933 wrote the paper "German Influences in the Architecture of the United States," now at the Burnham Library of Architecture at The Art Institute of Chicago. This paper, which was apparently intended for publication, contains brief biographical information on some of Chicago's German architects.

36. He was also the editor of the book *Living Architecture* (Chicago, 1930), to which he contributed the essay "Chicago Theater Building in Retrospect."

37. These included articles on contemporary German architecture, such as "Theater Planning – Here and There," *American Architect* 132 (Aug. 20, 1927), pp. 211-16, and "Sakralbau," *Western Architect* 37 (Sept. 1928), p. 185; or articles on historic German architecture, such as "Concerning North German Brick Architecture," *American Architect* 130 (Dec. 20, 1926), pp. 471-84; and "Patrician Houses of Old North Germany," *Western Architect* 36 (Mar. 1927), pp. 32-38.

38. Peter Behrens, "Administration Buildings for Industrial Plants," trans. Arthur F. Woltersdorf, *American Architect* 128 (Aug. 26, 1925), pp. 167-74, and idem, "Seeking Aesthetic Worth in Industrial Buildings," trans. Arthur F. Woltersdorf, *American Architect* 128 (Dec. 5, 1925), pp. 475-79.

39. These are in the Burnham Library of Architecture at The Art Institute of Chicago.

40. See [Henry W.] Hill and [Arthur F.] Woltersdorf, "Utilitarian Structures and Their Architectural Treatment," *American Architect* 96 (Nov. 10, 1909), pp. 183-85, and Arthur F. Woltersdorf, "An Expression on the Design of Factory and Warehouse Buildings," *American Architect* 99 (June 14, 1911), pp. 237-38.

41. On the Eastman Kodak Building, see Russell Sturgis, "Factories and Warehouses," *Architectural Record* 19 (May 1906), pp. 469-76.

Paris by the Lake: Sources of Burnham's Plan of Chicago

Joan E. Draper

Addressing the commissioners of Chicago's South Park Board in February 1897, Daniel H. Burnham first proposed a grand scheme "that will make Chicago so beautiful it will outrival Paris."[1] Twelve years passed before he completed the document that outlined his dream: the *Plan of Chicago*. What had begun as a relatively modest plan for a linear park stretching along the Lake Michigan shore from Chicago's downtown south to the site of the 1893 World's Columbian Exposition had grown tremendously in scope and ambition (pls. 70, 71). Burnham's 1909 plan, co-authored with Edward H. Bennett, proposed the transformation of the sprawling, chaotic metropolis into a world-class capital as grand as any in Europe. The architects, working with their sponsors from the Commericial Club of Chicago, proposed a series of interrelated public works projects that addressed the city's pressing needs for new parks and public buildings (fig. 1), for improved harbor and rail facilities, and for an integrated network of streets and highways.

As the most cursory inspection of the document and the drawings produced for it reveals, the imagery of the plan is explicitly European in its inspiration. Burnham and his associates emulated Paris and other Old World cities as they created their ideal vision of the future Chicago. Traditional aesthetic forms and ideals shaped the modern urban environment. Chicago was to become a "Paris by the Lake," as the newspapers put it. Yet the new city that the plan described in words and pictures constituted a recognizably American entity. This mixture of the old with the new and the foreign with the native has struck some historians as contradictory or paradoxical.

Carl Condit, for example, praised Burnham's plan for its prescient concern with motorized transit and for its regional scope, but described its symmetry and hierarchical arrangement as "surviving symbols of the mathematical harmonies underlying the divine order, a cosmos in which mankind by the nineteenth century had ceased to believe."[2] In his scheme the Chicago Plan is transitional, between Renaissance-baroque planning and modern planning. But this interpretation does little to illuminate the rhetorical function of the plan in its

own day, nor do criticisms of Burnham's historicism, which Thomas Hines has labeled "spiritual and intellectual indolence" and "a failure of nerve."[3] This attitude precludes any serious exploration of the nature and purpose of the Chicago Plan's European sources. If we discard modernist biases and refrain from judging according to later conceptions of planning, the apparent contradic-

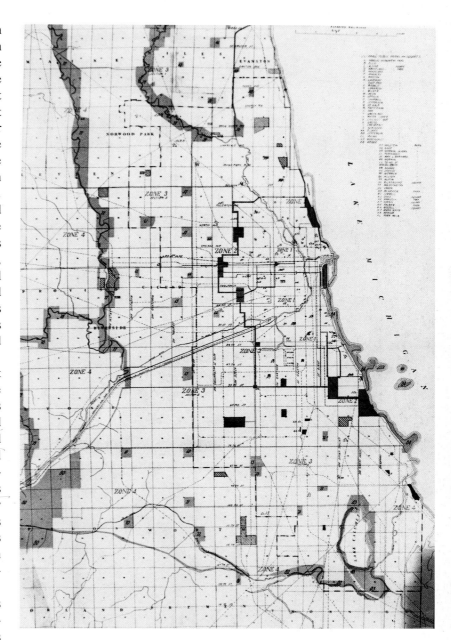

Fig. 1 Proposed Civic Center square (detail), 1908; from Plan of Chicago *(Chicago, 1909), pl. 139 (see fig. 8).*

Fig. 2 Dwight Heald Perkins, Proposed Metropolitan Park System for Chicago, 1904.

tions and paradoxes disappear. It becomes evident that the plan recast in more cosmopolitan terms the myths about Chicago's destiny and unity that are found in earlier booster literature. Like utopian fictions, the plan constructed an ideal on paper as a way of accommodating new experiences to old interpretations.[4]

This document was one response to the general recognition that Chicago's physical environment needed a major overhaul and that accomplishing this transformation would require tremendous resources and coordinated action. The specific origins of the plan are rightly traced to the 1893 World's Columbian Exposition, masterminded by Burnham and business leaders who later supported the plan. But it was not an isolated planning effort. Between 1890 and 1909, scores of documents issued from the pens of concerned individuals and representatives of various public agencies, although concrete results were few in number until later. These studies and plans dealt with almost every aspect of Chicago's physical environment.

In 1901, for example, the City Homes Association published its report on *Tenement Conditions in Chicago*. In 1902, the City Council's Committee on Local Transportation commissioned a study of the mass transit problem from consulting engineer Bion J. Arnold, who had designed and built the electric Intramural Railway for the 1893 Fair; this was only one in a series of such reports during these years.[5] In 1904, architect Dwight Perkins, who had worked for Burnham during the Fair years, produced a plan for a metropolitan park system, which incorporated the ambitious expansion schemes developed by Chicago's park districts during the previous decade (fig. 2).[6] The same year, studies of street paving problems and railway terminal consolidation appeared.[7] And in 1909, the Chicago Harbor Commission issued a report on port development in the region, the culmination of two decades of debate over rebuilding Chicago's inefficient harbor facilities.[8] Other individuals and groups concerned themselves with reforming everything from sewage disposal to civic art.

The 1909 plan drew upon some, but by no means all, of this accumulated documentation and dreaming, and it differs significantly in presentation, tone, and intent from these earlier Chicago planning reports. It is a visionary, not a technical document, intended to appeal to the public rather than to specialists. Its scope is comprehensive rather than focused on a single urban function, although it encompasses only the city's public realm, excluding elements then under private control such as housing and urban mass transit. The plan's aim was to rouse Chicagoans to the cause of planning and to

lay out with broad strokes an orderly set of proposed improvements. These public works projects – new streets and bridges, for example – were intended not only to make the metropolitan organism more efficient, but also to promote aesthetic and social unity throughout. In their arrangement and design, they would serve both functional and symbolic purposes, and in turn-of-the-century language the metaphors here were biological rather than cosmic.

This was an architect's plan and thus different from the efforts of contemporary engineers, landscape architects, lawyers, journalists, and social reformers. Those efforts, varied as they were, together constituted "city planning" in the United States around the turn of the century.[9] Burnham, Bennett, and other architects dominated one facet of the early planning movement; their values and methods are reflected in their plans. The architectural character of the Chicago Plan is evident in several ways. Like other City Beautiful plans of the day, it redesigned the physical environment rather than the processes by which the municipality could control city building. Its final chapter, a pragmatic analysis of the legal aspects of the Plan of Chicago, merely calls for establishing an advisory planning commission and for increasing the city's bonding powers (i.e., raising the debt ceiling).[10] A fluent text in the main body of the report convinces readers of the economic, social, and spiritual benefits of the projected improvements, but the plan communicates most effectively through pictures. In 164 pages there are 142 plates, including maps, photographs, and drawings; of these, 61 drawings were specially prepared for the Chicago Plan, many of them large perspective renderings in color, obviously intended for exhibition as well as publication (fig. 4; cat. no. 231).[11] Furthermore, the original volume in which the plan was presented to the public was handsomely designed and printed, the drawings carefully reproduced through the lithographic process.

This was planning through imagery. Burnham and his associates knew their recommendations could only be carried out by mobilizing public opinion. As lawyer Walter Fisher explained in his chapter on legalities:

Governmental powers in the United States, unlike those in many European countries, are defined by written constitutions, which would undoubtedly prevent the imitation here of some of the sweeping undertakings and arbitrary though effective methods of European city planning.[12]

Publicity and persuasion would have to bring about implementation of the plan, since significant legislative and administrative reforms could not be ex-

pected. Its content had to be accessible and its presentation graphic.

Burnham had learned the wisdom of this approach from New York architect Charles McKim during their collaboration on the Senate Park Commission Plan for Washington, D.C., in 1901. As Charles Moore, Burnham's biographer, recalled some twenty years later:

Plans and drawings, [McKim had] argued, mean nothing to the lay observer, and not much more to the professional. In order to carry conviction, drawings must be rendered. For this task the best illustrators in the country were none too good.[13]

Following the Washington precedent, the Chicago Plan drawings were rendered by experts and put on public display at The Art Institute of Chicago in 1909. That same year, the mayor appointed the Chicago Plan Commission, and during the next three decades this semi-official body worked assiduously and successfully to promote the plan.[14]

Burnham had left the 328-member Commission "a noble and logical diagram"[15] for the future Chicago rather than blueprints for specific boulevards, buildings, and parks. His talent lay in seeing the big picture and in mobilizing teams of experts who had professional skills he himself lacked. The 1909 Plan

Fig. 3 Bird's-eye view of proposed developments for Washington, D.C.; from Report of the Senate Committee on the District of Columbia . . . *(Washington, D.C., 1903).*

Fig. 4 Jules Guérin for Daniel H. Burnham and Edward H. Bennett, View of the railway station scheme west of the river, 1908 (cat. no. 231).

death he worked with the sons on park plans for Washington and Chicago.

Burnham had reorganized his office along corporate lines following the death of his partner John Wellborn Root in 1891. It became one of the largest and most successful architectural firms in the country, thus allowing its principal to enter the ranks of the city's business elite and to engage in planning work on a *pro bono* basis. In order to carry out the big commissions that paid the bills and brought him fame, Burnham gathered around him junior partners and head designers skilled in the language of academic classicism. Like other architect-magnates of his day, he hired Ecole des Beaux-Arts graduates.[18] For his own edification Burnham took four trips to Europe before 1909 to see buildings and sites that the younger men knew from school days. His second trip, in 1901, was probably the most instructive. In the company of McKim, Frederick Law Olmsted, Jr., and Charles Moore, he made an intensive seven-week study tour of the capitals of modern Europe. Their purpose was to prepare a plan for Washington that would restore the grandeur of L'Enfant's 1791 plan (fig. 3).[19]

So well received was the Senate Park Commission Plan that Burnham's expertise was soon much in demand throughout the country. To assist with

Fig. 5 Cassien-Bernard and Gaston Clément Cousin, Alexander III Bridge, Paris, 1896-1900.

Fig. 6 Edward H. Bennett, with Thomas G. Pihlfeldt and Hugh E. Young, engineers, Michigan Avenue Bridge, 1912-20.

Fig. 7 Edward H. Bennett, Pylon, Grant Park, c. 1915/27.

of Chicago benefited from his previous experiences. Experience, in fact, was Burnham's teacher rather than any academic training, which he lacked entirely.[16] His knowledge of planning came from a quick, intuitive grasp of organizing structures and of the essence of his colleagues' expertise. His service as Director of Works of the 1893 World's Columbian Exposition had demonstrated both Burnham's extraordinary organizational ability and his grasp of the power of classicism to impose order on a grand ensemble. Burnham delegated specific design tasks to cosmopolitan Eastern architects like Charles McKim and Richard Morris Hunt, and Charles B. Atwood of his own staff. Their skillful use of classical forms contributed to the Fair's much admired image of unity and harmony. The ensemble effect was equally attributable to Frederick Law Olmsted's site plan.[17] Burnham first collaborated with the distinguished landscape architect here, and after the elder Olmsted's

Fig. 8 Fernand Janin for Daniel H. Burnham and Edward H. Bennett, Proposed Civic Center square, 1908; from Plan of Chicago *(Chicago, 1909), pl. 139.*

several of the planning commissions he agreed to take on, Burnham hired Edward H. Bennett in 1903. Bennett, born in England, had graduated from the Ecole des Beaux-Arts in 1901 and then had gone to work for George B. Post in New York, following a European tour. He was recruited for the Chicago firm by Peirce Anderson, a Paris friend and the first Beaux-Arts man in Burnham's office. The younger architect fulfilled his apprenticeship in planning by assisting with Burnham's 1903 West Point Military Academy competition entry and by designing a series of new neighborhood parks for Chicago in collaboration with the Olmsted firm. Bennett then assumed day-to-day supervision of the San Francisco Plan work during 1904 and 1905, while Burnham traveled to the Philippines to prepare plans for Manila and Baguio. When the Chicago Plan effort commenced in earnest in September 1906, Bennett oversaw the operation of a separate office in the eighteenth-floor penthouse of the Railway Exchange Building (p. 452, fig. 18), where the Burnham firm was then located. From this aerie overlooking the city's lakefront, he supervised the work of the draftsmen and the collection of data from sources around the world.

After publication of the *Plan of Chicago* in 1909, and as Burnham's health declined, Bennett developed his own practice. He advised dozens of public and private clients throughout the United States (see cat. no. 238) and Canada, and assumed the role of consulting architect to the Chicago Plan Commission. For more than twenty years Bennett defended and elaborated the plan. In addition to designing architectural embellishments for bridges and parks, he joined Commission executives in negotiations to assure that various public and private agencies would build according to the guidelines they had established. Despite his status as a founder of city planning practice in the United States, Bennett's thinking never advanced much beyond the principles and practices developed under Burnham's tutelage. He continued to see the city as a growing organism that could be given perfect, but essentially static, order and form by the professional planner. A competent, but never original, architect, he repeatedly drew upon French precedents encountered during his student days as he designed Chicago's new public works. His Ecole training (see cat. no. 39) and the experience of the 1900 Paris Exposition Universelle (fig. 5) provided him with a wealth of detail with which to flesh out Burnham's plan in the years after 1909.[20] His designs for the Michigan Avenue Bridge (1912-20; fig. 6; see also cat. no. 237) and for pylons, columns, and balustrades in Grant Park (1915-c. 1930; fig. 7) are borrowings as literal as details sketched for the plan itself.

Bennett's was not the only Paris-trained hand to work on the original document. To render eleven of the colored perspectives, Burnham hired Jules Guérin, one of the Washington Plan artists. Despite his name, Guérin was an American. He had studied painting at the Ecole des Beaux-Arts and by 1900 had established a successful career as an illustrator, renderer, painter, and set designer from his New York studio. Guérin did not actually design anything in the Plan of Chicago, but his stun-

Fig. 9

ning, impressionistic views bring to life Burnham's big plan, giving it "magic to stir men's blood" (pl. 73). As Robert Bruegmann has remarked, "Guérin's technique was perfectly suited to the task of indicating large ensembles."[21]

Fig. 10

More conventional are the drawings of Fernand Janin, an Ecole des Beaux-Arts student brought from Paris to design the civic center for the plan (pls. 74, 75). Janin, who began his formal architectural training in 1898, was the brilliant pupil of the Ecole's most prominent *patron*, Victor Laloux. He and Bennett had become friends as fellow students in Paris. In 1905 the young Frenchman won the Premier Second Grand Prix;[22] his winning *château d'eau* project had no urbanistic applications, but certainly Janin knew the 1903 Grand Prix designs for *une place publique* by Léon Jaussely, Jean-Frédéric Wielhorsky, and Henri-Paul-Emile Joulie. The gigantic ensemble of five municipal buildings Janin designed to sit at the intersection of Congress and Halsted streets in Chicago (figs. 1, 8) combined elements of the scheme of Jaussely, the first-place winner (fig. 9), and of the two second-place projects by Wielhorsky (also in Laloux's atelier) and Joulie (fig. 10). Furthermore, the towering domed city hall that Janin designed to be Chicago's focal point is an overblown elaboration of his teacher Laloux's 1878 Grand Prix-winning cathedral design (fig. 11), which was itself a synthesis of the Panthéon in Paris and St. Peter's in Rome.[23]

Of all the proposed public works in the Chicago Plan, this was the most artificial. Unlike many other elements of the plan, a civic center on the West Side across the Chicago River never found a place on the Chicago Plan Commission's publicity agenda. From a practical standpoint, it was not required. While Burnham and his team prepared the plan, new city and county buildings were going up downtown, namely, Holabird and Roche's County Building of 1907, and the firm's City Hall of 1911 (see Klotz, fig. 6). A few blocks away stood the recently completed Post Office (later called the Federal Building) of 1905 by Henry Ives Cobb (figs. 12, 13). The idea of building a civic center had been discussed since 1900, with Grant Park on the lakefront being the most frequently mentioned location. In 1905, when an explosion made replacement of the adjacent city and county buildings a necessity, Mayor Edward F. Dunne, with support from the West Side alderman and residents, proposed moving city hall to Union Park, almost two miles due west of Courthouse Square, where the existing structures stood. His suggestion, however, met with opposition from North and South Side aldermen, who contended that by using modern building methods and by rebuilding on Courthouse Square, the city could more economically obtain a convenient structure of sufficient size. The mayor acquiesced, and the new steel-frame structures rose at their old locations.[24]

Fig. 9 Léon Jaussely, Plan of "Une Place Publique," Grand Prix de Rome, 1903; from Les Grands Prix de Rome d'Architecture (1906).

Fig. 10 Henri-Paul-Emile Joulie, Plan of "Une Place Publique," Grand Prix de Rome, 1903; from Les Grands Prix de Rome (1906).

Fig. 11 Victor Laloux, Elevation of a cathedral, Grand Prix de Rome, 1878; from Les Grands Prix de Rome (1891).

Fig. 12 Henry Ives Cobb, Dome of the Federal Building, Dearborn Street between Adams and Jackson streets, under construction.

Fig. 13 Cobb, Federal Building, 1905.

PLAN OF CHICAGO

86

provide. If in certain sections buildings for light manufactures abut upon these thoroughfares, the working people will then enjoy a maximum of fresh air and light; and so will work

with greatest effectiveness. The boulevard also affords appropriate sites for statues and fountains, and all other forms of adornment pleasing to the eye, making attractive the city. The smaller parks may well be adjacent to the boulevards, or may be expansions of them, thus providing for larger playgrounds, for places of assembly, and for displays of plants and flowers, and rare and beautiful trees, which appeal to the almost universal love of nature. The principle governing the grouping of boulevards and avenues is the establishment of through connection, so that one thoroughfare shall lead into another, and that circulation shall be

XCII. PARIS. THE AVENUE DU BOIS DE BOULOGNE, LOOKING TOWARDS THE ARC DE TRIOMPHE.

everywhere promoted but never impeded.

Along the curved avenues and the diagonals the architectural design should avoid the building up of the thoroughfare structure by structure, each one following the whim of its owner or the struggle for novelty on the part of its architect. Without attempting to secure formality, or to insist on uniformity of design on a large scale, there should be a constant display of teamwork, so to speak, on the part of the architects. The former days when each architect strove to build his cornice

XCIII. PARIS. THE TUILERIES GARDENS, AND CHAMPS ÉLYSÉES BEYOND, FORMING THE MAIN AXIS OF THE CITY.

higher or more elaborate than the adjoining cornice are giving place, happily, to the saner idea of accepting existing conditions when a reasonable line has been established. There is as

Fig. 14
Plan of Chicago, *p. 86.*

Clearly, the Chicago Plan's proposed civic center had symbolic rather than utilitarian value. The plan's authors stated that it would lie along the "backbone of the civic body" and at the "center of gravity" of an organically unified network of existing and proposed traffic arteries.[25] This monumental architectural ensemble, whatever form it ultimately took, would stand for the ideal of social harmony and would inspire civic unity, they claimed. Great public buildings

typify the permanence of the city, they record its history, and express its aspirations. Such a group of buildings as Chicago should and may possess would be for all time to come a distinction to the city. It would be what the Acropolis was to Athens, or the Forum to Rome, and what St. Mark's Square is to Venice — the very embodiment of civic life.[26]

Such sentiments, of course, did not originate with Chicagoans. Since before the turn of the century, municipal reformers across the country had advocated building architectural expressions of the "civic renaissance" they fostered.[27] Most of these

City Beautiful-era civic centers also featured monumental domed city halls flanked by symmetrical ranks of uniformly classical buildings housing other government offices, as well as libraries, museums, and auditoriums. And like the Chicago civic center, the vast majority of these projects in cities like Seattle and St. Louis never materialized. Even the few realized civic centers such as the one in San Francisco remained hopeful symbols of a social order that did not yet exist. Responding to the reformers' program, architects had designed these emblems of community life as "correctives" to the weakening of the fabric of society and to "the separation of men into self-seeking factions." They believed civic centers to be active agents of democracy and to be antidotes to problems resulting from mass immigration and strife between labor and capital. These beautiful and monumental groupings of public buildings would, on the one hand, force the ward bosses out of their neighborhoods, and, on the other hand, would inspire civic pride in the hearts of the masses — so they said.

That the forms these architects employed in designing civic centers originated in the despotic Old World troubled them not at all. They rejected the associationism of nineteenth-century picturesque styles and attempted to recreate an American neoclassical tradition suitable for their world. In the palaces and churches of Renaissance Europe they perceived the expression of order, harmony, and stability — values they shared with the politicians and businessmen who were often their clients.[28]

Burnham and Bennett also shared these attitudes. To them, Paris was the ideal model of urban order both aesthetically and functionally. The *Plan of Chicago* states:

City planning in the sense of regarding the city as an organic whole and of developing its various units with reference to their relations one to another, had its origins in Paris during the Bourbon period. Among great cities, Paris had reached the highest stage of development; and the method of this attainment affords lessons for all other cities.[29]

The French had laid out streets in their capital in advance of occupation. Their public and semi-public buildings had been provided with proper approaches. Furthermore, the French recognized that "the convenience and beauty of Paris bring large returns in money as well as in aesthetic satisfaction."[30] Burnham had used this last point to sell the idea of planning to Chicago's business leaders. In a speech before the Merchant's Club in April 1897, he noted:

You all know there is a tendency among our well-to-do people to spend much time and money elsewhere....

Fig. 15 Rue de Rivoli, Paris; from Auguste Vitu, Paris. 450 dessins inédits d'après nature *(1889).*

We have been running away to Cairo, Athens, The Riviera, Paris and Vienna, because life at home is not so pleasant as in the fashionable centers.... No one has estimated the number of millions of money made here in Chicago and expended elsewhere, but the sum must be a large one.[31]

This argument was repeated on the *Plan*'s last page. Burnham praised Emperor Napoleon III and Baron Georges-Eugène Haussmann, who had made Paris into a touristic and commercial capital: "The task which Haussmann accomplished for Paris corresponds with the work which must be done for Chicago."[32]

Given these sentiments, it is not surprising to find that images of Paris appear more frequently in the *Plan* than those of any other city. Out of forty-three maps, photographs, and drawings illustrating various praiseworthy aspects of European cities, fourteen are from Paris (fig. 14) and five from other parts of France. Vienna figures five times, London four times, Rome four times, and Berlin three times. In contrast, the only American cities illustrated are those that had been replanned by Burnham – Washington, Cleveland, and San Francisco. Other municipalities' recent improvement activities were summarized in two paragraphs of the text.

The plan as a whole does not demonstrate anything like a thorough knowledge of contemporary planning practice and theory, American or European. Borrowings and references, even to France, are selective and determined by pre-existing attitudes rather than by systematic study. In preparation for making the plan, Burnham and his associates had collected extensive data about Chicago and cities throughout the United States and the world. With assistance from the Secretary of State, he requested materials from American ambassadors and consuls abroad. Plans arrived from Amsterdam, Berlin, Brussels, Budapest, London, Madrid, Moscow, Paris, Rome, St. Petersburg, and Vienna.

From Paris, the largest collection of documents was secured. It included panoramic views, engravings of artistic street lamps, maps, books, and a specially prepared report on "The Expropriation of Property in France" by attorney Georges Barbey. Among the books sent were Auguste Vitu's *Paris. 450 dessins inédits d'après nature* (fig. 15), Paul Joanne's *Paris*, and an edition of the *Atlas municipal des vingt arrondissements de la ville de Paris*. Apparently, not every item requested arrived in Chicago, nor had all items received been asked for.[33] The majority of the materials were graphic or pictorial. A few of these images were reprinted in the *Plan of Chicago*. Considering illustrations of European precedents from other sources and various references and footnotes in the document, it is obvious that the authors depended upon materials that were easily obtainable and that supported con-

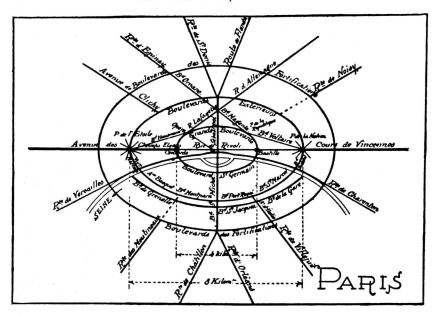

Fig. 16 Eugène Hénard,
"Theoretical Diagram of
the Streets of Paris," in
Etudes sur les transfor-
mations de Paris (1905);
from Plan of Chicago,
pl. 97.

clusions they had already reached. For the most part, the text refers to books and journals that might be found in the library of any well-read architect. These include, for example, Lanciani's *Ancient Rome* and three articles concerning Paris and Napoleon III that had appeared in *Architectural Record, Atlantic Monthly,* and *Century Magazine.*[34]

The one exception is Eugène Hénard's *Etudes sur les transformations de Paris,* a plan for modernizing the city's traffic circulation and open space systems, which appeared in eight installments between 1903 and 1906.[35] The French architect's innovative plan updated Haussmann's work. His principles of vehicular circulation were echoed in the Chicago Plan. Following his general circulation diagrams (fig. 16), Burnham and Bennett recommended concentric circuits of arterials and more diagonal streets penetrating the heart of Chicago and extending into the region (fig. 17), just as Hénard had proposed to Paris.

Given Burnham's emphasis on monumental public buildings, parks, and transportation systems, it is not surprising to find that planning efforts in England and German-speaking countries received little notice in the Chicago Plan. Neither Burnham nor Bennett had any first-hand knowledge of these activities other than what they had observed as tourist and student.[36] Generally, they found historical examples in Britain, Germany, and Austria more relevant than current ones. Their discussion of London, for example, centers on three points. The generous provision of large public parks, many of them former royal preserves, should be surpassed in the greater Chicago of the future. London's failure to enact Christopher Wren's 1666 rebuilding scheme following the great

fire had cost later generations millions for street construction, a lesson that Chicago should heed. And finally, the City of London's construction of housing for the poor might some day have to be imitated in Chicago "unless the matter shall be taken in hand at once."[37]

Other than urging strict enforcement of building regulations, the plan offers no solutions to housing problems, since the Commercial Club considered them outside its purview. The Garden City concept, England's most significant contribution to modern planning theory, is not mentioned, even in the historical overview chapter. Policies of decentralization and communal ownership of land advocated by Ebenezer Howard and the Garden City Association contradicted fundamental principles of the Chicago Plan's authors. The document was rooted in the assumption of the continuous expansion of the central city through the agency of its entrepreneurial citizens. Planning in this scheme of things facilitated rather than hindered growth and private profit.

The treatment of Germany and Austria is similarly brief. Dresden's Zwingerhof, Vienna's Ringstrasse, and Berlin's Spree Island, all shown in photographs, exemplified handsome groupings of public buildings around squares and gardens in the city center. Maps illustrating park systems in Berlin and Vienna were reproduced from a 1907 tract by Berlin architects that advocated regional planning, but the text of the Chicago Plan does not indicate that its authors had read this publication. Instead, they merely allude to the magnitude of the city planning movement in Germany and to the controversy over straight or curved streets.[38] Certainly, Burnham and Bennett were not unaware of Germany's strict land-use regulations and of the powers of its cities' professional planning bureaucrats. Several English-speaking authors had extolled German planning, although the tide of enthusiasm for German methods would not peak until the period from 1910 to 1914. Translations of papers by German planners and theorists had appeared in professional publications, and one of them, by Joseph Stubben, originally had been prepared for the International Engineering Congress at the 1893 World's Columbian Exposition.[39]

Had the architects wished to study German planning more thoroughly, they could have consulted a Chicago expert. George Hooker, Civic Secretary of the Chicago City Club since its founding in 1903, had made frequent trips to Europe and often wrote about municipal affairs at home and abroad. His library included numerous planning documents from around the world. Hooker was appointed to the Chicago Plan Commission in 1909, but his con-

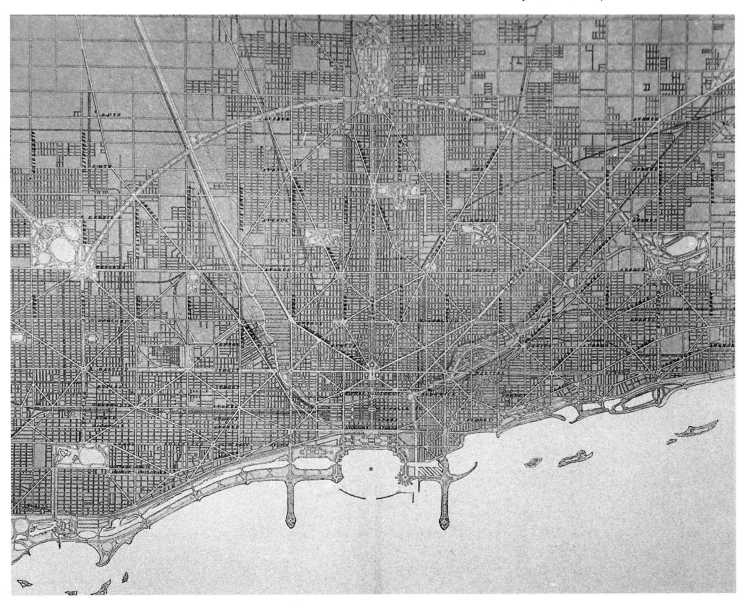

Fig. 17 Plan of a complete system of street circulation; from Plan of Chicago, pl. 85.

tribution before that date was limited to offering an opinion on the consolidation of Chicago's railway terminals.[40] To the plan's authors, his expertise on local transportation issues seemed more pertinent.

Indeed, every chapter of the plan shows evidence of a thoughtful study of local conditions and attempts to base projections on the data about Chicago gathered by Burnham's staff and Commercial Club members from people like Hooker. It also incorporated specific project proposals from men who had already studied various aspects of the city's physical development, but only those projects that supported the preconceptions of Burnham and his sponsors. For example, the Chicago Plan makes no mention of the March 1909 report of the Chicago Harbor Commission, despite the fact that Frederic A. Delano and Charles H. Wacker, two active Commercial Club members, also served on the Commission. That document called for the joint development of the lakefront between the mouth of the Chicago River and Jackson Park for parks and for a commercial harbor. The report tacitly recognized the conflict between park and harbor interests.[41] For its part, the Commercial Club "must be ready to present a plan to demolish the arguments of others," Wacker urged his colleagues at a 1908 club meeting.[42]

Their plan did just that. It expanded upon Burnham's first sketch (cat. no. 212), showing the future shoreline developed as a twenty-three-mile band of parks, with two small commercial piers projecting beyond, into the lake, near the mouths of the Chicago and Calumet rivers. In Grant Park, at the center of this park band, Burnham and Bennett placed a cultural center on axis with the proposed civic center to the west. This cultural center included formally landscaped gardens and a domed edifice for the Field Museum of Natural History, to

Fig. 18 View of the Chicago lakefront looking north, Sept. 1941.

be flanked by harmonious classical structures for the John Crerar Library and the Art Institute. This new Field Museum project replicated the structure then housing the collections, namely, the Fine Arts Building of the 1893 Exposition. The entire composition incorporated the major features of the Grant Park plan that Olmsted Bros. had presented to the South Park Commission in 1903.[43] More important than these specific details, however, was the manner in which the lakefront plan expanded upon the development of a park and parkway along the north shore of Lake Michigan to the suburb of Evanston and beyond (fig. 18). Since the late 1880s, the Lincoln Park District (serving the northern part of Chicago) and a group of Evanston residents, including Daniel Burnham himself, had been working to create a continuous chain of lakefront parks on filled land and a continuous lakefront pleasure drive from downtown Chicago to the northern suburbs.[44] Their efforts were only partially successful, but by the 1890s, Chicago's North Side shore featured a sheltered lagoon, bath and boat houses, and an outer drive. Here in small form

was what Burnham projected on a grand scale for the South Shore in the various plans he made between 1896 and 1908.

Chicago's lakeshore was and remains unique. Burnham's plans for it had no precedent in Paris or any other city. In this aspect, particularly, the Chicago Plan follows the architect's dictum: "the development of every city must lie along individual lines."[45] As the text of the document explains elsewhere:

Chicago has two dominant natural features: the expanse of Lake Michigan . . . and a corresponding area of land extending north, west, and south without hills or any marked elevation. These two features, each immeasurable by the senses, give the scale.[46]

These features and the predominant commercial character of the city determined the character of the plan.

The "Paris by the Lake" envisioned by Burnham resembled the European capital only at the level of its overall organization and in its details. This unified organic pattern that had been adapted from Haussmann and Hénard, Burnham believed, was essential for the growth and progress of any modern metropolis. The details, which he never claimed were original or final, were intended to suggest the level of civic beauty and amenity that Chicago might attain (pl. 76). The elements of the city so organized and embellished — the parks, the lakeshore, the river, the railway, and the street systems — these were *sui generis*. And the scale of the proposed undertakings only confirmed the Windy City's belief in its destiny: "Chicago within the lifetime of persons now living, will become a greater city than any existing at the present time," proclaimed the *Plan*.[47] Earlier booster literature had measured urban greatness in terms of numbers and regarded progress as the result of individual effort; the *Plan* spoke of civic unity, and it embodied greatness in works of civic art recognizable to citizens of Chicago and the world alike.

NOTES

The research for this article was carried out with support from the Graham Foundation for Advanced Studies in the Fine Arts and from the College of Environmental Design, University of Colorado, Boulder. My thanks go to both institutions.

1 *Chicago Tribune*, Feb. 11, 1897.

2 Carl W. Condit, *Chicago, 1910-29: Building, Planning, and Urban Technology* (Chicago, 1973), p. 65.

3 Thomas S. Hines, *Burnham of Chicago: Architect and Planner* (New York, 1974), p. 368.

4 See John James Pauly, "The City Builders: Chicago Businessmen and Their Changing Ethos, 1871-1909" (Ph.D. diss., University of Illinois, Urbana, Ill., 1979), pp. vii-xv, 223-44; and Carl S. Smith, *Chicago and the Literary Imagination* (Chicago, 1984), pp. 149-51.

5 Bion J. Arnold, *Report on the Engineering and Operating Features of the Chicago Transportation Problem*. Submitted to the Committee on Local Transportation of the City Council of the City of Chicago, 1902 (New York, 1905).

6 Chicago, Special Park Commission, *Report of the Special Park Commission to the City Council . . . of Chicago on the Subject of a Metropolitan Park System*. Report compiled by Dwight Heald Perkins (Chicago, 1904).

7 See John W. Alvord, *A Report to . . . the Commercial Club on the Street Paving Problem in Chicago* (Chicago, 1904); and Frederic A. Delano, *Chicago Railway Terminals: a Suggested Solution for the Terminal Problem* (Chicago, 1904). Alvord, an engineer, supervised grades and drainage for the 1893 Exposition. Delano belonged to the Commercial Club and served on the Chicago Plan Commission Executive Committee.

8 Chicago Harbor Commission, *Report to the Mayor and Aldermen of the City of Chicago by the Chicago Harbor Commission* (Chicago, 1909). See also Harold M. Mayer, *The Port of Chicago and the St. Lawrence Seaway* (Chicago, 1957).

9 On the early history of city planning in the United States, see Mel Scott, *American City Planning since 1890* (Berkeley, 1971); Giorgio Ciucci, et al., *The American City from the Civil War to the New Deal* (Cambridge, Mass., 1979); and Donald A. Krueckeberg, ed., *Introduction to Planning History in the United States* (New Brunswick, N. J., 1983).

10 Daniel H. Burnham and Edward H. Bennett, *Plan of Chicago*, ed. Charles Moore (Chicago, 1909), pp. 127-56. The chapter is by Walter L. Fisher, a lawyer and long-time leader of municipal government reform in Chicago.

11 Robert Bruegmann, "Burnham, Guérin and the City as Image," in *The Plan of Chicago: 1909-1979*, John Zukowsky, Sally Chappell, and Robert Bruegmann (Chicago, 1979), pp. 16-28.

12 Burnham and Bennett (note 10), p. 156.

13 Charles Moore, *Daniel H. Burnham: Architect, Planner of Cities* (Boston, 1921), vol. 1, p. 165. Also see Senate Committee on the District of Columbia and Park Commission, *The Improvement of the Park System of the District of Columbia*, 57th Cong., 1st sess. 1902, S. Rept. 166.

14 Thomas J. Schlereth, "Burnham's *Plan* and Moody's *Manual*: City Planning as Progressive Reform," in *The American Planner: Biographies and Recollections*, ed. Donald A. Krueckeberg (New York, 1983), pp. 75-99.

15 Moore (note 13), vol. 2, p. 147. The phrase is part of the frequently quoted injunction attributed by Moore to Burnham; although consistent with his style, he never actually uttered it in this form:

Make no little plans; they have no magic to stir men's blood and probably themselves will not be realized. Make big plans; aim high in hope and work, remembering that a noble diagram once recorded will never die, but long after we are gone will be a living thing, asserting itself with ever-growing insistency. Remember that our sons and grandsons are going to do things that would stagger us. Let your watchword be order and your beacon beauty.

16 Hines (note 3), pp. 3-16.

17 David F. Burg, *Chicago's White City of 1893* (Lexington, Ky., 1976), pp. 75-100; Hines (note 3), pp. 73-124.

18 Bernard Michael Boyle, "Architectural Practice in America, 1865-1965 — Ideal and Reality," in *The Architect: Chapters in the History of the Profession*, ed. Spiro Kostof (New York, 1977), pp. 315-16.

19 Moore (note 13), vol. 1, pp. 117-38, 141-72; vol. 2, pp. 1-2, 29-44.

20 Joan E. Draper, *Edward H. Bennett: Architect and City Planner, 1874-1954* (Chicago, 1982), pp. 7-42.

21 Bruegmann (note 11), pp. 17-24.

22 In 1910, after returning to Paris from Chicago, Janin was awarded the Grand Prix de Rome. See Donald Drew Egbert, *The Beaux-Arts Tradition in French Architecture* (Princeton, N. J., 1980), pp. 72, 191-92, pl. 26; E. Delaire, *Les Architectes élèves de l'Ecole des Beaux-Arts*, 2nd ed. (Paris, 1907), p. 300.

23 *Ecole nationale supérieure des beaux-arts: les concours du grand prix de Rome* (Paris, n. d.), vol. 2, pt. 2, pl. 188; vol. 2. pt. 3, pls. 499, 505.

24 *Chicago Record Herald*, Apr. 25, Apr. 26, May 18, May 23, July 1, 1905.

25 Burnham and Bennett (note 10), pp. 113, 115.

26 Ibid., p. 117.

27 See "Public Art in American Cities," *Municipal Affairs* 2 (Mar. 1898), p. 8; John DeWitt Warner, "Civic Centers," *Municipal Affairs* 6 (Mar. 1902), pp. 1-21; George Howe, quoted in "Municipal Art," *Architectural Record* 23 (1908), pp. 238-39.

28 The quotations are from J. G. Phelps Stokes, "Advantages to be Gained by Appropriate Groupings," in *The Grouping of Public Buildings*, ed. Frederick L. Ford, Municipal Art Society Bulletin 2 (Hartford, Conn., 1904). Also see Joan Elaine Draper, "The San Francisco Civic Center: Architecture, Planning and Politics" (Ph.D. diss., University of California, Berkeley, 1979), pp. 1-55.

29 Burnham and Bennett (note 10), p. 14.

30 Ibid., pp. 18, 80, 91.

31 Moore (note 13), vol. 2, p. 101.

32 Burnham and Bennett (note 10), p. 18.

33 Auguste Vitu, *Paris: 450 dessins inédits d'après nature* (Paris, c. 1890); Paul Joanne, *Paris* (Paris, 1897, and many other editions); *Atlas municipal des vingt arrondissements de la ville de Paris* (Paris, 1910, and many other editions). Correspondence concerning requests for European materials includes: Burnham to Huntington Wilson, February 5, 1907; Burnham to Elihu Root, July 15, 1907; John Ball Osborn to Bennett, April 7, 1908; Frank Mason to Bennett, July 21, 1908; Frank Mason to Elihu Root (copy), May 8, 1907; Edward H. Bennett Papers, Burnham Library, The Art Institute of Chicago. Burnham also received information and photographs from his son Hubert, then studying in Paris.

34 Rudolfo Amadeo Lanciani, *Ancient Rome in Light of Recent Discoveries* (Boston, 1888); Dr. Barry E. O'Meara, "Talks with Napoleon," *Century Magazine* n. s. 37 (1890), pp. 611-33, 778-93, 860-70; Edward R. Smith, "Baron Haussmann and the Topographical Transformation of Paris under Napoleon III," *Architectural Record* 22 (1907), pp. 121-33, 227-38, 369-85, 490-606; Stoddard

Dewey, "The Year in France: French Finance," *Atlantic Monthly* 102 (Aug. 1908), pp. 232-42.

35 Eugène Hénard, *Etudes sur les transformations de Paris*, 8 fascicles (Paris, 1903-1906). See also Peter M. Wolf, *Eugène Hénard and the Beginnings of Urbanism in Paris 1900-1914* (The Hague, 1968).

36 Bennett had left his home in Bristol, England, at sixteen. He worked for a London architect during 1897-99, between stints at the Ecole des Beaux-Arts.

37 Burnham and Bennett (note 10), pp. 21-22, 48, 109.

38 Ibid., pp. 20-21, 45-46, 113-15; Vereinigung Berliner Architekten und dem Architektenverein zu Berlin, *Anregung zur Erlangung eines Grundplanes für die städtebauliche Entwicklung von Gross-Berlin* (Berlin, [1907]).

39 J[oseph] Stubben, "Practical and Aesthetic Principles for the Laying out of Cities," *Transactions of the American Society of Civil Engineers* 29 (1893), pp. 718-36. On American and British interest in German planning, see George R. Collins and Christiane Crasemann Collins, *Camillo Sitte and the Birth of Modern City Planning* (New York, 1965), pp. 85-102; and John Robert Mullin, "American Perceptions of German City Planning at the Turn of the Century," *Urbanism Past and Present* 3 (1976-77), pp. 5-15.

40 Hooker to Burnham, October 27, 1906, and November 30, 1906, Bennett Papers (note 33). See, for example, George Hooker, "The German Municipal Movement," *Chicago Record Herald*, Jan. 30, 1904. Hooker, a Hull-House resident, knew Camillo Sitte and intended to translate his *Der Städtebau* (Vienna, 1889). Apparently, his intense involvement with Chicago affairs prevented the undertaking. His collection of bound articles and pamphlets concerning all aspects of European and American planning is now in the Regenstein Library, University of Chicago.

41 Chicago Harbor Commission (note 8), pp. 41-43.

42 Commercial Club of Chicago, Plan Committee Minutes, January 27, 1908, Bennett Papers (note 33).

43 Chicago, South Park Commissioners, *Report of The South Park Commissioners for a Period of Fifteen Months from December 1, 1906, to February 29, 1908, inclusive*, p. 8. A plaster model of this Olmsted plan for Grant Park was exhibited at The Art Institute of Chicago in 1908.

44 Michael H. Ebner, "Preserving Chicago's North Shore: Evanston, the Plan for Sheridan Road, and the Suburban Landscape" (Paper delivered at Northwestern University, Evanston, January 23, 1985), pp. 7-9. In 1889 Burnham lent his name to efforts to widen Sheridan Road, but by 1902 had joined a suit to stop its extension along the lakeshore. This route would have cut off his Evanston estate from the water. On Lincoln Park, see Chicago Park District, "Historical Register of the Twenty-Two Superseded Park Districts Compiled under the Supervision of the Division Secretary . . . by the Works Progress Administration," ed. Daniel F. Breen (Chicago, 1941), vol. 1, pp. 131-40 (typescript); and I. J. Brayan, *Report of the Commissioners and a History of Lincoln Park* (Chicago, 1899).

45 Burnham and Bennett (note 10), p. 29.

46 Ibid., p. 79.

47 Ibid., p. 4.

Chicago: A French View

Henri Loyrette

Writing to engineer Charles Mascar, who was to attend the 1893 World's Columbian Exposition, the French Consul in Chicago indicated that his compatriot need spend only a day or two in the center of the city staying at the Auditorium Hotel or the Palmer House. After that the Consulate would find him "something less of a hodgepodge in the vicinity of the Exposition."[1] That was what most French visitors to Chicago at that time attempted to do. The head of the French delegation, Camille Krantz, spent ten months, from March 1, 1893, to January 1, 1894, looking for an apartment that would be "well-situated," that is, "near the trains and trolleys" in order to have speedy access to Jackson Park where the Fair was located.[2]

Aside from the exhibitors themselves, very few Frenchmen made the trip to Chicago. There was, of course, the *silhouettiste* of the Eiffel Tower, eager to try his talents under new skies, who requested that he be sent.[3] Certainly there were other French architects who volunteered to work on the Exposition as well.[4] But few sought to remain any length of time. The advertisement in the *Génie Civil* on December 10, 1892, for "a French civil engineer based in Chicago, having a number of connections in America, who would like to represent French businesses dealing in machinery" was a rare exception.

The World's Columbian Exposition of 1893 (fig. 1) presented the French with a great opportunity to discover the capital of the Midwest; for many, however, it was an opportunity not taken. Preoccupied with visiting the Fair and seeing the exhibits relevant to their interests (figs. 2-4), and more intent on selling their products than on exploring the nearby city, most French visitors neglected the real city for the fabricated "White City" of the Exposition grounds.

The most extensive accounts of Chicago are provided by travelers who, in the tradition of a literary genre as popular then as it is now, published the journals of their visits to the United States. For the most part they came only once, stayed a short time, strolled up and down Michigan Avenue, visited the Auditorium Building, and drove out to the stock-yards.[5] Rare were those who, like Jacques Hermant and Paul Bourget, lingered in the city; rarer still were those whose curiosity prompted them to venture beyond the city limits.[6]

Although these accounts, often superficial and exaggerated, were the principal source of information for the French public, one must also consider the active role of several publications that sent special correspondents to cover the 1893 World's Columbian Exposition. In addition to these there were articles reprinted from foreign periodicals which, though biased, still provided some idea of what was going on in Chicago.

For the most part, American architecture was overlooked in the traditional (French) architectural reviews. When the subject was treated at all, it was more likely to be in relation to a New York building or East Coast mansion than to a commercial building in the Midwest. It is thus important to point out the efforts of the *Génie Civil*, "A

Fig. 1 World's Columbian Exposition, 1893 (demolished).

Fig. 2 René Dubuisson and Henri-Paul Motte, French Government Building, World's Columbian Exposition, 1893 (demolished).

Figs. 3/4 George B. Post, Manufacturers and Liberal Arts Building, French section, designed by Dubuisson and Motte, World's Columbian Exposition, 1893 (demolished).

Magazine Covering French and Foreign Industries," to inform its readers about American technology and production. Between 1899 and 1911 the *Génie Civil* published essays on skyscrapers, reviews of new publications, and reports on innovative projects such as the folding bridges on Weed Street[7] and Canal Street,[8] the canal constructions along the Illinois River,[9] the electric drawbridge on Van Buren Street,[10] and the Halsted Street bridge,[11] in articles illustrated with photographs, drawings, and detailed layouts. Scientific publications, such as E. Levasseur's *L'Ouvrier américain* (1898; two vols.), Paul de Rousier's *La Vie américaine* (1892), and Henri de Varigny's *En Amérique: Souvenirs de voyage et notes scientifiques* (1894), did not focus specifically on architecture, but devoted a number of studies to the realities of the American city.

Thinking that it might interest the readers of the *Génie Civil*, civil engineer Henri La Luberne submitted the following report, based on his observations during a month's visit to Chicago in 1891. The substance of his dry account was typical of descriptions being written at the time, although often in a more wordy or literary fashion.

The city of Chicago, completely destroyed sixteen years ago by one of the worst fires to ravage the New World, is now completely rebuilt, and stretches along the shores of Lake Michigan in an area greater than that occupied by Paris. The center of the city is the business district and the residential quarters are on the outskirts. The avenues run north and south, and are cut at right angles by streets running east to west. Among the avenues, certainly the most remarkable is Michigan Avenue [see fig. 5]. As wide as the Avenue de l'Opéra, shaded by rows of trees and lined on each side with stately residences, it is extravagant, perhaps, by European standards, but nonetheless has a charm of its own.[12]

Most of the time, chroniclers limit commentary to a discussion of the growth of the population and the rapid reconstruction after the Great Fire, a description of streets "thirty kilometers long, lined with houses twelve, fourteen, sixteen, eighteen, twenty, and twenty-two stories high" that are "veritable self-contained communities,"[13] the sprawling parks, and the disorder of the urban network.

The travelers had come to see the World's Columbian Exposition; they devoted their attention to the "White City," and passed over the real, noisy, and confusing city of Chicago nearby. But there was one attraction that surpassed all others, that had attained celebrity even in Europe: the Chicago stockyards.[14] Often visitors devoted entire chapters of their travel journals to detailed descriptions of the slaughter of hogs and cattle, the stench,

Fig. 5 3300 block of South Michigan Avenue, 1887.

Fig. 6 Bridge over the Chicago River at Randolph Street, with Butler Brothers Warehouse (1913) by D. H. Burnham and Co.

Fig. 7 Illinois Central Railroad Station at Van Buren Street, view looking northwest sometime after 1892.

the pools of blood, and the implacable, efficient, relentless machines of death.[15] Accompanying these descriptions, of course, were the inevitable philosophical reflections that such sights inspired:

It suddenly seemed as though I had before my eyes a symbol of life itself. . . . The workings of nature, our lives compared to those of these creatures, my awareness of time and of death was tinged with wonder before the power, the enormous scale of the flawless functioning of this vast operation.[16]

From her tour of North America, Sarah Bernhardt retained only two impressions of Chicago: the friendliness of Potter Palmer, owner of the Palmer House, and the "butchering of the hogs, a horrible and magnificent spectacle."[17]

Even the painter Camille Pissarro (who had not visited the city), remarked in a conversation about the Fair, "Who the devil wants to go to those butchers?"[18]

The novelist Paul Bourget saw in the stockyards the perfect illustration of everything that was both grand and base in the enterprising spirit of the Americans: "That colossal thrust of the imagination" harnessed to a "calculating and determined manipulation of the environment."[19] Paul de Rousiers more simply classified Chicago as the "meat capital" or "Pork'opolis," explaining the extraordinary development of the city with the statement that "in Chicago one can truthfully say, modifying a well-known expression: 'when the meat goes well, all goes well.'"[20] This image of Chicago

has persisted until the present day in the popular comic strip adventure book, *Tintin in America,* for example, where sides of beef are shown sliding down a conveyor belt to emerge a few feet down the line as links of sausage or corned beef. In a manner similar to the tales that later developed about prohibition and the "gangsterism" of Al Capone, these visual images of the stockyards tended to overwhelm and thus distort the outsider's impression of the city.

Those who did linger in Chicago discovered that it was unlike any other city they knew. Whereas New York or Washington retained some Old World characteristics, Chicago was the most purely "American" city on the continent. The French visitor was at once astonished, bewildered, and disoriented by the differences he found. The men were skinny and ill-mannered; the women were stout and easy prey for the foreigner (especially the Parisian) — marriages were made and unmade within the day.[21] It was also much less expensive to live in Chicago than in those East coast cities, which was not without its disadvantages. As one chronicler remarked, "The easy living attracts thousands of vagabonds, beggars, hoodlums, and other questionable characters that keep Chicago police busy."[22]

The unique flavor of Chicago could be captured by taking a ride through the city or viewing it from atop the Auditorium Building. Paul Bourget wrote in 1895 that:

After a few seconds the eye becomes accustomed to the panorama of this unusual landscape. From the tower platforms, six-story edifices look like little cottages, two-story houses appear flattened against the sidewalks, commercial buildings of fourteen, fifteen, and twenty stories seem to float like islands viewed from the mountaintop of Negropont.[23]

What struck one immediately in this bird's-eye view of the city was its incoherence, the juxtaposition of tall commercial buildings with wooden shanties, of vacant lots with neatly laid out blocks of buildings.

You walk along the sidewalks of streets that seem to have been improvised: here you have cobblestone, there asphalt, and even wooden planks covering swampy marshlands. The incoherence of this network of roads is reflected in the inconsistency of the buildings. One moment you are surrounded by tall building... next to these looming towers of Babel will be an empty lot, weedy and untended, where a cow grazes quietly. Further along, you have a series of tiny wooden shacks, scarcely adequate for a family. Next to this a Gothic church that has been converted to a store with a tin sign hanging outside; then the scorched remains of a fancy nightclub that burned down the week before. And so it goes: empty lots, shacks, churches, ruins.[24]

Incoherent and chaotic, these vivid images recall the phantasmagoric urban illustrations of Gustave Doré. For the traveler whose measure was his native France, Chicago was the very antithesis of Paris.

Not until the publication of Burnham's *Plan of Chicago* in 1909 (see essay by Draper) was atten-

tion drawn to (potential) similarities between Chicago and Baron Georges-Eugène Haussmann's Paris. Napoleon III's administrator and prefect confined his plans for the redesigning of Paris to the twenty districts of the capital, within which he created an orderly urban pattern of carefully calculated perspectives, without irregular projections and random empty spaces. In contrast, Chicago sprawled out endlessly, with neither beginning nor end, juxtaposing buildings with empty lots, and imposing edifices with shacks constructed of every kind of material. The most striking difference was that in the French capital all industry had been confined to areas outside the city limits since the 1860s, while in Chicago industry was everywhere apparent: in the numerous bridges with their "disgraceful iron framework" (fig. 6); in the railroad stations located at the very heart of the city (fig. 7); in the "smokestacks vomiting black smoke"; and in "the railroad tracks crisscrossing every neighborhood."[25]

The growth of the city was not controlled by codes and regulations; the city was in constant flux. It flaunted its disdain for aesthetic concerns. All of these factors invited unfavorable comparison with Paris.

Paris is above all an elegant city, but Chicago has no such pretensions, and is organized primarily from the point of view of development of its commercial and industrial activity. Anything appears justifiable that can usefully contribute to this result.[26]

9503

In France there was but one comparable phenomenon, the suburbs, pejoratively referred to as the "zone," the wide "belt" encircling Paris. Here, with the exception of tall office buildings, was found everything that embodied Chicago for the French traveler. It is no wonder, then, that the French architectural publications were silent regarding developments across the Atlantic, and that, in contrast, relatively elaborate descriptions could be found in the *Génie Civil*. For, indeed, the construction in Chicago could not help but interest the engineer who was continually on the lookout for new technological advances and oblivious to aesthetic considerations. He, in any case, would find what he was looking for in the "industrial Babel" (fig. 8).[27]

Down to the very smells and sounds, "the smoky fumes of industry, the bells of the locomotives,"[28] Chicago was the antithesis of Paris, and uniquely so. Compared to other American cities, Chicago had a special, innate quality that distinguished it from all others, making it the most American city, indeed the only truly American city on the continent. "Chicago is an amazing city," wrote the correspondent from the *Revue illustrée*. "It is the model *par excellence* of the American city, due to its vastness and the rapidity with which it has grown."[29] Paul de Rousiers went so far as to say, "[It is] ... the most active, the boldest, the most

American of all the cities in the Union."[30] The enthusiasm of the more chauvinistic Frenchmen, however, was dampened by the large percentage of the population with German origins. "The Germans claim that Chicago is the third city of the Empire — after Berlin and Hamburg — because there are over 600,000 of them there." This fact, notes economist Victor Cambon bitterly, is just one more negative aspect of "this unpleasant and pretentiously ugly human anthill."[31] The French found a typically Teutonic je ne sais quoi in this capital of the Midwest.

But the dense population and wide expanse of the city would not, in themselves, explain the uniqueness of Chicago. One must recognize the architectural originality of the city, regardless of the criticism it provoked. The Chicago School was not yet discussed, if one spoke of architecture at all, since critics commented that "the only truly architectural edifices are few,"[32] and that the only aesthetic intention that could be discerned was the representation of the "immense," the "extraordinary," the "mark of power."[33] In his official report following the World's Columbian Exposition, Jacques Hermant, architect of the French section of the Fair, noted more judiciously that Chicago, which he considered to be "the purest kind of commercial city," was clearly different from the cities of the East Coast with their European flavor, "a

Europe magnified and transformed, but Europe nonetheless.... Boston, New York, and Philadelphia remind one of the great English cities; San Francisco, which is becoming increasingly American, has a Spanish or Chinese flavor. Chicago *is* America."[34]

It was futile to look in Chicago for that which was so common in New York, "that terrible mania for styles of the past, that passion to copy historical forms."[35] On the contrary, "one immediately senses an energetic resistance to the importation of the European; the determination to create something original and make a purely personal statement without borrowing from others."[36] This endeavor, which was little understood by French observers, was discernible in intention and form, first, in the problem of the tall office building, in the work of the architect Louis Sullivan, and later, in the more general movement to abandon the use of historical forms in architectural designs.

The architectural terminology used by French writers and journalists varied: "colossal house," "tall house," "giant house," and "tall office building" were all employed. The term "skyscraper" was considered to be "a bit pretentious," and was not used.[37] In spite of the ambiguous use of the word "house" with its obvious domestic connotations, the definitions are much the same: a building of several stories containing offices. Jacques Hermant

is one of the very few French critics of the time to distinguish carefully between "residences" and "buildings."

Considered to be typically American, and therefore difficult to export, the "tall office building," as it was commonly called after the 1893 Fair, was perceived to be the most obvious manifestation of an indigenous architecture. Lyrical explanations abounded for the appearance of this phenomenon, this building type erected by "some impersonal, irresistible, and unconscious power, like the force of nature in the service of which man is but a docile instrument."[38] Similar remarks had been made about the Eiffel Tower, a triumph of the art of engineering, the pure product of the "fever of commerce."[39] For those who favored an evolutionary interpretation, the tall office building was a natural development in American architecture. These structures of iron, "necessitated by the great industrial development," succeeded the colonial log cabin and the humble house of brick and stone, and would subsequently be replaced by constructions in marble and granite, symbols of the "prosperity [that had been] achieved."[40]

A more straightforward view was offered by Jacques Hermant, who called the tall commercial building "the ideal structure, a temple to labor, where everything is planned and integrated in order to improve working conditions, making them

Fig. 8 View of Chicago lakefront, c. 1895, showing Illinois Central Railroad yards.

Fig. 9 Jenney and Mundie, New York Life Building, 37-43 South LaSalle Street, 1893-94.

The tall office building, constructed to fill the needs of commerce, and thus of man, had its counterpart in the suburban house designed for the family, the woman's domain, where "everything is done to satisfy her love of comfort and elegance."[43]

In the 1880s and early 1890s the tall office building was not regarded as having much of a future. Although architects and engineers had successfully solved the delicate problem of laying foundations on marshy soil, numerous difficulties remained, including the danger of fire, deterioration due to rust, and health considerations. The proximity of these towers prevented air from circulating and "deprived those below of any hope of catching a ray of sunlight; transforming the streets that are less than twenty meters wide into veritable cesspools, bringing to mind certain streets of old Paris."[44] French critics, responding to claims made by Chicago architect Dankmar Adler that such buildings would eventually exceed forty stories, predicted that it would never come to pass.

Actual construction methods received little attention in the French press; some writers did not find them very original, remarking simply that "the assembly of these steel skeletons closely resembles our way of constructing in France." "What strikes us as most American," continued the same journalist, "is that the builders are able to bring the iron framework to the site in enormously heavy sections (up to 22 tons)."[45] The only comments on construction methods were made in passing by journalist Henri de Varigny, who claimed to have made "scientific notes" on his trip to the United States: "Nowadays they often build by assembling large steel frames that they later join together and complete with bricks, for example."[46] Once again, it is Jacques Hermant who devotes one-fourth of his report to construction techniques and provides the most detailed description of American innovations:

It would be totally impossible to raise solid walls to such heights, which, in order to bear such colossal weights, would need to be unacceptably thick at the base. The engineers were therefore obliged to find another solution. Instead of connecting the floors to the facades and the supporting partitions layer by layer, the structure is assembled by joining steel pillars to form a skeleton. These pillars are then connected to thick steel beams that support the entire floor above. Therefore, they each have the same function and bear an identical weight, as the height of the stories is generally the same.[47]

For the most part, these office buildings were not distinguished from one another, but were described as being repetitive, and thus monotonous, invariably built according to the same procedures. "They always have the same powerful bases, the same patterns of windows as high as the eye can

as pleasant and agreeable as possible."[41] From an historicist point of view Hermant commented:

Just as ancient architecture has left us temples, basilicas, thermal baths, and amphitheaters that correspond to the principal needs and activities of the peoples of Greece and Rome; just as we have the church, the feudal castle, and town hall to represent the three major social components of the Middle Ages; just as the castles and palaces of the great century express the power of absolute monarchy — so are we obliged to recognize, in the products of the most American of all cities, design and construction techniques that answer the requirements of commerce, and are the very essence of the American genius.[42]

Such evolutionary theories were widely held at that time. Charles Garnier, the architect of the new Paris Opéra, spoke of his building, in ruins in the distant future, as being archeologically important to a study of the Second Empire.

see, the same ornament, the same materials of granite, marble, or brick used on the facade in continuously repeating patterns."[48] Aside from the Auditorium Building, unquestionably the shining star, few of these structures received more than passing notice. Exceptions to this were the New York Life Building (fig. 9) by Jenney and Mundie, and the Reliance Building (see Chappell, fig. 9), whose originality was briefly discussed in the *Génie Civil*: "They did away with the facing walls and replaced the facade with glass surfaces all the way to the top."[49] When Hermant refers to the Monadnock Building (fig. 10; pls. 15, 16), for example, it is to contrast it with the powerful structures of Sullivan: "Here [in the Monadnock Building] there is no regard for form or composition. It is not the work of an artist, who adapts with intelligence to particular conditions, keeping in mind all the consequences. It is, rather, the work of a builder, who, without the slightest concern, superimposes fifteen rigorously similar floors to form a block, and stops only when he judges that the block is high enough."[50]

For the interior this monotony seemed tolerable — the office spaces were scarcely alluded to. When it came to the exterior, even the least hostile critics grudgingly conceded that they "astonish without pleasing,"[51] and that it was therefore imperative to find some "aesthetic solutions" to embellish them. There were a few reporters, like P. Germain, an engineer from Saint-Etienne, who felt that the "'colossal houses' responded to a new challenge that architects seized with much daring and freedom"[52] and, in the best examples, perhaps "raw strength" could be considered to be "a principle of beauty."[53] Most, however, maintained that it was necessary to find a style and form to improve upon "these artistically unsatisfying"[54] constructions. Some felt that the architecture of the Waldorf Hotel in New York was the best solution;[55] for others it was in the systematic use of the Belgian Renaissance style;[56] but the most perceptive critics asserted that there could be only one solution — an "American style," as advocated by Louis Sullivan and captured so masterfully in his designs.

Sullivan

Of all the Chicago architects, Sullivan is the only one whose name was frequently cited in French journals, and the Auditorium Building, as has been indicated, was the only monument that was at all celebrated in late nineteenth-century France.

One might think that the French influence in his work, which seem so apparent today, played a role in this recognition; that the French felt themselves

Fig. 10 Burnham and Root, Monadnock Building, 53 West Jackson Street, 1890-91.

to be on familiar ground with Sullivan and the vocabulary of his ornament. But that does not seem to have been the case. There was never any allusion to his studies in Paris (see cat. nos. 27-33) nor to his connection to the French rationalist school, exemplified by the work of the students of Viollet-le-Duc, particularly Victor-Marie Ruprich-Robert. On the contrary, Sullivan was viewed as being typically American, even if one detected traces of other influences, such as the Roman-Byzantine style. In his early career such influences tended to weaken the originality of his work. Even if his designs were more moving than convincing, more impassioned, "especially when he is certain of the grandeur of his mission,"[57] than successful, Sullivan was considered the worthy pioneer of a modern art form that was commendable in spite of its occasional blundering and lack of taste.

Fig. 11 Louis H. Sullivan, Getty Tomb, Graceland Cemetery, 1890.

crates of plaster casts from the Transportation Building that he had made for the exposition in Chicago, as well as several casts from the Auditorium Building." André Bouilhet confirmed in February 1895 that these crates were "received last spring, and remain, I believe, in the street level hall." Unfortunately, we have lost all trace of them.

Although the Transportation Building (fig. 13; cat. nos. 125-27) was mentioned in most reports of the 1893 Fair, it provoked only the mildest interest in the French press. The correspondent from the *Revue Encyclopédique* viewed it as a flagrant mistake, the very symbol of the innumerable architectural aberrations rampant at such international fairs: "A Byzantine gate opens on to a depot of mail coaches, Pullman cars, and all sorts of coaches and hearses for all classes. Such is the absurdity which is the basis of this gigantic display of artistic pretention and of commercial and industrial competition."[58] Hermant, on the other hand, highly praised the Transportation Building, which distinguished itself from the mediocre parade of palaces and pavilions in a hodgepodge of styles that imitated the most hackneyed products of the Ecole des Beaux-Arts. "The architects attempted to play at a local Grand Prix de Rome," he wrote, "to pile the entablatures onto the columns and multiply the porticos along the arcades."[59] But in the face of such whiteness, two elements stand out unquestionably: "the audacious polychromy of the Transportation Building, and the somber tones of such wooden constructions as the Swedish Pavilion and the Navy restaurant."[60] Hermant was full of praise for the ingenious ornamentation of the Golden Portal of the Transportation Building, designed by Sullivan, calling it a "perfect example of American modern art," and praising it for its candor and daring which burst forth "in the midst of this old arsenal of columns and ornamental pediments."[61]

With a few exceptions, critics expressed similar appreciation for Adler and Sullivan's Auditorium Building. The usually verbose Lutaud, for example, commented only on its efficient design, while the *Revue Encyclopédique* referred to it in an attack on the "monstrous and extravagant monuments of Chicago."[62] Paul de Rousiers cited the Auditorium as a typical example of the tawdry fascination of the Americans with all that is colossal and of questionable taste: "The eye is annoyed by the excess of decoration, the incoherent eccentricity of architectural lines, the brutal aspect, and the piling on of expensive materials, all of which create a crude and discordant effect."[63] In general, however, the Auditorium was well received. Its multifaceted nature seemed to capture the very essence

An eloquent testimony to the flattering critical appraisal of Sullivan in France was the plaster cast of the door of the Getty Tomb (pl. 42) exhibited at the Columbian Exposition. The cast had been made under the supervision of André Bouilhet, manager of the Christofle firm. A year later, Sullivan made an electroplate of the same door, which he sold to the Union Centrale des Arts Décoratifs in October 1894 (figs. 11, 12). In the archives of the Union Centrale there is also a record of a gift which Sullivan, deeply touched by the French public's appreciation, made to that establishment. "Mr. Sullivan has sent to the Union Centrale three

Fig. 12 Sullivan, Cast of ornamental doorway from the Getty Tomb, made by N. Christofle, Paris, 1894 (cat. no. 124).

*Fig. 13 Adler and Sulli-
van, Transportation
Building, World's Co-
lumbian Exposition,
1893 (demolished).*

of the American lifestyle, which goes a long way toward explaining its fame. "The Auditorium is famous because within its four walls, it contains a theater seating six thousand people [fig. 14], a hotel with five hundred rooms, a department store, ten banks, twenty business offices, thirty studios, and many shops."[64]

In his assessment, Hermant was once again more responsive to the details of ornamentation than to the overall design. He considered the Auditorium to be the most comprehensive example of the new American style, and described it at length, remarking upon the restraint and delicacy of the decoration, the use of different materials, the lighting that brought out the polychromy. The polychromy was "novel, gentle to the eye, and absolutely charming,"[65] as well as being admirably suited to the auxiliary areas—the vestibule, stairways, reception areas, and dining rooms—creating the "impression of the palace anterooms of emperors of the East."[66] He lamented, however, that "this happy and inter-

esting endeavor" was unfortunately "incomplete," as the theater itself was "less appealing."[67] "The six illuminated tiers emphasize most cruelly the antediluvian nature of the design, and unfortunately bring out the bareness of this gigantic cave. The lower section, occupied by spectators, is arranged with charm, combining a sense of the practical with a subtle appreciation of tones, which is in disconcerting contrast with the brutality of the overall design."[68] In Hermant's view, Sullivan's big mistake was to believe that that which was suitable on a small scale could be applied to projects of great scale; Hermant also felt that Sullivan failed to understand that if he proceeded in that fashion his work would "inevitably become monotonous and inadequate."[69]

One cannot state too often that the World's Columbian Exposition of 1893 was a missed opportunity for the French. French opinion, loudly and widely proclaimed by the press, was that the Fair had hoped to imitate and surpass the Paris Exposi-

tion of 1889, and had failed in this enterprise. One must have the fervor, the narrow-mindedness, or the chauvinism of a Jacques Gréber to claim that the principal value of the 1893 Fair was that it indirectly "indicated the *great success of our Ecole des Beaux-Arts with regard to American students.*"[70] On the other hand, it could be claimed that one must deplore the fact that American architects did not follow the path they began in Paris in 1867; that they did not continue in the efforts they exhibited there to explore and develop a local architecture – the American building, the American school, "humble buildings whose stature and grandeur is moral, because in the midst of all this outdated opuamidst of all this outdated opulence, they symbolized the birth of a future."[71] With regard to the Paris Exposition of 1878, it was noted that the American facade on the picturesque rue des Nations eschewed all "suspicion of artificiality" and allowed "something natural and untamed"[72] to break through. After the expositions of 1889 and

1893, the American contribution to the 1900 Exposition merely confirmed the impression that the architects had abandoned the healthy precepts that had originally inspired them. As this opinion of Chicago architecture was generally held by French observers, it is no wonder that the architecture of the World's Columbian Exposition was so continually condemned for not being "original." The French visitor to Chicago had to be particularly attentive to appreciate the city's architecture, and it is not surprising that they were unable to recognize its merits as we perceive them today. One must allow, however, that they were not unaware of the new developments in construction and foundation techniques, nor did they fail to mention the "glass block" floors of the Hick Company or the decorative ironwork of the Winslow Brothers (fig. 15).[73]

Indeed, with their national pride in being "Mother of the Arts" (if no longer "Mother of the Arsenal"), the French did not accurately weigh the possible applications of these innovations. Ac-

Fig. 14 Adler and Sullivan, Auditorium Theater, Congress Parkway between Michigan and Wabash avenues, 1887-89, interior view.

Fig. 15 Winslow Bros. Company, Iron staircase in the Monadnock Building (Burnham and Root, 1890-91).

knowledging American superiority in designing the "convenient," and the "useful,"[74] they generally refused to see that "these people, proud of their practical sense, were imperceptibly and unconsciously developing an artistic sensibility alongside of and merging with the need for *comfort*. For the time being, this sensibility was confined to places that attracted the crowds, such as hotels, railroad stations, theaters, boats."[75]

"Let time take its course," the art critic Victor Champier remarked insightfully, and time has proven him right. But in this period at the end of the century, we must commend Paul Bourget and Jacques Hermant, who, in different ways, were able to recognize that, in spite of the extreme confusion that reigned, a unique local architecture could only develop after the encroaching "historical and architectural apparatus"[76] transplanted from the Old World had been swept away; that only then could the as-yet-undefined American truth be pursued. This deliberate primitivism, this "desire to return to native roots," this need to renew a design vocabulary that had been long abandoned, was remarked upon everywhere. It

was not only because it seemed to be a "rudimentary" architecture, as architect Paul Sédille proclaimed it, referring to the designs of certain American houses whose "rustic walls with enormous boundary stones seemed disproportionate to the logical and harmonious use of the materials."[77] Critics attacked the American's determination to break with conventional usage. "Primitive themselves, working for a primitive people, they are tempted above all to seek out effects of a lively and animated relief, deliberately rejecting any delicacy or subtlety in exteriors. They are not opposed to giving their facades a resistant quality that bears traces of the period, albeit recent, when the struggle with the native populations obliged the conquerors to remain on the defensive."[78] Despite these statements, we must recognize that this architecture was responding to new needs. The French architects, "paralyzed...by academic traditions and a collector's mania for repetitions and clutter,"[79] were unable to appreciate the originality of the structural and design solutions that some Chicago architects presented.

Thus, the Universal Exposition of 1900 was a glaring demonstration of an exhausted, repetitive art, in which the architects unflaggingly, tirelessly produced "brutal monuments whose eclectic parts borrowed from all styles and ages constituted generally the most abstract travesties of design that one can imagine."[80] Chicago was not to be the regenerative force that Africa or the Pacific Islands were to be for a Matisse or a Gauguin. American architecture, despised and neglected for some time, would be avenged later. Far from adapting it and modifying it to their needs, the French would be content to transplant it. By the end of the nineteenth century, Chicago, "this mosaic of a radical, almost barbaric civilization, with its unbridled energy discernible beneath the burst of industrial creativity,"[81] was already, for the better, and often for the worse, our own modern times.

NOTES

1 Paris, Archives Nationales, F 12, 4447.
2 Ibid., F 12, 4452.
3 Ibid., F 12, 4450.
4 Ibid., F 12, 4454.
5 Ibid., F 12, 4448.
6 A. Lutaud, *Les Etats-Unis en 1900* (Paris, 1896), p. 150.
7 *Le Génie Civil* 20 (1891-92), pp. 33-34.
8 Ibid., 24 (1893-94), pp. 337-38.
9 Ibid., 26 (1894-95), pp. 246-249.
10 Ibid., pp. 337-38.
11 Ibid., 28 (1895-96), pp. 82-84.
12 Ibid., 20 (1981-92), p. 45.
13 Henri La Luberne, "Chicago et l'Exposition américaine," *La Revue illustrée* 1 (1893), p. 338.
14 Lutaud (note 6), p. 158.
15 Paul Bourget, *Outre-Mer* (Paris, 1895), vol. 1, p. 175.
16 Ibid.
17 Sarah Bernhardt, *Ma double vie* (Paris, 1980), vol. 2, pp. 252-53.
18 Letter, Sept. 15, 1893, in Camille Pissarro, *Lettres à son fils Julien* (Paris, 1950).
19 Bourget (note 15), p. 171.
20 Paul de Rousiers, *La Vie américaine* (Paris, 1892), p. 70.
21 La Luberne (note 13), p. 341 f.
22 Lutaud (note 6), p. 161.
23 Bourget (note 15), p. 159.
24 Ibid., p. 162.
25 De Rousiers (note 20), p. 74.
26 Ibid.
27 Bourget (note 15), p. 159.
28 Ibid.
29 La Luberne (note 13), p. 337.
30 De Rousiers (note 20), p. 96.
31 Victor Cambon, *Etats-Unis – France* (Paris, 1917), pp. 33-34.
32 Lutaud (note 6), p. 158.
33 De Rousiers (note 20), p. 108.
34 Exposition Internationale de Chicago en 1893, *Comité 36, Génie Civil. Travaux publics. Architecture. Rapport de M. Jacques Hermant, architecte de la Ville de Paris* (Paris, 1894), p. 5.
35 Ibid., p. 24.
36 Ibid.
37 See *Le Génie Civil* 19 (1891), pp. 376-77; 20 (1891-92), p. 108; 24 (1893-94), pp. 5-6; 25 (1894), p. 115; 26 (1894-95), pp. 262-66.
38 Bourget (note 15), p. 160.
39 Ibid.
40 Exposition Internationale de Chicago en 1893, *Comité 21, Rapport* (Paris, 1894), p. 31.
41 Hermant (note 34), p. 6.
42 Ibid.
43 Hermant (note 34), p. 27.
44 Ibid., p. 10.
45 *Le Génie Civil* 20 (1891-92), p. 264.
46 Henri de Varigny, *En Amérique, Souvenirs de voyage et notes scientifiques* (Paris, 1894), p. 49.
47 Hermant (note 34), p. 15.
48 Ibid., p. 23.
49 *Le Génie Civil* 26 (1894-95), p. 263.
50 Hermant (note 34), p. 9.
51 *Exposition de Chicago. Rapport de M. Ernest Lourdelet, Membre-délégué de la Chambre de Commerce de Paris, Novembre 1893* (Paris, 1893), p. 10.
52 *Le Génie Civil* 19 (1891), p. 377.
53 Bourget (note 15), p. 161.
54 *Le Génie Civil* 24 (1893-94), p. 5.
55 Ibid., p. 6.
56 *Le Génie Civil* 25 (1894), p. 115.
57 Hermant (note 34), p. 8.
58 B. H. Gausseron, "Exposition de Chicago," *La Revue Encyclopédique* 3, 70 (Nov. 1, 1893), p. 1084.
59 Hermant (note 34), p. 32.
60 Ibid., p. 33.
61 Ibid., pp. 40-41.
62 Gausseron (note 58), p. 1062.
63 De Rousiers (note 20), p. 109.
64 La Luberne (note 13), p. 338.
65 Hermant (note 34), p. 25.
66 Ibid.
67 Ibid., p. 26.
68 Ibid.
69 Ibid.
70 Jacques Gréber, *L'Architecture aux Etats-Unis* (Paris, 1920), vol. 1, p. 32.
71 *L'Exposition Universelle de 1867 illustrée* (Paris, 1867), vol. 1, p. 86.
72 *Les Merveilles de l'Exposition de 1878* (Paris, 1878), p. 171.
73 Hermant (note 34), p. 59.
74 De Varigny (note 46), p. 65.
75 Victor Champier, "L'enseignement des Arts Décoratifs aus Etats-Unis d'Amérique," *Résumé de rapports de missions sur les institutions d'enseignement industriel et artistique à l'étranger adressé aux membres du congres, organisé par l'Union Centrale des Arts Décoratifs* (Paris, 1894), p. 59.
76 De Varigny (note 46), pp. 45-46.
77 Paul Sédille, "L'Architecture américaine jugée par un critique français," *Encyclopédie d'Architecture*, vol. 5, p. 11.
78 Hermant (note 34), p. 28.
79 Ibid., p. 8.
80 J. K. Huysmans, "Le Fer," in *Certains* (Paris, 1975), pp. 401-02.
81 Bourget (note 15), p. 164.

Shopping – Chicago Style

Neil Harris

It cannot be said that Chicago invented American shopping. Her boosters, eager to assign primacy to urban accomplishments, must acknowledge the innovators who worked elsewhere: A. T. Stewart of New York, John Wanamaker of Philadelphia, F. W. Woolworth of upstate New York, S. S. Kresge of Detroit, and Edward A. Filene of Boston, to name a few. Eastern towns and cities were spawning mercantile giants while Chicago was just a village.[1]

But if Chicago failed to initiate the shopping habit, the city nonetheless hosted some extraordinary adventures in marketing. They ranged from creating the most concentrated downtown retail section in the country to hosting the largest mail order houses in existence. Along with business growth came advances in commercial architecture and display.

As a monument to economic man, Chicago, by the 1860s, was boasting of the splendor of her commercial facilities. The move within a single lifetime from frontier outpost to world metropolis was not simply heady: it enshrined a set of contrasts, a before and after, that was measured by local retail and wholesale establishments as well as by railroad stations, parks, churches, and libraries. Because of

the breakneck speed of their economic take-off, Chicagoans valued the visible evidence of their attachment to finer things. By the late nineteenth century this usually meant the power to command European art and fashion. In great parallel movements the city's shopping world would exhibit the dichotomy characterizing much of American architecture: ingenuity of mind leading to a rationalization that prized simplicity, logic, and economy of operation on the one hand, and love of ornament and eclectic quotation on the other. The first sensibility projected a functionalist ethic; the second promoted historical reference and traditional display values. In the fifty years following the Great Fire, Chicago's shopping settings revealed that builders moved along both axes of this American grid. By the early twentieth century they were exporting some of their talent and experience to the rest of the country. In its downtown, Chicago powerfully endorsed the urbanity associated with European cosmopolitanism, but in a version unmistakably her own. Elsewhere in the city Old World motifs were less mediated, less self-conscious, and ultimately more traditional. By the 1920s the Loop, the chic Michigan Avenue sector, and the neighborhoods offered three versions of what city shop-

Fig. 1 State Street, view looking north from Madison Street, 1915.

Fig. 2 Milwaukee Avenue at Chicago Avenue, view looking southeast, 1915.

MARSHALL FIELD & CO.
WHOLESALE, CHICAGO

Fig. 3 Henry Hobson Richardson, Marshall Field Wholesale Store, Adams Street between Wells and Franklin streets, 1885-87 (demolished).

ping could be like, and three different interpretations of European memories or ideals. This essay focuses primarily on developments in the Loop, but what happened in the other two areas must constitute a decisive counterpoint.

Between 1871 and the 1920s Chicago became a colonizing power in her own right, annexing whole towns and villages. This spatial imperialism made her, for much of this period, America's second largest city in physical area as well as population. Just 36 square miles in 1870, Chicago reached practically her full portion, 207 square miles, by 1930, behind only New York and Los Angeles. By contrast, Philadelphia and St. Louis were geographically static for the 100 years following 1870, while the aggressive annexation patterns of southern and southwestern cities took place much later.[2]

Area and population growth aside, Chicago thrived by means of a sophisticated transportation system. Commuter railroads, trolleys, and elevated railroads traversed hundreds of miles of track in the city by the 1920s. In 1925 a total of 830 trains, electric and steam, served the commuting area. The whole system poured its energies into a "golden circle" served by what was known as the Union Loop. Created in 1897, the Loop linked each of the city's existing elevated systems to a track that circled the central business core. Indeed, according to one visitor, it practically forced such a movement: "Strictly speaking, the man who has no business in this section of the city had better look about and

arrange matters so that he has, or he has no business in Chicago."[3] While the city's mass transit corrupted politics for a generation, it created pools of buyers for the downtown emporia (fig. 1) and for the neighborhood centers that gathered around transfer points (fig. 2).

Transportation had established Chicago's initial mercantile character. By the 1870s steam railroads brought buyers to the city from throughout the Midwest, looking to stock their shops from huge new warehouses. These were becoming some of Chicago's most imposing structures. Before the 1890s wholesale business dwarfed retail for great merchants like Marshall Field. The annual or semi-annual trips of buyers from a huge area of the country climaxed in visits to the wholesale houses, best epitomized by Henry Hobson Richardson's Marshall Field Wholesale Store of 1885-87 (fig. 3). Famous at the time and much described by architectural historians, its massive rusticated granite facade was as appropriately a symbol for this city of commerce as its fortified ancestors that had served the dynastic conflicts of an earlier age.[4]

However expressive of mercantile strength and scale, warehouses like Field's served specialists and initiates better than they did a generalized public. To switch from a military to a religious vocabulary, they were the monasteries and chapter houses of the economic faith, the abbeys and friaries where members of the order gathered on professional business. The temples, cathedrals, and tabernacles would be located a few blocks to the east, on State

Street, for more dramatic reenactments of the ritual. But that took a little more time.

The warehouses did not require much external display. Customers knew where they were and came on specific errands. Favoring a compressed and economical presentation of merchandise, their large, well-lit floors had to support heavy weights. By the 1890s the old wholesaling district on Wabash Avenue had been succeeded by a new area, extending between Randolph and Van Buren streets on a north-south axis, and from Fifth Avenue to the Chicago River on the west. Here the Marshall Field, James H. Walker, J. V. Farwell, Carson Pirie Scott and Co., Henry W. King, Hiram Sibley, and C. M. Henderson warehouses stood like moored ships, their holds filled with an immense quantity of goods. Massive, unadorned facades and crowded interiors made up an inheritance that would soon be passed to Chicago's retail architecture.[5]

As selling spaces the warehouses were complemented, in the early years, by manufacturing salesrooms and jobbing showrooms. In buildings like that owned by John M. Smyth on West Madison (an elaborate, expensive facade dressed in Bedford stone on its first two stories, with a forty-foot arch and plate glass windows), furniture for home or office was marketed.[6] But none of these types was destined to house Chicago's most impressive selling environments. These would come in a series of carefully designed buildings erected during a twenty-five-year period starting about 1890. This spasm of construction and reconstruction made State Street the most crowded downtown shopping street in the country, perhaps the world, and gave Chicago much of her physical personality, bustle, and energy. In seven huge establishments the city provided one of the first great American shopping strips and a training ground for modern merchandising methods.

Chicago's early retail center, reflecting patterns of residence and transportation, was an east-west thoroughfare, Lake Street (fig. 4). Persuaded by the greater advantages of a north-south axis, the merchant-entrepreneur Potter Palmer purchased large portions of State Street, yielded twenty-seven feet in depth along his frontage to widen it, and encouraged other property owners to do the same. The erection of a large store building, palatial by contemporary standards, brought in Levi Z. Leiter and Marshall Field as partners (fig. 5).[7] The street's horse cars carried lots of buyers, and within a block or two the Madison Street lines provided access to the West Side. By 1870 only one of Chicago's seven largest wholesale or retail firms remained on Lake Street. The destruction caused by the Great Fire

did nothing to shake State Street's claims; it merely delayed the street's full development.

During the next few years downtown retailers extended their premises in makeshift sections, usually no more than four or five stories high, rarely of uniform style. The structure housing Field, Leiter and Co. (as it was known in 1881 when the partners went their separate ways) was large to begin with and had been rebuilt several times by 1879 because of fires; it had six stories and a basement. It was not

Fig. 4 Lake Street, view looking east from State Street, 1868.

Fig. 5 E. S. Jennison, Field and Leiter Store, northeast corner of State and Washington streets, 1873 (demolished).

Fig. 6 State Street, view looking north from Madison Street, 1905.

Fig. 7 State Street, view looking south from Lake Street, c. 1892.

Store, begun just after the fire by C. W. and Edwin Pardridge, had just 46 feet of frontage on State Street in its first location; Schlesinger and Mayer, moving in 1880 from the West Side to a corner store at State and Madison that contained 32,000 square feet, would control ten times this amount of space almost six years later.[9]

In scale and solidity the warehouses still dominated. Visiting Chicago in the 1880s, Charles Dudley Warner, journalist and novelist, told readers of *Harper's* that no other American city could show "business warehouses and offices of more architectural nobility." He invoked Florence and "the structures of the Medicean merchant princes." But the building he best remembered was Richardson's Marshall Field Wholesale Store on West Adams Street, unrivaled "in massiveness, simplicity of lines, and admirable blending of artistic beauty with adaptability to its purpose."[10]

State Street, by contrast, consisted of a series of lighter, relatively low buildings with irregular roof lines, differing architectural styles, and elaborate ornamentation, broken up by an occasional larger and still more elaborate mass like the Palmer House. Boosters made a virtue of necessity. Although John Flinn suggested, in 1893, that State Street might remind visiting Europeans of the Avenue de l'Opéra in Paris, Regent Street in London, or the Ringstrasse in Vienna, he admitted some problems. Parisian streets, by "reason of the uniformity of the style of architecture so closely adhered to during the last empire," undoubtedly presented "a more pleasing view at first sight" than did State Street (fig. 7). But, he added quickly,

only larger than most others but fussier, in what Chicagoans termed a "Parisian" style, flaunting its mansards, its cast-iron Italian Renaissance front, and a central pavilion with a glass dome (fig. 6).[8] It would be redone and expanded in the 1880s, as other merchants also enlarged their quarters on the street. But most started smaller than Field, Leiter and Co. Ernest J. Lehman opened his first general store on the west side of State Street in an area of little more than 1,200 square feet; the Boston

Fig. 8 William Le Baron Jenney, Siegel, Cooper and Co. Building (known as the Second Leiter Building; later Sears, Roebuck and Co.), State Street between Jackson and Van Buren streets, 1889-91.

Fig. 9 William Le Baron Jenney, The Fair store, Adams Street between State and Dearborn streets, 1890-91 (demolished).

such "uniformity in style soon becomes tiresome, and the visitor is half inclined to wish that it were broken here and there, no matter how."[11]

Whatever its other claims, State Street faced no problems of uniformity as yet. Ambitious and florid, it aped what it thought to be elegance of an international mode. But by 1893 important changes had already appeared, led by the first two retail stores that in scale and design would soon dominate the American idea of the Big Store. These were the work of William Le Baron Jenney: the second Leiter Building, completed in 1891 and occupied soon thereafter by Siegel, Cooper and Co., and The Fair Store, built for Ernest J. Lehman, whose first section was completed in 1891 on Dearborn and Adams streets, but which would soon be enlarged and extended, in the same style, to reach the west side of State Street (figs. 8, 9).[12]

Fig. 10 Louis H. Sulli-van, Schlesinger and Mayer Store (now Carson Pirie Scott), southeast corner of State and Madison streets, 1899-1904; exterior ornament.

ture that housed Siegel, Cooper and Co. claimed to occupy the largest retail floor area in the world. Extending 400 feet along State Street and 143 feet deep, it comprised 514,000 square feet of selling space, ten times the amount occupied by the firm five years earlier. Praised by guide books as "an example of good taste, munificence, and wisdom," it could have been subdivided had no single client been found. Instead, its 50,000-square-foot floors, sixteen feet high, gave a "dynamic impression of open and airy spaciousness."[13] It seemed to owe little to foreign precedent. A contemporary acknowledgment of its distinctiveness praised the building as "a commercial pile in a style undreamed of when Buonarotti [*sic*] erected the greatest temple of Christianity."[14] Even a visiting Parisienne recorded her astonishment at the store's affluence and luxury, its soda water fountain, and a museum of curiosities lurking on an upper floor.[15]

Jenney's other store building, The Fair, has received less consistent praise from historians by reason of its "profusion of tasteless ornament" and "incredibly heavy-handed details," including a band of rustication at the sixth story, huge pier capitals, an elaborate cornice, and an unhappy devotion to salmon-colored terracotta (see Klotz, fig. 1).[16] But these were surface "blemishes," and The Fair, with its final additions, laid claim to being the "largest mercantile establishment in the world," exceeding even the Bon Marché of Paris.[17] Its nine floors above ground also made it the tallest retail store constructed until then.

The two Jenney buildings brought Chicago something new. Marked by enormous floor size, impressive height, uniform tailoring, and somewhat severe, multiwindowed facades, they were organized for customer comfort. By the time of the World's Columbian Exposition in 1893, the struc-

The first two mammoth stores, the increased traffic, the population growth, the transport improvements — these stimulated other retailers.

Fig. 11 D. H. Burnham and Co., Marshall Field and Co. Store, State Street between Randolph and Washington streets, 1902-14.

Marshall Field and Co. embarked on a vigorous program of acquiring all contiguous property on its block, modernizing existing frontage, and constructing a nine-story addition on the northeast corner of its large site in 1892. Opening in the summer of that year, the Annex (fig. 12) was designed by Daniel Burnham, whose World's Columbian Exposition triumph lay just ahead. This clean, classical building, in Ann Van Zanten's words "both sumptuous and elegant in its demeanor," referred back to a Florentine palazzo.[18] Hinting at the dream of urbanity that would climax in his Chicago Plan fifteen years later, Burnham initiated his association with Marshall Field, an association that would lead his firm into the first ranks of department store planning.

Fig. 12 D. H. Burnham and Co., Marshall Field and Co. Annex, northwest corner of Wabash Avenue and Washington Street, 1892.

The Annex, however, was more vertical, more imitative, more self-consciously decorative than Jenney's buildings. It did not foretell the coming expansion of the State Street stores. Its more deliberate aping of European forms, however appropriate in Boston or New York, did not suit Chicago architects. It remained more mannered than the rest of Field's new complex, suggesting that while an ideal of elegance could be European, its vocabulary would have to be sifted through the warehousing tradition that was Chicago's wholesaling legacy. New York's new department stores on Sixth Avenue featured, at just this time, settings so ornate, encrusted, and elaborate that according to one historian they contributed to their own economic decline.[19] Chicago's "ladies' half mile" would be more austere and restrained, despite windows that vied "in array with those of any city on the face of the globe."[20]

Chicago stores, like the city's office buildings that helped inspire them, relied on massiveness and proportion rather than height or detail to achieve their effect. William Archer likened the relationship between Chicago's downtown and New York's "as the elephant (or rather the megatherium) to the giraffe.... There is a proportion and dignity in the mammoth buildings of Chicago which is lacking in most of those which form the jagged sky-line of Manhattan Island."[21] To be sure, Archer allowed, the midwestern city's smoky atmosphere resisted any but the most massive interventions.

By 1896 Field's Annex was up, the two Jenney buildings were well established, and Mandel Brothers' large store had begun to penetrate State Street from its location on Wabash and Madison, while Schlesinger and Mayer, the Boston Store, and Rothschild's in a new location at Van Buren and State were growing apace. All the actors had now arrived. The successful merchant, wrote the *Economist,* "must build for to-morrow rather than to-day."[22] Rental figures assumed incredible levels. C. D. Peacock, the jeweler, renting the corner of Madison and State from Marshall Field, was paying $40,000 a year for seven years, and $50,000 for each of the ninety-two years remaining on its ninety-nine year lease. "These figures would be startling," the *Economist* observed, "if one had not become accustomed to big talk in regard to property on the leading retail street in Chicago." Because of concentration Chicago valuations of central property led those abroad. In London or Paris there were "several localities of approximately equal importance."[23] Chicago had only one Loop. This placed a premium on size and compression, and the new stores and their additions were now rarely less than twelve stories in height, sometimes more, supported by two or three basement levels.

The early twentieth century brought completion to the State Street center, with the most celebrated of all of Chicago's big store buildings. Its height, bulk (with additions), and cellular window openings fit prevailing patterns, but its rounded corner entrance, sweeping lines, and extraordinary decorative details made it unique in Europe and America. This was Louis Sullivan's Schlesinger and Mayer store (see Klotz, fig. 25; in 1904, Carson Pirie Scott and Company), which opened its first new section in October 1903. Full-page newspaper advertisements reproduced both the building and its decorative schemes, the management pronouncing it "a perfect product of architecture," whose "vast interior spaces" were "flooded with daylight."[24] Like the other downtown stores,

Fig. 13 Marshall Field and Co. Store, atrium and dome.

Fig. 14 Marshall Field and Co. Store, interior.

Schlesinger and Mayer featured reading and writing rooms, rest rooms, a medical treatment room, art galleries, and elaborate restaurants. Its eating places, with tessellated floors and ceilings studded with jewels, presented a general ensemble of "refined simplicity."[25] It was probably the extraordinary iron grillwork, products of the imagination of Sullivan and architect George Elmslie and executed by Winslow Brothers, that had the most impact, enhancing display windows fronting on the "world's most crowded corner" (fig. 10; pl. 39). But beyond the sumptuous fixtures of rest and recreational areas, the interior had little to rival Sullivan's exuberant exterior, in addition, that is, to the large, open, well-lit floors that were now a normal element.

It was Marshall Field's rather than Schlesinger and Mayer that attempted to provide interior drama. Reversing the procedure of its neighbor it masked its theatrical spaces with a sober, somewhat monotonous facade (fig. 11). Turning again to Burnham, Marshall Field began in 1902 a five-year march along State Street from north to south, on a journey around its square block that would take more than a decade to complete. A huge white granite building, "severe in outline . . . of the most chaste simplicity," loomed up over the street, twelve stories in height. Its main entrance boasted four granite pillars, the tallest cut-stone monoliths "west of Karnak."[26] By the time of the extensive and formal opening in 1907, Marshall Field's contained 1,339,000 square feet, insisting that it had now become the largest store in the world. During an opening week, some two million people passed through the building, served by 7,000 employees. Everything about the structure was now colossal, and tied to advertising rhetoric: the 27,000 automatic fire sprinklers, the 35,000 electric lights, the 50 elevators and 12 entrances. Working with Ernest Graham of the Burnham firm, and Field executives like John G. Shedd, a committee prepared details with the care appropriate to a military campaign.[27] Newspaper ads were commissioned from distinguished illustrators like Alphonse Mucha, Edward Penfield, and Harrison Fisher. Thirty-five of the drawings were run by Chicago newspapers within the week, several featuring the Burnham building, enhanced by allegorical and typographical frames.[28]

Marshall Field's was the largest decorated warehouse Chicago had yet received. Burnham set a pattern his firm would repeat elsewhere. The store contained several great spaces, vertical and horizontal. In the southern portion a four-story atrium covered by a Tiffany mosaic dome ran above the first floor (fig. 13); another court, set within some upper floors, enhanced an elegant restaurant. Running parallel with State Street was a well-proportioned, white-columned main aisle some 385 feet long, constituting something of an indoor arcade, a special adaptation of a European form. Thousands "will naturally assume the privileged pleasures of wandering through this great aisle on their way up or down town in preference to walking along State

Street," predicted Field's promoters.[29] Field's main aisle, agreed Chicago's *Inter Ocean*, was "one of the show places of Chicago."[30] On either side stood carefully crafted plate glass and mahogany show cases, brilliantly lit by miniature incandescents, invisible because of their placement in shallow troughs. Corners were rounded to add space and avoid damaging merchandise (fig. 14). Dividing walls bore mirrors to create an even greater impression of cleanliness. Everything down to the Tiffany globes in the elevator cabs had been painstakingly worked out — better lighted cabs than any others in the city, Field's boasted.[31]

Wave after wave of publicity featured the new emporium in brochures, books, souvenirs, postcards, and advertisements. A visit to Field's retail store now replaced a visit to the warehouse as a must-see. This imposing, dignified, enormous envelope shielded a formidable selling machine, whose purpose was to multiply desire. Burnham began planning the new store while Harry Gordon Selfridge was Field's partner, and Selfridge found retailing more compelling an arena than wholesaling. It was Selfridge who insisted that Field's windows become the best decorated in the country, who tied the store to civic events like the World's Columbian Exposition, who initiated campaigns like counting the number of days until Christmas, and who organized the spectacular sets of openings.[32]

And it was Selfridge who took Burnham's decorated warehouse to Oxford Street in London (fig. 15), recreating — as much as fire regulations, complex building codes, and ancient leasing restrictions permitted — the great open spaces of the Chicago store.[33] Although Selfridge claimed to take his inspiration from the quickly dashed off drawing of an obscure architectural draftsman, he relied on Burnham's Chicago firm for some of his advice. He knew that he wanted "a noble building

on Greek lines, so designed that it could subsequently be harmoniously extended to cover much more ground than the original site."[34] The cellular frames Burnham favored could be almost indefinitely expanded. Chicago stores added section after section without interrupting the inexorable progress of their facades. Selfridge followed suit, copying Field's use of artistic newspaper advertisements for the formal opening. Coronations, royal visits, aviation meets — Selfridge tied his emporium to these London events just as Field's had linked itself to Chicago events. Selfridge's drew people inside without insisting on any *quid pro quo*. Chicago's stores were "free stores," and Selfridge took aim at the stodgy pomposity of older British establishments which, he believed, limited the ease and freedom of shoppers as it reduced the profits of shop owners.[35]

Burnham stores penetrated America as well as Britain. The firm built McCreery's in Pittsburgh, Alms and Doepke in Cincinnati, San Francisco's Joseph Fredericks and Co., Gimbel's and Wanamaker's in New York, and most impressive of all, the huge Wanamaker Store in Philadelphia, larger even than Field's.[36] This, said Burnham, was "the most monumental commercial structure ever erected anywhere in the world."[37] It was dedicated in December 1911, in the presence of the President of the United States, William Howard Taft. Like Field's it featured a great open court, this one dominated by a huge organ (fig. 16). Eastern eyebrows were raised by the choice of a Chicago architect for the job. But his logic soon prevailed.[38]

Burnham also invited inquiries from Canada. The "sort of building mentioned by you is strictly in our line," he wrote the Hudson's Bay Company in Winnipeg.[39] And the Burnham firm prepared a design for Eaton's of Toronto, featuring an immense rotunda and several versions of an impressive atrium (fig. 17; pl. 55; cat. nos. 223, 224).[40] Only the most majestic of Burnham stores sported this feature. But this Eaton's was never built.

Fig. 17 D. H. Burnham and Co., Perspective study of the interior atrium of the proposed Eaton's Department Store, Toronto, c. 1912 (cat. no. 224).

Fig. 18 Holabird and Roche, Mandel Brothers Store, northeast corner of State and Madison streets, 1912 (altered).

Fig. 19 State Street, view looking south from Washington Street; left to right: *W. W. Boyington, Columbus Memorial Building, 31 North State Street, 1893 (demolished); D. H. Burnham and Co., Stevens Store, 17 North State Street, 1912 (altered); Mandel Brothers Store; D. H. Burnham and Co., Reliance Building, 32 North State Street, 1895.*

While Burnham and his successor firm Graham, Anderson, Probst and White spread the Chicago-style store throughout the country, a local competitor dominated some other State Street projects.[41] Holabird and Roche now received commissions from three State Street stores, all with late nineteenth-century origins and all benefiting from the Loop's strategic location. All three projects were under way by 1911. The dream of Leon, Emmanuel, and Simon Mandel for "a castle in the air" became a reality in 1912, although none of the three brothers survived to see it.[42] Having already designed for Mandel Brothers an annex of unusual power and simplicity, featuring wide bays and huge glass windows — this covering portions of Wabash Avenue and Madison Street — Holabird and Roche produced a fifteen-story structure standing 307 feet

above ground (fig. 18). With huge granite pilasters at its base and an arcade of Corinthian columns at its top, it replaced a smaller, older building and helped make Mandel Brothers one of the three largest stores in the city. Some 6,500 square feet of plate glass were featured on a display frontage of almost 400 linear feet, a crucial statistic for Chicago stores.

A second undertaking for the Rothschild Store also opened in 1912. This was unusual, for it represented a single new structure, built all at once, into which the entire store moved. In a gleaming white coating of enameled terracotta, ten stories high with thirty-eight elevators and seven miles of aisles, the new store was distinguished by delicate detailing, including a projecting cornice, and arcaded lower floors allowed it a lighter appearance than some of its neighbors, although the *Chicago Record-Herald* stressed its massive character.[43] News reports also emphasized the unusual care taken to make it fireproof, its specially created ventilation system, and the solidity of its construction.

Simpler in appearance than the Rothschild Store, but no less distinctive, was a third Holabird and Roche project, a series of buildings for the Boston Store. Commenting on a section completed before 1912, Franz Winkler termed it "the architectural embodiment of the 'Chicago Idea' in commercial architecture." "Would anybody venture upon such extreme plainness in a like erection in New York or Boston?" he asked in the *Architectural Record*.[44] Only the essentials were provided and the building, like the other great stores, was flooded with light. Five years later Holabird and Roche contributed another of their flat, cellular commercial structures to the Boston Store, this the second tallest department store building in the city. The completed Netcher Building (named after the owner of the Boston Store) featured seventeen stories above ground and three basements, comprising among other things small workrooms for making candy, cigars, and ice cream, a full-sized tennis court on the roof, and a branch of the Chicago Public Library, appropriate to what had suddenly emerged as Chicago's second largest store. Its height was emphasized by converting the top of a tank house into a free observatory platform, 325 feet above the ground. Unlike the earlier sections this construction phase dignified itself with some serious decoration, featuring a colossal multistory colonnade running across its upper stories.[45]

In this the Netcher Building resembled a neighbor, the last of the Marshall Field complex, a non-connected building facing the central store across Washington Street, twenty stories in height and

housing a men's store on its lower six floors and
offices elsewhere. The blending of Chicago's commercial style with store architecture was here
epitomized. Except for its great display windows it
was indistinguishable from many other Loop
office towers, although its interior appointments in marble and fine woods carried out the theme of luxury
that the Burnham firm favored for mercantile
clients.[46]

By 1917 the shopping center that constituted
Chicago's Loop was complete, and the "Seven Sis-
ters" were ready for the world. Except for resurfac-
ing, interior remodelings, and some extensions,
there would be few changes during the next sixty
years.[47] It had taken only a quarter of a century,
from the sudden unveiling of the Jenney buildings
to the completion of the Boston Store, for State
Street to be draped in its stole of department
stores.

The height of these buildings testified to the
impressive land values. By 1920, in fact, the Loop
had a series of office towers that were little more
than vertical shopping centers, buildings like the
nineteen-story Stevens (fig. 19), built in 1912 by
D. H. Burnham and Co., and extended in the
1920s. "Think of It! Twelve Floors of Shops," ran
one advertisement in the 1920s, "There is no noise,
no scuffle, no stop-and-go signal, or dodging of
motor cars . . . always pleasant weather no matter
what the weather is outside."[48] Nearly 100 apparel
and accessory shops rented quarters in the building. The Stevens was not alone, nor was it the first
of its type. A 1920 visitor to Chicago found this

"light shop-keeping" fascinating, and recounted
the story of a local pharmacist who, forty years
before, had been "the first druggist to open a store
on the second floor of a business building not only
in Chicago but in the United States." Even large
banks had second-floor offices. This "mass of shopping," as Robert Shackleton put it, helped maintain "the compactness of the business section."[49]

Compactness, concentration, thematic contigui-
ty, all were features of Chicago shopping. Traders
and professionals sought their colleagues. Physi-
cians, dentists, attorneys, and accountants flocked
to particular buildings. Within the buildings themselves jewelers, silversmiths, parfumiers, and
watchmakers sought their own floors.[50] Wabash
Avenue featured "Piano Row," a string of instrument dealers whose showrooms abutted teaching

studios and recital halls, making the stretch something of a music center itself. Further south was Furniture Row, where manufacturers and jobbers could spread their wares out somewhat more economically. And within a couple of miles of the Loop, invading what had earlier been the city's best residential area, a series of car dealers had created an Automobile Row. The first auto showroom arrived on South Michigan Avenue by 1908. Three years later there were twenty-six of them between 22nd and 25th street, stimulating a tenfold increase in land values. By 1917 the four-block stretch contained fifty-five establishments devoted to the sales, servicing, and repair of automobiles. Distinguished local architects, including several who had worked on the great Loop stores, were brought in, among them Holabird and Roche; Jenney, Mundie and Jensen; Jarvis Hunt; and Howard Van Doren Shaw (fig. 20).[51]

Like the department stores, the auto showrooms synthesized utilitarian functionalism with gestures toward retailing refinement. If anything, the auto dealers preferred something more genteel. Touches of modeled ornament highlighted the large showroom windows; multicolored brickwork, enameled terracotta, cornices, and occasional balustrades suggested the dignity and financial scale of

the automobile purchases and hinted at the romance of motoring (fig. 21).

But the Near South Side showrooms fronting a smoothly paved boulevard hinted at something else, a future in which the massive downtown structures would less effectively dominate the area's retailing. The very compression that fed department store growth underscored the problem. Chicago flappers might be proud that they shopped "within the district that has been the center from the days when pioneer merchants built" the first stores; citizens at large might be pleased that unlike New York "where Chicago began she has continued...."[52] But complaints about extreme crowding were generations old. Trying to promote a southward business move, the *Economist* in 1910 condemned the "hellish conditions" of the Loop. "During the busy hours the downtown streets are worse than Dante's celebrated pipe-dream."[53]

As automobile ownership spread, the streets became still more clogged and the search for parking spaces became an urban quest with overtones of desperation; the whole Loop had only several hundred curbside spots.[54] Nevertheless, downtown stores continued to be built in Chicago in the 1920s, some of them, like Holabird and Root's Baskin Building (fig. 23), influenced by the elegant Art Deco facades promoted by Parisian architectural folios.[55] Dramatic lettering, black marble, polychromatic cast iron, all were now available. But the changes came generally in the form of smaller shops. Not in two decades had State Street hailed any "new major store merchandising inception," the *Economist* mourned in the 1920s. There "must be expansion – a Greater Loop," and expansion came.[56] But it was not the continuous southern march that Loop promoters hoped for. Instead, the decade saw a threefold erosion of Chicago's old downtown: to smart boutiques, specialty shops, and Paris-influenced stores on North Michigan Avenue, newly fashionable with construction of a double-deck bridge across the Chicago River (designed by Edward H. Bennett and built in 1920) and the opening of hotels and office buildings; to suburbs like Evanston and Oak Park, following the surge of population; and to neighborhood shopping centers already scattered throughout the North, West, and South sides. In all of these were European influences, perhaps more than in the tall, block-like department stores that represented Chicago's architectural heritage to the outside world.

The European strain found expression at its most cosmopolitan level on North Michigan Avenue. There were many versions. A remodeled Malabry Court connected nine large shops and a new resi-

Fig. 22 Graham, Anderson, Probst, and White, Marshall Field and Co. Store, 1700 Sherman Avenue, Evanston, Illinois, 1929; from The Architectural Work of Graham, Anderson, Probst and White *(London, 1933).*

dential unit with an open, slate-paved courtyard, tiled on three sides. Dormer windows, lanterns, whitewashed walls, and window boxes projected a French country atmosphere.[57] The Michigan Square Building, on the other hand, epitomized Continental sleekness; its arcade of dozens of shops was labeled a "miniature Rue de la Paix" by the *Chicagoan*.[58] Glass columns of futuristic design, a huge rotunda (fig. 24), and a dining area resembling "an outdoor European cafe" attracted a chic clientele. This was a merchandising style more directly imported, less vernacular than the Loop emporia of the pre-World War I years.

The borrowings were also evident in places like Lake Forest, Evanston, Oak Park, and Wilmette. Here, upper middle-class customers were served either with rustic Old World touches, as in Howard Van Doren Shaw's Lake Forest Market Square (see Wilson, figs. 21, 23),[59] or with dressy, fashionable, urbane stores like the Marshall Field outlets opened in 1929 in Evanston (fig. 22) and Oak Park.

Both designed by Graham, Anderson, Probst and White, they were almost identical with their dormer windows, elegant entries, and the traditional Field's clock – clearly designed for an upscale crowd.[60] They stood in direct contrast to the massive commercial blocks that continued to serve downtown shoppers.

But the third arena for mercantile dispersal was perhaps the most interesting synthesis of American need and European practice, and far older than the other two. This was found in the neighborhood centers spawned by the city's rapid transit system. Despite its spectacular lakefront wall, Chicago, by the 1920s, had become a city of cottages and apartments, clusters of small, walk-up three-flats, six-flats, and twelve-flats, that stretched for miles. Specialists like Henry A. Newhouse, Charles F. Sorenson, David Saul Klafter, B. Leo Steif and Ottenheim, Stern and Reichert had been erecting these types of residential buildings for decades. Costing only ten or fifteen thousand dollars, the

Fig. 23 Holabird and Root, Baskin Store, 133 South State Street, 1928 (altered).

Fig. 24 Holabird and Root, Michigan Square Building, 540 North Michigan Avenue, 1930 (demolished); interior of Diana Court.

*Fig. 25 Sailor and Hoff-
man, Building for Frank
Weber, southwest corner
of South Racine Avenue
and 82nd Street, 1927.*

flat buildings often incorporated stores into their ground floors.[61] Serving both as residences and investments for upwardly mobile members of Chicago's growing ethnic communities, these stores provided daily shoppers with basic needs: tailoring and shoe repair, candy and groceries, hair-cutting and stationery (fig. 25; cat. no. 153). Even in 1904 Chicago contained almost 7,000 retail stores. Twenty years later there were almost 45,000, 13,000 of them groceries, 7,600 candy and soft drink stores, 1,700 bakeries, and almost 3,000 clothing outlets.[62]

But not all local shopping was confined to these modest shops on the ground floors of flat buildings. By the 1920s Chicago contained something approaching two dozen shopping centers.[63] Where streets like Madison and Crawford, Halsted and 79th, Ashland and 47th, Lincoln, Belmont, and Ashland came together, clothing and furniture stores, restaurants, motion picture theaters, five-and-ten-cent stores, professional office buildings, and department stores clustered together, or ran down the principal avenues in ribbons. City visitors like Robert Shackleton found them offering lively scenes of promenading, eating, and entertainment.[64] Here store buildings with more pretensions than the narrow ground-floor shops of the side

streets flaunted elegant touches. Proud owners or developers put up combination shop and office structures faced with terracotta and laced with ornaments – swags, cartouches, urns, medallions, tiled lettering, cornices, mosaics – to enhance their dignity. These district facades were often fussier than the downtown stores, more directly if naively inspired by classical and baroque ornament, but they bore a standardized air. The architects chose the ornamental elements from manufacturers' catalogues, and the big district stores tended to resemble one another more clearly than they reflected any special Chicago or neighborhood character. Chicago's Midland Terra Cotta Company kept a rich assortment of molds, entrances, entablatures, and ornamental motifs (cat. no. 154).[65] The three-story buildings put up in 1927 by the architectural firm Rissman and Hirschfeld at Milwaukee and Kimball were typical of this ambitious neighborhood building type: ornamental iron lamps atop the structure, ten eighteen-foot display windows, walnut trim, elegant terracotta ornaments – these brought an Old World touch to local shoppers.[66]

But the big neighborhood stores may well have reflected European memories more than European architecture. The neighborhoods, filled with

recent immigrants and their children, were communities where bargaining might remain an element in the shopping ritual, where merchandising techniques were louder and less subtle than those downtown, built more around personal contacts than brands and luxurious appointments. Yiddish, Italian, Polish, and Hungarian could be the tongues of purchase. These were the people who shopped in stores like L. Klein's, "the West Side's Greatest Store." Located on Halsted and 14th Street, Klein's began in 1869 as a tiny ground-floor storefront that was transformed in the course of forty years into a four-story, 160,000-square-foot complex, decently but plainly finished in its exterior but hardly a building of architectural distinction.[67]

Paradoxically enough, Chicago may have reflected less European influence in its concentrated center than in its auxiliary areas. The warehousing model, so powerful by the late nineteenth century, reinforced by the office towers, and carried even further by mail order houses like Sears, Montgomery Ward (cat. no. 87), and Spiegel's, constituted the city's special contribution.[68] Through architects like Burnham; Holabird and Roche; Graham, Anderson, Probst and White; and Nimmons, Carr and Wright (designers of Sears retail centers; fig. 26),

Chicago exported her shopping landscape to the rest of the country. The extravaganzas of light and space created by Sédille, Jourdain, Binet, Messel, and others in Paris, Berlin, and Leipzig influenced Chicago designers as ideals.[69] But European eclecticism was probably more apparent in boutiques and special shops, auto showrooms and neighborhood centers. The details rather than the conception was foreign. Even the light courts of stores like Field's and Wanamaker's owed as much to the atria of older American office buildings as to European stores.[70]

In the period after World War II American architects would again develop a special shopping form. Regional shopping centers, in huge enclosed malls, spread from the Middle West to other metropolitan areas and then back across the Atlantic.[71] They, alas, testified not to urban vigor but to downtown deterioration. Profiting, however, from the suburban translation of this older urban type, cities like Chicago have begun a rescue campaign, constructing their own new vertical shopping centers and restoring some of their old ones. In retail commerce downtowns have found new sources of theater and ritual as well as economic support. The rejuvenation of Chicago's Loop would mark a major moment in this process of rediscovery.

Fig. 26 Nimmons, Carr and Wright, Sears, Roebuck and Co., Retail Store, 1900 Lawrence Avenue, 1925.

NOTES

1 There is no adequate, comprehensive history of American retailing. There are, however, biographies of major mercantile figures. Excellent references, as well as an interesting argument, can be found in William R. Leach, "Transformations in a Culture of Consumption: Women and Department Stores, 1890-1925," *Journal of American History* 71 (Sept. 1984), pp. 317-42.
2 Kenneth T. Jackson, *Crabgrass Frontier: The Suburbanization of the United States* (New York, 1985), treats the subject of municipal annexation, pp. 138-56. See particularly the tables, pp. 140-41. Chicago retained her third-place rank until 1950, but by 1980 had fallen to twentieth, behind cities like Jacksonville, Indianapolis, Anchorage, Memphis, and El Paso. The great wave of annexations that took place after 1950 shifted relationships between area size and population that for so long had been relatively stable among the leading cities. There were other cities which, like Chicago, grew consistently both in population and area for much of the late nineteenth and early twentieth centuries, but they never reached Chicago's level.
3 Charles Henry White, "Chicago," *Harper's Monthly* 118 (Apr. 1909), p. 730. White referred to "loop victims," a category of people who didn't want to go into the Loop but ended up there anyway, or who got lost once they arrived.
4 For a representative description of the building, see Monsignor Count Vay de Vaya, *The Inner Life of the United States* (London, 1908), pp. 172-73.
5 The area was evoked by G. W. Steevens, *The Land of the Dollar* (New York, 1897), p. 147, who referred to the "almost prehistoric effect" of the buildings, their "massive simplicity, something like the great cyclopean ruins of Mycenae or Tiryns."
6 Stores like these are described in E. E. Barton, *A Business Tour of Chicago, Depicting Fifty Years' Progress* (Chicago, 1887).
7 The shift in shopping centers is documented in several places, among them Homer Hoyt, *One Hundred Years of Land Values in Chicago, 1830-1933* (Chicago, 1933), pp. 88-90, 103-04; J. R. Hamilton, "State Street," in Chicago Association of Commerce and Industry, *Survey* (Chicago, 1925); and Harold M. Mayer and Richard C. Wade, *Chicago: Growth of a Metropolis* (Chicago, 1969), pp. 54-56.
8 Field's publicity literature featured prints and photographs of the various stores; they were also immortalized by innumerable postcards. A particularly concise and useful pictorial history is contained in a 1913 guidebook issued by the firm, *Marshall Field and Company,* a copy of which can be found in the Field Archives.
9 "The State Street Stores," *Economist* 15 (June 13, 1896), pp. 728-29, presents some comparative statistics on the size and growth of the city's major stores.
10 Charles Dudley Warner, "Chicago," *Harper's Monthly* 76 (May 1888), pp. 873-74. This was the third in a series Warner was doing for *Harper's* entitled "Studies of the Great West."
11 John J. Flinn, *The Standard Guide to Chicago,* World's Fair Edition (Chicago, 1893), p. 50.
12 These stores are described briefly by Carl W. Condit, *The Chicago School of Architecture: A History of Commercial and Public Building in the Chicago Area, 1875-1925* (Chicago, 1964), pp. 89-91. For contemporary comments on the expansion of The Fair, comparing it to the Bon Marché (which it exceeded in size), see "Great Mercantile Building," *Economist* 15 (Oct. 24, 1896), pp. 428-29.
13 Condit (note 12), p. 89.
14 *Industrial Chicago* (Chicago, 1891), vol. 1, p. 205, as quoted by Condit (note 12), p. 90.
15 Mme. Léon Grandin, *Impressions d'Une Parisienne à Chicago* (Paris, n. d.), pp. 209-12. The trip was made during the 1892-93 year, and the book was published shortly thereafter. For a careful and comprehensive picture of one major Paris department store, see Michael B. Miller, *The Bon Marché: Bourgeois Culture and the Department Store, 1896-1920* (Princeton, 1981).
16 The phrases are Condit's (note 12), p. 91. For more on The Fair and its building, see Timothy Barton, "A Fair to Remember," *Inland Architect* 30 (May/June 1986), pp. 62-66. See also Forest Crissey, *Since Forty Years Ago* (Chicago, 1915), for a history of the store. The Fair also penetrates American consciousness as the site of our most famous fictional excursion into shopping, Carrie Meeber's initiation into the world of high consumption in Theodore Dreiser's *Sister Carrie,* first published in 1900. For more on this and shopping culture, see Rachel Bowlby, *Just Looking: Consumer Culture in Dreiser, Gissing and Zola* (London and New York, 1985), ch. 4; Neil Harris, "The Drama of Consumer Desire," in Otto Mayr, ed., *Yankee Enterprise: The Rise of the American System of Manufactures* (Washington, D.C., 1981), pp. 181-216.
17 *Economist* 15 (Oct. 24, 1896), p. 428.
18 Ann Lorenz Van Zanten, "The Marshall Field Annex and the New Urban Order of Daniel Burnham's Chicago," *Chicago History* 11 (Fall and Winter, 1982), p. 135.
19 Robert A. M. Stern, Gregory Gilmartin, and John Massengale, *New York 1900: Metropolitan Architecture and Urbanism 1890-1915* (New York, 1983), p. 192. More precisely, it was the monumentality and the vastness of these new emporia that Stern cites as cause for their economic problems.
20 John Kendall, *American Memories: Recollections of a Hurried Run Through the United States During the Late Spring of 1986* (n. p., n. d.), p. 183.
21 William Archer, *America To-Day: Observations and Reflections* (London, 1900), p. 88. Archer concluded that better proportions were encouraged by the larger plots Chicago architects had to build upon.
22 "The State Street Stores," *Economist* 15 (June 13, 1896), p. 728.
23 *Economist* 15 (May 9, 1896), p. 574.
24 The quotation is taken from a full-page advertisement in the *Chicago Tribune* (Oct. 31, 1903), p. 5.
25 Another full-page advertisement run by Schlesinger and Mayer, *Chicago Tribune* (Oct. 7, 1903), p. 8. Among the features of the new building celebrated by the publicity were: its corner circular entrance; mahogany and marble fixtures; new combination arc and incandescent lights; the "largest and finest" display windows in the world; telephone booths; reading, writing, and rest rooms; an emergency medical aid room, and, for the opening week beginning October 12, 1903, 10,000 chrysanthemums.
26 These phrases are taken from the many promotional pamphlets published by Marshall Field and Co. Some can be found in the Field Archives, others in the Chicago Historical Society. They are frequently undated, making it difficult to refer with precision to a specific piece. Among the more glowing accounts of the building program is a thirty-one-page pamphlet, *Marshall Field and Co. Retail,* printed shortly after 1907. *The Store of Service,* a piece put out about 1920 when Field's downtown buildings were basically complete, also reviewed the history of the store. By this time, Field's covered almost two million square feet of retailing, and employed some 9,000, with another 4,500 hired during the Christmas season.
27 Only fragmentary records exist of all these conferences, but a tantalizing example in the Field Archives contains minutes for a planning meeting held in Shedd's office, November 14, 1905. The participants discussed, among other things, the cost of fixtures, the nature of the store's refrigeration system and fur vault, the role of the escalators (a controversial subject among department store planners), the size of the columns, and the location of the various departments. For a contemporary comment on the architectural planning of American department stores, and consideration of the need for visual coherence ("most shoppers are not clever, and everything must be made clearer than daylight..."), see John Lawrence Mauran, "The Department Store Plan," *Brickbuilder* 17 (Nov. 1908), pp. 252-55.
28 Reproductions of some of this art work can be found in *Inland Printer* 40 (Dec. 1907), pp. 397-99. Five years earlier, when the first portion of the new building opened, Field's had run a similarly elaborate campaign, purchasing seventy-five drawings for use in full-page advertisements. See "Some Unusual Advertising," *Inland Printer* 30 (Dec. 1902), pp. 415-17. Many artists were employed in both campaigns. Editorialists pointed to the advertisements as examples of the close and growing connection between art and commerce. See *Chicago Tribune,* "Art and Business," (Oct. 4, 1907), p. 8. The *Tribune* also praised the display methods of the downtown stores, which had apparently benefitted from the various foreign exhibitions presented almost fifteen years earlier at the World's Columbian Exposition.
29 *Marshall Field and Co. Retail* (note 26), p. 20.
30 *Centennial History of the City of Chicago: Its Men and Institutions* (Chicago, 1905), p. 182.
31 *Marshall Field and Co. Retail* (note 26), p. 26.
32 Selfridge's role in developing Field's retailing ventures is discussed in some detail by Robert W. Twyman, *History of Marshall Field and Company, 1852-1906* (Philadelphia, 1954) and Lloyd Wendt and Herman Kogan, *Give the Lady What She Wants* (Chicago, 1952).
33 Reginald Pound, *Selfridge: A Biography* (London, 1960), pp. 35-40, reviews his efforts to create the London store and recounts his encounters with British ordinances and building codes.
34 This story, and the encounter with Swales (Selfridge could not even remember his first name), was told by Selfridge in "Selling Selfridge," *Saturday Evening Post* 208 (Aug. 10, 1935), pp. 66-70. This was the second piece in a four-part series that ran every other week starting July 27 and ending September 7. Although Selfridge was vague about Swales, Francis S. Swales was active as an architect in Canada, England, and the United States, and was responsible for several articles and a number of fine renderings published during the twenties and thirties in *Pencil Points.* See the entries on Swales, and on R. Frank Atkinson, the architect responsible for much of the specific store planning in A. Stuart Gray, *Edwardian Architecture: A Biographical Dictionary* (Iowa City, 1986), pp. 93-95, 343. Gray also discusses the Selfridge building in a section entitled "Edwardian Shops and Stores in London," pp. 66-73.
35 Selfridge, "Selling Selfridge," *Saturday Evening Post* 208 (July 27, 1935), pp. 18-19, 51-53. Reputation, argued Selfridge, was more important to British shopkeepers "than turnover.... This cult of gentility was simply a reflection of the attitude of the British shopping public of those days.... They did not trouble to compare prices.... They were contemptuous of crowds and suspicious of cheapness," p. 53. All this Selfridge intended (and helped) to change. Americans took much interest in Selfridge's London adventure. For more on British shopping, see Alexandra Artley, ed., *The Golden Age of Shop Design: European Shop Interiors 1880-1939* (London, 1975); and Alison Adburgham, *Shops and Shopping 1800-1914* (London, 1964).
36 All these stores are illustrated in *The Architectural Work of Graham, Anderson, Probst and White, Chicago, and Their Predecessors D. H. Burnham and Co. and Graham, Burnham and Co.* (London, 1933), vol. 1, pl. 121-70. For comments on one of Burnham's San Francisco stores, and descriptions of contemporary department store buildings in that city, see A. G. David, "The New San Francisco," *Architectural Record* 31 (Jan. 1912), pp. 1-26. These were, on the whole, quite a bit smaller than the Chicago stores. For comments on contrasts between American department stores design, using (implicitly) the Burnham stores as models, and German department stores, see William L. Mowll, "The Architecture of the Modern German Department Store," *Brickbuilder* 23 (Sept. 1914), pp. 205-10.
37 Burnham is so quoted in Thomas S. Hines, *Burnham of Chicago: Architect and Planner* (New York, 1974), p. 303. Hines summarizes the Wanamaker projects Burnham undertook as well as the construction of Filene's in Boston, pp. 303-07. The Architectural Collection of the Chicago Historical Society contains another great Pennsylvania project by D. H. Burnham and Co., the plans for the Wood Street Building in Pittsburgh, which would become McCreery's Department Store. Sheet after sheet details the showcases, the paneling, the exact location and dimensions of stock cases, mirrors, staircases, elevators, washrooms, eighty-eight sheets of floor plans, fixture drawings, and architectural elevations. The extraordinary range of details, the scale, and the cost, suggested why retailers liked going to a large, experienced firm like Burnham's, that had a demonstrated capacity to plan these giant selling machines.
38 "The announcement that a Chicago architect has been selected to erect a great department store in Philadelphia and another in New York might cause surprise among laymen," observed the *Chicago Tribune,* "but in tall buildings Chicago has led." *Chicago Sunday Tribune* (Oct. 11, 1903), p. 18. The article went on to

compare tall buildings in New York and Chicago, to the detriment of the former.

39 Burnham to H. C. Burbridge, Chicago, Feb. 10, 1911, Burnham Letters, vol. 18, The Art Institute of Chicago.

40 Several of these sketches are in the Architecture Department of The Art Institute of Chicago.

41 Robert Bruegmann is currently preparing a history of the firm. For a preliminary assessment, see Robert Bruegmann, "Holabird & Roche and Holabird & Root: The First Two Generations," *Chicago History* 9 (Fall, 1980), pp. 130-65.

42 *Chicago Record-Herald* (Sept. 22, 1912), pt. 2, p. 5. The Mandel brothers had begun their first Chicago store in 1855, at 260 South Clark Street. The State Street store is today the home of Wieboldt's.

43 *Chicago Record-Herald* (Oct. 15, 1912), p. 16. This building would pass through various hands, eventually becoming the home of Goldblatt's. Four stories were added in 1928.

44 Franz Winkler, "Some Chicago Buildings Represented by the Work of Holabird and Roche," *Architectural Record* 31 (Apr. 1912), p. 313. In 1948, with the liquidation of the Boston Store, the building was changed to multiple commercial use and named the State-Madison Building. A brief history of the building is given by Frank A. Randall, *History of the Development of Building Construction in Chicago* (Urbana, Ill., 1949), p. 226. Indeed, Randall offers summaries of most of the buildings discussed in this essay.

45 The *Economist* 34 (July 1, 1905), p. 23, described in more detail one phase of the Netcher Building. Margaret Corwin, "Mollie Netcher Newbury: The Merchant Princess," *Chicago History* 6 (Spring 1977), pp. 34-43, presents the history of the Boston Store itself. The management of Marshall Field and Co. kept careful tabs on the building projects of their Loop rivals, compiling comparative statistics on square footage, linear footage of display windows, numbers of elevators, etc. The Field Archives contain a folder labelled "Construction: Building Statistics" that has a rundown of these features in the early 20th century.

46 This structure was erected in 1914.

47 A number of store additions were constructed in the twenties on State Street, including a large annex for Carson's and the Rothschild additions. And there were new specialty stores, and other commercial buildings. See, for example, "The Baskin Building, Chicago," *Architectural Record* 63 (Apr. 1928), pp. 403-05, for a discussion of one. But in basic form the department store district was complete by 1917, with the last elements of the Boston Store.

48 This advertisement ran in the *Chicago Tribune* (Oct. 4, 1926), p. 7. "Set in Michigan Avenue, these Twelve blocks of Admirable shops would stretch from Randolph Street to Roosevelt Road. . . ." That very same year State Street decorated itself with jewel-studded arches and an expensive new lighting system designed by a General Electric engineer, Walter D'Arcey Ryan. See *Chicago Tribune* (Oct. 10, 1926), p. 1; (Oct. 14, 1926), p. 1; (Oct. 15, 1926), p. 1. A special festival inaugurated the new lighting.

49 Robert Shackleton, *The Book of Chicago* (Philadelphia, 1920), pp. 73-74.

50 *Rand McNally's Souvenir Guide to Chicago* (Chicago, [c. 1912]), comments, p. 27 and passim, on this cluster system. "Some one has likened Chicago to a great exposition, with its large business interests grouped together as if on exhibition," p. 22.

51 For more on Chicago's Automobile Row, see Robert Pruter, "The Prairie Avenue Section of Chicago: The History and Examination of Its Decline" (M. A. thesis, Roosevelt University, 1976); and Peter B. Wight, "The Transmutation of a Residence Street," *Architectural Record* 27 (Apr. 1910), pp. 285-93. Chester H. Liebs, *Main Street to Miracle Mile: American Roadside Architecture* (Boston, 1985), pp. 75-86, outlines the history of auto showrooms and automobile rows.

52 Shackleton (note 49), pp. 15, 69.

53 *Economist* 43 (Apr. 30, 1910), p. 866.

54 Between 1908 and 1920 the number of automobiles in Chicago increased seventeen times, from 5,000 to 86,500; in the next ten years they quadrupled again. See Hoyt (note 7), pp. 205, 237. By 1926 almost 100,000 vehicles

were entering the central part of the city in a twelve-hour day.

55 "The Baskin Building, Chicago," *Architectural Record* 63 (Apr. 1928), pp. 403-05. Among the folios publicizing Parisian stores and store fronts were: Henry Delacroix and A. Lezine, *Boutiques* (Paris, n. d.); René Herbst, *Boutiques et Magasins* (Paris, n. d.); idem, *Modern French Shop-Fronts and Their Interiors* (London, 1927); and Roger Poulain, *Boutiques* (Paris, 1931). Holabird and Root also exploited traditional English Georgian design in the twenties, as in a combination set of shops, apartments, studios, and courtyards in Omaha. See "The Aquila Court Building at Omaha, Nebraska," *Through the Ages* 3 (Mar. 1926), pp. 29-33. A few years earlier a group of buildings on Michigan Avenue and Ontario Street had been remodelled by Chester A. and Raymond C. Cook into a courtyard-like center.

56 Joseph Wild, "State Street: A Greater Loop," *Economist* 70 (Sept. 1923), p. 527.

57 Anne Lee, "Malabry Court, Chicago—A Remodeled Building," *Architectural Record* 63 (Feb. 1928), pp. 97-104.

58 *Chicagoan* 7 (Aug. 3, 1929), p. 18. One major Chicago store influenced by continental chic was Saks Fifth Avenue, which opened in 1929, designed by Holabird and Root. See *Architectural Forum* 50 (June 1929), pp. 182-83, for some photographs. This "Shop and Store Reference Number" contains many examples, particularly from New York, of modernist facades and interiors, many of them influenced by European examples. Ely Jacques Kahn, "The Modern European Shop and Store," pp. 789-804, treats the subject broadly.

59 For Shaw's Lake Forest Market Square, see *Architectural Forum* 27 (Oct. 1917), pls. 65-68. Chicago was not alone in this kind of development. J. Clyde Nichols's Country Club Plaza in Kansas City was heavily influenced by traditional European architectural touches, even while it flirted with modern planning techniques. See Richard W. Longstreth, "J. C. Nichols, The Country Club Plaza and Notions of Modernity," *Harvard Architectural Review* 5 (1986), pp. 120-35. This development, in turn, heavily influenced a North Shore project, now in Wilmette, the Spanish Court, constructed in the twenties, also in modified Spanish style. It has been enlarged and reconstructed as the Plaza del Lago.

60 Photographs for these store facades, and interiors, can be found in *The Architectural Work of Graham, Anderson, Probst and White* (note 36), vol. 1, scattered among the fifty plates devoted to stores.

61 The names of these architects, and others like them, can be found in the thousands of flat projects described annually by the *Economist*. Both The Art Institute of Chicago and the Chicago Historical Society have examples of flat buildings that incorporated ground floor stores.

62 These figures are taken from L. M. Barton, *A Study of 81 Principal Markets* (Chicago, 1925), and J. R. Hamilton, "State Street," in Chicago Association of Commerce and Industry, *Survey* (Chicago, 1925). Barton was Secretary-Treasurer of The 100,000 Group of American Cities, who published his report. At this point he claimed Chicago, with a population of 2,968,000, to be the fourth largest city in the world.

63 These shopping centers are discussed comprehensively and precisely in Malcolm J. Proudfoot, "The Major Outlying Business Centers of Chicago" (Ph.D diss., University of Chicago, 1936). See also Mayer and Wade (note 7), pp. 344-46.

64 Shackleton (note 49), p. 89.

65 Store owners could also purchase more modest facades from manufacturers, who issued catalogues like *Kawneer Store Fronts: A Collection of Successful Store Front Designs* (Niles, Mich., [c. 1923]). The Midland Terra Cotta Company in Chicago issued, about 1925, a collection of stock terracotta pieces for various types of buildings, including stores. The Burnham Library of The Art Institute of Chicago has a copy. See particularly plates 16-17, 47-50. In some ways the eclectic quotations indulged in by neighborhood stores played an analagous role to the functions served by the architectural evocation of immigrant Roman Catholic churches in the city. See Edward R. Kantowicz, "To Build the Catholic City," *Chicago History* 14 (Fall 1985), pp. 14-27; and George A. Lane, *Chicago Churches and Synagogues* (Chicago, 1981).

66 Blueprints, drawings, elevations, and construction plans for the building can be found in Rissman and Hirschfeld, Job No. 271, Architecture Collection, Chicago Historical Society. B. Leo Steif, M. Spitz, A. H. Spitz, Alfred S. Alschuler, and other architects whose work is preserved by the Chicago Historical Society put up elaborate neighborhood stores at this time.

67 See the pamphlet put out by the store, *The L. Klein Reference Book: Compliments of The West Side's Greatest Store* (Chicago, [c. 1914]). A copy ist held by the Chicago Historical Society.

68 For more on Sears and retailing see James C. Worthy, *Shaping an American Institution: Robert E. Wood and Sears, Roebuck* (Urbana, Ill., 1984), pp. 81-105. For the building style that emerged as Sears expanded its regional mail order headquarters and stores, see George C. Nimmons, "The New Renaissance in Architecture, As Seen in the Design of Buildings for Mail Order Houses," *American Architecture* 134 (Aug. 5, 1928), pp. 141-48. Nimmons described buildings in Los Angeles, Minneapolis, Milwaukee, Detroit, Boston, and Memphis.

69 For comments on and descriptions of the European light courts, see Bernard Marrey, *Les Grands Magasins: Des origines à 1939* (Paris, 1979); Meredith L. Clausen, "La Samaritaine," *Revue de l'Art* 32 (1976), pp. 57-77; Mowll (note 36), pp. 205-10; and Julius Posener, *Berlin auf dem Wege zu einer neuen Architektur: Das Zeitalter Wilhelms II.* (Munich, 1979), pp. 453-81.

70 This point is made by Meredith L. Clausen, "Frank Lloyd Wright, Vertical Space, and the Chicago School's Quest for Light," *Journal of the Society of Architectural Historians* 44 (Mar. 1985), pp. 66-74.

71 For more on the evolution of the shopping center, see Liebs (note 51), ch. 1; and Neil Harris, "Spaced Out at the Shopping Center," *New Republic* (Dec. 13, 1975), pp. 23-26.

Paris of the 1880s and the Rookery

Meredith L. Clausen

Paris held a special appeal for Americans during the latter part of the nineteenth century. Students of architecture seeking professional training – first Richard Morris Hunt in 1845, then Henry Hobson Richardson in the 1860s, and Louis Sullivan in the 1870s – were drawn there specifically to study at the Ecole des Beaux-Arts, the most highly respected art academy in the world. As Napoleon III's grand plans transformed Paris, the French capital became particularly attractive to the American public which was seeking a model for its own cities.

In the years following the Civil War, Americans became preoccupied with defining their national identity. The 1876 Centennial Exhibition in Philadelphia encouraged an awareness of history, giving the public a sense of its own past and the country's uniqueness with respect to other nations. As the economy recovered after the depression of 1873, increasing numbers of Americans visited Europe, particularly France. Published sketches and accounts of such trips further stimulated public curiosity about and interest in European culture and civilization.

By the 1880s, what became known as the American Renaissance was in full swing.[1] This designation referred to a perceived affinity between the sixteenth-century Italian Renaissance, marked by a rebirth of culture founded on classical antiquity, and an analogous concern in America for a renewal of culture based on a revered past, especially European art and architecture of the seventeenth and eighteenth centuries. The underlying assumption was that the art of the past could provide inspiration for the emergence of a new art that was particularly American.

Freely appropriating images and forms from abroad, American artists, sculptors, architects, and writers modified and adapted what they drew from foreign sources to suit their own purposes. At the 1876 Centennial Exhibition many Americans, exposed to Old World culture for the first time, became aware of the differences between the European culture and their own. A sense of inferiority, especially in matters of art and taste, inspired a desire to develop a New World culture as refined as that of Europe. Well-to-do American travelers began to seek out the classical past as an important steppingstone to a better American future. A new cosmopolitan spirit emerged as they sought the best of everything – art, architecture, literature, music, and fine wines and cuisine. France especially beckoned as a source for the acquisition of the cultivation and urbanity they found lacking at home.[2]

Representative of this cosmopolitan spirit was John Wanamaker of Philadelphia, a merchant who specialized in men's clothing. Closely involved in the planning of the Centennial Exhibition, he was drawn to Paris by his interest in French style and retailing methods. When he returned to Philadelphia, he opened "a new kind of store," inspired by what he had seen abroad. Deriving much from the wide-open, well-lit spaces of newly opened stores in Paris, with their new techniques of display, Wanamaker provided a major impetus to the development of the American department store building.[3]

Chicagoans, too, felt the lure of Paris, the recognized capital of the world in taste and fashion (fig. 2).[4] With its boulevards brilliantly illuminated by newly installed electric light and thronged with pleasure-seeking crowds (fig. 3), Paris seemed a far cry from commercially bustling Chicago with its warehouses, meat-packing plants, and smokestacks. Perceiving their city as needing more of the urbanity of such established cultural centers, the more cosmopolitan-minded inhabitants of Chicago looked to the French capital for a model of civic order and artistic expression.

As Henry Van Brunt pointed out in an 1889 article in the *Atlantic Monthly,* addressing the issue as it pertained to architects, this did not mean that the more intelligent and better trained of them, particularly in Chicago, merely imitated, but rather that they appropriated for their own purposes what were recognized to be the great achievements of the past. Chicago, Van Brunt believed, was the major source of architectural reform in the West. Its

Fig. 1 Burnham and Root, Rookery, 209 South LaSalle Street, 1886-87, view of interior court.

Fig. 2 John Marin, The Opéra, Paris, etching, 1908; The Art Institute of Chicago, Gift of Mrs. Bruce Borland.

Fig. 3 Camille Pissarro, The Place du Havre, Paris, oil on canvas, 1893; The Art Institute of Chicago, Potter Palmer Collection.

situation was unique: on the one hand, it was free of the traditions and precedents imposed by an academy; on the other, it was endowed with an able body of young professionals trained in the East, their outlook broadened still further by study and travel in Europe — men who had the wisdom to recognize the artistic shortcomings of local traditions. Their merit, Van Brunt wrote, derived from something specifically Western:

[Its] independence of spirit, perhaps, its energy, enterprise, and courage, or a certain breadth of view, inspired by its boundless opportunities, [which] has happily enabled them to use this [European] inheritance without being enslaved by it. It would have been easiest for them to quote with accuracy and adapt with grace the styles of the Old World, to be scholarly, correct, academical, and thus to stand apart from the sympathies of the people, and to constitute themselves an aristocratic guild of art. They preferred to play the more arduous and nobler part; to become, unconsciously, ministers of an architectural reform so potent and fruitful, so well fitted to the natural conditions of the West, that one may already predicate from it the speedy overthrow of the temporary, experimental, transitional vernacular art of the country, and the establishment of a school which may be recognized in history as the proper exponent of this marvelous civilization.[5]

Theirs was an art that had developed beyond the stage of mere practical considerations to the point where "the whole satisfied the eye as a work of art as well as of convenience and strength."[6] But, Van Brunt suggested, because the architects of the West enjoyed greater freedom from the restraints of the European schools than those in the East, no established stylistic formulas interfered with the practical necessities of building in Chicago. A primary consideration in Chicago buildings, given their pressing need for natural light,[7] he noted, was that windows be large and frequent enough to accommodate this need (fig. 4), without regard for academic predilections for "the noble wall surfaces of Italian palaces and medieval monasteries, or . . . the buttressed or pilastered symmetries of the Old World." No attempt was made by Chicago architects to avoid the "enormous difficulty" in design imposed by the requirement of maximum interior light or broadly glazed modern shop fronts, and the use of vast single sheets of polished plate glass set in frames of iron and steel, "a condition important enough in itself to set at defiance nearly all the precepts of all the academies." It was this imperative, he noted, that if frankly accepted by the architect could create "the flower of a new art."[8] It was the ability to meet these requirements with grace rather than hostility that marked the work of the best architects of the West — including John Wellborn Root (1850-1891), principal designer of the Rookery (figs. 1, 8; pls. 10, 11).

Fig. 4 Holabird and Roche, Tacoma Building, northeast corner of LaSalle and Madison streets, 1887-89 (demolished).

Located in the heart of the city at 209 South LaSalle Street, the Rookery was conceived as a speculative office building. The commission was given to the firm of Burnham and Root in October 1885, but the lot did not become available until December. At that point, the financial backers, a company of East Coast real estate investors with Peter and Shepard Brooks of Boston as the principal stockholders, signed a ninety-nine-year lease with the city, which owned the site. Burnham was apparently in charge of the main layout of the building, which responded to the basic requirements of the client. The working out of the actual design and refinements of detail was left to Root, then principal designer for the Burnham and Root firm.

Root began designing the Rookery in the spring of 1886. The drawing up of the plans and construction of the building continued through 1887, with

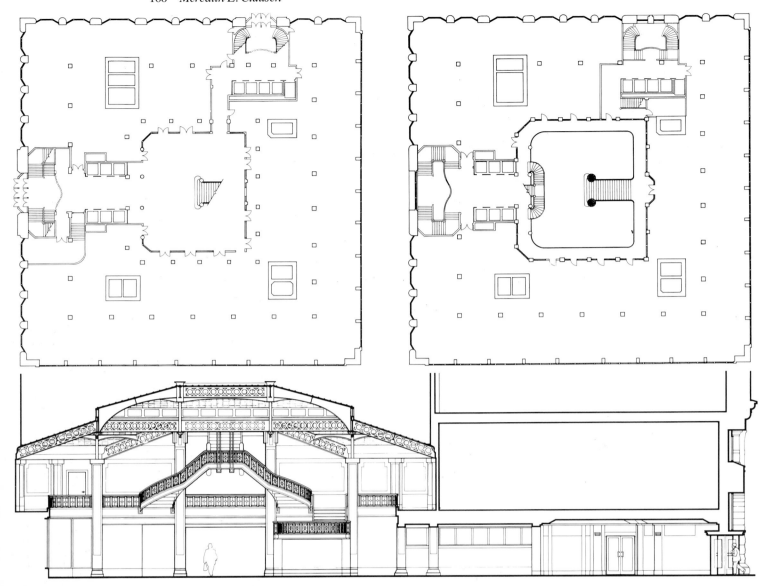

Figs. 5/6 Rookery, plans of first and second floors.

Fig. 7 Rookery, section looking west.

several revisions being made to the original scheme. The building, finished early in 1888, was thus contemporaneous with Henry Hobson Richardson's momentous Marshall Field Wholesale Store (1885-87; see Klotz, fig. 19). The dark red brick exteriors of the Rookery show the influence of Richardsonian Romanesque, embellished with Moorish/Byzantine accents. This was in keeping with the general tendency toward a new freewheeling eclecticism on the part of Americans noted by Van Brunt. The Rookery, however, went beyond the usual in synthesizing a wide range of elements from a variety of architectural styles and creating something genuinely new.

Both the Rookery's innovative rail-grillage foundation, which "floated" the building on a raft-like base, and its metal skeletal structure marked a technological advance over the more conservative and traditional load-bearing masonry of the Richardson building and William Le Baron Jen-

ney's Home Insurance Building (1884-85; pl. 14; see Larson, fig. 1), which it recalled stylistically. In the Home Insurance Building the use of metal supporting elements in the exterior walls began only above the rusticated masonry base, while in the Rookery these elements extended clear to the ground level, allowing Root to open the street level fully for display windows. Instead of using a heavy solid masonry base as did Jenney, Root poised the Rookery on a colonnade, anticipating the point-supports or stilted base of buildings of the later modernist era. This allowed interstices between supporting elements to be filled entirely with glass. Only the thickened corner piers and monumental rough-hewn masonry entrance anchor the building, proclaiming the Chicago School predilection for a substantial base.

Despite these technological advances, what contemporaries of the Rookery found remarkable was both its sheer size — it was considered the largest

8 Burnham and Root, Rookery.

office building in Chicago and perhaps in the nation — and its innovative, highly successful plan.[9] Above all it was the magnificent and elegant glazed interior court surrounded by spacious, well-lit offices on the building's periphery that brought Root and his firm its wide acclaim.

Traditional commercial buildings in Chicago followed a particular format: rooms were typically aligned along two sides of a long, enclosed central corridor, with a stairwell at one end. Depending on the site, the corridor either ran parallel to the street or at right angles to it. But the results were inevitably the same, as Charles Blackall pointed out in an 1887 article: inaccessible stairs, dark corridors, and poorly lit rooms. Because of Chicago's peculiar street system, which divided blocks into quadrants with narrow intersecting alleys, buildings lacked the light wells commonly used in other cities.[10] Since the alleys segregating the tall, densely packed buildings were narrow, buildings tended to be extraordinarily dark, especially on the lower stories. Providing a maximum amount of light and air — particularly important given that the development of a safe, comfortable artificial lighting system was still, in the early 1880s, in its infancy — was highly desirable.

The solution Root developed for the Rookery was ingenious. A huge, all-but-square structure of 168 by 178 feet, ten stories high with a basement below, the building occupied the site on the southeast corner of LaSalle and Adams streets, extending from the two streets to the intersection alleys in the rear. The main entrance, located in the center of the LaSalle Street facade, is defined by a monumental arch forming the base of a wide projecting bay. This opens onto a broad vestibule, with stairs on either side leading up to a mezzanine where they meet in the center of the building. Narrowing into a corridor flanked by three sets of elevators, the main level entrance hall continues under the centralized stair on the mezzanine above, emerging suddenly into a spacious, well-lit interior court (figs. 5, 6). Defined on all sides by a skeletal structure of metal devoid of confining walls and glazed overhead at the level of the second floor, the expansive sixty-two by seventy-one-foot interior court is flooded with light (fig. 7). Above the glass/iron roof at the second level of the court, the inner walls of the building, in contrast to the massive red brick masonry exterior facades, are thinned,

Fig. 9 Rookery, detail of bay with granite columns.

Fig. 10 Rookery, LaSalle Street entrance; revolving doors, side panels, and window frames and trim added c. 1930.

Fig. 11 Rookery, interior of light court.

sheathed only in a glazed white enameled terracotta that reflects light still further into individual office cells and onto the floor of the court below (fig. 11). On the floor of the court, a monumental staircase swells out on axis with the entrance, providing access to the mezzanine level above and adding to the drama of the enclosed space.

The street facades were more or less conventional: basically Richardsonian Romanesque in their heavy masonry, grouping of windows, dark red brick with terracotta trim, rusticated base, and monumental arched entrance (fig. 10). Bays on the ground floor, however, were defined by a sturdy colonnade formed by a series of polished granite columns on either side of the entrance; load-bearing as they were, these permitted the opening up of the walls for shop windows, substantially lightening the building in effect as well as matter (fig. 9). Above each display window, a tripartite projecting bay of plate glass held in place only by slender metal mullions, multiple tiers of windows rose in vertical bays, subsumed in the Richardsonian manner by arches at two levels. The building was capped by an attic story formed of paired rectangular windows set on a projecting cornice and surmounted by an ornamented terracotta parapet. The exotic brick and terracotta ornamentation was

NEUBAUTEN IN NORDAMERIKA.

Architekten: Burnham und Root, Chicago.

CHICAGO, Illinois.
Haupttreppe im Rookery-Kaufhause.

Erbaut 1885.

Fig. 12 Rookery, detail of rooks at LaSalle Street entrance.

Fig. 13 Rookery, interior court; from Paul Graef, Neubauten in Nordamerika *(Berlin, 1897-1905).*

Fig. 14 Rookery, interior showing stairway; as part of a remodeling of the court between 1905 and 1907, Frank Lloyd Wright encased cast-iron columns in marble, removed the electroliers, and added octagonal pedestals and lighting fixtures.

Fig. 15 Alexandre La-planche and Louis-Auguste Boileau, Bon Marché, rue de Sèvres, Paris, 1869-76 (altered); from Bernard Marrey, Les Grands Magasins (Paris, 1979).

far-reaching in its sources, including elements drawn from Moorish, Islamic, and Venetian buildings, as well as the Romanesque architecture of southern France.

In his detailing and in the use of the stately colonnade on the ground floor, Root went well beyond the practical requirements of the ordinary office building. The sumptuous polished granite columns, the delicate, finely carved detailing on stringcourses and cornices, spandrels, corner piers, entrances, and store windows, and even the rooks carved around the entrance added grace, artistry, even humor to the design, marking a departure from the pragmatism of the typical Chicago School commercial building. Root's incorporation of the rooks, from which the building took its name, alluded to the colony of pigeons that inhabited the old city hall, former occupant of the site, a light-hearted touch characteristic of the architect (fig. 12).

Root's work on the Rookery was consistent with his theory of architecture. In a symposium address to the Illinois State Association of Architects in 1887, Root discussed current tendencies of architectural design in America. Root began by referring to the French philosopher Hippolyte Taine's views on the difficulty of distinguishing lasting characteristics from the merely ephemeral in the art of a particular country. Commenting on the kaleidoscopic panorama of styles characteristic of American architecture, Root asked what qualities were truly indigenous. First, he noted, American architecture would probably continue to be catholic, borrowing freely "any new thing" because

it seemed better than the old. Rather than a conservative retention of traditional, merely imitative ways, however, he foresaw a constant striving in a wide range of new directions and ideas which would preclude the development of a single national style.[11] Whatever style was used (and here Root was referring to a particular historical style rather than style as the expression of an era), would "be taken and Americanized—that is, acclimatized and modified by local conditions." Second, it would be earnest, revealing the underlying seriousness of the American character. Softening this gravity was a humorous side, a lightness revealed in "grace of detail, or in delicacy of parts, or in occasional touches of fancy or even *whimsicalness*" [his italics]. And third, he predicted that American architecture would remain practical. This would not exclude structures of "purely decorative character," but rather each decorative detail would play some important, immediately recognizable functional role.

Given this basic pragmatism, Root feared it would be a long time before the nation would consider "with equanimity" spending large sums for buildings whose purpose was solely aesthetic. But in view of the accumulations of wealth and a national liking for display, a time would come when buildings both private and public would be erected "whose splendor will be phenomenal in the history of the world." Signs of this were already evident, he maintained, not only in the magnificent residences for the very rich but also in the "gorgeous trade-palaces" which were already dotting the country.[12]

Root's pragmatism in the plan and facade of the

Rookery was clear, as were his catholic taste, grace, and sense of humor. Splendor he saved for the interior. Although the light well in itself was not new to American architecture, or even to the firm of Burnham and Root, Root's use of it in the Rookery was striking.[13] The interior, with its grand, monumental stair and decorated ironwork, was extraordinarily refined for the time. Its elegant foliated electroliers and delicate skeletal balustrades, the lacy arabesques on the perforated risers of the stair, even the ornamented girders supporting the glazing overhead, created a light and graceful ensemble that enchanted visitors (figs. 13, 14).

In his obituary for Root, who died in 1891, Van Brunt commented on the "adventurous detail ... used with an amount of intrepidity that commands respect." He continues:

One may admire the audacity of the double iron staircase which supported by ingenious cantilevers, ramps with double curvature out into open space, meeting at a landing in the sky, as it were, from which the straight second run rises soberly backward to the stories above. One may admire this and wonder whether such an obvious *tour de force* is worth the study which must have been bestowed upon it. Even the imaginative prison visions in the famous etchings of Piranesi, with their aerial ladders and impossible galleries, present nothing more audacious.... The Rookery is not only a noted example of great fertility of design, but there is nothing bolder, more original or more inspiring in modern civic architecture either here or elsewhere than its glass-covered court.[14]

Nowhere except, perhaps, in Paris.

In the 1850s and 1860s, Napoleon III and his adroit collaborator Baron Georges-Eugène Haussmann had transformed Paris into the world capital of luxury and fashion. With its straightened and widened arteries that opened up the city and allowed it to move and breathe; tree-lined promenades, squares, and parks; and improved sanitation facilities, with new water and sewer systems, Paris became the most widely emulated model of modernity anywhere.

The city's international expositions, which drew tourists from around the world, furthered its reputation not only as a model of civic design but also as

Fig. 16 Bon Marché, interior staircase; from Marrey, Les Grands Magasins.

Fig. 17 Bon Marché, detail of exterior; from Marrey, Les Grands Magasins.

the fountainhead of style, fashion, and culture — indeed, as the epitome of refinement and artistic taste. The first international exposition to be held in Paris, in 1855, had introduced the public to the art of display, exposing it to now mass-produced luxury items and fostering in it the desire to buy.[15] Initiating among the bourgeoisie a revolution in attitudes toward consumption, the exposition did much to confirm the notion that Paris had indeed become what Haussmann called "the huge consumer market, the immense workshop."[16] By the 1880s, the life of the city was focused around its centers of trade: the newly established markets; broad, brilliantly lit boulevards lined with elegant small shops; glass-roofed, marble-walled arcades; and sumptuously decorated department stores.

The department store as a building type was a brand new institution, without precedent in the history of architecture.[17] Originating in Paris in the 1860s, it consisted of a large retail establishment

Fig. 18 Paul Sédille, Printemps, Paris, 1881 (demolished), interior light court; from Marrey, Les Grands Magasins.

offering a wide range of moderately priced, mass-produced goods, aimed primarily at the burgeoning middle classes. Typically a large, impressive building centrally located in the downtown area, it differed fundamentally from the traditional retailing spaces, including bazaars, glazed arcades, dry goods stores, and small specialty stores. Unlike any of these, the department store carried manufactured goods of all kinds, including foodstuffs, household wares, apparel, and toys, stocking them in semi-independent departments. Each department operated as a separate unit, with its own manager, buyer, and sales personnel, and each was responsible for developing its own marketing procedures. The store as a whole, however, was owned and operated by a single administration, thus streamlining management. In order to compete with the traditional small shop and the newer, fashionable glazed arcade, the management instituted certain marketing innovations such as fixed prices, free entrance, guaranteed returns, and free delivery. The department store's main advantage was in offering a wide range of goods under a single roof, enabling customers to satisfy all their shopping needs in one place.

The first true department store, as defined above, was Paris's Bon Marché. Beginning as a small men's shop in the 1820s, it expanded haphazardly over the years, gradually taking over spaces in adjacent buildings. In the 1850s, its proprietor, Aristide Boucicaut, began implementing the new economic policies that were to comprise the department store. Bolstered by his success, and inspired by the popularity of the 1867 International Exposition with its vast glass and iron exhibition halls, Boucicaut decided to erect a brand new store building.

Designed by Ecole-trained Alexandre Laplanche with the assistance of Louis-Auguste Boileau, it was a remarkably progressive building, five stories high, with monumental classical masonry facades, regular rows of exceptionally large plate-glass windows, and an internal structure entirely of iron (figs. 15, 16). The building was commissioned in 1867, the same year as the international exposition, with construction continued after the Franco-Prussian War of 1870. Louis-Charles Boileau, son of Louis-Auguste, assumed responsibility for the project, assisted by engineer Alexandre Gustave Eiffel, known for his structures erected for the 1867 Exposition. This was no mere coincidence: Boucicaut was clearly capitalizing on Eiffel's experience with new glass and iron structural systems, and their progressive display potentialities. Opening in 1876, the new Bon Marché department store building was further enlarged in

the 1880s and completed in 1887, by which time it covered virtually an entire city block.

The program was complex. What was needed was a large multistoried building with an internal structure that permitted a maximum amount of light and space throughout. Natural light was essential for the display of merchandise, since gas lighting was not only costly but posed a tremendous fire hazard. Ample, unencumbered space was equally important not only for the display of merchandise, but also for safe, easy circulation of the public.

Impressive facades were imperative (fig. 17). Recognized as vitally important in luring the casual passerby off the street, they needed to be eye-catching, easily identifiable, and memorable. Monumental arched entrances modeled after those of the 1867 International Exposition indicated that it was a building geared to the public; exceptionally large windows, especially on the street level, suggested a building destined for commercial uses. Turning the corners of the huge building block were domed rotundas that served as recognizable landmarks of the particular building type; at the focal point of a major traffic intersection, they drew the attention of crowds from all sides. The classical style of the building, especially the monumental

entrance defined by a huge, impressive Roman arch flanked by fluted Corinthian pilasters and embellished by classical statuary, was deliberately geared to attract the bourgeoisie. When delicate, ornamented filagree glass-and-iron marquees became fashionable in the 1880s, they too were added to the building, providing protection from inclement weather, as well as another touch of elegance.

The structure of the building was entirely of iron. Broadly spaced, slender iron columns obviated the need for internal walls, permitting the unobstructed flow of natural light throughout the building. Numerous glazed light courts penetrated down through all five stories of the building, funneling natural light into the deep interiors unreached by facade windows. Supplementing this light source was an artificial lighting system, first gas, then in the 1880s, as soon as it was available, electricity.

Although other facilities such as libraries, art galleries, restaurants, and medical clinics were included, the building was basically designed with but one function in mind: to sell. Attracting customers was essential, and in this the building itself played a fundamental role. Drawn by the sheer size of the store and its magnificently embellished facades, as well as its brilliant display of goods, the customer entering the building was drawn through

Fig. 19 Paul Sédille, Printemps, Paris, 1881 (demolished); from Marrey, Les Grands Magasins.

Fig. 20 John Eisenmann and George Horatio Smith, Cleveland Arcade, between Superior and Euclid avenues, Cleveland, 1888-89, interior view.

a labyrinth of display counters into its stunning light court. The effect of the multiple tiers of open metal galleries piled high with merchandise, the whole gilded, painted, and lavishly ornamented, was aimed at creating an atmosphere of luxury. A sumptuously decorated monumental double-revolutionary stair, resembling that of the newly opened Paris Opéra designed by Charles Garnier, invited customers to parade their finery under the admiring glances of spectators above, even as it lured them to the upper reaches of the store.

This dazzling space, comprised of tiers of lacy iron galleries and lightweight aerial footbridges, was the store's primary attraction. Like a vast metal and glass exhibition hall or colorful, bountiful Oriental bazaar, it was astonishing in both its novel spatial effects and in the sheer abundance of fine goods displayed. With the raw industrial nature of iron concealed beneath a layer of painted plaster richly ornamented with gilding and copper decor,

delicate arabesques of ornamental ironwork on railings and brackets, and brightly painted and stained glass ceilings, the building itself served as a theater, a magnificent stage set for merchandise and the public alike.

Decked out in its attractive new quarters, Bon Marché was soon rewarded by soaring profits; this drove its competitors to follow suit. Before long, other merchants began to enlarge their premises or erect new ones to make them comparable to the Bon Marché by including impressive interior courts and majestic monumental stairs. Among the most celebrated of Bon Marché's Parisian competitors was the Printemps department store. After fire destroyed the original quarters of this enterprise, architect Paul Sédille, known for his brilliant use of the polychromatic Venetian Renaissance style at the 1878 International Exposition, was commissioned in 1881 to exercise his skill on a new building for the store. Following the Bon Marché prototype, he built an impressively large, amply fenestrated multistoried building, with elaborately embellished monumental stone facades heightened by colorful mosaics, prominent domed corner rotundas, a metal-framed structure to insure maximum light and space, and magnificently decorated interiors (figs. 18, 19). Unlike the Bon Marché, however, Sédille's building had but one enormous skylighted court. Ringed by multiple tiers of galleries of open lacy ironwork, this vast interior space was criss-crossed by aerial staircases and footbridges, anchored in the center by a sumptuous monumental grand stair – decidedly Piranesian in effect, according to contemporaries. A much-flaunted tourist attraction when it opened, the Printemps building became widely known both at home and abroad. It was surely Printemps's great interior court, as much as anything, that served as a major inspiration for the glazed arcade of the vast Cleveland Arcade, built in Cleveland, Ohio, in 1888-89 (fig. 20).

In the summer of 1886, having completed the elevations of the two street facades of the Rookery begun in the spring of that year, Root took his wife and daughter on a trip abroad. While little is known about the details of the trip, it is certain that he visited Paris. Given his interest in the progressive technology of metal-framed structures – aroused earlier by his reading of Viollet-le-Duc – we have every reason to suppose that Root visited the celebrated Parisian department stores, then among the most structurally progressive buildings in the world. A comparison of the novel spatial effects in these buildings – the delicate decorative ironwork and monumental staircases that distinguish their interiors – with the interior of the Chicago Rookery suggests that Root must have been greatly impressed by these Parisian precedents.

The exteriors of the French models were, however, inappropriate for Root's purposes. Both the Bon Marché and Printemps were, after all, department stores dependent on flashy public appeal, whereas the Rookery was a speculative office building. Although the architects of the Parisian and Chicago buildings shared a common functional concern for maximizing light and space, their overall aims were different. Moreover, while the brilliantly colored scintillating mosaics and lavish sculptural decor of department stores like Printemps suited highly stylish Paris, they would have appeared wholly out of place in robust, still rough-hewn Chicago. More appropriate there, as Root well knew, were his massive, strongly textured Richardsonian exteriors, expressive of the aggressive spirit of Chicago's commercial and industrial establishments.

NOTES

1 For more information on the American Renaissance, see Richard Guy Wilson, *The American Renaissance 1876-1917* (New York, 1979).
2 On the lure of France for Americans at this time, see A. D. F. Hamlin, "The Battle of the Styles," *Architectural Record* 1 (1892), p. 270.
3 Meredith L. Clausen, "The Department Store," in *Encyclopedia of Architecture, Design, Engineering and Construction* (New York, forthcoming).
4 Walter Benjamin, "Paris, Capital of the Nineteenth Century," in *Reflections: Essays, Aphorisms, Autobiographical Writings*, trans. Edmund Jephcott (New York, 1978), pp. 146-62.
5 Henry Van Brunt, "Architecture in the West," *Atlantic Monthly*, (Dec. 1889), p. 777.
6 Ibid., p. 778.
7 On light and the Chicago School, see Meredith L. Clausen, "Frank Lloyd Wright, Vertical Space, and the Chicago School's Quest for Light," *Journal of the Society of Architectural Historians* 44, 1 (March 1985), pp. 66-74.
8 Van Brunt (note 5), p. 782.
9 C. H. Blackall, "Notes of Travel," *American Architect and Building News* (Dec. 1887), pp. 314-15; Thomas E. Tallmadge, *The Story of Architecture in America* (New York, 1927), p. 184; and idem, *Architecture in Old Chicago* (Chicago, 1941), p. 151.
   On the Rookery's progressive "floating" foundation, see Hasbrouck Hunderman Architects, *The Rookery:*

Program for the Restoration and Preservation of the Designated Features, for Continental Illinois National Bank (Chicago, 1984), p. 13. The construction techniques employed by Root in the foundation were similar to those used by French architect Jules Saulnier in his 1869 design for the Menier Chocolate Works. The degree to which Root might have been inspired by the iron-framed building that spanned the Marne River and was supported by masonry piers in the river's bed bears further research. See Gerald Larson's essay in this volume for more on the Menier Chocolate Works, and on the development of the iron skeleton frame in Europe and the United States. See also Carl W. Condit, *The Chicago School of Architecture: A History of Commercial and Public Building in the Chicago Area, 1875-1925* (Chicago, 1964), p. 7.
10 Blackall (note 9), p. 314.
11 John Wellborn Root, "What Are the Present Tendencies of Architectural Design in America?," in Donald Hoffmann, *The Meanings of Architecture: Buildings and Writings by John Wellborn Root* (New York, 1967), p. 208. For more on Taine and his theory of art, see Martha Pollak's essay in this volume.
12 Ibid., p. 208.
13 One precedent for the interior glazed court in the work of Burnham and Root can be found in the corporate headquarters they designed for the Chicago, Burlington & Quincy Railway Company. The building was commissioned in 1882 and built the following year, and its light court was remarkably large for its time. An expansive skylighted space, glazed at the top, rose unbroken

through all six stories of the building. Like the later design for the Rookery court, it was surrounded on all sides by tiers of office space facing galleries formed by openwork metal railings.
14 Henry Van Brunt, "John Wellborn Root," *Inland Architect and News Record* 16 (Jan. 1891), p. 87.
15 Benjamin (note 4), pp. 151-52. On the connection between exhibitions and department stores, see also Russell Lewis, "Everything Under One Roof: World's Fairs and Department Stores in Paris and Chicago," *Chicago History* 12 (Fall 1983).
16 Baron Georges-Eugène Haussmann, *Mémoires*, vol. 2, p. 200, cited in Françoise Choay, *The Modern City: Planning in the 19th Century* (New York, 1969), p. 16.
17 Clausen (note 3). See also Meredith L. Clausen, "The Department Store – Development of the Type," *Journal of Architectural Education* 39 (Fall 1985), p. 21; and Neil Harris's essay in this volume.

Solon Spencer Beman, Pullman, and the European Influence on and Interest in his Chicago Architecture

Thomas J. Schlereth

In a rare, and typically laconic, public speech delivered at the grand opening of one of his commercial buildings in 1903, Solon Spencer Beman (1853-1914) summarized his architectural philosophy and acknowledged his debt to European culture. Responding to a toast honoring him as the designer of the Beaux-Arts style United States Trust Bank in Terre Haute, Indiana, he quoted Mr. Pecksniff, an architect in Charles Dickens's novel, *Martin Chuzzlewit* (1844): "My friends ... my duty is to build, not speak; to act, not talk; to deal with marble, stone, and brick: not language."[1]

Beman's citation of a fictional architect's epigram is doubly significant. It reveals his lifelong interest in British life and letters, as well as his unpretentious personality as a Chicago architect. An ardent Anglophile, he preferred to let his buildings speak for themselves rather than to speak (or write) about them. Unlike his friends Louis Sullivan and John Root, Beman did not proclaim any architectural theory. Although he designed Pullman Water Tower (fig. 2) — the tallest building in the world for a time — he offered no pronouncements on high-rise aesthetics or engineering. An architect of two industrial towns, he never authored a treatise on urbanism or city planning. He would have been embarrassed at the idea of writing a memoir or an autobiography.

Other factors also account for Beman's obscurity in Anglo-American architectural history. Many of his nineteenth-century buildings, located in the urban core of various midwestern cities, have been demolished. For example, several of his most interesting Chicago projects, including Grand Central Station (1889-91; fig. 3), the Washington Park Club (1883), the Pullman Arcade (1881-83; fig. 4), the Bryson Apartments (1901), and most of his residences, have been destroyed. Few of the records of Beman's small Chicago firm have survived: scattered working and presentation drawings, fragmentary correspondence, and a personal scrapbook are the only documentary evidence of forty years' work.

In the late nineteenth century, however, S. S. Beman enjoyed a significant place in Chicago architecture. His work in the 1880s and 1890s was touted in the United States and abroad. Architectural critics ranging from Montgomery Schuyler to John Root championed his achievements. Frank Lloyd Wright and Louis Sullivan acknowledged his creativity. European architectural journals such as *Building News, British Architect,* and *The Builder* monitored and praised his designs.[2]

This case study of Beman's interaction with European architecture analyzes two projects: the model industrial town of Pullman, Illinois (1880-90), and several office complexes built in Chicago (1884-95) for the Studebaker Brothers Manufacturing Company and the Pullman Palace Car Company.

With the exception of the W. W. Kimball mansion (1889-90; fig. 5), a brilliant exercise in the chateau style, and his Beaux-Arts work, Beman's work was influenced primarily by British architectural theory and practice. It also was largely imitative. This midwestern architect often borrowed more than he originated, especially in his stylistic

Fig. 1 Solon Spencer Beman, Pullman Building, Michigan Avenue and southwest corner of Adams Street, 1883-84 (demolished), detail of court.

Fig. 2 Beman, Water Tower and Power House, Pullman, 1880 (demolished).

Fig. 3 Beman, Grand Central Station, southwest corner of Harrison and Wells streets, 1889-91 (demolished).

Fig. 4 Beman, Arcade Building, Pullman, 1881-83 (demolished).

Fig. 5 Beman, W. W. Kimball House, 1801 South Prairie Avenue, 1889-90.

treatment, and several of his Chicago projects owe part of their success to English precedents.

Born in Brooklyn in 1853, Beman was the first son of William Riley Beman and Sarah Ann Robbins, both descendants of British immigrants to Colonial America. In 1870 he was apprenticed to the New York architectural firm of Upjohn and Upjohn. Richard Upjohn's design of Wall Street's Trinity Church (1841-46), his important role in the ecclesiological movement in Britain and the United States, and the consistently high quality of his religious, residential, and public buildings made him indisputably one of the leading Gothic Revival architects of the Anglo-American world.

When Richard Upjohn (1802-1878) went into semiretirement in 1870, his son Richard Mitchell Upjohn (1827-1903), who had emigrated with his father from England in 1829 and had become his

partner in 1853, assumed the major responsibility for the family practice. In the seven years that Beman worked for the Upjohn firm, he performed the typical tasks required of the apprentice and was exposed to a wide range of building types and historical styles. He had the good fortune, for example, to help construct one of the most unabashedly exuberant High Victorian Gothic monuments of the Gilded Age: Richard M. Upjohn's magnum opus, the Connecticut State Capitol in Hartford (1875-78).[3]

While Upjohn gave young Beman his first architectural training, George M. Pullman gave him his first major architectural project. In 1879 Pullman commissioned Beman, then twenty-eight, to design an industrial community in Calumet, Illinois, outside Chicago, in collaboration with landscape architect Nathan F. Barrett.[4]

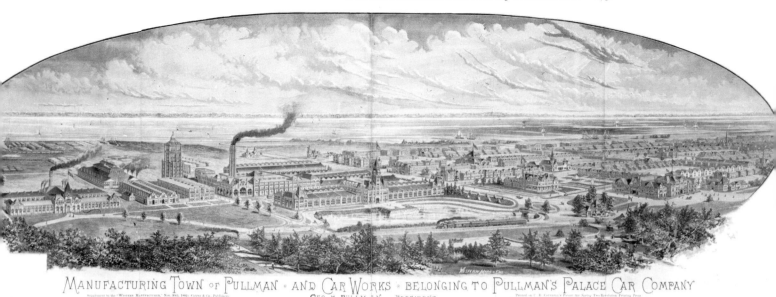

MANUFACTURING TOWN OF PULLMAN · AND CAR WORKS · BELONGING TO PULLMAN'S PALACE CAR COMPANY
GEO. M. PULLMAN   PRESIDENT

Pullman, a company town and an architectural and social experiment, was Beman's first major commission; it would also be his most famous, the project with which he would always be identified.[5] Pullman (fig. 6) was also the longest project on which Beman worked, for two decades later he was still building and rebuilding on the Calumet site.

Although architectural historians have alluded to various forms of American town planning as precedents for Beman's work at Pullman – from New England textile towns to Pennsylvania coal company towns and Robert Owen's utopian community at New Harmony, Indiana (1825-27) – few have examined its possible British forerunners.

In addition to Owen's first model community at New Lanark in Scotland, entrepreneurs such as Richard Arkwright at Cromford, Thomas Ashton at Hyde in Lancashire, Walter Milligan at Harden Bingley, Edward Ackroyd at Coply Halifax, John Richardson at Bessbrook, and George and Richard Cadbury at Bournville, all built factories, dwellings, chapels, and schools for their workers and tried to encourage the values they thought appropriate to the new industrial society.[6]

Saltaire, the model industrial town created in Yorkshire in 1851-71 by Sir Titus Salt, an innovative manufacturer of alpaca woolen goods, probably achieved the greatest commercial success and

Fig. 6 Pullman; from Western Manufacturer (Nov. 3, 1881).

Fig. 7 Saltaire Mills, near Bradford, England, 1851-71; C. F. Cheffins, lithographer.

Fig. 8 View of Pullman with plan; from Harper's New Monthly Magazine *70 (Feb. 1885).*

Fig. 9 Plan of Saltaire; from Leonardo Benevolo, The History of the City *(Cambridge, Mass., 1972).*

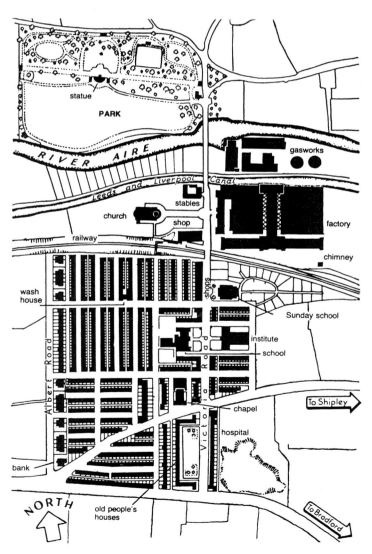

public acclaim of these nineteenth-century British ventures. Inspired in part by Benjamin Disraeli's *Sybil: or The Two Nations,* an 1845 novel in which the architectural features of a "Model Factory and Model Village" are sketched out in considerable detail, Salt established Saltaire (fig. 7) four miles north of the city boundaries of Bradford, commissioning the well-known firm of Henry Lockwood and William Mawson to build the town.[7]

George Pullman, whose conscience had been stirred by reading Charles Reade's *Put Yourself in His Place,* a social novel of 1870 set in the English industrial town of Hillsborough, seems likely to have visited Saltaire when touring Britain in 1873. Thomas Grant, a close friend of Pullman and a student of British and American industrial towns, claimed that the American industrialist and his architect had explicitly employed Saltaire as a prototype for the town they built on the Illinois prairie. Others, including French economist Paul de Rousiers, have also commented on the pronounced resemblances between Pullman and Saltaire.[8]

In any case, both plans called for the location of their model industrial towns on the edges of larger cities for several reasons, including the avoidance of municipal taxes and of building code restrictions. Important as well in these choices of location was the opportunity to place the factory-residential complexes in a pastoral setting where country air, light, and nature would create an ideal working environment. The architects of both towns engaged professional engineers to design modern sanitation, water, and gas supply systems; Be-

Fig. 10 Beman, Procter and Gamble Co., factory, Ivorydale, Ohio, 1885.

nezette Williams performed this service at Pullman.

The two towns were deliberately situated in immediate proximity to water and rail transport, thus ensuring the most efficient receipt and delivery of raw materials and finished products. Both communities were laid out in accordance with a geometrical plan, punctuated with public squares, gardens, and parks, and both plans called for residential, commercial, and recreational land usage (figs. 8, 9). In each case a primary building material (red brick for Pullman, ashlar stone for Saltaire) and harmonious architectural vocabulary (Italian Gothic for Saltaire, American Queen Anne for Pullman) were specified. Finally, both plans insisted on a fairly regular spatial perspective throughout the towns – a height of no more than two or three stories, periodically accented by vertical landmarks such as clock and water towers or factory chimneys.

In each model town, the client dictated the street names. Salt named most of his streets after himself, his spouse, and his family (Titus, Caroline, Mary, Helen, Ada) and his sovereigns (Victoria and Albert); Pullman called his town's main boulevard Florence Avenue after his daughter, and named its western thoroughfare after himself (Pullman, now Cottage Grove Avenue). He used most of the Beman/Barrett street pattern to honor Anglo-American heroes of technology: Robert Fulton, George Stephenson, James Watt, John Ericson, and Samuel Morse. Unlike Salt, who named streets after his architects, Pullman offered no such acknowl-

edgment of Beman and Barrett's planning achievement.[9]

Beman's Pullman commission was extensively surveyed and evaluated by both American and European observers. An English critic touring the Midwest in 1887 reported in the *London Times:* "No place in the United States has attracted more attention or has been more closely watched."[10] Indeed, the model town was so heavily visited by European tourists in the 1880s that it became necessary to place the industrial area off-limits. Among the curious were visitors like British social reformer William Stead and government officials like Monsieur Loudelet, sent by the French Ministry of Commerce to report on the success of the undertaking for possible imitation. The following comments by British observer Budgett Meakin are typical of the reaction to Beman's work. Praising the physical plan of Pullman as a progressive design concept suggestive of an "industrial park," Meakin noted:

Industrial structures were carefully grouped to expedite car building and segregated from residences by broad boulevards and ornamental walls. Their interiors were light and airy so as to improve morale and health, and consequently production. The shops' attractive, eclectic architecture was enhanced by surrounding greenery and an artificial lake.[11]

Beman, in collaboration with Barrett, laid out his residences and most public buildings on a grid plan. As London's *Pall Mall Gazette* pointed out, "one would expect . . . [this] American utopia should be regularly laid out, with streets appointed and set forth very commodious and handsome."[12] The plan's regularity was intentionally relieved by a market square, several parks, and a winding drive intended for Sunday outings. Beman also grouped several of his public buildings about two picturesque railroad stations.

Paul de Rousiers was equally impressed by the rationality and order of Beman's "scientific planning." He saw Pullman as a blueprint for instant town building of a scope and on a scale unprecedented among planners of modern industrial communities:

The planning of these workshops is remarkable, and every detail seems to have been considered. To cite one point, the buildings in which freight-cars are built are a series of vast sheds as broad as the cars are long. Opposite each car a large bay opens on the iron way and a car, as soon as it is finished, runs along the rails and leaves the shop. All the timber that forms a car is cut to the required size and is got ready for fitting together in a special department, whence it is brought along the same rails to the sheds where the car is built. Tiny little locomotives are running along the lines which are built in the spaces between the various workshops. Some are hauling magnificent Pullman cars, glittering with copper and gilding; others drag trucks of planks, joists, bolts and the iron needed in car-building. Everything is done in order and with precision; one feels that each effort is calculated to yield its maximum effect, that no blow of a hammer, no turn of a wheel is made without cause. One feels that some brain of superior intelligence, backed by a long technical experience, has thought out every possible detail.[13]

Beman's Pullman became known to Europeans not only through published accounts but also through graphics and models. Drawings and photographs of the site and its structures circulated in both the popular and professional press. A 100-foot scale model of Beman's achievement was exhibited at the World's Industrial and Cotton Centennial Exposition in New Orleans as early as 1884. Other models toured European world's fairs, such as the 1889 Paris exposition, with an enlarged exhibit prepared for display in Louis Sullivan's Transportation Building at the 1893 World's Columbian Exposition in Chicago. During that fair, the model town itself (only five miles away from the exposition site) served as an outdoor architectural museum for more than 10,000 foreign visitors.[14] Other fairs, in turn, publicized Beman's work abroad through awards like the one bestowed by the jury of the International Hygienic and Pharmaceutical Exposition held in Prague in 1896. The awards committee pronounced Pullman without peer in its domestic architecture, sanitation, public utilities, and civic buildings; it was judged nothing less than "the most perfect town plan in the world."[15]

Unfortunately, a decade of labor problems (a strike occurred at Pullman as early as 1885), the increasing paternalism of George Pullman toward the town and its inhabitants throughout the 1880s, and the violence of the 1894 strike temporarily discouraged other industrialists from undertaking similar experiments to procure social order through architectural planning. The failure of Pullman's social experiment, however, was not in any way linked to Beman's architectural design. On the contrary, American economist and social critic Richard Ely, echoing a view widely held in Europe as well, noted that "No other feature of Pullman can receive praise needing so little qualification as its architecture."[16]

Although it did not serve as the sole prototype for industrial towns of similar scale, Beman's Pullman had considerable significance for the Anglo-American planning tradition. Two legacies can be cited. The order and utility of the City Beautiful movement articulated in practice and theory, respectively, by the Columbian Exposition and the 1909 Burnham Plan for Chicago, espoused Beman's principles of urban design with its emphasis on parks, boulevards, and civic centers. The desire to show that industrialization was not necessarily married to urbanization paralleled the Garden City movement of Ebenezer Howard and made Pullman a forerunner of various efforts to resettle workers and industry in planned suburban communities away from major cities.

S. S. Beman continued to design industrial architecture and workers' housing after Pullman. In 1885, for example, William Procter and James Gamble commissioned him to design Ivorydale

Fig. 11 Beman, Rosalie Villas, Harper Avenue between 57th and 59th streets, 1884-90.

Fig. 12 Beman, Bryson Apartments, 4930 South Lake Park Avenue, 1901 (demolished); from Inland Architect and News Record 40, 4 (1902).

(fig. 10), a model industrial community for the manufacture of soap in Mill Creek Valley near the rural village of St. Bernard, seven miles outside Cincinnati, Ohio. At first an entire model town, including housing, was envisioned, but only a model factory and warehouse complex were actually built. Beman built Ivorydale in stone rather than brick (as at Pullman), but once again he situated the buildings of his manufacturing plant – twenty-eight in all – within a landscaped park setting.

Although he built no residences in Cincinnati, Beman became the chief architect of a south Chicago suburban real estate development later known as Rosalie Villas, a housing scheme of approximately fifty Queen Anne residences, each of which was to be unique in architectural style and yet affordable for middle-class families. Laid out between 1884 and 1890, Rosalie Villas (fig. 11) was sited adjacent to Frederick Law Olmsted's Midway Plaisance, connecting Chicago's Jackson and Washington parks, to provide residents with "proper entrance to a public pleasure ground."[17]

Named for Rosalie Buckingham, who later married Harry Gordon Selfridge, general manager of Marshall Field and Company and subsequently

founder of Selfridge's department store in London (see essay by Harris), Rosalie Villas received considerable publicity as the Hyde Park-Kenwood area's first planned community. As several interpreters have recognized, the Rosalie Villas project was meant to extend to middle-class residents a miniature version of the amenities that Beman had provided for skilled workers and their families in Pullman. As Gwendolyn Wright points out, the model suburb

also stands as a cautious exercise in an architect's idea of social reform: a middle-class neighborhood where each house was different from the others, yet a neighborhood which was to be a harmonious community. . . . Rosalie Villas and Pullman suggest that a few midwestern architects saw their designs in social as well as aesthetic terms.[18]

Beman returned to his interest in workers' housing in 1899 by submitting an invited design for high-rise, artisans' dwellings for the Shattuck Prize competition. For this limited competition Beman submitted several elevations of his proposed structures, a half-section of a side elevation, and a quarter-plan of a sample room arrangement. In one of his rare attempts to articulate verbally his objec-

Fig. 13 Beman, Bee Building, 17th Street at Farnham Street, Omaha, Nebraska, 1887 (demolished); from Inland Architect and News Record *12, 5 (1888).*

Fig. 14 Beman, Pullman Building.

tives for an architectural project, Beman included a description of the rationale behind his design. Various features were to characterize his model workers' apartments:

Abundance of direct light and pure air, the absence of closed courts and light shafts, provision for a strong circulation of air entirely around the apartments and a pleasant outlook for nearly all the living rooms; all toilet-rooms and staircases open directly to outside light air; separation of families by providing frequent staircases and entrances; courts opening to the street made of sufficient areas as to serve as recreation-grounds for children; staircases built of incombustible materials, enclosed with brick walls and made of easy ascent for the comfort of those occupying the upper stories.[19]

Although Beman received high praise for his Shattuck project, he never built the high-rise apartment complex. Instead he designed several apartment buildings for the middle class, particularly the Clinton and the Bryson buildings (fig. 12), on Chicago's South Side.

At the same time that Beman was developing industrial sites and planned communities for various American entrepreneurs, he began to receive commissions to design business blocks and sky-scrapers for downtown corporate headquarters. His commercial work was a distinctive phase of his career, tightly bracketed between his Pullman Building of 1885 and his final skyscrapers, the

Berger Building in Pittsburgh, Pennsylvania, and the J.M.S. Building in South Bend, Indiana, both completed in 1906. To midwestern railroad cities like Milwaukee, Wisconsin; Omaha, Nebraska; St. Paul, Minnesota; Grand Rapids, Michigan; and South Bend and Terre Haute, Indiana, he exported the commercial style acclaimed in Chicago.

His commercial architecture displayed the exceptional diversity typical of his other work. He began by building masonry, load-bearing structural systems exemplified by Milwaukee's Northwestern Insurance Company (1885) and Omaha's Bee buildings (1887; fig. 13), then made the transition to steel-frame structures within a few years of their introduction by Jenney, Holabird, and other Chicago architects. He experimented with all the stylistic idioms of the time, including Richardsonian Romanesque, High Victorian Gothic, and Chicago School commercial. He was at ease with the use of various sizes and hues of brick and masonry — as well as with more restrained monochromatic facades of white terracotta. He designed tall commercial towers, such as the Pioneer Press Building (1888; executed in the base-column-capital symmetry so often identified with Sullivan), as well as diminutive, squat blocks appropriate to the Main Street scale of the small midwestern city.[20]

Fig. 15 Pullman Building; from Building News *(Apr. 11, 1884).*

Fig. 16 Beman, Elevation of the Pullman Building (cat. no. 52).

Beman's first architectural foray into downtown Chicago came in 1883-84 with his Pullman Building, a ten-story office and apartment block (fig. 14) constructed opposite The Art Institute of Chicago at the corner of Michigan Avenue and Adams Street. Indebted for its U-shape form and floor plan to George B. Post's 1881 Mills Building in New York and for its recessed loggias and other upper facade detailing to Richard Norman Shaw's 1879 Albert Hall Mansions in London, the structure was one of the first tall commercial buildings erected along Chicago's Michigan Avenue.

Marked features of Beman's Adams Street elevation (fig. 16) included turrets at the building's corners and a series of colonnades flanking an elliptical granite entrance arch. From this grand portal, Beman constructed a skylit inner court extending back eighty feet. The court (fig. 1), like the dramatic interior design of the Arcade Building at Pullman, was something of a Beman trademark. His talent for designing interesting interior commercial spaces would be evident again in his Northwest Insurance Company Building in Milwaukee and in his stunning interior for the Grand Central Railroad Station in Chicago.

At the court's terminus, Beman placed a double granite and marble staircase leading to an elevator lobby and a reception parlor. Draftsman John Edelman, who had worked in Beman's office for several years, designed the exotic Egyptian elevator grilles and other interior decorations which, according to Hugh Morrison, strongly influenced the aesthetic of young Louis Sullivan's later ornamentation.[21]

The Pullman "hive," as locals dubbed the building, enjoyed a critical success in an opulent age that welcomed, as Thomas Tallmadge aptly put it, "a mix of the Romanesque Revival seasoned with a bit of the Queen Anne" in its commercial palaces.[22] One of the major "elevator buildings" that Tallmadge identified as the logical forerunner of the modern Chicago skyscraper, the Pullman office block brought Beman further local and even international notice. *Inland Architect* ran a handsome line-drawing perspective of the building as its first venture into centerfold, sepia-tone, print engraving. The editors were doubly proud when *Building News,* an architectural journal published in London, reproduced the illustration (fig. 15) and commented favorably on the superior status of Chicago architecture as represented by Beman's work.

To the Chicago builders who, in 1884, were in the midst of organizing the Western Association of Architects, this British recognition of one of their own signaled "that Western architecture has advanced to a stage where it can be favorably compared with that of Eastern cities, and that of Europe."[23] Championed as a symbol of local talent, Beman's Pullman Building was also frequently compared by later critics to the commercial work of John Root, particularly his Rookery Building (pls. 10, 11; see Clausen, fig. 8) constructed in 1886-87 on West Adams Street.[24]

S. S. Beman's architectural career was closely linked to the transportation industry. In addition to his extensive work on the town of Pullman and various railroad terminals and workshops, he also designed railroad car interiors, particularly for the Pullman Palace Car Company's special display at the 1893 World's Columbian Exposition. In 1885 he was engaged by the Studebaker Brothers Manufacturing Company, one of the few nineteenth-century wagon and carriage builders to make a successful transition to motorized automotive transport in the early twentieth century. Over the next two decades, Beman built factories, showrooms, investment properties, office buildings, music halls, and private residences for this important northern Indiana family firm. His Studebaker commissions extended over two cities: Chicago, which was the company's principal midwestern promotional and retail outlet, and South Bend, Indiana, the firm's factory center and corporate headquarters.

To mark the Studebakers' entry into Chicago's commercial architecture, Beman created, in the estimate of Montgomery Schuyler, "one of the show buildings of Chicago." Although Schuyler recognized that Beman's Romanesque facade (fig. 17) exuded a bit "too much of the palatial character of Devonshire Street and Wall Street to be fairly representative of the severity of commercial architecture in Chicago," he found the use of Romanesque, particularly in the arrangement of the first five stories, a "striking and well-studied feature, with every detail very good in itself and very well-adjusted in place and in scale."[25]

British Architect considered the building one of the "most well-designed American commercial structures," one that English builders would do well to emulate:

We have selected this building for illustration as a very good type of the best modern American business premises. . . . Moreover, we seriously believe there are comparatively few of its kind to be found in our English streets. Here is a street frontage in which the maximum of light has been obtained along with breadth of surface and dignified simplicity. We think it eminently satisfactory, and when we remember the fussy pilasters, mouldings, foliated spandrels, and gorgeous bosses of carving in some of our London streets, we are almost tempted to say too much of this modest and unaffected piece of American work. This is certainly the work we should apply for, were we in need of an architect for a London street.[26]

By 1895, the Studebaker firm had outgrown its Chicago headquarters and commissioned Beman to construct a new ten-story building (fig. 19) at 629 South Wabash Avenue. At the same time he was directed to turn the Studebakers' first structure on

Fig. 17 Beman, Studebaker Building, 410 South Michigan Avenue, 1885.

Fig. 18 Beman, Fine Arts Building, 410 South Michigan Avenue, 1896.

Fig. 19 Beman, Studebaker Building, 629 South Wabash Avenue, 1895 (altered).

Fig. 20 Beman, Fine Arts Building, interior.

Michigan Avenue into a cultural center, renamed the Fine Arts Building (fig. 18) in 1896.

Beman gave the structure that he had built only a decade earlier a noticeable facelift and a thorough interior remodeling. The domes, the attic, and the original facade of the eighth floor were removed and replaced by a three-story addition, which created a total of ten floors. This addition was faced with dark red syenite stone and topped with a flat stone and copper cornice. The two dark driveways at the street level were converted into main entrances for two new music halls on the main floor. The ground-level window-fronted spaces formerly devoted to the display of carriages were converted into three street-front shops.

The architect wrought the greatest changes within the building's interior (fig. 20). A structure initially devoted to commerce was transformed into an atelier of the arts. Beman filled the second through the tenth floors with studios, shops (such as Francis Fisher Browne's book store designed by Frank Lloyd Wright), and offices, all soundproofed and fireproofed. Here Anglo-American artistic exchange flourished: the magazines *Dial* and *Poetry* were first published in the building; English producer Maurice Browne introduced George Bernard Shaw's dramas to America in the building's Little Theatre; and here the British Arts

and Crafts movement received its first midwestern attention.[27] Beman's tenth-floor studios, intended for painters, sculptors, and architects (including Frank Lloyd Wright and Howard Van Doren Shaw), had skylights and twenty-three-foot-high ceilings to accommodate large drafting tables, canvasses, and sculptures. This floor also contained a hall connecting it to the dining room of Louis Sullivan's Auditorium Building next door.

A comparison of the Fine Arts Building with 629 South Wabash (fig. 19), the second office complex Beman designed for the Studebakers, provides a tidy demonstration of the evolution of the Chicago School's commercial architecture within a decade of a single architect's career. Unlike the load-bearing masonry construction of the first Studebaker building, the structural system of the later version was a steel cage. In fenestration, Beman abandoned his confused Romanesque arches for a brilliant exercise in the development of the Chicago window. These windows — flat and slightly behind the face of the thin terracotta piers that he permitted to run the full height of the structure — were separated at the building's floor lines by decorative iron spandrels.

Beman's skyscraper has been compared to Willis J. Polk's Hallidie Building (1915-17) and Sullivan's Gage Building (1898-99) for its adroit handling of steel and glass. "In this building," wrote Carl Condit, the ornament is "well subordinated to the overall form and structural lines" of the facade which was "a great open area of glass crossed by the thin lines of the molded piers and the narrow bands of the spandrels." In short, "the Chicago windows and the delicately articulated wall provide the fullest exploitation of steel framing that the Chicago School could show at the time."[28] Unfortunately, Beman's triumph has been badly mutilated. Although still standing with its parapet removed and its lower floors masked, the second Studebaker building is but a ghost of its former self.

S. S. Beman was responsible for many other structures in addition to those selected for discussion in this essay.[29] Some of these showed an indebtedness to European influences, including his famous residence built on Prairie Avenue for W. W. Kimball (1890; fig. 5) — opposite H. H. Richardson's Glessner House (1885-87; see Harrington, fig. 10) — modeled after the Chateau de Josselin, a sixteenth-century manor house in Brittany. His Pabst Building (1891) in Milwaukee, Wisconsin, with its flamboyant, Germanic guild hall tower, also embodies European references (fig. 21).

Prior to 1893 Beman had indulged in all the historic revival styles and especially delighted in the exuberant picturesque of the High Victorian era. In the early 1890s, however, he abandoned this eclecticism — a change evident, for example, in his design for Pullman for a second Market Hall (1894) to replace the 1881 structure that burned in 1892 (compare figs. 22 and 23).

Beman's career, in its final two decades, was almost totally dominated by Beaux-Arts classicism, beginning with his Mines and Mining and his Merchant Tailor buildings at the World's Columbian Exposition. He went on to contribute to the Beaux-Arts movement in the Midwest through a number of civic (fig. 24; cat. no. 82) and ecclesiastical (cat. no. 83) buildings. In short, he largely turned his back on the playfulness and diversity of the Queen Anne and the Romanesque for the sobriety and unity of the Renaissance and of classical antiquity. Whereas the England of Robert Shaw had prompted many of his designs throughout the 1880s, it was the Greece of Pericles in the fifth century B.C. that inspired his creations in the mid-1890s and thereafter.[30]

Throughout his career, Beman was an affable, dependable, hardworking, solid citizen of the Chicago architectural establishment. He lived the quiet, reserved existence of the middle-class Victorian professional man. His role in the city's building history was one of occasional innovator, highly

competent follower, and prolific exporter. His forte was versatility, the ability to turn out an impressive array of residences, factories, commercial blocks, skyscrapers, railroad stations, exposition buildings, and churches.

Quite properly many essays in this volume emphasize (in some cases for the first time) the French and German influences in Chicago's architecture. Beman knew of, and occasionally tapped, these design resources. Given his family background, however, his apprenticeship with Upjohn and Upjohn, the ancestry and aesthetics of many of his clients (Anglophiles such as George Pullman), and his frequent travels abroad, his own interaction was largely with British architecture. S. S. Beman's work, like that of, say, Isaac Scott and Howard Van Doren Shaw, reminds us of an established and continuing stream of Anglo-American architecture in the Chicago building story.[31] In his long (1870-1914) and productive career, Beman both drew upon this design vocabulary and cultural ethos and contributed to the dissemination of its influence.

Fig. 21 Beman, Pabst Building, East Wisconsin Avenue at Water Street, Milwaukee, 1891 (demolished); from Inland Architect and News Record 17, 2 (1891).

Fig. 22 Beman, Market Hall, Pullman, 1881 (demolished).

Fig. 23 Beman, Market Hall, Pullman, 1894 (partially demolished).

Fig. 24 Beman, Blackstone Memorial Library, 4904 South Lake Park Avenue, 1901-02; from Inland Architect and News Record 43, 3 (1904).

NOTES

1   See the report in S. S. Beman, Architectural Scrapbooks, Beman Manuscripts, Chicago Historical Society, p. 14.

2   Montgomery Schuyler, "Glimpses of Western Architecture: Chicago," in *American Architecture and Other Writings,* ed. William H. Jordy and Ralph Coe (Cambridge, Mass., 1961), vol. 1, pp. 265-66; "Address by Mr. Louis Sullivan, June 8, 1915," Louis H. Sullivan Manuscripts, Chicago Historical Society, p. 1; John Root, "Architects of Chicago," first printed in *America* 5 (Dec. 11, 1890), n. pag., reprinted in *Inland Architect* 16 (Jan. 1891), pp. 91-92, and in Donald Hoffmann, *The Architecture of John Wellborn Root* (Baltimore, Md., 1973), p. 236.

3   As one of his own draftsmen, Irving K. Pond, later noted, Beman apparently had a significant role in directing the actual construction of the building as well as "being charged at the same time with the cause of the local draughting." Irving K. Pond, "Pullman: America's First Planned Industrial Town," *Illinois Society of Architects Monthly Bulletin* (June-July 1934), p. 6.

4   S. S. Beman came to know George Pullman through Nathan Barrett. In 1874 Pullman had built Fairlawn, a spacious Queen Anne vacation retreat at Long Branch, a New Jersey shore resort that also included fashionable "summer cottage" residences designed by McKim, Mead, and White, Leopold Eidlitz, and Richard Morris Hunt. In the spring of 1879, he enlisted Barrett to landscape the property. On one of his expeditions to Long Branch, Barrett brought along Beman, who met the palace-car magnate. Beman sufficiently impressed Pullman to be invited out to Chicago to advise him in remodeling his Second Empire mansion on Prairie Avenue. Thus began a thirty-year architect-client relationship in which Beman designed practically everything Pullman wanted built.

5   See contemporary evaluations: Mrs. Duane Doty, *The Town of Pullman* (Chicago, 1893); Richard T. Ely, "Pullman, A Social Study," *Harper's New Monthly Magazine* 70 (Feb. 1885), pp. 452-66; Charles H. Eaton, "Pullman, A Social Experiment," *To-Day* 2, 1 (Jan. 1895), pp. 1-9. Among more recent appraisals, see Stanley Buder, *Pullman, An Experiment in Industrial Order and Community Planning, 1880-1930* (New York, 1967); Norbert J. Pointner, "Pullman: A New Town Takes Shape on the Illinois Prairie," *Historic Preservation* 22, 2 (Apr.-June 1970), pp. 26-35; Marie Christine Gaungneux, "Pullman City:

Une Cosmogonie Moderne," *Architecture, Mouvement, Continuité* 35 (Apr. 1974), pp. 122-28; William T.W. Morgan, "The Pullman Experiment in Review," *Journal of the American Institute of Planners* 20 (1954), pp. 27-29; Robert M. Lillibridge, "Pullman: Town Development in the Era of Eclecticism," *Journal of the Society of Architectural Historians* 12 (1953), pp. 17-22.

6 British industrial town builders have been studied by Colin and Rose Bell, *City Fathers: The Early History of Town Planning in Britain* (London, 1869); R. S. Fitton and H. P. Wadsworth, *The Strutts and Arkwrights, 1785-1883* (Manchester, England, 1958); and I. A. Williams, *The Firm of Cadbury, 1821-1931* (London, 1931). For an overview, see John Nelson Tarn, "Housing Reform and the Emergence of Town Planning in Britain before 1914," in *The Rise of Modern Urban Planning, 1800-1914*, ed. Anthony Sutcliffe (London, 1980), pp. 78-80.

7 "Sir Titus Salt," *Bradford Observer* 1 (1874), pp. 1-13; A. Holroyd, *Saltaire and Its Founder: Sir Titus Salt, Bart* (Bradford, England, 1873), n. pag.; J. M. Richards, "Sir Titus Salt; or, the Lord of Saltaire," *Architectural Review* 80 (Nov. 1936), pp. 213-18; Jack Reynolds, *Saltaire: An Introduction to the Village of Sir Titus Salt* (Bradford, England, 1976). On the town planning and architecture of Saltaire, see Robert Dewhurst, "Saltaire," *The Town Planning Review* 31, 2 (July 1960), pp. 135-44; R. Druiff, "Saltaire: Pioneer Factory Village," *Town and Country Planning* (May 1965); Henry Russell Hitchcock, *Early Victorian Architecture in Britain*, vol. 1 (New Haven, Conn., 1954), pp. 460-62.

8 Buder (note 5), p. 36, credits Pullman with twice reading the 1870 social novel set in a British industrial town as early as 1872. On Pullman and Saltaire, see Irving K. Pond, "Autobiography," ch. 5, I. K. Pond Manuscripts, William Clements Library, University of Michigan, pp. 2, 20; Pond (note 3), pp. 6-7; and Bessie L. Pierce, ed., *As Others See Us: Impressions of Visitors, 1673-1933* (Chicago, 1933), pp. 263-74.

9 Despite the similarities between Saltaire and Pullman – spatial plans and architectural design that reinforced values such as order, sobriety, efficiency, cleanliness, and social/economic mobility – there were marked differences as well. Both Salt and Pullman had their architects build churches, schools, and a library for their towns; but the attitude of George Pullman was that the company always had to make a minimum profit of eight percent, the town had to return six percent, and only those services that would be profitable would be provided. Sir Titus, however, being much more of a humanitarian, provided health care for his employees as well as retirement benefits, services that Pullman considered unprofitable. Sir Titus also sold vacant lots to workers who wished to build their own homes, something George Pullman felt would spoil "his town."

10 "A Visit to the States," *London Times*, article 29 (Oct. 21, 1887), article 30 (Oct. 24, 1887).

11 Budgett Meakin, *Model Factories and Villages: Ideal Conditions of Labour and Housing* (Philadelphia, Penn., 1905), pp. 285-89.

12 Quoted in Stanley Buder, "The Model Town of Pullman: Town Planning and Social Control in the Gilded Age," *Journal of the American Institute of Planners* 33 (Jan. 1967), p. 3.

13 Paul de Rousiers, *American Life*, trans. A. J. Herbertson (Paris, 1892), pp. 172-73.

14 Almont Lindsey, *The Pullman Strike: The Story of A Unique Experiment and of a Great Labor Upheaval* (Chicago, 1942), p. 57; "Visitor's Register for the Town of Pullman," Pullman Collection, Pullman Branch Library, Chicago, Illinois.

15 *Pullman Journal* (Feb. 6, 1897), p. 5, and (June 19, 1897) p. 5.

16 Ely (note 5); Meakin (note 11), p. 388.

17 *A Holiday at Rosalie Villas* (Chicago, 1888), n. pag.

18 Jean F. Block, *Hyde Park Houses: An Informal History, 1856-1910* (Chicago, 1978), p. 42; Gwendolyn Wright, *Moralism and the Model Home: Domestic Architecture and Cultural Conflict in Chicago, 1873-1913* (Chicago, 1980), pp. 74-76.

19 *American Architect and Building News* (Feb. 4, 1899), p. 39 and pl. 1206.

20 Thomas J. Schlereth, "Solon Spencer Beman, 1853-1914: The Social History of A Midwest Architect," *Chicago Architectural Journal* 5 (Dec. 1985), pp. 16-22.

21 Hugh Morrison, *Louis Sullivan: Prophet of Modern Architecture* (New York, 1935), p. 59.

22 Thomas E. Tallmadge, *Architecture in Old Chicago* (Chicago, 1941), p. 146.

23 *Inland Architect* 3, 1 (Feb. 1884), p. 6; 3, 4 (May 1884), p. 47; *Building News* (Apr. 11, 1884).

24 On Beman and Root, see Rand McNally, *Bird's-Eye Views and Guide to Chicago* (Chicago, 1883), pp. 154-55, and Tallmadge (note 22), pp. 144-45.

25 Schuyler (note 2), pp. 265-66.

26 *British Architect* (Jan. 29, 1886).

27 David Hanks, "Chicago and the Midwest," in *The Arts and Crafts Movement in America*, ed. Robert Judson Clark (Princeton, 1972), pp. 57-58.

28 Carl W. Condit, *The Chicago School of Architecture: A History of Commercial and Public Building in the Chicago Area, 1875-1925* (Chicago, 1964), p. 145.

29 For a selected checklist of Beman's major buildings and projects, see Schlereth (note 20), pp. 29-31.

30 Schlereth (note 20).

31 For other scholarly assessments of the Anglo-American tradition in Chicago architecture, see particularly this volume's essays by Elaine Harrington and Richard Guy Wilson.

International Influences on Henry Hobson Richardson's Glessner House

Elaine Harrington

"Richardson's finest urban residence" is how architectural historian James O'Gorman has characterized the South Side Chicago house designed by Henry Hobson Richardson (1838-1886) for industrialist John Jacob Glessner (1843-1936).[1] But before we turn to the house and its furnishings, both showing evidence of more than one influence from abroad, it is useful to look briefly at the prior development of the city and at selected examples of earlier residential architecture.

Chicagoans have long provided their architects with challenging design problems and opportunities to create comfortable and fashionable dwellings. At no time was this more evident than during the last quarter of the nineteenth century, when Chicago's leading entrepreneurs, department store owners, meat-packers, lumber dealers, agricultural implement manufacturers, and other business-

men commissioned large residences expressive of their achievements and ambition. Not surprisingly, many of these residences demonstrated the European traditions of architecture that prevailed on the East Coast (from which most early Chicagoans had come) and the European architectural training and heritage that new immigrants brought with them directly to the city.

Before the Great Fire of 1871, the three branches (main, north, and south) of the Chicago River shaped the urban development, both residential and commercial, of the city. For many reasons, including the location of the terminus of the Illinois and Michigan Canal and, later, of the various railroads coming into Chicago, the central business district, known as the Loop, emerged in the area south of the main branch and east of the south branch of the river. First called the Loop after a

Fig. 1 Henry Hobson Richardson, detail of front entrance to J. J. Glessner House, 1800 South Prairie Avenue, 1885-87; photo by George Glessner, c. 1888.

Fig. 2 Architect unknown, Henry B. Clarke House, 1836; now located at 1855 South Indiana Avenue.

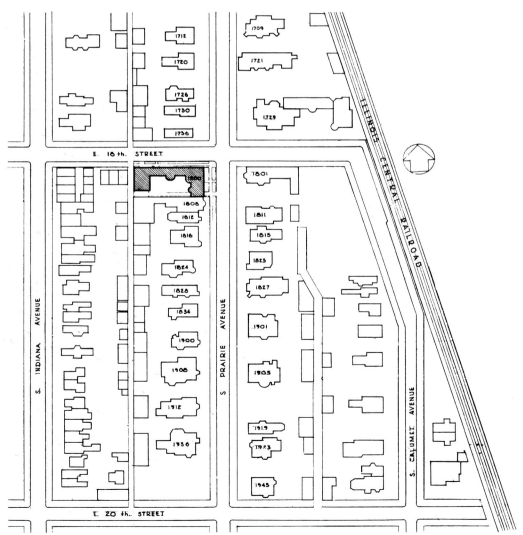

Fig. 3 Michigan Avenue looking north, 1863, with a view of Michigan Terrace designed by W. W. Boyington. Engraved by Raoul Varin after a view by Edwin Whitefield, published by A. Ackermann and Son, 1929.

Fig. 4 Site plan of Prairie Avenue from Historic American Buildings Survey. *Among the residences on Prairie Avenue near the Glessner House were 1729, Pullman House (J. M. Dunphy, 1873; Palm House and stable added by S. S. Beman, 1892); 1801, W. W. Kimball House (Beman, 1889-90); 1811, Coleman-Ames House (Cobb and Frost, 1886-90); 1905, Marshall Field House (Richard Morris Hunt, 1871-73).*

Fig. 5 *Richard Morris Hunt, interior of library of Marshall Field House, 1905 South Prairie Avenue, 1871-73 (demolished).*

Fig. 6 *Burnham and Root, Max A. Meyer House, 2009 Prairie Avenue, 1888 (now demolished); from Paul Graef,* Neubauten in Nordamerika *(Berlin, 1897-1905).*

circuit of horse-drawn streetcars of the 1850s, the area developed further following the erection of the Union Loop Elevated Railroad in 1897.

The Chicago River and its branches had defined the city's development from the outset. Traffic flowing into and out of the Loop from the early residential areas to the west and north had to pass through the tunnels and over the bridges of the main and south branches. As river traffic increased, land traffic was frequently delayed, especially because the pivot mechanism used by most of the bridges often failed to function properly. This encouraged the growth of a residential district on the South Side, which offered faster access to the Loop.[2]

Early residences on the South Side included the Greek Revival house of the Henry B. Clarke family (fig. 2) and the Italianate Terrace Row on South Michigan Avenue designed by architect W. W. Boyington (fig. 3). The Clarke House is now the city's oldest surviving residence and a fine example of the Greek Revival architecture that prevailed in the country from the 1820s through the 1850s. Indeed, Henry B. and Caroline Clarke were early settlers in Chicago in 1835 and brought with them a taste for homes in this style from New York State. These designs made direct reference to the democratic ideals associated with classical Greece and that country's nineteenth-century struggle for independence. Americans felt passionate about both. While the architect is unknown, the house displays

NEUBAUTEN IN NORDAMERIKA.

Architekten: Burnham und Root, Chicago.

Erbaut 1888.

CHICAGO, Illinois.

Wohnhaus Max Mayer an der Prairie-Avenue.

Fig. 7 Pre-19th-century building outside the walls of Abingdon Abbey, England; photograph was owned by the Glessner family.

Fig. 8 Richardson, Glessner House, 18th Street facade.

Fig. 7 Pre-19th-century building outside the walls of Abingdon Abbey, England; photograph was owned by the Glessner family.

Fig. 8 Richardson, Glessner House, 18th Street facade.

Greek-derived detail typical of nineteenth-century carpenters' pattern book designs.³

The eleven attached Terrace Row townhouses of 1856 show another early international influence fashionable in the 1840s and 1850s, the Italianate, distinguished by brackets under the eaves and classical round-arched window headings. The space-saving, attached design of these houses was the architect's response to their central location in the rapidly growing city. Located on South Michigan Avenue between Congress and Harrison streets (now the site of the Congress Hotel), Terrace Row attracted well-to-do residents seeking the convenience of ready access to the heart of the city. In contrast, the Clarke home, with its broad porticoed facade, was a country house built by an upper-middle-class family. Later the city grew around it.

As early as the 1860s a scattering of modest houses appeared close to Lake Michigan on what would become Prairie Avenue (fig. 4), two miles south of the Loop. Wealthy families turned to this

Fig. 9 Courtyard of Glessner House; photo by George Glessner, c. 1888.

area after their North and West Side residences had been destroyed by the Great Fire. The site was all the more attractive because it was not covered with rubble and debris like the fire-wasted land to the north. Moreover, the area south of the Loop along the lake was a popular residential location for businessmen because they could reach their offices in the Loop quickly without having to cross the river. Within a decade, Prairie Avenue, transformed by arching elm trees, had become "the sunny street that holds the sifted few." It would remain a choice residential area up to World War I.[4]

Among the most striking residences built on Prairie Avenue, at the southwest corner of 18th Street, was Glessner House, designed by the Boston architect H. H. Richardson for the Glessner family in 1886 (figs. 1, 10). Both in its exterior and interior features, it was and remained distinct in every way from the other substantial residences on the street. Its highly individual character perhaps can be most clearly appreciated when it is compared to some of the neighboring homes on Prairie Avenue, above all the 1873 residence designed by Richard Morris Hunt (1827-1896) for Marshall Field, Chicago's leading merchant.

By 1871, Hunt, the first American to train at the Ecole des Beaux-Arts in Paris, headed the busiest architectural firm in New York, known for its noteworthy commercial buildings. In the late 1860s Hunt began to design ornate mansions for wealthy clients in New York City, as well as along the Hudson River, in Boston, and in Newport.

The Prairie Avenue home for the Field family, one of the first on the street, was under construction at the time of the Chicago Fire and was completed in 1873. The house was designed by Hunt in the French Second Empire style, its flat red brick panels set off by sandstone horizontal divisions at foundation, stringcourse, and cornice, with vertical emphasis given by the sandstone-framed windows. The metal balconies at second-floor level reinforced the French aspect of the house. Its mansard roof set a tone and theme that would be followed by many other architects and clients on the street. Indeed, several existing homes on Prairie Avenue and nearby were soon remodeled and given new raised mansard roofs.[5]

On the interior, French style mixed with other furnishings of the day. For example, Second Empire and French Renaissance chairs were used in

Fig. 10 Richardson, Glessner House; photo by George Glessner, c. 1888.

the Fields' library (fig. 5), which had an English style fireplace with tiles under the mantle and a stained art glass panel above. It is of paramount importance to realize, however, that in their American incarnations these styles differed quite considerably from the various originals that inspired them.[6]

Later residences quoted even more directly from the French, with references to historic chateaux. While some social historians have questioned the appropriateness of building chateaux in an American industrial city, in their time they were seen as fitting settings for the lives of successful entrepreneurs who were the American equivalents of European aristocracy.

The Chicago architectural firm of Burnham and Root turned to yet another European source – the Flemish – for inspiration for the townhouse they designed in 1888 at 2009 Prairie Avenue for the Max A. Meyer family (fig. 6). Its decorated front entrance derives from the French Flamboyant Gothic.[7] A contemporary street-scape depicts the building flanked by typical Prairie Avenue neighbors – a mid-century Italianate on the left and a three-storied mansard on the right (pl. 28). The following year the firm would design a handsome, small, French style chateau with finialed dormers (cat. no. 72) at 434 Elm Street on the North Side for William J. Goudy.

A larger-scaled chateauesque limestone mansion was built at 1801 Prairie Avenue in 1890 for

piano and organ magnate W. W. Kimball. Designed by architect Solon S. Beman, it featured external elements, including a carved gable and front door frame, drawn from the Chateau de Josselin in Brittany (see Schlereth, fig. 5).[8] Oak paneling, featuring angels' heads and other carved decorations in sixteenth-century Francis I style, dominated the first-floor interiors.

The individuality of Richardson's adaptations of European elements in the Glessner house is all the more striking in light of the direct stylistic importations by the architects of the surrounding houses. Hunt and Richardson differed in their approaches both to buildings and clients: Hunt provided his clients with as large and exquisite a French chateau or Second Empire style mansion as they desired, while Richardson gave his clients a building that met their needs and simultaneously reflected his own aesthetic.[9] He combined elements and characteristics from French and English buildings he admired into a new whole with the intention of creating a new American architecture. As a contemporary English writer noted, "[He] represented all that was noblest, most original, and most hopeful in American architecture."[10] Writing some years later, an American critic maintained that the "power of simplification and unification...was the essential gift of Richardson, and which was quite independent of his fondness for Romanesque detail, for exaggerated voussoirs [the stones of an arch] and dwarfed columns."[11]

Commissioned in 1885, designed in 1886, and completed in 1887, the house for the Glessner family gave Richardson the opportunity to realize his ideas in a residence that was highly modern for its time. Complex ideas of plan and space are integrated with aspects of several historic styles. These are likely to have been drawn from a variety of sources, especially Richardson's travels and his extensive library. One might see a connection, for example, between the Southern French Romanesque aspect of the massive front and side entrance arches of the Glessners' house and the architect's student tours of Paris and its environs in the 1860s and his 1882 travels on the Continent. In a similar vein, some of the stone details on the exterior of Glessner House evoke the spirit of details found in Henri Revoil's *Architecture romane du midi de la France* (1873), which Richardson is known to have owned.[12] Richardson's ability to absorb and transform, rather than copy, elements from other sources contributed to the power and impact of his work.

The entire 18th Street elevation derived from a picturesque English structure, built much like a great English barn, located just outside the Abbey walls in Abingdon, near Oxford (figs. 7, 8). John Glessner reported that when Richardson visited the Glessners in 1885 to discuss the design of their prospective home he noticed "a small colored photograph of Abingdon Abbey" in the library. Turning to Frances Glessner (1848-1932), the architect asked, "Do you like that?" When she replied in the affirmative, he responded, "Yes? Then I'll make that the key note to your home. Give it to me, please."[13] Although the plan remained relatively fixed following this meeting, the elevations of the house received several refinements. A gable over the entrance disappeared, the roof lines of the Prairie Avenue and 18th Street facades were resolved, and a complex window for the major stair was simplified (pl. 29; cat. no. 66).

So impressed was Richardson with what he saw on his 1882 European tour, he later confided to Glessner, that he "wanted to send for Norcross his builder and Evans his stone carver to show them some really good work" from these early buildings seen on his travels.[14] O. W. Norcross and John Evans, who were based in Massachusetts, maintained a long association with Richardson, and both were involved with the building of Glessner House — the Norcross firm as general contractor, and Evans as carver of stone details, including the interlace of acanthus leaves in the arch over the front door. While the exterior of the house appears plain and massive, it actually features a good deal of restrained ornament in cut granite.

The main facade on elegant Prairie Avenue, with

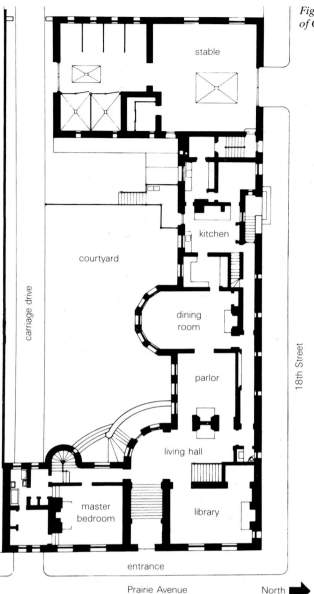

Fig. 11 First-floor plan of Glessner House.

its apparent New England five-bay width and center entrance, is balanced but not symmetrical, as an additional width is part of the building at the south end, with the porte-cochère at grade and dressing rooms on the first and second floors. The windows fronting on Prairie Avenue are larger than those on the subsidiary 18th Street facade, where the narrow windows provide light to the service passage but are small, to keep out cold and noise. At second floor level on both facades, decorative column capitals with acanthus and geometric designs — each one different from the next — enrich the window openings of the principal rooms. From the ground to shoulder height the walls are battered, although this treatment is halted at the servants' arched door on the side.

The rough-hewn granite of the exterior is from Milford, Massachusetts, and has a delicate pink-gray color. The tonal harmony continues with red-

Fig. 12 Interior of J. J. Glessner home on 261 West Washington Street, showing Isaac E. Scott bookcase, c. 1879.

brick-colored mortar and the terracotta of the roof tiles. (The building was carefully cleaned in 1984, so the original granite color and surface with mica and feldspar flecks can once again be appreciated.) Richardson specified that above the pink-gray granite of the batter of the foundation there should be a rough-cut pink marble for the remainder of the facade. It appears, however, that the Glessners had reservations about the marble, and after Richardson's death in 1886, they chose to use granite for the entire facade.[15]

A clinker-fired Chicago common brick, with limestone window sills and lintels, gives the courtyard facade a more informal aspect. There are three curved projections enclosing a spiral staircase, the entrance from the courtyard to the house, and the bay of the dining room with the conservatory above. The windows onto the courtyard are generous in size and number, and the courtyard attic dormer windows have jerkin head gables, a roof window treatment used in French country buildings (fig. 9).

It is not just the exterior appearance of Glessner House that makes it architecturally important, but also its innovative floor plan and how well it func-

tioned in both horizontal and vertical zones. Designed both for small family groupings and for large entertainments, the house was organized around the inner courtyard on the south. Richardson put large windows there, he said, so that "the sun would...pour in."[16] This was important in Chicago's latitude, as this structure was the family's residence for six months of the year. From May to October the Glessners lived in their summer home, The Rocks, in New Hampshire.

The interior of the south half of the Prairie Avenue portion of the house was taken up with the family's own rooms: the schoolroom at grade with a door to the courtyard; the master bedroom and dressing rooms on the first floor, with the two children's bedrooms directly overhead – all three levels communicating with a spiral stairway. The curved wall in the first-floor living hall encouraged the visitor to turn to the right upon entering the house from the broad entrance stair.

Richardson arranged the public rooms of the house along the 18th Street spine of the house, with the library in the corner, then the parlor and dining room facing the sunny courtyard, and the kitchen rooms beyond. A large attached coach house, the bulk of which extended along the alley at the back of the site, helped create the private courtyard. On both the first and second floors along the 18th Street north wall, servants' passages allowed the everyday life of the house to run smoothly and provided a buffer against the cold Chicago winter wind and the noise and dirt from the side street. The windowless north wall of the house next door created the southern edge of the Glessners' courtyard (fig. 11).

The architectural significance of Glessner House lies in its resolution of issues that challenged architects of the time. With great sophistication Richardson's design for Glessner House synthesized many of the basic attributes of modern architecture: a zoned plan, interrelated space, integrity of material, and coherence of expression. Its unusual appearance made it a topic of conversation at the time of its construction, but it is of larger interest to the history of American residential architecture because its architect and its design link the house to the beginnings of the modern movement.

Richardson was striving to make an urban house for an American family whose tastes and enjoyments paralleled his own – a love of music, books, fine dinners, and good company. On his 1882 tour of Britain and the Continent, Richardson had met some of the leading figures of the English Arts and Crafts movement.[17] His enthusiasm for their work, particularly that of William Morris and William

DeMorgan, was shared by his clients, as the interior of their house on Prairie Avenue would show.

Richardson died April 27, 1886, after the design for the house had been finished. In the course of the design work, the two families had become friends. John Glessner recalled, "From what he [Richardson] told me and what his young men said afterwards, I am convinced that this house of ours is the one of all that he built that he would have liked most to live in himself."[18] The completion of the house was carefully overseen by the architects in Richardson's successor firm, Shepley, Rutan and Coolidge.[19] The Norcross Brothers, generally regarded as the first general contracting firm in the country, were responsible for construction.

Interior

Like their architect, the Glessners were interested in the Aesthetic and Arts and Crafts movements, which grew out of English social and artistic reforms.[20] The Glessners' interest in these movements had been stimulated by lectures on art, especially after they met Isaac E. Scott (1845-1920) at one of them in 1875. A designer of buildings, furniture, and decorative accessories, Scott was a highly accomplished craftsman, particularly well known for his skill as a carver. In the same year they ordered their first piece of furniture from him, a large bookcase, Modern Gothic in style, which looked much like the designs of English tastemakers Charles Locke Eastlake and Bruce J. Talbert (pl. 32). Architectural in character, the walnut piece had a Gothic roof line and was embellished with cameo carving in holly and ebonized wood, a technique perfected by Scott and other furniture designers in Chicago.[21]

Two years later, the Glessners hired Scott to make improvements to the interiors of their Italianate home on Chicago's West Side at 261 West Washington Boulevard. Scott went on to make many pieces of furniture for the family, including most of the furniture in the master bedroom,[22] and some forty picture frames, as well as mantlepieces, ceramics, metalwork, and, later, embroidery designs. On the back of one of the picture frames from this period appeared Scott's stamp: Isaac E. Scott/Medieval/Wood and Metal Worker/Chicago, Ill.[23]

Scott constructed most of these furnishings of solid walnut. He ornamented them with carvings, both stylized and naturalistic, using a vocabulary of leaf and flower designs, accented with birds and reptiles in high relief. He also used floral, avian, and reptilian designs on the ceramics he made for

Fig. 13 Peter B. Wight, interior of the library of Eliphalet W. Blatchford House, 375 North LaSalle Street, 1875 (demolished).

the family at the Chelsea Keramic Works near Boston in 1879. He had formerly been a modeler of terracotta ornament and sculpture at the Chicago Terra Cotta Company.[24] Scott's work indicates familiarity with English aesthetic motifs as well as with design of Japanese origin. Although he was in business with architect Frederick W. Copeland from 1873 to 1875, according to the entries in the Glessner family journals they dealt only with Scott.[25] Even though the Glessners commissioned no more major pieces from Scott after they engaged Richardson to design their house, he remained a friend and frequent guest of the family until his death.[26]

During the 1870s and 1880s the Glessners continued in their quest for knowledge about English design and added many volumes to their library — often in the American editions — by Eastlake, Talbert, and William Morris, as well as *The House Beautiful* by American tastemaker Clarence Cook. They followed a certain pattern in enlarging their interest. After their initial introduction to a field, idea, or form, they pursued the subject by reading, by attending lectures, and by acquiring examples of the type. It was during this period that they bought

Fig. 14 Living hall of Glessner House; photo by George Glessner, c. 1888.

Fig. 15 Library of Glessner House in 1923.

many books on Japanese art and life, having acquired a large piece of Kutani ware in green tones in the 1870s. They displayed this piece on top of the large Scott bookcase in their library.

Examination of this room (fig. 12) in their earlier house on Washington Boulevard reveals a smaller bookcase by Scott, over which hangs the ebonized frame that carried his stamped label, a library table made by him, an ebonized chair and a Windsor chair, oriental carpets on the floor, and decorative wallpaper treatments on the walls and ceilings. The mixture of the English-derived Scott pieces and the Japanese ceramic and Japanesque ebonized wood, combined with a gesture toward the Colonial Revival[27] in the form of the Windsor chair, suggests the already rich and inclusive interests and tastes of the Glessners. These would be further expanded after 1886 in the furnishing of their more famous Prairie Avenue home.

The range of Scott's work from interior architectural elements through furniture, picture frames, ceramics, and embroidery suggests that the Glessners may have come to share his concern for the whole environment, from dwelling to dinner napkin — an approach that would come to full fruition in their relationship with Richardson and his firm. It appears that after they met Richardson the Glessners ordered no further large pieces from Scott, though he created some handsome embroidery designs for them. At any rate, no large piece of Scott furniture appeared in the principal receiving rooms — living hall, library, parlor, and dining room — of their new home.

Another example of a comprehensively designed Chicago interior contemporary with the Glessners' Washington Boulevard home was Peter Bonnet Wight's "Ulmenheim" (pl. 6) built for Eliphalet W. Blatchford, a prominent lead manufacturer, at 375 North LaSalle Street. Of particular interest is the library, for which Wight designed bookcases in the Eastlake taste (fig. 13).[28] While the Blatchford library is larger than the Glessners', the two represent similar aims in the creation of a unified space. There is a further connection between Scott and Wight in that furniture designs by Wight, as well as by architect William Le Baron Jenney, were executed in Scott and Copeland's workshop during the 1870s.[29]

The Glessners moved into their new home on December 1, 1887. In decorating and furnishing it they blended their Isaac Scott pieces in Modern Gothic with new furniture commissioned elsewhere. Clarence Cook's *House Beautiful* was clearly much consulted.[30] The predominant tone of the

interior, however, was set by the profusion of Arts and Crafts fabrics, wallpapers, fireplace tiles, lamps, chairs, ceramics, and embroideries from William Morris's firm in England.

Some of the major functional furniture for the principal first-floor rooms was designed by Charles Coolidge and Francis Bacon (1856-1940) and made by the A. H. Davenport Company (1880-1908). Coolidge was responsible for the Colonial Revival oak library table and oak dining room chairs (cat. no. 70), a blend of Colonial Revival and American Arts and Crafts. Bacon, earlier employed in Richardson's office, had become chief designer for Davenport and was responsible for the Glessners' hall chairs in the Arts and Crafts manner and the Steinway piano case. This furniture merged with Scott's pieces and the ebonized Japanesque chairs from the Herter Brothers (1865-1905) in New York.

It was altogether a very artistic mix and a distinct contrast to the furnishings favored by most of the Glessners' neighbors. The firm of A. H. Davenport had provided assistance in the decoration of the George M. Pullman House diagonally across the street from the Glessners', and the Herter Brothers had assisted with the decoration of the Marshall Field House close by on Prairie Avenue, as well as

with that of the castle that Potter Palmer had built on the Near North Side. The general interior appearance of these houses was in the mode of the French eighteenth century.

The difference between the interior character of the Glessner house and its neighbors can perhaps be attributed to the influence of Cook's *House Beautiful*. Many of the decorative elements used in the house, including the picture rails, embroidered hangings created by the William Morris workshop, Japanese ceramics, and newly popular American antiques, were highly recommended by Cook, who was also a strong advocate of the kind of Modern Gothic furniture made by Scott and the type of Anglo-Japanese art furniture that the Glessners purchased from the Herter Brothers.

Visitors to the Glessners' house were first ushered into what was known as the "living hall" (fig. 14; pl. 30) emulating the generous space to be found in English country homes. The fine quarter-sawn oak paneling was highlighted by terracotta red in the plastered horizontal wall space above the plate rail and by a light yellow-buff painted ceiling. In addition to the very large Morris Hammersmith rug in tones of red and blue,[31] the highly patterned portières were of a Morris woven woolen called Peacock and Dragon. This textile is significant be-

Fig. 16 Parlor, or living room, of Glessner House in 1923.

Fig. 17 Dining room of Glessner House in 1923.

Fig. 18 Master bedroom of Glessner House; photo by George Glessner, c. 1888.

cause it is of the same pattern as the cloth that hung in front of two alcoves flanking the fireplace in Richardson's own library in Brookline, Massachusetts, where the Glessners had sat as they talked over the plans for their house with their architect.

Indeed, the library in the Glessners' new home looked much more like Richardson's, with its fireplace, beamed ceiling, built-in bookcases at shoulder height, and massive library table, than it did like the library of the Glessners' former home (fig. 15). The new oak library table designed by Coolidge featured large drawers at each end within the apron of the piece, providing storage for the etchings and engravings the Glessners collected.

Adjacent to the library and over the front door was a small alcove lined with cork for the display of these prints. Richardson's own bedroom had walls covered in cork, convenient for pinning up architectural plans and drawings when he worked in that room (as he often did toward the end of his life).[32]

Other furnishings in the library included two Herter Brothers' armchairs and, by 1923, a table lamp by W. A. S. Benson (c. 1890) from the Morris Company. A small Morris Hammersmith carpet lay in front of the fireplace, and Morris woven wool draperies with a Bird and Vine pattern on a terracotta background hung at the front windows over matching window-seat cushions. The book-

shelves displayed many ceramics, including Japanese pieces,[33] and a splendid Gallé vase in tones of red and gold caught the light in the narrow window facing north. The books stored and used here supported the Glessners' many shared interests in the visual arts and music; the wild flowers, beekeeping, and cooking that were important to Frances Glessner; the Chicago imprints that interested John Glessner as a member of the Caxton Club; and the biographies, novels, and travel books that formed family reading. Several books in the Glessners' library dealt with color theory and had been read by Mrs. Glessner in 1883 and, later, in 1887, when she was preparing to decorate her new home.[34]

On the other side of the living hall from the library was the parlor, which in 1887 had yellow flowered wallpaper; rose and pale orange draperies of woven damask, called Kennett, from the Morris Company; and embroidered silk hangings in delicate colors against a sea-foam-color background as portières at the doorways on either side of the fireplace. The embroidery design was from the Morris firm, and possibly embroidered by Mrs. Glessner or the Chicago Decorative Arts Society.[35] The parlor in which the concert parlor grand Steinway (with its mahogany case designed by Francis Bacon) had been installed also served as

a music room. Mrs. Glessner played the piano, and so did many guest artists of the Chicago Symphony who were entertained by the family, including Ignace Paderewski and Fannie Bloomfield Zeisler. The Glessners were early supporters of the Symphony, and musical entertainments were often held in their house.

In 1893, the Glessners remodeled their parlor (fig. 16). They had Englishman William Pretyman, the Chief of Color of the World's Columbian Exposition, change the wall treatment from flowered yellow paper to a burlap stenciled in metallic colors. They also replaced the milky optic glass lampshades on the brass sconces in this room with pearlescent shell shades that took on rich colors when lit.

The oak paneling in the dining room (fig. 17; pl. 31) determined its Colonial Revival character. The Coolidge-designed oak chairs, with acanthus carving on the two armchairs, owed their overall

configuration to the same American Windsor chair sources as Richardson's earlier designs for library chairs, but featured a lighter Chippendale line in the crest rail that presaged the Art Nouveau (cat. no. 70). The dining room table, which had been rectangular in the Glessners' former home, was now a large round one. Richardson did not like extension tables and had a black oak oval dining table in his own dining room which John Glessner enjoyed. This may have influenced the Glessners' choice of table shape and size. There was also a smaller table in the room. A clearer link with their architect's house is the plate rail, much like one in Richardson's dining room, described by Glessner as follows:

There was a narrow shelf running around the walls, about 20 inches below the ceiling and less than six feet above the floor and this held a few rare plates and a number of iridescent [lustre] DeMorgan tiles, the gift of Mr. DeMorgan himself.[36]

Fig. 19 Second-floor living hall of Glessner House in 1923.

Fig. 20 Corner guest room of Glessner House; photo by George Glessner, c. 1888.

Fig. 21 Fanny Glessner's bedroom in 1923.

Above the plate rail was a compressed wallpaper of Japanese leather, paper stamped with a pattern, colored, and then gilded. The ceiling was gold leaf, a surface that would have made for handsome reflections from the wall sconces and table candles during a winter dinner. The fireplace surround was decorated with Isnik tiles purchased from Lockwood De Forest of New York. A photograph of this interior shows a tablecloth with embroidery designed by Scott. The pattern for this is dated 1894 and is one of several designs made up in white glossy pearl cotton on linen in tones of red and light blue.

The master bedroom, located to the left of the front door, completed the principal rooms on the first floor (fig. 18). In 1887 there were William DeMorgan tiles on the fireplace, purchased through the Morris Company, and the day bed at the foot of the master bed was covered in a pink and salmon-colored printed velvet from Thomas Wardle, Morris's silk dyer.[37] The wallpaper was a poppy pattern from the English firm of F. Arthur.[38] The major pieces here – the wardrobe, bookcase, bedstead, and mirrored dressing chest in Mrs. Glessner's dressing room – had been made by Isaac Scott for the family's former home. By 1923 the paper had been changed to the Morris Company pattern of Lily and Pomegranate, with Windrush-printed-cotton from the Morris firm used for the draperies, and an Acanthus pattern in three tones of red on the upholstered wing chair. A piece of Japanese obi sash fabric with applied European lace was used as a cover on the bedside stand.

The Glessners placed the large Scott bookcase in the upper living hall (fig. 19), complete with its large companion Kutani ware plate on top. The carpet was another Morris handwoven design, and the Colonial Revival chairs sported seat cushions covered in red Utrecht velvet from the Morris Company. Pictures and a French faience bowl, in frames carved by Scott, hung on the walls. By 1923, the oak paneling up to the chair rail and the oak woodwork framing a total of five doorways and five windows were accented by Morris draperies in the Bird and Vine pattern.

Photographs taken throughout the home in 1923 show changes in wallpaper and textile treatments since the initial decoration of the house in 1887. But the style remained consistently English in tone, with a strong inclination to William Morris patterns. The Morris theme prevailed in the corner guest bedroom in 1887 (fig. 20) with Rose and Thistle chintz at the windows, Sunflower wallpaper, and chair upholstery of African Marigold. The carpet is also attributed to Morris, one of the less expensive types marketed by his firm. A Scott pil-

grim vase was part of a display of ceramics on the mantle. By 1923, the draperies were Cherwell, a printed velveteen in gold and tan tones by the Morris Company, and the wallpaper was the firm's Double Bough.

In daughter Fanny's bedroom by 1923 (fig. 21), the wallpaper was Blossom from the Morris firm, with chairs and daybed covered in African Marigold. Son George's bedroom also had Morris Company wallpaper in 1887, namely in the Poppy pattern. Whatever the changes in the individual rooms, in wallpaper patterns, or in textiles, the interior of the Glessners' house was at all times rich with a variety of colors, textures, and treatments.

The Romanesque elements of Richardson's work influenced other residences in Chicago as well, including the Coleman-Ames House at 1811 Prairie Avenue designed by Henry Ives Cobb in 1890, and the Granger Farwell House at 1623 Prairie Avenue by Burnham and Root from around the same time.

The Colonial Revival influence evident in the interior woodwork and furniture of Glessner House also appeared elsewhere in Chicago, as in the mantle designed by the firm of Jenney and Mundie for the home of Mr. A. Poole at 89 Pine Street, on the North Side (c. 1890; cat. no. 74). This mantle featured paneled wood, an overmantle mirror, and ceramic tiles surrounding the fireplace opening.

The Classical Revival, distinguished by freely drawn classical proportion and ornamentation, gained influence in Chicago around the turn of the century. In 1901 the Glessners hired Shepley, Rutan and Coolidge to design two attached townhouses for their adult children in the block north of their Prairie Avenue house. The brick houses are Classical Revival in appearance and demonstrate the firm's direction away from the Romanesque forms that it had continued to favor in the early years after Richardson's death.[39]

The Glessners' preference for Arts and Crafts architecture persisted long after Richardson's death, as can be seen in the improvements they asked Shepley, Rutan and Coolidge to make on various buildings on their property, The Rocks, in New Hampshire. Isaac Scott had originally designed the main house in 1883, as well as barns, rustic gazebos, and a bee house. (In the same year he designed a commercial building in Chicago for John Glessner's business.) After the Glessners met Frederick Law Olmsted through Richardson, they asked him to lay out, landscape, and create scenic drives at The Rocks.

Several Arts and Crafts style buildings were erected on and near The Rocks through the Gless-

ner connection by Chicago architect Herman Von Holst (1874-1955) of Shepley, Rutan and Coolidge.[40] In 1904 Von Holst designed a shingled house for Mrs. Glessner's brother, George Macbeth, in a village near The Rocks (pl. 37). Called Glamis, it was distinguished by strong horizontal lines, a low-angled roof line, and overall use of shingles (fig. 22). Its site, opening up on mountain vistas, had been carefully chosen by Olmsted's son, Frederick Law Olmsted, Jr., who had been George Glessner's roommate at Harvard in 1890. Describing the house in a local newspaper for the benefit of his neighbors, Macbeth had explained that one should

make the house a part of the landscape, not an obtrusive part, not too conspicuous, a part of the earth and rocks around it, locate it thus, a long, not high, rambling house; it just fits in the trees and rocks. . . .

Von Holst did indeed create an organic design for his client, fitting it into the landscape. In Macbeth's words:

Von Holst joined the rooms together, put the windows to see out of, just right, utility within, to spare as much labor and care as possible, a place for the family and some friends.[41]

It was the standard rationale of the American house from Andrew Jackson Downing to Frank Lloyd Wright.

In 1906 Von Holst designed the first of several additions to The Rocks. A combination saw mill and pig pen, his initial effort there bore the hall-marks of Arts and Crafts styling, exemplified by the use of that movement's characteristic lettering on the front of the building. In 1907, Von Holst designed an addition to Scott's 1884 stone and shingle horse and carriage barn and, in 1908, a house for George Glessner. Situated on the Glessners' property, George's house, The Ledge, was characterized by Prairie School lines.

A graduate of the Massachusetts Institute of Technology in 1896, Von Holst worked in the Chicago office of Shepley, Rutan and Coolidge until he opened his own practice in Chicago in 1905. He taught architectural design at the Armour Institute and was known for his watercolor renderings. When Frank Lloyd Wright went to Europe in 1909, he contracted with Von Holst to take over his architectural practice in Oak Park until his return.[42] The work for the Macbeth and Glessner families in New Hampshire, accomplished early in Von Holst's career, forged a link from Richardson's legacy and firm to Frank Lloyd Wright.[43]

After Richardson's death, Romanesque ideas and ideals continued to surface in the work of other American architects, with mixed results. When Richardson's theories and examples were followed, emulating his own earlier search for a new American architecture, the results were impressive, as in Adler and Sullivan's Auditorium Building. But his ideas fell out of favor when unskilled imitators applied Romanesque decoration like so much crusty wallpaper to buildings of poor design.

Fig. 22 Herman Valentin Von Holst, George Macbeth House, "Glamis," Bethlehem, New Hampshire, 1904.

Richardson's works were published in American architectural journals, like the *American Architect.* This publication, which he himself edited in 1874 and 1875 under its former title, *New York Sketch-book,* featured heliotype photographs of Richardson's works through 1898.[44]

His work was noted as well in European publications, such as the German *Deutsche Bauzeitung* in 1892, the English *Magazine of Art* in 1894, and the Dutch *De Opmerker* in 1893 and 1896.[45] The Dutch architects H. P. Berlage and K. P. C. de Bazel seem to have been influenced by Richardson in their designs for the Amsterdam Stock Exchange (1898-1903), and a project for an Architects Association Building (1897), respectively.[46]

In England, the work of C. Harrison Townshend, especially the large arched opening of the Bishopsgate Institute of 1892 and the molded character of the tower of his Horniman Museum of 1896 (both in London), show Richardsonian elements, as does his Whitechapel Art Gallery of 1901 (also in London). The massing of the Congregational Church and School in London, by John Sulman, dating from 1880-82, and J. K. Kroeger's project for the Church of St. Jacob in Dresden, Germany, both recall the massing of Richardson's Trinity Church in Boston of 1872-77.[47]

In Finland, the romantic nationalism of the turn of the century, as seen in the architecture of Lars Sonck, shows direct application of Richardson's example. In Helsinki, the Eira Hospital of 1905, made of squared rubble granite and stucco, demonstrates kinship with Glessner House in its large entrance door arch, and in the rear court, where, sheltered by the two wings of the building, a rounded stair tower is to be found in a comparable location to the rounded stair tower in the Glessner courtyard.[48]

That the Glessner house was known abroad is suggested by a letter from the noted Italian archeologist Rodolfo Lanciani, who in 1890 thanked the Glessners for photographs of their house, noting "I like the style so much."[49]

The Glessners' houses, in Chicago and New Hampshire, reflected aspects of various European influences. Scott's work on the interior of the Washington Boulevard house showed strong English Arts and Crafts design. Their Richardson house on Prairie Avenue showed a masterful use of French Romanesque, English picturesque antecedents, and American Colonial Revival. The work Von Holst performed for the family in New Hampshire showed the full realization of American Arts and Crafts, drawn from the English Arts and Crafts movement and from Richardson's own work, as well as relating to the work of Wright. Not only did these architects bring international influences to the buildings they designed in America, but, in the case of Richardson, his creative use of these influences would travel back to Europe and would also inform the work of Sullivan, Wright, and Root in Chicago.

NOTES

1   Conversation with the author, October 1985.
2   By 1871 there were twenty-seven bridges and two tunnels (under Washington and LaSalle streets) in Chicago for vehicular traffic across the Chicago River. Bessie Louise Pierce, *A History of Chicago: Volume II, from Town to City, 1848-1871* (Chicago, 1940), pp. 322-23.
3   For more on the Greek Revival, see Talbot Hamlin, *Greek Revival Architecture in America* (Oxford, 1944; 2nd ed. New York, 1964).
4   Arthur Meeker, *Prairie Avenue* (New York, 1949), p. 3.
5   Paul R. Baker, *Richard Morris Hunt* (Cambridge, Mass., 1980), pp. 232-34.
6   Chicago residences tended to mirror the changes in architectural styles taking place in the country at large, often influenced by ideas from abroad, particularly France and England. It is helpful to know the style names used to characterize Chicago city residences either wholly or in part: Greek Revival, inspired by classical archeological sites, 1820-1850; Italianate, with classical decorations, 1840-1880; Stick style, with European wood antecedents, 1860-1880; Eastlake, with spindles and incised decorations as advocated by English designer Charles Locke Eastlake, 1870-1890; Renaissance styles of French and Italian derivation, in use from before the Civil War to the 1880s; Second Empire, of French origin, 1860-1890; High Victorian Gothic, with English-style polychromy stone work, 1860-1890; American Queen Anne, of English origin, 1875-1900; Colonial Revival, from America's own

heritage, 1885-1930; chateauesque, taken from French chateaux, 1870-1905; Romanesque, both Richardsonian and the Romanesque of southern France and Spain, 1870-1895; Shingle style from New England and England, and as adapted by Richardson, 1880-1895; Prairie style from Frank Lloyd Wright and his followers, 1895-1920; and the bungalow from India, by way of American Craftsman influence 1880-1940.
7   For more on the work of Burnham and Root, see, for example, Donald Hoffman, *The Architecture of John Wellborn Root* (Baltimore, 1973).
8   For more on Beman, see the essay by Thomas Schlereth in this volume.
9   Elaine Harrington and Kevin Harrington, "H. H. Richardson and the Glessners: An Architect and his Clients," *Perspectives on the Professions* 3 (Dec. 1983), pp. 8-11.
10 Horace Townsend, "H. H. Richardson, Architect," *Magazine of Art* 17 (1894), p. 133.
11 Montgomery Schuyler, "An Architectural Pioneer Review of the Portfolios Containing the Works of Frank Lloyd Wright," *Architectural Record* 31 (Apr. 1912), p. 429.
12 Mariana Griswold Van Rensselaer, *Henry Hobson Richardson and His Works* (Boston, 1888), pp. 26-34; John J. Glessner, "For Contemplated Paper on Richardson, Housebuilding, and c. 1890-1914" (unpublished notes, 1914), Glessner House, Chicago Architecture Foundation, p. 62; James F. O'Gorman, "Documentation: An 1886 Inventory of H. H. Richardson's Library, and Other Gleanings from Probate," *Journal of the Society of Architectural Historians* 41 (May 1982), p. 154.

13 Glessner (note 12), p. 17.
14 Glessner (note 12), p. 63; Van Rensselaer (note 12), pp. 29, 33. Both mention sending for Evans and Norcross, but only van Rensselaer specifies buildings meaningful to Richardson.
15 Frances Macbeth Glessner and John J. Glessner, "Journals (1879-1921) of Frances Glessner, with Occasional Entries by Her Husband, John J. Glessner," Chicago Historical Society. See the undated newspaper article from the *Chicago Tribune,* inserted in June 1886 at p. 142.
16 Glessner (note 12), p. 35.
17 In London he met Edward Burne-Jones (Pre-Raphaelite painter and stained glass designer), William Morris (arts and crafts designer), William DeMorgan (ceramics designer), and R. Phinney Spiers (architect), as well as other "unapproachables of England"; Glessner (note 12), pp. 62-63. He also toured the home of architect and critic William Burges; Van Rensselaer (note 12), p. 28. For more information on the Arts and Crafts movement, see Richard Guy Wilson's essay in this volume.
18 John J. Glessner, *The Story of a House* [1923] (Chicago, 1978), p. 4.
19 The principals were George Shepley (1860-1903), Charles Rutan (1857-1914), and Charles Coolidge (1858-1936). The firm maintained an active Chicago office from c. 1888 to c. 1905.
20 See Doreen Burke, ed., *In Pursuit of Beauty: Americans and the Aesthetic Movement* (New York, 1986); Wendy Kaplan, et al., *"The Art that Is Life": The Arts and Crafts Movement in America, 1875-1920* (Boston, 1987).
21 For more on Chicago furniture designers and

Chicago as a furniture-making center, see Sharon Darling, *Chicago Furniture: Art, Craft, and Industry, 1833-1983* (Chicago and New York, 1984).

22 Scott's drawings for the master bedroom furniture are in Glessner House, Chicago Architecture Foundation.

23 Stamped label on back of engraving framed by Scott, c. 1878. Glessner House, Chicago Architecture Foundation.

24 Sharon S. Darling, *Chicago Ceramics and Glass: an Illustrated History from 1871-1933* (Chicago, 1979), p. 49. See also Gerald Larson's essay in this volume for more on the Chicago Terra Cotta Company.

25 Glessner Journals (note 15).

26 David Hanks, *Isaac E. Scott: Reform Furniture in Chicago, John Jacob Glessner House* (Chicago, 1974).

27 Alan Axelrod, ed., *The Colonial Revival in America* (New York, 1985).

28 Sarah Bradford Landau, *P. B. Wight: Architect, Contractor, and Critic, 1838-1925* (Chicago, 1981), pp. 35-38.

29 Darling (note 21), p. 166.

30 Clarence Cook, *The House Beautiful* (New York, 1881). This is the Glessner edition; Cook's book was first published in 1877.

31 This carpet is now in the collections of The Art Institute of Chicago, 1974.524.

32 Glessner (note 12), p. 22.

33 Michael D. Baron, "The Japanese Influence in America as seen in the John Jacob Glessner House" (unpublished ms., 1983), copy at Glessner House, Chicago Architecture Foundation.

34 Paul A. Carnahan, "The Book in the Domestic Environment: The Glessner Family Library, Chicago 1886-1893" (University of Chicago, M. A. thesis, 1986), p. 51.

35 Glessner Journals (note 15), November 23, 1888: "My new Morris curtains embroidered by the Dec. Art Soc. came home Tuesday and are very beautiful." While it is not clear which room these curtains were for, the indication is that some Morris firm designs were being embroidered outside the house.

36 Glessner (note 12), pp. 9-10.

37 Linda Parry, *William Morris Textiles* (New York, 1983), p. 48.

38 Catherine Lynn, *Wallpaper in America from the Seventeenth Century to World War I* (New York, 1980), p. 459.

39 Plans and elevations in the collection of Glessner House, Chicago Architecture Foundation.

40 His father was head of the Department of History of the University of Chicago and a friend of the Glessners; Carnahan (note 34), p. 70.

41 George Macbeth, Letter to the *Littleton Republic Journal* (Littleton, N. H., Sept. 22, 1904), photocopy in Glessner House Collections.

42 Contract Between Herman Von Holst and Frank Lloyd Wright, September 22, 1909. A copy of the contract, supplied in 1951 by William Gray Purcell, is in the collections of The Art Institute of Chicago.

43 David Van Zanten, "Early Work of Marian Mahony Griffin," *Prairie School Review* 3 (1966), pp. 1-2, 5-23, 27.

44 Mary N. Woods, "The *American Architect and Building News*" (Ph. D. diss., Columbia University, 1982), p. 263.

45 Karl Hinckeldeyn, "Henry Richardson und seine Bedeutung für die amerikanische Architektur," *Deutsche Bauzeitung* 26 (Feb. 6, 1892), pp. 64-66; A. W. Reinink, "American Influences on Late Nineteenth-Century Architecture in The Netherlands," *Journal of the Society of Architectural Historians* 29 (1970), pp. 163-74; Horace Townsend, "H. H. Richardson, Architect," *The Magazine of Art* 17 (1894), pp. 133-38.

46 Dimitri Tselos, "Richardson's Influence on European Architecture," *Journal of the Society of Architectural Historians* 29 (May 1970), pp. 156-62.

47 Roger Dixon and Stefan Muthesius, *Victorian Architecture* (New York, 1978), p. 232; Nikolaus Pevsner, *Pioneers of Modern Design* (Harmondsworth, Eng., 1960), pp. 164-65; Tselos (note 46), p. 159.

48 Juhani Pallasmaa et al., *Lars Sonck, 1870-1956, Arkkitehti/Architect* (Helsinki, 1981), pp. 68-69.

49 Letter from Rodolfo Lanciani to J. J. Glessner, June 6, 1890, Glessner House, Chicago Architecture Foundation.

Chicago and the International Arts and Crafts Movements: Progressive and Conservative Tendencies

Richard Guy Wilson

The animating spirit of some of Chicago's turn-of-the-century residential and commercial architecture must be sought not only in that locality, but beyond the boundaries of the Middle West in the larger context of the international Arts and Crafts movement. In Chicago as elsewhere, Arts and Crafts was an ethos rather than a specific style, hence Chicago Arts and Crafts architecture ranges from the low-slung, wide-eaved Prairie style houses designed by Frank Lloyd Wright (figs. 1, 2) and others to the high-gabled, plaster and half-timber English cottages created by Howard Van Doren Shaw as well as Pond and Pond (fig. 3).

In accordance with the Arts and Crafts movement's emphasis on life-enhancing spaces, buildings were not designed simply as shells but were carefully crafted and embellished with such treasured detailing as leaded glass windows, inglenooks, and specially designed furniture. As in the case of the exterior design, the interior references were wide-ranging, from reproductions of vernacular furniture to plain oak Mission chairs, or the grace-fully curved Austrian Secessionist style furniture of George Mann Niedecken (fig. 4). This coexistence of the progressive and the conservative, the native and the cosmopolitan, illuminates the ecumenical spirit of the Arts and Crafts movement in Chicago and indicates the international context from which it sprang.

The origins of the Arts and Crafts movement can be traced to moralistic attitudes toward industrial and production design espoused in mid-nineteenth century England by, among others, Augustus Welby Northmore Pugin, and, later, John Ruskin and William Morris. Pugin, Ruskin, and Morris rejected many aspects of modern industrial civilization, but especially the rapid proliferation of machine production and the resulting lack of connection between labor, product, and consumption. They saw this as the basic cause of the growing alienation of workers from the rest of the society. In the eyes of both the English and American followers of the Arts and Crafts philosophy, the ideal society was the medieval one. What they

Figs. 1/2 Frank Lloyd Wright, Evans House, 9914 Longwood Drive, 1908, interior of dining room and view of exterior.

HOUSE AT LASALLE ILL. POND'POND ARCHITECTS CHICAGO.

Fig. 3 Pond and Pond, Perspective study of a house in LaSalle, Illinois, 1901-04 (cat. no. 84).

Fig. 4 George Mann Niedecken, Perspective rendering of the interior of the Bresler Art Gallery, 129 Milwaukee Street, Milwaukee, c. 1904 (cat. no. 170).

looked to was a romantic, hazy past in which, they believed, communitarian values, handicraft, and nature existed in a symbiotic relationship.[1]

This movement, while having its origins well before 1850, did not receive its formal designation until 1888, when Walter Crane founded the "Arts and Crafts Exhibition Society" in London. More oriented toward the decorative arts than architec-

ture, the Society nevertheless showed work by such leading architects as Philip Webb, William R. Lethaby, Charles R. Ashbee, Edwin L. Lutyens, and Charles F. A. Voysey, along with that of other designers like Morris (its president from 1890 to 1896) and Crane. By the 1890s the views of the English group had been slightly modified, and while a medieval-inspired handicraft communitarianism still remained the ideal, most of its members, including Morris, had come to accept the machine as a means for saving drudgery. Gradually, Arts and Crafts followers shifted the focus of their concern from the use of machines to the way in which they were used, condemning the capitalist society that exploited both machines and men to turn out imitative products in historical styles. However, the fundamental interest of the Arts and Crafts movement was not in style, but in achieving a sense of "rightness," a favorite term. Thus, a house should belong to its locality and not be an intruder, and equally important, its furnishings should be in harmony with its exterior. This allowed considerable latitude in design, so that buildings by English Arts and Crafts designers ranged from modernized versions of the half-timbered Elizabethan to Free Georgian and to rock-hewn organic masses and concrete structures.

Morris's Arts and Crafts philosophy went on to have an international impact, especially in Western Europe. In many countries it merged with similar movements reflecting dissatisfaction with the existing order in design. In France, Eugène Emmanuel Viollet-le-Duc developed a nationalistic philosophy that held the Gothic period to have been the high point of French civilization and banished classicism — particularly as taught by the Ecole des Beaux-Arts — as a pagan invader. The notion of a strongly nationalistic design, based upon or inspired by indigenous sources and yet neither imitative nor revivalist, inspired later generations of architects and designers such as Eduard Cuypers in the Netherlands, Eliel Saarinen in Helsinki, Otto Wagner in Vienna, Peter Behrens in Germany, Siegfried Bing in Paris, and Victor Horta in Brussels. These design movements — whether Art Nouveau, Secession, Jugendstil, or Prairie School — were all branches of the Arts and Crafts movement as developed by Morris and his followers in England.[2]

The American relationship to this international Arts and Crafts movement is complex and leads in a couple of directions. On the American side there are roots going back to the 1840s and the picturesque designs of Andrew Jackson Downing and Alexander Jackson Davis, who were the architectural equivalents of the painters of the Hudson River School and the transcendentalists of poetry and philosophy. This picturesque Stick style — as it is known today — provides an immediate background to the architectural developments of the later 1870s and the 1880s and the earliest work of Wright and his contemporaries. Working in what is known today as the Shingle style, though at the time as the modernized colonial or Queen Anne, American architects on the East Coast such as McKim, Mead and White fused the latest English fashion with native American developments. This wooden architecture with its continuous volumetric skins of shingles, although begun as a resort style, became the basis for American suburban building and a foundation for the Chicago Arts and Crafts.[3]

As has been pointed out by a number of historians, the connection of Chicago architecture and design to the international Arts and Crafts movement was both direct and long lasting.[4] Joseph Twyman, an English designer and decorator who claimed friendships with William Morris and Christopher Dresser, arrived in Chicago in 1870 and began to preach the gospel of reform in the crafts for the home. For a time he sold English reform style wallpapers for the firm of John J. McGrath. In 1898, he went to work for the Tobey Furniture Company, where he established a Morris Memorial Room, reputedly containing objects from Morris's own home.

"Tobey's New Furniture," introduced in 1900, was characterized by a simple and rectilinear geometry that could also be found in the work of William Morris and his English cohorts. In 1903 Twyman, together with Professors Richard G. Moulton and Oscar Lovell Triggs, established a William Morris Society to propagate Morris's artistic and social ideals. However, the Society did not survive Twyman's death in 1904.

Another link between English Arts and Crafts and design developments in Chicago was the work of Walter Crane. When Crane lectured in Chicago in December and January of 1891-92, his work was exhibited at the Art Institute. Two years later, the work of decorator Charles F. A. Voysey, another Englishman, was displayed at the 1893 World's Columbian Exposition. Charles R. Ashbee's work was shown in Chicago in 1898 and again in 1900, when he came to the city to lecture. Ashbee met Frank Lloyd Wright at that time, and the two men developed a friendship that was maintained by correspondence and renewed on Ashbee's next trip in 1908. In 1910 Wright asked Ashbee to write an introduction to a book on his work that the Berlin publisher Ernst Wasmuth was issuing as a supplement to a larger portfolio just published. These two publications made Wright's work available to a wide international audience and greatly influenced the future direction of European modernism.[5]

Chicago architects also had connections to the larger international Arts and Crafts movement through publications and travel. The *International Studio*, a London-based magazine, carried the work of the Austrian, German, and other "new art" movements, along with that of the British.

Other magazines such as the British *Academy Architecture* and *The Architectural Review,* and the German *Decorative Kunst* and *Moderne Bauformen,* were available in America and were eagerly devoured by progressive designers. Chicago designers like Howard Van Doren Shaw and George Maher were exposed to the movement in their travels abroad. George Mann Niedecken, one of Chicago's leading interior designers, studied in London, Berlin, and Paris, and his designs of the early 1900s bear marked traces of the Parisian and the Austrian decorative art of this period.[6] William Gray Purcell, a young architect from the Sullivan office, visited H. P. Berlage, the leading Dutch Arts and Crafts designer, in Amsterdam in 1906 before going on to Scandinavia to study vernacular architecture. A few years later the Dutch designer visited the Midwest on a lecture tour arranged by Purcell.[7]

The St. Louis World's Fair of 1904 provided another opportunity for Americans to see examples of the latest European decorative arts. Especially popular were the Austrian Pavilion by Ludwig Baumann and interiors by Joseph Urban, and the German exhibit in the Varied Industries building, designed by Josef Maria Olbrich (fig. 5) and other

leading Secessionist architects. Wright was impressed by the German work in particular, and dispatched some of his staff, including Francis Barry Byrne, to see the exhibit. Chicago architect Irving K. Pond, reveling in the rich, soft colors of the German exhibit, wrote an enthusiastic article for the *Architectural Record,* observing: "Everywhere the scheme of design is broad and simple."[8] The "Secessionist" label gained a certain currency in America and was applied by some critics to the work of Wright, Sullivan, and Walter Burley Griffin, though with the qualification that it was not a particular style so much as a stress on simplicity that linked Continental and midwestern designers.[9]

The founding of the Chicago Arts and Crafts Society at Hull-House in October 1897 occurred shortly after the Boston Arts and Crafts Exhibition of April 1897 and the establishment of the Boston Society of Arts and Crafts that June.[10] An important center of Arts and Crafts activities in the Chicago area, Hull-House (fig. 6) had been founded as a settlement house by Jane Addams and Ellen Gates Starr on the model of Toynbee Hall in London. It was on a visit to Toynbee Hall that Addams and Starr became familiar with the work of Ash-

*Fig. 5 Josef Maria Ol-
brich, Library room of
the German Building,
Louisiana Purchase Ex-
position, St. Louis, 1904
(demolished); from*
Deutsches Kunst-
gewerbe St. Louis *(Ber-
lin, 1904).*

*Fig. 6 Pond and Pond,
Additions to Hull
House, Halsted Street
west of Polk Street, c.
1907 (demolished).*

bee, who had established the Guild School of Handicraft there.

The primary purpose of both Toynbee Hall and Hull-House was not to produce goods, but to enrich people's lives through handicrafts. This interest in social reform brought together at Hull-House not only artists, craftsmen, and the immigrant populations they were meant to serve, but also politicians and educators. It was from the ranks of all of these that the founders of the Chicago Arts and Crafts Society were drawn.[11]

The Chicago Arts and Crafts Society included architects Frank Lloyd Wright, Robert C. Spencer, Jr., Dwight Perkins, Myron Hunt, and Irving and Allen Pond, among others, many of whom also had ties with the Chicago Architectural Club which had been established in 1895. In turn, members of the Architectural Club – including Howard Van Doren Shaw, George Niedecken, Elmer Grey, Birch Burdett Long, Arthur Huen, Richard Schmidt, Hugh M. G. Garden, Herman Von Holst, and Louis Sullivan – were also sympathetic to the Arts and Crafts movement.[12] Common interests and overlapping membership led the two organizations to exhibit jointly at Art Institute shows for a number of years. Both Chicago and English Arts and Crafts

work was displayed at these shows, culminating in the 1902 exhibit which was almost entirely devoted to the Arts and Crafts. Louis Sullivan designed the frontispiece to the catalogue and contributed both objects and drawings to the exhibition. Frank Lloyd Wright was represented by sixty-five items ranging from furniture to glass and scarves.[13]

A number of the architects who belonged to both the Society and the Club were also members of a more informal group called the "Eighteen," many of whom occupied or even shared offices at Steinway Hall. This group, which included Wright, the Ponds, Long, Spencer, Hunt, Perkins, and Griffin, met at mealtimes to discuss architectural theory, as well as their own work. They were joined in time by other Chicago architects, including George and Arthur Dean, Garden, Schmidt, Huen, and Shaw. By influencing the annual exhibitions of both the Arts and Crafts Society and the Architectural Club, the interests and views of this circle of architects changed the direction of American architecture and design.[14]

The intense discussion about design issues prompted by the interactions among this core of people ultimately found expression in a number of important lectures and publications. Among these

Fig. 7 Frank Lloyd Wright, Unity Temple, Lake Street at Kenil-worth Avenue, Oak Park, Illinois, 1906.

Fig. 7 Frank Lloyd Wright, Unity Temple, Lake Street at Kenil-worth Avenue, Oak Park, Illinois, 1906.

were Elmer Grey's "The Architect and the 'Arts and Crafts'"; Irving Pond's "The Life of Architecture"; Louis Sullivan's *Kindergarten Chats*; Robert Spencer's articles on farm houses; and, of course, Frank Lloyd Wright's essays, "In the Cause of Architecture" and "The Art and Craft of the Machine."[15]

The issue of the machine in relation to the Arts and Crafts movement was a major concern of a number of these essays. Some historians have claimed that there was a fundamental difference of opinion between the Chicago Arts and Crafts group and their English counterparts, with the Americans tending to be more positive toward the machine.[16] As noted earlier, however, even such a crucial figure in the English Arts and Crafts movement as William Morris moderated his position to one that accepted a role for some mechanization in reducing the drudgery of manual labor. This was also the stance of the Chicago Arts and Crafts Society, which had as one of its objectives:

to devise lines of development which shall retain the machine in so far as it relieves the workman from drudgery, and tends to perfect his product; but which shall insist that the machine no longer be allowed to dominate the workman and reduce his production to mechanical distortion.[17]

Concerns over the effects of machine production led one member of the Chicago Arts and Crafts Society, Oscar Lovell Triggs, a political radical who taught English at the University of Chicago, to found the Industrial Art League (1899-1904). Triggs saw the League as a means of bringing about "democratization of art" and organized manual

training workshops modeled after medieval guilds as he understood them. His statements on the issues of the machine and the worker could have been written by William Morris:

The function of the machine is clearly to do most of the mechanical work of the world, and all its drudgery. The ideal machine is automatic; the better and more perfect the machine, the more able is it to dispense with an operator. For the present at least the machine is calculated to do the lower kind of work, and to render serviceable to the world the less skillful and less intelligent workmen. The higher the work, the more of intelligent design necessary for a product, the greater is the need for skilled craftsmen to initiate and execute a given design.[18]

Frank Lloyd Wright, in his lecture "The Art and Craft of the Machine," delivered at Hull-House in 1901, took a stand that he believed to be radical when he disclosed that:

In the years which have been devoted in my own life to working out in stubborn materials a feeling for the beautiful, a hope has grown stronger with the experience of each year, amounting now to a gradually deepening conviction that in the Machine lies the only future of art and craft – as I believe, a glorious future; that the Machine is, in fact, the metamorphosis of ancient art and craft; that we are at last face to face with the machine – the modern Sphinx – whose riddle the artist must solve if he would that art live – for his nature holds the key.

Wright went on to explain that his own aesthetic of plain simple forms and surfaces owed a great debt to Morris, noting:

William Morris pleaded well for simplicity as the basis of all true art. Let us understand the significance to art of that word – SIMPLICITY – for it is vital to the art of the machine.

A Home in a Prairie Town

BY FRANK LLOYD WRIGHT

This is the Fifth Design in the Journal's New Series of Model Suburban Houses Which Can be Built at Moderate Cost

Wright was looking for confirmation of his own aesthetic of rectilinear simplicity. He admired machines that cut wood — or treated metal or lithographs — in plain, simple ways that resulted in plain, simple, rectilinear shapes. But Wright revealed a source of his aesthetic when he wrote that wood "has been universally abused and maltreated by all peoples but the Japanese."[19] Ultimately Wright's essay confirms and rationalizes his own aesthetic preferences for simplicity, preferences which he found corroborated in certain machine-like processes.

The point of difference between the American and English use of the machine ultimately lay in the realm of aesthetic judgments. Ashbee pointed out the contrast in an essay in *The House Beautiful*; he found Wright's work too brutal, and criticized his Unity Temple (fig. 7) and Larkin Company Building because they "rigidly excluded" anything that "savored of hand detail." Ashbee claimed, "We do not object to good standardized machine forms, but we prefer the craft when we can get it, and we will not have machine-made detail or machine-made ornament of any sort."[20]

Fig. 8 Frank Lloyd Wright, "A Home in a Prairie Town"; from Ladies Home Journal *(Feb. 1901).*

A Fireproof House for $5000

Estimated to Cost That Amount in Chicago, and Designed Especially for The Journal

By Frank Lloyd Wright

Fig. 9 Frank Lloyd Wright, "A Fireproof House for $5000"; from Ladies Home Journal *(Apr. 1907).*

One Side of the House, Showing the Trellised Extension

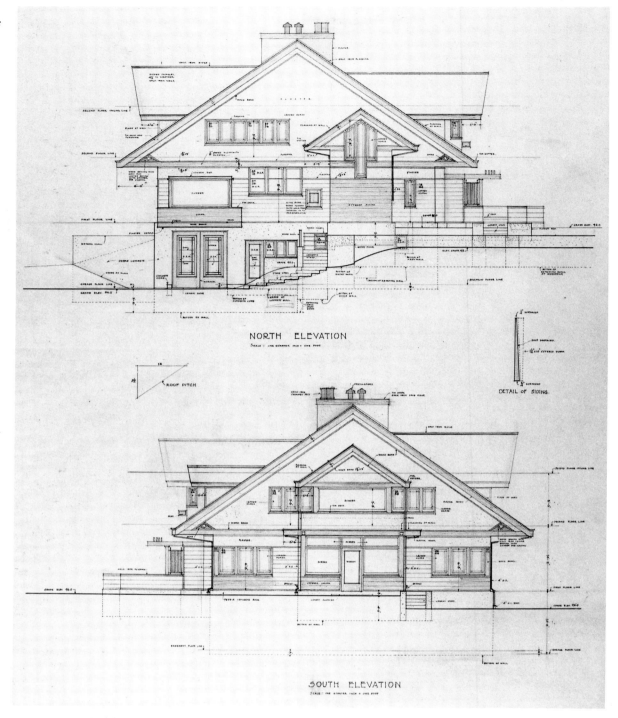

The relationship between architecture and craftsmanship perplexed a number of Chicago architects. Elmer Grey's notion of the architect was that "he is more of an overseer and less a craftsman — or rather his craftsmanship more largely consists of the overseeing of the work of other craftsmen." Grey's term for this relationship was "co-operative fellowship" or "practical socialism"; like many of the Chicago Arts and Crafts architects, he placed the architect above the other craftsmen.[21]

By the early 1900s what has been identified as the Prairie School of architecture emerged in the Chicago area. Its leading figure was clearly Wright, although some architects also looked to Louis Sullivan as a spiritual and theoretical leader. From Wright's office came designers such as Walter Burley Griffin, Marion Mahony, Francis Barry Byrne, William Drummond, and others. This group sought to apply William Morris's principles in their work.

The February 1901 issue of *Ladies Home Journal* carried a design by Wright titled "A Home in a Prairie Town" (fig. 8). Wright himself referred to his work as being "thoroughly saturated with the spirit of the prairies."[22] Most of the prairie houses were actually located in the growing suburbs of Chicago; only after 1910, as the movement dispersed, did rural cities and towns receive examples of Prairie School work. The prairie served as a metaphor, offering the promise of a new society and a new art, freed from stultified Old World and East Coast traditions. The concept of democracy, continually invoked by Sullivan and Wright, played a large role in the prairie metaphor. Walt Whitman, their favorite poet, had prophesied that a new man would arise out of the western prairies – the American Adam, who would need a new art and architecture to create a new democratic society. In a very profound sense, the *Kindergarten Chats* of Sullivan, Wright's "The Art and Craft of the Machine," and the buildings these two architects designed conveyed the spirit of the new democratic society. Irving K. Pond summed it up in 1918 when he wrote: "The horizontal lines of the new expression appeal to the disciples of this school as echoing the spirit of the prairies of the great Middle West, which to them embodies the essence of democracy."[23]

In fact, the houses of the Prairie School in many ways represented the new middle class. While some of them were commissioned by the wealthy, the most important work of the Prairie School architects was created for middle-class clients. Most of these houses were based on the balloon-frame construction common from the mid-1800s onwards. Wright's famous "Fireproof House for $5,000" (fig. 9; published in the *Ladies Home Journal* in 1907) and the house Vernon Watson (later a partner of Thomas Tallmadge) designed for himself in Oak Park, Illinois, in 1904, both derived from this type. Both Wright's and Watson's designs are essentially rectilinear in form and plan. Their distinction as prairie houses arises from their low pitched roofs, their extended eaves, their horizontal banding and trim, the banking of their windows, and their integrated living spaces.[24]

These houses and others, like the Amy Hunter House in Flossmoor, Illinois (1916; fig. 10), designed by William Gray Purcell and George Grant Elmslie, were seen at the time as part of the bungalow movement. Purcell, in particular, wanted to create an alternative to the low quality, builder-designed middle-class house, and designed a number of houses that were essentially bungalows.[25] The bungalow – with origins in India and elsewhere – was viewed as a new housing type that offered a decent, low-cost housing alternative for the middle class. Built with one or two stories, and characterized by low eaves, the bungalow was heavily promoted by American Arts and Crafts

Fig. 11 Gustav Stickley, Bungalow; from The Craftsman *(Apr. 1907).*

propagandists. As it developed a regional orientation, the bungalow drew upon ranch cabins in California, Cape Cod cottages, saltboxes, and even Colonial style houses in the East. In the Midwest, Prairie houses were frequently classified as bungalows. Henry Saylor, author of *Bungalows* (1911), describing a house by Tallmadge and Watson, wrote:

Their use of the strong horizontal line, as being most in keeping with the flat plains of the Central West, has brought about almost a new style in the architectural types of the world. There is no copying of the bungalow from India in this type.[26]

Strangely, the prime promoter of the bungalow and, indeed, of the entire Arts and Crafts movement in America, Gustav Stickley, practically ignored the Prairie School, as did his periodical, *The Craftsman* (fig. 11). The major exception was the publication of several articles by Louis Sullivan. Carl K. Bennett, the president of the National Farmers Bank in Owatonna, Minnesota, was so impressed by Sullivan's articles that he commissioned him to design a new bank building, probably Sullivan's finest late work (see Weingarden, figs. 1, 20, 21).[27] Stickley also published an article by Purcell and Elmslie and several pieces by Oscar L. Triggs. Aesthetically there is a clear relationship between Stickley's *Craftsman* furniture and the furnishings designed by Prairie architects, and in many cases Stickley's furniture was used in Prairie houses. Early in his career, Stickley had been heavily influenced by Harvey Ellis, who also was seen as a spiritual forefather of the Prairie School, so Stickley's lack of recognition of the Prairie School architects is difficult to understand.[28] Perhaps he saw their work as too extreme and too much of a challenge to his cozy domesticity to find it appealing.

Fig. 12 Walter Burley Griffin, Perspective view of Joshua Melson House, 56 River Heights Drive, Mason City, Iowa, 1912.

was exemplified in the Prairie School enclave at Rock Crest-Rock Glen at Mason City, Iowa (pl. 49). The eighteen-acre area, including limestone cliffs bordering a creek on one side and sloping into gentle glens on the other, was close to downtown. It had been bypassed and declared unusable as a building site because it had formerly been a quarry, and then used as a trash dump and factory site. In 1908 Frank Lloyd Wright obtained commissions for a bank and hotel from two Mason City businessmen, J. E. E. Markley and James Blythe. Subsequently, he received two house commissions for Mason City. He completed the first, but the second, for Joshua Melson, sited on the limestone cliffs, had not progressed beyond the drawing stage when Wright gave up his architectural practice in Chicago and departed for Europe with the wife of a client (ostensibly to oversee the production of the Wasmuth publications).

Melson, who still wanted to build, approached two former Wright associates, Marion Mahony and Walter Burley Griffin. The latter designed a scheme in which the site would be bounded by a string of houses along both the cliffs and the surrounding roads. A rough-faced ashlar limestone from the quarry would be used as a unifying element in the houses and also in low terrace walls and gate posts. Most of the houses were designed with their service facilities — kitchen, pantry, and garage — oriented toward the street, and the main living spaces and vistas directed toward the open central space. A large community green, more properly described as a prairie river landscape, occupied the center of the site. The rendering in gouache and ink on green satin by Marion Mahony displays an oriental sensibility: the vegetation is exotic and is presented as flat planes of color in a hazy atmosphere. The rendering expresses the Prairie School attitude to nature — not a raw, untamed nature, but a harmonious middle landscape of domestic bliss. Pastoral in setting, the Rock Crest-Rock Glen development was suburban; modern technology was banished and yet made possible the reclaiming and remaking of the landscape. Melson, along with Markley and Blythe, and another local businessman, W. J. Holahan, signed an agreement to purchase, clean up, and use the site for residential purposes only.[29]

Of the sixteen houses projected in the Griffin-Mahony proposal, only eight were built. Griffin was involved in about four of them, the prize being the primitivistic Melson House (fig. 12), which appears as an extrusion of a hollowed-out portion of the limestone cliffs. In plan the Melson House follows Wright's $5,000 house scheme. Just as construction began on some of the Rock Crest-Rock

Of course not all of the Prairie School commissions were for inexpensive middle-class dwellings. For example, Wright was approached to design a substantial house for Henry Ford in Dearborn, Michigan, and other Prairie School architects were certainly not averse to such commissions (pl. 48). The designs for these grand Prairie style buildings generally shared the rectilinear geometric character of the smaller houses, being composed of a series of interrelated planes and spaces.

An underlying goal of the Arts and Crafts movement, whether in England or Chicago, was to reestablish what the industrial revolution had appeared to rip apart: the integration of communities into a harmonious relationship with nature. This mission

Fig. 13 Elmer Grey, Perspective sketch of a summer house for Frank Gordon Bigelow, Fox Point, Wisconsin, 1900.

Fig. 14 Francis Barry Byrne with Walter Burley Griffin (?), Elevation study for the proposed C. A. Dakin House, Mason City, Iowa, c. 1912 (cat. no. 187).

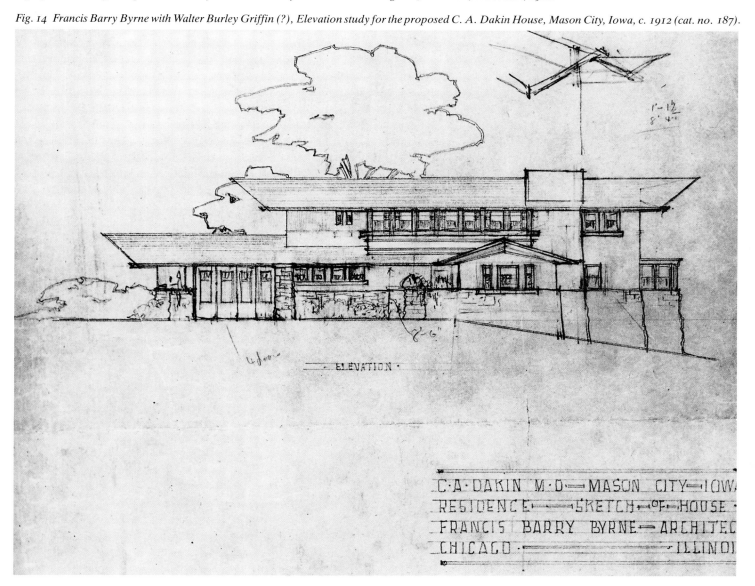

Fig. 15 Frank Lloyd Wright, Nathan G. Moore House and Stable, 333 Forest Avenue, Oak Park, Illionois, 1895 (rebuilt 1923).

Rock Crest-Rock Glen, one of the largest ensembles of Prairie School houses in the United States, indicates the type of community envisioned by the Prairie School: a group of harmonious, yet distinct, single-family houses located in a domestic landscape. It also illustrates that after 1910 much of the major Prairie School architecture was constructed outside of Chicago, in smaller cities and towns. The ideals of the Arts and Crafts movement seemed more capable of realization away from metropolitan centers.

The Prairie School was, however, only one expression of the Arts and Crafts movement in Chicago; other stylistic tendencies developed out of the interactions within the Arts and Crafts Society, the Eighteen, and the Architectural Club. Even Frank Lloyd Wright's work showed elements of other styles, as was evident in the house he designed for Nathan G. Moore in Oak Park (1895; fig. 15). A very non-Wrightean steep pitched roof and half-timbering was combined with Sullivanesque-Gothic ornament. Similarly, Arthur Huen, a member of the Eighteen and the Architectural Club, designed the Prairie School style Bridesmaid house in Des Moines, Iowa (1899-1900), complete with Niedecken furniture, but later adopted a more conservative, even revivalist style.[30] The work of Elmer Grey, also a member of these groups, showed some traces of the horizontal line and geometry of the Prairie School, but his major inspiration seems to have come from vernacular structures such as barns. His design for a summer home at Fox Point, Wisconsin (1900; fig. 13), has small elements of half-timbering, but the prominent form is the large, shingled, barnlike roof. Grey moved to southern California in 1903 and, with Myron Hunt, another Chicago Arts and

Glen houses, Griffin won the Australian capital competition and consequently left the works competition to Barry Byrne, another Wright office alumnus (see essay by Van Zanten). Byrne oversaw the Griffin work and designed several more houses, including a mausoleum for Melson's wife. The C. A. Dakin House, designed by Byrne and never built, featured long horizontal roofs and clipped gable ends (fig. 14). The local limestone was to have been used for the base and piers of the house. Apparently Byrne had a disagreement with the Mason City clients and was discharged. Several more houses exhibiting Prairie School characteristics were erected in the area by local architects and builders.

Fig. 16 Robert C. Spencer, Jr., U. F. Orendorf House, Canton, Illinois, 1905; from Western Architect *(Apr. 1914).*

Fig. 17 Howard Van Doren Shaw, Mentor Building, northeast corner of Monroe and State streets, 1906.

Fig. 18 Hall of Ragdale.

*Fig. 19 Study of Rag-
dale, showing architect's
desk (see cat. no. 100).*

Crafts architect, designed a number of buildings with Arts and Crafts features, as well as a number of Classical Revivalist buildings.[31]

Robert Spencer, a prominent member of all three Chicago organizations, effectively shows the transitional and multivalent character of the Chicago Arts and Crafts movement. Spencer had been a partner of Wright's in the mid-1890s and also one of his early publicists. Some of his designs were pure Prairie School, solidly geometrical with an avoidance of foreign references. And yet Spencer could design with equal facility houses with a strong, medieval English aspect, such as the high-roofed Orendorf House at Canton, Illinois (1905; fig. 16). On the interior the furnishings combined some traditional elements with Art Nouveau and

Mission style patterns. The den, featuring plain wood trim, an inglenook, and stenciling, could have fit into any English Arts and Crafts dwelling.[32]

Of this group of Chicago Arts and Crafts designers who lie outside the strict Prairie School mode, Howard Van Doren Shaw stands out most prominently. Thomas Tallmadge (of Tallmadge and Watson) summed up Shaw's position as "the most rebellious of the conservatives and the most conservative of the rebels."[33] Shaw's early commercial work, like the Nyberg Motor Company and the Mentor buildings (fig. 17), Chicago, followed the Sullivan tradition of decorating a rectilinear structural frame.[34] In domestic architecture Shaw tended to follow English precedent as in his own house, Ragdale, in Lake Forest, Illinois (1897-98; fig. 20), and his Donnelly Printing Building in Chicago has strong English features. A twin-gabled, stucco-covered building, with a protruding second floor bay over an inset entry, Ragdale has all the earmarks of a Voysey house. Indeed, the exterior of Ragdale is remarkably close to Voysey's own house, the Orchard, at Chorlywood in England, and it might be thought that Shaw cribbed his design, except that the Orchard dates from 1899, after Shaw had designed his own house. Nevertheless, Ragdale shows some Voysey or other English Arts and Crafts influences, including the hearts used to decorate the shutters.[35]

On the interior Ragdale also displays an English influence, though once again it has been transformed into Shaw's personal expression. The front hall (fig. 18), at cross-axis to the entry, serves as both a room unto itself and as a corridor that opens widely into the living room and dining room. Trimmed in plain-surfaced oak, with a high wainscoting, it contains window seats; the cove ceiling is in plain plaster. The most remarkable feature is the leaded glass screen separating the hall and dining room, which recalls similar features in Lutyens's houses of nearly the same date.[36] The screen suggests that the house incorporates fragments of earlier buildings and creates an interior world totally separate from the exterior. The remainder of the interior was equally based on Arts and Crafts principles, and included furniture that a contemporary writer described as having "a slight touch of the long lines of the Art Nouveau, but none too much."[37] The writer probably was referring to the furniture designed by Harvey Ellis and made by Gustav Stickley, as well as to Shaw's own designs for the settle and the desk with elegant uprights (fig. 19; pl. 33), recalling the work of the British Arts and Crafts designers Arthur H. Mackmurdo and Charles Rennie Mackintosh.[38]

Shaw would go on to exploit more thoroughly than any other Chicago designer the more conservative Arts and Crafts idioms. He was eclectic in

Fig. 20 Howard Van Doren Shaw, Shaw House, "Ragdale," 1230 North Green Bay Road, Lake Forest, Illinois, 1897-98.

that he chose easily from the past and the present, but he was neither an archeologist nor a dogmatist. He preferred English-based design idioms, but he would adopt French provincial and even Italian design elements when it suited his purpose. And his sense of shelter was never expressed in broad horizontal roofs, but in tall, steeply pitched roofs that covered and anchored a house to the ground (fig. 22; pl. 36).

Shaw's most important single work, Market Square in Lake Forest (1912-17), showed his sense of community and also what the machine (in the form of the motor car) was doing to the suburb. The scheme is an open, tree-lined square surrounded on three sides by buildings with shops on the ground floor and apartments, studios, and offices above. The open end of the square fronts on a main road that connects Lake Forest with Chicago and also gives onto the station for the commuter railroad. Buildings on the site were demolished to create the ensemble that was intended to eliminate automotive congestion, provide park-

ing, and create an atmosphere conducive to shopping. In addition, a building to serve as a clubhouse and gymnasium for the town was located at the end behind the square, and the YMCA and YWCA were given space within it and adjoining buildings.

Stylistically, Market Square suggests a number of modes. Peter B. Wight, the Chicago architect and critic, noted in 1917: "There is some resemblance to the old towns of Flanders and Germany of the fifteenth and sixteenth centuries. But there is no copying."[39] In addition one finds there is English half-timbering, Dutch roofs and gables, and American Colonial elements. The tower on the north side (fig. 21) resembles the towers George Maher sketched in Lucerne in 1891 (cat. no. 37), well before Shaw set out on his first European jaunt. Yet Shaw's tower is not a copy, nor does it duplicate the tower on the south side (fig. 23). Rather, the different elements assembled and interwoven with different materials — wood, plaster, tile, and brick, along with pieces of sculpture, Roman Doric columns, and oriel windows — create a

Fig. 21 Howard Van Doren Shaw, Market Square, Lake Forest, Illinois, 1914-15, view of north side.

Fig. 23 Market Square, view of south side.

Fig. 22 Howard Van Doren Shaw, Phi Delta Theta Fraternity House, 309 East Chalmers Street, Champaign, Illinois, 1923.

fantasyland image highly appropriate to the Arts and Crafts ethos. Market Square was possibly the first automobile shopping center designed and erected in America; it expressed the spirit of domestic tranquility and community that the Arts and Crafts movement sought to foster.

Subsequent writers have seen a wide gulf between the seemingly conservative imagery of a Howard Van Doren Shaw and the apparently progressive imagery of a Walter Burley Griffin.[40] Their architectural imagery was different, yet along with their contemporaries, Wright, Huen, the Ponds, Grey, Spencer, and others, they were perceived at the time as part of the same movement. The term "Prairie School" was a later creation, and while Wright used the word "prairie" in connection with some of his houses and as a metaphor for freedom, at the time all of these architects, along with Sullivan, were referred to as the "Chicago School," or the "New School of the Middle West," or simply as "Western."[41]

In spite of individual differences, a unity of purpose was common to most of these Chicago Arts and Crafts architects. They based most of their work on residential and, in particular, suburban models, seeking to return the everyday life of Americans to a more harmonious mode. Taking as a guide the ideals and, at times, the idioms of William Morris and other European Arts and Crafts designers, the architects of Chicago created their own midwestern movement. Although Louis Sullivan and Frank Lloyd Wright dominated the Chicago movement, on occasion, architects like Spencer, Grey, and Shaw were equally capable of creating compelling images. Conservative and progressive ideals and images existed side by side, and the difference between the two ultimately became blurred. For, to use the words with which Frank Lloyd Wright began his 1908 essay "In the Cause of Architecture," "Radical though it be, the work here illustrated is dedicated to a cause conservative in the best sense of the word."[42]

NOTES

1 For background on the English Arts and Crafts movement, see Gillian Naylor, *The Arts and Crafts Movement* (London, 1971); and Peter Davey, *Architecture of the Arts and Crafts Movement* (London, 1980).

2 See Ian Latham, ed., *New Free Style, Arts and Crafts-Art Nouveau-Secession* (London, 1980); Gabriel P. Weisberg, *Art Nouveau Bing, Paris Style 1900* (New York, 1986); Frank Russell, ed., *Art Nouveau Architecture* (London, 1979).

3 For background on the American Arts and Crafts, see Richard Guy Wilson, "American Arts and Crafts Architecture: Radical Though Dedicated to the Cause Conservative," in *The Art that is Life: The Arts and Crafts Movement in America* (Boston, 1987), pp. 101-31; idem, *McKim, Mead and White, Architects* (New York, 1983); Vincent Scully, Jr., *The Shingle Style and the Stick Style: Architectural Theory and Design from Richardson to the Origins of Wright*, rev. ed. (New Haven, Conn., 1971); and Doreen Bolger Burke, et al., *In Pursuit of Beauty: Americans and the Aesthetic Movement* (New York, 1986).

4 I am indebted, as is any historian who deals with this subject, to the writings of H. Allen Brooks, *The Prairie School: Frank Lloyd Wright and His Midwest Contemporaries* (Toronto, 1973); idem, "Chicago Architecture: Its Debt to the Arts and Crafts," *Journal of the Society of Architectural Historians* 30 (Dec. 1971), pp. 312-17; and Sharon Darling, *Chicago Furniture: Art, Craft and Industry, 1833-1983* (Chicago and New York, 1984).

5 Alan Crawford, "Ten Letters from Frank Lloyd Wright to Charles Robert Ashbee," *Architectural History* 12 (1970), pp. 64-76; idem, *C. R. Ashbee: Architect, Designer and Romantic Socialist* (New Haven, Conn., 1985). The titles of Wright's German publications were: *Ausgeführte Bauten und Entwürfe von Frank Lloyd Wright* (Berlin, 1910), known popularly as the "Wasmuth Portfolio"; and *Frank Lloyd Wright: Ausgeführte Bauten* (Berlin, 1911) with an introduction by C. R. Ashbee, known popularly as the "small Wasmuth."

6 Cheryl Robertson, *The Domestic Scene (1897-1927): George M. Niedecken, Interior Architect* (Milwaukee, Wisc., 1981).

7 Leonard K. Eaton, *American Architecture Comes of Age: European Reaction to H. H. Richardson and Louis Sullivan* (Cambridge, Mass., 1972), pp. 208-10.

8 Irving K. Pond, "German Arts and Crafts at St. Louis," *The Architectural Record* 17 (Feb. 1905), p. 121. See also, Gustav Stickley, "The German Exhibit at the Louisiana Purchase Exposition," *The Craftsman* 6 (Dec. 1904), pp. 488-506; and Brooks (note 4), p. 91.

9 C. Matlack Price, "Secessionist Architecture in America," *Arts and Decoration* 3 (Dec. 1912), pp. 51-53.

10 Karen Evans Ulehla, *The Society of Arts and Crafts, Boston: Exhibition Record 1897-1927* (Boston, 1981), pp. 4-5.

11 The founding membership list and constitution were published in *Catalogue of the Eleventh Annual Exhibition by the Chicago Architectural Club* (Chicago, 1898); see also Jane Addams, *Forty Years at Hull-House* (New York, 1935); and "Chicago Arts and Crafts Society," *Hull-House Bulletin* 1 (Dec. 1, 1897).

12 The origins of the Club go back to 1885 and the Chicago Architectural Sketch Club. See Wilbert R. Hasbrouck, *Chicago Architectural Journal* 1 (1981), pp. 7-14; and John Zukowsky, "The Chicago Architectural Club, 1895-1940," *Chicago Architectural Journal* 2 (1982), pp. 170-74.

13 The Art Institute of Chicago, *The Chicago Architectural Annual* (Chicago, 1902).

14 H. Allen Brooks, "Steinway Hall, Architects and Dreams," *Journal of the Society of Architectural Historians* 22 (Oct. 1963), pp. 171-75. See also Frank Lloyd Wright, *An Autobiography* (New York, 1977), pp. 147, 155.

15 Elmer Grey, "The Architect and the 'Arts and Crafts,'" *Architectural Record* 21 (Feb. 1907), pp. 134-37; Irving K. Pond, "The Life of Architecture," *Architectural Record* 18 (Aug. 1905), pp. 144-60; Robert Spencer, "American Farmhouses," *Brickbuilder* 9 (Aug. 1900), pp. 179-86; idem, "The Farmhouse Problem," *Annual of the Chicago Architectural Club* (Chicago, 1900), pp. 38-40; Frank Lloyd Wright, "The Art and Craft of the Machine" (1901), reprinted in *Frank Lloyd Wright: Writings and Buildings*, ed. Edgar Kaufmann and Ben Raeburn (New York, 1960), pp. 55-73; and idem, "In the Cause of Architecture," *Architectural Record* 23 (March 1908), pp. 155-222, reprinted in *Frank Lloyd Wright on Architecture*, ed. Frederick Gutheim (New York, 1941), pp. 31-45.

16 Brooks (note 4), p. 20. I am indebted to Debora Fulton for help on the problem of the machine in the Arts and Crafts movement.

17 Constitution (note 11), n. p.; see also "Notes," *The House Beautiful* 3 (Dec. 1897), p. 29.

18 Oscar Lovell Triggs, *Chapters in the History of the Arts and Crafts Movement* (Chicago, 1902), p. 193. Triggs wrote extensively, with articles in *The House Beautiful* and *The Craftsman*.

19 Wright, "The Art and Craft of the Machine" (note 15), pp. 55, 64-66.

20 Charles R. Ashbee, "Man and the Machine, The Soul of Architecture, II," *The House Beautiful* 28 (July 1910), pp. 55-56; Ashbee wrote three other articles for *The House Beautiful*, which appeared in June, August, and September, pp. 23-25; 88-90; 109-11.

21 Grey (note 15), p. 132.

22 Nancy K. Morris Smith, ed., "Letters, 1903-1906, by Charles E. White, Jr., from the Studio of Frank Lloyd Wright," *Journal of Architectural Education* 25 (Fall 1971), p. 104.

23 Irving K. Pond, *The Meaning of Architecture: An Essay in Constructive Criticism* (Boston, 1918), p. 175. Pond was critical of this horizontality as "running counter to the laws of nature."

24 H. Allen Brooks, "Percy Dwight Benteley at La Crosse," *The Prairie School Review* 9 (Third Quarter, 1972), pp. 6-8; and Richard Guy Wilson and Sidney K. Robinson, *The Prairie School in Iowa* (Ames, Iowa, 1977), pp. 6-7. See also "The Work of Tallmadge and Watson, Architects," *Western Architect* 22 (Dec. 1915), reprinted in H. Allen Brooks, ed., *Prairie School Architecture: Studies from "The Western Architect"* (Toronto, 1975), pp. 268-89.

25 On Purcell and Elmslie, see David Gebhard, "William Gray Purcell and George Grant Elmslie and the Early Progressive Movement in American Architecture from 1900 to 1920" (Ph. D. diss., University of Minnesota, 1957); and Brooks (note 24), pp. 80-129.

26 Henry Saylor, *Bungalows* (New York, 1911), pp. 40-41. See also, Robert Winter, *The California Bungalow* (Los Angeles, 1980); and Clay Lancaster, *The American Bungalow: 1880-1930*, (New York, 1985).

27 Mary Ann Smith, *Gustav Stickley, The Craftsman* (Syracuse, 1983), pp. 134-35; Louis H. Sullivan, "Reply to Mr. Rederick Stymetz Lamb on 'Modern Use of Gothic: The Possibility of New Architectural Style,'" *The Craftsman* 8 (June 1905), pp. 336-38; idem, "The Architectural Discussion: Form and Function Artistically Considered," ibid. 8 (July 1905), pp. 453-58; idem,

"What is Architecture? – A Study of the American People," ibid. 10 (May, June, July, 1906), pp. 142-49, 352-58, 507-13; Carl K. Bennett, "A Bank Built for Farmers: Louis Sullivan Designs a Building Which Marks a New Epoch in American Architecture," *The Craftsman* 15 (Nov. 1908), pp. 176-85.

28   Smith (note 27), pp. 57-72; William Gray Purcell and George G. Elmslie, "The American Renaissance," *The Craftsman* 21 (Jan. 1912), pp. 430-35; Oscar Lovell Triggs, "The Workshop-School," *The Craftsman* 3 (Oct. 1902), pp. 20-32; "The New Industrialism" (Nov. 1902), pp. 93-106; "A School of Industrial Art" (Jan. 1903), pp. 215-23; "The Play Principle," 4 (June 1903), pp. 286-94. See also *A Rediscovery: Harvey Ellis, Artist, Architect* (Rochester, N. Y., 1972).

29   Longer considerations of the Mason City development and the Melson House can be found in Wilson and Robinson (note 24), pp. 10-16; Robert E. McCoy, "Rock Crest-Rock Glen: Prairie School Planning in Iowa," *Prairie School Review* 5 (Third Quarter, 1968), pp. 5-39; and Brooks, *The Prairie School* (note 4), passim. See also Walter Burley Griffin, "Trier Center Neighborhood, Winnetka, Illinois," *Western Architect* 19 (Aug. 1913), pp. 75-76, reprinted in Brooks, *Prairie School Architecture* (note 24), pp. 16-17.

30   Wilson and Robinson (note 24), pp. 4-5; Wesley Shank, "The Residence in Des Moines," *Journal of the Society of Architectural Historians* 29 (Mar. 1970), pp. 56-59; Robert Spencer, Jr., "Country Houses," *House Beautiful* 19 (Dec. 1905), p. 23.

31   "House of Herbert Underwood, Esq., Fox Point, Wisc., Mr. Elmer Grey, Architect, Milwaukee, Wisconsin," *American Architect* 72, 1319 (Apr. 6, 1901), p. 8. Grey's drawings are at the University of California, Santa Barbara.

32   "Three Houses by Mr. Robert C. Spencer, Jr.," *Architectural Record* 18 (July 1905), pp. 40-50. On Spencer, see Brooks, *The Prairie School* (note 4), pp. 91-98 and passim; William Gray Purcell, "Spencer and Powers, Architects," *Western Architect* 20 (Apr. 1914), pp. 35 and passim, reprinted in Brooks, *Prairie School Architecture* (note 24), pp. 191-219.

33   Thomas E. Tallmadge, "Howard Van Doren Shaw," *Architectural Record* 60 (July 1926), pp. 71-73. On Shaw, see also Leonard K. Eaton, *Two Chicago Architects and their Clients: Frank Lloyd Wright and Howard Van Doren Shaw* (Cambridge, Mass., 1969); Richard Guy Wilson, *The AIA Gold Medal* (New York, 1984), pp. 47-59, 156-57; Julie L. Vosmik, "The Early Domestic Architecture of Howard Van Doren Shaw" (M. A. thesis, University of Virginia, 1982).

34   Illustrated in Thomas Tallmadge, "The 'Chicago School,'" *Architectural Review* 15 (Apr. 1908), p. 73.

35   Duncan Simpson, *C. F. A. Voysey: An Architect of Individuality* (New York, 1979), pp. 87-88; and Susan Dart, *Evelyn Shaw McCutcheon and Ragdale* (Lake Forest, Ill., 1980).

36   The Lutyens house reference is the upstairs hall at Munstead Wood for Gertrude Jekyll, 1893-1897, illustrated in Lawrence Weaver, *Houses and Gardens by Sir Edwin Lutyens* (London, 1913), p. 18.

37   "'Ragdale.' The Country Home of Mr. Howard Shaw, Lake Forest, Illinois," *Architectural Review* 11 (Jan. 1904), p. 25.

38   Both the Ellis chair and the Shaw desk are now in the collection of The Art Institute of Chicago.

39   Peter B. Wight, "The New Market Square at Lake Forest, Illinois," *Western Architect* 26 (Oct. 1917), p. 30; this article is the most extensive contemporary description of the development. See also Susan Dart, *Market Square, Lake Forest, Illinois* (Lake Forest, Ill., 1984).

40   Brooks, *The Prairie School* (note 4) and Eaton (note 33) are but two of many examples.

41   On the history of terminology, see Brooks, *The Prairie School* (note 4), pp. 7-13; and idem, "Chicago School: Metamorphosis of a Term," *Journal of the Society of Architectural Historians* 25 (June 1966), pp. 115-18. See also Hugh Garden, "A Style of the Western Plains," in Henry Saylor, *Architectural Styles for Country Houses* (New York, 1919), pp. 101-11.

42   Wright, "In the Cause of Architecture" (note 15), p. 31.

Louis H. Sullivan's Ornament and the Poetics of Architecture

Lauren S. Weingarden

Introduction:
A method for reading Sullivan's verbal and visual texts

Throughout his career Louis Sullivan wrote literary texts to explain his own design process and to comment on the architecture of his time.[1] He sought to fulfill both purposes with a critical method that at once deconstructed and reconstructed a nineteenth-century architectural discourse on the ontology of style. In his written work, Sullivan denigrated nineteenth-century historical copyism in order to realign American architecture with current conditions and timeless origins. But, as he explained, this critical method was contingent not only on written texts.

Sullivan also believed architecture should be read as a visual text. In one essay, "What is Architecture: A Study in the American People of Today" (1906), he observed that both the makers and viewers of nineteenth-century American architecture had lost "the gift for reading" past and present styles as "records" of "the thought of a people."[2] He further argued that the American people had failed to achieve a distinctive style with which to record their thought because both maker and viewer had severed their bonds with nature and the forces that shaped it. According to Sullivan, such a bond was recorded in all past "living" styles. He attributed the current aberrations to a prevailing "illogical gap between the theoretical and the practical." To close such a gap, he instructed the reader of his written text on how to become a reader of his visual texts.

Sullivan devised his reading instructions on the assumption that "the art of reading" is synonymous with "an art of interpretation." He thus explained that the reader-viewer should first learn to interpret the "book" of nature as a "symbol" of "its own creative energy and equipoise." Next, the reader-viewer should apply analogous interpretative methods to judge whether the parts and the whole of an architectural composition are "symbols" of both the artist's and nature's creative processes. In other words, Sullivan advised the reader-viewer to read his completed works of art as "PHILOSOPHY, POETRY AND AN ART OF EXPRESSION [sic]."[3]

Although Sullivan provided written instructions for reading the textual features of his visual texts, he did not leave instructions for reading his written texts. For this reason, modernist critics and historians have assumed much of Sullivan's writing to be lyrical, autobiographical discourses on non-architectural issues and have focused on the "functionalist" aspects of his architectural theory and designs.[4] But what these viewers have missed is that Sullivan used a metaphorical language for both his written and visual texts, intending his writings and buildings to co-function as exegesis and criticism. Without an understanding of how this metaphorical language works, we can understand neither the textual coherence of his theory and practice nor the symbolic function of his architectural schemes.

The first part of this essay addresses the way in which Sullivan appropriated linguistic models from nineteenth-century natural science and transcendentalist philosophy and poetry to explain how stylistic development originates in, and coincides with, continuity and change in nature. Specifically, it shows that Sullivan found in the scientific writings of English philosopher Herbert Spencer and the American transcendentalists Ralph Waldo Emerson and Walt Whitman a shared desire to make nature the focal point of present events and eternal laws.[5] Sullivan thus used the language of science because it provided a model for describing natural growth and decay. Likewise, he used the language of transcendentalist philosophy as a means for reconciling these scientific explanations of nature's apparent reality with metaphysical concepts of nature's hidden ideality. Sullivan found in poetry an exemplary model for using a symbolic language of nature's forms to re-present philosophy's conceptual synthesis of the real and ideal. In that Sullivan wanted his architecture to be considered co-equal with science, philosophy, and poetry, we shall see that he contributed to this nineteenth-century discourse on the language of nature by extending each of these verbal models and language-making procedures to architecture.

Fig. 1 Louis H. Sullivan, National Farmers Bank, 101 Cedar Street North, Owatonna, Minnesota, 1906-08, detail of exterior ornament.

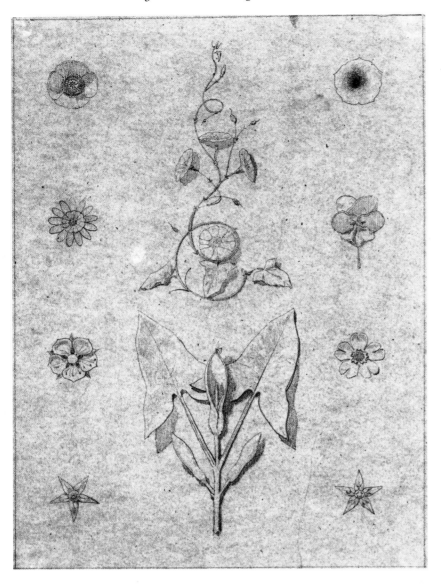

Fig. 2 Louis H. Sullivan, Sketch copy of composite ornament from Ruprich-Robert, Flore Ornamentale, *c. 1880 (cat. no. 108).*

Sullivan's verbal methods for reading, interpreting, and articulating a primal language of nature can be discerned in his use of metaphor as a literary feature and in his paraphrasing of scientific, philosophical, and poetic texts. Since he concurrently formulated a visual language of nature's text, his metaphorical and language-making procedures can also be demonstrated by verbal and visual references to aesthetic texts. The second part of this essay will show that Sullivan used John Ruskin's symbolic readings of nature and of Gothic ornament as guides to formulate an original, natural language of ornament in order to articulate what Sullivan called a "Poetic Architecture."

Sullivan's Concept of Style: The primal language of nature

Notwithstanding his visual dialogue with historical traditions, Sullivan sought to direct the nineteenth-century search for architectural renewal away from stylistic copyism and back to nature. It is in relation to his search for this primal, natural language of architecture that Sullivan's verbal references to the texts of Spencer, Emerson, and Whitman must be examined. He used these texts to compose "organic" analogies between nature and architecture in order to explain stylistic development and the artistic process. As we shall see, in Sullivan's verbal and visual language for an "organic system of ornament," the discourses of natural science and transcendentalist philosophy and poetry converge.

It is well known that Sullivan highly esteemed Herbert Spencer's writings on the theory of evolution.[6] What has not been investigated is how Sullivan adapted to his artistic ends a general theory of evolution, rather than a more limited biological one, through Spencer's application of the scientific "law of evolution" to metaphysical and sociological problems.[7] As the titles of Spencer's works suggest, in *First Principles of a New System of Philosophy; A System of Synthetic Philosophy* (1864) and *Illustrations of Universal Progress; A Series of Discussions* (1878) Spencer proposed the "universal law" of progressive evolution as the preeminent cause of all natural and human change. Assuming that "all is motion; all is rhythm," he described the evolutionary life cycle as the persistent interaction of conflicting forces of matter and motion, the cause of incessant growth and decay. Spencer characterized intervals within this cycle as phases of maturity; that is, when an organism achieves a relative stability, or dynamic equilibrium, between matter and motion.

Spencer's dialectical patterns of evolutionary growth and decay provided Sullivan with a strategy with which to move from stylistic copyism to organic representation. Sullivan signaled such a move in "Style," an essay written in 1888, in which he claimed, "Style is ever thus the response of the organism to the surroundings."[8] In this essay he described the linguistic function of style by combining a biological analogy with a nineteenth-century romantic exegesis of the creative process. Significantly, Sullivan shared this scheme with literary and pictorial artists who considered the completed work of art to be a symbol or metaphor of the original, albeit spiritual, source of inspiration. Sullivan thus made the artistic process parallel to nature's process. As he explained, a "true" work of art correlates with "style" as a "symbol or arbitrary sign" of "the soul [of nature, the artist, and the work of art], the inscrutable impelling force that determines an organism and its life."

In this essay Sullivan introduced a poetic model to explain the symbolic function of style and to describe his symbol-making procedures. Here,

Fig. 3 John Ruskin, "Abstract Lines"; from The Stones of Venice, *4th ed. (1886), vol. 1, pl. 7.*

again, he rejoined art with nature. Sullivan concluded by instructing the reader to contemplate the life cycle of the pine tree as a metaphor for stylistic "growth and decadence." He did so in order to disengage the reader's concept of style from the "grosser material envelopings" most vulnerable to decay. Rather than studying these external time-bound forms, Sullivan argued, the artist should seek style in nature's "poetic" text of "commonplace and simple things" so as to discern the "identity and spiritual nature" of a more profound reality beyond surface appearances. Subsequently Sullivan applied this poetic function to his "organic system of ornament." In doing so he called attention to his American transcendentalist lineage.

Sullivan combined a linguistic concept of style and a metaphoric concept of language by way of transcendentalist philosophical and poetic discourses. For Sullivan, as for his transcendentalist predecessors, poetry served philosophy as a language of symbols with which to connote spiritual reality. Given their shared literary assumptions, we

Fig. 4 Sullivan, Design for a ceiling, 1876 (cat. no. 110).

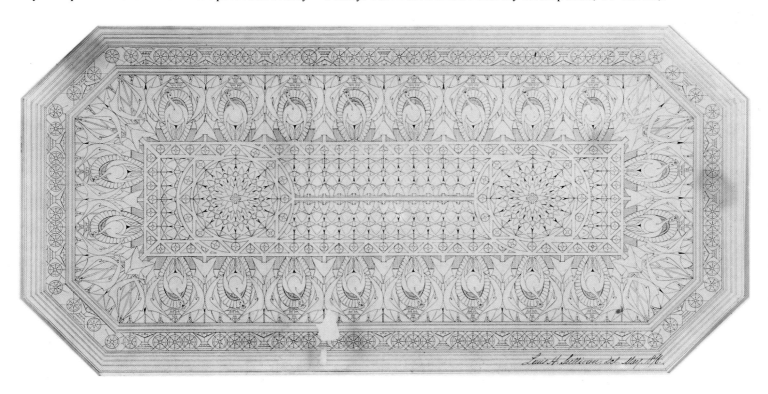

can examine how Ralph Waldo Emerson's theory of correspondences and Walt Whitman's poetry and prose facilitated Sullivan's translation of verbal into visual metaphors.

Sullivan directed his own symbol-making procedures to a problem posed by Emerson: how to sustain America's spiritual progress within a society increasingly dominated by material and technological progress.[9] Emerson urged innovators in both the mechanical and fine arts to become prophets for "transcendental democracy" and thus fulfill America's manifest destiny as "Nature's Nation."[10] Nevertheless, Emerson used the poet as a paradigm for instructing artists and artisans in every medium on the means for revealing the spiritual continuum between all things natural and manmade. As Emerson explained, the poet, who constantly recultivates the imagination in nature, uses words as analogues of all natural appearances and, in turn, as symbols of the "Divine Mind."

Fig. 5 Sullivan, Elevation study of a stair rail balustrade, c. 1880 (cat. no. 109).

Guided by Emerson's prescripts, Whitman further developed symbol-making as an American literary technique. In both the structure and imagery of his poetry and prose, Whitman converted apparently contradictory images of rural and urban existence, organic and mechanical forces, and individual and collective experiences into symbols of the "Kosmos" and its contingencies, the "Me" and the "Not-Me."[11]

Sullivan used Whitman's example to fulfill the Emersonian mission through the medium of architecture.[12] Specifically, Sullivan formulated a symbolic mode of ornament in two ways that drew on the form and content of Whitman's poems. On the one hand, Sullivan made ornament analogous to poetic expression in its relation to a recent technological event – the steel frame of the skyscraper as well as the socio-economic motivation for its construction. On the other, Sullivan renamed the triadic structure of Whitman's world view as the "Infinite Creative Spirit," an absolute generative force, and its contingent elements, the "objective" and the "subjective." He then correlated these terms with the geometric and botanical components of his ornament.

In the essay "Ornament in Architecture" (1892), Sullivan explained how he transformed poetic procedures for symbol-making into an architectural means of representation. He began his essay by asking, "Why do we need ornament?" He first answered this question by suggesting a moratorium on ornament so that the poet-architect could rediscover the beauty and primal meanings of "pure and simple," "elemental" forms, what he regarded as objective, logical articulations of "man's relation to nature and to his fellow man." But for Sullivan, designing reductivist geometric mass-compositions was merely the first phase in making rational construction artistic. At this stage, Sullivan declared, ornament "is mentally a luxury, not necessary." But it was with just this "luxury" that Sullivan, the poet-architect, was concerned. He thus argued that ornament satisfies an emotional necessity, "a craving to express . . . romanticism." Sullivan expressed this romanticism verbally and visually by conceiving ornament as "a garment of poetic imagery" with which to clad "strong, athletic and simple [tectonic] forms."[13] Viewing such statements in relation to his designs for skyscrapers, we can see that Sullivan renewed ornament as the subjective, organic counterpart to the objectively rendered mass-composition and underlying skeletal steel cage. For commercial architecture – as for other building types – he arranged the whole composition to represent the "Infinite Creative Spirit."

In his last written treatise, *A System of Architec-*

Fig. 6 Sullivan, Ornamental design, April 6, 1881; Michigan Historical Collections, Bentley Historical Library, University of Michigan.

Fig. 7 Sullivan, Ornamental scroll from the Jeweler's Building, 15-19 South Wabash Avenue, 1881-82 (cat. no. 111).

tural Ornament According with a Philosophy of Man's Powers (1922-23; 1924), Sullivan explicitly conjoined verbal and visual statements to demonstrate the symbolic function of his ornament, his evolutionary design process, and his theory of stylistic change (pls. 40, 41; cat. nos. 157-64).[14] In two short essays, "Prelude" and "Interlude," Sullivan rehearsed his theoretical and philosophical systems. For the main part of the treatise, he demonstrated these systems in twenty plates of ornamental designs. In the individual plates he verbally described and visually illustrated the design process as a developmental synthesis of "subjective-organic" and "objective-inorganic" elements into "mobile equilibrium."[15] In his use of such a verbal terminology, Sullivan continued to invoke Herbert Spencer's scientific theory of evolution.

Sullivan also invoked Spencer's evolutionary model of dialectical synthesis to explain his symbolic means of representation. Throughout the treatise he identified abstract geometric forms and "mechanical" axial patterns as symbols of the "objective-inorganic." Conversely, he identified botanical motifs and growth patterns with the "sub-

jective-organic." Finally, to show how the artist freely "manipulates" both the symbolic imagery of nature and human "logic," Sullivan began his "organic-inorganic" transformations in two alternative ways. He either initiated a "morphology" of composition with the "seed-germ" and other rudimentary botanical forms, or he began with straight, curved, angular, and undulating lines arranged in parallel, radial, and axial patterns.

Sullivan extended these verbal-visual analogies to align his new style with the eternal and time-bound origins of both ancient religions and modern science. He recorded how primitive societies had used similar, albeit simpler, more abstract geometric symbols to bring "the transcendental [into] physical, tangible and even psychic reality." He then asserted that modern society had evolved a more complex scientific and metaphysical comprehension of nature. Therefore, more intricate patterns replaced the earlier forms to reproduce the generative cosmic rhythms that have always inspired artistic creation. Given this historical perspective, Sullivan visually recorded his own realignment with the "universal," "primitive origins" of all true art from all times and places. By opposing and then combining the linear order of geometry with the organic efflorescence of plant motifs derived from his own scientific studies, he used both timeless and indigenous natural forms to depict "the universal power, or energy which flows everywhere at all times, in all places, seeking expression in form."[16]

Sullivan developed his symbolic mode of ornament and, by extension, his primal language of architecture out of a conceptual dialogue with the past, as well as out of a critical dialogue with the present "battle of the styles." In "Emotional Architecture as Compared to Intellectual: A Study in Objective and Subjective" (1894), he recast his evolutionary theory of stylistic change and his linguistic concept of style into a historical survey of architecture from pre-classical through medieval times.[17] He guided the reader back to the non-Western and primitive origins of Western styles, styles he considered to be the representations of a society's intuitive religious and mythic responses to natural conditions.

Turning last to the Gothic style, Sullivan juxtaposed this medieval mode with the ancient Greek style as paradigms of the primal language of objective and subjective representation. He identified the Greeks' structural statics and their love of pure form with "intellectual" responses to nature and an objective world view. Conversely, he associated Gothic structural dynamics and naturalistic ornament with emotional responses and a subjective world view. But now Sullivan emphasized the contrasts between the Greek and Gothic styles to show how each historical position was "too one-sided."

That the Gothic architecture, with sombre ecstatic eye, with its thought far above with Christ in the heavens, seeking but little here below, feverish and overwrought, taking comfort in gardening and plant life, sympathizing deeply with Nature's visible forms, evolved a copious and rich variety of incidental expressions but lacked the [Greeks'] unitary comprehension, the absolute consciousness and mastery of pure form that can come alone of unclouded and serene contemplation, of perfect repose and peace of mind.

In concluding his comparative analysis, Sullivan speculated on a synthesis of each world view and correlated means of expression:

I believe . . . that the Greeks knew the statics, the Goths the dynamics, of the art, but that neither of them suspected the mobile equilibrium of it: neither of them divined the movement and the stability of nature.[18]

It was with such a stylistic synthesis that Sullivan reconceived Emerson's view of America's manifest destiny in architectural terms. Sullivan prophesied for American architecture a synthesis of all "living art" and "the necessary [objective and subjective] elements of a great *Style*" (original emphasis). For Sullivan, such an American achievement would constitute a universal means of organic representation, signifying humanity's artistic and subsequent spiritual renewal in nature. He thus identified how the new style, what he called "the true, Poetic Architecture," re-presented "subjectivity and objectivity, not as two separate elements but as two complementary and harmonious phases of one impulse, that have always constituted and will always constitute the embodied spirit of art."[19]

In view of Sullivan's eventual synthesis of an objective and subjective means of representation in his mature style of ornament, we turn next to his early involvement with and transition from the Gothic style.[20] It was in this phase of his development, dating from 1873 to 1885, that he devised a formal analogy to and visual dialogue with a style he regarded as a "subjective-organic" representation of nature.

Sullivan's Formal Development: Renewing the natural language of style

Sullivan's earliest training in Gothic Revival ornament most singularly shaped his development of an innovative mode of ornament. In tracing Sullivan's formal development, Paul Sprague has documented the stylistic sources of and artistic influences upon his ornament. What follows expands on Sprague's observations to show how Sullivan reshaped the Gothic style into a network of formal and artistic analogies with nature.[21] In particular, it shows that Sullivan followed John Ruskin's method for extracting and combining abstract and realistic elements of design from Gothic motifs. Sullivan later retained this method to demonstrate the "organic" underpinnings of his mature ornament.

In *The Seven Lamps of Architecture* (1849) and in *The Stones of Venice* (1851-53) Ruskin presented a symbolist interpretation of the "organic" form and content of Gothic imagery. It is likely that the naturalistic connotations Ruskin attributed to Gothic ornament reinforced, if not mediated, similar descriptions Sullivan found in a variety of other nineteenth-century historical architectural treatises and handbooks on ornament.[22] Among these texts, Owen Jones's *Grammar of Ornament* (1854) was also important for conveying to Sullivan the "organic" principles of Gothic design.[23] Likewise, Victor-Marie Ruprich-Robert's *Flore Ornamentale* (1879) reaffirmed the naturalistic meanings of such principles without making historical references (fig. 2).[24]

While the formative influence of Jones's and Ruprich-Robert's treatises on Sullivan's early development has received scholarly attention, his

Fig. 8 Sullivan, Sketch of a column capital from the Wineman House, 2544 South Michigan Avenue, c. 1882; The Avery Architectural Library, Columbia University.

Fig. 9 Adler and Sullivan, Glazed terracotta relief panel from the Scoville Building, 619-31 West Washington Street, 1884-85 (demolished); The Saint Louis Art Museum.

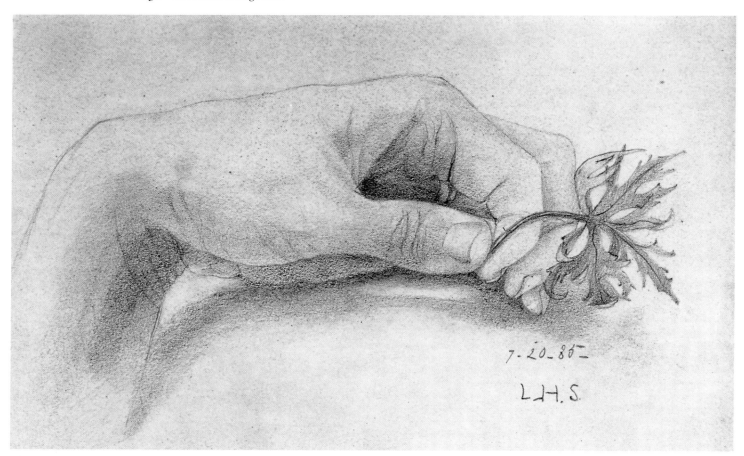

Fig. 10 Sullivan, Sketch of a hand with a leaf, July 20, 1885 (cat. no. 114).

equally strong and enduring connections with Ruskin's treatises have not. This oversight may be due to the fact that Sullivan once referred to Ruskin condescendingly, and that neither Sullivan nor his contemporaries explicitly associated Ruskin with Sullivan's work.[25] But throughout his written work, Sullivan paraphrased passages from Ruskin's *The Seven Lamps of Architecture* and *The Stones of Venice,* especially the chapters on "The Nature of Gothic" and "The Material of Ornament."[26] These verbal references, together with visual references to Ruskin's written and illustrated descriptions of Gothic naturalism, must count as concrete evidence of Sullivan's direct debt to Ruskin's treatises. Such references also indicate Sullivan's engagement in a Ruskinian discourse within American transcendentalist aesthetics, art education, and practice.[27]

Sullivan selected from Ruskin's texts those concepts and methods that informed his own Emersonian task in alleviating the objective, mechanistic conditions of architectural composition. Among Ruskin's lyricized and pictorial accounts of the Gothic craftsman's design process, Sullivan would have found definitions of ornament in relation to architecture that reaffirmed his transcendentalist concepts and symbol-making methods of poetic expression. For example, in *The Seven Lamps of Architecture,* Ruskin illuminated the subject of his treatise with the "lamp of sacrifice" by qualifying only ornamented structures as a true art form. Within this first lamp he defined architecture to be

that art which, taking up and admitting, as conditions of its working, the necessities and common uses of the building, impresses on its form certain characters venerable or beautiful, but otherwise unnecessary."[28]

Ruskin grounded this qualification in the moral and psychological impact of the art form on the viewer. He thus excluded from his definition of architecture what he called the "technical and constitutive elements [of] Building" or, simply, "construction."[29]

Sullivan's assertion that ornament is "mentally a luxury, not a necessary," indicates his ongoing verbal engagement with Ruskinian concepts.[30] But Sullivan went beyond adapting Ruskin's theoretical position on the relationship of ornament to construction for his own use; he also adapted from Ruskin artistic procedures for designing a symbolic mode of ornament derived from nature. Ruskin described such procedures in "The Nature of Gothic," in which he explained how the medieval craftsman transformed "the wayside herbage" into a symbol or "Mental Expression" of the spiritual bond between the maker and nature.[31]

Ruskin's technical description of Gothic "Naturalism" is what is important for evaluating Sullivan's formal dialogue with Ruskin's treatises. In "The Nature of Gothic," Ruskin rehearsed his discourse on "Naturalism" (taken, in turn, from his treatise on painting), to explain how the medieval craftsman integrated an abstract with a realistic depiction of organic life.[32] He thus surveyed the historical origins of abstraction in Gothic design. First, he observed that in the earliest Gothic designs crude and imperfect rendering of the natural model caused distortions, what Ruskin sanctioned as the inevitable yet audacious sign of an emerging "living art."[33] He then demonstrated how such distortions were relieved by the more realistically portrayed "wandering of the tendril and the budding of the flower." Finally, he observed that the Gothic craftsmen subsequently perfected imperfection, making distortion into an abstract element of design for symbolic and formal ends. Ruskin identified this Gothic fusion of the abstract and real as "Naturalism." For Ruskin, "Naturalism" is at once the symbolic "Mental Expression" of the artist's "intense affection" for nature and the artistic means for re-presenting nature in the obdurate materials of architecture.[34]

According to this double view of the creative process, Ruskin outlined, categorized, and illustrated the abstract principles of Gothic design in terms of a linear symbolism (fig. 3). In "The Material of Ornament," Ruskin reconceived the medieval craftsman's symbol-making design process. Assuming that the medieval craftsman felt nature to be imbued with an eternal divine presence, Ruskin explained that all visible forms and vital forces of nature became the "proper materials of ornament." He defined such "materials" as "whatever God has created and its proper treatment . . . in accordance with or symbolical of His laws."[35] Guided by his rule that beauty in nature is determined by the frequency and visibility of its forms, he asserted that "all perfectly beautiful forms must be comprised of curves; since there is hardly any common natural form in which it is possible to discover a straight line."[36] Ruskin restated his preference for using curved lines as a means of organic expression in recording the vital, incessant flux of nature. As in the portrayal of concrete appearances, he observed that "the essential character of Beauty depends on the expression of vital energy in organic things [found in] lines of changeful curve, . . . expressive of action, of force of some kind."[37]

Fig. 11 Sullivan, Sketch of an ornamental detail, c. 1885 (cat. no. 115).

Fig. 12 Ruskin, "Ornaments from Rouen, St. Lo, and Venice"; from The Seven Lamps of Architecture *(1848; rpt. 1886), pl. 1.*

We can now examine just how Ruskin's discourse on Gothic "Naturalism" mediated Sullivan's adaptations from both nature and art. Extant decorative schemes, architectural fragments, preparatory studies, and finished drawings provide material for reviewing Sullivan's visual engagement with Ruskin during this transitional phase of his development. We shall read this engagement in three ways: in Sullivan's "subjective-organic" transformations of Gothic Revival and medieval Gothic motifs; in his artistic re-presentation of natural motifs; and in his mode of representing an ornamental design and its "natural" model.

Sullivan first practiced designing "conventionalized" Gothic Revival ornament as an apprentice in the Philadelphia office of Furness and Hewitt in 1873.[38] From that time, until about 1880, he closely followed the traditionally static and rigid forms of conventionalized botanical motifs (fig. 4). He then began to modify these forms with Ruskinian techniques. For example, Sullivan's drawing for a balustrade (1880; fig. 5) shows that while his Gothic Revival motifs of 1880 strongly resemble Frank Furness's decorative motifs for the Pennsylvania Academy of Design (1871-76) and the Guarantee Trust and Safe Deposit Co. (1873-75), these similarities are of a particular kind.[39] That is, Sullivan's designs emulate Furness's conventionalized botanical patterns dominated by curvilinear substructures.

Similar references to Ruskin and Furness persist in Sullivan's drawings from 1881 to 1883. Sullivan's modifications of Furness's Gothic Revival motifs, seen in a drawing of 1881 (figs. 6, 7), invoke formal descriptions analogous to Ruskin's views of "wandering tendrils" in the original models of Gothic "Naturalism" (fig. 8).[40] As in the other 1881-83 designs, Sullivan arranged scrolling, scalloped, and radiating fan-shaped leaves, rosettes, and buds into asymmetrical patterns of curved, spiraling lines. With this dominating curvilinear element, however, Sullivan infused the 1881-83 designs with an organic integrity and dynamic expansion lacking in Furness's more compact and axial patterns.

By 1884 Sullivan increasingly submerged conventionalized Gothic Revival elements into networks of curved lines and more realistic motifs; he developed such "subjective-organic" elements in two ways. He began to render curvilinear configurations more broadly, more abstractly, and more variously than he had done earlier in the 1881-83 designs. In addition, he developed a more realistic rendering of botanical forms. Sometimes he combined these forms with abstract geometries; sometimes he did not.[41]

A new imagery appears in Sullivan's more abstract, curvilinear designs of 1884. The inception of this imagery can be seen in a drawing dated May 6, 1884, in which Gothic Revival motifs are subsumed by curvilinear forms (cat. no. 113).[42] In the drawing, a profusion of scrolls terminated by smooth-faced bulbous orbs surrounds an asymmetrically placed bud and a profiled scalloped leaf; the whole unfurls from a single stalk. What distinguishes this scheme from the 1883 motifs is that the scrolls are more numerous, and a single, dominant, sweeping, yet receding, curve enframes the entire image.

Sullivan further developed these curvilinear forms in what became his most original design to that date. In this scheme he extended an enframing scroll and undulating whiplash forms from a dominant, central orb. Because this motif is independent of historical styles, yet still distinct from Sullivan's mature style, we can conveniently refer to the combination of orb-scroll-whiplash as the "1884 motif."[43] This distinction is also suggested by the pediments of the Scoville Building (1884-85; fig. 9) and the chimney panel relief from the Rubel House, both in Chicago (1884; cat. no. 112); Sullivan used this motif extensively during 1884 for both commercial and residential designs.

In 1884 Sullivan recombined a variety of curvilinear forms to produce a more sinuous composition, characteristic of the greater "movement, fluidity, and naturalism" that informs his mature work.[44] Thus, the May 6, 1884, drawing and the related "1884 motif" reliefs represent a formal continuum between Sullivan's more derivative style and the early phase of his mature style. But an equally important developing symbolism connects the earlier and later works. The changes that result in the "1884 motif" need to be considered in the context of Sullivan's search for a symbolic means of representation; these changes are also evidence of his experiments with Ruskin's abstract principles of organic design.

Sullivan would have found in Ruskin's "The Material of Ornament" a symbolism of curvilinear forms and of undulatory lines pertinent to his own symbol-making procedures. Here Ruskin explained that "undulatory lines" answer an artistic need to introduce "some representation of water to explain the scene of an event, or as a sacred symbol."[45] Sullivan's whiplash forms evoke both aquatic motion and organic expansions of roots and tendrils. These references to Ruskin's symbols of "vital energy" are especially pronounced when the complete "1884 motif" is correlated with Sullivan's verbal descriptions of natural events. In his earliest writings, Sullivan used the artist's return to nature as a literary topos to suggest the natural origins of a new style. As in *Kindergarten Chats* (1901-02; 1918), his most complete statement of this theme, Sullivan relocated the architectural student in the midst of a forest or, occasionally, in front of an open seascape to witness at first hand the macrocosm in the microcosm; that is, the cyclical drama of nature's growth and decay as the outworking of an ineffable evolutionary force. In the context of his efforts to make analogies between verbal and visual forms, the "1884 motif" can be recognized as Sullivan's first overt attempt to create an original symbolism for what he considered the cause of all morphological change — the "Infinite Creative Spirit."

Fig. 13 Ruskin, "The Acanthus of Torcello"; from The Stones of Venice, 4th ed. (1886), vol. 2, pl. 2.

Beginning in 1885, Sullivan turned more directly to nature rather than to completed styles (cat. no. 116). In the course of that year, he verbally alluded to this turn by invoking Ruskin's medieval artist in the essay "Characteristics and Tendencies of American Architecture" (1885). Here he wrote that although the modern architect may be troubled by practical realities in realizing "an insuppressible yearning toward ideals," the artist-architect must nurture such ideals in "the wayside, yielding refreshing odors and the joy of color to the plodding wayfarer."[46] Evidently, at the inception of his mature phase, Sullivan continued to use Ruskin as a guide in relocating the origins of a new style in nature. In both his more realistic depictions of vegetation and his mode of representing how the real becomes the ideal, Sullivan proceeded in the spirit of Ruskin's Gothic craftsman rather than in imitation of Gothic forms.

Ornamental studies dating from 1885 show that Sullivan extended both the organic form and symbolic connotations of the abstract whiplash and curves from the "1884 motif" to a more realistic portrayal of vegetal motifs (figs. 10, 11).[47] This shift from organic abstraction to botanical realism indicates that he probably realized the limited communicative value of suggestive, albeit elusive, symbolic imagery.[48] Indeed, Sullivan's realistic renderings of spikey-edged and sinuous, fleshy leaves recall Ruskin's drawings of thistle and acanthus leaves before and after they became stone-carved ornament (figs. 12-15). At the same time, Sullivan used realistic plant imagery to make reference to the primeval vegetation of the American landscape.

These 1885 studies also reveal how Sullivan rearranged the real according to an abstract ideal. Whether using curves or straight lines and angles, he retained an underlying geometric order both as a unifying device and as a symbolic motif. These formal changes bring the 1885 drawings closest to the mature style he first fully realized in 1886-89 with the decorative schemes for the Auditorium Building.[49] Coincidently, Sullivan began to use a mode of graphic representation that further connects his procedures with Ruskin's and, in turn, with the Gothic craftsman inspired by nature.

A number of Sullivan's studies dating from his transitional phase in 1885 follow Ruskin's method of showing how the natural model undergoes a process of abstraction as it is carved in stone and integrated into the architectural fabric. Ruskin variously depicted the natural and the carved motif with three schemes: in paired juxtaposition; in separate stages of sequential transformations; and in fully organicized ornamental and vegetal unities that encroach upon architectural boundaries

Fig. 14 Adler and Sullivan, Carved wood relief from the Auditorium Building, c. 1888-89.

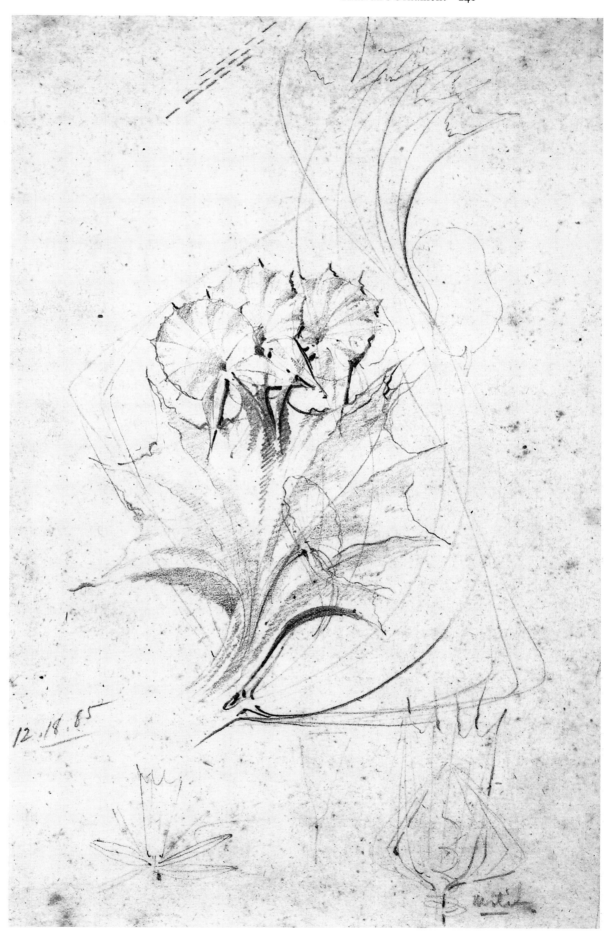

12.18.85

Fig. 15 Sullivan, Ornamental study, Dec. 18, 1885; The Avery Architectural Library, Columbia University.

Fig. 16 Ruskin, "Part of the Cathedral of St. Lo, Normandy"; from The Seven Lamps of Architecture (1848; rpt. 1886), pl 2.

(fig. 16). Likewise, in his ornamental studies (as in the plates of his treatise), Sullivan frequently placed small-scale realistic sketches of plants and/or geometric notations above or below and to the side of the finished study. In this way he recorded his process for extracting geometry from nature and, then, for transforming the original natural model into an ornamental form.[50]

Sullivan made similar references to Ruskin in preparatory and working drawings for the Auditorium Building reliefs and in the finished work. He repeated scrolling acanthus leafs superimposed on linear spiraling forms in the corbels, newel posts, and arches of the Auditorium Theater, Cafe, and Hotel lobbies (figs. 17, 18). Sullivan here represented the morphological transitions of the natural model in relief form just as Ruskin had

illustrated such a conversion in Plate 1 of *The Seven Lamps of Architecture* and Plate 2 of *The Stones of Venice* (figs. 12, 13). Similarly, in the graphic versions of these motifs, such as the drawings for ornamental arches, Sullivan depicted realistic vegetation and abstract scroll motifs as a vital unity, a unity in tension with inert architectural enframements. Sullivan's arrangement is a variation of Ruskin's more completely organicized scheme in Plate 2 of *The Seven Lamps of Architecture*. Finally, an analogous organic transformation unfolds in the working drawings for ornamental lightbulb sockets — but in a reverse and sequential order (fig. 19). In this and later examples, Sullivan initiated vegetal growth with an abstract order, developing his organic ornamental motif within the segments of radial axes (figs. 1, 20, 21).

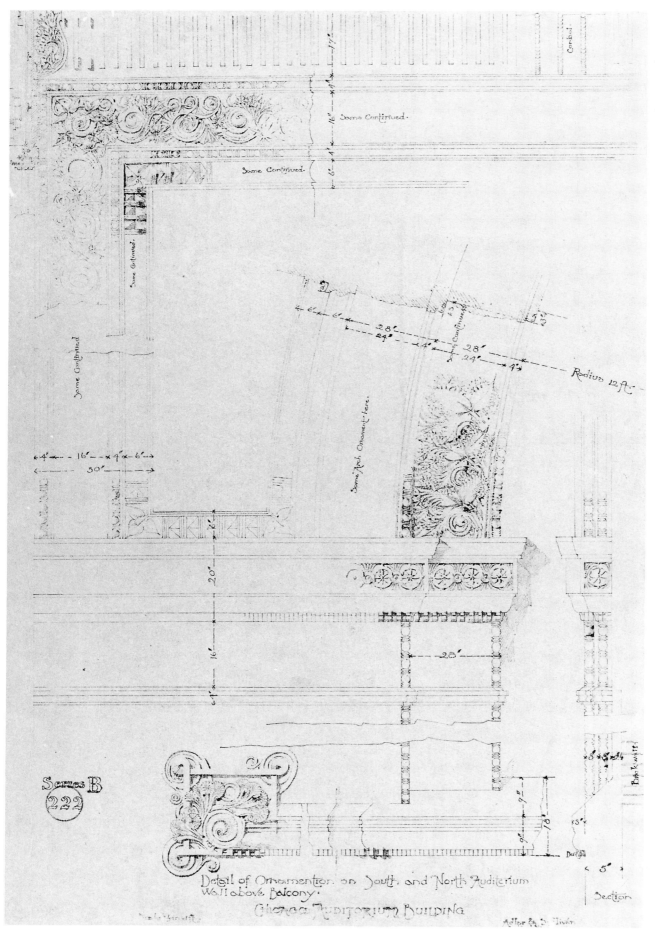

*Fig. 18
Adler and Sullivan,
Working drawing
for the ornamentati[on]
of the north
and south wall abo[ve]
the balcony,
Auditorium Theate[r]
c. 1887
(cat. no. 118).*

Detail of Ornamentation on South and North Auditorium Wall above Balcony.

Chicago Auditorium Building

Series B
222

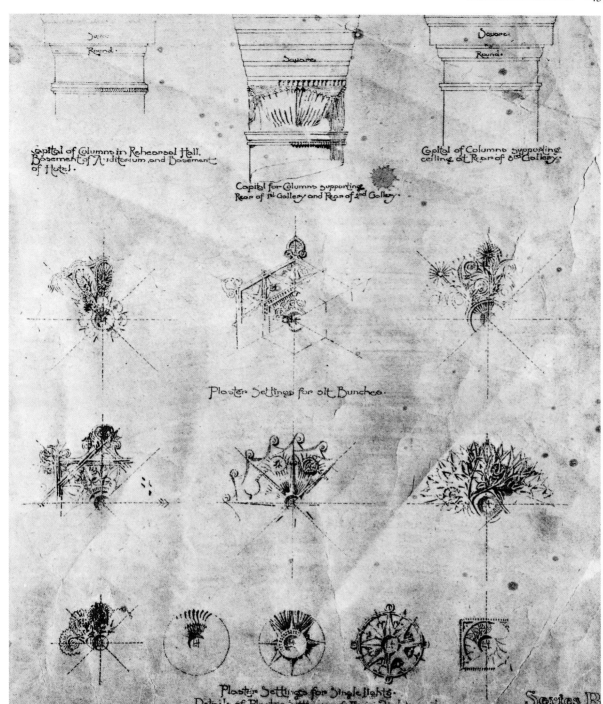

Fig. 19 Adler and Sullivan, Working drawing for the Auditorium Building, c. 1887; The Art Institute of Chicago.

From the design of the Auditorium Building until the definitive exegesis of his system of architectural ornament in 1922-23, Sullivan refined this graphic mode of presenting the evolutionary sequences of his design process. Plates 2 and 10 of *A System of Architectural Ornament* (fig. 22) are especially revealing of how Sullivan's ornament indicated his return to nature by way of science and art. Sullivan made explicit his return to nature by way of science by adding the inscription "Remember the Seed Germ," and by including references to Asa Gray's *School and Field Book of Botany* and Edmund Beecher Wilson's *The Cell in Development and Heredity* (see Plate 5 for the latter). At the same time he made implicit his coincident return to nature by way of art. If we read these references according to Sullivan's verbal and visual analogies, we can see how he used patterns of sequential and curvilinear growth to record his own realignment with Gothic naturalism by way of John Ruskin.

The Ruskinian Gothic line of development is only one side, even if the dominant one, of Sullivan's conception of a new American style. In the

plates of his treatise, he also recorded his reunion of Gothic naturalism with classical rationalism, a tradition he inherited from French academicism. How he evolved a neo-Platonic symbolism from this classical tradition must be the subject of another study. This essay has limited itself to a study of Sullivan's evolutionary theory of stylistic change to show how he recorded that theory in his transition to and attainment of a new mode of ornament. It has also demonstrated that we can recover the original reciprocity between Sullivan's theory and practice by using a linguistic model of interpretation. With this model, new evidence has emerged from known documents. This evidence reveals how Sullivan made artistic choices and devised formal procedures according to his search for an indigenous style grounded in and representative of nature.

Fig. 20 Sullivan, National Farmers Bank, Owatonna, Minnesota, exterior.

Fig. 21 Terracotta relief ornament for the National Farmers Bank.

Fig. 22 Louis H. Sullivan, "Fluent Parallelism," 1922; from A System of Architectural Ornament *(1924), pl. 10.*

FLUENT PARALLELISM
[NON-EUCLIDIAN]

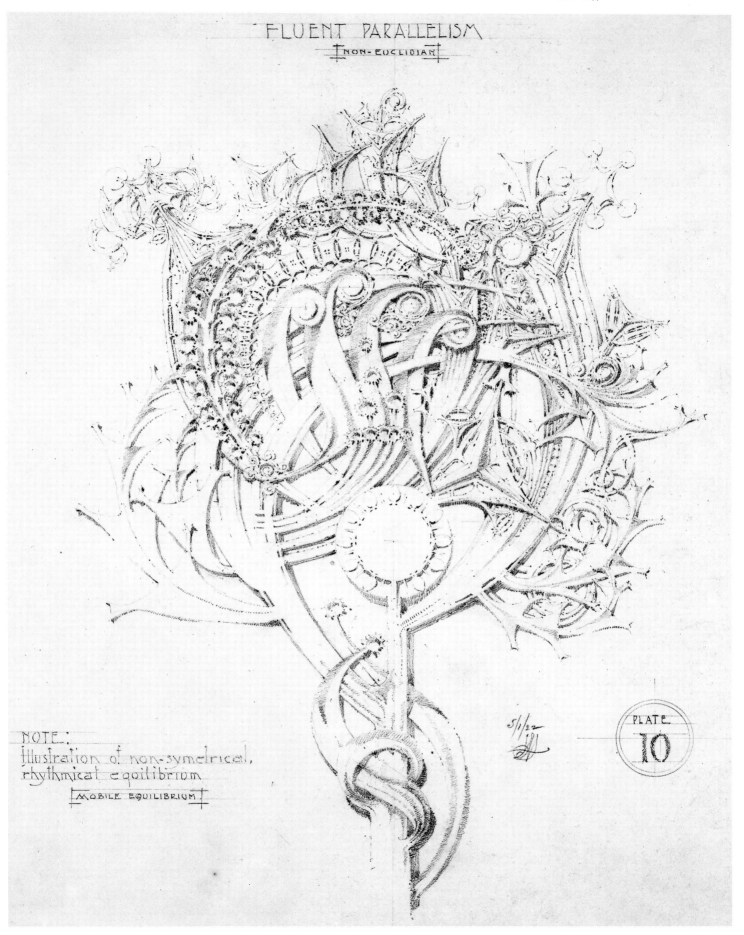

NOTE:
Illustration of non-symetrical, rhythmical equilibrium
[MOBILE EQUILIBRIUM]

5/1/22

PLATE
10

NOTES

1 Sullivan's earliest known writings on ornament and architecture appear in the "Lotos Club Notebook" (1872-82; New York, Avery Architectural Library, Columbia University). This "Notebook" contains the records of athletic events and reading programs for "Club" members, as well as architectural sketches by Sullivan and John Edelmann. Willard Connely transcribed a notebook essay on "distemper decoration" written by Edelmann and introduced (and possibly coauthored) by Sullivan; see Willard Connely, *Louis Sullivan as He Lived: The Shaping of the American Architecture* (New York, 1960), pp. 77-79.

2 Louis H. Sullivan, "What is Architecture: A Study in the American People of Today" (1906) in *Kindergarten Chats and Other Writings,* ed. Isabella Athey (New York, 1947), pp. 228-29.

3 Ibid., pp. 239-41.

4 In *The Autobiography of an Idea* (New York, 1924), Sullivan recalled that only a few of his like-minded colleagues understood the architectural ramifications of one of his earliest and most esoteric papers, "Inspiration: A Poem in Prose," when he presented it to the 1886 annual convention of The Western Association of Architects (see pp. 301-02). "Inspiration" was published as "Essay on Inspiration" in *Inland Architect and Building News* 8 (Dec. 1886) and as a brochure by Inland Architect Press (1886; rpt., Chicago, 1964).

5 Which books Sullivan read and owned can be determined partially from the "Lotos Club Notebook" reading list, his *Autobiography* (note 4), a list of books (now at the American Institute of Architects, Washington, D.C.) he left at his vacation home in Ocean Springs, Mississippi (microfilm; The Art Institute of Chicago) and an auction list of books. Williams, Barker and Severn Co. *Auction catalogue No. 5533,* Chicago, Nov. 29, 1909. Burnham Library, The Art Institute of Chicago. Now in David S. Andrew, *Louis Sullivan and the Polemics of Modern Architecture* (Chicago, 1985), appendix 2, p. 162. What books Sullivan retained or acquired after 1909 can be inferred partly by his tendency to paraphrase other authors.

6 Frank Lloyd Wright claimed that Sullivan "loved Walt Whitman's 'Leaves of Grass' and read Herbert Spencer," adding that Sullivan gave him works by both authors; see *Genius and the Mobocracy* (New York, 1949), p. 72; *An Autobiography* (New York, 1943), p. 103. Spencer's *Synthetic Philosophy* and *Illustrations of Universal Progress* appear on Sullivan's 1877 reading list in the "Lotos Club Notebook" (note 1). In his *Autobiography* (note 4), Sullivan named Spencer and Darwin with other nineteenth-century evolutionists in whose "theories of evolution he found much food for thought" (pp. 254-55). Here Sullivan also praised Spencer's notion of a "beneficent power" as the "primal" causative force underlying all growth and decay (p. 225).

7 Sullivan's metaphysical understanding of the theory of evolution is closer in both concepts and terminology to Spencer's philosophical writings than to Darwin's more mechanistic, scientific – albeit atheistic – descriptions and theory of evolution. Sullivan's upbringing among New England transcendentalist literary and religious leaders shaped his receptivity to Spencer. For an account of Spencer's popularity among transcendentalist intellectuals (especially because he acknowledged both a deity and religion), see Stow Persons, "Evolution and Theology in America," in *Evolutionary Thought in America,* ed. Stow Persons (New Haven, Conn., 1968), p. 424. For a treatment of Sullivan's appropriations of Darwin's and Spencer's theories of evolution, see Lauren Weingarden, "Louis H. Sullivan's Metaphysics of Architecture (1885-1901): Sources and Correspondences with Symbolist Art Theories" (Ph.D. diss., University of Chicago, 1981).

Modernist architectural historians have not made the distinction between Spencer's and Darwin's concepts of evolution. Therefore, Sullivan's theory of organic expression, and its corollary, "form follows function," have been traditionally associated with a "mechanistic-rationalist" interpretation. See, for example, Donald Drew Egbert, "The Idea of Organic Expression and American Architecture," in *Evolutionary Thought in America*, pp. 361-63. Paul Sprague, in "Louis Sullivan and his Chief Draftsmen" (Ph.D. diss., Princeton University, 1969), pp. 14-20, 40-41, attempted to correct such a misunderstanding by pointing to Sullivan's metaphysical idea of function as a "vitalistic," immaterial creative force, a force most effectively represented in his ornament. He did not, however, attempt to describe Sullivan's symbolic means of representation. See also note 16 below.

8 Louis H. Sullivan, "Style," a paper read at the Chicago Architectural Sketch Club, April 9, 1888; published in *Inland Architect and Building News* 11 (May 1888), pp. 59-60. In this essay, Sullivan reformulated his earlier poetic dramatization of the artist's creative process in nature, presented in "Inspiration" (note 4).

9 Sullivan enriched this American tradition with an investigation of nineteenth-century German idealist philosophy, a pursuit which began in 1876; see Sullivan, *Autobiography* (note 4), pp. 206, 249. Although writing in 1923, he disclaimed the philosophical abstractions of the Germans. Sullivan did acknowledge Arthur Schopenhauer's science of aesthetics as being relevant to his own artistic project (p. 209). We know from Sullivan's auction list (note 5) that he owned Schopenhauer's *Essays.* Beginning with "Inspiration" (1886) Sullivan consistently used the terms "objective" and "subjective" to describe the artistic transformations of the ideal into the real. These passages, together with Sullivan's anti-materialist statements, strongly suggest Sullivan's direct access to Schopenhauer's idealist aesthetic system and philosophy of pessimism presented in *The World as Will and Idea,* trans. R. B. Haldane and J. Kemp (London, 1883-86). For a discussion of late nineteenth-century idealist aesthetics and the discourse of objective-subjective representation, see Richard A. Shiff, "The End of Impressionism: A Study in Theories of Artistic Expression," *Art Quarterly* (Autumn 1978), pp. 338-78; and Weingarden (note 7).

10 For Emerson's discussions of the artist's prophetic mission and creative process, see "Art" (1836) and "The Poet" (1844) in *Ralph Waldo Emerson: Essays and Lectures,* ed. Joel Porte (New York, 1983), pp. 431-40, 445-68; and "Thoughts on Art" (1841) in *The Literature of Architecture,* ed. Don Gifford (New York, 1966), pp. 99-110.

11 See, for example, Walt Whitman, "Preface," *Leaves of Grass* (1855) and "Democratic Vistas" (1870) in *Walt Whitman: Complete Poetry and Prose,* ed. Justin Kaplan (New York, 1982), pp. 1-26, 929-94.

12 Sullivan first acknowledged Whitman as his literary mentor when he sent the poet a copy of "Inspiration" and asked him for a critical appraisal; see letter to Whitman, February 9, 1887, in Sherman Paul, *Louis Sullivan: An Architecture in American Thought* (Englewood Cliffs, N.J., 1962), pp. 1-3. In his essay "The Tall Office Building Artistically Considered" (1896), Sullivan clearly indicated that in designing skyscrapers he wanted to make a philosophical statement. See *Kindergarten Chats* (note 2), pp. 202-13, esp. 206; revised as "Form and Function Artistically Considered," *The Craftsman* 8 (July 1905). See also Lauren S. Weingarden, "Naturalized Technology: Sullivan's Whitmanesque Skyscrapers," *Centennial Review* 30 (Fall 1986), pp. 480-95.

13 Louis H. Sullivan, "Ornament in Architecture" (1892), in *Kindergarten Chats* (note 2), pp. 187-90.

14 In 1922 the Burnham Library of The Art Institute of Chicago commissioned Sullivan to record his philosophy and design process of ornament; see John Zukowsky and Pauline Saliga, "Late Works by Burnham and Sullivan," *The Art Institute of Chicago Museum Studies* 11, 1 (Fall 1984), pp. 73-74. The completed work was published in 1924 by the American Institute of Architects as *A System of Architectural Ornament According with a Philosophy of Man's Powers.* George Grant Elmslie, Sullivan's chief draftsman from 1893 to 1909, donated the original drawings for the volume to the Burnham Library in 1931.

15 In the drawing for Plate 3 Sullivan used the Spencerian term "Mobile Equilibrium," in the published work he used "Mobile Geometry"; perhaps he made this change to emphasize the synthesis of opposite phenomena. Elmslie, writing about Sullivan's "organic" system of ornament illustrated in the treatise, also used Spencerian terminology. See Elmslie's essay of 1935 entitled "Sullivan's Ornamentation," reprinted in *American Institute of Architects Journal* 6 (Oct. 1946), pp. 155-58.

16 Sullivan, "Interlude," *A System of Architectural Ornament* (note 14). In *Kindergarten Chats* (note 2) Sullivan provided a similar definition of "form follows function," correlating "function" with the "Infinite Creative Spirit" and "form" with the material embodiment of the immaterial. Likewise, Sullivan connected the "objective" and "subjective" symbolism with the primary elements of architecture – the pier, lintel, and arch. See *Kindergarten Chats* (note 2), pp. 46, 120-24; 160-76.

17 Sullivan, "Emotional Architecture as Compared with Intellectual" (1894), in *Kindergarten Chats* (note 2), pp. 191-201, esp. pp. 196-97.

18 Ibid., pp. 200-201.

19 Ibid., p. 194.

20 Expanding on Sprague's observations, Narciso Menocal has also pointed to medieval Gothic "sources" of Sullivan's architectural compositions and ornamental designs, and to Viollet-le-Duc's discussions of Gothic construction and drawings of Gothic ornament; see Narciso G. Menocal, *Architecture as Nature: The Transcendentalist Idea of Louis Sullivan* (Madison, Wisc., 1981), pp. 18, 24, 45-51. Sullivan owned Benjamin Bucknall's translation of Viollet-le-Duc's *Discourses on Architecture* (1889; rpt., New York, 1959) and *Dessins inédits de Viollet-le-Duc* (Paris, 1884). See also notes 5 and 22.

21 Because of their formalist methods, Sprague denied and Menocal may have overlooked Sullivan's artistic engagement with Ruskin; see Sprague (note 7), pp. 64-65.

22 Sullivan's 1909 auction list included a wide range of historical studies of architecture and ornament, from antiquity through the nineteenth century, including monographs on works by his contemporaries. While Owen Jones's and Ruprich-Robert's treatises are not on this list, Habert-Dys's *Fantaisies Decoratives* (Paris, 1886) is. This treatise must be counted among those visual sources that Sullivan used to formulate an imagery of geometric and naturalistic motifs.

As cited in note 20, Sullivan owned Viollet-le-Duc's *Discourses on Architecture.* Here, too, Sullivan would have been verbally and visually informed that the Gothic masons derived ornamental imagery from "local flora" and then made the natural model "sober and rational" by subordinating ornament to the geometric contours and dynamic forces of Gothic construction; see Viollet-le-Duc, *Discourses on Architecture* (note 20), vol. 1, pp. 270-71.

23 For a discussion of the technical influence of Jones's design principles on Sullivan's ornament, see Sprague (note 7), pp. 65-68 and *The Drawings of Louis Henry Sullivan: A Catalogue of the Frank Lloyd Wright Collection at the Avery Library* (Princeton, N.J., 1979), pp. 4-5, hereafter noted as *Avery*. In his *Autobiography* (note 6) Frank Lloyd Wright recalled that in 1888 Sullivan had trouble recalling Jones (pp. 91-92). However, Sullivan's 1885 foliage sketches from nature (Avery Nos. 19-24) and the Samuel Stern door panel relief (*Louis H. Sullivan Architectural Ornament Collection: Southern Illinois University at Edwardsville* [Edwardsville, Ill., 1982], hereafter noted as *SIU*, figs. 21-22) suggest that Sullivan used Jones's "Leaves from Nature" (Owen Jones, *The Grammar of Ornament* [1854], pls. 91-92) as examples for returning from abstraction to a closer approximation of nature. Furthermore, Jones's thirty-four design principles, transcribed from *The Grammar of Ornament,* immediately preceded Sullivan's descriptive essay of the Auditorium Building decorations; see *Industrial Chicago* 2 (Chicago, 1891), pp. 487-91.

24 For Sullivan's ongoing involvement with Ruprich-Robert's *Flore Ornamentale,* see Theodore Turak, "French and English Sources of Sullivan's Ornament and Doctrines," *Prairie School Review* 2 (Fourth Quarter 1974), pp. 6-17; and for Sullivan's contact with this treatise while apprenticed to Frank Furness in 1873, see James O'Gorman, *The Architecture of Frank Furness* (Philadelphia, 1972), pp. 35-36. In a paper presented to the "Louis Sullivan Session" of the 1984 Midwest Art History Association Annual Meeting, David Van Zanten suggested that while Sullivan was in Paris as a student at the Ecole des Beaux-Arts (1874-75) he may have traced Ruprich-Robert's motifs before these plates were bound in book form.

25 See, for example, Sullivan, "The Young Man in Architecture" (1900), in *Kindergarten Chats* (note 2), pp. 214-23, quotation, p. 215.

26 Throughout this essay, references to John Ruskin, *The Seven Lamps of Architecture* will be cited from the reprint of the 1849 edition (New York, 1979). References

to John Ruskin, *The Stones of Venice* 1, 2 will be cited from Vols. 9 and 10, respectively, Library Edition of *The Works of John Ruskin*, ed. E. T. Cook and Alexander Wedderburn (London, 1903-12). Citations will refer to chapter title, short book title, paragraph, and page.

27 For a discussion of Ruskin's influence on American art education and transcendentalist aesthetics, see Roger Stein, *John Ruskin and Aesthetic Thought in America: 1860-1900* (Cambridge, Mass., 1967). Sullivan would have come into direct contact with Ruskinian theory and design during his apprenticeships with Frank Furness (see O'Gorman [note 24], pp. 20-21) and with William Le Baron Jenney (1874) (see Turak [note 24], p. 6). John Edelmann's Gothic Revival designs (see Donald Drew Egbert and Paul Sprague, "In Search of John Edelmann," *American Institute of Architects Journal* 45 [Feb. 1966], pp. 35-41) and John Wellborn Root's visual and verbal dialogue with Ruskin's organic concepts of design (see John Wellborn Root, "Architectural Ornamentation" [1885] in *Meanings of Architecture*, ed. Donald Hoffman [New York, 1967], pp. 16-21) suggest that the emerging Chicago School provided Sullivan and his colleagues with a forum in which to discuss Ruskin's works. Sullivan particularly admired two of Henry Hobson Richardson's works, the Brattle Square Church (1870-72; Boston) and the Marshall Field Wholesale Store (1885; Chicago). These two designs closely follow Ruskin's descriptions of the sublime discussed in "The Lamp of Power," *The Seven Lamps of Architecture* (note 26).

28 Ruskin, "The Lamp of Sacrifice," *The Seven Lamps of Architecture* (note 26), par. 1, p. 16.

29 Ibid., "Introductory," p. 10.

30 See Sullivan's similar Ruskinian statement regarding the expressive function of ornament in *Kindergarten Chats* (note 2), pp. 233-34.

31 Ruskin, "The Nature of Gothic," *The Stones of Venice* 2 (note 26), pars. 4-6, pp. 182-84; pars. 68-69, pp. 235-37.

32 Ibid., pars. 41-65, pp. 215-33. Here Ruskin compared Gothic builders and their creative process for developing an ornament of "vegetation" with three kinds of pictorial artists and representation – the "Purists," "Sensualists," and "Naturalists" – and concluded that Gothic builders ranked highest with the "Naturalists" since both groups "unite fact with design" (see par. 64, pp. 231-32).

Since Ruskin's "Naturalism" has been mistaken by architectural historians for a theory of mimesis, scholars have dismissed the influence of Ruskin's drawings of ornament on Sullivan and his mentors. (See, for example, Sprague [note 7], pp. 64-65; and O'Gorman [note 24], pp. 20-21.) Conversely, Stein observed the attraction of American art educators, critics, and theorists to Ruskin because of the way he harmonized spiritualism and materialism in his aesthetics; see Stein (note 27), pp. 82, 88-89.

33 See also Ruskin, "The Lamp of Life," *The Seven Lamps of Architecture* (note 26), pars. 5-13, pp. 146-53.

34 Ruskin, "The Nature of Gothic," *The Stones of Venice* 2 (note 26), pars. 10, 22, 25, 42-44, 68-69, pp. 189-91, 202-4, 215-17, 235-37. See also "The Lamp of Life," *The Seven Lamps of Architecture* (note 26), pars. 5-13, pp. 142-53.

35 Ruskin, "Material of Ornament," *The Stones of Venice* 1 (note 26), par. 17, p. 265.

36 John Ruskin, "The Lamp of Beauty," *The Seven Lamps of Architecture* (note 26), par. 6, p. 104. Ruskin also correlated curved lines with organic representation and straight lines with inorganic rectilinear or crystalline geological formations, inappropriate imagery for ornament. See also "Material of Ornament" (note 35), par. 20, p. 268.

37 Ruskin, "Material of Ornament" (note 35), par. 20, p. 268.

38 For a discussion of Sullivan's apprenticeship with Furness, see Sprague (note 7), pp. 55-58, and *Avery* (note 23), pp. 4-5.

39 See *Avery* (note 23), fig. 14 (ornamental design, March 2, 1881); and Sprague (note 7), pp. 78-81. Sullivan designed similar motifs for the reliefs of the Jewelers' Building (1881; *SIU* [note 23], figs. 3-4), Revell Building (1881; *SIU*, fig. 6), and the Borden Block (1881).

40 See Sullivan's reliefs for Rosenfeld Building (1882; *SIU* [note 23], fig. 7), Bloomenfeld Residence (1883; *SIU*, fig. 9), Knisely Store (1883; *SIU*, fig. 11), and Barbe Residence (1884; *SIU*, figs. 12-15).

41 See note 23.

42 Sprague placed this drawing within the transitional phase of Sullivan's development (*Avery*, note 23), p. 29. It should also be noted that the "bud" formation in the May 6, 1884, drawing strongly resembles Viollet-le-Duc's renderings of "fleurons" from the ornament of Notre Dame in *Dessins inédits* (note 20).

43 Sullivan introduced the whiplash configuration in 1883; e. g. the pediment relief of the Hammond Library (*SIU* [note 23], cat. no. 17).

Other examples of the "1884 motif" can be seen in the elevations of the Ann Halsted Flats (1884; 1885 addition); the Rubel Residence (1884), and the Lindauer Residence (1884). This motif was variously distributed on the exteriors and interiors as cast-terracotta reliefs and as carved wood reliefs for door and window insets and pilaster or column capitals (*SIU* figs. 15-16; cat. nos. 27-41). As in the Scoville Building, for the attic story pediments and spandrels of the Troescher Building elevation (1884-85), Sullivan enlarged the scale of the 1884 motif and rendered it in higher relief (illustrated in Sprague [note 7], figs. 241-42). For a history of the Scoville Building, see Paul Sprague, "Sullivan's Scoville Building, A Chronology," *Prairie School Review* 2 (Third Quarter 1974), pp. 16-23.

44 Sprague (note 7), p. 173; Sprague also observed the water-like motion of the undulating forms. If we account for the symbolic value of the curvilinear formations, the "shift" from the more abstract designs of 1884 to the more realistic renderings of 1885 is not as abrupt as Sprague later suggested in *Avery* (note 23), p. 31.

45 Ruskin (note 35), par. 125, p. 232.

46 Sullivan, "Characteristics and Tendencies of American Architecture" (1885) in *Kindergarten Charts* (note 2), pp. 177-81; quotation p. 181.

47 In "Characteristics and Tendencies" (note 46) Sullivan also inferred that in 1885 he had arrived at a "plastic alphabet [with which] to identify [his] beliefs [comprised] of the simplest combination of terms" (p. 179), a statement that accounts for the inscription of "Alphabet" on an ornamental study dated December 18, 1885 (*Avery* [note 23], no. 23; see also no. 24, ornamental design dated September 30, 1885). As seen in the drawing, Sullivan now used an alphabet of geometric and realistic motifs.

48 Sullivan arrived at a similar realization in his written work, developing a more didactic, issue-oriented rhetorical style after the highly esoteric "poem in prose" style of the 1886 version of "Inspiration" (note 4).

49 The working drawings for the Auditorium Building (reproduced in hectograph prints) are attributed to Frank Lloyd Wright, hired as Sullivan's draftsman for this decorative scheme. As Sprague has explained, these working drawings are either redrawings of Sullivan's smaller pencil sketches to scale or ink tracings of these pencil drawings or of Sullivan's own scale drawings. In either case, during 1888-90, Sullivan closely supervised Wright, and Sullivan often detailed important parts of the Auditorium Building decorations. See Sprague (note 7), pp. 116-17; *Avery* (note 23), p. 35; and no. 35, figs. 20-21.

50 See *Avery* (note 23), nos. 15-17 B.

Vignole.

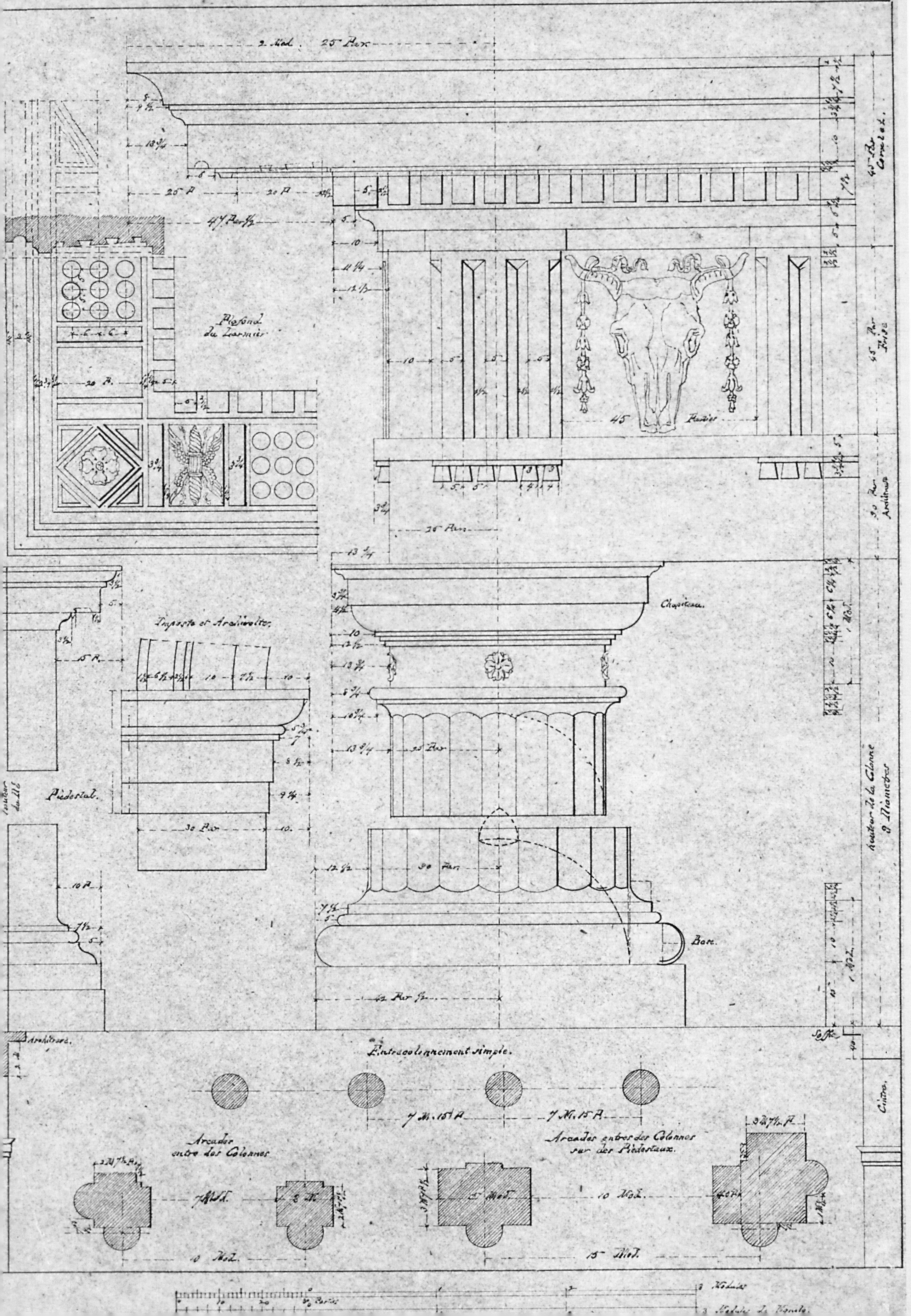

Plafond du Larmier
Imposte et Archivolte
Piédestal.
Chapiteau.
Base.
Corniche
Frise
Architrave
Hauteur de la Colonne 9 Diamètres
Entrecolonnement simple.
Arcades entre les Colonnes
Arcades entre les Colonnes sur des Piédestaux.
Cintre.
Modules

Sullivan and the Orders of Architecture

Martha Pollak

This essay deals with European, particularly French, influences on two aspects of Louis H. Sullivan's work. First, it discusses his Beaux-Arts training in the United States and Paris as a draftsman in relation to several drawings in the collection of The Art Institute of Chicago (cat. nos. 27-33). Second, it posits some plausible connections between Sullivan's later architectural theories and the writings of a number of seminal European thinkers represented in his personal library.

Among the drawings of Louis Sullivan preserved at The Art Institute of Chicago is a set of sheets illustrating the Doric and Tuscan orders of architecture after a French edition of Vignola (fig. 1; cat. nos. 27-29). It is not entirely clear whether Sullivan executed these particular sheets while at the Massachusetts Institute of Technology's School of Architecture in 1872-73 or, slightly later, in 1875 at the Ecole des Beaux-Arts in Paris, but we know from his autobiography that the drawing of the five orders of architecture was compulsory at MIT and had provoked him to rebellion. He rejected the "eternal verities" implicit in the use of the "correct" orders, and although he learned to draw well and accurately, his reception of this classical education was almost entirely negative:

Louis had gone at his studies faithfully enough. He learned not only to draw but to draw very well. He traced the "Five Orders of Architecture" in a manner quite resembling copper plate, and he learned about diameters, modules, minutes, entablatures, columns, pediments and so forth . . . with the associated minute measurements and copious vocabulary, all of which items he supposed at the time were intended to be received in unquestioning faith, as eternal verities. And he was told that these "Orders" were "Classic," which implied an arrival at the goal of Platonic perfection of idea.[1]

As part of his introduction to architecture at MIT, Sullivan studied the basic method of drawing under William R. Ware and his assistant, Eugène Létang, a graduate of the Ecole des Beaux-Arts. In his *Autobiography of an Idea*, Sullivan expressed a great deal of contempt for both of his instructors, almost blaming them for failing to fire his imagination the way his high school teacher Moses Woolson had done:

He reflected with a sort of despair that neither immaculate Professor Ware nor sweaty, sallow, earnest Eugene Letang was a Moses Woolson. Ah, if but Moses Woolson had been versed in the story of architecture as he was in English Literature, and had held the professorship; ah, what glowing flame would have come forth to cast its radiance like a rising sun and illuminate the past.[2]

Sullivan, like many students of architecture who feel a vocation to build, experienced a revulsion at the seemingly pointless educational process. At the time of his studies, this teaching method had been institutionalized for at least 175 years. The method

Fig. 1 Louis H. Sullivan, Elevation study of a Doric pedestal, base, capital, and entablature after a French edition of Vignola, c. 1875 (cat. no. 28).

Fig. 2 Charles Fürst, Elevation study of the Greek Doric order from the Parthenon, Athens, March 28, 1870 (cat. no. 9).

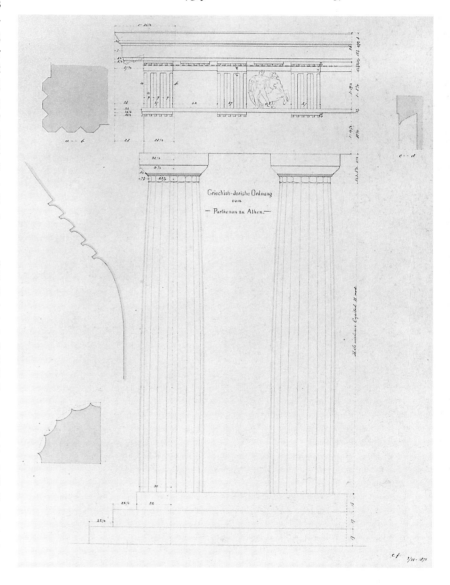

Griechisch-dorische Ordnung vom — Parthenon zu Athen.—

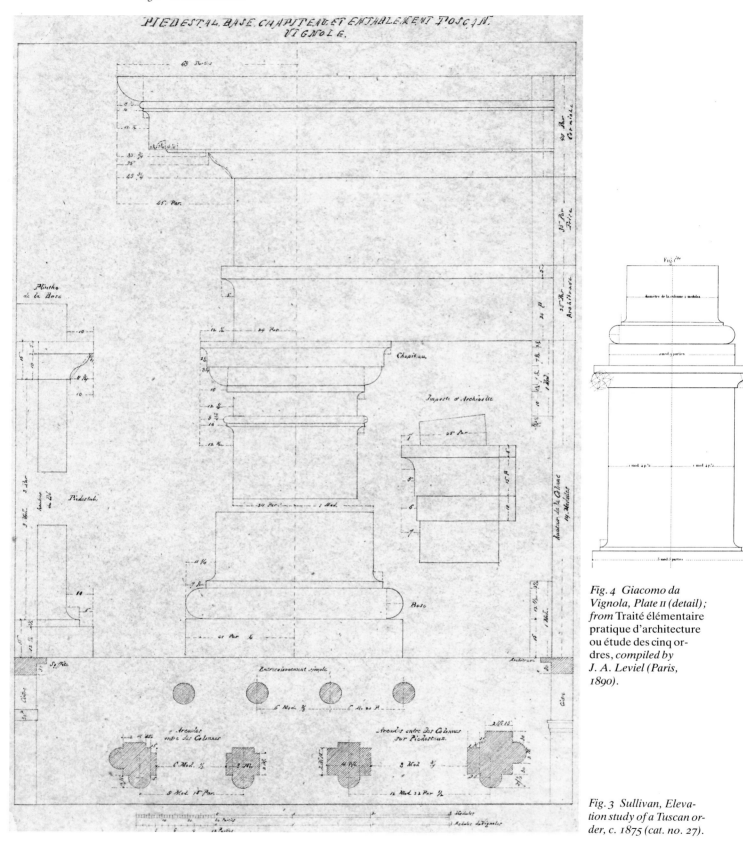

Fig. 4 *Giacomo da Vignola, Plate II (detail); from* Traité élémentaire pratique d'architecture ou étude des cinq ordres, *compiled by J. A. Leviel (Paris, 1890).*

Fig. 3 *Sullivan, Elevation study of a Tuscan order, c. 1875 (cat. no. 27).*

was dependent on two widely accepted assumptions. The first was that classical architecture and the composition of the orders was the principal object lesson of the history of building. The second assumption, implicit in the first, was that the inheritance of historic architectural forms should be used as a treasure house and a quarry for inspiration. Architecture was supposed to suffer from not being a truly mimetic art; its practitioners solved this apparent problem by creating, and then in-

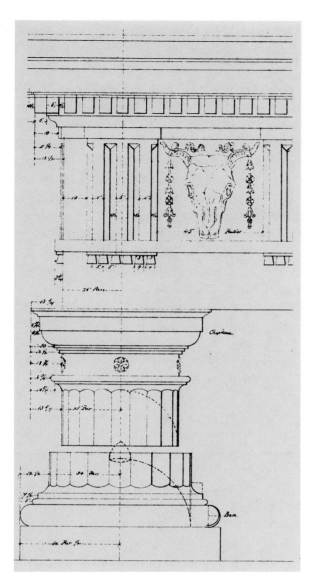

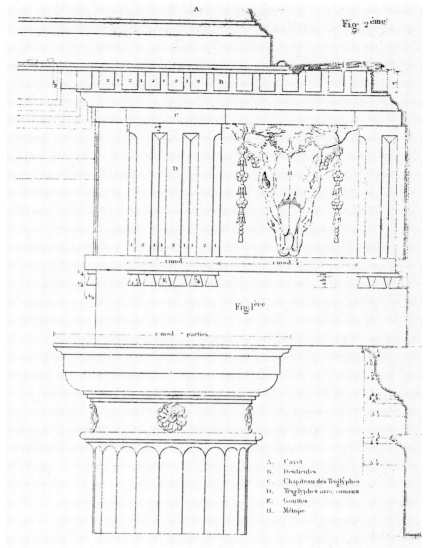

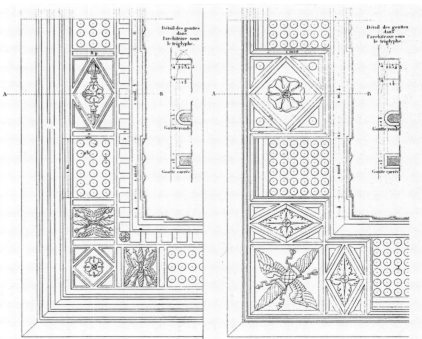

Fig. 5 Sullivan, detail of fig. 1.

Fig. 6 Vignola, Plate XIV (detail); from Traité élémentaire pratique d'architecture.

Fig. 7 Vignola, Plate XVI (detail); from Traité élémentaire pratique d'architecture.

Fig. 8 Sullivan, Elevation study of a variant Doric order, c. 1875 (cat. no. 29).

stitutionalizing, a process of introversion or self-referential eclecticism.

This imitative approach was formulated, as Henry Millon has shown, by Filippo Juvarra (1678-1736) at the Sunday Architecture School of the Academy of St. Luke in Rome:

Students would have been required to assemble their own album of plates on sheets of the same size by drawing after the authors assigned by Juvarra. To do so, portions would usually have to be taken from several plates in each treatise, then assembled and composed on one or two sheets in such a way that the various prescriptions could be easily compared.[3]

Though it could become mechanical and reductive, the technique evolved by Juvarra — an eminent draftsman and one of the most inspiring teachers at the Academy — could encourage a critical, comparative, and analytic approach to the inherited corpus of architectural writing and composition. A comparison of Sullivan's drawings with a copy of Vignola reveals both the limitations and the stimulating potential of the classical Juvarrian method.[4]

The undeniable tedium of this traditional study of the orders could generate work of an equivalent dullness. This potential danger may be seen if we compare Sullivan's drawings with similar plates executed by the architect Charles J. Fürst, taken from architectural theorists such as Vicenzo Scamozzi (1552-1616) and from measured existing buildings in Rome and in Athens (fig. 2; cat. nos. 9-12). Fürst's sheets are doomed by his basic misunderstanding of the meaning of the columns: he does not realize that they are a modular, proportional system. Thus he draws the entire shaft of the column, compounding his error by drawing two columns, with a continuous entablature above them. This is not at all Sullivan's problem. His sheets, at least three of them, are rigorous, disciplined, economical, and beautifully composed, and thus show that the classical architectural education could be worthwhile.

Sullivan integrates elements from several different plates in his original drawings. For his sheet illustrating the Tuscan order, Sullivan combined elements from Plates II, IV, and VII of the French edition of Vignola (figs. 3, 4).[5] The resulting composition is rich in detail, while providing a clear outline of the Tuscan order. The drawing is as austere as the Tuscan order itself, and minutely labeled with numbers and letters. For the less adorned version of the Doric order, Sullivan adopted parts of Plates XIII, XIV, and XVI (figs. 5-7).[6]

The Mutular Doric was principally collaged from Plates XV and XVI (figs. 8, 9).[7] The fourth sheet (fig. 10) seems unfinished in comparison with the other three. It illustrates the cornice and entabla-

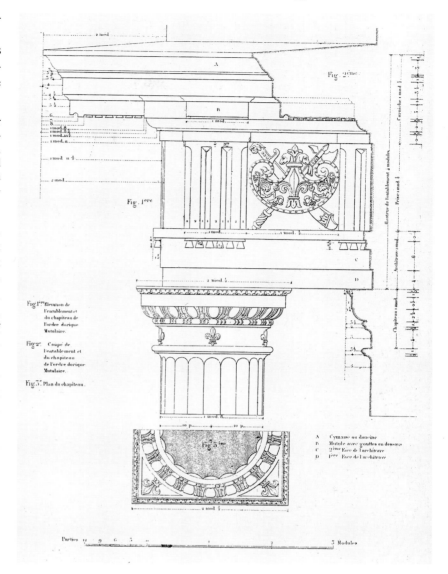

ture of the Corinthian or the Ionic order — since only a sketch for the capital is shown, we cannot be certain which one it is. Sullivan diverged from his model in one fundamental aspect: he did not draw the profiles of any of his details. In the engraved plates the trace of the profile was used to visually separate the main drawing representing the order from the edge of the sheet. This also helped in the separation of dimensions and label from the line drawings. Sullivan did not use any legends, and his labels are placed immediately next to the drawing. There are many instances in which the instruments he used to trace the various curves can be only too clearly discerned, giving away the hand of a beginner and indicating their likely creation while he was a student at MIT. Since Sullivan omitted the textual explication included in Vignola, his sheets are longer. Thus he had a larger surface on which to range the elements of the order, including the plans of the arcades at the bottom. His sheets have a lively, artisanal quality.

Fig. 9 Vignola, Plate xv; from Traité élémentaire pratique d'architecture.

Fig. 10 Sullivan, Elevation study of a detail of a classical frieze and entablature, c. 1875 (cat. no. 30).

Sullivan's education at MIT was followed, after a one-year hiatus, by a period of study in Paris during which he prepared for, and then successfully passed, the examination for admission to the Ecole des Beaux-Arts. Before beginning his architectural studies in the atelier of Emile Vaudremer (following the footsteps of his MIT instructor Eugène Létang), Louis Sullivan went on a trip to Italy. His interest in Italian painting and architecture had been whetted, he tells us, by his encounter with the French cultural historian Hippolyte Taine (1828-1893), who had been a professor of aesthetics and of the history of art at the Ecole des Beaux-Arts for twenty years.

During his preparatory work he had discovered three small volumes by Hippolyte Taine devoted to the Philosophy of Art in Greece, in Italy, and the Netherlands. From these works he derived three strong impressions, novel shocks: First, that there *existed* such a thing as a Philosophy of Art; second, that according to M. Taine's philosophy the art of a people is a reflex or direct expression of the life of that people; third, that one must become well acquainted with that life in order to see into the art. All this was new and shining.[8]

Taine's discussion of Michelangelo had such an effect on Sullivan that he traveled to Rome to see the Sistine Chapel, where he had a quasi-mystical and ecstatic revelation:

In the volume on Italy... occurred a statement which struck Louis as of most sinister import for him: It alarmed him. It was to this effect: That, concerning the work of Michael Angelo in the Sistine Chapel, the Last Judgment was *obviously* done on *momentum,* as compared with the vigor of the ceiling. Now Louis had never trusted the care of his eyesight to anyone, nor did he now propose to entrust it in M. Taine's keeping. . . . It was his pride that he could see. But, could his eye detect so subtle a change in the work of a great artist as was implicated in the word *momentum* and which M. Taine had said was *obvious*? . . . He must go to Rome, to verify; for the worth of his whole scheme seemed to rest in this delicate balance. It was vital. There must be no doubt. He *must,* beyond question, be sure of the quality of his eyesight. To Rome he went, quaking but courageous. [T]hen a cumulating agony ended forever in a supreme moment of relief; and Louis knew, once and for all, that he could see anything that eye could see.[9]

Sullivan's assignment of the role of *cicerone* to Taine in his description of this significant experience may have come after the fact, when he was recalling the event in later years. But in any case, whether Sullivan read Taine just before going to Italy, during his trip, or later that year, he had become acquainted with this philosopher at an early date.[10] The charismatic and admired Moses Woolson, Sullivan's first-year teacher at the Latin High School in Boston, had announced that "the best existing history of English literature was written by a Frenchman, one Hippolite [sic] Taine by name."[11] In that lecture, Taine's name had become associated with the concept of culture, an idea that was entirely novel to young Louis and provided him with the revelation that "culture ... signified the genius of a people ... their culture was their own expression of their inmost selves."[12] Thus Taine was praised as a man of vision who brought about a synthesis between philosophy and literary inquiry. Since the appraisal was made by Woolson, whom Sullivan trusted entirely, it seems likely that Taine's *Philosophy of Art* (1867) would have had an *a priori* credibility for the young traveler. An 1868 edition of Taine's *English Literature* was in Sullivan's library when it was auctioned in 1909.[13]

Taine's stormy and unconventional academic career may also have been a sympathetic model for the impulsive Sullivan. Taine had remained peripheral to university circles, from which he was excluded because of his political and philosophical beliefs.[14] He had been a student at the Jardin des plantes (also known as the Muséum d'histoire naturelle) where he had become a follower of Etienne Geoffroy Saint-Hilaire (1772-1844), an important pre-Darwinian anatomist, and of Georges Cuvier (1769-1832), the eminent paleontologist and the former director of the museum.[15] The *Philosophy of Art* emerged from Taine's lectures at the Ecole des Beaux-Arts delivered in 1864.

There are several points in Taine's *Philosophy* that seem to have strongly influenced Sullivan's thinking about architecture, and helped in the formulation of the ideas expressed in his autobiography. The significance of the cultural context and Sullivan's reaction to it have been mentioned above. Taine summarized this concept in his compiled lectures by saying, "The work of art is determined by a condition of things consisting of all surrounding social and intellectual influences."[16]

His definition of art reads like a capsulized history of form, or aesthetics:

At first we thought the art aimed solely at an imitation of *the visible exterior of things*. Next, separating mechanical imitation from intelligent imitation, we found that what we wish to reproduce in the visible exterior of things is the *relationship of parts*. Finally, remarking that relationships are, and ought to be, modified in order to attain the highest results of art, we proved that if we study the relationships of parts it is *to make predominant an essential character*. No one of these definitions destroys its antecedent, but each corrects and defines it.[17] (Taine's italics)

Taine's notions of the "visible exterior of things," the "relationship of parts," and the "essential character" are recognizable in Sullivan's search for ideal form. In Paris, he very quickly realized that the education at the Ecole des Beaux-Arts, based on the use of a plan as the principal design tool, would not help him to discover what he wished to know. While Sullivan thought that the plan "beautifully set forth a sense of order, of function, of highly skilled manipulation," he was overcome by "the hovering conviction that this Great School, in its perfect flower of technique, lacked the profound animus of a primal inspiration."[18]

His reading of Taine provided Sullivan with a theoretical basis for his ruminations on art, architecture, talent, and the meaning of form. It also may have introduced him to some of the scientific and philosophical thinking current in France, which he could have explored further in contemporary encyclopedias such as the *Grand dictionnaire universel* by Pierre Larousse, started in 1866. Larousse's publication was an intellectual event of the second half of the nineteenth century, matched in importance only by the publication of the *Encyclopédie* a century earlier (1751-1765). The Larousse made available a corpus of critical analyses of the works and lives of illustrious men, among them Taine and the scientists Etienne Geoffroy Saint-Hilaire and Georges Cuvier. Taine's *English Literature* was only one of the 274 lots listed in the catalogue of November 19, 1909, which accompanied Sullivan's library to the auctioneer's block. (Ironically, we owe a knowledge of Sullivan's collection of books and household objects to his unfortunate insolvency.) The books identified in the auction catalogue suggest the breadth of Sullivan's intellectual horizon, his great curiosity and eclectic interests.[19] This catalogue has been mined by scholars of Sullivan's oeuvre in order to shed light on his temper and inclinations, as they influenced the shaping of Sullivan's architectural convictions.

Among these books is a treatise on physiognomy by the eighteenth-century Swiss theologian and

Fig. 11 Portrait of Johann Wolfgang von Goethe; from Johann Kaspar Lavater, Physiognomische Fragmente *(Leipzig, 1775-78).*

Fig. 12 Portrait of Johann Kaspar Goethe; from Lavater, Physiognomische Fragmente.

poet Johann Kaspar Lavater (1741-1801). This work occupies a singular place in Sullivan's collection because of its subject: physiognomy. Entitled *Essays on Physiognomy,* it is one of the earliest publications owned by Sullivan, and has not been considered before by the historians who have analyzed his possible readings of such authors as Nietzsche, Whitman, and Schopenhauer. Lavater was a philosopher, poet, and orator, as well as a Protestant theologian. He is the author of numerous volumes of poetry, sermons, and theological writings through which he exercised a great cultural influence, not only in his native Zurich, in Switzerland, but also in Germany and England.[20] His most important work is the *Physiognomische Fragmente,* published in Leipzig in four volumes between 1775 and 1778. It was published in London between 1789 and 1798 in three volumes under the title *Essays on Physiognomy Designed to Promote the Knowledge and the Love of Mankind.*[21]

The book appeared amidst extraordinary expectations, since Lavater enjoyed a great following as pastor and spiritual leader throughout German-speaking central Europe and beyond. The volumes were magnificently illustrated, with around 800 engravings in the English edition. In its own day it was considered a work of immense psychological interest; it fascinated the *demisavants* and gave great satisfaction to the multitude. The few who dared criticize it were rejected as envious detractors. But by 1869 the entry on Lavater in Larousse pronounced this judgment on his work: "An attempt to establish precise laws about the relation between the soul and the physiognomic is an enterprise worthy of a mystic carried away by his imagination, it is throwing oneself on a path as dangerous as it is conjectural."[22]

Lavater's intention, declared in the subtitle to this work, was to portray human nature through an analysis of its physical aspects. This aesthetic interest was premised on his belief that exterior form is the reflection and symbol of character. In his analysis of the external aspect of man, Lavater hoped to find each man's inner essence, an enterprise that can be traced back through Renaissance and neoclassical physiognomies to Aristotle's concept of substantial form, which he identified with energy and the dynamic element of existence. This nonaccidental component — "by form I mean the essence of each thing"[23] — was the aim of Lavater's search; he implacably opposed the belief "that everything in Man depends on education, culture, example, and not in original organization and formation."[24]

While Lavater was greatly admired for his charismatic personality and as the founder of a new physiognomy, his greatest enemy in his own lifetime was ridicule, since European thinkers were divided between physiognomists and non-physiognomists. But his goal was far from contemptible — nothing less than the reconstruction of human nature according to a spiritual but scientific theory of the unity of soul and body. The fundamental idea in the *Essays on Physiognomy* was that "the character of the soul is expressed in the whole outward frame, but more especially mirrored in the face,"[25] and therefore the human form must be regarded as a harmonious work of art, produced by the hand of the master artist, Nature. This "doctrine of harmony" also found expression in the work of Geoffroy and Cuvier. Geoffroy's research in zoology and anatomy led him to develop the theory of the "unity of organic composition," which posited that there was a single, consistent structural plan basic to all animals. This theory synthesized the principles of elective affinities, inequality of development, fixity of connections, and balance of organs.[26] Cuvier founded the science of paleontology. His theory of the "correlation of forms," which allowed him to reconstruct a skeleton from small remaining fragments,[27] was a translation into the natural sciences of Lavater's hypothesis of the "perfect cohesion of beings."[28] Although Geoffroy and Cuvier were close friends and collaborated on anatomical research, they clashed in a public debate in the Academy of Sciences in 1830. The debate addressed some of the same theological and physiognomic issues that had concerned Lavater decades earlier, though in different terms.

By the latter part of the nineteenth century Lavater's science was being treated as no more than eccentric and antiquated occultism. Recent work, however, places his contribution within an important cultural-spiritual tradition of intellectual history, and his influence on nineteenth-century French literature was undeniably strong.[29] Both

Fig. 13 Sullivan, Sketch
of a grotesque head,
January 26, 1878 (cat.
no. 106).

Fig. 14 Sullivan, Sketch
of a man's face in profile,
November 2, 1878 (cat.
no. 107).

Balzac and George Sand were among the admirers of Lavater.[30]

In searching for a closer link between Lavater's and Sullivan's theories, we turn once again to the architect's library. In a work by Herman Grimm entitled *The Life and Times of Goethe,* an entire chapter is dedicated to an analysis of the relationship between Goethe and Lavater, who were frequent correspondents.[31] According to Goethe, Lavater was "a unique, gifted individual, . . . the flower of humanity, the best of the best."[32] Goethe was seduced by Lavater's personal magnetism and brilliance into becoming a joint editor of the *Physiognomische Fragmente*: "He undertook to publish it, making himself, in a measure, responsible for the whole thing."[33] His own portrait and that of his father are among the engravings in the treatise (figs. 11, 12). While very much impressed by Lavater, thoroughly involved with him and his work on physiognomy, and even influenced by his style of writing, Goethe eventually rejected him. Grimm's discussion of their relationship is colored by the negative judgments made by Goethe in old age.[34] Earlier, Goethe had written of his relationship with Lavater in *Dichtung und Wahrheit,* part of which Sullivan owned as a collected German edition of Goethe's works.[35] Sullivan does indeed seem to have had strong interests in German culture and ideas, perhaps whetted by his friend John Edelmann, or, more likely, his own German grandfather.[36]

Goethe's studies in the neo-science of physiognomy were part of his wider interests in poetry, philosophy, and the natural sciences. He pursued the latter upon his arrival in Weimar, where he formulated the concept of the *Urpflanze,* the archetypal plant out of which all other plants can be developed according to natural law, and to which all plants can be traced back.[37] Goethe, like Taine, had a strong intellectual commitment to science and a great interest in the implications of scientific method and discovery for philosophy. He demonstrated this by following closely the famous debate between Geoffroy and Cuvier, finding it more absorbing than the stormy political events of the 1830 Revolution in France.[38]

While others have commented on Sullivan's romanticism, possibly nourished by readings from Goethe, the influence of his interest in physiognomy on his writing and architectural design has not been broached until now. And yet this interest is evident throughout his autobiography. By the time Sullivan wrote *Autobiography of an Idea,* physiognomy had been widely popularized in French literature, notably by Honoré Balzac, who had a wide audience. When Sullivan describes his mother's parents — "Henri List . . . 6 feet tall, well proportioned, erect carriage, and topped by a domical head, full, clean-shaven face, thick lips, small gray eyes, beetling brows and bottle-nose. . . . Her mother . . . was Swiss-French. . . . But her long Florentine nose suggested, unmistakably, an Italian strain" — his emphasis on the head clearly embodies Lavater's belief that the face is the mirror of moral character.[39]

Indeed, all the people who are important to Sullivan's spiritual and emotional life are described in thorough detail, including a lengthy analysis of cousin Minnie, and of the architects Edward Burling and Dankmar Adler (later Sullivan's partner). Of Burling, Sullivan wrote that "he was an incredible, long and bulky nosed Yankee, perceptibly aging fast, and of manifestly weakening will," while Adler was "a heavy-set, short-nosed Jew, well bearded, with a magnificent domed forehead which stopped suddenly at a solid mass of black hair. He was a picture of sturdy strength, physical and mental."[40] This association between appearance (form) and moral character (content) and his numerous sketches show Sullivan to have been a physiognomist (figs. 13, 14).[41]

Among the theories and views discussed above, Cuvier's seem to be the most directly relevant in a discussion of the European influences on Sullivan's work. Cuvier appears to have influenced the thinking of a wide range of people through his work at the Jardin des plantes. The architect and theorist Gottfried Semper was indebted to Cuvier, whose exhibition of animal skeletons partly inspired the taxonomic system through which Semper sought to establish a typology of architecture.[42] Cuvier's doctrine had a powerful impact on Viollet-le-Duc as well, and no architect active in the second half of the nineteenth century entirely escaped his influence.[43]

While Geoffroy's debate with Cuvier concerned technical matters of vital importance to zoologists, paleontologists, and anatomists, Geoffroy's "philosophical anatomy" and Cuvier's "functionalist anatomy" carried wider implications whose impact

Fig. 15 Sullivan, Schlesinger and Mayer Store (now Carson Pirie Scott), southeast corner of State and Madison streets, 1899-1904; section of a screen (cat. no. 136).

Fig. 16 Sullivan, Schlesinger and Mayer Store; interior showing wooden screen.

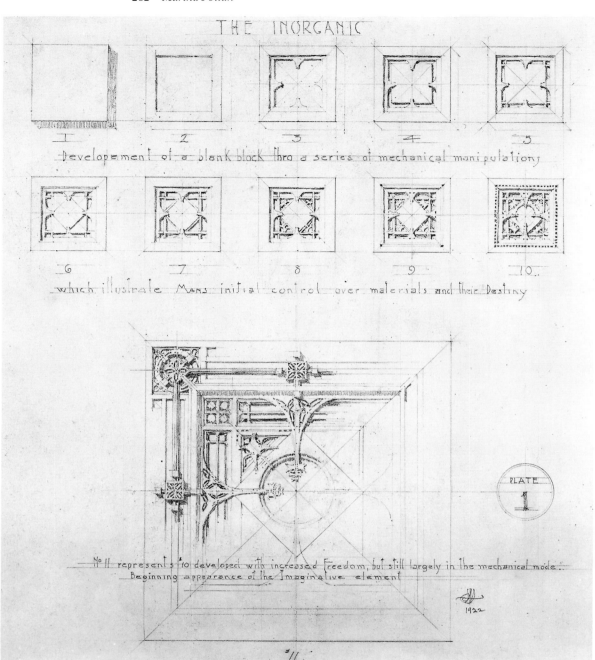

THE INORGANIC

Development of a blank block thro a series of mechanical manipulations;

which illustrate Mans initial control over materials and their Destiny

No 11 represents 10 developed with increased freedom, but still largely in the mechanical mode. Beginning appearance of the Imaginative element

PLATE 1

1922

Fig. 17 Sullivan, "Development of a blank block through a series of mechanical manipulations," 1922; from A System of Architectural Ornament *(1924), pl. 1 (cat. no. 157).*

Fig. 18 Sullivan, "Impromptu," 1922; from A System of Architectural Ornament, *pl. 16 (cat. no. 163).*

echoed through literature, philosophy, and, eventually, architecture. This scientific controversy crystallized the key issues of early nineteenth-century natural science by proposing two polarized interpretations of animal structure, one explained "by morphological laws," the other "explained primarily by reference to function."[44]

Geoffroy proposed that science ignore the form and function of the parts in favor of the "principle of connections" that was at the core of the science of morphology. His concepts were essentially evolutionary and paved the way for Darwin's theories. His theory freed scientists to search for general laws of animal organization, whereas Cuvier defined the scientist's role as one of gathering positive facts.[45] There were two key elements in Cuvier's functionalist dictum: "that the animal's needs sufficed to determine its structure," and that "the Creator was free to produce the appropriate organ."[46] According to Cuvier, the single principal organs, at least in large animals, are those visible through dissection, rather than those visible on the exterior. The corollary to this is that the function which determines the form of the animal is internal to it. Thus, not only does function itself determine the more complex, asymmetrical forms, but those forms are invisible.[47] Cuvier seems to have belonged to the camp that was highly critical of Lavater and contemptuous of his theories concerning physiognomy.[48] Nonetheless, there is a strong phi-

IMPROMPTU!

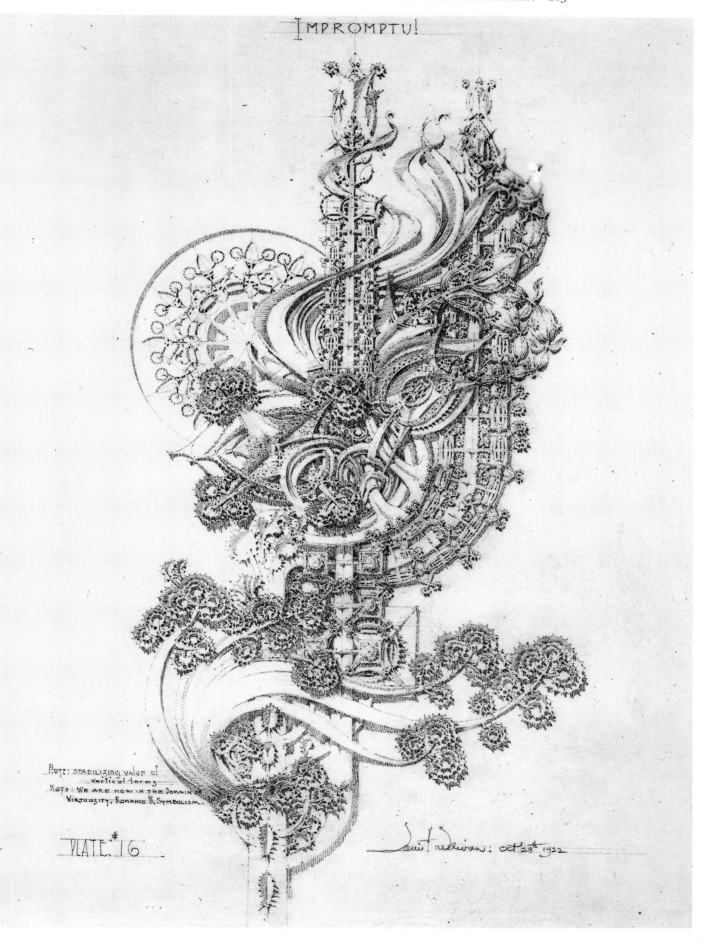

Note: STABILIZING VALUE OF
      vertical forms
Note: WE ARE NOW IN THE DOMAIN
      VIRTUOSITY, ROMANCE & SYMBOLISM

PLATE #16

Louis Sullivan: Oct 23rd 1922

losophical similarity between the basic assumption of both Cuvier and Lavater that exterior appearance, of both humans and animals, is only a reflection of inner essential qualities and functions that are invisible, hidden from the naked eye.

We know from his autobiography that Sullivan was a great reader; therefore, it seems logical that he was aware of Cuvier's work and the debate with Geoffroy.[49] Sullivan's dictum "form follows function" is considered to be the essence of his contribution to modern architecture. Cuvier would certainly have been in accord with this statement, given his own functionalist theories as outlined above. Cuvier's construct might actually be used to interpret Sullivan's architectural output, and his ornament in particular (figs. 15, 16). I would like to suggest that beyond the use of the motto "form follows function" as a catch-all for the materialist quality of his tall buildings, Sullivan was fascinated by the consideration that the principal organs of the anatomy were single and asymmetrical. With this idea firmly in mind, he designed the most comprehensive and beautiful ornamental system of modern architecture, which, when applied to the surface of a building, was to illustrate the true nature of the functions within. As epitomized by *A System of Architectural Ornament* (figs. 17, 18; pls. 40, 41; cat. nos. 157-64), he rendered the invisible visible. In his driven quest for honesty in architecture, Sullivan integrated Lavater's claim that appearance is a mirror of the soul and the moral character with Cuvier's functionalist theory. In his search for essential form, he thus synthesized in a personal and creative manner the apparently contradictory, or incompatible, conclusions of the founder of physiognomy and the founder of paleontology.

The most seductive of the abilities ascribed to Cuvier was the ease with which he could reconstruct an entire skeleton from the smallest bone fragment (through his previous knowledge of the possibilities).[50] This was not an entirely new notion, since Diderot had been credited with the ability to establish whether a man was healthy or deformed by observing a single knuckle of his finger.[51] Both of these anecdotes refer to a powerful pervasive topos that has an equivalent in architecture. Composition in Greek classical architecture, and by extension in ancient Roman and Renaissance architecture, was based upon the orders of architecture. The orders imply the use of a modular proportional system in the design of buildings. The module is the diameter of the shaft at the base of the column. Thus one drum from the column's shaft suffices for the reconstruction of an entire building. The laborious study of the orders, continued even after the impossibility of perfect absolute proportions had been demonstrably argued,[52] provided the adepts with an understanding of ancient architecture and training in building design as a system of related parts.

The seemingly unrelated threads in Sullivan's intellectual and artistic background are thus reconnected. He drew inspiration and support for his tendency toward the concept of organicism from apparently contradictory sources. His classical education in the orders, albeit brief, had a profound impact on him. His voracious reading outside the discipline of architecture, suggested by the contents of his library, could have led him to the great scientific debates of his century. Sullivan developed his own architectural theories from a fusion of the polarized traditions of classicism and organicism, and gave them expression in his buildings and drawings. Concerned with function in his morally felt endeavor to design an architecture of democracy, he relied on both a study of the orders and a Cuvier-inspired functionalist theory. His fervid personal need for an integrated architecture of genius was fulfilled by this synthesis, which he achieved through his system of organic ornament.

NOTES

I wish to thank Professor Leo Schelbert, University of Illinois at Chicago; Daniel F. Goujet, Maître de Conference, Muséum d'histoire naturelle; Professor David Hull, Northwestern University; Prof. James G. Turner, University of Michigan; and Timothy Samuelson, Commission on Chicago Historical and Architectural Landmarks, for their timely advice and generous help in the preparation of this essay. I am deeply indebted to Professor Marco Diani, Northwestern University and CNRS (Paris), for sharing with me his research in nineteenth-century French intellectual history.

All translations from the French are the author's.

1 Louis Sullivan, *The Autobiography of an Idea* (1924; rpt., New York, 1956), p. 186.
2 Ibid., p. 189.
3 Henry A. Millon, *Filippo Juvarra: Drawings from the Roman period 1704-1714* (Rome, 1984), pt. 1, p. xxiv.
4 The edition of Vignola I have used for this comparison is: Vignole, *Traité elémentaire pratique d'architecture ou étude des cinq ordres*, comp. by J.-A. Leveil (Paris, 1891).
5 The bottom of the shaft, base, plinth, capital, and entablature of the model were from Plate ii. The top of the shaft, capital, and entablature were modeled on Plate iv. It is from this plate that he borrowed the simple intercolumniation, whereas the plan of the arcade on columns and the arcade on columns above pedestals, and the details of the cornice, were inspired partially by Plate vii.
6 From Plate xiii he borrowed the bottom of the shaft, base, plinth, and pedestal of the order, and the geometrical derivation of the fluting of the shaft. The cornice, entablature, capital, and the top of the shaft were drawn from Plate xiv, as was the elevation of the impost of the archivolt. Finally, the plan of the projecting cornice was drawn from the figure on the left of Plate xvi.
7 Sullivan omitted the metope in the frieze, and replaced the stylized lily in the echinus and on the abacus with rather impressionistic rosettes. The plan of the cornice was modeled on the figure on the right of Plate xvi. The base of the order and the studies for the fluting were most likely modeled on plates that are now missing. The most striking aspect is the relative carelessness with which the naturalistic elements of the decoration are drawn. This is especially evident in the leaves of the cornice and the rosettes of the echinus.
8 Sullivan (note 1), p. 233.
9 Ibid., p. 234.
10 Louis Sullivan, Notebook, Ms. f. 190, Avery Architectural Library, Columbia University, New York. In the "Lotos Club Notebook," a manuscript series of notes kept by Sullivan, his friend John Edelmann, and other members of the club, there is an entry listing 31 books read in 1875 by Louis Sullivan, or by all the members of the club, perhaps at his suggestion. It was not until the fall of 1875 that Sullivan returned to Chicago. Taine's *Philosophy of Art*, the first book on the list, and supposedly begun on January 5, was thus read while he traveled in Italy, not before.
11 Sullivan (note 1), p. 167.
12 Ibid.
13 Williams, Barker and Severn Co. *Auction catalogue No. 5533*, Chicago, Nov. 29, 1909. Burnham Library, The Art Institute of Chicago. Now in David S. Andrew, *Louis Sullivan and the Polemics of Modern Architecture* (Chicago, 1985), appendix 2, p. 162. This volume of Taine was lot 29 in the auction catalogue.
14 For a succinct biography and analysis of the work of Taine, see André Creson, *Hippolyte Taine, sa vie, son œuvre* (Paris, 1951). For an evaluation by a contemporary see Pierre Larousse, *Grand dictionnaire universel du xix siècle* (Paris, 1866-79), vol. 14, p. 1408.
15 For a discussion of the role of the Museum of Natural History in scientific circles of the nineteenth century, see William Coleman, *Biology in the Nineteenth Century, Problems of Form, Function and Transformation* (New York, 1971), pp. 3-14.
16 Hippolyte Taine, *Philosophy of Art* (London and Paris, 1867), p. 158.
17 Ibid., p. 63.
18 Sullivan (note 1), p. 240.
19 See note 13.

20 Larousse (note 14), vol. 10, pp. 266-67.
21 The English edition was translated from the French edition, published in The Hague in four volumes between 1781-1803, and titled *Essais sur la physiognomie, destiné à faire connaître l'homme et à le faire aimer*.
22 Larousse (note 14), vol. 10, p. 267.
23 W. Tatarkiewicz, "Form in the history of aesthetics," in Philip Wiener, ed., *Dictionary of the History of Ideas* (New York, 1973), vol. 2, pp. 216-25.
24 J. K. Lavater, *Essays on Physiognomy Designed to Promote the Knowledge and the Love of Mankind*, 3 vols. (London, 1789-98), vol. 1, Fragment 116.
25 Herman Grimm, *The Life and Times of Goethe* (Boston, 1880), pp. 167-83. (Lot 78 in the auction catalogue for Sullivan's library; see note 13).
26 Larousse (note 14), vol. 8, p. 1180.
27 Ibid., vol. 5, p. 693.
28 Grimm (note 25), pp. 167-83; Toby A. Appel, *Philosophical Anatomy and the Cuvier-Geoffroy Debate* (Chicago, 1986), introduction. I am indebted to Professor David Hull of the Northwestern University Department of Philosophy for bringing this work to my attention, and for lending me the typescript. F. Baldensperger, *Etudes d'histoire littéraire* (Paris, 1910), vol. 2, pp. 51-91.
29 For estimates of Lavater, see Kamal Redwan, *Die Sprache Lavaters im Spiegel der Geistesgeschichte* (Goppingen, 1972); Christian Janentzky, *Lavaters Sturm und Drang* (Halle, Germany, 1916); and, more recently in art history, Barbara M. Stafford, "'Peculiar Marks': Lavater and the Countenance of Blemished Thought," paper presented at the 1986 meeting of the College Art Association.
30 Appel (note 28), ch. 6.
31 See note 25. Their correspondence is in *Goethe und Lavater*, ed. Heinrich Funck (Weimar, 1901).
32 Grimm (note 25), p. 167.
33 Ibid., pp. 167-83.
34 Ibid., p. 180. In his conversations with J. P. Eckermann, Goethe said of Lavater that "He lied to himself and to others."
35 Lot 147 in the auction catalogue (note 13).
36 Sullivan reports in his *Autobiography* ([note 1], pp. 11-12) that his grandfather, Henri List, taught Greek in Geneva. Sullivan also passes on the family legend that List was a rebellious priest in Germany. List's exact academic titles and earlier life remain shrouded in mystery.
37 Goethe's view of nature was fundamentally organic. In *Faust* he condemns the analytical scientist: "The parts in his hand he may hold and class/But the spiritual link is lost, alas!" quoted in G. N. G. Orsini, "Organicism," in Wiener (note 23), vol. 3, pp. 421-27.
38 Appel (note 28), intro., ch. 5.
39 Sullivan (note 1), p. 11.
40 Ibid., pp. 142, 252.
41 A similar idea is expressed by N. G. Menocal in *Architecture as Nature, the Transcendentalist Ideal of Louis Sullivan* (Madison, Wisc., 1981), p. 63: "Sullivan believed that the outward appearance of a work of nature is the image of its essence. A design could thus be made to express the heroic soul of a building, it could portray its transcendant individuality in the same way that a picture of a human being could be the best expression of that person's physical and moral character." Menocal does not make any reference to physiognomic or anatomic models, however.
42 Wolfgang Herrmann, *Gottfried Semper: In Search of Architecture* (Cambridge, Mass., 1984); and review by Rosemarie Bletter in the *Times Literary Supplement*, Jan. 24, 1986.
43 See the essay by Joseph Rykwert, "Architettura e organicismo dall'organon al funzionale," in *L'Avventura delle idee nell'architettura 1750-1980*, ed. J. M. Lampugnani (Milan, 1985), pp. 103-19.
44 Appel (note 28), p. 5.
45 Ibid., ch. 5.
46 Ibid., p. 6.
47 Rykwert (note 43), p. 108.
48 See the letter from Charles Villers to Georges Cuvier, Metz, 1802, in Baldensperger (note 28), pp. 67-68.
49 There is a long entry on Cuvier in Larousse (note 14), which in outline form reads like a list of Sullivan's concerns as seen in his own writing. His knowledge of Cuvier may well have been more than a second- or third-hand

acquaintance, since he read, or at least owned, the writings of several authors who were close to the biological debate and concerned with the implications of scientific controversy for the understanding of nature and human life.
50 Larousse (note 14), vol. 5, p. 693.
51 Grimm (note 25), p. 175.
52 By Claude Perrault in *Ordonnance des cinq espèces de colonnes selon la méthode des anciens* (Paris, 1683), preface.

From Homes to Towers: A Century of Chicago's Best Hotels and Tall Apartment Buildings

C. W. Westfall

At the time of Chicago's birth, the American hotel was considered more a public meeting place for local men of affairs than a stopping-off place for travelers.[1] The early hotels on the Chicago River — at first rustic, then increasingly sophisticated — defined the program followed for a century by hotels wishing to occupy first place among competitors. This required that the table and entertainment be the best in town. The bar, dining room, lobby, and parlors had to attract both the city's men of affairs and the most prominent visiting celebrities. The building itself had to be one of the grandest in town, more splendid than the most recent municipal or county government edifices. And its name, rather than evoking something eastern or foreign, had to have local significance.

During the 1860s hotels began to accommodate families and to serve as long-term residences for those who preferred a hotel to a temporary house during extended business trips. Once proper ladies began to stay in hotels, it became essential to provide a separate entrance for them, with a route to the upper floors shielded from the gaze of men

lounging about in the public rooms. This feature was discarded only in the present century.

It was during this period that Potter Palmer, the city's most successful drygoods merchant, became influential in Chicago's hotel business. Palmer was the first Chicagoan to recognize that the greater part a hotel played in a city's commerce, the more it would prosper. His entry into the hotel business was part of a larger real estate venture to reorganize the city's core. Between the aging but bustling harbor and retail district along the Chicago River and the mansions extending southward a few blocks from the mudflats leading to the lakefront, Palmer first built a grand retail palace that he leased to his former partner, Marshall Field. Shortly after, in 1870, he opened the first Palmer House, a luxurious, mansarded eight-story hotel, designed by John M. Van Osdel, at Quincy Street, three blocks beyond Marshall Field's. Soon Palmer began to build a new hotel, again designed by Van Osdel, which would take up most of the State Street frontage in the block north of the Palmer House.

Fig. 1 Marshall and Fox, Blackstone Hotel, northwest corner of Balbo Street and Michigan Avenue, 1908.

Fig. 2 W. W. Boyington, Grand Pacific Hotel, northeast corner of LaSalle and Jackson streets, 1870; rebuilt 1872 (demolished); from Rebuilt Chicago (Chicago, 1873).

Fig. 3 John M. Van Osdel with Charles M. Palmer, Palmer House III, southeast corner of State and Monroe streets, 1872 (demolished); from Rebuilt Chicago.

The year before the first Palmer House opened, the transcontinental railroad link that would assure Chicago's future prosperity was completed. The course of railroad construction in the United States meant that no regularly scheduled service ever extended from one coast to another, with the result that trains bound across the continent had to stop in Chicago, making it the nation's busiest terminal city. In Europe, and particularly in England, the railroad companies built stations to include hotels, a practice not followed in the United States. Terminal cities needed hotels, however, and Palmer's hotels were among the many built to handle the anticipated increase in travelers passing through Chicago. Chicagoans usually sited these hotels with disregard for the location of the city's many railroad terminals, with one exception, the Grand Pacific Hotel, which was completed in 1871.

The backers of the hotel included leading stockholders in the railroads using the Van Buren Street Station at the foot of LaSalle Street on the edge of the central city (fig. 2).[2] Designed by Chicago's other major hotel architect, William W. Boyington, the Grand Pacific Hotel rose six stories and covered half a block. Like Van Osdel, Boyington favored the newly fashionable Second Empire Parisian style that had replaced the staid Italianate in

popularity. This style was characterized by a five-part facade, usually of stone, carrying an elaborate bracketed cornice often topped by a mansard with pavilions at the center and the corners. The facades were distinguished by a mixture of arched and linteled windows of several sizes, variations in floor heights, and a plethora of pilasters and columns.

These new hotels were larger, more carefully planned, and better equipped than their Chicago predecessors. They had a greater number and variety of guest rooms, with accommodations ranging from small rooftop rooms for hotel staff and guests' servants to elaborate suites equipped with separate toilets. They had a greater variety of public rooms with more sumptuous furnishings, lavish staircases, dining rooms, and kitchens able to satisfy both the refined appetites of travelers from the East Coast and the prodigious demands of the robust men of the West. The hotels also contained conveniences that were only then being perfected: elevators, steam heat, electric call boards, extensive running water, and telegraph (and soon telephone) connections to the front desk, the city, and the world. None of the hotels, however, was fireproof.

The Grand Pacific Hotel's 500 rooms were nearly finished, Van Osdel's second Palmer House was well under way, and competitors were preparing or ready for their inaugural festivities when the Great Fire destroyed the hotels and the rest of the central area of the city in October 1871. Now, instead of competing for guests, the proprietors fought to be the first to reopen. By rebuilding according to the same plans that had guided construction before the fire struck, a new Grand Pacific opened in June 1873,[3] with the third Palmer House following only a few months later. (Van Osdel's second Palmer House building had not been completed when it was destroyed by the fire.)

Although it reopened last, the Palmer House won first place in the hotel world (fig. 3). It was reported that immediately after the fire, Potter Palmer went to Europe accompanied by his architect to study "thoroughly the merits of such buildings as the Grand Hotel [1862] and Hotel du Louvre [1855] in Paris, Langhams [1864] in London, and the Beau Rivage d'Angleterre [1865] and the Grand Hotel de la Paix [1872], Geneva," to consult architects about fireproofing and to order materials.[4] Having started late, Palmer had to make haste if he was to benefit from legislation Congress had passed on April 5, 1872, allowing a rebate of import duties on materials other than lumber "actually used in buildings erected on the site of buildings burned" by the fire within a year of the act's passage. The imported glass and the 500 tons of iron beams Palmer had bought in Belgium were rushed into place by a crew of 350 men whose labors were extended to eleven at night by electric arc lights playing on the "huge structure, that stood out in the artificial light like a great skeleton" (fig. 4).[5] Although his name is traditionally assigned to it, Van Osdel had less responsibility for this Palmer House design than he had had for the first two.[6] Eight stories high and filling even more of the block than the uncompleted, burnt hulk it replaced, the new Palmer House contained 700 rooms, 16 stores, 60 offices in its entresol, a lavish lobby, stairs, and public rooms, not to mention the basement barbershop, which had silver dollars embedded in the floor. To boast of its resistance to fire, Palmer extended a dare to anyone who wished to risk a test: "If only the room burns, you pay; if the hotel burns, I pay!" The Palmer House set the standard for opulence for a generation and remained the city's largest hotel well into the next century.

The city's first apartment buildings were an outgrowth of the city's best hotels. From the beginning Chicago had resisted multifamily residences of any kind. The first ones, known locally as flats, were low enough not to need elevators. These flats had been built as an expedient after the fire, and until

Fig. 4 Palmer House under construction at night, 1872; from Rebuilt Chicago.

the turn of the century, being substitutes for houses, they did their best to disguise themselves as single-family residences. Then and later, in the residential fringes, the image of a town guided those who built block upon block of two- and three-story houses and two-, three-, and four-story flats. Only in the central commercial area where the hotels were built did the building boom of the 1880s begin to replace the features of a town with those of a city of ever-taller commercial buildings.

Chicago's first apartment buildings — a term used locally to refer to buildings tall enough to call for an elevator — were meant to attract families that could afford to buy a residential house if they chose to do so. The first were built in the 1880s, well after Boston and New York had seen their first buildings of this kind.[7] They appeared in the straggling district between the developing commercial core and the expanding residential fringe, and their designs betrayed the same lack of definition as their locations. In their provision of public dining rooms and parlors and in their exterior form, these apartment houses were like hotels that had been subdued to suggest the greater privacy of a residence. In the configuration of the individual units and their location away from commercial hotels, they were like residences. As a result, they were neither clearly

commercial structures in a city, as hotels were, nor residences in a neighborhood, as mansions and lesser houses were. This ambiguity would haunt most of Chicago's better apartment buildings.

Very little is known about the first apartment building, the Walton, completed in 1879. The Mentone, designed by Lawrence G. Hallberg in 1882, acknowledged non-Chicago precedents for this type of building, displaying a formal resemblance to Richard Morris Hunt's Stuyvesant Apartment House in New York and the influence on it of Viollet-le-Duc's work. In 1889 the Mentone underwent a financial reorganization. Two stories were added to its original six, and it was modified to provide more hotel services.[8]

The largest among the first three Chicago apartment buildings, the seven-story Ontario Flats of 1880, designed by the flourishing firm of Treat and Foltz, more clearly fit local design patterns than the Mentone, as most of the better apartment buildings tended to do (fig. 5).[9] Each floor contained apartments with two and three bedrooms (as well as a maid's room), whose plans resembled those used during the previous half-dozen years for the few larger, better flats built in Chicago (fig. 6). The Ontario Flats' brick and stone construction materials and the design of its entrance portico, incised decoration, and metalwork ornament acknowledged both current French fashion and one of the prevalent styles of Chicago residences; but its size,

Fig. 5 Treat and Foltz, State Street elevation of the Ontario Apartments, 1880 (cat. no. 76).

Fig. 6 Treat and Foltz, Isometric drawing of the Ontario Apartments, 1880 (cat. no. 75).

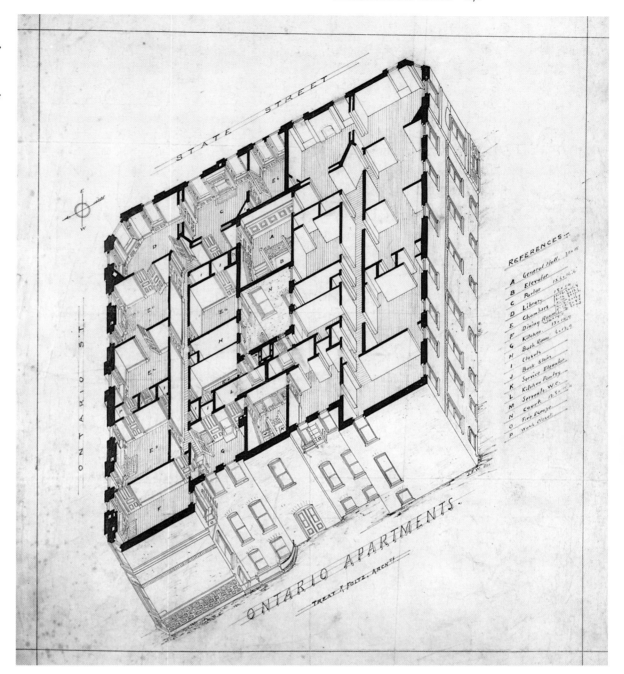

massing, and general composition made it much too large for a residence, and the public dining room was appropriate to a hotel rather than a private home.

Similarly lacking in clear functional definition were some hotels built in the early 1880s. Their location in the central area on Michigan Avenue overlooking the lake and their lavish parlor and dining rooms suggested that they were meant for transient visitors, but the upper stories contained apartment-like suites for long-term residents. The most pretentious of these was the Hotel Richelieu. Opened in 1885, the hotel was the venture of H. V. Bemis, a local man who had accumulated a fortune in brewing and grain trading and had spent it on

horse racing and the hotel overlooking Lake Michigan. Bemis, whose efforts to erect the lavish Richelieu earned him the nickname "Cardinal," hoped the hotel would raise the level of taste in Chicago. The six-story building was packed with works of art collected in Europe and America, and offered the city's most exquisite board and wine list. Managing the enterprise was Henry Clair, a former assistant to A. T. Stewart, the only person in the drygoods business with whom Palmer and Marshall Field had not tried to compete and the operator of a string of luxury hotels in New York City and East Coast resorts.[10] The Richelieu, said one report, "is one of the most perfectly appointed and elegant hotels in America . . . [and] combines the ease of boarding with the content and order of a well-ordered and beautiful home."[11] But it lasted less than a decade. Unlike projects that found a more enduring place in the city's life, it had not adequately adapted its importations to local sensibilities and had failed to ally itself clearly with either the private homes of the town or the hotels of the city.[12]

The next year saw the construction of the first unambiguously residential apartment building, albeit with a very specialized appeal. In 1886 Burnham and Root, a new firm with a growing reputation based on its designs for commercial buildings and mansions, designed two buildings that merged commercial and residential programs. Reported to be "the largest structures of this class erected west of New York, and... well planned for apartment purposes,"[13] the larger of the two, the Argyle (fig. 7), was on Michigan Avenue near the Richelieu but nearer the junction of the commercial core and residential fringe. The *Chicago Tribune* announced, "It will be a rich man's house. Nothing in the way of architectural contrivance and beauty of decoration will be spared." Its ground floor held two large restaurants approached by wide halls and large lobbies. Above, continued the report, were two apartments on each floor with very large rooms; those on the second and third floors divided into suites of three rooms, each suite equipped with bathroom, storeroom, and wine cellar to make it especially suitable for bachelors.[14]

The other apartment building, the Pickwick, was farther south and squarely in the midst of an exclusive residential district. Of the building's two entrances, one faced Michigan Avenue on the building's short end, which was set back twenty feet in line with that avenue's mansions. The exteriors of the two buildings had projecting bays, ornamental brickwork, and terracotta. Both buildings shared design characteristics with the most recently built mansions, although they were tall and narrow in shape rather than cubic.

The high architectural quality of these two buildings, combined with their scale (but not their mass), suggested the comforts of home rather than the transient and commercial nature of their predecessors. This set them apart from the inexpensive apartment buildings, most of them cheapened versions of the Mentone and the Richelieu, proliferating along the heavily traveled cable car routes running south from the Loop and extending the commercial city into the residential town.

Burnham and Root's Argyle and Pickwick apartment buildings provided lesser architects with a new formula, but only indirectly. The intermediary was Adler and Sullivan's great Auditorium Building (1887-89).[15] A small group of wealthy Chicagoans built the Auditorium to serve the city in the same way that Paris's opera, hotels, and salons served its citizens. Assembled within a single hull were a splendid auditorium for opera and its attendant social display; a 400-room hotel offering sumptuous accommodations for guests; a bar; banquet halls suitable for important festive and civic occasions; and a commercial office section to help finance the operation. A booster publication crowed, "the Auditorium Hotel may be taken as a type of the best class of the Chicago Hotels; or it would be if any of them equalled it."[16] As a resort for men of standing, its only rivals were their own mansions and their private clubs which, like hotels, were a special kind of public, although restricted, residence offering them homes away from home.

Three versions of Sullivan's design for the Auditorium's massive exterior are known, two in renderings and a third in the finished form. The earliest rendering shows how Sullivan first considered resolving the problem of investing the building with a single character although it contained a variety of functions — an unusual but not a unique problem. Next door was S. S. Beman's brand new Studebaker Wagon Company Building, which contained a factory and warehouse on the upper floors and fancy showrooms on the lower floors that gave the building's facade its principal character. Three blocks to the north was George M. Pullman's headquarters (see Schlereth, fig. 14), a giant stone structure whose design suggested that it was as much a baronial stronghold as it was an office building and that gave no hint of the seventy-five bachelor apartments on the upper floors.[17] Similarly choosing one aspect of the building to be dominant, Sullivan had the Auditorium's hotel activities dictate the design's character. Its orientation responded specifically to its site: the commercial block faced the city's commercial center, the hotel portion took its place along Michigan Avenue south of the Argyle and the hotel row developing along the lakefront, and the auditorium was inserted between the hotel and the offices, with its side-street entrance made visible by its projection outward and upward from the building's mass. This disposition emphasized the hotel facades, and thus the hotel, rather than the auditorium or commercial office block, functions.

In this hotel-like guise, Sullivan gave the building the characteristics of the latest fashion. Had he attempted to have his building allude to the current premier hotel in Chicago, he would have played its design off against the Palmer House. That he did not do so suggests that he or the backers of the Auditorium considered the Palmer House design

THE ARGYLE APARTMENT BUILDING, CHICAGO.

Fig. 9 Adler and Sullivan, Auditorium Building, 1887-89.

Fig. 10 Adler and Sullivan, Standard Club, Michigan Avenue at 24th Street, 1887 (demolished); the six-story structure at the left was added by Adler and Sullivan in 1892.

unfashionable. Perhaps it was out of date in a world in which fashion was an index of social standing, or perhaps it represented, both literally and figuratively, the aristocratic social circle that the more democratic Auditorium enterprise was to replace or supplement. Instead of referring to the Palmer House, Sullivan's earliest scheme (fig. 8) shows oriels, dormers, a pitched roof, variations in texture and in silhouette, and a number of other devices that did two things at the same time: they alluded directly to the character of the city's best mansions of the moment, and they reduced the block's scale and increased its apparent solidity while providing as much picturesque character as the site and program allowed. Sullivan thus presented the building as the vast, overgrown mansion or club its promoters wanted it to be.

The design that was built was substantially different (fig. 9). The lower floors of the first two schemes survived virtually intact, as did the multistory arcade borrowed from Beman's neighboring building, but the rest of the final design was dramatically different from its earlier versions. Perhaps this change was in response to John Root's taunt about an excess of ornament, or perhaps it acknowledged the power that H. H. Richardson's austere design for Marshall Field's Wholesale Store had over Sullivan. Whatever the reason for the change, nothing about the finished exterior "allows one to identify its mainly 'cultural' character.... To use Sullivan's own way of putting it, this is a case where the function *auditorium* did not generate the form *auditorium*. The form is *office building*," conceived as a kind of "architectural manifesto: it was the first building in which he [Sullivan] tried consciously to be 'modern'...."[18] This thesis holds for the block as a whole, even with the substitution of the words "hotel" or "club" for the word "auditorium." The point is that the final building looks more at home among the buildings accommodating the anonymous activities of a commercial democracy than those serving the personal ones of a town.

Whatever Sullivan's final intent, his achievement was incomplete. The building did retain contact with its residential predecessors, particularly in the ruggedness of the lower floors, which remained relatively unaltered from the first rendering to final construction. The rugged blocks forming arched and linteled openings were fashionable just then and were found in any number of residential structures. Adler and Sullivan acknowledged this when they used them in combination with the rhythms of the Auditorium's upper stories to convey a sense of domesticity in their Standard Club (fig. 10; pl. 34) of 1887 on Michigan Avenue.

But that was not enough to domesticate the huge building. While the Auditorium retains contact with the town of houses, it also beckons towards the city of blocks, and finally to that of towers. That is, while the final design of the lower floors suggested that the building was the city's great public hotel and club, its blocky form sanctioned the use of efficient massing for the apartment buildings that would soon be built in great numbers up and down the lakefront. Similarly, its suggestion that a building need not convey a sense of its use but merely possess a towerlike character presaged the towering forms of the commercial city's modern buildings, buildings that were less distinctive for being residential or commercial buildings than for being towers.

Blocky buildings clearly responding to the commercial programs of Chicago entrepreneurs would quickly fill the central area of the city. Whether purely commercial or commercial residences like hotels or apartment buildings, they were unlike structures serving similar purposes elsewhere. Chicagoans resisted looking beyond their own residential districts for sources for these large commercial residences. Chicago had not transformed its com-

*Fig. 11
Clinton J. Warren, Virginia Hotel, northwest corner of Rush and Ohio streets, 1888-89 (demolished).*

mercial core from a town to a city in order to fulfill a predetermined program or a large vision of what the new central city of the continent should look like. It did not ape other cities and draw its building designs from the East Coast and from abroad. Instead, the transformation occurred unwittingly and unintentionally. As a result, these new, large, multifamily residences, whether apartments or hotels, remained largely innocent of imported characteristics. They retained many of the domestic aspects of Chicago's earlier homes, perpetuating a sense of the old town as they contributed to the image of the new city.

The transformation was accelerated by the choice of Chicago as the site of the 1893 World's Columbian Exposition. Chicago prepared for the Exposition by rushing to provide accommodations for Fair visitors, as well as homes for the city's population. Most of the new flat buildings were sprinkled among mansions along the streets paralleling the boulevards between the Loop and the Fair's site in Hyde Park, where they loomed above and interspersed themselves among their low-lying, long-established domestic neighbors. Others were built elsewhere, for Chicagoans whose numbers were constantly increasing. One example of this new residential building type is Treat and Foltz's Cleveland (or Goudy) Flats on the North Side (1890-91).[19] This four-story building containing thirty-two apartments was brick, with stone arched entrances and bays in sheet metal, a material so common it was called "Chicago granite."

Taller buildings based on the Argyle, the Pickwick, and the Auditorium also proliferated.[20] Their external homogeneity stands in contrast to the heterogeneity of their predecessors, few of which have the formal characteristics of this group of buildings. The new buildings tended to have a relatively flat silhouette and planar walls, usually of brick rather than stone. Like the Auditorium, buildings with a more direct appeal for transient trade tended to have a large, inset balcony above the entrance; however, they generally retained the oriels and bays that Sullivan eliminated from his final design for the Auditorium.

Internally, the better buildings displayed a heterogeneity belied by their exteriors. Because of a continuing inability to decide whether the character of a hotel or of a residence should predominate, each building apparently tried to be all things to all people. The facilities and flexibility praised at the Argyle appear to have provided the model for these buildings, and Clinton J. Warren, who was working for Burnham and Root when that building had been designed, was often the architect of the best of them.

In 1889, Warren designed the most notable of the new group, the very large Virginia Hotel (fig. 11; also known as the McCormick Apartment House), which opened to great acclaim on May 1, 1890, the first day of the city's traditional six-month lease season. Sited on the southern edge of "McCormickville," the North Side area filled with McCormick family members made rich by the reaper, it was built and inhabited by Leander McCormick, a person of impeccable social standing. The Virginia, as its promotional brochure proclaimed, recognized that "one of the growing tendencies of the present time in the large cities is the constantly increasing number of families making their permanent homes in hotels,"[21] and established the large multifamily residence as a place in which Chicago's most respectable people could live.

Gadgetry and appointments rather than appearance were emphasized to boost the building's attractiveness. A press release stressed that it was

fireproof, heated by steam, lighted by electricity, and furnished with all the accommodations and luxuries of the most modern buildings of that class. Mr. R. Hall McCormick [Leander's brother] has personally inspected a number of apartment houses in this city and in New York with a view of getting all their best features, and it is intended that the new structure shall be better than anything else of the kind ever erected in Chicago. There will be 400 rooms, divided into 54 suites.

The building offered a telephone and gas-log fireplaces in each apartment, billiards and bowling in the basement, and a "parlor floor" with public reception rooms and restaurants so that a family could "rely upon the public tables for their food." The apartments also had kitchens in which either gas or coal could be used for cooking.[22] Most rooms had outside exposure, but some were lit and ventilated only by narrow courts open to the street.

Another half-dozen buildings designed by Warren were variations on the Virginia. The last was the eight-story Plaza Hotel, which Warren designed for himself and a partner on the North Side in 1891. He retired from his career as an architect in order to manage its 150 rooms.[23]

The national depression of 1893 affected Chicago despite the success of the Fair, and construction of hotels and apartment buildings virtually ceased even before the Exposition closed. Nearly a decade passed before full-scale building activity resumed, with residential construction during the interval largely limited to mansions and country houses commissioned by the wealthy. The designs for these buildings revealed a radical change in attitude toward the home and its design. Gone were the unprecedented, home-grown styles used by Burnham and Root, the idiosyncratic approach of Sullivan, and the derivatives of recent French and English modes. Instead, these buildings demonstrated that the World's Columbian Exposition had legitimized the various polished classical styles often encountered in the interiors – though not the exteriors – of post-Auditorium, pre-Exposition hotels and apartment buildings. This style of interior decoration moved to the exterior as Chicago's new buildings evoked times and places distant from the newly settled West.

And yet, as Herbert Croly, an acute observer from the East, noted, the new century in Chicago brought forth the admirable, "severely simple apartment house," indicating that a sound, local convention guided the city's designers.[24] That convention, benefiting from two decades of frenzied building followed by a period of reflection, was combined with a new interest and skill in using traditional styles to produce designs for tall buildings that were strictly indigenous, distinctly residential, and clearly identifiable as either a hotel or an apartment building. Before long these two types of buildings were joined by a third, the residential hotel – a calculated combination of the two and therefore unlike the Argyle Apartment Building and the Virginia Hotel, in which the combination had been haphazard and unresolved. All three kinds of building were now distinct in program, interior arrangement, exterior appearance, and position within the urban fabric.

The forms established for hotels and apartment buildings around the turn of the century and for residential hotels soon thereafter would remain standard for the next half-century. The wealthy came to accept these buildings as suitable places of residence. As more of these buildings were erected, architects could contrive interior and ex-

terior designs that were precisely aimed at a particular clientele. They no longer had to borrow from or allude to the styles of private mansions; they could instead draw on the existing forms of large residential buildings, ranging from the best social hotels to residential hotels and tall apartment buildings.

Foremost among the designers of all three kinds of the city's large residential buildings between

Fig. 12 Marshall and Fox, Marshall Apartments, 1100 Lake Shore Drive, 1905 (demolished); from A Portfolio of Fine Apartment Homes *(Chicago, 1928).*

Fig. 13 Plan of Marshall Apartments; from Directory to Apartments of the Better Class along the North Side of Chicago *(Chicago, 1917).*

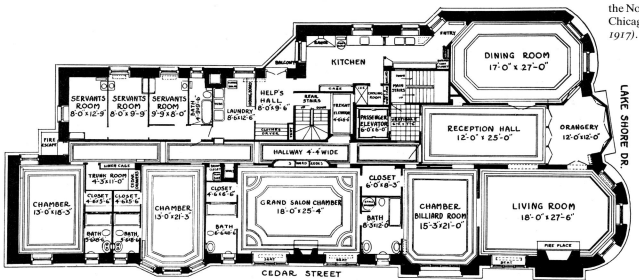

Fig. 14 Marshall and Fox, 1550 North State Parkway, 1911; from A Portfolio of Fine Apartment Homes.

out. While under construction, the Raymond was hailed as one of the "projects of the year"; even before opening, it was cited as setting a high standard that other buildings in the area would have to match.[26] Marshall's second essay in the type was the nearby nine-story Marshall Apartments of 1905, the first apartment building on North Lake Shore Drive at the foot of the Gold Coast (fig. 12). "It was the almost unanimous opinion of real estate men and builders," declared a 1912 report, "that the Lake Shore Drive was primarily a thoroughfare for exclusive residences and that the class of people that resided there would not take kindly to the apartment house idea." The Marshall "is particularly notable," the report continued, "because of its distinguished tenants. Among these may be noted Joy Morton, who was one of the first to take an apartment after he had inspected the plans. . . . It will be but a question of a few years until this famous drive is dotted with stately apartments."[27] Morton's role at the Marshall resembled that of Leander McCormick at the McCormick Apartment House — his living there assured the building's social status. Marshall and his father built the Marshall as an investment, and because it enjoyed a larger site and more ample budget than the Raymond had done it set the measure for the next generation of practice.

The arrangement of the plan in the Marshall's eight full-floor apartments perfected that of the Raymond and established the standard for creating homelike qualities within the limited confines of a tall building (fig. 13). Its exterior also became canonic. Although its general massing resembled that of the Argyle, the Pickwick, and hundreds of other similar buildings, its actual design drew directly on a Georgian and American Colonial-inspired mansion a few blocks away, designed in 1892 by Charles McKim for banker Bryon Lathrop.

Marshall worked in several other versions of the classical as well: the French of Louis XIV, XV, and XVI; the refined Adamesque; and the Italian of the High Renaissance, as interpreted through the best of French academic teaching. Until the closing years of the 1920s, a Chicago builder who used the Beaux-Arts classicism that was popular in other cities, rather than one of the versions Marshall favored, did so at potential financial risk.

Marshall designed and owned the acknowledged leader among all of Chicago's luxury apartment buildings, the building at 1550 North State Parkway of 1911 (fig. 14). In Chicago it is described as French (an association Marshall cultivated by labeling his plans in that language), but from a New York perspective it has more in common with the "severely simple apartment house" Herbert Croly

1900 and the Great Depression of the 1930s was Benjamin Howard Marshall.[25] A Chicagoan who was largely self-taught, Marshall designed mansions for a decade on the South Side before he expanded his practice to include designs for apartments and hotels. He was the city's best at endowing hotels with an exotic and luxurious ambiance, and he was unsurpassed in investing expensive apartment buildings with an unambiguously domestic aspect both inside and out.

Marshall's first luxury apartment building, the eight-story Raymond of 1900, provided a model plan that replaced the confusion, darkness, and cramped space of previous plans with an orderly division of public, private, and service areas, an expansive interlocking of rooms, and a proper regard for light and air. Potter Palmer, the largest landowner in the North Side lakefront area, attempted to block its construction, as he believed that it would undermine the value of the residences he had built throughout the area. However, Harry Raymond, an investment and insurance man, won

admired. Its plan possesses clarity and grace with each floor devoted to one huge, clearly zoned apartment. Its service areas are clustered on one side and use a narrow light well for ventilation. Dominating the plan is a unified suite of public rooms running across the front of the building, overlooking Lincoln Park. The bedrooms, each with a generous bath and dressing area, face the lakefront with the view thought to be guaranteed (it was not, as things turned out) by the presence of a mansion on each of the two intervening blocks. Marshall used materials and design elements that had come to be associated with Chicago buildings. The building's steel frame supports a terracotta curtain wall with shallow relief, except around the extensive but simple fenestration, where inset balconies increase the depth of the relief. The facade's relative spareness combines with the grass-and-shrub-framed street-level setback to fit the building into the conventional Chicago mode, distancing it from the relationship of building to boulevard in the grand Parisian style, a point emphasized by an entrance that is minuscule relative to the size of the building, but appropriate for a residence.

Soon after establishing a new, high standard for apartment houses, Marshall did the same for the city's best hotels. In 1908 he designed the Blackstone (fig. 1; pl. 84), Chicago's first luxury hotel to depart internally and externally from the precedent set by the Auditorium Hotel (fig. 9). John and Tracy Drake, sons of the proprietor of the Grand Pacific Hotel, built it on the South Michigan Avenue site of their father's house, a few blocks south of the Auditorium Hotel. It was aimed at the same kind of clientele that Palmer had drawn to his hotel and that McCormick had sought for the Virginia Hotel, rather than at the travelers whom the founder of the Drake dynasty had sought to lure to the Grand Pacific. It quickly became the center of Chicago's most exclusive social activities, accommodating the coming-out parties and balls that Chicago's social leaders had formerly hosted in their homes.[28] The Louis XV details presented in gilt-touched plaster inside the Blackstone and in bronze, marble, terracotta, and elaborate electrical candelabra outside, established a new style for elegant social settings in Chicago.

The Blackstone was the first of a plethora of new hotels, most meant for travelers, scattered throughout the central area of the city before World War I. Some were designed by Marshall, some by other architects, like Holabird and Roche's La Salle Hotel (fig. 15), yet all resembled it in one way or another. To expand their offerings, the Drakes planned an annex, with the lower seven floors devoted to banquet and ballrooms, and a

gallery passageway and "new art hall" atop the Blackstone Theater that Marshall had built for the Drakes in 1910, immediately west of the hotel.[29]

America's entry into the war intervened, and when civilian construction resumed, the Drakes turned to the North Side for their expanded operations. The Burnham and Bennett Plan of Chicago of 1909 showed how a new bridge and boulevard would link the Loop with the North Side Gold Coast, which was gradually replacing the South Side as the city's exclusive residential district. The Drakes placed their new hotel on a site overlooking Lake Michigan at the point where the new Michigan Avenue joined Lake Shore Drive. The bridge and the hotel both opened in 1920. The Drakes returned to a Chicago tradition of selecting a local name for the hotel, in this case their own, and they commissioned Marshall to do the design (fig. 17).

The Drake Hotel has a thirteen-story H-plan tower rising above a two-story podium which contains shops opening onto the lobby, as well as a full complement of dining, social, and reception

Fig. 15 Holabird and Roche, LaSalle Hotel, northwest corner of LaSalle and Madison streets, 1909 (demolished).

Fig. 16 Holabird and Roche, Perspective rendering of the lobby with proposed decoration, Palmer House, 17 East Monroe Street, 1925 (cat. no. 249).

rooms. Although it was built in conjunction with other projects designed to fit into the Burnham and Bennett Plan, it contradicted the very essence of that plan. The Plan pictured a city whose central area, extending as far as the Drake's site, would be filled with blocks of buildings with facades that would provide a decorous variety in their detailing while their homogeneous massing formed a unified impression.[30] The Drake did the opposite: it treated its portion of the block as a convenient podium for a building standing independent of its neighbors and finished on each side, whether that side was street frontage or merely an interior lot line. Although as an isolated building the Drake is an excellent design, it was unlike the Blackstone and most of the other hotels and tall apartment buildings it resembled that were unambiguously a part of the city, and especially of the city pictured in the Burnham and Bennett Plan. The character of its design left it to equivocate between being a freestanding residence in a town (though it was much too large for that) or a giant building in a giant city (though it was too inward-looking to form a city block). Later practice would show that it was an

Fig. 17 Marshall and Fox, Drake Hotel, southeast corner of Michigan Avenue and East Lake Shore Drive, 1919.

Fig. 18 Holabird and Roche, Stevens Hotel (now Chicago Hilton and Towers), 720 South Michigan Avenue, 1927.

Fig. 19 Marshall and Fox, South Shore Country Club, 7059 South Shore Drive, 1906-15, interior of solarium.

Fig. 20 South Shore Country Club, interior of grand ballroom.

isolated object in the kind of city Sullivan had envisaged, the kind being built by aggressive entrepreneurs willing to fragment an existing city.

The Drake's design presaged the demise of the spirit animating the 1909 Plan. It suggests either that the city's premier hoteliers and the architect of its most luxurious residences did not understand the civil and design implications of the Burnham and Bennett Plan, or that the image the Plan portrayed no longer gripped their imagination, or that they were no longer willing to be governed by it. Whatever the reason, the builder and architect of the Drake Hotel reached back to an earlier configuration that had been used since the 1890s for apartment buildings and hotels on rectangular sites like the one occupied by the Drake.[31] The H-shaped configuration, to be sure, allowed light and air into rooms situated far from the lot line, but it also gave the building a conspicuous and independent presence. This was less problematic in the earlier period, when the building was only twice the height of its residential neighbors. But when a building has a broad setback as exaggerated as that of the Drake, when it is as large as the Drake, and when it is surrounded — as the Drake was and was intended to be — by large neighboring structures built to compose a city, it rends the fabric of a city.

But that very rent in the fabric is appealing as far as the entrepreneur is concerned, for it becomes an advertisement, calling attention to the building. As the promotional brochure for the Virginia Hotel proclaimed in 1890, that building's

lofty walls tower far above surrounding edifices, and, as the walls in the rear, as well as on the street fronts, are faced with red pressed brick, it presents a uniformly finished appearance on all four sides. It is of commanding importance, and punctuates the progress of improvements in the beautiful section of the city in which it is located.[32]

The Virginia shared its red pressed-brick facades with the residences of its period, just as the Drake's limestone cladding and its design based on Italian Renaissance forms linked it with a domestic imagery that had been increasingly fashionable since the turn of the century. The use of limestone here for the Blackstone's replacement as the arbiter of elegance established a new fashion in the best apartment buildings and in the next series of hotels, just as its massing would subsequently be used whenever a site was large enough.

Among the new hotels of the decade of the 1920s was the fourth Palmer House, built between 1924 and 1927 with facades of brick above a limestone base. Holabird and Roche designed and supervised

construction on the building which covered more than half a city block with its three basements and twenty-five stories including extensive service areas and 2,268 guest rooms. It replaced a building whose style was clearly out of fashion and whose equipment was out of date, but it did not assume the premier position its predecessor had once enjoyed in the city's social life. Nevertheless, its grand and gracious second-story reception lobby and connected banquet room and ballroom remain among the city's most elegant (fig. 16; cat. no. 249).

In 1927, the same architects completed the Stevens Hotel (fig. 18; pls. 86, 87), a building that had been projected since World War I to be the world's largest hotel. Once again, Holabird and Roche followed the canons Marshall had established at the Blackstone in designing its interior arrangement and contriving its exterior appearance. However, only construction techniques developed after the Blackstone's completion provided the experience required to produce this huge, twenty-five-story hotel stretching across the frontage of an entire long block. It turned out to be the largest of the many hotels that Chicagoans recognized as being for transients, and that foreign publications found notable for their size and efficiency.[33] This hotel remains as the southernmost of the series of

hotels stretching southward three-and-a-half nearly solid blocks from the Auditorium Hotel, and it enjoys the magnificent view of Lake Michigan that has long attracted important hotels to this street.

As far back as the early 1860s, guests in boarding houses north and south of the city's built-up area had enjoyed the lake's cooling breezes in the hot summers and bracing sport during the winter season. After the turn of the century, the wealthy staked their claim to the lake by means of exclusive clubs. In 1905 Jarvis Hunt built a stone and shingle clubhouse on the extensive North Side grounds of the elite Saddle and Cycle Club,[34] and in 1906 Benjamin Marshall built the first phase of a Mediterranean-style villa for the South Shore Country Club (figs. 19, 20), just south of Hyde Park.

The grandest of such facilities, however, was Marshall's Edgewater Beach Hotel, a club-like resort accessible to anyone able to pay the moderate cost of a room. Its first phase was begun in 1915, immediately north of the Saddle and Cycle Club and a mere nine miles north of the center of the Loop, easily reached by the elevated public transit system.[35] Marshall expanded the eight-story building in 1919, and in 1923 added another one to the south. The new building reached eighteen stories in a series of steps, one of which was topped by a radio

studio. A pair of transmitting towers was intended for the roof (they were apparently not built), while a 200-car garage, reached through the lobby and placed beneath a terrace with enclosed lounges, connected the building to the original section (fig. 21). The pair of reinforced concrete buildings with pink walls, red tile roofs, and blue stencil patterns in the interiors were vaguely evocative of the Mediterranean, although the massing was purely local. From the beginning the complex's 1,000-foot beach promenade led up to an outdoor dancing terrace, which opened into a dining room with a sliding skylight that could be opened when Chicago's changeable weather permitted. The grounds included gardens, children's playgrounds, a lighted tennis court convertible to a skating rink in the winter, and a nine-hole putting golf course. In 1927 Marshall added the nineteen-story Edgewater Beach Apartments (pl. 85) at the north end of the extensive acreage. This was a more elegant building, meant less for vacationers than for residents desiring both the services of a hotel and the privacy of a home, which is just what a residential hotel offered.

Others had anticipated Marshall in building residential hotels. In the years just before World War I, when enough Chicagoans began leading less family-oriented lives, builders responded by developing two kinds of residential hotels catering to different social classes. The new buildings were situated in already established apartment building enclaves — some near the lake in Hyde Park, but most of them north of the Gold Coast, stretching to and beyond Marshall's Edgewater complex.

One type was designed for young people, married or single, who were entering the new white-collar employment market in Chicago's changing economy. The builders, assuming that this group would enjoy proximity to the beaches, offered buildings with balconies, loggias, and rooftop dining and dancing in settings suggesting Mediterranean villas. The first of these was probably the Eastwood Beach Apartments, a six-story block of 1916 by John Nyden. It contained eighty suites, a few with two main rooms but most with a large room and a tiny entrance nook called, grandly, a "reception hall"; another small room called a "breakfast room, with complete equipped kitchenette"; a bathroom with a "porcelain tiled bath with shower"; and a large closet called a "dressing room" and equipped with a clothes press, dresser, and "Marshall-Stearns sanitary portal bed" that folded out into the large room to convert it from a living room to a bedroom. The building offered, "in fact, all the conveniences of a modern club or hotel with residential privacy."[36]

The other type was directed at the more prosperous and established. The first of these was the Parkway Hotel of 1916. Designed by Walter W. Ahlschlager to suggest a Renaissance palace, the eleven-story building with 225 rooms promised to be the

ideal residential hotel of Chicago . . . intended to serve its patrons in any season of the year. It will contain every improvement, every device designed for good service, with an atmosphere of refinement and taste so pleasing to those desiring accommodations of a superior standard of excellence. . . . Every room has a private bath; one-half have a shower. A ballroom is provided for dancing, afternoon and evening. Special arrangements can be made for banquets, dinners, teas, card parties, dances, etc. Marinello shop, barber shop, drug store, billiard room and cigar stores are in the building.[37]

World War I interrupted the momentum of construction activity in Chicago, but recovery failed to bring forth new kinds of buildings. As had been the case after the Great Fire of 1871, the scramble to build produced more of the same kinds of buildings that had begun to gain acceptance before the interruption of construction. Facing rapid inflation in building costs and straitened incomes on the part of renters who sought a social life outside the home, postwar builders made certain adjustments in these buildings. Henceforth they would construct larger buildings holding smaller apartments whose appeal was increased by new labor- and space-saving

gadgets such as gas or electric refrigerators and hideaway beds that folded out of closets to convert sitting rooms into bedrooms.

Fig. 23 Robert DeGolyer with Walter T. Stockton, 1120 North Lake Shore Drive, 1924.

For most of the hotels and apartment buildings built after the World's Columbian Exposition, some form of the classical style provided the basis for the design. Classicism apparently evoked the desired association with the civilized form of urban life these buildings were thought to provide. But a number of mansions and country houses from 1893 on drew from various versions of the Gothic, especially English Gothic, and Tudor, because these styles were taken to be more homelike.

The first luxury apartment building to do so was built in the Tudor style in 1910 at 1130 North Lake Shore Drive (fig. 22). The building was a near neighbor and worthy competitor to its predecessor, the Marshall. Howard Van Doren Shaw was both the designer and one of eight owners who all resided in this nine-story building.[38] Shaw was notable for producing inventive designs for people

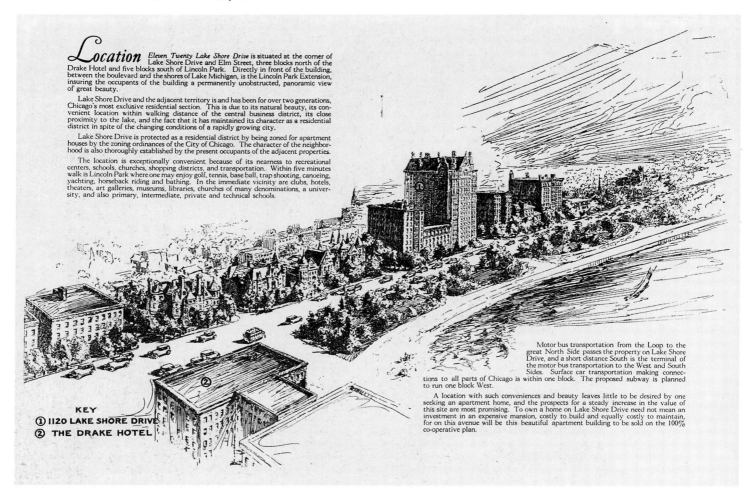

Location Eleven Twenty Lake Shore Drive is situated at the corner of Lake Shore Drive and Elm Street, three blocks north of the Drake Hotel and five blocks south of Lincoln Park. Directly in front of the building, between the boulevard and the shores of Lake Michigan, is the Lincoln Park Extension, insuring the occupants of the building a permanently unobstructed, panoramic view of great beauty.

Lake Shore Drive and the adjacent territory is and has been for over two generations, Chicago's most exclusive residential section. This is due to its natural beauty, its convenient location within walking distance of the central business district, its close proximity to the lake, and the fact that it has maintained its character as a residential district in spite of the changing conditions of a rapidly growing city.

Lake Shore Drive is protected as a residential district by being zoned for apartment houses by the zoning ordinances of the City of Chicago. The character of the neighborhood is also thoroughly established by the present occupants of the adjacent properties.

The location is exceptionally convenient because of its nearness to recreational centers, schools, churches, shopping districts, and transportation. Within five minutes walk is Lincoln Park where one may enjoy golf, tennis, base ball, trap shooting, canoeing, yachting, horseback riding and bathing. In the immediate vicinity are clubs, hotels, theaters, art galleries, museums, libraries, churches of many denominations, a university, and also primary, intermediate, private and technical schools.

Motor bus transportation from the Loop to the great North Side passes the property on Lake Shore Drive, and a short distance South is the terminal of the motor bus transportation to the West and South Sides. Surface car transportation making connections to all parts of Chicago is within one block. The proposed subway is planned to run one block West.

A location with such conveniences and beauty leaves little to be desired by one seeking an apartment home, and the prospects for a steady increase in the value of this site are most promising. To own a home on Lake Shore Drive need not mean an investment in an expensive mansion, costly to build and equally costly to maintain, for on this avenue will be this beautiful apartment building to be sold on the 100% co-operative plan.

KEY
① 1120 LAKE SHORE DRIVE
② THE DRAKE HOTEL

within and beyond his circle of wealth and standing — though not in the way Louis Sullivan, Frank Lloyd Wright, and others were. Investors looking for a profit and wealthy householders looking for a place to live tended to avoid architects who departed from historical precedents.

An exception to this was Schmidt, Garden and Martin, one of the few large firms able to do both innovative work allied with the Prairie School style and orthodox commercial buildings, as well as luxury flats and apartment buildings for investors resistant to innovation. In 1910 Buckingham Chandler, a developer who wished to build "the ideal apartment building" on a cramped Gold Coast site, turned to that firm. The result was the six-story Chandler Apartments (it received a seventh in 1914) with fourteen- and fifteen-room apartments. Chandler described the venture as

[t]he engrafting of the Parisian apartment, with its attractive court and fountain, on the sturdy commercialism of the Chicago product, and the combining with all the comforts and care in planning found in our well-to-do American homes.... [The exterior] is English Renaissance of the time of Charles II and James II, a period made memorable by Sir Christopher Wren, the architect, and Grinling Gibbons, the great woodcarver.[39]

The same orthodoxy prevailed even when the investor was himself a person known for innovation — in this case, Hugh Garden. In 1915 Garden designed and built his own eight-story luxury building. The venture was risky because its lakefront site was five miles north of the Loop and three miles beyond other tall apartment buildings on the North Side, then limited to the Gold Coast. His choice of the Tudor style for the facade was apparently an effort to make his investment safer.[40] When he sold the Garden Apartments at a handsome profit a few years later, it had already attracted even more luxurious neighbors, most of them in some version of classical styles.

A similar use of a conservative Tudor style in an innovative building is seen in Robert DeGolyer's 1120 Lake Shore Drive of 1924 (fig. 23). This was the first of the giants to be raised in the Gold Coast, the first to have a bulk defined by the zoning code enacted in 1923, and the first large Gold Coast luxury venture financed as a cooperative building and offered for sale to members of the public who, by purchasing shares, would live in apartments they owned. New York's apartment buildings, which were greater in number, larger in size, and more densely packed into larger sections of the

Fig. 24 North Lake Shore Drive, from a real estate development brochure.

Fig. 25 Rissman and Hirschfeld, 3520-30 North Lake Shore Drive, 1924.

city's fabric than their Chicago counterparts, had for decades been financed in this way. In Illinois, however, between the fire of 1871 and World War I, state legislation (endorsed by Chicago real estate interests) had precluded the formation of corporations for the purpose of developing land.

The new method of financing, coinciding with the new zoning code modeled on New York's ordinance of 1916, allowed the kind of building embodied by the Drake to become dominant in Chicago. The building's mass could be predicated on what the market might absorb, what a corporation might be willing to finance, and what the zoning code permitted. Before long, apartment buildings were no longer thought of as they had been before the Fair — as residential compromises within a town structure and therefore disguised as houses or designed as overgrown clubs or dislocated hotels. Nor were they conceived of as they were pictured in the Burnham and Bennett Plan — as building blocks that would accumulate to form a unified city. Instead, their designers would look inward from the boundaries of their sites, packing the lots efficiently with buildings conceived of more as independent objects than as parts of a whole. The resulting form would be more a tower than a block and would

stress its independence from its neighbors, as the sales brochure's picture of DeGolyer's building did by having it loom above its smaller neighbors — Shaw's and Marshall's first two buildings on the lakefront and another by Marshall, the Stewart, from 1912 (fig. 24).

During the rest of the decade, dozens of buildings like 1120 Lake Shore Drive were punched upward into the skyline, designed by architects adept in the specialized skills that made these ventures profitable. The most active designers included Marshall, who almost always did the best and most expensive buildings and did them well; William Ernest Walker, Marshall's near peer in the earlier part of the period; DeGolyer, the most prolific and competent for buildings slightly lower in standing;[41] Ahlschlager, for the grand, flashy, and innovative; the firms of Fugard and Knapp, and McNally and Quinn, which provided many sound buildings for the wealthier and middle classes; firms such as Rissman and Hirshfeld (fig. 25), Hooper and Janusch, Huszagh and Hill, Leichenko and Esser, and others that did workmanlike jobs for less pretentious buildings; and B. Leo Steif, Raymond Gregori, and Philip Maher, whose activity was filled with promise when the

Great Depression of the 1930s suspended building operations for more than a decade.

On the exteriors of their buildings, these architects followed the strong conventions unique to Chicago, occasionally including details to suggest the Gothic or the Tudor, though more often some version of the classical. Later in the decade, after 1927, their forms ceased to refer to some previous style and instead demonstrated a modernistic independence. Inside, the architects crammed an increasing number of small, efficiently arranged, and well-equipped apartments. Most years saw the construction of one or two buildings with very large apartments; but a Gold Coast location, liveried doorman, and favorable press reports and gossip did more than exterior appearance or generous interior spaces to indicate the higher social and economic standing of the residents. Such a luxury building, actually far north of the Gold Cast property, is Peter J. Weber's Harbor Apartment Building at 3400 Sheridan Road (pl. 89), with an exterior that is a revised, heavier version of Marshall's 1500 North State Parkway. Across the street from the Garden Apartment Building, it was begun in 1919, but a shortage of materials delayed its opening until 1921, when a roster of millionaires began to move into its ten- to sixteen-room apartments.[42]

The sheer accumulation of these buildings changed the formal character of the city. The central area became more densely concentrated with commercial blocks, some with towers above the twenty-story cornice line, a feature first allowed by the 1923 zoning ordinance. The residential areas spread ever farther toward the horizon, with three-story flats closer in and houses farther out, both of which allowed Chicago's essentially townlike character to remain intact by having grassy setbacks and often side yards or open courts. But in a thin ribbon along the North Side lakefront and in isolated clusters in Hyde Park, Chicago became a collection of isolated towers. Increasingly belonging neither to the flatland of Chicago's homes nor to the blocky city of commerce in Chicago's heart, the tall apartment zone became the harbinger of post-1950 Chicago, which merged the American and European experiences of the 1910s and 1920s to produce buildings independent of a past, having a place within neither town nor city, and more the product of technology and economics than of civil design or concern for domesticity.

NOTES

1   David Watkin, "The Grand Hotel Style," in *Grand Hotel* (New York and Paris, 1984), p. 15. Many stories by George Ade, the turn-of-the-century Chicago author, acknowledged this aspect of hotels in his fables.

2   For its ownership, see Alfred T. Andreas, *History of Chicago*, 3 vols. (Chicago, 1884-86), vol. 2, p. 509. La-Salle Street was rapidly developing as the West's banking and commodities trading center. In 1885, when W. W. Boyington's Chicago Board of Trade Building opened at the foot of LaSalle in the block directly in front of the rail terminal, the hotel traded its distinction of being a center for travelers for a reputation as host to plungers and tycoons. In 1875, the hotel came under the proprietorship of John B. Drake, about whom more is said below.

3   See David Lowe, *Chicago Interiors: Views of a Splendid World* (Chicago, 1979), pp. 14-15, for plan and section and interior and exterior photographs.

4   It is not clear who the architect was or whether this trip included an architect. For additional information, see note 6. "Our Great Hotels: The Palmer House," *Land Owner* 5 (June 1873), p. 115. The dates in brackets are the dates given in Watkin (note 1), index.

5   "Palmer's Grand Hotel," *Land Owner* 5 (Mar. 1873), p. 82. This issue included a front-page wood engraving of the night work, indicated that as protection against fire, the kitchen was in a separate building, and reported, "Each iron beam taken up the elevator cost $69 in gold, and the rebate amounted to over $10." Extensive debate, found in *The Congressional Globe*, delayed passage of the Act of Congress until the ashes of the fire had been cool for six months.

6   *Land Owner* 5 (June 1873), p. 115, stated, "The building has been for the past two years under the control of the talented young architect, Mr. C. M. Palmer, whom Mr. P. Palmer considers a very superior architect, both as designer and constructor." Charles M. Palmer was no relation to Potter Palmer. Thomas Tallmadge, *Architecture in Old Chicago* (Chicago, 1941), p. 113, also names C. M. Palmer, who had an office in the Palmer House

entresol. Andreas, vol. 3, p. 64, states: "The plans for this building were, to a considerable extent, conceived, if not completed, abroad. Mr. Palmer, with a view to its erection, visited the chief cities of Europe, in company with one of the leading architects of this city. The general style of the building, both in its exterior and its more important features of interior arrangement, is largely the embodiment of modern French ideas, particularly in the *entresol*, which is strikingly Parisian in appearance."

7   For example, the Hotel Pelham in Boston was built in 1857, and the Stuyvesant Apartments in New York in 1869.

8   The press reported, it "will be one of the handsomest and best finished structures of the character in Chicago or the West.... The structure will contain 12 compartments or flats, of 8 and 9 rooms each, exclusive of pantries, closets, and bath-rooms, the principal rooms of which will be finished handsomely with hardwood and veneered panels. A commodious passenger elevator will run up the center of the building, and a freight elevator will have a place in the rear of the building. Two shafts for light and ventilation will be placed in the structure for the comfort and convenience of servants and others occupying inside rooms.... The style of the structure is intended to be a modern treatment of Gothic as near as may be to comport with harmony, which is the main point aimed at." "Apartment House," *Chicago Tribune* (Oct. 8, 1882), p. 18.

9   Frank A. Randall, *History of the Development of Building Construction in Chicago* (Urbana, Ill., 1949), p. 94, gives the permit date as August 3, 1880. Its original plans, dated to June and July, 1880, are now in The Art Institute of Chicago's Department of Architecture. In 1892, Treat and Foltz were preparing plans for converting it to a hotel with two more stories and an addition on the property to the north; *Economist* (Apr. 16, 1892), p. 574. The two stories were not added, but plans at the Art Institute show that various alterations were made and that the four-story residence to the north was joined to the building and incorporated into its operations, which included expanded public dining facilities.

10   The description in Andreas (note 2), vol. 3, pp. 355-

56, conveys the period's inability to find a way to characterize Bemis's undertaking.

11   Charles Eugene Banks, *The Artistic Guide to Chicago and the World's Columbian Exposition* (1893), p. 157. Even a generation later, it was recalled with fondness: "Nothing since has ever quite filled its place for the cosmopolitan traveler." Paul Gilbert and Charles Lee Bryson, *Chicago and Its Makers* (Chicago, 1929), p. 134, ill. p. 138.

12   Another similar, noteworthy example was the six-story Beaurivage Bachelor Apartments built at Michigan and Van Buren in about 1875, replaced after a fire in 1882, and converted to a hotel in 1891. Rand McNally and Company's *Bird's-Eye Views and Guide to Chicago* (1898), reprinted in Randall (note 9), p. 174, said it was "Chicago's first 'French flats,' or fashionable apartment building," a claim that the lack of clear definition of terminology and of dates for this building make impossible to verify. The 1880 edition of Chicago's *Elite Guide* listed residents for fifteen flats, including its then-owner, J. K. Fisher, and the architect Peter B. Wight. A photograph appears in Gilbert and Bryson (note 11), p. 294.

13   *Inland Architect* 9, 3 (1887), p. 28, where it is wrongly stated that both were eight stories and meant for fifteen families each. See also Donald Hoffmann, *The Architecture of John Wellborn Root* (Baltimore and London, 1973), pp. 98-99.

14   *Chicago Tribune* (Jan. 31, 1886), p. 20.

15   The best source of information is still Hugh Morrison, *Louis Sullivan: Prophet of Modern Architecture* (1935; reprinted New York, 1962), pp. 85 ff.

16   *Chicago and Its Resources Twenty Years After* (Chicago, 1892), p. 15. This publication saw the Auditorium Hotel's three rivals among "the world's famed hotels" as the Grand Pacific, the Palmer House, and the Richelieu. It is noteworthy that in 1912 and earlier, the Auditorium's tower was used as the logo for *The National Hotel Reporter*, one of the period's trade newspapers; illustrated in "Hotel Association of Chicago," *Hotel Monthly* 20 (June 1912), p. 43.

17   The ten-story building was begun in 1883 with its

giant entrance facing Adams Street, a feature that allied the building with the Loop's commercial structures rather than with its neighboring hotels. See *Industrial Chicago: The Building Interests* (Chicago, 1891), vol. 1, pp. 178-79. After 1888, Irving K. and Allen B. Pond, who designed innovative model flats for Jane Addams at Hull-House, lived on the eighth floor and had their office on the sixth.

18 David S. Andrew, *Louis Sullivan and the Polemics of Modern Architecture* (Urbana and Chicago, 1985), pp. 86-87, 91.

19 Among the many buildings mentioned in a review of buildings on the North Side is this one, called the Cleveland Apartment House, and owned by the late W. C. Goudy. The review (*Economist* [July 14, 1894], pp. 71-72) mentioned that it paid fourteen to sixteen percent the first two years. The building's plans are at The Art Institute of Chicago.

20 An early, misleading notice of some aspects of these buildings is in Sigfried Giedion, *Space, Time and Architecture: The Growth of a New Tradition*, 3rd ed. (Cambridge, Mass., 1956), pp. 375-79. The only review of these buildings, itself quite partial, is in Carl W. Condit, *The Chicago School of Architecture: The History of Commercial and Public Building in the Chicago Area, 1875-1925* (Chicago, 1964), pp. 148-59.

21 [E. S. Hand], *The Virginia: A Description, with Illustrations, of the new Hotel lately erected at the Gateway to the fashionable North Side of Chicago* (New York, 1890), n. pag. Daniel Bluestone, who found this publication in the Library of Congress, kindly brought it to my attention. The McCormick clan used the building as an extension of their residences in the area; see, for example, the remarks in Emmett Dedmon, *Fabulous Chicago* (New York, 1953), pp. 132-33.

22 *Economist* (Dec. 29, 1888), p. 8. Another source noted, "It is furnished with the largest individual electric-light plant in the city, and contains fifteen steam engines ranging from ten to two hundred and fifty horse-power each"; *Daily News Almanac* (Chicago, 1891), p. 358. *Industrial Chicago* (note 17), vol. 1, p. 243, called special attention to the laundry rooms on the top floor and noted that "the flats are divided into parlor, library and dining room, and are so arranged that they can be made into one room."

23 It was reportedly designed with eleven shops along the commercial street and, above, 150 apartments ranging from two to seven rooms; *Economist* (Sept. 26, 1891), p. 534; (Oct. 17, 1891), p. 678; (Jan. 30, 1892), p. 162; (Apr. 16, 1892), p. 576; *Daily News Almanac* (1892), p. 382. A glimpse of its lobby is found in Lowe (note 3), p. 21.

24 Herbert Croly, "Some Apartment Houses in Chicago," *Architectural Record* 21 (1907), pp. 119-30.

25 For specific information not provided here, see C. W. Westfall, "Benjamin Henry [lapsis for Howard] Marshall of Chicago," *Chicago Architectural Journal* 2 (1982), pp. 8-27, which includes a list of Marshall's buildings, and which examines the relationships between Marshall's designs for residences, apartment buildings, clubs, and hotels. Charles Fox, mentioned below, was a long-time partner of Marshall. See also Robert F. Irving, "Benny Marshall: The Dreams That Money Could Buy," *Inland Architect* 22 (Feb. 1978), pp. 14-17; and Carl John Sterner, "The Marshall-Walton Papers," *The Library Chronicle of the University of Texas at Austin* 9 (1978), pp. 61-65.

26 See *Economist* (Sept. 8, 1900), p. 276; (Sept. 17, 1900), p. 304; (Sept. 29, 1900), p. 362; (Dec. 31, 1900) p. 807; and (Mar. 2, 1901), p. 249.

27 Raymond Thompson, "Apartment Houses on Chicago's Lake Shore Drive," *The Apartment House* 2 (Aug. 1912), pp. 16-17.

28 Arthur Meeker, *Chicago, With Love* (New York, 1955), pp. 129, 131, 273.

29 In 1912, the Hotel Association of Chicago, founded in 1898, boasted thirty-eight hotel members accounting for 12,000 rooms, 8,000 of which were in fireproof buildings. The hotels are pictured in "Hotel Association of Chicago," *Hotel Monthly* 20 (June 1912), pp. 40-43. Information about the annex to the Blackstone Theater comes in part from the 1916 preliminary drawings in the collection of Marshall drawings at the University of Texas.

30 For a similar analysis stressing the importance of establishing a reciprocity between building and street in

designs by Burnham and Root from the late 1880s and 1890s, including the Argyle and the Pickwick, see Mario Manieri-Elia, "Towards an 'Imperial City': Daniel H. Burnham and the City Beautiful Movement," in *The American City: From the Civil War to the New Deal*, trans. B. L. La Penta (Cambridge, Mass., 1979), p. 13.

31 As an example of a case where a smaller site allowed only half of an H-plan, which backed up to an alley but presented finished facades along all the other sides, see the 1893-94 five-story Tudor building designed by Treat and Foltz, described in *Economist* (May 6, 1893), p. 634; for the configuration of this building, see *Sanborn Atlas of Chicago* (New York, 1925). vol. 14. Another example was the seven-story South Side Kenwood Apartment Building, planned by Charles S. Frost in 1892 but not finished until 1895; *Inland Architect* 21, no. 2 (1893), p. 16, and later plate for a plan and rendering; for a photogravure, see *Inland Architect* 43, no. 2 (1899).

32 Hand (note 21), n. pag.

33 Two examples of foreign publications noting Chicago hotels are the following: Fritz Kunz-Düsseldorf, *Der Hotelbau von Heute* (Stuttgart, 1930), which discussed the Stevens Hotel, and *Neuzeitliche Hotels und Krankenhäuser* (Berlin-Charlottenburg, 1930), which devotes pp. 11-29 to a description of the Bismarck Hotel.

34 A Gold Coast resident reported, "*The* clubs are the Casino and the Saddle and Cycle." Quoted with original emphasis in Harvey Warren Zorbough, *The Gold Coast and the Slum* (Chicago, 1929), p. 50. The Casino, located near the Drake, was the first Chicago club to admit both men and women to membership.

35 For photographs, see "The Edgewater Beach Hotel, Chicago, Ill.," *American Architect* 112 (Sept. 26, 1917), pp. 233-34, and additional plates.

36 A. J. Pardridge and Harold Bradley, *Directory to Apartments of the Better Class along the North Side of Chicago* (Chicago, 1917), p. 114; see also *Modern Type of Apartment Hotels Thruout United States* (Chicago, 1917), n. pag. For the building permit, see *Economist* (July 8, 1916), p. 104.

37 Pardridge and Bradley (note 36), p. 88; *Economist* (Aug. 26, 1916), pp. 417, 430; for the addition, see *Economist* (May 18, 1918), p. 924. An early brochure put out by the Lott Hotel Company, which built and operated it and the other similar hotels, explained: "The tremendous demand for hotel accommodations is found to be due to the large number of residential guests, who have given up their private homes. . . . The high cost of fuel, food and other commodities coupled with the desire of this class of people to be relieved of various home inconveniences is bringing about this change in the mode of living." *Apartment Hotels: The Belden, The Webster, The Parkway* (Chicago, n. d.), n. pag.; copy in Chicago Historical Society. Its success brought forth an addition from 1919, also designed by Ahlschlager, which added 163 suites of four rooms each.

38 *Economist* (Feb. 12, 1910), p. 342; (Apr. 23, 1910), p. 839; and (Oct. 19, 1918), p. 646. In 1922 Shaw designed, and then moved into, the thirteen-story Georgian cooperative at 2450 Lakeview (extant) which occupies only a portion of the site and allows each of the twelve very large apartments a view to Lake Michigan across Lincoln Park. Like his neighbors, Shaw considered this to be merely his town apartment, while Ragdale in Lake Forest was his home.

39 Buckingham Chandler, "'33 Bellevue Place' — An Ideal Realized," *The Apartment House* 1 (Oct. 1911), pp. 14, 15; the publication includes plans and renderings.

40 Within a year all but one of its seven thirteen- to fourteen-room, four-bath apartments were reported rented for $5,400 per year on leases of five years or more; *Economist* (Mar. 31, 1917), p. 699.

41 One of his early larger buildings, from 1917, was 200 E. Pearson, six stories, ten apartments, one of the few in Chicago with a direct prototype, in this case the Palazzo Farnese in Rome; one of its residents was Ludwig Mies van der Rohe. For it, see Pardridge and Bradley (note 36), pp. 68-69, which includes a rendering and a plan.

42 See, for example, *Economist* (July 26, 1919), p. 213; (Aug. 23, 1919), p. 389; building permit published September 23, 1919, p. 545; (Jan. 22, 1921), p. 203; (Apr. 15, 1922), p. 860.

As if the Lights Were Always Shining: Graham, Anderson, Probst and White's Wrigley Building at the Boulevard Link

Sally Chappell

The design of the Wrigley Building by one of Chicago's most conservative firms reflects a number of traditional influences: a creative adaptation of ideas from the European classical tradition; the legacy of the Chicago commercial style of the 1880s; the heritage of the World's Columbian Exposition of 1893; new developments in the terracotta industry; the challenge of contemporary architecture in New York; and a predisposition toward civic-mindedness on the part of leaders of the Chicago business world. Last, but not least, of course, was the quality that breathed life into the confluence of these many elements, the spirit that transformed the Wrigley Building project from an additive mixture to a new synthesis: the inspired pen of a gifted architect.

Ask people on the streets of Chicago to name their favorite building, and the immediate response is likely to be "The Wrigley!" (figs. 1, 2). Everyone loves this sparkling tower on the river — office workers, construction workers, lawyers, and taxi drivers. Tourists gather in its flowery fountain courtyard to photograph each other, so that they can carry home a souvenir of the apex of Michigan Avenue.

Although the place where Michigan Avenue meets the Chicago River was a jumble of lofts and factories in 1920 (fig. 3), Chicagoans were quick to predict that the Wrigley Building and the just-completed bilevel bridge across the river would be the "new gateway of the Greater Chicago." Indeed, they boasted that the space would soon be "as famous as the Place de la Concorde in Paris" (fig. 5). While this prediction proved to be inflated, the subsequent erection of the London Guarantee and Accident Building (1923, now called the Stone Container Building) on the southwest corner; of the 333 North Michigan Building (1927-28) on the southeast corner (fig. 4); and of the Tribune Tower (1925) and the Equitable Building (1965) on the

Fig. 1 Graham, Anderson, Probst and White, Wrigley Building, 410 North Michigan Avenue, 1919-21 (before later addition).

Fig. 2 Left, Wrigley Building, with later addition, 1924, and right, Howells and Hood, Chicago Tribune tower, 435 North Michigan Avenue, 1925.

Fig. 3 Wrigley Building, with surrounding industrial buildings, 1921.

Fig. 4 Left, Holabird and Root, 333 North Michigan Avenue Building, 1928, and right, Alfred S. Alschuler, London Guarantee and Accident Building (now Stone Container Building), 360 North Michigan Avenue, 1923.

Fig. 5 "New Gateway of the Greater Chicago."

splayed site on the northeast corner transformed the intersection into a vantage point from which the present viewer is treated to a lively river panorama of Chicago's diversified architectural heritage.

It is a site also rich in other associations with Chicago history. It was at this spot that Jacques Marquette and Louis Jolliet made their first portage west of the Great Lakes, and it was here that La Salle planted the flag of France. Fort Dearborn stood on this site, and it was here that Ouilmette first invited Black Partridge, Chief of the Potawatomi, to a Christmas party. Cyrus Hall McCormick built a reaper plant on the east side of the river in 1847, and Jean Baptiste Point du Sable lived on the site of the Wrigley Building. Since the space is architecturally noteworthy and a repository of local history, landmark designation is currently being written for a Michigan Avenue Bridge Historic District, with its principal tall buildings.

While the skyscraper tower is common in Chicago now, the Wrigley Building was a startling novelty when erected in 1919-22, for the city was then a vast grid of office blocks. The daring height and slender form of the Wrigley were both a threat and a challenge to the traditional four-square character of the city.

To understand this, one must first look at the history of both urban planning and the tall office building. The Wrigley Building epitomizes a period

ONE HUNDRED THOUSAND DOLLARS GIVEN JOINTLY BY WILLIAM WRIGLEY JR AND FERGUSON FUND TRUSTEES TO EMBELLISH FOUR MICHIGAN AVE. BRIDGE HOUSES, MARKS FIRST STEP IN MAKING THIS GATEWAY AS FAMOUS AS THE PLACE DE LA CONCORDE IN PARIS.

of American architecture when a number of significant elements came together and were transformed by the imagination of the chief designer, Charles G. Beersman (1888-1946), into a unique synthesis.

The client, William Wrigley, Jr., was head of the Wrigley Company, successful manufacturer of chewing gum. Wishing to build a headquarters for the company worthy of its international standing,

Wrigley engaged the Chicago architectural firm of Graham, Anderson, Probst and White. Graham assigned the commission to Beersman, one of the firm's promising young designers.

Trained at the University of Pennsylvania by teachers who transmitted the traditions of the Ecole des Beaux-Arts, Beersman won the Le Brun fellowship for a year of travel in Europe. Around 1919 he joined Graham, Anderson, Probst and White. Ernest R. Graham, like his former chief, Daniel H. Burnham, admired the work of the "Beaux-Arts boys from the East,"[1] and the two had hired a string of them, beginning with Charles B. Atwood and Peirce Anderson. Under the circumstances, Graham's choice of Beersman was an especially good one, for the Wrigley site offered tremendous opportunities and challenges that only a talented designer could meet.

Solving the problem of the shape of the land, "cockeyed all the way around,"[2] was crucial (fig. 7). Michigan Avenue north of the river is slightly to the right of Michigan Avenue south of the river. The bridge, and the section of the street that connects the two parts of Michigan Avenue at the eastern border of the site, thus ran on a slight diagonal. East North Water Street on the north side was also on a diagonal, and so was the river bank on the south. Either one made a virtue of these limitations or one failed utterly, creating a dead spot in the center of Chicago. The whole architectural office was involved in talks lasting several weeks, and Beersman played with one idea after another. The project presented a special challenge because of the triangular nature of the plot, which made it unsuitable for the standard cubic office block in the firm's repertoire; indeed, nothing massive and unwieldy seemed right for that reflecting spot by the water. Beersman mulled over his past experience – his training, his travels, his knowledge of New York, and his familiarity with the building capacity of Chicago.

Finally, a spark of inspiration ignited his imagination, and the lofty, majestic structure we see today emerged on his drawing board (fig. 6). Although many architectural designs are the product of teamwork, Charles F. Murphy, a long-time member of the firm, emphasized that "the Wrigley was Charlie Beersman's."[3]

Of the four corners at the junction of the river and Michigan Avenue, the northwest corner chosen by William Wrigley, Jr., in 1918, was by far the best. Because of the shift in the street from the south, the Wrigley Building now seems to stand right in the middle of Michigan Avenue, its position giving it a commanding view in all directions (fig. 8). As one contemporary put it:

THE WRIGLEY BUILDING

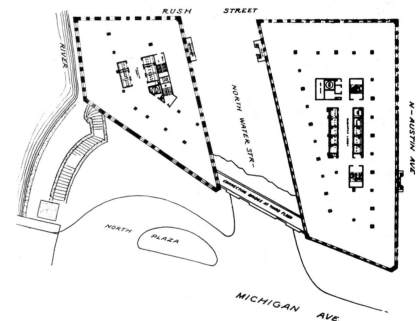

At a distance of about a mile one becomes suddenly conscious of the new presence ... one can see the tower in all the airy grace of its many pinnacles and turrets, much as one might glimpse the towers of some distant castle set on a rock long before he has seen its base. ... Perhaps the most impressive view of all is that obtained from the surface of the river, west of Rush Street, where the three stories which are below the street level are visible, and the whole vast pile seems enhanced in height by its quivering reflection in the river.[4]

A writer for the old *Chicago Post* wrote that from Roosevelt Road

[the tower is] like a phantom castle in a fairy tale. At Adams Street it becomes recognizable as the boulevard's climax. Beyond Madison it dominates the whole picture,

Fig. 6 Left to right, *Ernest R. Graham, Peirce Anderson, Edward Probst and Howard J. White, with model of the Wrigley Building, 1922.*

Fig. 7 Wrigley Building, site plan; from a promotional brochure distributed by the building's operating managers.

Fig. 8 View of Michigan Avenue Bridge and North Michigan Avenue, with Wrigley Building and Tribune tower.

stealing admiration from its companion wonder, the link bridge.[5]

From the newly developed vantage points to the north, wrote another contemporary, the building seems "a huge, sharp, dominating prow, for the Wrigley Building is only five feet wide at that point, it seems to cut the air and to be slowly bearing down on the spectator with an awful majesty quite overpowering."[6] The bend in the line of the street indeed gave unusual prominence to this "strategic, conspicuous location with no equal in the city," and the river doubled the impact by reflecting the image to the west and by providing a generous foreground to the southeast. But if the irregularly shaped lot posed a problem, the solution gave Beersman the polygonal ground plan that inspired the prow shape at the northeastern point. All of this would have been lost if he had tried to impose the standard Burnham office block here, one of those great cubes that had grown out of the Chicago street grid. Yet in many other respects the Wrigley Building is rooted in the Chicago commercial style that emerged after the Great Fire of 1871.

Structurally the building is like those older models — steel-framed on bedrock caissons with glass windows between the supporting piers. Horizontally it is articulated in the same tripartite manner — base, shaft, and capital. Were it not for the tower the building would take its place in the long line of Daniel Burnham's works — like a cross between the Rookery and the Reliance buildings.

The Reliance Building (1895; fig. 9) was itself a product of factors that emerged in the 1890s — the commercial style and the World's Columbian Exposition of 1893. It was at the first Chicago World's Fair that the French-inspired Beaux-Arts architecture caught the public imagination, as did the notion of the "White City." The buildings of the Fair dazzled all who came to see them, and became the embodiment of "America the Beautiful," the fulfillment of the dream of alabaster cities. Based on a mixture of hemp and plaster sprayed with whitewash, the whiteness of the Fair was ephemeral. Not until the terracotta industry manufactured large panels suitable for exterior cladding could the architect transform this vision into a lasting reality. Atwood, with his design for the Reliance Building, was the first to do so. The Wrigley was a direct descendant of the Reliance.

It was both the transparency and the whiteness of the Reliance Building that struck a new note. Looking at an early drawing of the Reliance, architectural historian William H. Jordy thought that Atwood "must have seen it as a shimmering, substanceless textile of light and slight shadow; a thing of space rather than stuff. How remote this gossamer conception is from the burly Chicago blocks of the preceding decade."[7] Although Beersman narrowed the expanses of glass seen in the Reliance in favor of more classical solidity, he continued the use of the color white to give an airy, light quality. In this he followed the example of many architects of the period. The special refinement in the Wrigley Building was the unusually lively quality of the play of light. Here Beersman's Beaux-Arts training in watercolors and the painterly arts helped him create a subtle movement. Six different shades of a special enamel finish were baked on the terracotta, varying from gray to pale cream and getting progressively lighter toward the top. The result is "as if the sun were always shining on its upper reaches,"[8] as one contemporary put it. The effect prompted another writer of the period to exclaim that the Wrigley seems to soar "from mists and fog to clear skies."[9]

The Wrigley Building not only incorporates painterly effects, but other Beaux-Arts characteristics as well. As the French phrase it, a building must be *bien disposé*. To be "well disposed" a building must take every advantage of its site, among other requirements. The Wrigley Building meets the rest of the city with urbanistic grace at every level. A plaza is set aside on Michigan Avenue and a courtyard offers a parklike respite between the north and the south sections. The plaza is linked to the river below by a curving staircase leading to a stepped terrace provided by the city.

William Wrigley, Jr., who served on the Chicago Plan Commission, was interested in the development of the city. When the new north section of the building was being designed, Wrigley agreed to have it set back from the lot line so that the east front of that section would be on a continuous line with the south section. Later, he and the trustees of the Ferguson Fund together donated $100,000 for relief sculptures to adorn the four pylons on the Michigan Avenue Bridge that had been designed by Edward H. Bennett and that opened in May 1920 (see Draper, fig. 6; cat. no. 237).[10]

Without the civic connections of his client, Charles Beersman would not have had the opportunity to design the felicitous connections between the two sections of the building and the way the building meets the river and the street. This spirit of civic obligation was strongly felt by the Chicago entrepreneurs who were commissioning the important urban buildings of the period. But the Wrigley Building is also an example of the cooperation between the private and the public sectors. The river embankment, staircase, and plaza, as well as the wide sidewalk areas, legally still belong to the city of Chicago, as does the plaza over East North Water Street. The city of Chicago agreed to repair any broken pavement; the Wrigley Company agreed to keep the area free of debris and snow and to maintain the plantings. Over the years the city made various agreements permitting the erection of bridges connecting the two sections at the third floor (1924) and the fourteenth floor (1931). To this day the Wrigley Company pays the Municipal Department of Revenue an annual fee for right-of-way permits.[11]

Another of Beersman's precepts, learned from teachers who had been trained at the Ecole des Beaux-Arts, was that a building must be *bien distribué*. The rooms must be proportioned and arranged in a manner that is logical for their use. While the offices in the upper stories of the Wrigley Building are usually ample, with their regularity reflected in the businesslike grid of the windows on the exterior, the lobby would have seemed rather

Fig. 9 D. H. Burnham and Co., Reliance Building, 32 North State Street, 1895.

meager to Beersman's Parisian predecessors, considering that the client wanted this to be the most spectacular building in the city. After the lowering of the ceiling in a subsequent remodeling, the feeling of the lobby is even more cramped compared to other public spaces created by the firm in this period. In general, the subdivisions of the middle portion, or shaft, are the standard office warrens of any contemporary building, except for the corner spaces with their polygonal aspect and the tower rooms with their airy openness on all four sides.

The building would earn good marks from a traditional jury for being well composed. The interior arrangement is expressed on the exterior, and in the words of a contemporary critic:

[The tower] is adroitly designed to spring, not from the expanse of flat roof, which would have been bald and abrupt, but from a cluster of lesser roofs, parapets, spires and pinnacles. This softens the effect and makes a more

Fig. 10 Andrew Noble Prentice, Sketch of the Giralda Tower, Seville, 1889.

Fig. 11 McKim, Mead, and White, Madison Square Garden, Madison Avenue between 26th and 27th streets, New York, 1887-90 (demolished); tower.

harmonious sky line than if it leaped into space stark and sheer from the main roof.[12]

The observation room in the tower of the Wrigley Building was at that moment the highest point in the city. The upper part of the tower, the little circular temple together with its cupola, rising to 398 feet, had to be purely ornamental and unoccupied, however, because the building height limit in Chicago from 1920 to 1923 was 260 feet.

In designing the Wrigley Building, Beersman found inspiration in two separate sources. For the shape he turned to the Giralda Tower in Seville (originally a Moorish structure started by Aben Yuqub Yusuf, but rebuilt as part of a church after an earthquake in 1568, when Renaissance forms were added to the top). For the ornament he

turned to the style commonly called Francis I, after the French king whose influence made it popular throughout Europe. The Spanish reference seemed suitable because the use of glazed tile had a long pedigree there, going back to the Moorish occupation, and the Wrigley Building also was to be covered in glazed tile. And indeed, as Beersman must have hoped, the Wrigley tower has become for Chicago what the Giralda is for Seville (fig. 10). The following passage from a contemporary guidebook could easily be substituted for a description of the Wrigley Building in Chicago:

The Giralda has a pervasive presence throughout the city, and keeps appearing, in whole or in part, from the most unexpected corners of the town. If you look out from the top of the Giralda you see . . . a wide and beautiful view of the city and the peaceful river flowing to the port which gives Seville its outlet to the sea.[13]

Beersman changed the silhouette of the tower and altered its massing, however, perhaps because he found the Giralda's first setback, where the Renaissance forms are placed over the medieval remains, too severe. Comparing the two towers, the Giralda seems sober and weighty compared to the light, confectioners' quality of the Wrigley.

Another influence was certainly contemporary architecture in New York. Graham, Beersman, and Wrigley were keenly aware of the changes in the Manhattan skyline. Skyscraper towers had appeared in the lower Broadway area before the 1893 Fair gave Chicagoans a taste for flat roofs and uniform cornice lines. The Tribune Building (1873-75), designed by Richard Morris Hunt, was among the first of these tall New York icons of big city life and was eventually followed by a succession of what Winston Weisman calls "mounted towers," such as McKim, Mead and White's Madison Square Garden of 1887-90 (fig. 11), Ernest Flagg's Singer Building of 1908, and the Woolworth Building, designed by Cass Gilbert in 1911-13 (fig. 12).[14]

Chicago boasted some early examples of "mounted towers." In the days before the World's Fair of 1893, Louis Sullivan had given Chicago two, the Auditorium Building and the Schiller Theater, and there were others in the Central Manufacturing District, atop railroad stations as well as other buildings. The taste for Beaux-Arts classicism that came with the Fair, however, dominated the vision of everyone involved with it and influenced the work of nearly every Chicago architect for the next twenty-five years. Chicago buildings were sedate, monumentally enduring, and classical in their repose compared to New York's restlessly vertical skyscrapers.

Some Chicagoans must have felt that the Woolworth Building with its blocky base and slender tower demonstrated a successful neo-Gothic combination of the office building and the tower, but to Graham and to Anderson, who was still the firm's chief designer, the neo-Gothic was not acceptable. It was perhaps only when William Mitchell Kendall of McKim, Mead and White designed New York's Municipal Building in 1913, with its combination of a tower and the classical style, that the men in Graham's office accepted the possibility of having the best of both worlds – dignity and great height, a synthesis of aspiring monumentality. Their young colleague, Beersman, would give this combination concrete expression in Chicago.

The decoration of the building reflected more traditional French architectural thought, which held that a building should pay homage to the past by displaying historic ornament. However, this ornament had to be appropriately designed; it could not be merely copied. Beersman adapted the sixteenth-century use of urns and floral ornament in low relief favored by Francis I to adorn the roofline and frame the windows and arched doorways of the Wrigley Building. In general, the festive air of the building embodied the optimism of the era and the hope that World War I had indeed marked a final farewell to arms. In giving form to these aspects of the spirit of his time and place, Beersman was also following the precepts of the European classical tradition.

Before leaving the subject of the design, a word should be said about how the designer gave unity to the two separate parts of the structure, for the site for the northern section was not acquired until after the completion of the southern section. The new part was cast in a similar style, clad in the same glazed terracotta and united to the older building by a decorative three-story screen at the upper Michigan Avenue level. In addition, by taking advantage of the bilevel street system created by the concurrent construction of the bilevel bridge, the architects designed a plaza on the level above East North Water Street, although this was not developed into its present form until 1957. The basket arches of the glassed-in screen at its entrance, however, were in the 1924 design. The resulting shelter provides a welcome respite from Chicago's weather, a function not fulfilled by any other plaza in the Windy City.

In the words of contemporary Joseph I. Karl, the 1924 structure completed the plans of William Wrigley, Jr.,

[for] impressive and artistic embellishment of its commanding property overlooking the north plaza of the Michigan Avenue bridge . . . making Chicago his civic debtor. . . . The two diverse plots used, though separated by the width of a street, have, by the wonderful way they

have been handled, been united in one improvement of marvelous balance and unity.[15]

Karl also noted that the new north section of the building, even if it stood alone, would in itself be "a remarkable building project." Following the original in its delicate setback above the cornice at the top of the block section, the annex, too, has a tower, but one that is deliberately modest, respecting the older building's dominance. The two stand side by side as fraternal, not identical, twins. The taller, southern building with its tower seems stately; the shorter, northern building seems monumental. In their mutually complementary juxtaposition, each is self-sufficient, but subservient to the life of the whole. This seeming subservience of the "annex" is all the more noteworthy when one learns that it has nearly double the site area of the original – 21,000 square feet compared to 11,000. Like the earlier building, the north unit rises sixteen stories to a height of 210 feet from plaza to crowning parapet; then comes the square tower or apex rising to a height of 300 feet, compared to the nearly 400 feet of the south unit.

Fig. 12 Cass Gilbert, Woolworth Building, 223 Broadway, New York, 1911-13.

The main entrances in the buildings are similar. Both doorways rise to the third-story stringcourse line, leading to tall marble-floored entrances, which, in turn, lead to the elevator lobbies. In the south section there are six passenger elevators, and in the north section there are nine. Two enclosed stairways, adjoining the elevator space, provide service between floors. All utility stacks and pipes are at the center of each of the buildings. The corridors, extending east and west from the elevators at each floor, are lined with marble, and mahogany doors and trim are used throughout. From the first, three floors were rented to merchants, a bank, and a restaurant, a tradition that continues to this day.

Other outstanding features at the time included an observation room with telescopes for viewing the surrounding city. The observatory was exciting to contemporaries for its "bird's-eye view" of Lake Michigan and its "airplane view" of the surrounding landscape stretching for miles. A guide, "prepared to answer all questions," was on hand. Still there is the original tower clock, with faces on all four sides (fig. 14). Each dial is twenty feet in diameter; the redwood hour hands are seven-and-one-half feet long, and the minute hands are eleven-and-one-half feet long. The movements are reliable, precise enough to run the city by, and regulated by automatic electric controls.

The cladding of the Wrigley Building reflected the general practice of the firm in this period. On the lower two floors, near the river and adjoining the lower level streets, the blocks are limestone, scored and provided with a border and with recessed joints. This use of rustication is an echo of the age-old masonry tradition, in which the heaviest and thickest part of a building was at the bottom, where the wall had to bear the most weight. In the Wrigley Building, however, this masonry style is also related to the workaday part of the building, to the sections along the waterfront where bulk materials are delivered, and to the alleys where goods are dispatched. Above, beyond the sidewalks at the upper level of Michigan Avenue, as the cladding changes to terracotta, the whole mood of the architecture changes to a lighter, more festive spirit. When the piers reach the height of the cornice they are adorned with eagles in flight and vine-covered vases against the skyline. In the many transitions that follow as the building narrows and soars to its final pinnacle, the architects provided terracotta wreaths of flowers, arcading, dentils, and other classical moldings, and above the clock tower an open circular temple topped by a finial. If one searches for precedents for this freely decorated building, erected in an eclectic period in the history of architecture, one has to mention not only the Giralda Tower but also the Monument of Lysicrates (334 B.C.) in Athens (fig. 13).

Over the years the terracotta cladding of the Wrigley Building has continued to embellish the center of Chicago with its shimmering light. While the beauty of the material has fulfilled its earlier promise, the durability, unfortunately, has not. The surface has had to be washed at great expense every year and early on developed fine cracks "like old porcelain."[16] By 1974 the problems that terracotta-clad buildings faced had become more serious. In October of that year, a chunk falling from the cornice of a building at 22 West Madison Street killed a passerby. The city immediately put six teams of specially trained building inspectors to work. They came up with a list of 2,600 Chicago buildings faced with terracotta, of which 1,100 had observable faults.

It was soon ascertained that the chief enemy of terracotta is water. When rain gets in through the mortar joints and seeps down to the shelf-iron (a five-inch-wide angle-iron supporting the tiles at each floor), rust builds up, decreases the normal expansion space, and puts pressure on the terracotta, causing it to crack. In cold weather freezing water causes more pressure. By 1979 the crew at the Wrigley Building had replaced 10,000 of the total 200,000 tiles on the buildings. They took out each piece above and below the old shelf-iron and cleaned it of rust, then treated it with a metal preservative or replaced it and installed new terracotta around it.

It was a costly, meticulous operation. As decorative pieces were removed, often in fragments, each piece was marked, glued back together, and sent off to Gladding McBean, a tile company in Lincoln, California, at the time the only major manufacturer of terracotta left in the United States. At this stage of the restoration, efforts were made to match the different shades of white by making six different glaze formulas. By the time the replacements came back, the crew had to hunt again for exactly the place each piece belonged.

The new locations were covered with mortar, and the holes in the top of each tile were aligned with stainless steel rods (which replaced the old iron rods), then anchored to the building's structural steel. The rods were hooked to hold the tile in place, and then the terracotta piece was fitted into the fresh mortar.[17]

In subsequent years the decision was made to replace the china-like pieces with plastic replicas. The first phase of this major alteration began in April 1984 with the replacement of 350 weather-worn finials. The originals ranged from thirty inches to ten feet in height, and from 150 to 2,500 pounds in weight (cat. no. 253). In all there were eighteen different types and sizes, some very ornate. The plastic replacements, molded from forms cast around the originals, weigh about as much as the terracotta and are impervious to weather.[18] Today the lions' heads, scrollwork, and flowery fiberglass urns seem at home on the Wrigley Building, except that their color scheme was not graded to the original subtle spectrum that evolved through six different shades from gray to titanium white as it went up the building. The new plastic has a uniform cream color at all levels.

Interestingly enough, the image of the building was rarely used to advertise Wrigley products. Occasionally a drawing of the tower appeared in the *Chicago Tribune,* but it was there to tout the restaurant or the observation tower. There seems to have been a deliberate effort to separate the corporate offices from the basis of the Wrigley Company's business – the manufacture of chewing gum. In a similar way, the image of the Woolworth Building in New York was separated from the source of the family's fortune. The modern schism between the end and the means is evident in both buildings, and it is tempting to think that the lower the product is on the socially acceptable scale the higher the client wished to go on the architecturally acceptable scale, and the more he wished to separate the imagery of the two.

It could be argued, however, that Wrigley was emboldened by the commercial success of his electric sign in teeming Times Square in New York City. The largest of its kind, the sign was 250 feet long, 70 feet high, made up of 17,286 bulbs depicting a pair of peacocks, splashing fountains, and turning spearmen (fig. 15). If William Wrigley, Jr., wanted no such obvious commercial devices for the Wrigley Building in Chicago, the structure could, in a more abstract sense, be an advertisement for Wrigley – not for the chewing gum, but for the company. Perhaps Wrigley also hoped to gain dignity for Spearmint, Doublemint, and Juicy Fruit gum by associating them in the public mind with the clean, white, airy building in Chicago. The advertisements of the period were replete with pictures of healthy families and children with sparkling teeth. As David Van Zanten has pointed out, the 1920s was a period when the movies and glossy illustrated magazines created a visually overheated world in order to sell products and, inevitably, architecture was bent to this commercial purpose.[19]

Whatever his motives, Wrigley spared no expense in the erection of his building on Michigan Avenue. For comparison, the Federal Reserve Bank of Kansas City, a bank office building the

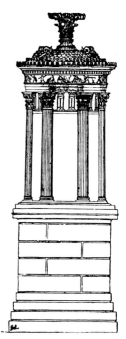

Fig. 13 Monument of Lysicrates, Athens, 334 B. C.; from James Fergusson, A History of Architecture in All Countries *(New York, 1907).*

Fig. 14 Wrigley Building, clock tower.

firm built in the same period, cost $0.867 per cubic foot, while the Wrigley Building cost $1.228 per cubic foot for the south section, $0.835 for the north, or an average of $0.978 per cubic foot for both. Another office building across the river from the Wrigley Building, the Builders Building, constructed in 1927, also by Graham, Anderson, Probst and White, came in at $0.622 per cubic foot. When one also considers the amount of potential rentable office space Wrigley sacrificed in setting the building back from the lot line and not building to the height limit, the combination of corporate image-making and civic-mindedness seems even stronger.[20]

Emphasis on advertising was one of William Wrigley, Jr.,'s three key policies. After keeping cash reserves at a high level and maintaining the good will of wholesalers and jobbers, he believed in advertising. "The Wrigley Review" in 1927 was one of the first coast-to-coast radio programs, and Wrigley was the first sponsor of the famous "Guy Lombardo and His Royal Canadians" show. The company always had an extensive advertising schedule to keep up with the demands of its founder. But the Wrigley Building was not only a highly visible "ad" for the company. As his son Philip K. Wrigley explained in an interview:

I think I explained to you about his boyhood ambition of building a house on a hill. It was pretty much the same thing in Chicago. He just wanted to have something that he had created. He was creative by nature and it was his and it was different, and it was in a prominent location. . . . Dad had always had pictures of things on his letterhead, going back to when telephones were very rare. They finally got a telephone in the office, and the letterhead at that time had a picture of a telephone on it which boasted, we have a telephone – this is the number. . . . As I say, we have a lot of tenants that have offices in the Wrigley Building that use a picture of the building on their letterhead as "this is our Chicago office." . . . It is a landmark. Something that is interesting is the BOAC using a picture of Big Ben in London and the Wrigley Building Clock. There are two pictures and they are reversed. It is a full page ad in magazines which says "BOAC From Chicago to London," and vice versa from London to Chicago, and it used the towers and the clocks as the symbols [of the two cities].[21]

While the Wrigley has continued to appear as a symbol for Chicago to the present day, there was a time in the 1950s and 1960s when the building's reputation, like that of many other great works of the 1920s, suffered from modernist architectural criticism. It was either not included or given only slight notice in the architectural books of that period. One writer quipped that it was a building that refused "to go to school — in this case, the Chicago school of architecture," but asserted its uniqueness and charm in spite of that.[22] As late as 1980 a local guidebook declared that "the building achieved fame through traits other than architectural merit."[23]

No analysis of the Wrigley Building is complete without comparing it to the modern architecture emerging in Europe at the same time. Next to the asymmetrical, flat-roofed, unornamented buildings taking shape during the post-World War I era in Europe, when Continental architects expressed something of the utopian vision shared by those who hoped that art and technology could bring a better way of life for all classes, the Wrigley Building is traditionally axial, flagrantly ornamented, and given over to consumerist theatricality, not one bit a part of any new social order or new social vision.

The building is not without its faults. Some of the cornice-line ornament is oversimplified and the lobby space is underscaled. There are no other major interior spaces for public use, and the river-edge development is minimal. In a balanced judgment, however, these shortcomings are outweighed by the stunning relationship of the building to its site, its grand proportions, the sensitive treatment of its cladding, and the amenities of its interior offices. If the building's reputation was eclipsed briefly in the heyday of modernism, and if some compromises had to be made over the terracotta cladding, the Wrigley Building's final claim to fame — its dramatic, gleaming nighttime illumination — had improved gloriously over the years (fig. 1).

The 1922 rental brochure described the "revolving light at the tower's tip serving as a beacon to the mariners on the lake as well as the navigators of the air," noting that "the building is lighted from hundreds of flood lights on adjacent buildings, as well as its own roof, so that at night, too, it stands forth in an ethereal beauty."[24] Contemporary reporters noted that the lantern carrying the revolving light was visible for twenty miles out on Lake Michigan and from all quarters of the city.[25] And a critic writing for *Architecture and Building* in 1921 accounted for this striking effect by explaining to his readers that

the light is projected by powerful X-ray reflectors, using 500-watt lamps mounted on the roof of the Kirk Building on Michigan Avenue. . . . increasing in intensity with the height until the tower stands out "one blaze of glory". . . . The turrets and other ornamentation on the top of the tower are brought out in relief by smaller X-ray reflectors which use 250-watt lamps. The installation of the exterior lighting equipment . . . consists of 123 reflector units, each using 500-watt lamps and 37 reflector units with 250-watt lamps. Total current consumption is 70,750 watts. This installation is said by lighting men to be one of the finest of its kind ever attempted.[26]

Fig. 15 Electric sign advertising Wrigley's Spearmint Gum, Times Square, New York.

Certainly it was a great popular success: among the first, if not *the* first of its kind, and hence very influential in the succession of lighted buildings in the 1920s.

When the old warehouse supporting the front floodlights was demolished in 1970, a new battery of lamps was mounted on the East Wacker Drive side, twice as powerful as the old incandescent lights. The whole structure is now lit by 118 1,000-watt metal halide bulbs mounted on Wacker Drive, and the effect of ascending brightness is achieved by placing four more banks of lights near the top. Three of these have 16 500-watt quartz lights, one at the seventeenth floor, one at the nineteenth floor, one at the peak. The fourth, to illuminate the west side, is placed on top of the swimming pool at the River Plaza Building. This bank contains 16 1,000-watt quartz lights because of its greater distance.[27] Except during World War II and for a brief period during the energy crisis of the early 1970s, the Wrigley has continued to brighten the night skyline of Chicago.

Light is a powerful vehicle of expression. When electricity was first used as an architectural medium at the World's Columbian Exposition of 1893, it dazzled everyone who saw it. The arc lights, incandescent lights, and colored flood lights turned the daytime wonder of the Fair into a nighttime magic that no one who saw it ever forgot. William Wrigley, Jr., and Ernest R. Graham were there as young men, and carried the impression with them to their maturity when the chance to do the same for a permanent structure in Chicago presented itself in the Wrigley Building.

Giving the inert mass of architecture vitality against the oblivion of the night, the lighted Wrigley Building carried a message of postwar optimism to Chicagoans of the 1920s as they walked across the Michigan Avenue Bridge. Sixty years later, Chicagoans may regard the nightly vision of the Wrigley somewhat differently. Since the dawning of the atomic age, its continually reappearing splendor has carried a message of hope for life, for city lights ever after.

NOTES

Research for this paper was made possible by grants from the Graham Foundation for Advanced Studies in the Fine Arts, DePaul University, and through the courtesy of William Surman, President, Graham, Anderson, Probst and White. The author wishes to thank Robert Bruegmann for making helpful critical suggestions.

1 Interview with Charles F. Murphy, June 22, 1981.
2 F. K. Plous, Jr., "The Dowager of Michigan Avenue," *Chicago Sun-Times* (July 23, 1972).
3 Interview (note 1).
4 "New Wrigley Building, Chicago's Tallest Structure," *Fort Dearborn Magazine* (Mar. 1921), n. pag.
5 Quoted in Plous (note 2).
6 "Wrigley Building, Chicago, Ill.," *Architecture and Building* 53 (Dec. 1921), p. 95.
7 William H. Jordy, *American Buildings and Their Architects*, vol. 3, *Progressive and Academic Ideals at the Turn of the Twentieth Century* (New York, 1972), p. 60.
8 "New Wrigley Building" (note 4).
9 "Wrigley Building" (note 6), p. 95.
10 The reliefs were added to the pylons in 1928 by sculptors James Earle Fraser and Henry Hering. The Ferguson Fund was established in 1905 from the bequest of Benjamin Franklin Ferguson, a respected and successful Chicago businessman. The Art Institute of Chicago has the

responsibility of administering the Fund, which is to be used for "the erection and maintenance of enduring statuary and monuments, in the whole or in part of stone, granite, or bronze, in the parks, along the boulevards or in other public places, within the city of Chicago, Illinois, commemorating worthy men or women of American history." Quoted in an article by William M. R. French, the first director of the Art Institute, in *Bulletin of the American Association of Museums* 8 (1914), p. 128.
11 Linda Hanrath, Corporate Librarian, William Wrigley, Jr., Company, letter to the author, Sept. 19, 1986.
12 "Wrigley Building" (note 6), p. 95.
13 *All Sevilla* (Barcelona, 1981), pp. 6-7.
14 Winston Weisman, "A New View of Skyscraper History," in *The Rise of an American Architecture*, ed. Edgar Kaufmann, Jr. (New York, 1970).
15 Joseph I. Karl, "Wrigley Buildings Attract Anew," *Real Estate News* 19, 1 (Jan. 1924), p. 1.
16 "The Wrigley Building," *Chicago Tribune* (Sept. 15, 1968).
17 "Facelift: Sprucing up the Wrigley Building," *All Around Wrigley* (Summer 1979), p. 11.
18 Bob Olmstead, "Plastic s-tile Wrigley," *Chicago Sun-Times* (April 25, 1984).
19 David Van Zanten, "Twenties Gothic," *New Mexico Studies in Architecture* (1982), pp. 19-23.
20 In the end, Wrigley sacrificed considerable rental

space for a combination of aesthetic, civic, and advertising reasons. Although built after a 1924 ordinance allowing greater height and volume had taken effect, the north building was constructed to conform to the lower cornice line of the south building. Four potential floors were lost. At 16,000 square feet per floor, this space would be worth about $1,600,000 in annual rental fees in 1986 dollars.
21 Paul McClelland Angle, interview with Philip K. Wrigley, 1966, transcript in the Chicago Historical Society.
22 Plous (note 2).
23 Ira J. Bach, *Chicago's Famous Buildings*, 3rd. ed. (Chicago, 1980), p. 53.
24 The 1922 rental brochure is located in the Wrigley Archives.
25 "New Wrigley Building" (note 4).
26 "The Wrigley Building at Night," *Architecture and Building* 53 (Dec. 1921), p. 95.
27 Robert Bruegmann, "Relighting the Skyline," *Inland Architect* 26 (1982), p. 54.

When Worlds Collided: European and American Entries to the Chicago Tribune Competition of 1922

Robert Bruegmann

After more than sixty years, Plate 196 in the book of entries to the Chicago Tribune competition remains as enigmatic as ever.[1] Above a stepped base, a gigantic Doric column soars into the sky against a backdrop of dramatically raking clouds (fig. 1). Although it is beautifully drawn and rendered in a way that makes it look almost plausible, it is still hard to believe that Viennese architect Adolf Loos was serious. Did he really believe that conservative Chicago businessmen would relish the idea of looking out over the sober buildings of their city through the fluting of a polished black granite Doric column more than 400 feet high?

There is not a trace of irony in Loos's own description, however.[2] He stated that he wanted to create an image so striking that it would come to represent Chicago the way cathedrals and major public monuments did European cities. Chicago building laws ruled out the creation of the world's highest building. He might have created a starkly contemporary building resembling those being designed by some of his avant-garde colleagues in Germany, but he rejected this idea, stating that such novelties quickly became unfashionable. So he resorted to a form that he said was both inherently beautiful and had venerable historic and architectural associations.[3] Besides, Loos argued, the use of such historic forms as building terminations was not uncommon in America. The top of the most famous American commercial building of its era, the Woolworth Building in New York, for example, was modeled after the sixteenth-century Butter Tower of Rouen Cathedral.[4] It is also known that Loos even tried to work out, although none too successfully, some of the practical problems inherent in a skyscraper with circular office floor plans.[5]

His avant-garde colleagues in Europe were surely startled.[6] Since the turn of the century they had

Fig. 1 Adolf Loos, Perspective rendering of entry for Chicago Tribune competition; from The International Competition for a New Administration Building for the Chicago Tribune *(Chicago, 1923), plate 196.*

Fig. 2 Saverio Dioguardi, Perspective rendering of entry for Chicago Tribune competition; from International Competition, *plate 248.*

been united in an attempt to create a new architecture no longer dependent on what they considered an outworn academic tradition. Many of his contemporaries were especially scornful of the literal use of classical forms and ornamentation. Loos himself had already created some of the most abstract and unornamented buildings of the century. How could he, of all people, select such a literal classical element for the basis of his design? And then blow it up to such a grand scale and put it on a classical base with an entrance surmounted by what unmistakably resembled figurative allegorical sculpture? This was too much. Were he serious, it would have put Loos's entry in a category with some of the most *retardataire* entries in the competition, for example, the scheme by the Italian Saverio Dioguardi (fig. 2), in which a Roman triumphal arch was enlarged to the scale of a skyscraper.[7]

The objection to the scheme on urbanistic grounds was more fundamental. Loos's entry seemed to signal an acceptance of the existing American city and a desire to create for it new monuments using old forms on a wholly new scale. The European avant-garde might have conceded that New York and Chicago were exciting but they also viewed these cities as nightmares of chaotic growth and uncontrolled private exploitation of the land, often in blatant disregard of the common good.[8] How could a European like Loos, especially one from Vienna where the monuments of church and state still dominated the cityscape, succumb to the kind of blatant commercialism that made it possible for Frank Woolworth, head of a nickel and dime empire, to build a headquarters that completely overshadowed the nearby New York City Hall? How, moreover, could a reader of the venerable newspapers of Europe take seriously a frontier enterprise like the Chicago Tribune, which laid claim to being the world's finest newspaper? Or, finally, how could anyone accept the notion that the mere expenditure of vast sums of money was all that was necessary to produce the "most beautiful and distinctive office building in the world" that was called for in the competition?

Even Loos's biographers have been unable to make up their minds on this project. Some of them have taken it as a serious proposal and have advanced exceedingly ingenious and improbable rationalizations on its behalf. For the most part, however, even Loos's most ardent admirers have found it impossible to accept the project as a serious design effort. Surely, they suggest, it was intended as a satiric commentary on America, its capitalistic values, and the swaggering language of the newspaper. Or perhaps it was an elaborate joke of the kind practiced by the Dadaist circle in Paris that Loos was just entering.[9]

The confusion surrounding the Loos entry is symptomatic of the entire Tribune competition enterprise. On the surface, everything was clear. The program was admirably concise. Architects of all nations were invited to compete for $100,000 in prize money. In addition a group of well-known American architects was invited to compete, and each would be paid $2,000 for participating. Each of the competitors was asked to submit the same materials: six drawings, including a ground-floor and typical floor plan, two elevations, a section, and a perspective from the southwest. The jury, to be composed of four officers of the Tribune company and Chicago architect Alfred Granger, was to select the best scheme. The site (fig. 3), a plot with 100 feet of frontage along newly created Michigan Avenue, was carefully described, as were the client's program requirements and the restrictions imposed by the Chicago building laws.[10]

The Tribune insisted that, above all, the competition must be international. It would rise above national divisions and prejudices to demonstrate the universal validity of architecture in the modern city. With few practical restrictions imposed on them, the architects would be free to concentrate on aesthetic concerns. Architects of all nations, it implied, would be on an equal footing and would be judged by the same standards. Finally, the Tribune would publish the results for all to see, allowing readers the world over to make up their own minds.

In fact, what the Loos entry seems to suggest is that the architectural languages used by designers in various parts of the world were as diverse and fundamentally different one from another as their spoken languages. The result was to make the Tribune competition not so much an international display of talent and skill but an exercise in mutual incomprehension. This was most marked in the entries from parts of the world where the problem of the skyscraper was most actively debated: in the United States, especially Chicago and New York, on the one hand, and in northern Europe, especially Berlin and Amsterdam, on the other hand.

From the viewpoint of the competition jury and most American writers, the American entries were greatly in advance of all others, with the possible exception of the entry by Finnish architect Eliel Saarinen.[11] From the point of view of writers in the German architecture journals, all the winning entries and the vast majority of those from the United States were *retardataire*, derivative, and socially irresponsible, and only a few European proposals were worthy of serious consideration.[12]

It is not the purpose of this essay to restate the arguments of each side. Instead it focuses on one of the most fundamental differences between the Americans and their European colleagues: their ideas on the relationship of architecture to business and society in the context of the modern city.

1. *The Americans*

For many American competitors, the tall office building was a building type with which they were familiar. They understood the economic conditions that demanded from tall office buildings the maximum amount of rentable space. They also understood the countervailing force of public opinion that was wary of the new scale, the loss of light and air to the street, and possible fire and safety hazards posed by the huge new buildings. Starting as early as the 1880s, these concerns had led many municipalities to pass increasingly restrictive development legislation.[13] These laws governed the use as well as the height and bulk of buildings throughout the city. A comprehensive package with restrictions of both kinds was called zoning. The first and most famous of these had appeared in New York in 1916. In 1922 Chicago did not yet have a zoning ordinance, but fairly stringent height restrictions had been incorporated in the city's

building laws since the 1880s.[14] The wording of these laws and the way in which they were spelled out in the Tribune's program was very matter-of-fact. The occupied portion of the Tribune's building, for example, could only rise 260 feet above the street level; unoccupied parapet walls, dormers, cupolas, and towers could rise above this up to an ultimate height of 400 feet on the condition that they had a floor area considerably smaller than that of the main block.[15]

As in other cities around the country, Chicago's building laws were enacted primarily for practical reasons, to guarantee light and air to the street and to ensure that the fire department could effectively combat fires. But any American architect who read the debates on these laws in the professional journals would have realized that they also embodied definite aesthetic intentions. The provisions for non-occupied elements above the main cornice were clearly intended to encourage diversity of massing and ornamentation in commercial buildings. The setback provisions that would be contained in the 1923 zoning law were also, in part, motivated by a desire to reduce the monotony caused by the earlier height limits that produced streetscapes with endless rows of buildings rising sheer from the sidewalk to an idential cornice height. The model for both kinds of provision came

Fig. 3 View of the site chosen for the Chicago Tribune building, 1922; photograph was supplied to each entrant.

from European cities, especially Paris, in which height regulations and setback provisions had long been common.[16] What made the American situation so different was that the scale had been vastly enlarged.

Most of the American entries accepted the approach implied by these laws and by the Tribune's program materials. The result was a series of projects with a lower block sixteen to twenty stories high filling the permitted occupiable building envelope. In most cases, a three- or four-story base was created at street level to accentuate the entranceway and public spaces. Above this the next twelve to sixteen floors hardly varied from one project to the next, whether the nominal style was Gothic, classical, or exotic, since the Tribune's program, calling for large, well-lit floors, practically dictated plans that filled the entire envelope and relatively thin walls filled with large windows. The variety came mostly above the cornice line of the main block, where the architects placed their towers, domes, and other decorative features. The great challenge was to make a graceful transition between the bulky lower sections and the much

slimmer upper features. In most cases the solution was to place at the corner of the lower block finials, turrets, pyramids, or statues, all of which were decorative and were thus allowed to extend beyond the established building envelope rather than cutting into rentable space. These decorative elements helped to continue the momentum of the rising vertical lines from the lower to the upper portions of the building. In some cases the architects went further and sacrificed a little of the full permitted volume of the main block so as to set back the building several times, creating a telescoping effect that made the transition between base and top less abrupt.

Because the top of the building was not bound by functional requirements and would be visible from great distances, it was the part that would most clearly characterize the building and its occupant to the general population. For this reason it was the place where architects lavished the greatest amount of attention and ornament. This priority is clear even in the arrangement of the entries in the Tribune's publication of the project. Preceding publication, they had apparently been arranged first by country, then in alphabetical order according to the last name of the architect within each country. Indeed, vestiges of this original organizational system remain. This order was clearly modified, however, so that projects that contained similar terminal features could be grouped together, presumably to allow readers the most relevant comparisons. Thus, on successive pages, one finds polygonal Gothic openwork crowns, circular Roman temples, oriental or Islamic domes, obelisks, columns, illuminated spheres, and so on.

The vast majority of the American entries implied an acceptance not only of the office building program, but also of the general configuration of the American city's business districts. This led to structures with blocky massing filling the envelope below, and a display of architectural pyrotechnics above. Given this perspective, it is easy to understand why the scheme by Raymond Hood and John Mead Howells triumphed.[17] It fulfilled admirably all these expectations. It offered a good office building plan with a large rectangle of open space surrounding the elevator and utility core, and with a nearly uniform window spacing. The transition to the tower was made by the spectacular device of flying buttresses that carried upward the structural lines of the lower mass and visually linked it to the ornamental tower. The architects wrote that this top could be floodlit at night to create an even more dramatic effect. It was a skillful solution to a perplexing problem. The style was Gothic, justified by the architects on the grounds that it allowed a good

expression of the vertical steel structural columns (fig. 5; pls. 94, 96; cat. no. 270).

Although the architects did not mention it, it was also, as noted earlier, the style of the Woolworth Building in New York (designed by Cass Gilbert, 1911-13), the country's tallest and most prestigious office building at that time. The entry also bore some resemblance to a 1918 scheme commissioned from several prominent Chicago architects for the development of North Michigan Avenue.[18] But it was clear from Hood and Howells's description that the choice of style was not a major issue. The flying buttresses used to create the transition between the blocks suggested the literal use of Gothic precedents. But a glance at the shaft and base reveals that there was very little that was explicitly

Gothic below the buttresses, and in fact Hood and Howells would never again use such overt historic references.

Some of the other American entries pointed in this same direction. The most influential of these was probably the one submitted by Bertram Goodhue, America's most influential architect of the era that immediately preceded the competition. Goodhue proposed a blocky scheme in which virtually all historic references were eliminated and the ornament was strictly subordinated so as to emphasize the dramatic sculptural mass (fig. 6). It was perhaps a little bald in appearance, but it would be highly influential in the design of the great setback skyscrapers of the 1920s and in the development of visionary schemes for entire cities, using the setback as a basic ordering device (fig. 4).[19]

2. *The Europeans*

As a whole, the European entries were more heterogeneous than those of the Americans. This is hardly surprising, since few of the European architects had first-hand experience with the skyscraper and had not been exposed to the debate that had gone on for several decades in the United States concerning its role and appearance in the city. A number of Europeans sacrificed American business practicality altogether in order to make a more monumental form. The entry by Dioguardi is of this type. While this architect undoubtedly displayed considerable skill in creating a powerful and dramatic building silhouette, the interior spaces and their fenestration would have been eccentric, to say the least, and the elevator service fiendishly complicated. Projects like this had very little impact on future architecture, however, because they undoubtedly already seemed hopelessly old-fashioned and impractical to Europeans and Americans alike.

Considered more progressive were the entries inspired by the moderate avant-garde of the prewar years. The famous German architect Peter Behrens had been advocating high buildings since the early teens.[20] Along with other important architects such as Alfred Messel, Paul Bonatz, and

Fig. 7 Walter Fischer, Perspective rendering of entry for Chicago Tribune competition; from International Competition, *plate 221.*

Fig. 8 J. Braham and R. Kastelleiner, Skyscraper design, first prize entry for the Bahnhof Friedrichstrasse competition, Berlin, 1921; from Wasmuths Monatshefte 7 *(1922-23).*

Fig. 9 K. Paul Andrae, "Das größere Berlin VIII," 1913/20; from Wasmuths Monatshefte 7 *(1922-23).*

Wilhelm Kreis, he had also been moving away from elaborate nineteenth-century ornamentation toward more condensed, simpler massing and stripped forms. The entry by Walter Fischer of Magdeburg provides a good example of this approach (fig. 7). His entry, like most of the American ones, was practical, filling the envelope with floor after floor of well-lit office spaces. But his treatment of the facades was quite different from that of most of the Americans. A hint of the Gothic was created by recessing the windows and pulling forward the piers, extending them above the roof lines and opening front and sides with great vertical windows. Fischer went further than almost any American in transforming historic prototypes into something new. German critics rightly remarked that this building had a Gothic feeling without resorting to the use of literal Gothic details, such as the buttresses in the first-prize entry by Hood and Howells.[21] This was even reinforced by Fischer's drawing style. In his perspective, shadows vigorously rendered with diagonal strokes created an atmospheric effect that emphasized the texture rather than the details. Both the massing and treatment of the facades, as well as the drawing technique, seem to have been inspired by the moderate wing of the German postwar Expressionist movement. Fischer's entry was perfectly representative of the kind that had been winning the numerous German competitions for high buildings in the early 1920s. It was similar in spirit to the winning entry submitted by Braham and Kastelleiner of Kassel in the famous Friedrichstrasse competition for a skyscraper in Berlin (fig. 8). It also resembled several other well-publicized schemes by prominent German architects of the day.[22]

It appears that for many progressive German architects the skyscraper represented one of the most interesting challenges modern architecture could offer. German architectural periodicals of the early 1920s, such as *Wasmuths Monatshefte* or *Deutsche Bauzeitung*, but especially those on city planning, notably *Stadtbaukunst alter und neuer Zeit,* were filled with articles discussing how the skyscraper could be tamed to fit into the context of the historic German city center. Some architects such as Max Berg hoped to use the new building type as a tool in the effort to create an alternative, non-capitalistic society. The skyscraper might be used as a "Stadtkrone," or City Crown, bringing citizens together and symbolizing the secular, socialist city in the way the cathedral and palace had functioned for the medieval city. Others were content to work within the capitalist status quo but wished to curb the ability of individual landowners to endanger the public welfare. By careful plan-

Figs. 10/11 B. Bijvoet and J. Duiker, and Max Taut, Perspective renderings of entries for Chicago Tribune competition; from International Competition, *plates 238 and 229.*

ning, some of these architects felt, skyscrapers could be controlled and used in those places where they would legitimately serve as focal points for whole urban compositions. Others, such as K. Paul Andrae, worked out schemes for skyscraper cities based on the new American setback ideas (fig. 9).[23] What almost all these moderate German architects and critics had in common was their opposition to what appeared to them to be the unplanned prolif-

eration of excessively large and overly ornamented skyscrapers in the American city.[24]

This critical view was shared by more radical German architects of the early Weimar years, but because they had even less patience with existing conditions, their proposed remedies were more brutal. This wing was represented in the Tribune competition by the team of Walter Gropius of Weimar and Adolf Meyer of Berlin, Max Taut of

Berlin, and the team of Bijvoet and Duiker of Holland. Although they shared a number of ideas, notably the conviction that old architectural forms were totally inadequate to express the new age, each project took a somewhat different approach. Bijvoet and Duiker seem to have based their entry (fig. 10) on the experiments being carried out by the Dutch De Stijl movement and the work of Frank Lloyd Wright, who was very popular in

Europe in the teens and twenties. In Max Taut's project (fig. 11), on the other hand, the crystalline transparency of the building seems to reflect the Expressionists' fascination with glass, although it rejects vigorously any of their interest in picturesque effects. The entry by Gropius and Meyer, finally, although influenced by De Stijl and by Russian Constructivism, seems most clearly based on the forthright expression of structure (fig. 12;

Figs. 12/13 Walter Gropius and Adolf Meyer, and Jarvis Hunt, Perspective renderings of entries for Chicago Tribune competition; from International Competition, *plates 197 and 118.*

Fig. 14 Eliel Saarinen, Detail of elevation of upper floors of entry for Chicago Tribune competition; from International Competition, *plate 15.*

Fig. 15 Saarinen, Detail of section through upper floors; from International Competition, *plate 16.*

pl. 93). A number of authors have suggested that Gropius was trying to reestablish a continuity with the work of certain late nineteenth-century Chicago architects such as Burnham and Root and Louis Sullivan. Although this work had been mostly forgotten in the United States, Gropius and his avant-garde colleagues in Europe were at the moment rediscovering it.[25] It appears that Gropius took the structural bay module of the existing four-story printing plant, seen at the right side of his perspective drawing, as a point of departure for his project. Curiously, though, his tower was to have had a structural system of reinforced concrete, the favorite material for the European avant-garde, rather than of steel, which had been the material almost universally used in Chicago.[26]

What seems to have motivated the authors of all three of these schemes was their almost total rejection of the assumptions made by most of the Americans and moderate Europeans. All three, for example, shunned the use of a crowning decorative feature. Even though each used some kind of

tower that, judging from the perspective drawings, must have extended above the limit of occupiable space, they treated these elements like the office floors below.[27] This was probably done in part because these architects considered any kind of ornament unnecessary, and, given their left-wing views, found historic ornament particularly offensive since it represented the decadent trappings of bourgeois taste and consumerism. Their political views also dictated their rejection of the traditional hierarchy of buildings as an institutionalization of the class structure of capitalist society. Thus, Gropius and Meyer could echo an industrial building like a printing plant in their design for a prestigious office building. A comparison with the entry of Chicago architect Jarvis Hunt is instructive. Hunt, who had been responsible for the design of the printing plant just two years before, submitted a design for the tower that was clearly meant to be in strong contrast to the printing plant and much more monumental, since it was for a headquarters building primarily housing offices (fig. 13).[28]

From a broader perspective, the radical European entries also imply a sharply negative estimate of the American city.[29] Although they made some of the same criticisms of American cities as did their more moderate German colleagues, the extremists proposed a much more drastic remedy. Instead of trying to create well-integrated tall buildings as the focal point of compositions embracing the lower buildings of the historic town centers, they were prepared to disregard the old city altogether. Indeed, their submissions appear to be designs for the first buildings in some city of the future.

A preliminary drawing by Max Taut is interesting in this regard. It shows his tower from the rear with the printing block redesigned in a more "modern" style, but with no other buildings visible, implying that Taut had in his own mind cleared the entire district of existing structures. At just this moment colleagues of Taut and Gropius were in fact preparing a number of schemes for new districts and whole new cities that made a point of breaking completely with the patterns of the traditional city, sweeping away the chaos created by development over long periods and substituting great isolated towers linked by railroads and superhighways. This was clearly a vision inspired by the Italian Futurists and the Russian Constructivists, and curiously, it was not very different from some of the scenes found in American science fiction fantasies.[30]

3. Eliel Saarinen

The one entry that seems to have had some success in bridging the chasm between the Old World and the New was that submitted by Finnish architect Eliel Saarinen. Even the harshest European critics admitted that his was the best of the "Gothic" designs, and a surprising number of American writers claimed that he had understood the American spirit better than had any of the native competitors.[31] His was the only entry that received attention from all quarters and praise from most, and it instantly propelled its author into prominence in the United States. It is the contention of this essay that Saarinen succeeded in great part because he was able both to understand how the American city had come to be the way it was, and to suggest a plausible new vision of what it might become.

Fig. 16 Saarinen, Perspective rendering; from International Competition, *plate 13.*

At first glance the Saarinen entry resembled many of the American entries (fig. 16). It is not clear how well he knew American office building practice or whether he knew any Americans who might have helped him in his design.[32] He obviously knew something about this subject, since a preliminary elevation study appears to have been based at least in part on the front elevation of the Woolworth Building.[33] But unlike many of the American contestants, Saarinen used this as a point of departure only. In his final and much refined scheme, the building's telescoping pyramidal composition is much more fully worked out than in most of the American schemes. He avoided monotony by using a rectangular plan for the base of the building and the upper setbacks and giving the first setback a cross-shaped plan. In all of this Saarinen followed good academic principles. His most conspicuous success involved the difficult task of integrating the masses. He accomplished this in part by projecting vertical ribs in front of the window plane and carrying them above the various roof lines to create finial-like projections. Saarinen probably learned this treatment from moderate German Expressionists like Hans Poelzig, Max Berg, or Walter Fischer, or he may have developed it on his own. The same is true of the slashing diagonal drawing style seen in his perspective, which, as in the case of the Fischer entry, emphasized the massing but drew attention away from distracting details. The round arches and some of the sculpture, on the other hand, seem to have been his own creations, although probably derived from the late nineteenth-century Romanesque revival. Whatever the origin of the individual parts, Saarinen's great achievement was to fuse them into a personal style that was largely ahistoric, yet sufficiently monumental for the very conspicuous site and client.

Saarinen also seems to have found a way of creating a heraldic device at the top of his building that, more than those of any of the other prize-winning entries, was also integral with the inhabited block below. He proposed for his crowning feature a large single room, presumably serving as an open observation station, whose mural-covered upper walls were carried on an open arcade. Seen from the exterior, the piers of the arcade continued the lines of the main block into the top of the tower, while the voids of the arches provided a visual separation. It was perhaps a less dramatic terminating feature than the buttresses of Hood and Howells, but it was a subtler and more unified composition (figs. 14, 15).

The final reason that Saarinen's proposal met with such approval is only hinted at in the drawings.

Almost alone among the competitors, his perspective seems to show the structure flanked by other large office buildings filling out the street line but lost in shadow higher up, presumably where they stepped back from the street. Unlike most of the Americans who tacitly accepted the assumption that their task was to design for a single site, or the Europeans, who so disliked the American city that they created ideal projects with no actual site, Saarinen seems to have been willing to work on a single site that could serve as a prototype for the whole city. How this was to be accomplished he suggested more fully in a publication almost simultaneous with that of the Tribune competition. In 1923 the magazine *American Architect* contained a project by Saarinen for the Chicago lakefront in which two buildings similar in appearance to his Tribune tower formed part of a vast urban complex to be located in Grant Park (fig. 17; pl. 95).[34]

Fig. 18 Reinhard and Hofmeister; Hood, Godley, and Fouilhoux; Corbett, Harrison, and MacMurray, Rockefeller Center, Fifth Avenue between 49th and 50th Streets, New York, 1929-39.

Fig. 17 Saarinen, Project for lakefront development in Chicago, 1923; from American Architect *124 (Dec. 5, 1923).*

This scheme answered a number of questions about his Tribune tower project and guaranteed that it would be seen in a larger context. Saarinen, who had worked in Finland as much as planner as architect, made his attitude toward Chicago clear in his description of the lakefront scheme. He obviously disliked much of the disorder and uncontrolled development he found there, but, unlike many of his more extreme European colleagues, he realized that fundamental changes in the American economic and political system were unlikely. Accepting this, he hoped to bring a greater degree of order to the most prominent and public part of the city, the central lakefront, and in so doing, to set an example for the rest of the urban area. His scheme was an ideal one, based on his belief in the power of a good idea, not a detailed prescription of how the city and private property owners might be coerced into accepting it.

In all of these assumptions, his attitudes closely followed those of Daniel Burnham, and Saarinen readily acknowledged his admiration for that architect's famous 1909 Plan of Chicago. Saarinen's own scheme implied that most of Burnham's plan would be left untouched, that he merely intended to graft a new element onto it. What Saarinen seems to have been doing was to use Burnham's own logic but to push it further in an attempt to bring it up-to-date.

Saarinen started with the transportation problem. To remove the chaotic sprawl of railroads that usurped the lakefront, Saarinen proposed the creation of a large station under Grant Park. This would service the existing lakefront lines after they had been electrified and depressed, as well as lines that would be brought from the West Side to the lakefront through new underground tunnels. Even more pressing was the problem of the automobile. Still primarily a plaything for the rich when Burnham started his plan, it had become, in the intervening years, a major factor in the city. Saarinen proposed to remove much of the congestion from the Loop by creating a huge underground garage and a high-speed roadway leading to it, running below grade directly along the north-south axis of the park. Commuters to the Loop could use this garage, then walk to their offices.

Above ground Saarinen proposed a monumental grouping of low buildings forming courtyards and arcades in the park framing two skyscrapers, one at each end of the north-south axis. Although his towers would have been the tallest and most conspicuous in Chicago, neither would represent church or state, on the traditional European model. The northern one, the only one to which he assigned a function, was to serve as a hotel, perhaps in recognition of Chicago's central role as a secular marketplace and transportation hub.

This scheme, like his Tribune tower project, represents a highly effective synthesis of ideas. In it, Saarinen turned decisively away from the influence of planners like Camillo Sitte, who proposed small-scale, often picturesque urban effects, toward the grandiose monumentality of nineteenth-century French urban planning and the contemporary American ideal of the City Beautiful.[35] But Saarinen's dramatic expression of automobile transportation and the use of widely spaced setback skyscrapers were new ideas. This scheme, combining forthrightly modern scale and transportation elements with academic Beaux-Arts planning, was especially effective because of Saarinen's polite, respectfully phrased presentation.

Like the Tribune tower entry, the lakefront scheme remained a paper project. It was never seriously considered by public officials in Chicago. Still, Saarinen's ideas were obviously much discussed. It is difficult, though, to judge the effect of Saarinen's designs on subsequent American architecture and city planning precisely because he was so in tune with developments in the United States in the early 1920s. It has been suggested that specific buildings such as the Pacific Telephone Company's headquarters in San Francisco designed by Timothy Pflueger, the American Radiator Building in New York by Raymond Hood, and the 333 North Michigan Avenue Building in Chicago by Holabird and Roche, as well as whole complexes such as Rockefeller Center (fig. 18) in New York, were directly influenced by the Saarinen scheme. But it appears that Saarinen was not so much the inventor of a new means of expression as the most successful synthesizer and popularizer of new ideas coming from Europe and the United States.[36] Clearly, it was not novelty that made Saarinen's Tribune tower entry so famous in its day. It was the widespread perception that this entry was the one that best fulfilled the Tribune's hope of commissioning a work of art that could transcend national borders and speak to the imagination of people in many lands.

NOTES

1 The competition was set out in Howard L. Cheney, *Program of Architectural Competition for the Administration Building of the Chicago Tribune*, a booklet published by the Tribune in 1922. All of the entries plus analyses and indexes appeared in a book also published by the Tribune, *The International Competition for a New Administration Building for the Chicago Tribune* (Chicago, 1923). This book has been reprinted by Rizzoli in a somewhat abbreviated form as volume I of *Tribune Tower Competition* (New York, 1980).

2 Loos's description is found in Ludwig Münz and Gustav Künstler, *Der Architekt Adolf Loos* (Vienna, 1964), pp. 175-77. Translated in Münz and Künstler, *Adolf Loos, Pioneer of Modern Architecture* (New York, 1966), pp. 393-94.

3 Loos's entry may also have been inspired by the pun on the meaning of the word "column" as it is used in a newspaper.

4 Paul Gerhardt of Chicago and Mathew L. Freeman submitted schemes with columns projecting from a more or less conventional building block.

5 On Loos's attempt to make his office floors practical, see the plan reproduced in Münz and Künstler (note 2), p. 393.

6 For a typical reaction, see Ludwig Hilberseimer, *Contemporary Architecture, Its Roots and Trends* (Chicago, 1964), p. 165.

7 A very interesting discussion of this and the other Italian entries to the competition is found in Giorgio Muratore's "Métamorphose d'un mythe 1922-43: le gratte-ciel américain et ses reflets sur la culture architecturale italienne," *Archithese* 18 (1976), pp. 28-36.

8 On European views of American skyscrapers, see note 22.

9 Manfredo Tafuri, in Giorgio Ciucci, et al., *The American City: From the Civil War to the New Deal*, trans. Barbara Luigia La Penta (Cambridge, Mass., 1979), pp. 402-3. Benedetto Gravagnuola, *Adolf Loos, Theory and Works* (New York, 1982), p. 174.

10 Michigan Avenue had been a key element in the 1909 Burnham Plan of Chicago. It was created by widening an older roadway, Pine Street, that ran north from the river, and joining it to the Loop via a new double-level bridge. From the beginning, the landowners hoped to create a great commercial boulevard, the equal of any in Europe, and they attempted to impose restrictions to maintain architectural consistency. As early as 1918, the merchants' association commissioned a group of architects to draw up a scheme that might suggest the architectural development on the avenue. This work, by Andrew Rebori, Holabird and Roche, and others, was reported in *American Architect* 114 (Dec. 11, 1918), pp. 691-99, 701. On the development of the boulevard, see John Stamper, "The Architecture, Urbanism, and Economics of Chicago's North Michigan Avenue, 1830-1930" (Ph.D. diss., Northwestern University, 1985).

11 See, for example, Irving K. Pond, "High Buildings and Beauty, Part I," *Architectural Forum* 38,2 (Feb. 1923), pp. 41-44; Thomas E. Tallmadge, "A Critique of the Chicago Tribune Building Competition," *Western Architect* 32,1 (Jan. 1923), pp. 7-8.

12 The most extensive review was that of Gerhard Wohler, "Das Hochhaus im Wettbewerb der Chicago Tribune," *Deutsche Bauzeitung* 58 (July 5, 1924), pp. 325-30; (July 16, 1924), pp. 345-47. See also the discussion in Werner Hegemann, "Das Hochhaus als Verkehrsstörer und der Wettbewerb der Chicago Tribune," *Wasmuths Monatshefte* 8 (1924), pp. 296-309. More recently, Manfredo Tafuri has published an extended study of the competition in Ciucci, et al. (note 9), pp. 390-419. See also Reyner Banham, *Theory and Design in the First Machine Age* (New York, 1967), pp. 268-69.

13 On American building restrictions, see the excellent book by Seymour Toll, *Zoned America* (New York, 1969).

14 At the time of the competition a zoning law for Chicago was under consideration, and would be passed by 1923. It was modeled in part on the famous New York law of 1916. The New York law in turn had been based on earlier height regulations, such as the ones in force in Chicago. Some discussion of zoning in both cities, although inaccurate in details, can be found in Carol Her-

selle Krinsky, "Sister Cities: Architecture and Planning in the Twentieth Century," in John Zukowsky, David Van Zanten, and Carol Herselle Krinsky, *Chicago and New York: Architectural Interactions* (Chicago, 1984), pp. 58-60.

15 Its total floor area could be no more than 3,600 square feet, that is to say, the square footage of all its floors could not exceed about one-third of the building's ground floor area. This accounts for the fact that in many entries the tower is composed of a single great room or a few very high rooms that would take the building up to the maximum height without going over the square footage. It seems that a number of competitors either did not understand this regulation, or that they got around it by designing what looked like office floors but were understood to be merely storage areas or room for expansion if the building laws were ever changed.

16 On the aesthetic bases of zoning, see, for example, Irving K. Pond, "Zoning and the Architecture of High Buildings," *Architectural Forum* 35 (Oct. 1921), pp. 131-34.

17 On this entry, see Walter H. Kilham, *Raymond Hood, Architect* (New York, 1973), pp. 57-60; Leon V. Solon, "The Evolution of an Architectural Design," *Architectural Record* 59,3 (Mar. 1926), pp. 215-25; Robert A. M. Stern with Thomas P. Catalano, *Raymond Hood* (New York, 1982), pp. 7-8, 34-35.

18 On Michigan Avenue, see Stamper (note 10).

19 On architects' responses to the zoning laws see Carol Willis, "Zoning and Zeitgeist, the Skyscraper City in the 1920s," to appear in a forthcoming issue of the *Journal of the Society of Architectural Historians*.

20 The debate on high buildings in the city among the European avant-garde is being studied by Francesco Passanti, who, in his work on Le Corbusier, has described the debt of the young Swiss architect to both Peter Behrens and the French architect August Perret.

21 Wohler (note 12), p. 347.

22 The Friedrichstrasse competition was the one to which Mies van der Rohe submitted his famous glass skyscraper design. On this competition, see Adolf Behne, "Der Wettbewerb der Turmhaus-Gesellschaft," *Wasmuths Monatshefte* 7 (1922-23), pp. 58-67; Max Berg, "Hochhäuser im Stadtbild," *Wasmuths Monatshefte* 6 (1921-22), pp. 101-20.

23 A drawing by Andrae was published in *Wasmuths Monatshefte* in 1922-23 with a caption stating that it was drawn in 1913. Even if its date is not as early as claimed, this project shows that some Europeans were working along the same lines as their American counterparts in imagining how the city of the future, incorporating the new setback ideas, would look.

24 The difference between German and American practice is summarized in a most concise way in a pair of articles in the *Journal of the American Institute of Architects* (Sept. 1923), pp. 365-71: "Skyscrapers in Germany" by the German Walter Curt Behrendt, and "Skyscrapers in America," by the American George C. Nimmons. See also "Zur Entwicklung des Hochhauses in Deutschland," *Deutsche Bauzeitung* 55 (Mar. 5, 1921), pp. 89-95; and Martin Machler, "Zum Problem des Wolkenkratzers," *Wasmuths Monatshefte* 5 (1920-21), pp. 191-94, 260-63.

25 On the rediscovery of the Chicago School by Europeans, see Lewis Mumford, "New York vs. Chicago in Architecture," *Architecture* 56 (Nov. 1927), pp. 241-44.

26 Letter of 1958 from Gropius to Morton Frank published in Reginald R. Isaacs, *Walter Gropius der Mensch und sein Werk* (Berlin, 1983-84).

27 On the bulk restrictions applying to the tower, see note 15.

28 In fact, it appears that Hunt (Plate 118 in the Tribune's book of entries) went so far in his desire to be monumental that he disregarded the competition program and thus severely jeopardized his chances of winning one of the prizes. Although the program demanded floors that virtually filled the site, Hunt elected to give his building a semicircular plan in the portion that faced Michigan Avenue, sacrificing a great deal of floor space.

29 One of the best expressions of this can be found in the writings of their colleague Ludwig Hilberseimer in his "Das Hochhaus," *Das Kunstblatt* 6, 12 (1922), pp. 525-31.

30 The famous drawings by Mies van der Rohe for the Friedrichstrasse competition clearly show his desire to break as decisively as possible with the existing street-

scape. "Hochhausproject für Bahnhof Friedrichstrasse," in *Frühlicht* 1 (1922), pp. 122-24. The best known of these urban schemes, of course, is the contemporary city for 2,000,000 people by Le Corbusier, but Hilberseimer was apparently working on a related scheme at this time as well. Francesco Passanti is currently studying these schemes (note 20).

31 On the Saarinen entry, see Irving K. Pond (note 11), pp. 42-43; Pond, "Eliel Saarinen and his Work: A Word of Appreciation and Greeting," *Western Architect* 32,7 (July 1923), pp. 75-76; Walter Creese, "Saarinen's Tribune Design," *Journal of the Society of Architectural Historians* 6 (July-Dec. 1947), pp. 1-5; Albert Christ-Janer, *Eliel Saarinen, Finnish Architect and Educator* (Chicago, 1979), pp. 57-59, 147; David G. DeLong, "Eliel Saarinen and the Cranbrook Tradition in Architecture and Urban Design," in *Design in America: The Cranbrook Vision* (New York, 1983), pp. 47-52. The most euphoric comments were by Tallmadge (note 11) and later in his *Story of Architecture in America* (New York, 1927), pp. 290-95; and in the famous piece by Louis Sullivan, "The Chicago Tribune Competition," *Architectural Record* 53 (Feb. 1923), pp. 151-57. For the European point of view, see Wohler (note 12), pp. 345-46.

32 The Tribune's book of entries lists Dwight G. Wallace and Bertell Grenman of Chicago as associated architects, but these men seem to be mentioned nowhere else in the literature on Saarinen.

33 The preliminary elevation is remarkably similar, for example, to that of the design submitted by Richard Yoshijiro Mine of Urbana, Ill., which also clearly descended from the Woolworth elevation. On this see John Zukowsky, Pauline Saliga, and Rebecca Rubin, *Chicago Architects Design: A Century of Architectural Drawings from The Art Institute of Chicago* (Chicago, 1982), p. 82.

34 Eliel Saarinen, "Project for the Lake Front Development of the City of Chicago," *American Architect* 124 (Dec. 5, 1923), pp. 487-514.

35 On Saarinen's earlier urban schemes, see the excellent analysis by Marc Treib in his "Urban Fabric by the Bolt," *Architectural Association Quarterly* 13 (Jan.-June 1982), pp. 43-58, and "Eliel Saarinen as Urbanist: The Tower and the Square," *Arkkitehti* 3 (1985), pp. 16-31, 92-95.

36 A good compendium of these designs, which clearly shows the centrality of the Saarinen scheme in the development of the tall building, can be found in Francisco Mujica, *History of the Skyscraper* (New York, 1930).

Walter Burley Griffin's Design for Canberra, the Capital of Australia

David Van Zanten

On May 23, 1912, King O'Malley, Minister for Home Affairs of the Commonwealth of Australia, pronounced Chicago architect Walter Burley Griffin winner of the international competition for the design of a federal capital at Canberra.[1] The choice of the thirty-six-year-old architect, landscape designer, and former office manager for Frank Lloyd Wright is puzzling, especially if one considers the architects engaged for similar projects in other parts of the British Empire at that time.

During the latter decades of the nineteenth century and in the years just prior to the outbreak of World War I, the extensive British Colonial holdings were reorganized and developed into a consistent imperial system. The task was immense, and was carried out sometimes brusquely, as by Cecil Rhodes in southern Africa, sometimes grandly, as by Lord Curzon in India. But it took on a different character in Australia.

The British vision of a permanent worldwide empire manifested itself in florid declarations, splendid ceremonies, and elaborate buildings. Among the largest of these rhetorical gestures were the plans for two monumental capital complexes: the Pretoria Union Buildings in South Africa and New Delhi in India.[2] Built between 1910 and 1913, Pretoria was the work of Herbert Baker (1862-1946), who called himself Cecil Rhodes's architect, and who went on to a most successful architectural career in Africa, India, and England.[3] The 1912 plan for New Delhi was the work of another British architect, Edwin Landseer Lutyens (1869-1944), aided by Baker. Both were subsequently knighted for their efforts. How and why did the Australians come to choose an obscure American architect to develop the plan for their capital city of Canberra?

Writing in Chicago seventy-five years later, we cannot know the answer to this question with certainty. We can, however, explore the suggestive thought that Griffin's design was imbued with a directness and simplicity (what might loosely be termed "democracy") that was quintessentially Chicagoan and, incidentally, also appropriate to a certain conception of Australia particularly connected with O'Malley.

Griffin had been born in 1876 in Maywood, Illinois, a suburb just west of Oak Park, the son of George Walker Griffin, an insurance broker, and Estelle Malvina Burley, an active social worker. He continued to live in Maywood until he settled in Australia in 1914. Griffin attended Oak Park High School and the University of Illinois, graduating with a Bachelor of Science in Architecture in 1899. There he had been inspired by the emerging Chicago School of design led by Louis Sullivan and Frank Lloyd Wright. He worked for Wright in the Oak Park Studio from 1901 to 1905, where he executed his first major independent commission – the William H. Emery House in Elmhurst, Illinois (1901-02) – in Wright's Prairie style. There he became friends with the Prairie School architects William Drummond, Francis Barry Byrne (who took over Griffin's practice when he left for Australia in 1913), and Marion Mahony. The last of these was one of Wright's principal draftsmen and, in 1911, became Griffin's wife. Late in 1905 Griffin set up on his own. His victory in the Canberra competition seven years later was his first great opportunity.

O'Malley (c. 1858-1953) was an amazing character. He was an American, born, he believed, in Canada, who had immigrated to Australia in 1886. After engaging in various small business ventures, he was elected as a Labour party member to the first Commonwealth Parliament in 1901. First as a member, then as a minister, he pursued a number of issues with celebrated enthusiasm: the suppression of drunkeness; rights for illegitimate children; the erection of a transcontinental railroad to Perth; the establishment of a popular savings bank – the Australian Commonwealth Bank; and the founding of Canberra. He resigned in 1916 in protest over the imposition of conscription to sustain the Australian contribution to World War I.[4]

O'Malley's style, however, was his essence. He was something of Abraham Lincoln and something of Will Rogers. He was tall and wore odd clothing. He enjoyed jokes, especially on himself. He could talk to anyone – addressing them as "brother" and "sister" – and rarely missed an opportunity to do so. He saw the world of men with crystalline clarity

Fig. 1 Walter Burley Griffin, Competitive design for the federal capital city of the Commonwealth of Australia, Canberra, 1912; plan.

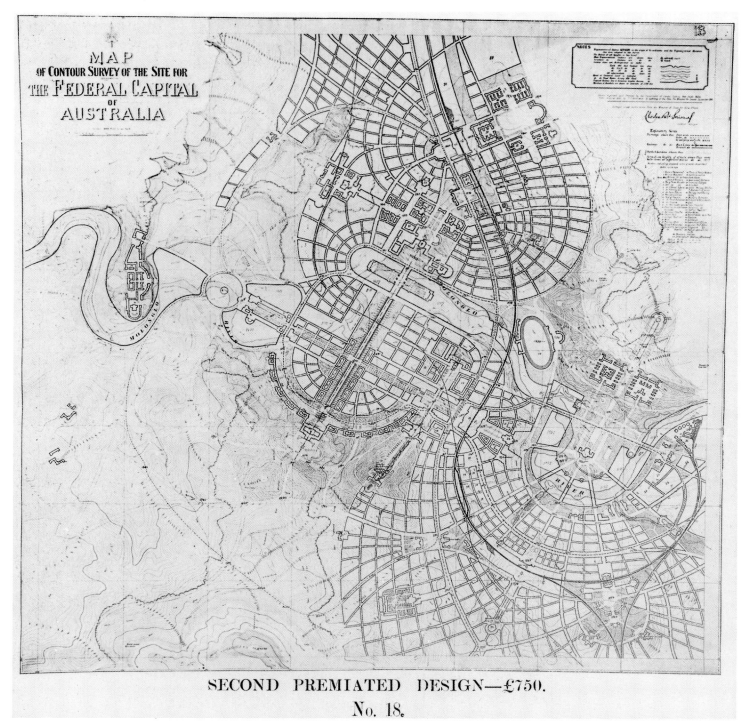

SECOND PREMIATED DESIGN—£750.

No. 18.

Fig. 2 Eliel Saarinen, Competitive design for Canberra; plan (drawn over topographic map), 1912.

and worked to improve it with such directness that he often succeeded.

Although at first cavalier with Griffin's plan, he became Griffin's friend and supporter during his second term as minister (1915-16), and in the 1920s moved into a Griffin-designed house at Castlecrag, a suburb of Sydney.

The Competition

Following the establishment in 1788 of the first British settlement in what would become the col-

ony of New South Wales, five more colonies were founded on the Australian continent. In 1900, after a decade of negotiations, the six separate colonies became states federated into the Commonwealth of Australia. One provision of the Act of Federation was that the government should be settled in a newly founded city to be located not less than 100 miles from Sydney in the state of New South Wales. A series of acts passed between 1908 and 1910 set the site of the future capital near the settlement of Canberra, about halfway between Sydney and Melbourne in the state of Victoria. Situated on the

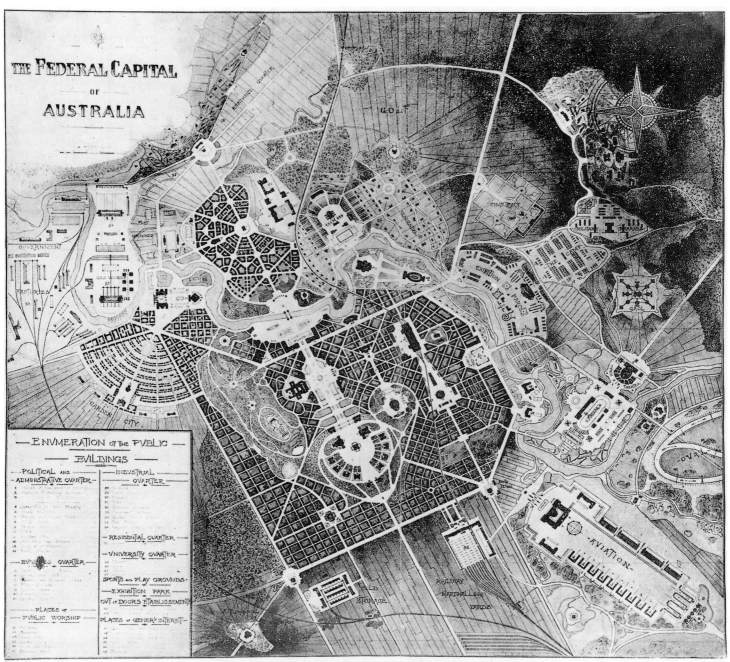

THE FEDERAL CAPITAL

OF

AUSTRALIA

ENVMERATION of the PVBLIC
BVILDINGS

POLITICAL and
ADMINISTRATIVE QVARTER

INDVSTRIAL
QVARTER

RESIDENTIAL QVARTER

VNIVERSITY QVARTER

BVSINESS QVARTER

SPORTS and PLAY GROVNDS

EXHIBITION PARK

OVT of DOORS ETABLISSEMENTS

PLACES of
PVBLIC WORSHIP

PLACES of GENERAL INTEREST

THIRD PREMIATED DESIGN—£500.
No. 4.

sluggish Molonglo River seventy miles from the sea, the settlement was in a valley of rolling pasture land sharply defined by mountains and blessed with a dry and pleasantly Mediterranean climate.

The federal government took possession of the site on January 1, 1911, and Colonel David Miller, Secretary of the Department of Home Affairs, proposed an international competition for an urban plan from which a final plan might be developed. An entirely separate competition was to be held for the design of the Parliament buildings. King O'Malley, Minister for Home

Affairs in the Labour government of Prime Minister Andrew Fisher, approved the idea, and on April 30, 1911, the first competition was announced over his signature.

Specific materials were made available for prospective competitors in Wellington, Ottawa, Pretoria, and Cape Town, as well as in London, Paris, Berlin, Washington, New York, and Chicago. These included a contour map of the site, a full-circle panoramic painting of the valley and the mountains beyond, basic topographical information, and a list of public functions to be accommo-

Fig. 3 Donat-Alfred Agache, Competitive design for Canberra; plan, 1912.

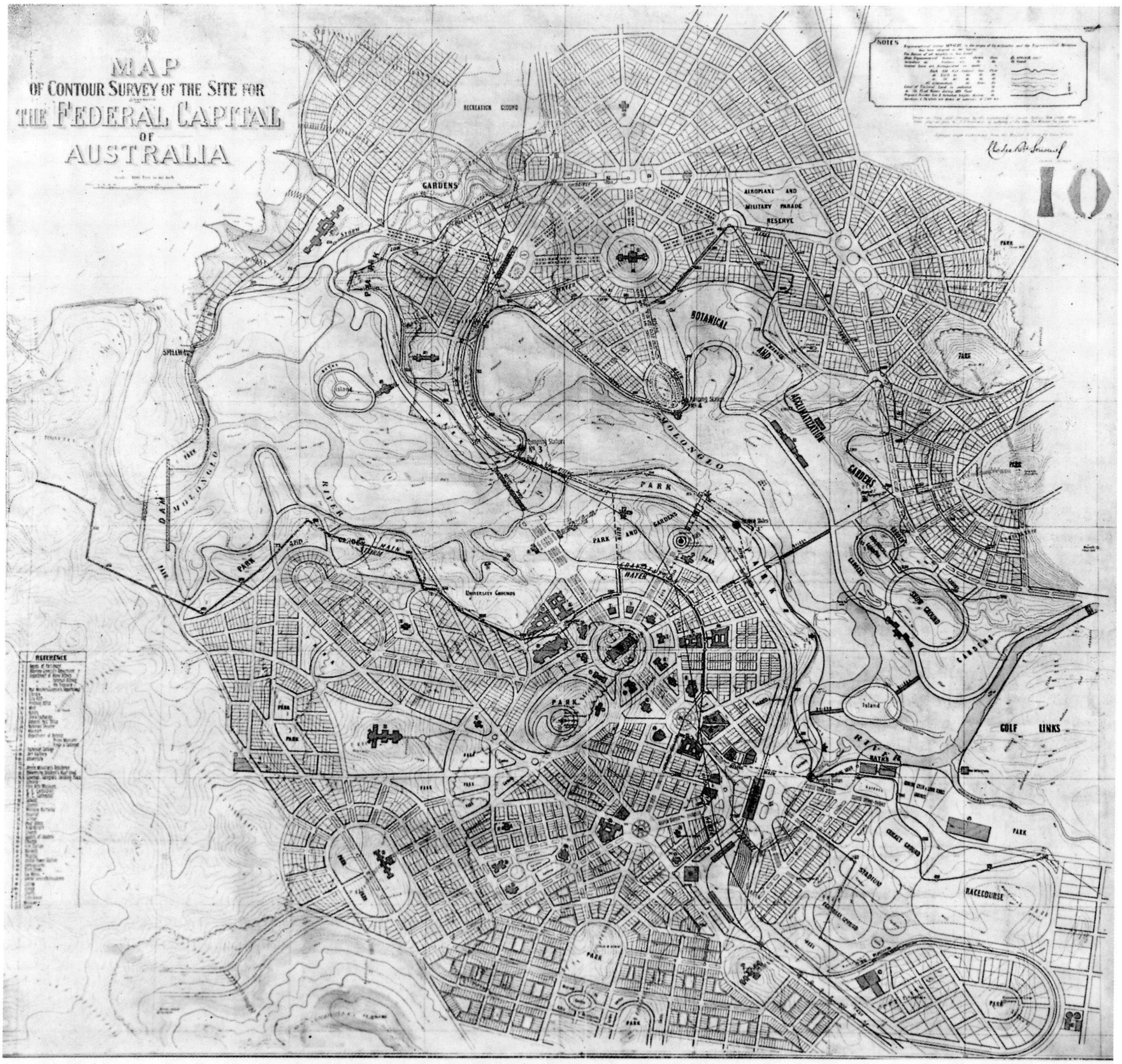

DESIGN No. 10.

Fig. 4 W. Scott Griffiths in partnership with Charles Gibbon Coulter and Charles Henry Caswell, Competitive design for Canberra; plan, 1912.

dated. It was proposed that the designers provide an "ornamental water" by damming the Molonglo River. O'Malley was quoted as declaring that:

The Federal Capital should be a beautiful city, occupying a commanding position, with extensive views, and embracing distinctive features which will lend themselves to the evolution of a design worthy of the object, not only for the present, but for all time, consequently the potentialities of the site will demand most careful consideration from a scenic standpoint, with a view to securing picturesqueness, and also with the object of beautification and expansion.[5]

The Design Board was to consist of an engineer, an architect, and a licensed surveyor — all as yet unnamed — reporting to the Minister, who would make the final adjudication without appeal. The drawings would become the property of the Australian government, which would lay out the city using whatever suggestions in the plans seemed useful. Projects were to be in hand at the Ministry in Melbourne by January 31, 1912; the awards would be: first prize, £1,750; second, £750; and third, £500.

Architectural competitions at the turn of the cen-

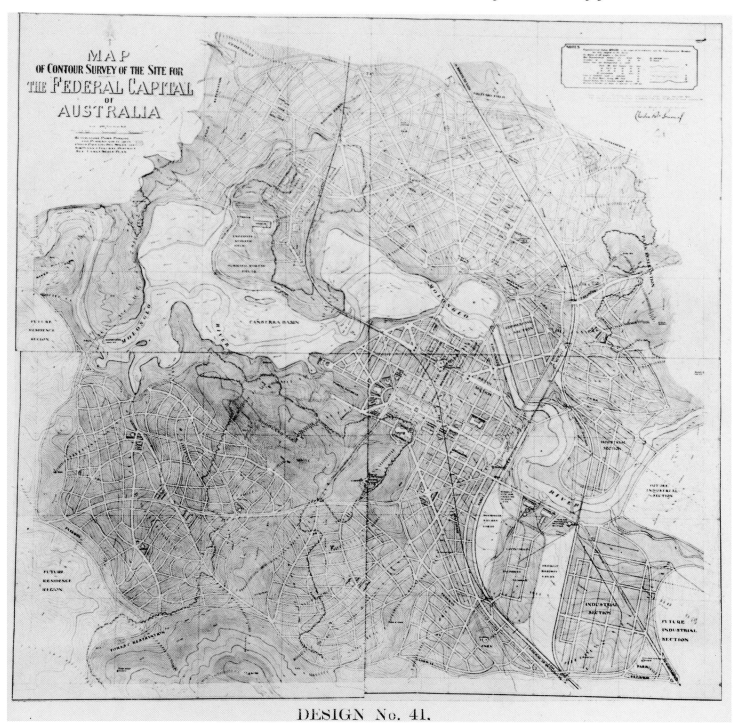

MAP
OF CONTOUR SURVEY OF THE SITE FOR
THE FEDERAL CAPITAL
OF
AUSTRALIA

DESIGN No. 41.

Fig. 5 Arthur C. Comey, Competitive design for Canberra; plan, 1912.

tury were a matter of bitter controversy because the prize winners were often not employed to carry out their designs; instead, they were paid off and forced to watch their ideas bowdlerized by others.[6] That appeared to be precisely what O'Malley and Miller were preparing to do. This suspicion, combined with comparatively low prize money,[7] provoked strong objections from the Victoria and New South Wales Institutes of Architects. Their protests were endorsed by the Royal Institute of British Architects in London, which finally boycotted the competition, ethically barring its members —

virtually all of the distinguished designers in the Empire — from competing.[8] The American Insitute of Architects expressed disapproval, but believed that it could not prohibit participation in competitions sponsored by foreign countries.[9]

In spite of this inauspicious start, 137 submissions arrived in Melbourne by the deadline and were set up impressively in the ballroom at Government House for inspection. The Design Board, officially announced on March 2, 1912, consisted of James Alexander Smith, past president of the Victoria Insitute of Engineers, John Kirkpatrick, ar-

MAP
OF CONTOUR SURVEY OF THE SITE FOR
THE FEDERAL CAPITAL
OF
AUSTRALIA

DESIGN No. 81.

Fig. 6 Nils Gellerstedt in collaboration with Ivan Lindgren and Hugo du Rietz, Competitive design for Canberra; plan, 1912.

chitect, and J. M. Coane, licensed surveyor, all distinguished Australian practitioners.[10] They reported a split judgment on May 14, 1912.[11]

Smith and Kirkpatrick awarded the first, second, and third prizes to the projects of Walter Burley Griffin of the United States, Eliel Saarinen of Finland, and Donat-Alfred Agache of France, respectively (figs. 1-3). Coane awarded the prizes to the projects of W. Scott Griffiths (in partnership with Charles Gibbon Coulter and Charles Henry Caswell) of Sydney; to Arthur C. Comey of Cambridge, Massachusetts; and to Nils Gellerstedt

(with his collaborators Ivan Lindgren and Hugo du Rietz) of Stockholm (figs. 4-6). Smith and Kirkpatrick also requested that two other designs, that of Harold Van Buren Magonigle of New York and that submitted by the firm of Schanfelberg, Rees and Gummer of London, be cited for special merit (figs. 7, 8). O'Malley approved the majority decision, and on May 23, 1912, Griffin was declared the winner of the competition for the design of the capital city of Australia.

The *New York Times* carried the announcement on Friday, May 24, 1912, editorialized about it on

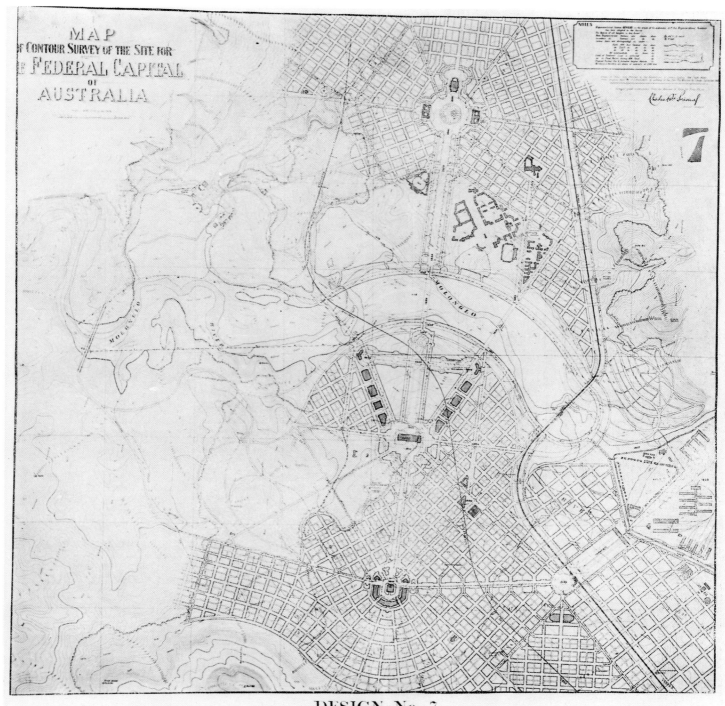

DESIGN No. 7

May 25, and devoted a full page to the project and Griffin's ideas in its Sunday magazine of June 2. The article in the latter quoted Griffin at length:

I do not know whether I shall be called to Australia to superintend the construction of the new city. I hope so. I rather expect I shall. It would be only fair to me. There is nobody in the world who can work out my ideas like myself.

I do not know what type of architecture I should adopt. I have planned a city not like any other city in the world. I have planned it not in a way that I expected any governmental authorities in the world would accept. I have planned an ideal city – a city that meets my ideal of the city of the future.

I am what may be termed a naturalist in architecture. I do not believe in any school of architecture. I believe in architecture that is the logical outgrowth of the environment in which the building in mind is to be located. I have been planning houses in Chicago to meet Chicago's needs. They do not accord with the ordinarily accepted types of houses. . . . I have tried to make them answer the needs of Chicago climatically and topographically.

It is of course difficult to describe such buildings. They are not like the buildings of any school. . . . Our National architecture is yet to be evolved. When it is evolved it will be an architecture that will meet the requirements of the

Fig. 7 Harold Van Buren Magonigle, Competitive design for Canberra; plan, 1912.

DESIGN No. 35.

Fig. 8 Schanfelberg, Rees, and Gummer, Competitive design for Canberra; plan, 1912.

climate and exactly along what architectural lines it will fall remains to be seen.

I have never been in Australia, but I have an idea what the climate of Australia is. Consequently I have a vague idea what sort of architecture I should recommend for the future Australian capital. But I am not prepared yet to go into details regarding it. Australia is a newer country than the United States. It has no architectural traditions. Its ideals of architecture are not influenced by any imported schools.... I think in such a country, untrammeled by traditions, I ought to be able to evolve a very beautiful architectural type adapted to the needs of the climate and harmonizing with the topography. I should like to try it.

The professional world was surprised and a bit condescending about the success of the little-known architect — except in the Midwest, where Griffin's triumph was seen as wonderful vindication of local architectural achievement. The project drawings were published in most of the prestigious national and international journals, although accompanied by very little critical comment. Griffin became a minor celebrity, being asked, for example, to present his plan at the American Civic Association meeting in Baltimore in December 1912. But O'Malley and Miller made no further

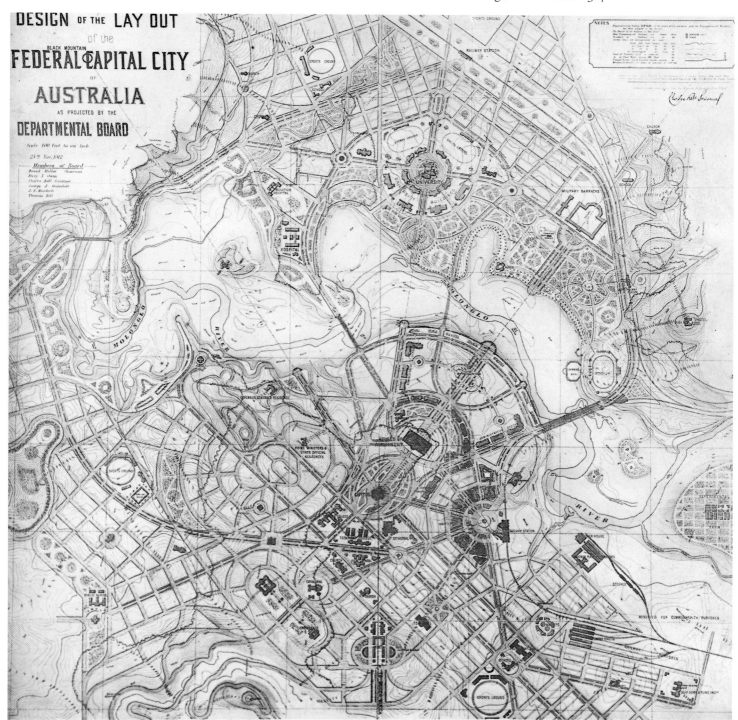

DESIGN OF THE LAY OUT
of the
BLACK MOUNTAIN
FEDERAL CAPITAL CITY
OF
AUSTRALIA
AS PROJECTED BY THE
DEPARTMENTAL BOARD

contact with Griffin, and on November 25, 1912, their department presented a strange composite plan for Canberra using some of Griffin's as well as other architects' suggestions (fig. 9). This provoked another professional outcry and a lengthy letter from Griffin to O'Malley, requesting that he be permitted to supervise the execution of his design, both because of the cavalier treatment of the projects and because of the distressing quality of the result.

At this point the Labour government fell and the Liberal party led by Joseph Cook came to power.

The new Minister for Home Affairs, W. H. Kelly, responded to the continuing architectural commotion by telegraphing Griffin on July 25, 1913, inviting him to come to Australia. Griffin accepted at once and arrived in Sydney on August 19. He made a great stir. He addressed the Institute of Architects of both New South Wales and Victoria. The chief professional journal, *Building,* published his lectures, his explanation of the Canberra scheme, his portrait, and a profoundly laudatory profile, "Walter Burley Griffin, Rebel." He visited the site, conferred with government officials, and

Fig. 9 Departmental Board of the Ministry for Home Affairs, Design of the layout for the federal capital city of Australia, Canberra, November 1912.

finally, on October 18, was named Federal Capital Director of Design and Construction for a term of three years. His wish to carry out his design, expressed so earnestly to the reporter for the *New York Times,* seemed about to be fulfilled. Griffin revised his scheme, which he had conceived in Chicago without any firsthand knowledge of Canberra, and then, on November 15, left again for America to put his affairs in order before settling in Australia.

Back in Chicago from his first trip to Australia, Griffin arranged for his former associate in Wright's Oak Park Studio, architect Francis Barry Byrne, to supervise his American affairs, which now embraced promising commissions for buildings at the University of New Mexico and a new city at Mossmain, Montana, as well as a number of large residences, including the development of Rock Crest-Rock Glen in Mason City, Iowa (cat. no. 186).

Fig. 10 Griffin, Competitive design for Canberra; plan drawn over topographic map, 1912.

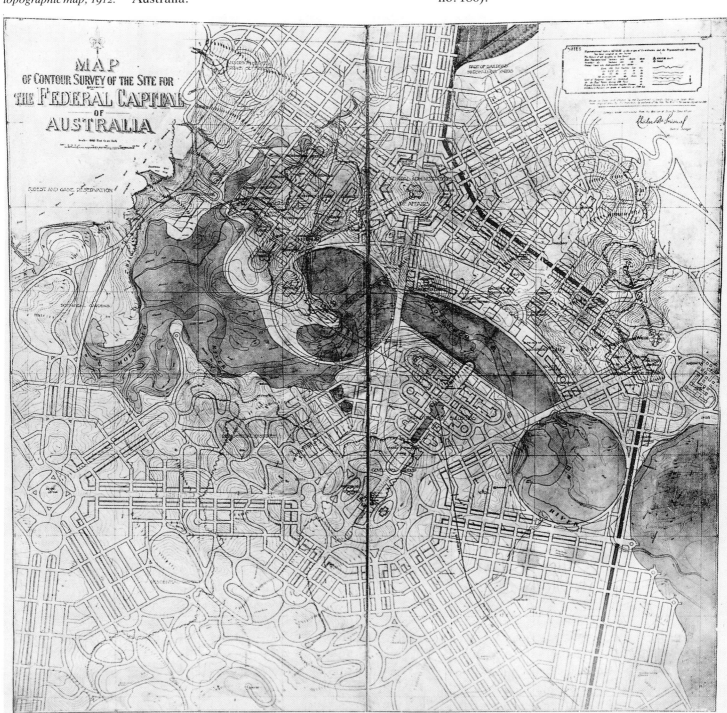

FIRST PREMIATED DESIGN—£1,750.
No. 29.

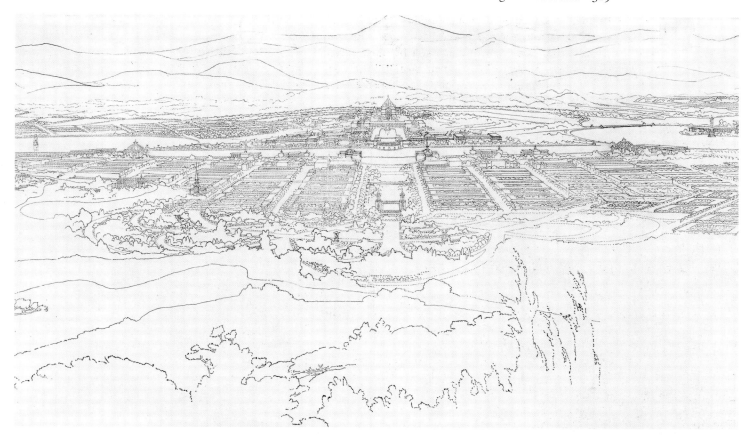

Fig. 11 Griffin, Bird's-eye view of Canberra from Mt. Ainslie, c. 1911-12 (cat. no. 184).

Before leaving Australia, early in November 1913, Griffin had drawn up the guidelines and a program for the competition for the design of the Parliament House buildings to be erected in Canberra. After his departure these guidelines were accepted by the Australian cabinet, and a telegram dated February 5, 1914, informed Griffin that the jury would consist of an English, an American, a French, and a German architect, meeting in London under the chairmanship of an Australian designer.[12] On February 15, Griffin departed Chicago for Europe to select the jurors and lecture on and publicize the competition. In a telegram of March 15 to the Australian government he proposed Sir John James Burnet, Louis Sullivan, Victor Laloux, and Otto Wagner as jurors, with the respected Anglo-Australian architect John Sulman to serve as chairman. These men were formally notified of their appointment on June 25, and the competition was announced on June 30.

In addition to their other qualifications it seems most likely that Wagner was chosen principally because of his "modernism" (his *Moderne Architektur* had been translated by Griffin's architecture professor, Nathan C. Ricker, for his students at the University of Illinois); Burnet because of his adoption of reinforced concrete in business buildings like the Kodak House on Kingsway in London (1910-11); and Laloux surely because of his impressive Gare du Quai d'Orsay (1896-1900) in Paris (now the Musée d'Orsay)[13] and because his atelier at the Ecole des Beaux-Arts was the one most popular among American architecture students.

In a letter to the Minister for Home Affairs dated June 9, 1914, Griffin summarized his activities in America and Europe on behalf of the Canberra project.[14] In San Francisco, upon his arrival, he had been requested to provide a model of his design for Canberra for the Panama-Pacific Exposition, which he executed with Australian funds. While in Chicago he had received a similar request from the authorities in charge of the Exposition Internationale Urbaine in Lyons, France, being organized by Mayor Edouard Hérriot, and had had a second set of his competition drawings rendered for this. He also delivered fifteen lectures to civic and professional groups in Chicago, Milwaukee, and St. Louis, while declining other invitations further afield.

In London he had met with Sir John James Burnet and presented the Canberra plan before the Royal Institute of British Architects. In Paris he had talked with Victor Laloux and acquiesced to the request of Louis Bonnier, Inspecteur général des travaux d'architecture de Paris and president of the Société des architectes diplômés par le gouvernement, to provide renderings of his house designs for an exhibition that took place between June 20 and July 13 at the Musée des Arts Décoratifs.[15] In Germany he had met with the two architectural publishers: Hoffmann in Stuttgart, and Wasmuth in Berlin. In Vienna he had met with Otto Wagner. At each of these stops he had examined municipal facilities and conferred with technical authorities.

From Griffin's correspondence with Wagner, which is available to us,[16] we catch a glimpse of what they focused on. The first note from Wagner to Griffin, dated March 11, 1914 (presumably soon after they had met), notes that he had been able to find nothing about the work of the English Arts and Crafts designer William R. Lethaby and thus could not give an opinion of its artistic merits. Next is a letter of April 10, 1914, from Griffin, listing the members of the jury and stating in German (strangely enough, for he did not speak the language) that Lethaby was in sympathy with "our program" (*unserem Programm*). Burnet, he said, was as well, although his only work that demonstrated this was his Kodak House. On April 23, 1914, Wagner replied, saying that he would translate the competition program into German and publicize it, and would also ask Burnet for information about Kodak House. On May 5, 1914, Wagner wrote Griffin again, stating that he had finished the translation, but that he took exception to a clause specifying that "harmony of style" should be sought. In place of this he proposed saying that they "recognize the evolution of the style of our own age and only want true artists to participate in the competition, true artists *never copy anything*" (Wagner's emphasis). On June 26, Wagner received a garbled telegram informing him that George Temple-Poole had replaced Sulman on the jury. Here the correspondence ends.

Griffin returned to Australia on May 12, 1914. On August 4, Britain declared war on Germany and Austria-Hungary, and Australia immediately followed suit. With the outbreak of war the Canberra project, including the competition for the Parliament House buildings, lost its impetus, and the new political situation meant that Wagner was now the citizen of an enemy state.[17]

In the course of the next five years, Griffin's involvement petered out to a dreary end. Lionel Wigmore and Donald Leslie Johnson have documented the details of Griffin's progressive frustration as Colonel Miller and Colonel Percy T. Owen (Miller's appointee as Director General of the Works at Canberra) denied Griffin effective control of the construction of the project.[18] Finally, in December 1920, Griffin withdrew from it completely.

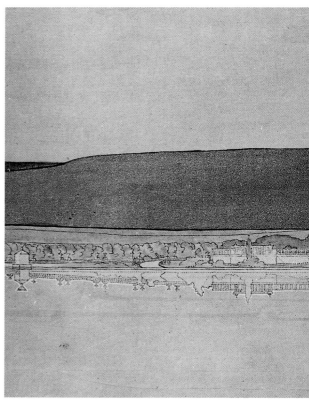

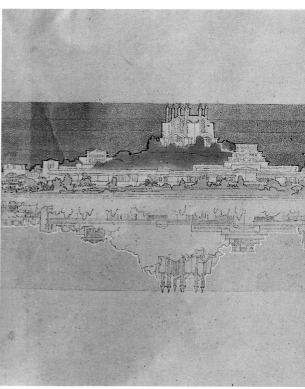

Griffin's Design

A city's plan is a complex and changing thing. Griffin's project for Canberra exists in three slightly different forms. First came the drawings and explanatory essay with which he won the competition of 1912 (figs. 10-13). The perspective drawings in this indicate the buildings with which it might be

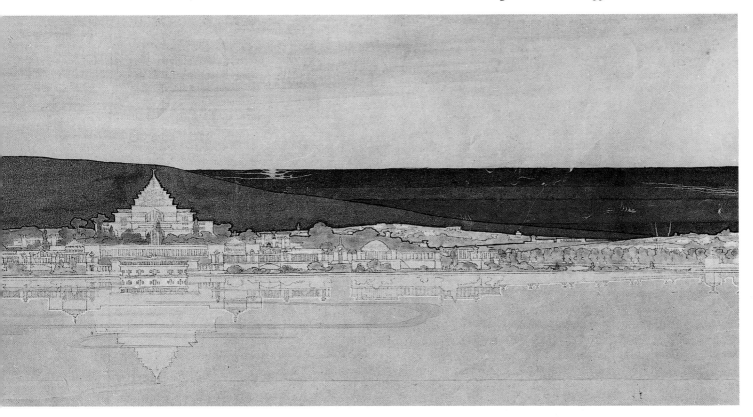

filled out in a monumentalized version of the Prairie style to be executed in reinforced concrete. Second came the revised map and explanatory text made in October 1913, at the end of his first Australian visit. Third is a formal working plan, drawn up in 1918 after work at the site had begun and published, in a revised form, by the committee of architects that succeeded him in 1925.[19] For the purposes of this essay, it is the first, most pristine of these, that we shall analyze.

In the topography of the site Griffin recognized a natural axis running southwest from Mount Ainslie to Bimberi Peak, directly over a low hill, Kurrajong, around which curled the meandering

Fig. 12 Griffin, Elevation of Government Building on Kurrajong Hill, 1912.

Fig. 13 Griffin, Cathedral and Military Academy, seen from Kurrajong Hill, 1912.

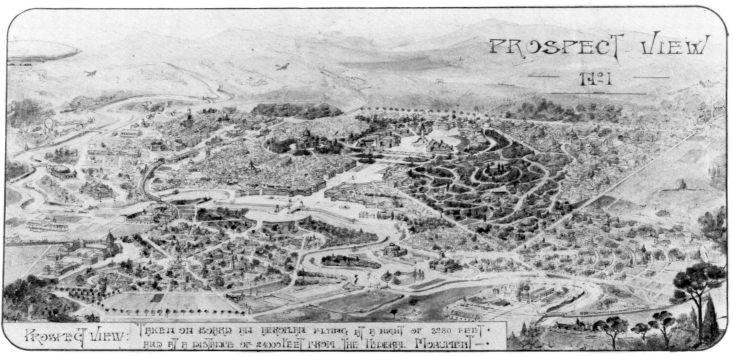

Fig. 14 Agache, Competitive design for Canberra; air field, 1912.

Fig. 15 Agache, Competitive design for Canberra; general view, 1912.

Molonglo River. Crossing this axis at right angles, he perceived a second, minor axis from the peak of Black Mountain, southeastward down the Molonglo flood plain. He constructed his plan upon this natural infrastructure. The Parliament House buildings were placed on Kurrajong, spreading horizontally up the major axis toward the Molonglo, disciplined by an octagonal grid of streets spreading down its slopes and sending diagonal, axial avenues up a valley due northward, out over the flood plain westward and southeastward. Griffin dammed the river, as the program had suggested, and with earthworks formed a string of lakes down the cross axis, around the valley front of Kurrajong. He then carried two of the diagonals of the Kurrajong grid across this lake on bridges, framing the space between two hexagonal nodes, one the city's business district with the main railroad station, the other the municipal government center.

Between the business district and the government center, Griffin ran a broad avenue paralleling the minor axis with the city's cultural institutions — museums of art and natural history, a theater, an opera house, a stadium, and a gymnasium — spread out in parkland along the lakeshore facing Kurra-

PROSPECT VIEW

Nº II

PROSPECT VIEW:
TAKEN ON BOARD AN AEROPLANE
FLYING AT A HIGHT OF 820 FEET
AND AT A DISTANCE OF 6000 FEET
FROM THE FEDERAL MONUMENT

THIS VIEW IS 4 TIMES
LARGER THAN THE GENERAL
PERSPECTIVE (Nº I)

jong. This avenue opens at its center into a tree-lined boulevard carrying the major axis up the slopes of Mount Ainslie to a public park and casino. Around this triangular core of three multi-axial grids, Griffin carried his axes out – where topography permitted – to coalesce in further octagonal and hexagonal units: a manufacturing center to the north; an exclusive residential suburb to the west; and three "agricultural garden cities" to the southeast. A university was laid out below Black Mountain, beyond the business district, on the minor axis to the west, and a military encampment and academy were sited behind the municipal center to the east. In his views of the city, marvelously rendered in a flat Japanese style by Griffin's architect-wife Marion Mahony, the street pattern appears filled out with buildings in picturesque, monumental groupings, geometricized for execution in reinforced concrete.

Neither the majority nor the minority reports of the Australian board of adjudicators included analyses of the projects. With the exception of *Der Städtebau* and the Swedish journal *Arkitektur,* none of the professional journals of the day examined the plans comparatively. Looking at them today, one longs for contemporary guidance; they

are a puzzling group. To begin with one is struck by the simplicity and effectiveness of the American projects as opposed to the complexity and confusion of the other schemes. Magonigle, Comey, and Griffin (figs. 1, 5, 7) establish a single, consistent pattern, orient it to the axis connecting Ainslie and Bimberi peaks, and place the capitol, commercial center, and cultural buildings at clear points of emphasis. These designs can be read at a glance. In contrast, the Griffiths plan (fig. 4) seems chaotic; the Agache design – for all its cleverness in including a garden city, a gas works, government factories, an exhibition park, and a large airfield – seems scattered and unresponsive to the site (figs. 3, 14-16); and Saarinen's plan appears hypnotically elaborate (figs. 2, 17-20).

The German critic Wernecke, writing in *Der Städtebau,* picked out the Gellerstedt plan for close analysis, and one can see that, in spite of its apparent complexity, there is a monumental axis from the railroad station square to the Parliament building dome and that the center of the city is neatly embraced in a defining boulevard (fig. 6). But this, perhaps, is the exception that proves the rule: Gellerstedt and his collaborators elaborate their scheme in such detail, and with so many inflections

Fig. 16 Agache, Competitive design for Canberra; parliamentary group, 1912.

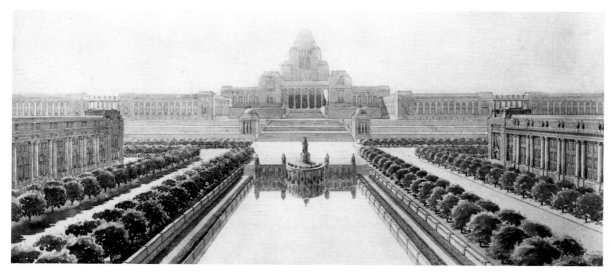

Figs. 17/18 Saarinen, Competitive design for Canberra; Parliament Building, 1912.

Fig. 19 Saarinen, Competitive design for Canberra; general view, 1912.

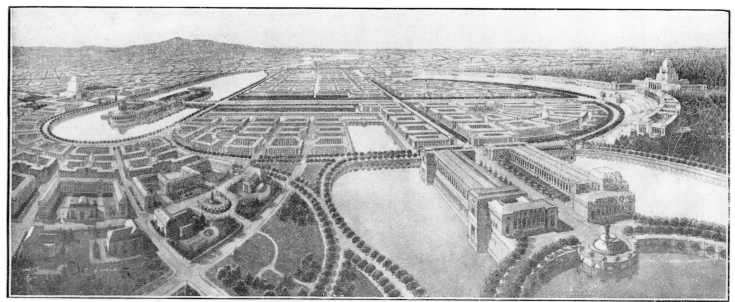

in response to imagined complexities of function and topography, that they appear to be projecting an ancient European city onto this piece of blank Australian ground rather than imposing an organizing pattern that might fill itself in later by degrees.[20]

The American projects include few details beyond those specified in the program; they are basic organizing grids. Among these Griffin's is the clearest and most elastic, both in its system of axes and octagonal nodes and in its monumental tableau centered on the lakes with the parliamentary and cultural groups mirroring each other beneath the silhouettes of Mount Ainslie and Bimberi Peak. Its octagonal and hexagonal grid spreads across the valley floor like the simple, orthogonal patterns of western American cities.

These American projects for Canberra are in the Beaux-Arts style, that is, worked out on a regular, symmetrical system of straight, monumental axes intersecting at one or more starlike points of emphasis at which the principal buildings are sited. Beaux-Arts city planning had been established in the United States with the Court of Honor of the 1893 World's Columbian Exposition in Chicago (see Loyrette, fig. 1) and by the subsequent expositions in Buffalo (1901), St. Louis (1904), and San Francisco (1915). It had later been magnificently applied by the Exposition's Director of Construction, Daniel Burnham, in his projects for the replanning of Washington (1901-02), Cleveland (1902-03), San Francisco (1905), Manila and Baguio in the Philippines (1905), and, finally, Chicago itself (1909). This last plan was published as a book and hotly debated around 1910, when Griffin, Magonigle, and Comey were conceiving their Canberra designs.[21] Burnham's work was but the main thrust of a broad movement for the establishment of monumental city planning in the United States, forwarded by Beaux-Arts architects like Charles Follen McKim, John Mervan Carrère and his partner Thomas Hastings, Edward H. Bennett, and John Galen Howard. Conferences were held, books published, and plans commissioned and sometimes – as in the cases of San Francisco and Philadelphia – partially carried out.

Although American in inflection, the Beaux-Arts movement was French in origin, taking its name from the chief Parisian architecture school, the Ecole des Beaux-Arts. At the turn of the century, that institution was famous for teaching a particularly clear method of architectural organization based on a system of symmetrical monumental axes. This was most clearly manifested in the elaborate designs for single buildings produced by the students at the Ecole, but it could easily be ex-

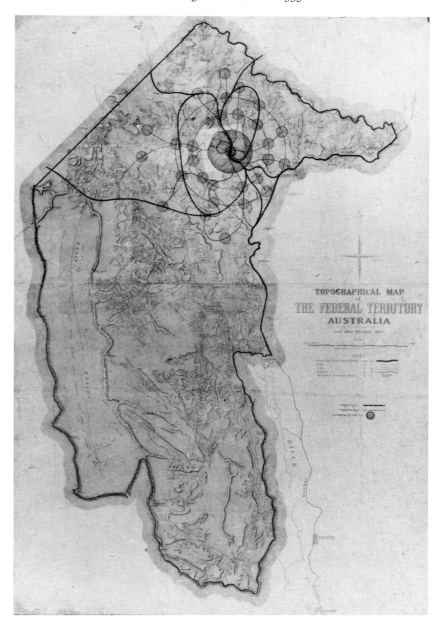

tended to urban complexes, as it was by Emile Bénard in his celebrated winning project in the competition for the design of the University of California at Berkeley (1899).[22] Beaux-Arts principles had informed the dramatic rebuilding of Paris during the Second Empire (1852-1870) and made the city the model (along with Washington, D.C., laid out by the Frenchman Charles L'Enfant in 1791) for Burnham and his friends.

In 1912 another highly regarded alumnus of the Ecole, Ernest Hébrard, produced a project comparable to the Canberra designs, an International World Center, a city to be constructed *ex novo,* dedicated to intellectual cooperation (fig. 21).[23] Like Griffin and the American Beaux-Arts planners, Hébrard centered his composition on a star of avenues, in this case radiating from a skyscraper Tower of Progress, with a broad central

Fig. 20 Saarinen, Competitive design for Canberra; regional plan with satellite cities, 1912.

avenue flanked by cultural institutions leading from it to the spreading, domed Temple of Arts, and beyond to an ornamental basin, a stadium, and the sea. A grid of residential streets organized by repeated stars of diagonal avenues extended out across the countryside of the ideal, flat site. This was a serious project at a time of utopian world organizations like the World Court at The Hague, supported by a widespread movement, and Hébrard's scheme was widely published and discussed. But what critics realized was that for all its abstract geometric coordination, the sequence of spaces did not produce an orchestrated progress toward the chief natural feature, the sea, and that the buildings were impossibly far apart and over-scaled. "We feel enervated rather than inspired by such vast units," A. Trystan Edwards wrote of Hébrard's project in the London *Architects' and Builders' Journal.*[24] In comparison, Griffin's Canberra plan is far more inviting and humanly scaled.

The Capitals of the British Empire

Comparison with the plan of Hébrard is only formal, however. The design of Canberra was a very specific project — the creation of a capital for an important unit of the British Empire. Its equivalents were the contemporaneous plans for the capital complexes at Pretoria and New Delhi. These were not simply patterns of streets but elaborate symbolic statements — ones subtly modified by the different natures of imperialism in South Africa, India, and Australia.

Pretoria came first and is the work of the remarkable imperial architect, Sir Herbert Baker. He had had a typical English architectural upbringing: raised in rural Kent; trained at the Royal Academy by George F. Bodley, Richard Norman Shaw, and George Peto; admiring Ruskin, Morris, and Jekyll. But in 1892 he moved to Capetown, South Africa, and was caught up in the vision of a British Empire embracing the Dutch Boer republics (the Orange Free State and the Transvaal) to the north and stretching all the way to Cairo. After much agitation and the war of 1899-1902, the republics were appropriated by the British, but with the concession of self-government to a larger Union of South Africa and the establishment of the seat of executive government in the old Boer capital of Pretoria, high in the mountainous interior. This was codified in the Act of Union passed on May 31, 1910.

Baker was immediately commissioned to design a suitable complex of capital buildings for the government ministries. In his *Architecture and Personalities* (1944), Baker explains that he rejected sites on the flat plain within the city in order to locate the structure dramatically halfway up the barren hillside of Meintjes Kop to the south, with planted terraces reaching down to the valley (figs. 22, 23). The main building itself was divided into two blocks joined by a long, open, semicircular colonnade reaching back into the hillside, pinned at its ends by two tall domes. This unprecedented shape was to symbolize the union of the English and Boer colonists and to provide an amphitheater for public ceremonies. Beyond the veil of columns, Baker proposed a Hall of Fame in the form of a dome or classical temple, from which an arduous *via sacra* might lead to a small Temple of Peace at the top of the ridge. In the end, only the main building was erected, and without much of the terracing planned below it to face the city.

The style is that of the Anglo-Dutch classical baroque of the seventeenth century, specifically that of Christopher Wren in the Royal Hospital at Greenwich. The detailing is simple, if academic, and inflected with local tropical elements. The siting is superb. Baker later recalled that the symbolism was profoundly admired by Cecil Rhodes as well as by the Boer generals, Louis Botha and Jan Smuts. Baker was an imperialist of his friend Rhodes's stamp: a believer in the English destiny to organize the world and harness the peoples of the earth, with Europeans in command, and natives in support. He was also an artist of symbols, in the simple but earnest manner of a sincere Anglican.[25] His Union Buildings are possessed of a daunting conviction. During World War I, Baker was pleased to relate, his amphitheater was the setting for two splendid ceremonies, one celebrating General Botha's conquest of German Southwest Africa, the other marking General Smuts's victory in German East Africa (renamed Tanganika).

In comparison, the plan for New Delhi, set on a rolling desert plain, seems immense but anticlimactic. The origins of that plan were very different from those of Canberra or Pretoria. It was not to symbolize a political reorganization; that came with the Montagu-Chelmsford reforms of 1919 and necessitated the erection of an asymmetrically sited, round parliament building that spoiled the clarity of the scheme. On the contrary, Delhi was the old Mughal capital of their Indian empire. In 1877, it had been the site of the splendid Durbar at which Queen Victoria was proclaimed Empress of India. Her successor, Edward VII, was similarly honored at a Durbar organized by the Viceroy of India, Lord Curzon, in 1903. On this occasion more than one hundred thousand participants knelt and paraded amid the temporary pavilions set up on the plain north of the city.

VUE GÉNÉRALE À VOL D'OISEAU.

FAÇADE GÉNÉRALE SUR LE CENTRE ARTISTIQUE

Fig. 21 Ernest M. Héb-rard, An International World Centre, 1912; bird's-eye view and elevation.

In 1911 Viceroy Lord Hardinge organized an even more spectacular Durbar, at which George V announced the intention to establish a permanent capital at the Delhi site to symbolize in stone the replacement of the Mughal dynasty by the British monarchy. A Town Planning Committee was set up by the Anglo-Indian authorities, and the well-connected and respected Edwin Lutyens was placed in charge of the design. In 1913 Baker was called from South Africa to assist Lutyens. Their design was published in a three-volume report completed in March 1913.[26]

The plan for New Delhi expressed the orientalized power of the British King. It displayed a Beaux-Arts system of interconnecting axes with public buildings, embassies, and official residences on its spacious acres. (A restricted habitation quarter was set along the northern edge.) There is one dominating axis, the two-mile ceremonial route named King's Way, which terminates in Lutyens's domed Durbar Hall (fig. 24). Around that chamber, and enclosing it, was the huge Viceregal residence, the symbol of Britain's absolute power

assigned to the King's deputy. Flanking the axis and enframing the Viceroy's palace are Baker's two spreading secretariats, in which the entire administration of the subcontinent was to be located. Queen's Way, a cross-axis halfway down the ceremonial road, leads to the railroad station plaza and onward to old Delhi. One critic remarked that the plan seemed laid out for "a perpetual Durbar." Before the constitutional reform of 1919, the only consultative element in the plan was a council chamber inside the Viceroy's house.

How different this all was from Canberra! Lord Hardinge requested the winning plans of the Australian competition in 1912 for examination by his Town Planning Committee. How strange they must have seemed![27] Australia was a very different place and O'Malley a very different man. The initiative for the Australian federation had come from the Australians themselves. They had chosen Canberra's architect by an open competition — one scorned by the profession in Britain and won by a clever young Yankee. Pretoria's and New Delhi's architects had been appointed by the Colonial ad-

Fig. 22 Sir Herbert Baker, Union Buildings, Pretoria, 1910-12; view showing statue of General Louis Botha.

Fig. 23 Baker, Union Buildings, Pretoria, 1910-12; aerial view.

ministration with the approval of the profession in London. This was reflected in the urbanistic results. The plan for Pretoria was an optimistic symbol of the Anglo-Boer union, purportedly spontaneous but in fact imposed by military force, and the plan for New Delhi was the proud expression of British dominion over an alien race. The plan for Canberra, by contrast, was for a place in which to live, promenade, and enjoy cultural and athletic exercises. It is modest, open, and pleasant.

Comparison with the plans for Pretoria and New Delhi makes it evident that one key is the treatment of the capitol building itself. Although the design of the Parliament House buildings was relegated to a separate competition, the plan for Canberra needed to take these projected buildings into account, and Griffin laid them out in some detail. His proposal is unconventional. Griffin's Houses of Parliament occupy low buildings below the brow of Kurrajong, with the administrative offices terracing down to the lake. At the peak of Kurrajong, in a park and flanked by the prime minister's and governor general's residences, is an unfamiliar stepped pyramidal structure which Griffin described as "the general executive headquarters and official headquarters for popular official and social functions and ceremonials."[28] All the major axes of the city plan emanate from its open sides. As an archive and hall of fame it is a remarkable belvedere, completely commanding the city. As a ceremonial hall, its interior would be visible to an immense crowd in the park and along the axes. Where the plan for Pretoria is heroic and that for New Delhi ceremonial, Griffin's plan for Canberra is open and festive, in the manner of the American world's fair complexes at Chicago and St. Louis.

Personalities

Griffin's scheme seems profoundly and unselfconsciously democratic. The spreading out of the cultural buildings in a park along the lakefront, facing the parliamentary group, the casino in the park projected up the sides of Mount Ainslie, and, most importantly, the attractively laid out suburban neighborhoods bespeak an enjoyment of common social activities and the outdoors that informal peoples like Midwesterners and Australians, we imagine, would appreciate for their capital. The simplicity of Griffin's plan, next to the grandiose projects for new or rebuilt cities by his European contemporaries like Saarinen, Baker, Hébrard, and Lutyens, leads one back to his formative experiences in Chicago at the turn of the century.

We have noted that Griffin had grown up in suburban Chicago, had been trained at the University of Illinois, and had worked for Frank Lloyd Wright. This was an extraordinary place and moment in time for a young architect to be trained and to set up practice. It was when Sullivan was still a mighty force – if now more as a writer than as a builder – and Wright a coming one. A bright constellation of young designers gathered about both architects, Griffin and Marion Mahony prominent among them.

More importantly, however, Chicago itself was the new American metropolis, rivaling New York and virtually reinventing architecture. Here there was a new kind of architect – a planner and engineer as much as an artist – a new manner of building – the steel-framed skyscraper – a new style of design in the work of Sullivan and Wright, and a new scale of planning in the projects of Daniel Burnham. One spoke proudly of a Chicago style in the circles of Sullivan and Wright around 1900, but beyond that there was a whole world of Chicago building that extended from the rudiments inculcated at the University of Illinois to the visions of whole rebuilt cities in Burnham's brochures.

Griffin's first Australian friend and supporter, the publisher George A. Taylor, noted that one of Griffin's most formative experiences went back to 1893, when at the age of fourteen he was profoundly impressed by the Court of Honor at the World's Columbian Exposition. Combined with that riveting vision was a profound interest in landscaping and botany. He had devoted the few electives allowed him in the Illinois architecture program to horticultural courses,[29] and he practiced landscape design from the outset, with the laying out of the Eastern State Normal School at Bloomington, Illinois, in 1907.

Otherwise, Griffin designed suburban houses and subdivisions, trying to develop street patterns and house sitings that would complement the natural topography, while arranging several suburban communities to further neighborhood cooperation. The *Western Architect* wrote of these designs in 1913:

Always there is that consideration in his town planning problems of the convenience and happiness of all its citizens with no thought for any special class advantages. In his commutual developments there is, too, a beautiful spirit of neighborliness displayed in that each member considers always the wishes of every other and his grounds are so laid out and his house so designed that it becomes not a thing of joy to him alone but an integral part of a symmetrical plan which adds to the beauty and value of his neighbors' belongings, bringing deeper satisfaction to himself and contributes to the material progress and beauty of the city in which he lives. In all the projects described and illustrated herein Griffin's spirit is so clearly shown that if one were never to meet him they would know the character of the man.[30]

Fig. 24 Sir Herbert Baker and Sir Edwin Lutyens, Viceroy's House and Ministries Building, New Delhi, 1913-30; view showing Republic Day parade; from Robert Grant Irving, Indian Summer *(New Haven, 1981).*

He had a grander vision too. A Chinese delegate to the 1904 St. Louis Fair (officially the Louisiana Purchase Exposition) had him draw up a plan for a new city near Shanghai to replace the old, a project now lost but which Griffin later cited as a precedent for his Canberra scheme. Around 1910 his architecture began to emancipate itself from the influence of Wright, becoming more abstract and monumental in its forms, and displaying Pueblo and Mayan motifs (fig. 12). He experimented with structural techniques using reinforced concrete. He started to receive commissions for public buildings and complexes and treated them in a monumental, geometric manner, translating dramatic, exotic shapes and spaces into the rigid planes of concrete. He claimed that he had followed the political evolution of Australia from the foundation of the Commonwealth in 1900 and was both philosophically and artistically ready when the competition for the design of Canberra was announced in 1911.

The Louisiana Purchase Exposition of 1904 (fig. 25), to which Griffin's Chinese client was a delegate, had tremendous impact on the incipient Chicago School and on Frank Lloyd Wright. Wright was so struck by the extensive German display of architecture and design, dominated by the new, modern work of Josef Maria Olbrich, that he gave his staff at the Oak Park Studio a vacation to go and see it for themselves. Griffin was in the studio and, since his brother Ralph lived in St. Louis, surely took advantage of the opportunity to visit the Fair. His Canberra plans indicate that it

was not just the German pavilion that impressed him. The ensemble of the Exposition, laid out by Cass Gilbert, is a refinement of the 1893 Columbian Exposition scheme, with a series of exterior spaces organized in three axes radiating from an elaborately crowned Festival Hall situated on a hill at their apex. This is clearly the immediate source of the central zone in Griffin's plan for Canberra: the triangle embracing the parliamentary group and the two municipal centers. In both plans the composition spreads out from an open, pyramidal hall, with two lateral diagonal axes carried out to organize a line of monumental buildings facing back toward the hall, which is isolated from them but mirrored in an artificial basin occupying the central axis. The Columbian Exposition may have excited Griffin's first architectural ambitions, but it is the St. Louis Exposition that seems to have focused his urbanistic conceptions. Significantly, Griffin referred to the lake at Canberra as the "Court of Honor reservoir."

There were clearly several elements to Griffin's intellectual predispositions when he conceived Canberra: a midwestern liberal concern for community; a Chicago School effort to develop a new architecture appropriate to function and environment; and a romantic excitement in the new industrial city, given shape by Burnham's Court of Honor and the St. Louis Fair. These elements, in fact, had emerged in Chicago with considerable individual refinement and in a fragile alliance just around 1910. The central factor was Burnham's second great gift to the city, his *Plan of Chicago* (pls. 70-78; cat. nos. 227-36), published by the Commercial Club in 1909, its magnificent drawings on display at the Art Institute, with political support for its execution in the process of being orchestrated.

The Chicago Plan itself, for all the grandiosity of its public squares and monuments, also embraced more practical issues such as transportation, neighborhood development, and a regional park system. Chicago's progressive philanthropists, brought together first at Hull-House, then after 1903 in the large City Club of Chicago, debated the plan and offered counterproposals that emphasized the more down-to-earth, democratic problems.[31] Addresses on urban problems were arranged by leading American and European planners and garden city advocates, including Dr. Albert Suedekum of Berlin (November 1910), Raymond Unwin (June 1911), Thomas Mawson (November 1911), Jacob Riis (January 1910), Henry Hornbostel (March 1912), and Jarvis Hunt (January 1913). The activist George Hooker was named Civic Secretary of the Club in 1903 and in 1911 founded a City Planning

Committee with landscape architect Jens Jensen as chairman and with Wright's assistant William Drummond and architect Dwight Perkins (Marion Mahony's cousin) as members. Membership lists do not survive for this period, so it is unclear whether Griffin himself joined, but it was not an exclusive club. The City Club organized discussions, mounted exhibitions, and finally, in March 1913, organized a competition for an ideal neighborhood plan for a quarter-section in Chicago's outer districts. The winning project by Wilhelm Bernhard was in the new Chicago School style, leaning toward Griffin rather than Sullivan or Wright. Also submitted was a project by Drummond, advised on by Griffin, and a non-competitive plan by Wright.[32] This was followed in 1914 by the competition for a neighborhood center. (Griffin sent a copy of this competition program to Otto Wagner in Vienna.) For a moment just before World War I, all the components of the Canberra plan seem to have been together and the subject of active debate in Chicago.

If the origin of Griffin's solution is clear, what was the source of the resonance it inspired in Australia? It was still no ordinary plan. In its clarity, sincerity, and urbanistic gracefulness it was a remarkable summation and transformation of the ideas discussed among the crowds at the City Club. The idealism and unselfconscious joy that Griffin expressed to the *Times* reporter upon winning the competition appears again in the letter he addressed to King O'Malley on January 21, 1913, when he heard that his plan had been altered.

I had entered this Australian event to be my first and last competition, solely because I have for many years greatly admired the bold radical steps in politics and economics which your country has dared to take, and which must, for a long time, set ideals for Europe and America ahead of the possibility of their accomplishment. . . .

The plan I submitted was, whatever it may have been also, first and last an expression of functions. Regardless of the fact that the bulk of most modern designers' work takes account directly of precedent and prototypes, and has expressed itself in endless tiresome copy and repetition, I maintain and follow in my practice the conviction that these steps are irrelevent, if not unscientific, and that our work is a matter of adapting topography and materials straight toward the needs or functions these are to serve, just exactly as with mechanics and engineering, though the elements of the problem, especially social and esthetic, are decidedly different. . . .

My work has been previously best known in connexion with the development in this country of a type of architecture that is independent of classic, Gothic, or any other historic, or academic basis, and also free from effort to be original, eccentric, or striking, further than results from the contrast between the borrowed finery of applied academic architecture and a straightforward adaptation of present day labour-saving economic constructive methods and materials to the essential, but

often new, functions of our more complex activities. This, in other words, is to treat architecture as a democratic language of everyday life, not a language of an aristocratic, especially educated cult.[33]

After he came to know Griffin, O'Malley remarked that he had not invited him to Australia from the start because it would have been seen as "one Yank bringing out another."

Upon Griffin's arrival in Australia in 1913 he made no bones about his ideas, and some Australians responded. He lectured at the Institutes of Architects of Victoria and New South Wales on democracy, the model of engineering and scientific method, and the necessity of inventing new architectures for new environments. He reiterated these themes and applied them to his Canberra plan in a series of articles in *Building* magazine. The editor, George A. Taylor, prefaced the essays with a ringing declaration of support:

Griffin is a modern evangelist with the gospel of commonsense construction. The ill-ventilated home, the badly built city, produce the soul-crushed individual. The mean street makes the mean man, the sickly woman, the anemic child and the tottering nation.

The world wants rebels in its architecture, as well as in its Art, Theology and Science.

Then shall the people better realise that hymn of mental freedom that is swinging around the universe.

From the earth in the thundering roar of the locomotive and the whirring of the mighty machines; from the sea in the throbbing of the mammoth liners and swift swish of the submarine; from the air in the hum of the aeroplane and the singing spark of the wireless wave rises a paean of praise to the Great Creator for the infinite scope he gives the human intellect.[34]

Fig. 25 Cass Gilbert, Festival Hall, Louisiana Purchase Exposition, St. Louis, Missouri, 1904; from Walter B. Stevens, The Forest City (St. Louis, 1904).

Aftermath

So far we have been addressing O'Malley's competition and Griffin's first Canberra plan. This was the simple, exciting part of the story. There was also the aftermath, documented by Lionel Wigmore and Donald Leslie Johnson. When Griffin established himself definitively in Melbourne to take up his duties as Director of Design and Construction, he found the existing staff in the Ministry of Home Affairs unsympathetic. Colonel David Miller had appointed his friend Colonel Percy T. Owen Director General of the Works at Canberra, and they had proceeded with grading and initial staking-out with only selective regard for Griffin's plan. A long, acrimonious struggle ensued.

In 1916-17 a Royal Commission examined the situation, and Parliamentary Paper 153 for the Session 1914-16 was published documenting the charges and countercharges. In October 1919, Griffin's second three-year term ran out and his appointment was extended only quarterly. In December 1920, he withdrew from the project entirely, refusing to serve on the committee of architects that replaced him. Miller and Owen's hostility may have been bureaucratic resistance to outside interference, but it also might have gone deeper. James Weirick has pointed out that both had fought for the Empire in South Africa. They must have found it difficult to serve under a Yankee pacifist in the creation of the symbolic capital of their Australian Commonwealth.[35]

Griffin stayed in Australia, although he never gave up his American citizenship. He had a circle of enthusiastic friends and, beginning in 1920, they worked together to develop Castlecrag, a picturesque promontory projecting into Sydney Harbor, built up with houses for the Griffins and their friends (including O'Malley) in the style of the buildings in the Canberra competition renderings. Times were hard after the Great Depression struck in 1929, but Griffin produced an extraordinary series of designs for municipal incinerators during the 1930s. In 1935 he visited Lucknow, India, to design a university library, and found such a sympathetic and supportive situation that he and Marion established themselves there for two last years of tremendously productive work. Then Griffin died suddenly in February 1937. Marion returned to the United States, where she spun out utopian ideas and wrote a biography of her husband, *The Magic of America,* before dying in 1962.[36]

In the 1950s, having survived the Great Depression and six years of war, Australians once again turned their attention to the Canberra project. In 1951 the Federal Congress on Regional and Town Planning met in Canberra, with the city itself as its major theme. In 1957 the National Capital Development Commission came into being to study Canberra's development. In 1958, Peter Harrison, an admirer of Griffin's original vision, was appointed Chief Town Planner. Harrison set out to restore the essence of Griffin's plan. In 1963 the Molonglo was dammed, the lake filled, and appropriately named Lake Burley Griffin. Today, finally, the permanent Parliament House is under construction on top of Kurrajong. With the issues and personalities of the earlier years forgotten, the basic strengths of Griffin's original plan have come to be recognized.

The plan for Canberra is an extraordinary but characteristic episode in the history of Chicago design. Like so many productions of that city's architects at the turn of the century, it is simple and practical, yet romantic — and nonetheless unified and effective. The pattern is clear and topographically powerful, yet theatrically dramatic in the government group envisioned terracing up Kurrajong and disarmingly festive in the cultural buildings laid out along the lakeside facing that tableau. In its genre it is the equivalent of Sullivan's skyscraper type, Wright's Prairie School house, and Burnham's conception of a world's fair: a part of the Chicago vision of the modern city.

NOTES

Several friends have been tremendously helpful during my research on this project: Porter Mansfield, who found and photocopied the Australian government publications on Griffin's connection with Canberra; Joan Draper, who read the manuscript and made numerous important criticisms and additions; James Weirick in Canberra, who reviewed again his extensive Griffin research with me; Sharon Irish, who shared her research on Ernest Hébrard and looked up Griffin's academic record at the University of Illinois; Craig Miller, who advised me on Eliel Saarinen's part in the story; Joanna Walker in Pretoria, who shared with me her research on Herbert Baker; Terence McCarthy, the Australian Consul-General in Chicago, who provided many pieces of information and advice; and Henri Loyrette, who helped with Griffin's French contacts.

1   A basic bibliography of Griffin and Canberra would include: Donald Leslie Johnson, *The Architecture of Walter Burley Griffin* (South Melbourne, Australia, 1977); David Van Zanten, *Walter Burley Griffin, Selected Designs* (Palos Park, Ill., 1970); James Birrell, *Walter Burley Griffin* (Brisbane, Australia, 1964); and Lionel Wigmore, *The Long View: A History of Canberra, Australia's National Capital* (Melbourne, Australia, 1963). Griffin's papers and drawings have been split up between the Mitchell Library, Sydney; The Art Institute of Chicago; the Avery Architectural Library, Columbia University, New York; the New-York Historical Society; and the Mary and Leigh Block Gallery, Northwestern University, Evanston, Illinois.

2   There were, of course, other smaller projects elsewhere in the British Empire, especially at Ottawa. A competition for the design of the monumental group of ministry buildings there was announced in 1913, the jury to be presided over by T. E. Collcutt, past president of the R.I.B.A., along with the Canadian architects H.G. Russell and J.O. Marchand. The deadline for submissions was January 2, 1914, later extended to April 2. (*Builder* [Sept. 19, 1913], p. 287; [Nov. 7, 1913], p. 486; *Journal of the Royal Institute of British Architects* 20 [June 28, 1913], p. 612.) Nothing seems to have come of this: by letter of December 20, 1913, Edward Bennett of Chicago – Daniel Burnham's assistant on his urbanistic projects – was retained to produce a general project for this group as well as a report on the replanning of the whole city, which he submitted in January 1915. See the Ottawa papers in the Bennett collection, Burnham Library, The Art Institute of Chicago. Also, Joan E. Draper, *Edward H. Bennett: Architect and City Planner, 1874-1954* (Chicago, 1982).

3   See Herbert Baker's autobiography, *Architecture and Personalities* (London, 1944). Further information has been provided me by Joanna Walker. See also Baker's *Cecil Rhodes by his Architect* (Oxford, 1934).

4   On O'Malley, see Dorothy Catts, *King O'Malley: Man and Statesman* (Sydney, Australia, 1957).

5   See the Australian government publications: *Preparation of Competitive Designs for the Federal Capital City of the Commonwealth of Australia*, 1911, Federal Capital City; *Report of Board Appointed to Investigate and Report to the Minister for Home Affairs in Regard to Competitive Designs*, 1912, Federal Capital City Designs; *Report of Board Appointed to Investigate and Report as to Suitability of Certain Designs for Adoption in Connexion with Lay-Out of Federal Capital*, 1912, Parliament of the Commonwealth of Australia, paper 153 of the session of 1914-15-16, Federal Capital; and *Documents Necessary to Complete Parliamentary Paper No. 153 of Session 1914-15-16 Laid on the Table of the House of Representatives on 16th June, 1915*. All of these are available in the library of the Graduate School of Design at Harvard University. Griffin's competition drawings are preserved at the Australian Archives, Canberra. Griffin's line layout drawings are located in the Department of Architecture, The Art Institute of Chicago.

6   Both the A.I.A. and the R.I.B.A. were working to ameliorate competition regulations at the turn of the century. See, for example, Charles Moore, *Daniel H. Burnham: Architect, Planner of Cities* (Boston, 1921), vol. 1, pp. 98 ff.

7   In comparison, the prizes awarded in the Hearst competition for Berkeley were: first prize, $10,000; second, $4,000; third, $3,000; fourth, $2,000; fifth, $1,000.

Griffin's recommendations for the Canberra Parliament building competition were: first prize, £2,000; second, £1,500; third, £1,000; fourth and fifth, £500; sixth and seventh, £250 (*Parliamentary Paper 153* [note 5], p. 9, letter of Nov. 20, 1913).

8   See *Journal of the Royal Institute of British Architects*, 3rd ser., 8 (July 29, 1911), p. 642; 19 (Nov. 11, 1911), p. 24; 19 (Dec. 9, 1911), p. 115; 19 (May 11, 1912), p. 490. Also the *Times* (London) April 22, 1912, a letter from the R.I.B.A. explaining its action.

9   The A.I.A.'s stance is explained in *American Architect* 102, 1910 (July 31, 1912), pp. 39-40; see also Johnson (note 1), p. 17.

10   All profiled in *Australian Dictionary of Biography* (Melbourne, 1983).

11   The Board's report was published by the Australian government (see note 5).

12   In the Australian government publications (note 5).

13   James Weirick emphasizes the importance of the Gare du Quai d'Orsay. Griffin himself cites Kodak House in a letter to Otto Wagner of April 10, 1914.

14   *Parliamentary Paper 153* (note 5), pp. 37-39.

15   Louis Bonnier, *Musée des Arts Décoratifs...du 20 Juin au 13 Juillet 1914 ... Exposition d'esquisses d'Architecture de l'Architecte Americain Walter-Burley Griffin Organisée par l'Union Centrale des Arts Décoratifs et par la Société des Architectes diplômés par le Gouvernement*, brochure with introductory remarks.

16   These letters are in the possession of the author.

17   There was an abortive effort to revive the competition in 1916: *Journal of the Royal Institute of British Architects*, 3rd ser., 23 (Aug. 26, 1916).

18   *Parliamentary Paper 153* (note 5) for the session of 1914-15-16 documents Griffin's pleas and problems closely.

19   Johnson (note 1), pp. 24-25.

20   Joan Draper makes this observation of American Beaux-Arts planning in general in her 1979 Berkeley doctoral dissertation, "The San Francisco Civic Center: Architecture, Planning and Politics."

21   Published in the celebrated volume *Plan of Chicago* by Daniel H. Burnham and Edward H. Bennett, edited by Charles Moore (Chicago, 1909; republished 1970).

22   Illustrated handsomely in the publication of the winning projects, *The International Competition for the Phoebe Hearst Architectural Plan for the University of California*, (n.p., n.d.), n. pag.

23   Published by the Société Internationale pour Favoriser la Création d'un Centre Mondial, led by Hendrik C. Anderson, *La Conscience Mondiale* (Rome, 1913). See Giuliano Gresleri and Dario Matteoni, *La Citta' Mondiale: Andersen, Hébrard, Otlet, Le Corbusier* (Venice, 1982). I owe this latter reference to Sharon Irish.

24   A. Trystan Edwards, "Creation of a World Centre of Communication," *The Architects' and Builders' Journal* (Jan. 28, 1914), pp. 82-85. Joan Draper (note 20) points out that Bénard's scheme for the Berkeley campus inspired at least one similar observation in the San Francisco *Bulletin*, Oct. 22, 1899.

25   Among Baker's publications is *The Church House: Its Art and Symbolism* (London, 1940).

26   The first, second, and final *Report of the Delhi Town Planning Committee*, published as British Parliamentary Papers, cited in Robert Grant Irving, *Indian Summer: Lutyens, Baker and Imperial Delhi* (New Haven, 1981), pp. 384-85.

27   Ibid., p. 87. Lord Denman, the Governor General of Australia, proudly mentioned Lord Hardinge's request in his speech at the commencement ceremony of the work of Canberra, March 12, 1913; Wigmore (note 1), p. 63.

28   Quoted from Griffin's original typescript (p. 14) a copy of which I owe to the kindness of the Australian Archives.

29   Griffin's record of courses at the University of Illinois shows him to have taken Horticulture 4 and Horticulture 5 during the fall of his senior year. These were virtually the only electives the architecture program allowed.

30   *Western Architect* 20, 8 (Aug. 1913), p. 66.

31   See David P. Handlin, "The Context of the Modern City," *The Harvard Architecture Review* 2 (1981), pp. 77-89. The Club's records are deposited at the Chicago Historical Society. The Club published a regular *Bulletin* with the texts of talks delivered. See also Gwendolyn Wright, *Moralism and the Model Home* (Chicago, 1980).

32   Alfred B. Yeomans, ed., *City Residential Land Development* (Chicago, 1916).

33   *Parliamentary Paper 153* (note 5), pp. 5-7.

34   George A. Taylor, "Walter Burley Griffin, Rebel," *Building* (Oct. 1913), pp. 47-49; Donald Leslie Johnson, "Walter Burley Griffin: An Expatriate Planner at Canberra," *Journal of the American Institute of Planners* 39, 5 (Sept. 1973), pp. 326-36, explores Taylor's somewhat radical, bohemian roots, as well as the fact that he was the principal architectural publisher in Australia until 1930.

35   Wigmore and Johnson (note 1) flesh out the story of the six-year battle between Griffin and Miller and Owen, documented in part in *Parliamentary Paper 153* (note 5).

36   Copies of *The Magic of America* can be found in the Burnham Library, The Art Institute of Chicago, and the New-York Historical Society.

Chicago: A Personal View

Stanley Tigerman

The efforts of heroes do not inevitably result in success. In fact, heroism is more often associated with failure than with its opposite. This relationship is especially true in Chicago, where heroes fall victim to success. Chicago is also a city of disillusionment. In 1924 Louis Sullivan, in a cry of despair, denounced the 1893 Columbian Exposition: "The damage wrought by this World's Fair will last for half a century from its date, if not longer."[1] In 1985 the city of Chicago canceled its plans for a 1992 World's Fair that was to have celebrated not only the five-hundredth anniversary of the discovery of America, but also the one-hundredth anniversary of the event that announced Chicago's coming of age, the same event that Sullivan decried. As the architects of the Columbian Exposition conferred legitimacy upon earlier epochs by their choice of a neoclassical style, so do their postmodern Chicago descendants in their search for a referential language of architecture. It seems as if Chicago architects both then and now suffer a sense of disillusionment with the present.

If one recognizes that disillusionment with the present is accompanied by curiosity about the absent, that is, by the focusing of critical energies toward the memory of an earlier time, then the fascination with "legitimate" architecture of former epochs is certainly what Sullivan was referring to when he voiced his disapproval. Yet it was the mute cry of the unheard hero. Indeed, if nothing else, Sullivan was resoundingly a hero, a figure cast in the mold of other émigrés to the city on the lake whose fortunes have been chronicled by writers from Theodore Dreiser to Saul Bellow. The tortured protagonists of fiction have had their counterparts in architecture. Louis Sullivan and Frank Lloyd Wright — and perhaps even Ludwig Mies van der Rohe himself in the next generation — all desperately attempted to remain heroic and free of the pressures of culture, though continually faced with the aura of the kind of success sought after by Chicago's early commercial and entrepreneurial barons, the Potter Palmers, the Fields, the Swifts, the Armours.

In this nation of practically minded souls accustomed to synthesizing otherwise unusable concepts, reason and utility have always been the stuff of American success. Unfortunately, the result of this synthesizing tends to leave the rationale for a concept mute and inaccessible. The danger of failure can conceivably be avoided by remaining practical and useful, but it is the condition of being heroic that, like a siren's song, leads the architect into uncharted waters, calling him to his eventual demise.

Certainly, Sullivan and Wright (and Mies) were each called, and each ultimately failed. I contend that the specter of failure was raised by Sullivan in 1924 when his review of the entries to the Chicago Tribune tower competition confirmed for him that architects were again under the spell of the classical language of architecture, which had already dominated the 1893 Columbian Exposition. What so enraged Sullivan was the fact that nearly all of the American entries to this seminal event were solidly grounded in either neoclassical or Gothic Revival styles. For Sullivan to perceive that his efforts had indeed garnered almost no followers, no acolytes, no disciples — that his influence was virtually nonexistent within his own time — must have filled him with an overwhelming sense of despair. If, by being heroic, one dares to inhabit the realm of the unknowable future, surely Sullivan must have been distressed to see that the only speculations about such things in 1923 were engaged in by the European architects who submitted entries to the Tribune competition (see, for example, those by Walter Gropius and Adolf Meyer and by Max Taut; see Bruegmann, figs. 11, 12). On his native soil, with his peers seemingly deaf to his challenge, Sullivan had failed. Robbed of the courage and optimism necessary to move ahead in the way that is essential for adventuresome architectural production (John Entenza once referred to Mies van der Rohe as "willing" his buildings into existence),[2] Sullivan's last few declining months in Chicago were disastrous. Like the protagonist of Upton Sinclair's *The Jungle,* Sullivan, almost anonymously, collapsed in frustration and failure in a cheap, South Side hotel. Only much later was his star to rise as that of the much maligned, misunderstood authentic hero of his era. But it is the destiny of the

Fig. 1 View of Chicago, looking north, c. 1935.

failed hero to be elevated only after death, at which time it is safe for all to honor him. Instead of having to contend with heroism while it is present, it seems easier to deal with it once it is securely distanced from us.

Even as Sullivan was crying out in despair, however, signaling the beginning of the end of heroism in Chicago architecture, another kind of architect was arising in this inland capital of the prairie. This architect seemed to understand thoroughly the kind of architecture that was needed to dispel the déclassé image of Chicago around the world and to replace it with historically referential, and hence creditable, architecture. This kind of architect was rooted in usefulness, yet he combined with it the capacity to elaborate pretensions and conceits architecturally in celebratory ways. This architect of accommodation was Daniel H. Burnham, the role model for the generation of architects who followed. Burnham not only successfully combined utility with visions of legitimate architectural forms – especially those like classicism which always denoted credibility – but he was also able to carry out the planning implications that he (and others) had merely proposed at the Columbian Exposition. Burnham's descendants – among them, David Adler, Benjamin Marshall, and Howard Van Doren Shaw, and, for that matter, all manner of large-scale firms like Holabird and Root; Graham, Anderson, Probst and White; and even Skidmore, Owings and Merrill – came of age just as Chicago was needing their services to achieve architectural parity with other American cities.

Sullivan's legacy, the heritage of heroism, was claimed by his foremost student, Frank Lloyd Wright, whose influence was also seriously diminished by the Tribune Competition. Wright's concepts were no longer seen as paradigmatic as they had been at the turn of the century, for the new generation of Chicago architects took for granted that they had to speak the accepted language, not oppose it. Wright was not, of course, without influence: one thinks of the center of gravity of De Stijl or of the Bauhaus; and certainly the European career of Mies van der Rohe was informed by the 1910 Wasmuth exhibition and subsequent publication of Wright's drawings. A populist extension of Wright's influence in this country was manifested in the open planning of California style domestic architecture (most notably after World War II), but Wright never shaped the high art of architecture and its later practitioners as he doubtless hoped to do. In all events, Wright had already left Chicago, where his earliest, most optimistic work had risen. He no longer seemed welcome, though perhaps his eccentric personal and domestic behavior, more than anything else, contributed to this. In any case, there didn't seem to be a lot of room for a hero in a city more interested in success.

The generation of architects that followed the highly productive building period of the 1920s was not particularly engaged in major architectural exploration. By the time American architectural production was again in full swing in the frenetic 1950s, the careers of many Chicago architects had been terminally disrupted by one decade of disillusionment brought on by the Great Depression and another spent in, or recovering from, a war of apocalyptic proportions. The displacement of strong beliefs in one's own time brought with it a loss of innocence that pervaded Chicago architecture. Utility seemed to be all that mattered in architectural production, and the position of the hero appeared to be permanently vacated.

But was not Mies himself essentially heroic? That is, by virtue of being the first to go against the grain, especially when he began his explorations into the possibilities implicit in the expression of the exposed structural frame, as in Promontory Apartments (1946-49) and 860-880 Lake Shore Drive Apartments (1948-51). Such revolutionary buildings seemed extraordinary in light of conventional architecture, with its masonry facades with "punched" openings, simulating the classical language again. Of course, Mies and his peculiar brand of heroism also ultimately failed in Chicago, since the cadre of disciples who utilized Miesian expression did so reductively in their search for practical application apart from theoretical investigation.[3]

Sullivan, Wright, and Mies were all first-generation Chicagoans: Sullivan fresh from Boston, Wright down from the hills of Wisconsin, and Mies self-exiled from Germany. All were removed from their native grounds. They were all displaced persons, who, though they may have longed for what was lost or missed, were conditioned by a state of uneasiness with the present that brought their individual heroism sharply into focus. It is difficult to become successful while residing in a strange and foreign place; it is almost more natural to react in such a way that one's efforts are misconstrued as attempts at being heroic. Sullivan, Wright, and Mies all acted in ways not always consonant with their locality, Chicago, and the responses of others to their architectural texts must surely have further isolated them and reinforced their sense of exile.

On the other hand, Burnham's successors and the well-mannered, respectable firms that were the very models of utility capitalized on the inventions of the heroes they displaced. To Chicago's everlasting credit as the capital of normative American

Fig. 2 View of Chicago, looking northwest, showing Grant Park and Buckingham Fountain, c. 1929.

pragmatism, the city expunges, where necessary, any fringe element considered unusable. At the same time, it transforms conceptual inventiveness into the grist from which utilitarian commodities are made. The genius of America lies in its ability to transform heroism into success, putting ideas to practical use, making the unusable usable.

While innocence is inexorably linked to the optimistic acts of the hero, knowledge, and with it skepticism, is required to be practical. There is little doubt that Chicago now suffers from an apparently terminal case of loss of innocence. The Chicago architects of the 1960s and 1970s who tried to expand on the useful aspects of Mies's architecture knew that usefulness has its appropriate rewards. Their brand of historicism was as mimetically contrived as that of any neoclassical or postmodern architect bracketing the one-hundred-year period between the great fair that was and the one that, apparently, will never be. A society conditioned by a loss of innocence is basically uninterested in and skeptical about abstraction. Anything not comfortably referential and familiar is put a safe distance away. Nothing in particular guided the ways in which Sullivan, Wright, and Mies forged into the future, except their own individual courage. But in order to produce work considered useful, the succeeding generation of architects de-voted to following the careers of these three heroes had to remove whatever features they felt were inexplicable or unnecessary. In so doing, they reduced invention to convention. These mimetically inclined disciples also displaced the originals to whom they had originally deferred. The heroism of Sullivan, Wright, and Mies was marked by their inability to distance themselves from their work. Their visceral attachment to architectural production made each of them ultimately vulnerable to failure. They were revered in the very ways religious leaders are revered, and they failed so that we might succeed — as we go about displacing the intrinsic characteristics of each as we see fit and replacing them with our precious notions of utility, something that we understand thoroughly and that society accepts implicitly. Ultimately, then, we spare society the difficult task of analyzing the essential nature of the work of the hero.

NOTES

1 Louis H. Sullivan, *The Autobiography of an Idea* (New York, 1924), p. 325.
2 Spoken at the Arts Club of Chicago in 1966, upon the occasion of Mies's receipt of the gold medal from the Chicago chapter of the American Institute of Architects.
3 See Stanley Tigerman, "Mies van der Rohe and his Disciples, or The American Architectural Text and its Reading," in *Mies Reconsidered: His Career, Legacy, and Disciples*, ed. John Zukowsky (Chicago, 1986), pp. 99-107.

Plates

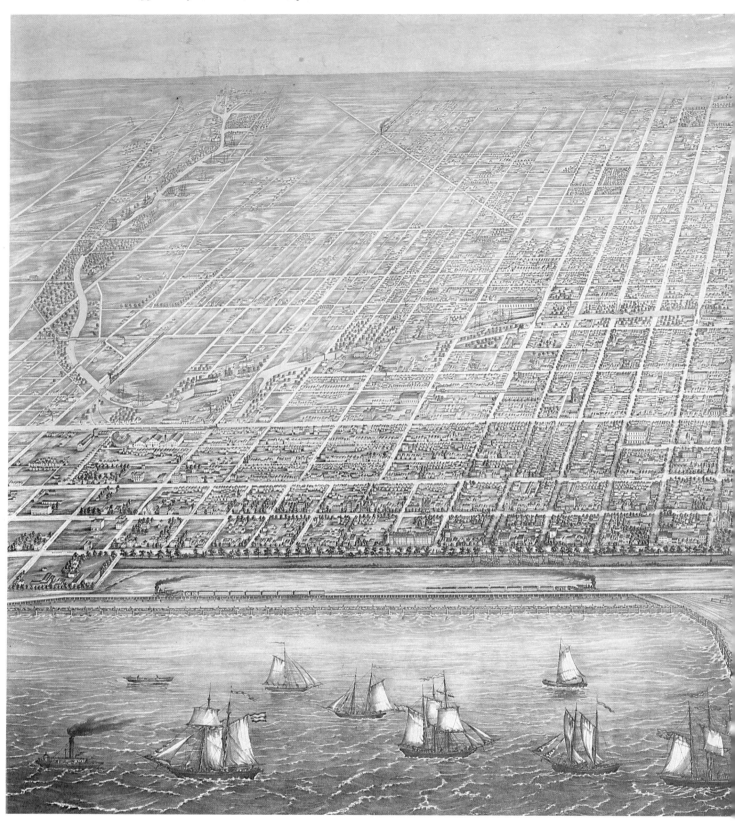

1   I. T. Palmatary and Charles Inger, Bird's-eye view of Chicago, 1857 (cat. no. 3)

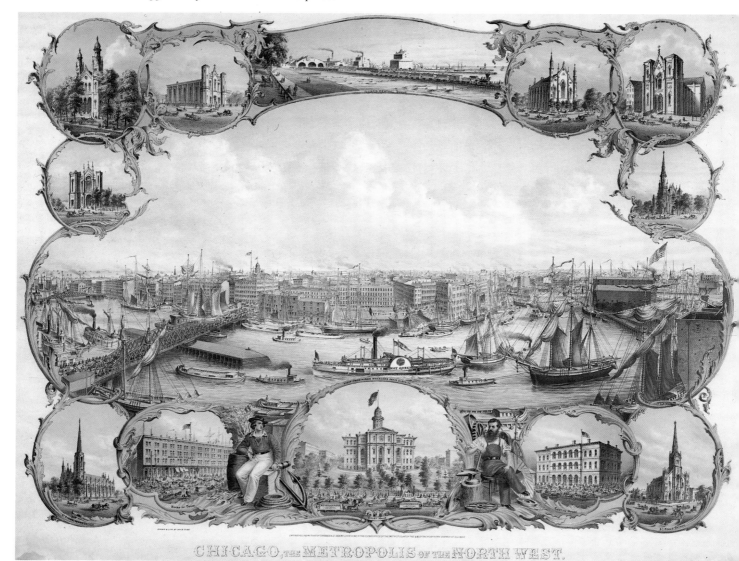

CHICAGO, THE METROPOLIS OF THE NORTH WEST.

4   CHARLES FÜRST, Rendered elevation
of a villa, c. 1870 (cat. no. 13)

2   LOUIS KURZ, Chicago, the Metropolis
of the Northwest, 1864 (cat. no. 4)

3   JOSHUA SMITH, Chicago as
seen after the great conflagration, 1871
(cat. no. 5)

5   NATHAN RICKER, Rendered elevation of a mansard roofed villa, 1872 (cat. no. 25)

P. B. WIGHT, Rendered elevation and partial section of the Eliphalet W. Blatchford House, 1875 (cat. no. 20)

7 CARTER, DRAKE AND WIGHT,
Perspective rendering
of the Lenox Building, delineated
by John Wellborn Root, 1872
(cat. no. 18)

8   CARTER, DRAKE AND WIGHT,
Perspective rendering
of the Stewart-Bentley Building,
delineated by
Daniel H. Burnham, 1872 (cat. no. 17)

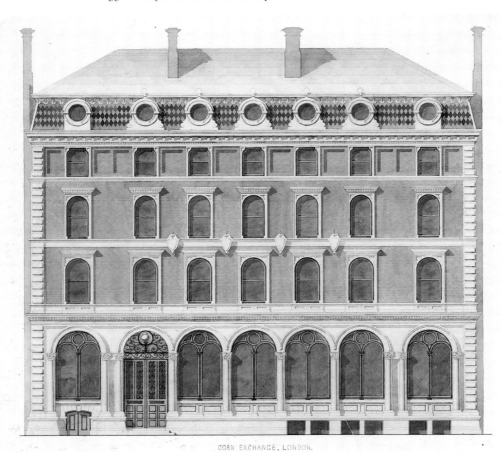

CORN EXCHANGE, LONDON.

9
NATHAN CLIFFORD RICKER,
Rendered elevation of
the Corn Exchange, Londo
1872 (cat. no. 24)

10   BURNHAM AND ROOT,
Elevation of the Rookery,
1885 (cat. no. 58)

11   BURNHAM AND ROOT,
Rookery,
209 South LaSalle Street,
1885-87, exterior

12/13   ADLER AND SULLIVAN
Stock Exchange Trading Roo
(1893-94), reconstructed
in 1976-77 at The Art Institut
of Chicago
(see cat. nos. 129-31)

14   L. PRANG & CO.,
Poster of Home Insurance Bui
c. 1885/86 (cat. no. 55)

THE CHICAGO BUILDING OF THE HOME INSURANCE CO.

OF NEW YORK

/16   HOLABIRD AND ROCHE,
93 addition to Monadnock Building
Burnham and Root, 1891),
West Jackson Blvd., exterior
d detail

17   D. H. BURNHAM AND CO.,
Fisher Building, 343 South Dearborn Street, 1896,
exterior detail

18/19   PETER J. WEBER, Elevation of an addition
to the Fisher Building, 1906 (cat. no. 239)

20   HOLABIRD AND ROCHE,
Perspective rendering of
the McClurg Building, 1899
(cat. no. 63)

21-24   J. W. Taylor, Panorama of Chicago, 1913 (cat. no. 96)

25   ADLER AND SULLIVAN, Auditorium Building, northwest corner of Michigan Avenue and Congress Parkway, 1887–89, exterior

26   HENRY IVES COBB, Newberry Library, 60 West Walton Street, 1892, detail of main entrance

27   ADOLPH CUDELL AND ARTHUR HERCZ,
Perspective rendering
of Francis J. Dewes House, 1896
(cat. no. 79)

8   BURNHAM AND ROOT,
erspective rendering
f the Max A. Meyer House, 1888
cat. no. 73)

29 H. H. RICHARDSON, Perspective rendering of the J. J. Glessner House, 1885/87 (cat. no. 68)

30 H. H. RICHARDSON, Perspective rendering of the living hall and stairs of the J. J. Glessner House, 1886/87 (cat. no. 69)

31   H. H. Richardson, J. J. Glessner House, interior of dining room with furniture by Charles Coolidge (cat. no. 70)

32   Isaac E. Scott, Cabinet-bookcase for the J. J. Glessner family, c. 1875 (cat. no. 23)

33   HOWARD VAN DOREN SHAW, Architect's desk, from "Ragdale," 1897 (cat. no. 100)

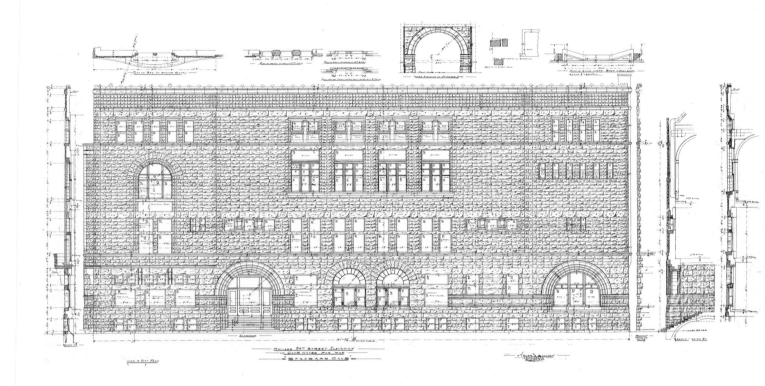

34   ADLER AND SULLIVAN, Revised 24th Street elevation, partial section, and other details of the Standard Club, 1887 (cat. no. 117)

35   CHARLES S. FROST, Perspective rendering of the Calumet Club, 1893 (cat. no. 78)

36   HOWARD VAN DOREN SHAW, Perspective view of Phi Delta Theta Fraternity House, Champaign, Illinois, 1922 (cat. no. 105)

37   HERMAN VALENTIN VON HOLST, Perspective rendering of "Glamis," Bethlehem, New Hampshire, 1904 (cat. no. 86)

38   HOLABIRD AND ROCHE, Perspective rendering of the University Club, 1908 (cat. no. 85)

39 LOUIS H. SULLIVAN, Carson Pirie Scott and Company, southeast corner of State and Madison streets, 1899, detail of main entrance

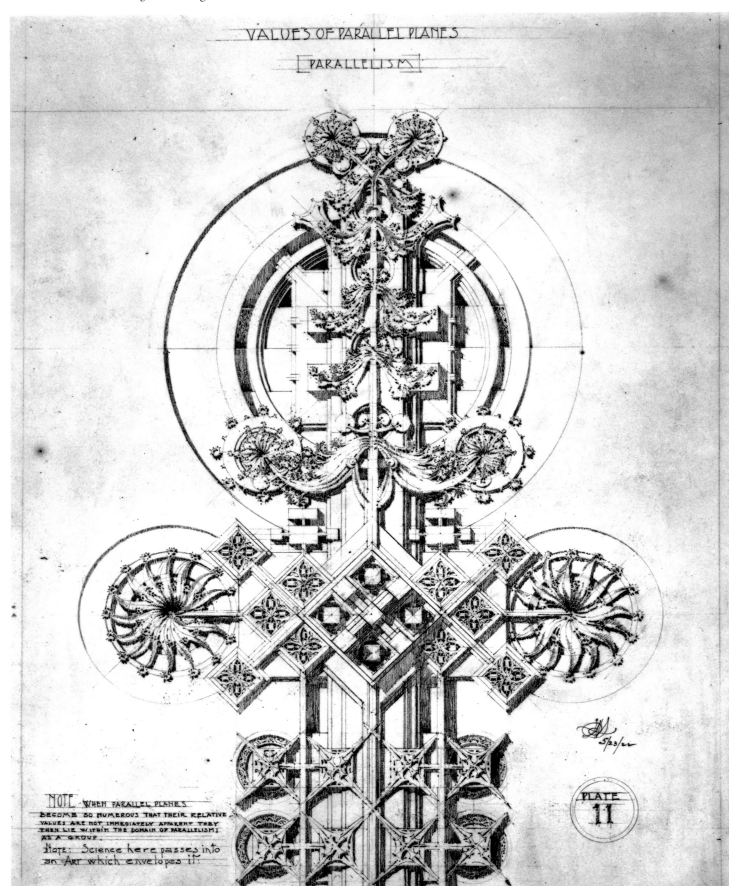

40 LOUIS H. SULLIVAN, "Values of parallel planes," 1922 (cat. no. 160)

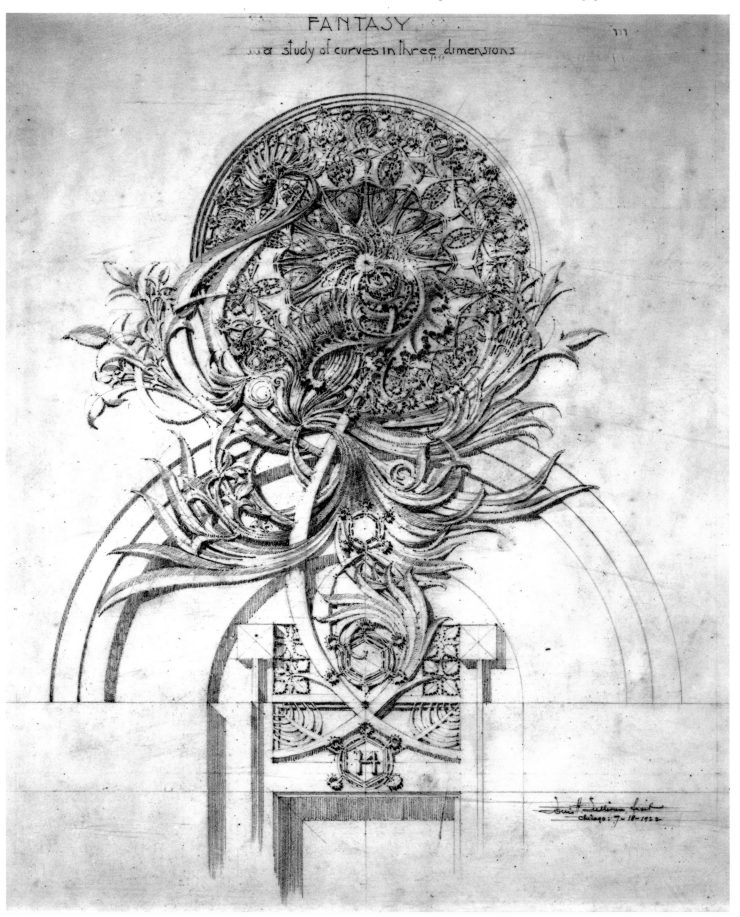

41   Louis H. Sullivan, "Fantasy, a study of curves," 1922 (cat. no. 162)

42   LOUIS H. SULLIVAN,
Getty Tomb, Graceland Cemetery, 1890

43   LOUIS H. SULLIVAN, Perspective rendering of
St. Paul's Methodist Episcopal Church, Cedar Rapids,
Iowa, 1910 (cat. no. 142)

44   LOUIS H. SULLIVAN, South elevation of
St. Paul's Methodist Episcopal Church, 1911 (cat. no. 144)

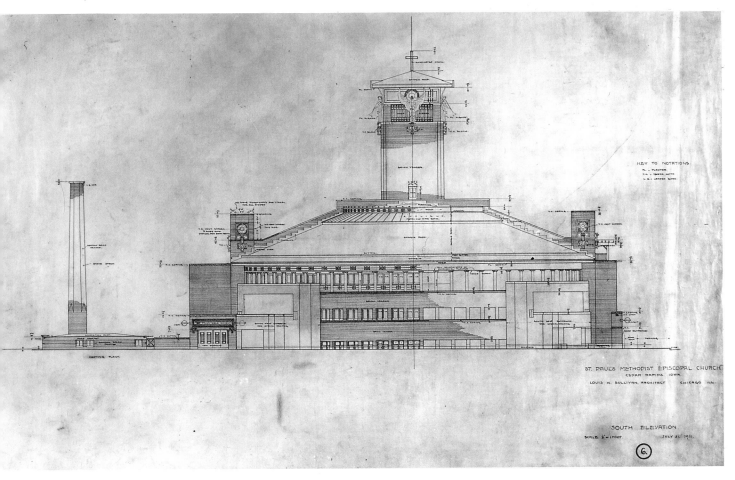

THE FRANCIS APARTMENT BUILDING BUILT FOR THE TERRE HAUTE TRUST CO IN 1895 ✦ DIVIDED INTO THREE ✦ FOUR ✦ AND FIVE ROOM APARTMENTS ✦ EXTERIOR OF YELLOW FIRECLAY ROMAN BRICK ✦ CORNICE AND DADO CREAM WHITE VITREOUS TERRA COTTA BOND STONE COURSES BASE AND WATER TABLE OF BUFF BEDFORD ✦ FINISHED IN QUARTERED WHITE OAK ✦ PAINTED WALLS TILED BATHS MARBLE AND MOSAIC ENTRANCES

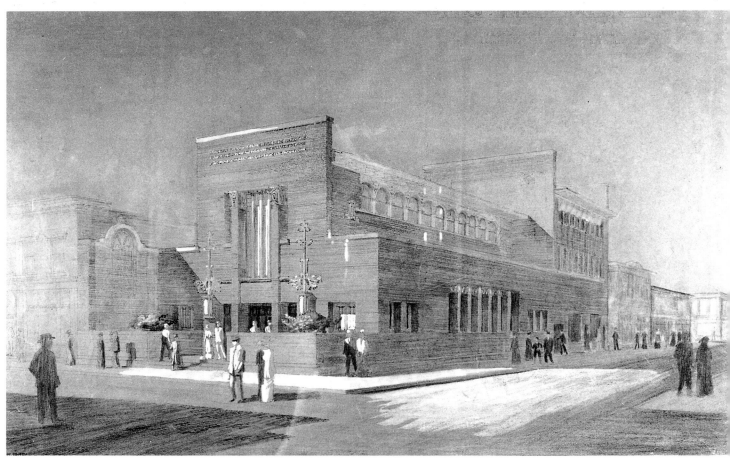

45   FRANK LLOYD WRIGHT, Perspective rendering
of the Francis Apartments, 1895 (cat. no. 166)

46   PURCELL, FEICK AND ELMSLIE,
Perspective rendering of the proposed First National Bank
of Mankato, Minnesota, 1911 (cat. no. 147)

47   ALFONSO IANNELLI with FRANK LLOYD WRIGHT,
Head of a Sprite from Midway Gardens, Chicago, 1914
(cat. no. 192)

48   GEORGE MANN NIEDECKEN,
Presentation rendering of the proposed interior of the
Henry Ford House, c. 1910 (cat. no. 182)

49   WALTER BURLEY GRIFFIN AND
MARION MAHONY GRIFFIN, Bird's-eye view of
Rock Crest / Rock Glen, c. 1912 (cat. no. 186)

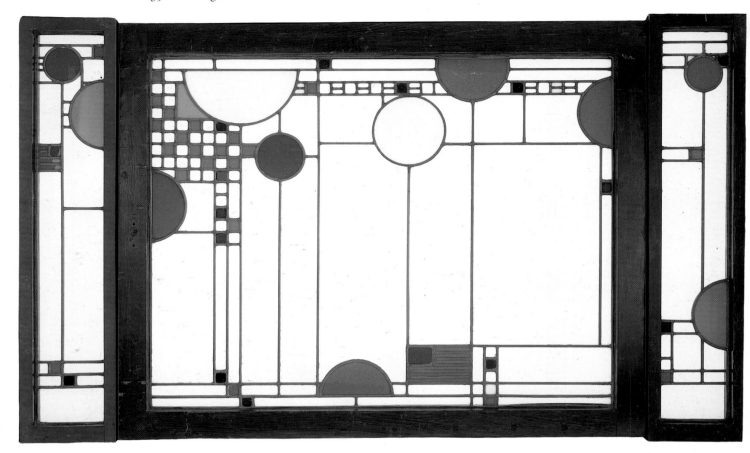

50 FRANK LLOYD WRIGHT, Triptych window from a niche in the Avery Coonley Playhouse, 1912 (cat. no. 183)

51 FRANK LLOYD WRIGHT, Interior view of the Avery Coonley Playhouse, 1912

52 FRANK LLOYD WRIGHT, Dining room furniture from the Robie House, 1909 (cat. no. 176)

53 FRANK LLOYD WRIGHT, Robie House, Interior view of the dining room, c. 1910

To D.H. Burnham
with my Compliments
Jules Guérin

54   D. H. Burnham
and Co.,
Perspective rendering
of the Flatiron Building,
New York, 1902
(cat. no. 214)

55   D. H. Burnham
and Co.,
Perspective study
of the proposed
colonnade of Eaton's
Department Store,
Toronto, 1912
(cat. no. 220)

56   D. H. Burnham and Co.,
Perspective rendering of
the proposed addition to the 1891
Land Title and Trust Co. Building,
Philadelphia, 1900 (cat. no. 214)

57
GRAHAM, ANDERSON,
PROBST AND WHITE,
Continental Illinois
National Bank and Trust
Co. Building, 231 South
LaSalle Street, 1924,
second-floor interior

58   D. H. BURNHAM
AND CO., Railway
Exchange Building
(now Santa Fe Center),
224 South Michigan
Avenue, interior of
lobby

59   D. H. BURNHAM AND CO.,
Perspective rendering
of the Conway Building, c. 1912/14
(cat. no. 225)

60
Lewis Edward Hickmott,
World's Columbian Exposition (detail),
1894 (cat. no. 210)

61   THURE DE THULSTRUP,
Perspective view of the
lakefront at the World's Columbian
Exposition, c. 1893 (cat. no. 211)

62   JOHN WELLBORN ROOT,
Design for a proposed Fine Arts Museum,
c. 1890 (cat. no. 199)

63   PETER J. WEBER, Perspective view
of the Chocolat Menier Pavilion, 1893 (cat. no. 203)

COMPETITIVE DESIGN FOR THE CHICAGO PUBLIC-LIBRARY BUILDING.

Perspective View from the South East

P. B. Wight, Architect.
Chicago.

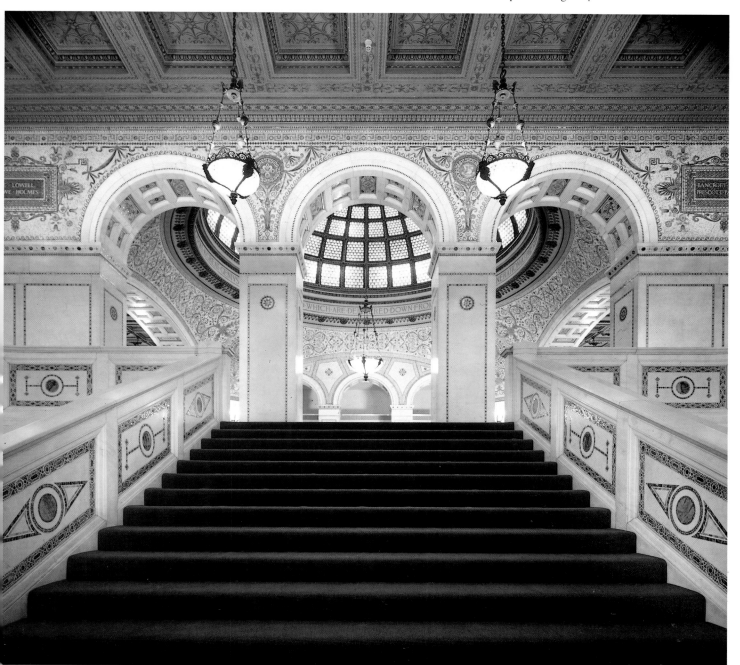

64   P. B. Wight, Perspective rendering of a
competitive design for the Chicago Public Library, 1891
(cat. no. 198)

65   Shepley, Rutan and Coolidge,
Chicago Public Library, northwest corner of Michigan Avenue
and Washington Street, 1891-97, exterior

66   Shepley, Rutan, and Coolidge,
Chicago Public Library, interior of mosaic staircase

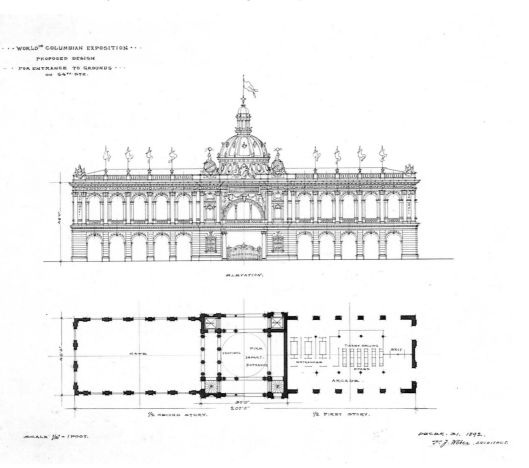

···WORLD'S COLUMBIAN EXPOSITION···

PROPOSED DESIGN

··· FOR ENTRANCE TO GROUNDS ···
ON 64TH STR.

67 PETER J. WEBER,
Proposed design for entrance
to grounds on 64th Street,
World's Columbian Exposition,
1892 (cat. no. 201)

68 PETER J. WEBER,
Proposed design for entrance
to grounds on 60th Street,
World's Columbian Exposition,
1893 (cat. no. 202)

69 Jules Guérin for
DANIEL H. BURNHAM AND
EDWARD H. BENNETT,
Rendered elevation of the
proposed Civic Center, 1908
(cat. no. 234)

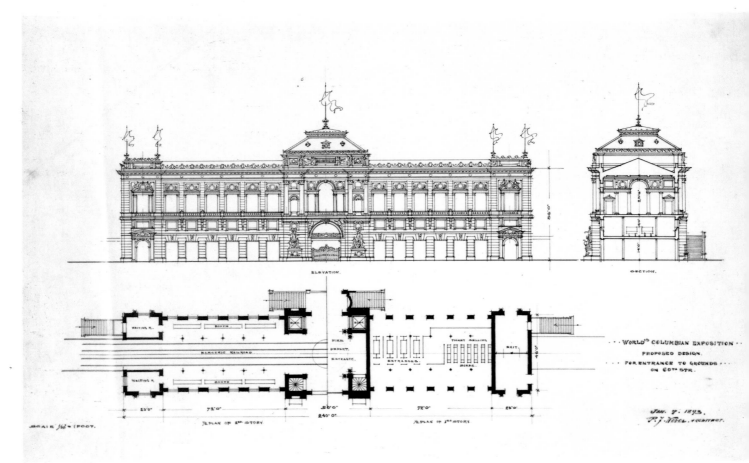

70/71   Jules Guérin for DANIEL H. BURNHAM AND EDWARD H. BENNETT,
View of Chicago from Jackson Park to Grant Park (cat. no. 227)

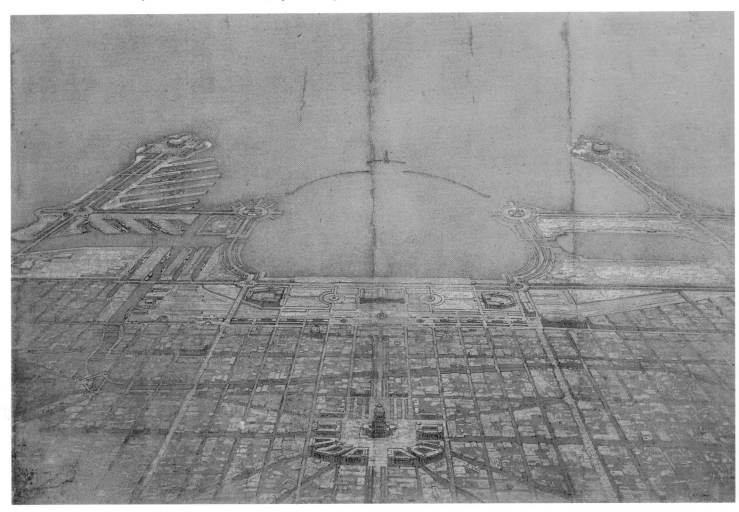

72   Jules Guérin for DANIEL H. BURNHAM AND EDWARD H. BENNETT,
View of the proposed development of the City Center (cat. no. 236)

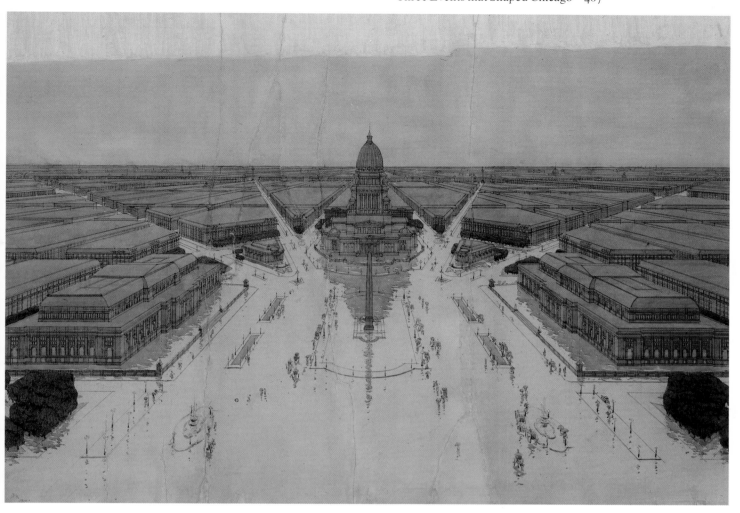

73   Jules Guérin for DANIEL H. BURNHAM AND EDWARD H. BENNETT,
View west of the proposed Civic Center Plaza (cat. no. 232)

74   Attributed to Fernand Janin for
DANIEL H. BURNHAM AND EDWARD H. BENNETT, Plan of
the business center of Chicago, c. 1908 (cat. no. 233)

75   Fernand Janin for
DANIEL H. BURNHAM AND EDWARD H. BENNETT, Elevation
of the proposed Civic Center (detail), 1908 (cat. no. 235)

76   Chris. U. Bagge for DANIEL H. BURNHAM AND EDWARD H. BENNETT,
View of Michigan Avenue looking towards the south, c. 1908 (cat. no. 230)

77   Jules Guérin for DANIEL H. BURNHAM AND EDWARD H. BENNETT,
Rendering of the proposed boulevard to connect the north and south sides of the river (cat. no. 229)

78 Jules Guérin for Daniel H. Burnham and Edward H. Bennett, View of Chicago looking west (cat. no. 228)

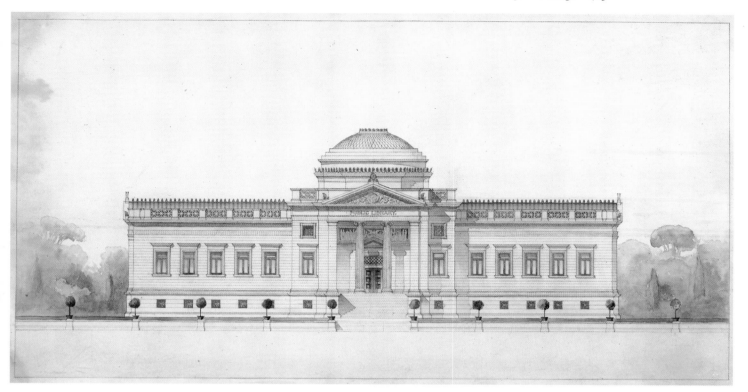

79 RICHARD YOSHIJIRO MINE,
Rendered elevation of a proposed War Memorial,
1921 (cat. no. 46)

80 AUGUST C. WILMANNS,
Rendered elevation of a public library,
c. 1896 (cat. no. 80)

81 PETER J. WEBER,
Perspective rendering of a
skyscraper in the Chicago School style,
1910 (cat. no. 240)

82   PETER J. WEBER,
Perspective rendering of a skyscraper
in the classical style, c. 1910/15
(cat. no. 241)

83   FROST AND GRANGER,
Perspective rendering of an addition
to St. Luke's Hospital, c. 1904
(cat. no. 91)

84   MARSHALL AND FOX,
Perspective study of the Blackstone Hotel,
Theater, and proposed annex, c. 1911/15
(cat. no. 242)

85   MARSHALL AND FOX,
Perspective rendering of the Edgewater
Beach Apartments, 1927 (cat. no. 251)

86 HOLABIRD AND ROCHE,
Stevens Hotel
(now Chicago Hilton and Towers),
720 South Michigan Avenue, 1927,
exterior

87 HOLABIRD AND ROCHE,
Stevens Hotel, interior of great hall

88 GRAHAM, ANDERSON, PROBST
AND WHITE, Wrigley Building,
410 North Michigan Avenue, 1921-2
exterior

89   PETER J. WEBER,
Perspective rendering
of 3400 North Sheridan Road,
c. 1915/17 (cat. no. 245)

90   WILLIAM DRUMMOND,
Competitive entry for
the Chicago Tribune tower,
1922 (cat. no. 258)

91   HOLABIRD AND ROCHE,
Competitive entry
for the Chicago Tribune tower, 1922
(cat. no. 264)

COMPETITION
FOR
THE NEW TRIBUNE BUILDING

92   RICHARD YOSHIJIRO MINE,
Competitive entry
for the Chicago Tribune tower, 1922
(cat. no. 255)

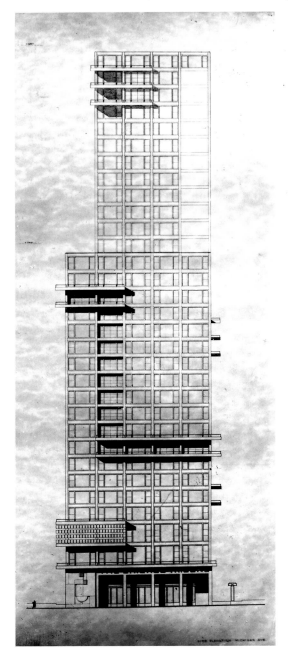

93   WALTER GROPIUS, Competitive
entry for the Chicago Tribune tower, 1922
(cat. no. 256)

94   RAYMOND HOOD OF HOWELLS AND HOOD,
Perspective study of competitive
entry for the Chicago Tribune tower,
1922 (cat. no. 269)

95   ELIEL SAARINEN, Perspective
study of the Chicago Lakefront Project, 1923
(cat. no. 276)

Evanston Illinois 1923

96   Wrigley Building and Tribune tower, view from the Wacker Drive embankment of the Chicago River

Catalogue

John Zukowsky

*Note. Dimensions are given in centimeters with height preceding width.
Lenders to the exhibition are indicated as such, and all donations to The Art Institute of Chicago are credited as gifts of their respective donors.*

I. Chicago: The Historic Context

Although Chicago was visited by French missionaries and explorers in the late 1600s, it was not settled until more than a hundred years later by fur traders, among whom was British-born John Kinzie (1803-1865). Often considered the "father of Chicago" because his house and investments were among the largest in the village, Kinzie became an important real estate speculator and village leader. Chicago was grid-planned in 1830, and incorporated in 1833 as the village grew with the prospect of the building of the Illinois and Michigan Canal. But it was the meteoric rise of the railroads that transformed this flat site on Lake Michigan into a national transit hub. Chicago blossomed, then, from the fortified village of Fort Dearborn (fig. 1) of 1803 (rebuilt in 1816 after being burned 1812) into a prairie city within the next half century. The prints and views on display are intended to survey this rapidity of growth within the grid. This expansion was partly accomplished through the development of the balloon frame — inexpensive, milled construction that enabled the quick erection of buildings.

Chicago's disastrous fire of October 8-10, 1871, created an urgent need and a tremendous opportunity for architects, and they settled here from eastern cities such as Boston and New York and from places in faraway

Fig. 1 Bird's-eye view of Ft. Dearborn, 1803.

Europe, particularly Germany. In rebuilding the city, these architects helped to develop successful solutions for fireproofing a steel structure, thereby making possible the tall office building, or so-called "skyscraper," that typified Chicago's commercial buildings in the next two decades.

1. Inger and Bodtker and Co., lithographers. Chicago in 1820, with a vignette of John Kinzie, printed 1867. Colored lithograph on paper, 53 x 66. Lent by the Chicago Historical Society.

2. Cutaway model of a balloon frame, c. 1835. Wood, approx. 40 x 40 x 60. Constructed in 1987 by Richard Tickner for The Art Institute of Chicago.

3. I. T. Palmatary, delineator, and Charles Inger, lithographer. Bird's-eye view of Chicago, 1857, published by Braunhold and Sonne. Lithograph, framed, 141.5 x 229. Lent by the Chicago Historical Society. (See plate 1.)

4. Louis Kurz. Chicago, the Metropolis of the Northwest, 1864. Colored lithograph on paper, 59.4 x 74. Lent by the Chicago Historical Society. (See plate 2.)

5. Joshua Smith, photographer. Chicago as seen after the great conflagration, 1871. Photoprint, 23.5 x 80. Lent by the Chicago Historical Society. (See plate 3.)

6. Kurz and Allison. Chicago in early days, 1779-1857, published 1893. Colored lithograph on paper, 55 x 70.3. Lent by the Chicago Historical Society.

7. Shober and Carqueville, lithographers;

Louis Klinckerfues and Jacob Richter, architects and engineers. Bird's-eye view of Chicago in 1879 taken 2000 ft. above the crib. Toned lithograph on paper, 65 x 99. Lent by the Chicago Historical Society.

8. Model of Chicago's business district under reconstruction in 1872. Mixed media, approx. 397 x 397. Constructed in 1987 by Richard Tickner for The Art Institute of Chicago.

Cat. no. 7

z

Fig. 2 Fürst and Rudolph, John York Building, 1888 (demolished).
Fig. 3 The Illinois Board of Examiners in P. B. Wight's Office, 1898; from Illinois Society of Architects, Handbook for Architects and Builders (1898). Illinois was the first state to require architects to be licensed.

PETER B. WIGHT, Secretary.　W. H. REEVES.　DANKMAR ADLER, President.　W. CARBYS ZIMMERMAN.　PROF. N. CLIFFORD RICKER.

II. European Foundations of Chicago Architecture: Germany and France

Chicago buildings both before and after the 1871 fire were designed in a variety of revival styles that could be found throughout the United States. Nonetheless, the city's architecture can be said to be essentially Franco-Germanic in character. The German influence is directly seen in the work of immigrants who, with thousands of their countrymen, left Germany after the unsuccessful revolutions of 1848. Charles Fürst (fig. 2) and Augustus Bauer are two of these, with Bauer the first to arrive here from Germany in 1853. Fürst's designs, probably student work, are among the rare drawings to survive from this early period of Chicago. Bauer and his partner Robert Loebnitz numbered among their German clients in the city the wagon-maker Peter Schuttler.

In addition to people who designed and built the city, German methods of architectural education and German ideas of international design were brought to the University of Illinois in the mid-1870s by Nathan Clifford Ricker (fig. 3), who reshaped the curriculum at that school. German magazines such as *Architektonisches Skizzenbuch* and *Deutsche Bauzeitung* found their way into the libraries of various Chicago architects such as Peter B. Wight who copied plates as drawing exercises. These publications gave local architects the latest in European design, and, as with Wight's 1875 stenciling for the Ottawa, Illinois, Opera House, which was copied from an English design published in *Building News,* supplied Chicagoans with tangible sources of inspiration for their projects. Wight himself patented a system of fireproofing, and his firm, Carter, Drake and Wight, executed a number of commercial buildings in the city during the 1870s when he gave a start to Chicago's later greats Daniel H. Burnham and John Wellborn Root. Although almost all of Wight's buildings have been demolished and are documented only in drawings, a few commercial structures designed by others shortly after the 1871 fire still survive. The Delaware Building (fig. 4) by Wheelock and Thomas is one of the most notable examples, being recently restored.

But an equal, if not greater, influence on Chicago's architecture came from France. French influence was widespread in the United States after the Civil War, especially after architects trained at the Ecole des Beaux-Arts in Paris — like Richard Morris Hunt, the first American architect to study there — returned to this country to practice. Among the Chicagoans who studied at the Ecole were Louis H. Sullivan, William Augustus Otis, Edward H. Bennett, and John A. Holabird. They and others either con-

tinued to copy buildings from publications, or they visited Europe and other foreign locales to see great architectural treasures, sketching monuments in order to experience, first-hand, the best of the past and to retain that knowledge for future reference and inspiration. Daniel H. Burnham's 1896 views of Algiers, for instance, stress the waterfront and "big picture" view, prefiguring his later interest in large-scale planning. Frederick P. Dinkelberg's 1878 view of St. Peter's in Rome serves to remind

Fig. 4 Wheelock and Thomas, Delaware Building, 36 West Randolph Street, 1874.

us that he used that major monument as a source of inspiration for the dome of his 35 East Wacker Drive Building (fig. 5) of 1926. C. Herrick Hammond's sketches of Parisian sites recall that Paris served as an international capital of western culture and architecture in the early 1900s. Its Alexander III Bridge of 1899 influenced the design of pylons in Chicago's Grant Park from the second decade of the twentieth century. French influence on architectural education became even more pervasive when the drawing techniques of the Ecole were transplanted to American schools, such as the Architecture School of Armour Institute of Technology, which was housed in The Art Institute of Chicago from the 1890s until 1938 when Ludwig Mies van der Rohe arrived as its director, changed the curriculum from a French-based one to a German, Bauhaus-oriented program, and subsequently moved the school to its current location at 35th and State streets, the Illinois Institute of Technology in the 1940s. During Armour's heyday as a Beaux-Arts school, students such as James Edwin Quinn, Milton Herman, and Paul McCurry were taught to prepare elaborate renderings even from architectural elements that were on display at the Art Institute. After Norman J. Schlossman graduated from Armour Institute in 1922, he traveled to Europe to see and sketch its monuments. Schlossman's sketches serve as a record of reconstruction after World War I, and they remind us of the interruption of active architectural interchange between Chicago and Europe during the years 1914-18. Even the University of Illinois in downstate Champaign-Urbana became infected by this Francophilia in design techniques, as witnessed in the elaborately rendered work of Japanese émigré Richard Yoshijiro Mine in 1921. Chicago architects, who were trained in America, and whose design work relates to either Jugendstil or the Arts and Crafts movements, such as George Maher and Howard Van Doren Shaw, also made the grand tour to Europe to see and sketch their favorite buildings.

A. German Architects and Engineers: The Beginnings of a Chicago School of Architecture.

9. Charles Fürst. Elevation study of the Greek Doric order from the Parthenon, Athens, drawn March 28, 1870. Ink and wash on paper, 59.8 x 45. Gift of Mrs. Marie Fürst Florence to The Art Institute of Chicago. (See Pollak, fig. 2, p. 251.)

10. Charles Fürst. Elevation study of the Roman Doric order from the Baths of Diocletian, Rome, drawn April 1, 1870. Ink and wash on paper, 59.8 x 45. Gift of Mrs. Marie Fürst Florence to The Art Institute of Chicago.

11. Charles Fürst. Elevation study of a Renaissance Doric order from Scamozzi, drawn June 5, 1870. Ink on paper, 59.8 x 45. Gift of Mrs. Marie Fürst Florence to The Art Institute of Chicago.

12. Charles Fürst. Elevation study of a Greek Ionic order from the Temple of Minerva Polias, Athens, drawn May 23, 1870. Ink and colored ink on paper, 59.5 x 45. Gift of Mrs. Marie Fürst Florence to The Art Institute of Chicago.

13. Charles Fürst. Rendered elevation of a villa, c. 1870. Ink and colored ink on paper, 45 x 60.3. Gift of Mrs. Marie Fürst Florence to The Art Institute of Chicago. (See plate 4.)

14. Bauer and Loebnitz. Elevation of the Peter Schuttler House, 287 West Adams Street, Chicago, 1873-74 (demolished). Pencil and ink on paper, 62.7 x 53.8. Gift of Arthur Woltersdorf to The Art Insitute of Chicago.

15. Peter B. Wight. Rendered elevation of a gardenhouse from Hildebrandt's Villa on a canal near Berlin by Kirhoff, drawn by A. V. Keller, copied by Wight c. 1860 from the *Architektonisches Skizzenbuch* 11, 3 (1853). Pencil and watercolor on paper, 22.7 x 28.5. Gift of Peter B. Wight to The Art Institute of Chicago.

16. Peter B. Wight. Elevation sketch of a show window in Frankfurt, designed by Ritter and drawn by A. Schultz, copied by Wight c. 1860 from the *Architektonisches Skizzenbuch* 7, 5 (1852). Pencil on paper, 16.3 x 22.5. Gift of Peter B. Wight to The Art Institute of Chicago.

17. Carter, Drake, and Wight. Perspective rendering of the Stewart-Bentley Building, 112-114 Dearborn Street (now 30-32 North Dearborn Street), Chicago, delineated by Daniel H. Burnham, 1872 (demolished). Ink and watercolor on paper, 55.9 x 29. Gift of Peter B. Wight to The Art Institute of Chicago. (See plate 8.)

18. Carter, Drake, and Wight. Perspective rendering of the Lenox Building, 88-90 Washington Street (now 59 West Washington Street), Chicago, delineated by John Wellborn Root, 1872 (demolished). Ink and wash on paper, 51.2 x 25. Gift of Peter B. Wight to The Art Institute of Chicago. (See plate 7.)

19. Peter B. Wight. Rendered elevation of the Epic Poetry stencil for the Opera House, Ottawa, Illinois, c. 1875, copied from Henry Stacy Marks's lunettes for the Gaiety Theatre, London, published in *Building News* (March 19, 1869). Gouache and pencil on paper, 55.9 x 41.2. Gift of Peter B. Wight to The Art Institute of Chicago.

20. Peter B. Wight. Rendered elevation and partial section of the Eliphalet W. Blatchford House, "Ulmenheim," 375 North LaSalle Street, Chicago, 1875 (demolished). Ink and watercolor on paper, 51 x 63. Gift of Peter B. Wight to The Art Institute of Chicago. (See plate 6.)

21. Peter B. Wight. Decorative tiles from the Blatchford House, c. 1875. Terracotta, each 12.7 x 12.7 x 4. Gift of Thomas Blatchford to The Art Insitute of Chicago.

22. Peter B. Wight. Butternut wall cabinet from the Blatchford House, c. 1875. Wood, 106.8 x 82.5 x 59.5. Lent by the More Collection.

23. Isaac E. Scott. Cabinet-bookcase for the J. J. Glessner family, Chicago, c. 1875. Walnut, with holly and ebonized wood decoration, 218.5 x 177.8 x 36.8. Lent by Glessner House, Chicago Architecture Foundation. (See plate 32.)

Cat. no. 14   Cat. no. 15

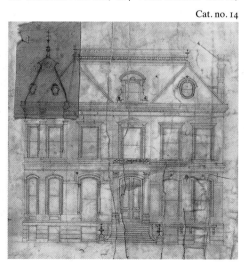

Cat. no. 19

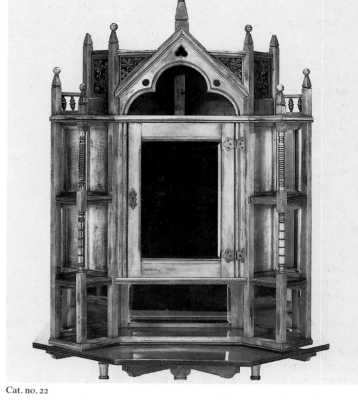

Cat. no. 22

Cat. no. 26

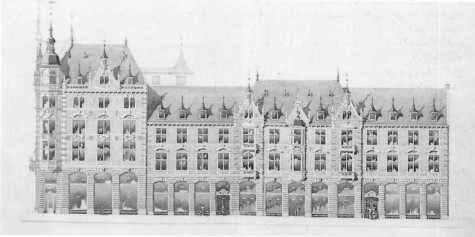

24.   Nathan Clifford Ricker. Rendered elevation of the Corn Exchange, London, February
22, 1872. Watercolor on paper, 47 x 62.3. Lent
by the University Archives, University of
Illinois at Urbana-Champaign. (See plate 9.)

25.   Nathan Clifford Ricker. Rendered elevation and first-floor plan of a Mansard roofed
villa, March 14-30, 1872. Watercolor on paper,
45.7 x 50.7 and 63.5 x 47. Lent by the University
Archives, University of Illinois at Urbana-
Champaign. (See plate 5.)

26.   Peter J. Weber. Rendered elevations of a
new Ratskeller in Halle, on the Saale River,
Germany, c. 1880-85. Ink and watercolor on
paper, each approx. 69 x 98. Gifts of Bertram
Weber to The Art Institute of Chicago.

B. French Concepts of Architectural Education: The Ecole des Beaux-Arts and Beaux-
Arts schools in the Midwest, and continuing
education through European travel.

27.   Louis H. Sullivan. Elevation study of a
Tuscan order after a French edition of Vignola,
c. 1875. Ink on tracing paper, 30.5 x 20.3. Gift of
George Grant Elmslie to The Art Institute of
Chicago. (See Pollak, fig. 3, p. 252.)

28.   Louis H. Sullivan. Elevation study of a
Doric pedestal, base, capital, and entablature
after a French edition of Vignola, c. 1875. Ink
on tracing paper, 30.5 x 20.3. Gift of George
Grant Elmslie to The Art Insitute of Chicago.
(See Pollak, fig. 1, p. 250.)

29.   Louis H. Sullivan. Elevation study of a
variant Doric order after a French edition of
Vignola, c. 1875. Ink on tracing paper, 30.5 x
20.3. Gift of George Grant Elmslie to The Art
Institute of Chicago. (See Pollak, fig. 8, p. 254.)

30.   Louis H. Sullivan. Elevation study of a de-
tail of a classical frieze and entablature, c. 1875.
Pencil on tracing paper, 20.5 x 20. Gift of
George Grant Elmslie to The Art Institute of
Chicago. (See Pollak, fig. 10, p. 256.)

31.   Louis H. Sullivan. Sketch inscribed "Deja
le violaneux commence a roeler son instrument," February 26, 1875. Ink on paper, 27 x
21. Gift of Andrienne Sullivan to The Art Institute of Chicago.

32.   Louis H. Sullivan. Sketch of a man and a
woman (a painter and his model), March 29,
1875. Ink on paper, 33.8 x 25.7. Gift of George
Grant Elmslie to The Art Institute of Chicago.

33.   Louis H. Sullivan. Elevation study of an
entablature after Ruprich-Robert, *Flore Ornamentale,* c. 1880. Pencil on tracing paper, 27 x
20.4. Gift of George Grant Elmslie to The Art
Institute of Chicago.

34.   Frederick P. Dinkelberg. Perspective
view of the interior of St. Peter's, Rome, probably copied from an engraving or published
view, 1878. Ink on paper, 73.5 x 60. Gift of the
estate of George F. Killinger to The Art Institute of Chicago.

Fig. 5 Giaver and Dinkelberg, with Thielbar and Fugard, Jewelers Building (later Pure Oil Building), 35 East Wacker Drive, 1926.

Cat. no. 34

Cat. no. 33

Cat. no. 37

Cat. no. 39

Cat. no. 41

Cat. no. 35

Cat. no. 38

35.   William Augustus Otis. Elevation sketch of the chateau at La Clayette, Soane et Loire, 1880. Ink on paper, 22.3 x 31. Gift of William Augustus Otis to The Art Institute of Chicago.

36.   Irving K. Pond. Elevation sketch of the Nassaurhaus, Nuremberg, c. 1890. Ink on paper, 35.5 x 25.5. Gift of the estate of Irving K. Pond to The Art Institute of Chicago.

37.   George Maher. Perspective sketches of buildings in Granada, Lucerne, Rome, and Cologne, 1891. Ink on paper, each approx. 25.3 x 19. Gifts of Violet Wyld and the Kenilworth Historical Society to The Art Institute of Chicago.

38.   Daniel H. Burnham. Two views of Algiers, 1896. Pencil and watercolor on paper, each 17.6 x 25.2. Gift of Daniel and Hubert Burnham to The Art Institute of Chicago.

39.   Edward H. Bennett. Rendered elevation of the Royal Portal, Chartres Cathedral, 1896. Pencil and watercolor on paper, 95 x 61. Lent by Mr. and Mrs. Edward H. Bennett, Jr.

40.   C. Herrick Hammond. Perspective sketch of Notre-Dame, Paris, August 8, 1904. Ink on paper, 12.5 x 16.4. Gift of James W. Hammond to The Art Institute of Chicago.

41.   C. Herrick Hammond. Perspective sketch of the Alexander III Bridge, Paris, August 22, 1904. Ink and watercolor on paper, 18.5 x 13.8.

Gift of Mary Hammond Rodman in memory of James Wright Hammond to The Art Institute of Chicago.

42.   John A. Holabird. Perspective sketch of the entrance to a French garden, c. 1912. Watercolor on illustration board, approx. 36.3 x 23.5. Gift of John A. Holabird, Jr., to The Art Institute of Chicago.

43.   John A. Holabird. Four perspective sketches: Baths of Caracalla, St. Peter's in Rome, St. Maria della Pace, and the Farnese Palace, 1913. Pencil on note paper, each 19 x 12.6. Gifts of John A. Holabird, Jr., to The Art Institute of Chicago.

44.   James Edwin Quinn. Rendered elevation of an arbor, a student drawing for the School of

Cat. no. 47

Cat. no. 50   Cat. no. 48

the Art Institute – Armour Institute of Technology, November 16, 1914. Ink, pencil, and watercolor on paper, 15.5 x 10. Gift of James Edwin Quinn to The Art Institute of Chicago.

45.   Howard Van Doren Shaw. English travel sketchbook, 1920. Pencil on paper, 15.5 x 10. Gift of Susan Dart McCutcheon and John T. McCutcheon, Jr., to The Art Institute of Chicago.

46.   Richard Yoshijiro Mine. Rendered elevation of a proposed War Memorial, a student drawig for the University of Illinois at Champaign-Urbana, 1921. Ink and wash on paper, 54.6 x 93.9. Gift of Richard Yoshijiro Mine to The Art Institute of Chicago. (See plate 79.)

47.   Milton Herman. Rendered elevation and section of a window, a student drawing for a freshman project at the Armour Institute of Technology, 1922. Ink and watercolor on paper, 91 x 61. Gift of Paul McCurry to The Art Institute of Chicago.

48.   Paul McCurry. Rendered elevation and section of a fifteenth-century Gothic fireplace from Laon (showing the coat of arms of Pierre II de Fontette) in The Art Institute of Chicago, a student drawing for a junior project at the Armour Institute of Technology, 1924. Ink and watercolor on paper, 96 x 64. Gift of Paul McCurry to The Art Institute of Chicago.

49.   Norman J. Schlossman. Perspective sketch of the tower of Soissons Cathedral, under repair after being damaged in the First World War, December 9, 1922. Pencil on paper, 32.8 x 25.6. Gift of Norman J. Schlossman to The Art Institute of Chicago.

50.   Norman J. Schlossman. Perspective sketch of the interior of Soissons Cathedral, under repair after being damaged in the First World War, December 9, 1922. Pencil on paper, 32.8 x 25.5. Gift of Norman J. Schlossman to The Art Institute of Chicago.

III. Major and Minor Masterpieces

Northern Europe continued to serve as a major point of reference for Chicago. Architect Solon Spencer Beman used Victorian England as a source for his model town of Pullman, Illinois, from 1879 and the Pullman Building of 1884. Others like Burnham and Root drew on French sources for their landmark Rookery of 1885. Burnham and Root later received international recognition, particularly, in German publications of the 1920s, for their severe, unornamented Monadnock Building. But the loft spaces of that building contrast with their Rookery plan, which uses a courtyard formula based, in part, on French atrium and department store design. This light-court solution and "square-donut" plan became a trademark of later office buildings by Burnham and Root, D. H. Burnham and Co., and successor firms. But they and others such as Henry Ives Cobb, Charles S. Frost, and Otto H. Matz owe much of the appearance of their rough-faced, boldly Romanesque structures to Boston architect Henry Hobson Richardson. His Romanesque buildings in Chicago achieved international prominence. Of special importance are the landmark Glessner House, the Marshall Field Wholesale Store, and the less well known Franklin MacVeagh House (figs. 6, 7), the latter two unfortunately now demolished.

William Le Baron Jenney's famed Home Insurance Building of 1884 (now demolished) and the Chicago School skeletal work of firms such as Holabird and Roche have been featured in numerous publications and exhibitions on Chicago architecture, as have the works of Howard Van Doren Shaw and Irving K. Pond and his brother Allen B. Pond. But it should be remembered that a number of lesser lights actively practiced in Chicago, among them Germanic immigrants and their descendants, such as Alfred S. Alschuler, Frederick Baumann, Adolph Cudell (pl. 27; fig. 8), Fritz Foltz, Arthur Hercz, Edmund C. Krause, Richard Schmidt (fig. 9), Herman Valentin Von Holst, August C. Wilmanns, and Arthur

Figs. 6/7 H. H. Richardson, Franklin MacVeagh House, 1400 North Lake Shore Drive, 1885-87 (demolished); exterior and view of dining room and palm court.

Woltersdorf (fig. 10). Along with their more famous colleagues, these less well known architects shaped the cityscape with structures ranging from minor masterpieces to background buildings. As with their more famous counterparts, their buildings and architectural styles changed with the times and reflected shifts toward classical detailing, particularly in the late 1890s after the success of the World's Columbian Exposition. In any case, their inclusion helps us to place major designers within the more accurate context of Chicago's built environment. Consequently, we can more easily assess the achievements and impact of Chicago's architectural heroes in the next three sections: Louis H. Sullivan, Frank Lloyd Wright, and Daniel H. Burnham. Each of these three exhibition sections functions as a mini-monograph, presenting a survey of the architect's works in relation to some of his followers.

Fig. 8 Cudell and Hercz, Frances J. Dewes House, 503 West Wrightwood Avenue, 1896; parlor/front entrance vestibule.

Fig. 9 Richard E. Schmidt, Montgomery Ward Building, 6 North Michigan Avenue, 1898 (altered).

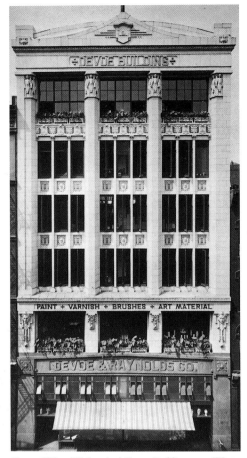

Fig. 10 Hill and Woltersdorf, Devoe Building, 14-16 West Lake Street, 1912-13 (demolished).

51. Solon Spencer Beman. Preliminary elevation of the Main Car Shop, Pullman, 1879-80. Pencil on paper, 66 x 228. Gift of Pullman, Inc., to The Art Institute of Chicago.

52. Solon Spencer Beman. Elevation of the Pullman Office Building, southwest corner of Adams Street and Michigan Avenue, Chicago, 1884 (demolished). Ink on linen, 100 x 110. Gift of Jeremy Beman to The Art Institute of Chicago. (See Schlereth, fig. 16, p. 182.)

53. Solon Spencer Beman. Detail sketch for a Pullman Car, c. 1892-94. Pencil on tracing paper, 52 x 74. Gift of Bates Lowry to The Art Institute of Chicago.

54. William Le Baron Jenney. Model of the Home Insurance Building, northeast corner of LaSalle and Adams streets, Chicago, 1884 (demolished). Mixed media, 38 x 38 x 51. Constructed in 1987 by Richard Tickner for the Deutsches Architekturmuseum.

55. L. Prang and Co., lithographers. Poster of the Home Insurance Building, c. 1885-86. Colored photolithograph, 84 x 65.5. Lent by the Deutsches Architekturmuseum. (See plate 14.)

56. H. H. Richardson. Perspective sketch of the Marshall Field Wholesale Store, Adams at Franklin Street, Chicago, c. 1885 (demolished). Pencil, black crayon, and red wash heightened with white, 29 x 50.6. Lent by Houghton Library, Harvard University. Chicago showing only.

57. H. H. Richardson. Perspective study of the corner of the Marshall Field Wholesale Store, c. 1885. Pencil on tracing paper, 45 x 54.6. Lent by Houghton Library, Harvard University. Chicago showing only.

58. Burnham and Root. Elevation of the Rookery, 209 South LaSalle Street, Chicago, 1885. Colored hectograph print, 61.2 x 72.6. Gift of D. H. Burnham, Jr., to The Art Institute of Chicago. (See plate 10.)

59. Burnham and Root. Elevation of the grand staircase of the Rookery, 1885-86. Colored hectograph print, approx. 71 x 101.5. Gift of D. H. Burnham, Jr., to The Art Institute of Chicago.

60. Burnham and Root. Model of the Rookery, 1885-86. Mixed media. Constructed for the Deutsches Architekturmuseum.

61. Charles S. Frost. Elevation and section of the Chicago and Northwestern Railroad Station, Wisconsin Avenue, Milwaukee, Wisconsin, 1889 (demolished). Hectograph, ink, and colored ink on linen, 73.5 x 89. Lent by Mr. and Mrs. Dale Cowel.

62. Holabird and Roche. Elevation of the Tacoma Building, northeast corner of LaSalle and Madison streets, Chicago, c. 1888-89 (demolished). Sepia print, 121.3 x 79.5. Lent by the Chicago Historical Society, gift of Holabird and Root.

63. Holabird and Roche. Perspective rendering of the McClurg Building, 218 South Wabash Avenue, Chicago, 1899. Sepia print, 77.5 x 46.5. Lent by the Chicago Historical Society, gift of Holabird and Root. (See plate 20.)

Cat. no. 70

Cat. no. 56

Cat. no. 66

Cat. no. 72

Cat. no. 71, detail

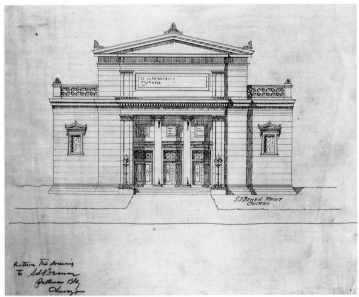

Cat. no. 74

Cat. no. 83

64.   Holabird and Roche. Elevation and section of the terracotta details, lower levels of the Adams Street addition to the Marquette Building of 1893, 140 South Dearborn Street, Chicago, 1905. Watercolored hectograph print, 96.5 x 61. Lent by the Chicago Historical Society, Gift of Holabird and Root.

65.   H. H. Richardson. Presentation plan of the J. J. Glessner House, 1800 South Prairie Avenue, Chicago, May 1885. Pencil and watercolor on tracing paper, mounted on board, 29.6 x 65.5. Lent by the Houghton Library, Harvard University. Chicago showing only.

66.   H. H. Richardson. Preliminary elevation of the Prairie Avenue facade of the J. J. Glessner House, c. 1885. Pencil, ink, and watercolor on buff paper, 59 x 69.8. Lent by the Houghton Library, Harvard University. Chicago showing only.

67.   H. H. Richardson. Detail of the 18th Street facade of the J. J. Glessner House. Pencil on tracing paper, 23.5 x 26. Lent by the Houghton Library, Harvard University. Chicago showing only.

68.   H. H. Richardson. Perspective rendering of the J. J. Glessner House, c. 1885-87. Ink on Bristol board, 16.5 x 40.5. Lent by Glessner House, Chicago Architecture Foundation. (See plate 29.)

69.   H. H. Richardson. Perspective rendering of the living hall and stairs of the J. J. Glessner House, 1886-87. Ink on tracing paper, 62.2 x 40.7. Lent by Glessner House, Chicago Architecture Foundation. (See plate 30.)

70.   Charles Coolidge. Armchair and side chair for J. J. Glessner, 1887. Oak; armchair, 99.7 x 66 x 53.3; side chair, 97.3 x 53.3 x 45.8. Lent by Glessner House, Chicago Architecture Foundation. (See plate 31.)

71.   John Wellborn Root of Burnham and Root. Preliminary perspective studies of St. Gabriel's Church, 4501 South Lowe Street, Chicago, c. 1886. Pencil and watercolor on paper, 42.5 x 100.5. Gift of John Wellborn Root, Jr., to The Art Institute of Chicago.

72.   John Wellborn Root of Burnham and Root. Perspective rendering of the William J. Goudy House, 434 Elm Street, Chicago, c. 1889 (demolished). Pencil and wash on paper, 53 x 45.5. Gift of Dr. and Mrs. Stanton Fletcher to The Art Institute of Chicago.

73.   Burnham and Root. Perspective rendering of the Max A. Meyer House, 2009 Prairie Avenue, Chicago, 1888 (demolished). Watercolor on paper, 63.5 x 40.6. Lent by Mr. and Mrs. Dale Cowel. (See plate 28.)

74.   Jenney and Mundie. Rendered elevation and section of a mantel (no. 3) for Mr. Abraham Poole, 89 Pine Street, Chicago, c. 1890 (demolished). Pencil and watercolor on paper, 28.2 x 35.8. Gift of Elmer C. Jensen to The Art Institute of Chicago.

75.   Treat and Foltz. Isometric drawing of the Ontario Apartments, State and Ontario streets, Chicago, delineated by J.F.W., 1880 (demolished). Ink on linen, 65.4 x 45.8. Gift of J. Arthur Scott to The Art Institute of Chicago. (See Westfall, "From Homes to Towers," fig. 6, p. 271.)

76.   Treat and Foltz. State Street elevation of the Ontario Apartments, 1880. Ink on linen, 72 x 75. Gift of J. Arthur Scott to The Art Institute of Chicago. (See Westfall, "From Homes to Towers," fig. 5, p. 270).

77.   Treat and Foltz. Elevation of the Goudy Flats, 501-507 Fullerton Parkway, Chicago, c. 1890. Ink on linen, 59 x 94. Gift of J. Arthur Scott to The Art Institute of Chicago.

78.   Charles S. Frost. Perspective rendering of the Calumet Club, northeast corner of Michigan Avenue and 20th Street, Chicago, delineated by T. O. Frankel, 1893 (demolished). Ink on linen, 77.5 x 125. Lent by Mr. and Mrs. Dale Cowel. (See plate 35.)

79.   Adolph Cudell and Arthur Hercz. Perspective rendering of the Francis J. Dewes House, 503 Wrightwood, Chicago, delineated by Lawrence Buck, 1896. Watercolor and pencil on paper, 64 x 98. Lent by the Chicago Historical Society, gift of Mr. Arthur Hercz and Mrs. Greta Hale. (See plate 27.)

80.   August C. Wilmanns. Rendered elevation of a public library, c. 1896, exhibited in the Chicago Architectural Club. Watercolor on paper, 46 x 85. Anonymous gift to The Art Institute of Chicago. (See plate 80.)

81.   August C. Wilmanns. Rendered plan of a public library, c. 1896, exhibited in the Chicago Architectural Club. Watercolor on paper, 46 x 85. Anonymous gift to The Art Institute of Chicago.

82.   Solon Spencer Beman. Elevation, plan, and detail of the Blackstone Library, 4904 South Lake Park Avenue, Chicago, 1901-02. Ink on linen, three sheets, 70 x 89, 54 x 94, and 38.4 x 67.2. Gifts of Jeremy Beman to The Art Institute of Chicago.

83.   Solon Spencer Beman. Two elevations of the First Church of Christ Scientist, 4019 South Drexel Boulevard, Chicago, 1897. Ink on linen, 48 x 45, 57.5 x 75.5. Gift of Jeremy Beman to The Art Institute of Chicago.

84.   Pond and Pond. Perspective study of a house at LaSalle, Illinois, 1901-04, exhibited in the Chicago Architectural Club. Pencil and watercolor on paper mounted to board, 13.5 x 23.8. Gift of the estate of Irving K. Pond to The Art Institute of Chicago. (See Wilson, fig. 3, p. 210.)

85.   Holabird and Roche. Perspective rendering of the University Club, Michigan Avenue and Monroe Street, Chicago, 1908. Watercolor, pastel, and pencil on board, approx. 160 x 122. Lent by the University Club, Chicago. (See plate 38.)

86.   Herman Valentin Von Holst. Perspective

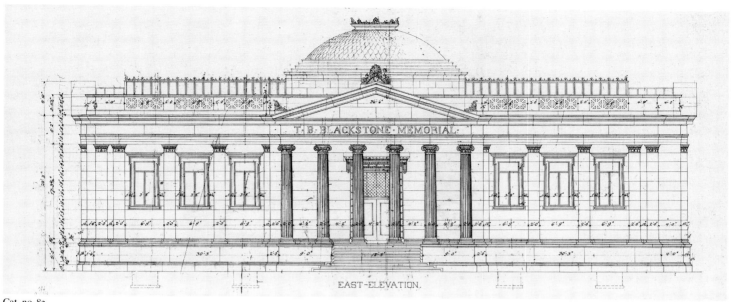

T·B·BLACKSTONE·MEMORIAL·

EAST-ELEVATION.

Cat. no. 82

Cat. no. 87

Cat. no. 93, detail

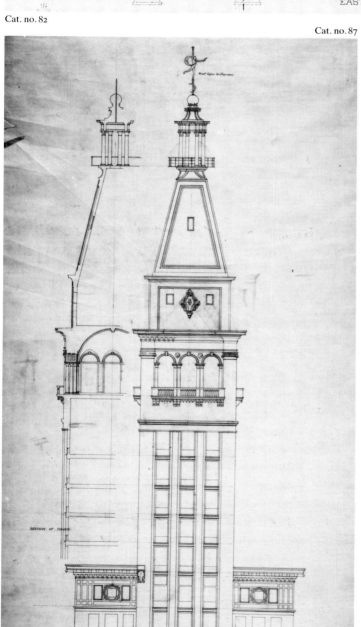

rendering of "Glamis," Bethlehem, New Hampshire, for George Macbeth, 1904. Pencil and watercolor on paper, 21.3 x 43.8. Restricted gift of Mr. and Mrs. David Hilliard to The Art Institute of Chicago. (See plate 37.)

87. Richard Schmidt. Elevation of the Montgomery Ward Tower, 6 North Michigan Avenue, Chicago, c. 1898 (altered). Ink on linen, 106 x 48. Gift of Schmidt, Garden, and Erikson to The Art Institute of Chicago.

88. Richard Schmidt. Elevation of Michael Reese Hospital, 2789 South Ellis Avenue, Chicago, c. 1905 (altered). Ink on linen, 106 x 73.3. Gift of Schmidt, Garden, and Erikson to The Art Institute of Chicago.

89. David E. Postle and John Fischer. Elevation of an eighteen-story building, c. 1900. Pencil on paper, 191 x 107. Gift of Helen E. Fischer to The Art Institute of Chicago.

90. Frederick Baumann. East and west elevation of a proposed monument, possibly for the Department of Agriculture Monument Competition, c. 1900. Ink and red ink on linen, 78.5 x 58.6. Gift of Bertram Weber to The Art Institute of Chicago.

91. Frost and Granger. Perspective rendering of an addition to St. Luke's Hospital, 1439 South Michigan Avenue, Chicago, c. 1904. Ink on linen, 86.5 x 71.5. Lent by Mr. and Mrs. Dale Cowel. (See plate 83.)

92. Edmund C. Krause. Elevation and partial section of the Majestic Building, 16-22 West Monroe Street, Chicago, September 4, 1904. Ink on linen, 211 x 88.8. Department of Architecture Purchase, The Art Institute of Chicago.

93. Edmund C. Krause. Elevation details of the terracotta for the Majestic Building, 1904. Ink on linen, 211 x 94. Gift of David Fleener to The Art Institute of Chicago.

94. Marshall and Fox. Ohio Street elevation of a warehouse for A. C. McClurg and Co., 457-77 (now 330-350) East Ohio Street, Chicago, November 28, 1907 (demolished). Ink and colored ink on linen, 63.5 x 92. Lent by the University of Texas at Austin, Architectural Drawings Collection. (See Westfall, "Buildings Serving Commerce," fig. 4, p. 80.)

95. Marshall and Fox. Details, including wall section and elevation of the corner pavilion, for a warehouse for A. C. McClurg and Co., November 28, 1907. Ink and colored ink on linen, 95 x 61.5. Lent by the University of Texas at Austin, Architectural Drawings Collection.

96. J. W. Taylor, photographer. Panorama of Chicago, 1913. Six photographs, 20.5 x 152.5. The Burnham Library of Architecture, The Art Institute of Chicago. (See plates 21-24.)

97. Arthur Woltersdorf of Woltersdorf and Bernard. Perspective rendering of Driscoll's Danceland, Madison Street, Chicago, 1910-15 (demolished). Pastel and pencil on paper, 16.2 x 56. Gift of Arthur Woltersdorf to The Art Institute of Chicago.

98. Alfred S. Alschuler. Facade elevation of the Ilg Electric Ventilating Co. Building, 2850 North Pulaski Road, Chicago, July 31, 1919. Ink on linen, 79 x 127.8. Gift of Friedman, Alschuler, and Sincere to The Art Institute of Chicago. (See Westfall, "Buildings Serving Commerce," fig. 12, p. 86.)

99. Alfred S. Alschuler. Michigan Avenue elevation of the Hudson Motor Car Co. showroom and service station, 2220-28 South Michigan Avenue, Chicago, February 15, 1921 (demolished). Ink on linen, 105 x 60.5. Gift of Friedman, Alschuler, and Sincere to The Art Institute of Chicago.

100. Howard Van Doren Shaw. The architect's desk from "Ragdale," 1230 North Greenbay Road, Lake Forest, Illinois, 1897. Oak, 243.5 x 147.5 x 64. Lent by Alice Ryerson Hayes. (See plate 33.)

101. Howard Van Doren Shaw. Deer-headed andirons and pitchfork-poker from a private residence, c. 1900. Brass and iron; andirons, each 66 x 96.5 x 66; poker, 106.7 x 15. Lent by John and Susan Dart McCutcheon.

102. Howard Van Doren Shaw. Sketch of a bell tower, c. 1919-20. Pencil and colored pencil on black bordered "In Memoriam" stationery, 20.5 x 15.8. Gift of Susan Dart McCutcheon and John McCutcheon, Jr., to The Art Institute of Chicago.

103. Howard Van Doren Shaw. Sketches of details for the Charles Hutchinson Apartment, 2450 Lakeview Avenue, Chicago, c. 1924. Pencil on Paper, 22.8 x 15.1. Gift of Susan Dart McCutcheon and John McCutcheon, Jr., to The Art Institute of Chicago.

104. Howard Van Doren Shaw. Sketch elevation and plan of the Catherine and Jessica Colvin House, 1350 North Lake Road, Lake Forest, Illinois, 1922 (unexecuted). Pencil on tracing paper, each approx. 43 x 56. Gift of Susan Dart McCutcheon and John McCutcheon, Jr., to The Art Institute of Chicago.

105. Howard Van Doren Shaw. Perspective view of the Phi Delta Theta Fraternity House, Champaign, Illinois, 1922. Pencil on tracing paper mounted on illustration board, 34 x 53. Gift of Susan Dart McCutcheon and John McCutcheon, Jr., to The Art Institute of Chicago. (See plate 36.)

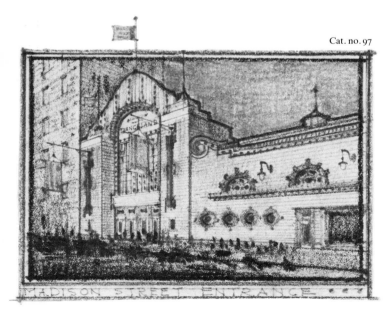

Cat. no. 97

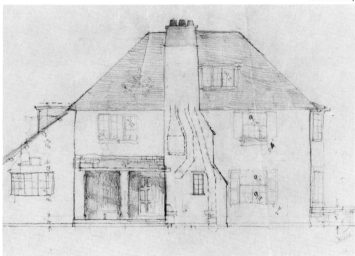

Cat. no. 104

Fig. 11 Dankmar Adler, Isaiah Temple (now Ebenezer Missionary Baptist Church), 4501 South Vincennes Avenue, 1898-99.

Fig. 12 Parker N. Berry, Interstate National Bank, 13310 Baltimore Avenue, Hegewisch, Illinois, 1917-18 (demolished).

IV. Louis H. Sullivan's Architecture and Ornament: An American Architecture

Louis H. Sullivan's education at the Ecole des Beaux-Arts in 1875 and his exposure to European rationalists, particularly Viollet-le-Duc, and to French and German philosophers conditioned his attitude toward ornamental and architectural design. He strove to create a distinctly American architecture whose ornament was based on the underlying geometry of natural forms, and whose tripartite facade composition of base, vertical shaft, and capital he related to the compositional elements of a classical column. Sullivan himself was decorated and honored by French professional societies, and cast examples of his work are found in French collections — witness the Getty Tomb (pl. 42) and the casts of ornamental gates in the Musée des Arts Décoratifs in Paris. But, in addition to that Francophilia, his German partner Dankmar Adler drew upon the best that Germanic countries had to offer in planning and designing two of their masterpieces of theater design: the Auditorium of 1887-89 and the Schiller Theater of 1892 — the latter unfortunately now demolished. Both theatres owe much to reform principles developed by architect Gottfried Semper and composer Richard Wagner.

After Adler and Sullivan dissolved their partnership in 1895, Adler continued to design mostly industrial buildings, synagogues (fig. 11), and their related schools. Sullivan also turned from the tall office buildings that the two together had previously done. But Sullivan's impact can be found in several much more modest projects in Chicago and throughout the Midwest, especially in small rural banks — which have been likened to jewel boxes — that he and his followers Parker N. Berry (fig. 12), Homer Grant Sailor, William Gray Purcell, and George Grant Elmslie designed for towns in Minnesota, Iowa, Illinois, Wisconsin, and Ohio. Sullivan-like ornament was manufactured by Midland Terra Cotta and other local companies, and this bootlegged decoration can be found on numerous small commercial buildings throughout Chicago's neighborhoods. On a more legitimate note, Sullivanesque ornament was also created by Healy and Millet, who were the decorators for some of his projects, notably the Chicago Stock Exchange Trading Room of 1894. Even more than this legacy, Sullivan left us his masterpiece of ornamental design theory in *A System of Architectural Ornament According with a Philosophy of Man's Powers*. This book was published just before his death in 1924, but the exquisite drawings were commissioned, in part, by The Art Institute of Chicago in 1922.

106. Louis H. Sullivan. Sketches of five grotesque heads, dated January 26, 28, 29, 30, February 6, 1878. Pencil on paper, each approx. 19.5 x 10.4. Gift of Andrienne Sullivan to The Art Institute of Chicago. (See Pollak, fig. 13, p. 259.)

107. Louis H. Sullivan. Sketch of a man's face in profile, initialed and dated November 2, 1878. Pencil on paper, 22 x 14.2. Gift of George Grant Elmslie to The Art Institute of Chicago. (See Pollak, fig. 14, p. 259.)

108. Louis H. Sullivan. Sketch copy of composite ornament from Ruprich-Robert, *Flore Ornamentale*, c. 1880. Pencil on tracing paper, 27.5 x 20. Gift of George Grant Elmslie to The Art Institute of Chicago. (See Weingarden, fig. 2, p. 230.)

109. Louis H. Sullivan. Elevation study of a stair rail-balustrade, c. 1880. Pencil on tracing paper, 21 x 13.6. Gift of George Grant Elmslie

to The Art Institute of Chicago. (See Weingarden, fig. 5, p. 232.)

110. Louis H. Sullivan. Design for a ceiling, 1876. Ink on paper, 40 x 73.5. Gift of George Grant Elmslie to The Art Institute of Chicago. (See Weingarden, fig. 4, p. 231.)

111. Dankmar Adler, Architect. Jeweler's Building, 15-19 South Wabash Avenue, Chicago, 1881-82. Ornamental scroll designed by Louis H. Sullivan. Cast iron, 22.5 x 10 x 4. Gift of Richard Nickel to The Art Institute of Chicago. (See Weingarden, fig. 7, p. 233.)

112. Adler and Sullivan. Copy of a "sunburst" chimney panel from the Rubel Residence, 320 South Ashland Avenue, Chicago, 1884 (demolished). Plaster, 56.5 x 55.2 x 23. Copied from an original red terracotta fragment in the collection of the Southern Illinois University at Edwardsville.

113. Louis H. Sullivan. Ornamental designs, May 6, 1884. Pencil on paper, 34.7 x 21.2. Lent by the Avery Architectural and Fine Arts Library, Columbia University.

114. Louis H. Sullivan. Sketch of a hand with a leaf, July 20, 1885. Pencil on paper, 25 x 20.3. Gift of Andrienne Sullivan to The Art Institute of Chicago. (See Weingarden, fig. 10, p. 236.)

115. Louis H. Sullivan. Three sketches of ornamental details, c. 1885. Pencil on paper, each approx. 35 x 21.5. Lent by Mr. and Mrs. Joseph A. Guyer. (See Weingarden, fig. 11, p. 237.)

116. Louis H. Sullivan. Ornamental design, October 19, 1885, inscribed "18 Sept. 1913 to Earl H. Reed." Pencil on paper, 19.8 x 14. Gift of Earl H. Reed to The Art Institute of Chicago.

117. Adler and Sullivan. Revised 24th Street elevation and partial sections of the Standard Club, Michigan Avenue, Chicago, September 19, 1887 (demolished). Ink on linen, 67.5 x

Cat. no. 113

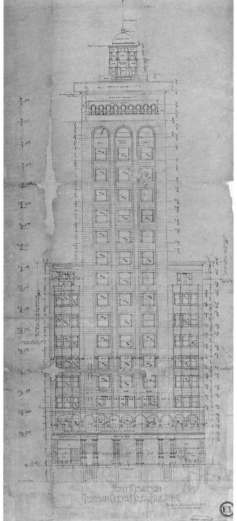

Cat. no. 122

137.5. Gift of Friedman, Alschuler, and Sincere to The Art Institute of Chicago. (See plate 34.)

118.   Adler and Sullivan. Working drawing for the ornamentation of the north and south wall above the balcony, Auditorium Theater, 70 East Congress Street, Chicago, attributed to Frank Lloyd Wright, c. 1887. Hectograph print, 68.9 x 47.3. Gift of George Grant Elmslie to

The Art Institute of Chicago. (See Weingarden, fig. 18, p. 244.)

119.   Adler and Sullivan. Two door plates with handles from the Auditorium Building, c. 1888-89. Brass, each 37 x 12.5 x 7. Gifts of Dr. and Mrs. Edwin DeCosta to The Art Institute of Chicago.

120.   Adler and Sullivan. Design for their office window, Auditorium Building, c. 1883. Hectograph print on paper, 35.5 x 21. Lent by Mr. and Mrs. Joseph A. Guyer.

121.   Adler and Sullivan. Ceiling panel from the Barber Shop, Auditorium Building, c. 1888. Plaster, 91.4 x 91.4 x 2.54. Lent by Timothy Samuelson.

122.   Adler and Sullivan with Baumann and Cady. Facade elevation of the Schiller Theater, 64 West Randolph Street, Chicago, 1891 (demolished). Hectograph print, 100 x 40.5. Gift of Balaban and Katz to The Art Institute of Chicago.

123.   Adler and Sullivan. Ornamental detail from the Schiller Theater, 1891. Plaster, 99 x 81 x 4. Gift of the Commission on Chicago Architectural Landmarks to The Art Institute of Chicago.

124.   Adler and Sullivan. Cast of ornamental doorway from the Getty Tomb, Graceland Cemetary, Chicago, 1890, made by N. Christofle, Paris, 1894. 233 x 105. Lent by the Musée des Arts Décoratifs, Paris. (See Loyrette, fig. 12, p. 131; see also plate 42.)

Cat. no. 127

125. Adler and Sullivan. Sketch for ornamental fresco of the Transportation Building, World's Columbian Exposition, Chicago, c. 1891 (demolished). Pencil on tracing paper, 45.7 x 44.6. Lent by the Avery Architectural and Fine Arts Library, Columbia University.

126. Adler and Sullivan. Model of the Golden Portal of the Transportation Building, World's Columbian Exposition, 1893. Resin cast, approx. 36 x 41. Constructed in 1986 by Richard Tickner for the Musée d'Orsay.

127. Adler and Sullivan. Lunette from the Transportation Building and the Albert Sullivan Residence, 4575 South Lake Park Avenue, Chicago, c. 1892-93 (both demolished). Plaster, 66 x 132.5 x 15. Copied from an original in the collection of the Southern Illinois University at Edwardsville.

128. Three medals awarded to Louis H. Sullivan by the Union Centrale des Arts Décoratifs,

Cat. no. 130

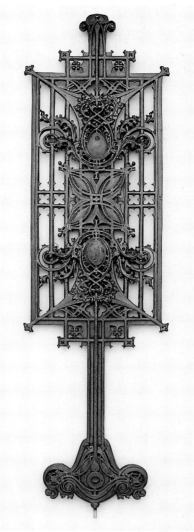

Cat. no. 137

1894. Gold, silver, bronze, each 5 diameter. Gift of George Grant Elmslie to The Art Institute of Chicago.

129. Adler and Sullivan. Elevator grill from the Stock Exchange Building, 30 North LaSalle Street, Chicago, 1892-94 (demolished). Cast and wrought iron, 212 x 104. Gift of Kenneth Newberger to The Art Institute of Chicago.

130. Adler and Sullivan. T-plate from the elevator grills of the Stock Exchange Building, 1892-94. Stamped copper, 40.7 x 44.2. Gift of Sudler and Co. to The Art Institute of Chicago.

131. Adler and Sullivan. Section of stenciling from the Trading Room, Stock Exchange Building, executed by Healy and Millet, 1892-94. Oil on canvas, 143.7 x 305.4 x 1. Gift of Mr.

and Mrs. Arthur Dubin to The Art Institute of Chicago. (See also plates 12, 13.)

132. Louis H. Sullivan. Sketch of the Eliel Apartment Building on Adler and Sullivan Stationery, November 28, 1894. Pencil on paper, 27.4 x 20. Lent by the Avery Architectural and Fine Arts Library, Columbia University.

133. Louis H. Sullivan. Detail of the facade of the Gage Building, 18 South Michigan Avenue, Chicago, 1898 (altered). Cast iron, 91.5 x 85. Gift of Mr. and Mrs. L. Lattin Smith to The Art Institute of Chicago.

134. Louis H. Sullivan. Elevation study for an ornamental lunette, possibly for the Gage Building, c. 1899. Pencil on paper, 16.8 x 18.2. Lent by the Avery Architectural and Fine Arts Library, Columbia University.

135. Louis H. Sullivan. Window detail from the Schlesinger and Mayer Store (now Carson, Pirie, Scott), State and Madison streets, Chicago, 1899. Terracotta, 27 x 45.7 x 15.2. Lent by Timothy Samuelson.

136. Louis H. Sullivan. One section of a screen from the Schlesinger and Mayer Store, 1899-1904. Wood, 35.5 x 35.5 x 2.5. Gift of George Fred Keck to The Art Institute of Chicago. (See Pollak, figs. 15, 16; pp. 260-61.)

137. Louis H. Sullivan. Baluster from the Schlesinger and Mayer Store, designed by George Grant Elmslie, 1899-1904. Cast iron, 89 x 25. Gift of Carson, Pirie, Scott to The Art Institute of Chicago.

138. Dankmar Adler. Elevation study for the west facade of the Isaiah Temple (now Ebenezer Missionary Baptist Church), 4501 South Vincennes Avenue, Chicago, May 16, 1898. Ink on linen, 71 x 93. Gift of Friedman, Alschuler, and Sincere to The Art Institute of Chicago.

139. Dankmar Adler. Alternate west elevation of the Isaiah Temple, c. 1898-99. Ink on linen, 63.5 x 82.6. Gift of Friedman, Alschuler, and Sincere to The Art Institute of Chicago.

140. Dankmar Adler. Elevation of an organ screen with Sullivanesque ornament for the Isaiah Temple, August 10, 1898 (unexecuted). Ink on linen, 37 x 48. Gift of Friedman, Alschul-

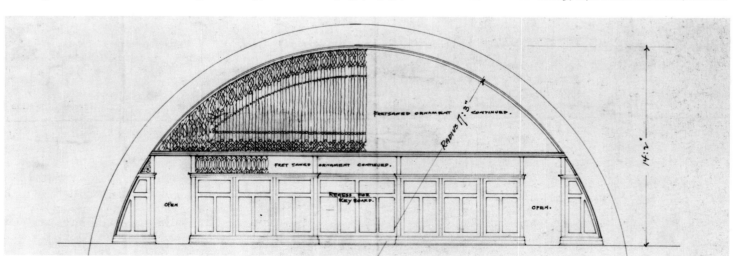

Cat. no. 140, detail

Cat. no. 143

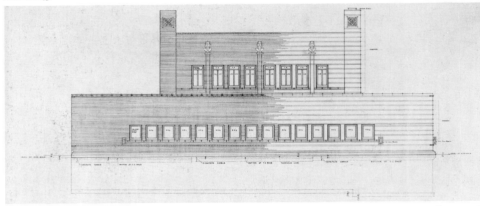

Cat. no. 146   Cat. no. 148

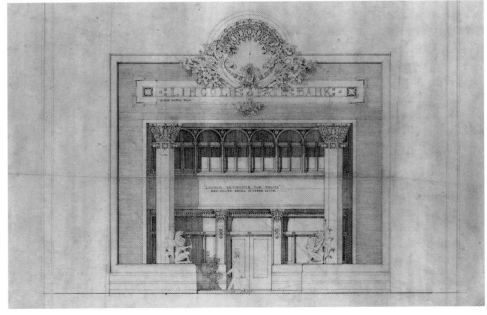

er, and Sincere to The Art Institute of Chicago.

141. Dankmar Adler. Elevation of an organ screen with Greco-Roman ornament for the Isaiah Temple, October 12, 1898. Ink on linen, 56 x 54. Gift of Friedman, Alschuler, and Sincere to The Art Institute of Chicago.

142. Louis H. Sullivan. Perspective rendering of St. Paul's Methodist Episcopal Church, 1340 Third Avenue, Cedar Rapids, Iowa, c. 1910 (executed differently). Watercolor on paper, 56 x 89. Lent by the Cedar Rapids Museum of Art. (See plate 43.)

143. Purcell, Feick, and Elmslie. Perspective rendering of proposed St. Paul's Methodist Episcopal Church, 1910. Ink on linen, 65 x 79. Lent by the Northwest Architectural Archives, University of Minnesota.

144. Louis H. Sullivan. South elevation of St. Paul's Methodist Episcopal Church, July 31, 1911 (executed differently). Ink on linen, 62 x 102.5. Gift of William Gray Purcell to The Art Institute of Chicago. (See plate 44.)

145. Louis H. Sullivan. Ornamental details from St. Paul's Methodist Episcopal Church, drawn July 31, 1911. Ink on linen, 62 x 102.5. Gift of William Gray Purcell to The Art Institute of Chicago.

146. Louis H. Sullivan. East elevation of the Peoples Savings Bank, 101 Third Avenue, Cedar Rapids, Iowa, July 14, 1910. Ink on linen, 69 x 102.5. Gift of William Gray Purcell to The Art Institute of Chicago.

147. Purcell, Feick, and Elmslie. Perspective rendering of the proposed First National Bank of Mankato, Minnesota, drawn September 12, 1911. Watercolor, colored pencil, and ink on paper, 59.7 x 77.5. Lent by the Northwest Architectural Archives, University of Minnesota. (See plate 46.)

148. Parker N. Berry. Elevation study of the proposed Lincoln State Bank, Chicago, 1912. Pencil on tracing paper, 33.3 x 51.6. Gift of Homer Grant Sailor, Jr., to The Art Institute of Chicago.

149. Parker N. Berry. Presentation rendering of the proposed Adeline Prouty Old Ladies Home, Princeton, Illinois, 1917. Ink on paper, 51.5 x 61. Lent by Deborah and Helmut Jahn.

150. Louis H. Sullivan. Three elevation studies for the Farmers and Merchants Union Bank, James Street and Broadway, Columbus, Wisconsin, 1919. Pencil on paper, various sizes. Gifts of J. Russell Wheeler to The Art Institute of Chicago.

151. Louis J. Millet. Sketch inscribed "Bon-Jour a Vous," sent to Sullivan from Millet, February 18, 1921. Pencil and colored pencil on paper, 27.4 x 12.8. Gift of Robert Kueny and the University Archives of the University of Wisconsin-Parkside to The Art Institute of Chicago.

152. Louis J. Millet. Sketch inscribed "Tombstone design," c. 1921. Pencil on paper, 16 x 21.3. Gift of Robert Kueny and the University

Cat. no. 152, detail

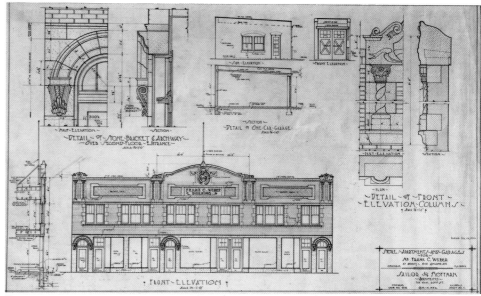

Cat. no. 153

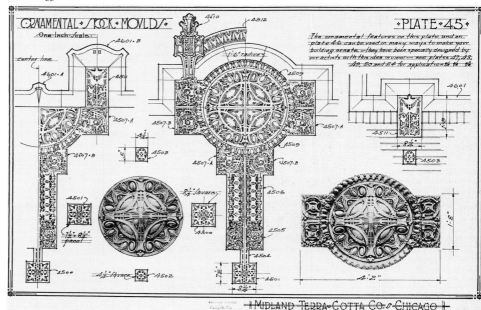

Cat. no. 154

Archives of the University of Wisconsin-Parkside to The Art Institute of Chicago.

153. Homer Grant Sailor of Sailor and Hoffman. Elevations and plans for stores, apartments, and garages for Frank C. Weber, 8151 South Ashland Avenue, Chicago, 1926 (demolished). Ink and colored ink on tracing paper, 57 x 91.5. Gift of Homer Grant Sailor, Jr., to The Art Institute of Chicago.

154. Midland Terra Cotta Co. Four presentation plates for stock ornament in Sullivan's style from a promotional brochure, c. 1922-25. Offset print, 25 x 36.2. The Burnham Library of Architecture, The Art Insitute of Chicago.

155. Louis H. Sullivan. Sketch of preliminary ornamental design, proposed monument for the National Terracotta Society, January 25, 1921. Pencil on blue paper, 15.2 x 14. Gift of Robert Kueny and the University Archives of the University of Wisconsin-Parkside to The Art Institute of Chicago.

156. Louis H. Sullivan. Elevation study for a proposed monument, exhibition pylon, National Terracotta Society, April 4, 1923. Pencil on paper, 28 x 21.5. Gift of Robert Kueny and the University Archives of the University of Wisconsin-Parkside to The Art Institute of Chicago.

157. Louis H. Sullivan. "Development of a blank block through a series of mechanical manipulations," 1922, plate 1 from *A System of Architectural Ornament, According with a Philosophy of Man's Powers,* 1924. Pencil on strathmore, 57.5 x 73.5. The Art Institute of Chicago. (See Pollak, fig. 17, p. 262.)

158. Louis H. Sullivan. "Manipulation of the organic," 1922, plate 2 from *A System of Architectural Ornament. . .,* 1924. Pencil on strathmore, 57.7 x 73.5. The Art Insitute of Chicago.

159. Louis H. Sullivan. "The values of parallel axes," 1922, plate 7 from *A System of Architectural Ornament. . .,* 1924. Pencil on strathmore, 57.7 x 73.5. The Art Institute of Chicago.

160. Louis H. Sullivan. "Values of parallel planes. . .," 1922, plate 11 from *A System of Architectural Ornament. . .,* 1924. Pencil on strathmore, 57.7 x 73.5. The Art Institute of Chicago. (See plate 40.)

161. Louis H. Sullivan. "Interpenetration. . .," 1922, plate 13 from *A System of Architectural Ornament. . .,* 1924. Pencil on strathmore, 57.7 x 73.5. The Art Institute of Chicago.

162. Louis H. Sullivan. "Fantasy, a study of curves. . .," 1922, plate 14 from *A System of Architectural Ornament. . .,* 1924. Pencil on strathmore, 57.7 x 73.5. The Art Institute of Chicago. (See plate 41.)

163. Louis H. Sullivan. "Impromptu," 1922, plate 16 from *A System of Architectural Ornament. . .,* 1924. Pencil on strathmore, 57.7 x 73.5. The Art Institute of Chicago. (See Pollak, fig. 18, p. 263.)

164. Louis H. Sullivan. Untitled ornamental design, 1922, plate 18 from *A System of Architectural Ornament. . .,* 1924. Pencil on strathmore, 57.7 x 73.5. The Art Institute of Chicago.

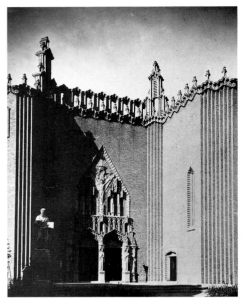

Fig. 13 Frank Lloyd Wright, Detail of the entrance to the Francis Apartments, 4304 South Forrestville Avenue, 1895 (demolished).

Fig. 14 Frank Lloyd Wright, Detail of the Alphonso Iannelli sculptures of Midway Gardens, Cottage Grove Avenue and 60th Street, 1914 (demolished).

Fig. 15 Francis Barry with Alphonso Iannelli, St. Thomas the Apostle Church, 55th and Kimbark, 1924.

Fig. 16 Frank Lloyd Wright, Imperial Hotel, Tokyo, 1915-16 (demolished).

V. Frank Lloyd Wright and the Prairie School: International Interactions

Frank Lloyd Wright is undoubtedly America's most famous architect and Sullivan's most famous student. Wright, whose early ornament is Sullivanesque (fig. 13) and who called Sullivan his "lieber Meister," continued his teacher's search for an American architecture in the development of the Prairie School of residential design and its unique relationship to, and reflection of, the gently rolling landscape of the Midwest and Wright's native Wisconsin. But there are foreign roots to this movement beyond the rationalism of Viollet-le-Duc that relate to Japanese spatial traditions, Jugendstil design in Germany and Austria, and the English Arts and Crafts movement. Interior architectural designers such as George Mann Niedecken, who trained in Vienna, and sculptors such as Italian émigré Alphonso Iannelli collaborated with Wright on a number of commissions, most notably Niedecken's interiors of the renowned Robie House of 1909 and Iannelli's sculptures for the 1913 Midway Gardens (fig. 14; now demolished). Thomas E. Tallmadge, Vernon Watson, and William Drummond also built houses influenced by the spatial and decorative features of Wright's Prairie style.

Wright himself exported this "American" house style to Europe with a 1910 publication of his work in Berlin called *Ausgeführte Bauten und Entwürfe von Frank Lloyd Wright*. A Berlin exhibition concurrent with this publication influenced a range of German architects such as Mies van der Rohe, who later remarked, "Here finally was a master-builder drawing upon the veritable fountainhead of architecture, who with true originality lifted his architectural creations into the light. Here, again, at last, genuine organic architecture flowered. . . . His influence was strongly felt even when it was not actually visible." This influence ranged from the open space planning of Mies van der Rohe and Walter Gropius to the Prairie-influenced designs of J. J. P. Oud and Robert van T'hoff in Holland. And, as regards the Orient, Wright himself had the opportunity to

build there his famed Imperial Hotel (fig. 16; now demolished) of Tokyo, 1915, and a number of other buildings such as the Aisaku Hayashi House (1917) in Tokyo, the Tazaemon Yamamura House (1918) in Ashiya, and the Jiyu Gakauen Girls' School (1921) in Tokyo.

Three of Wright's former employees also exported the Prairie style as well. Walter Burley Griffin and his wife, Marion Mahony, moved to Australia after winning the 1912 competition to plan Canberra, and together designed a number of projects in Melbourne and Sydney. Francis Barry Byrne, a specialist in Prairie-influenced ecclesiastic design (fig. 15), built the church of Christ the King in Cork, Ireland, in 1927. Thus, if we consider that Wright is an extension of Sullivan in many ways, then the international impact of Wrightian design is Sullivan's most important legacy as well.

165. Frank Lloyd Wright. Ornamental baluster from the Roloson Apartments, 3213-3219 South Calumet Avenue, Chicago, 1894. Terracotta, 43 x 20 x 20. Lent by the Deutsches Architekturmuseum, Frankfurt.

166. Frank Lloyd Wright. Perspective rendering of the Francis Apartments, 4304 South Forestville Avenue, Chicago, 1895 (demolished). Brown pen and cream wash on tracing paper, 30 x 43. Lent by the Royal Institute of British Architects, British Architectural Library, Drawings Collection. (See plate 45.)

167. Frank Lloyd Wright. Circle block from the dado, Francis Apartments, 1895. Terracotta, 45.7 x 44.4 x 10.1. Lent by Timothy Samuelson.

168. Frank Lloyd Wright. Circular vent cover from the Francis Apartments, 1895. Cast iron, 97.5 diameter. Gift of The Antiquarian Society of The Art Institute of Chicago through the Mrs. Robert Hixon Glore Fund.

169. Vernon Watson of Tallmadge and Watson. Elevations and sections of the Vernon Watson House, 143 Fair Oaks Avenue, Oak Park, Illinois, 1904. Ink on linen, 46 x 66.7. Gift of the estate of Vernon Watson to The Art Institute of Chicago.

170. George Mann Niedecken. Perspective rendering of the interior of the Bresler Art Gallery, Milwaukee, Wisconsin, c. 1904. Ink on linen, 48 x 74. Restricted gift of the Thomas J. and Mary E. Eyerman Foundation to The Art Institute of Chicago. (See Wilson, fig. 4, p. 210.)

171. George Mann Niedecken for Frank Lloyd Wright. Rendering of a desk for the Avery Coonley House, 300 Scottswood Road, Riverside, Illinois, c. 1907. Ink and watercolor on paper, 27.9 x 39.4. Gift of Mr. and Mrs. James Howlett to The Art Institute of Chicago.

172. George Mann Niedecken for Frank Lloyd Wright. Perspective studies of hall chair designs for the Avery Coonley House, c. 1908. Ink and watercolor on tracing paper, 24.7 x 15, and pencil on paper, 26.4 x 13.5. Purchase, Department of Architecture, The Art Institute of Chicago.

173. Frank Lloyd Wright. Window from the Avery Coonley House, 1908. Leaded glass, 111.5 x 52. Gift of Mr. and Mrs. James Howlett to The Art Institute of Chicago.

174. Frank Lloyd Wright. Window from the Evans House, 9914 Longwood Drive, Chicago, 1908. Clear, opaque, and mottled glass (green and white), 105.2 x 94.8. Gift of Mr. and Mrs. F. M. Fahrenwald to The Art Institute of Chicago.

175. Frank Lloyd Wright. Library table from the Evans House, 1908. Oak, 73 x 91 x 168. Gift of Mr. and Mrs. F. M. Fahrenwald to The Art Institute of Chicago. Chicago showing only.

176. Frank Lloyd Wright. Dining room furniture from the Robie House, 5757 Woodlawn Avenue, Chicago, 1909. Table: oak, colored glass, and ceramic tiles, 141.3 x 249.4 x 135.8; chairs: oak and leather, 133 x 43.2 x 50.2. Lent by the David and Alfred Smart Gallery, the University of Chicago. (See plates 52, 53.)

177. Frank Lloyd Wright. Window from the Robie House, 1909-10. Clear and colored leaded glass, 124.5 x 76.8. Lent by the David and Alfred Smart Gallery, the University of Chicago.

178. Frank Lloyd Wright. Cutaway model showing the dining room and living room of the Robie House, 1909. Constructed in 1986 by Richard Tickner for the Musée d'Orsay.

179. George Mann Niedecken for Frank Lloyd Wright. Perspective rendering of proposed living room decorations, the Robie

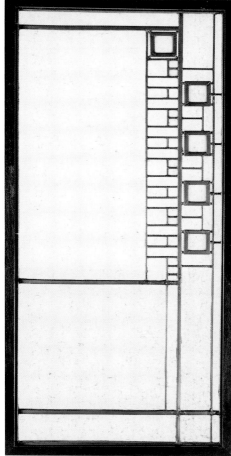

Cat. no. 173

House, 1909-10. Pencil and watercolor on buff paper, 26.1 x 79.4. Lent by the Milwaukee Art Museum Collection, gift of Mr. and Mrs. Robert L. Jacobson.

180. George Mann Niedecken. Armchair from the Robie House (see cat. no. 179). Lami-

Cat. no. 169, detail

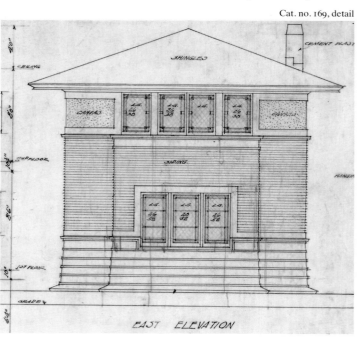

EAST ELEVATION

Cat. no. 171

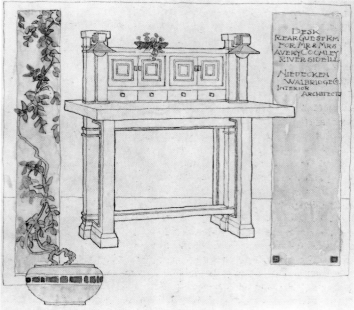

nated oak, 100.3 x 80 x 78.7. Lent by the David and Alfred Smart Gallery, the University of Chicago.

181. *Ausgeführte Bauten und Entwürfe von Frank Lloyd Wright* (Berlin, 1910). Burnham Library of Architecture, The Art Institute of Chicago.

182. George Mann Niedecken of Niedecken-Walbridge Co. Interior Architects. Presentation rendering of the proposed interior of the Henry Ford House, Dearborn, Michigan, c. 1910. Pencil and watercolor on a linen scroll, 51 x 224. Restricted gift of the Thomas J. and Mary E. Eyerman Foundation to The Art Institute of Chicago. (See plate 48.)

183. Frank Lloyd Wright. Triptych window from a niche in the Avery Coonley Playhouse, 350 Fairbanks Road, Riverside, Illinois, 1912. Clear and colored leaded glass; center panel, 89.5 x 109.3; side panels, 91.5 x 19.8. Restricted

gift of the Walter E. Heller Foundation and Dr. and Mrs. Edwin J. DeCosta to The Art Institute of Chicago. (See plates 50, 51.)

184. Walter Burley Griffin and Marion Mahony Griffin. Bird's-eye view of Canberra from Mt. Ainslie, c. 1911-12. Ink on linen, 61.5 x 233.5. Gift of Marion Mahony Griffin through Eric Nicholls to The Art Institute of Chicago. (See Van Zanten, fig. 11, p. 329.)

185. Walter Burley Griffin and Marion Mahony Griffin. Plan of Canberra, 1912. Ink on linen, 104 x 76. Gift of Marion Mahony Griffin through Eric Nicholls to The Art Institute of Chicago.

186. Walter Burley Griffin and Marion Mahony Griffin. Pespective rendering of Rock Crest/Rock Glen, Mason City, Iowa, c. 1912. Lithograph and gouache on green satin, 59 x 201. Gift of Marion Mahony Griffin to The Art Institute of Chicago. (See plate 49.)

187. Francis Barry Byrne, with Walter Burley Griffin (?). Elevation study for the proposed C. A. Dakin House, Mason City, Iowa, c. 1912. Pencil and colored pencil on paper, 39.5 x 43.2. Lent by the Chicago Historical Society, gift of Mrs. Annette C. Byrne. (See Wilson, fig. 14, p. 219.)

188. Augustus Fritsch with Walter Burley Griffin and Marion Mahony Griffin. Perspective rendering of Newman College, University of Melbourne, Swanston Street, Melbourne, Australia, c. 1915-17. Lithograph and gouache on beige satin, 48 x 118. Gift of Marion Mahony Griffin through Eric Nicholls to The Art Institute of Chicago.

189. William Drummond. Perspective study for a Prairie School apartment building, c. 1914. Ink on linen, 61 x 89. Lent by the Chicago Architecture Foundation.

190. Frank Lloyd Wright. Model of Midway Gardens, Cottage Grove Avenue and 60th Street, Chicago, Illinois, 1914 (demolished). Constructed in 1986 by Richard Tickner for The Art Institute of Chicago.

191. Alfonso Iannelli. Elevation study for Sprite sculpture, Midway Gardens, drawn March 28, 1914. Pen and ink on prepared board, approx. 33 x 20. Lent by the Metropolitan Museum of Art, gift of Scott Elliott in memory of Alex Sutherland.

192. Alfonso Iannelli with Frank Lloyd Wright. Head of a Sprite from Midway Gardens, 1914. Plaster, 54 x 24 x 29. Gift of the Thomas J. and Mary E. Eyerman Foundation to The Art Institute of Chicago. (See plate 47.)

193. Alfonso Iannelli with Frank Lloyd Wright. Four Sprite studies for Midway Gardens, 1914. Plaster, each approx. 27. Lent by Seymour H. Persky.

194. Purcell and Elmslie. Two elevations of the Amy Hunter House, 1441 Braeburn Road, Flossmoor, Illinois, drawn by G.G.E. (George Grant Elmslie) and F.A.S., December 20, 1916. Ink on linen, 62.4 x 88.9. Lent by the Northwest Architectural Archive, University of Minnesota. (See Wilson, fig. 10, p. 216.)

195. Francis Barry Byrne with Alfonso Iannelli. Perspective rendering of the exterior of St. Francis Xavier High School, 808 Linden Avenue, Wilmette, Illinois, 1923. Pencil on tracing paper, mounted on paper, 41.5 x 66. Restricted gift of the Thomas J. and Mary E. Eyerman Foundation to The Art Institute of Chicago.

196. Francis Barry Byrne. Initial sketches for the church of Christ the King, Cork, Ireland, labeled "Sketched on shipboard enroute to Ireland — first stage of idea," c. 1927. Pencil on paper, 15.2 x 22.9. Lent by the Chicago Historical Society, gift of Mrs. Annette C. Byrne.

197. Francis Barry Byrne with J. R. Boyd Barrett. Elevation of the entrance of the church of Christ the King, 1928. Pencil on tracing paper, 100 x 69. Lent by the Chicago Historical Society, gift of Mrs. Annette C. Byrne.

Cat. no. 197

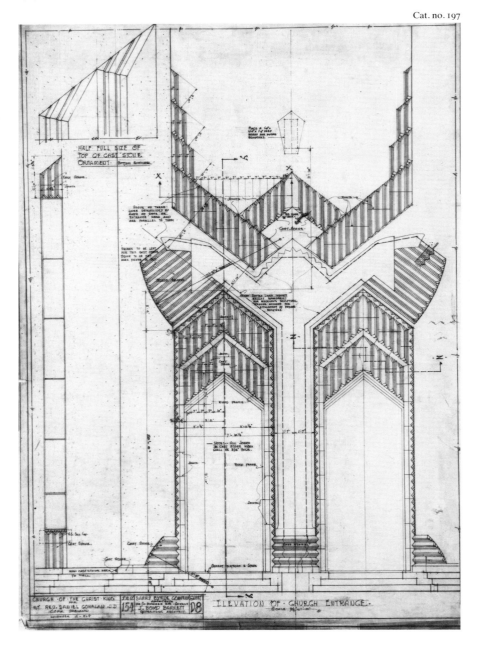

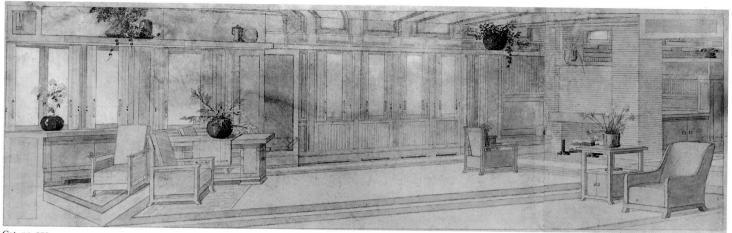

Cat. no. 179

Cat. no. 188

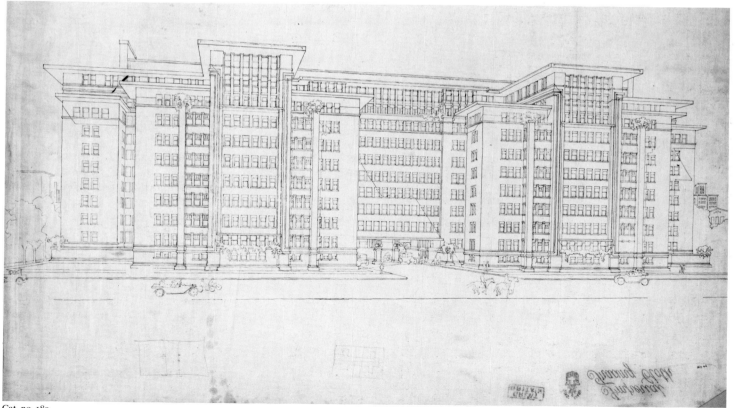

Cat. no. 189

VI. Paris on the Prairie: Burnham's Vision of Chicago

Unlike Sullivan and Wright, Daniel H. Burnham has only recently and somewhat reluctantly been admitted into the heroes' circle. This is partly because Sullivan and Wright, in the eyes of Modernist architects, consciously strove to create an American architecture that was unique to this country, even though they, as Burnham, drew on European sources. Yet Burnham's architecture and planning is no less American than theirs, and his impact on Chicago and the world is, perhaps, greater. When Burnham's partner John Wellborn Root died in 1891, he was consulting architect for the World's Columbian Exposition of 1893 under Burnham's supervision as Director of the Works. In addition to employing a number of East Coast architects and planners to design major buildings and spaces for the fair, Burnham also brought other architects to Chicago to take the place of his deceased partner. In doing this, he was the first American architect to organize his office on a corporate model, with himself as president and with various vice-presidents of design and construction. The most prominent of these assistants was Charles B. Atwood, who had a team of designers that included German architect Peter J. Weber and Atwood's New York colleague Frederick P. Dinkelberg. They and others within the Burnham organization, such as Beaux-Arts-trained Peirce Anderson, designed some of Burnham's most famous structures across the nation: among them, the addition to the Land Title and Trust Company Building (fig. 17), Philadelphia, 1900; the Flatiron Building in New York from 1902; and, in Chicago, the Railway Exchange Building (fig. 18) of 1903-04, to which Burnham moved his corporate offices; and the Conway Building of 1912. All have classical details based on French or Roman examples. In the case of atrium department stores such as the proposed but unexecuted Eaton's Department Store, shown here, they use French planning principles. But retail buildings such as Eaton's,

Marshall Field's in Chicago, and Selfridge's in London can be said to be more American than European in their technology and scale. The fire-proofed steel frame and the frequent use of mass-produced details of terracotta and other materials mark them as a development from earlier 1880s buildings.

Burnham's planning schemes display much the same hybridization. He began his experience with large-scale planning as Director of the Works at the World's Columbian Exposition. The fair's administration was modeled, in part, on the experiences of the 1889 World's Fair in Paris. The classical architecture and uniform tones and cornice lines of the so-called "White City," grouped around a central Court of Honor, manifested European origins and Beaux-Arts planning principles. Burnham's ability to coordinate large projects was further refined in his work on the Plan of Washington, D.C. (1902), the Cleveland Civic Center, plans for Manila and Baguio in the Philippines, and the San Francisco Plan (all from 1905). This last project was prepared with the assistance of Edward H. Bennett, a young English immigrant trained at the Ecole des Beaux-Arts who was to become the co-author of Burnham's planning masterwork – the acclaimed *Plan of Chicago* (1909).

In the Chicago Plan, Burnham and Bennett compiled information on various European cities such as Rome, Vienna, Berlin, Budapest, and especially Paris. Newspaper articles at the time recognized that the plan would make Chicago a "Paris by the Lake," with the construction of grand boulevards comparable to those implemented by Baron Georges-Eugène Haussmann in the French capital during the mid-nineteenth century. Burnham even brought Frenchman Fernand Janin to Chicago to work on some of the drawings for the plan. Jules Guérin, a renderer born in St. Louis and trained as a painter at the Ecole des Beaux-Arts, prepared a number of the drawings, as did members of Burnham's own staff.

Some of the presentations make direct reference to cultural buildings in Paris such as the Opéra of 1860-75 by Charles Garnier which appears, transplanted, on Michigan Avenue (see pl. 76; cat. no. 230). It is no

Fig. 17 D. H. Burnham and Co., Addition to the Land Title and Trust Co. Building, 1400 Chestnut Street, Philadelphia, 1900-04.

Fig. 18 D. H. Burnham and Co., Railway Exchange Building (now Santa Fe Center), 224 South Michigan Avenue, 1903-04.

Fig. 19 Henry Ives Cobb, Ryerson Physical Laboratory Building of the University of Chicago, 1100-14 East 58th Street, 1894.

surprise that this type of image appears in the *Plan of Chicago*. The World's Columbian Exposition gave Chicago an impetus for expanding and improving the city's cultural and educational facilities, private and public. Buildings such as The Art Institute of Chicago and Chicago Public Library (pls. 65, 66), both by Shepley, Rutan and Coolidge, and the

Henry Ives Cobb structures at the University of Chicago (fig. 19) are more or less directly related to the World's Fair. Moreover, Burnham himself was an avid supporter of the arts, seeing historic and cultural sites as closely connected to the commercial success of a city like Paris or Chicago. His own architectural vision of Paris on the Prairie included

Fig. 20 Exhibition of the Chicago Plan drawings in Düsseldorf, August 1910; from Charles Moore, Daniel H. Burnham *(1921).*

THE CHICAGO PLAN EXHIBITED AT DÜSSELDORF, AUGUST, 1910

Fig. 21 D. H. Burnham and Co., Orchestra Hall, 220 South Michigan Avenue, 1904.

ning exhibits in 1910 in Düsseldorf (fig. 20) and London. It was at the London Town Planning Conference of that year that Burnham is supposed to have uttered his oft quoted exhortation, "Make no little plans; they have no magic to stir men's blood and probably will not be realized."

When Burnham retired soon thereafter, he referred planning requests to his assistant Bennett, whose earlier involvement on the Chicago Plan enabled him to implement some of Burnham's ideas over the next two decades. Bennett became a leading proponent of the City Beautiful movement, designing buildings, boulevards, and street fixtures based on French and Roman classical prototypes, adapting their forms to the modern technology of steel and concrete in Chicago and throughout North America, even in small urban locations such as Cedar Rapids, Iowa.

In addition to Bennett, other architects followed suit in altering and adapting French classical sources for Chicago's needs. Rapp and Rapp designed numerous movie palaces in the early twenties, based on French and Spanish Renaissance prototypes. Marshall and Fox built a number of hotels and apartments in the city, two of which were specifically French in inspiration but Chicago multistory in construction: the Mansard-roofed Blackstone Hotel (1908) and the 1911 apartment building at 1550 North State Parkway. The latter's classical details and bay windows make a good comparison with Peter Weber's drawing of a similar apartment house at 3400 North Sheridan Road from 1917. Holabird and Roche's Palmer House of 1925, though elaborately decorated in various French period styles from Renaissance through Empire, was renowned in Europe because of its sophisticated plan and steel construction as published in Richard Neutra's book *Wie baut Amerika?* from 1927. The Austrian-born Neutra received on-the-job training with Holabird and Roche on this project, as well as design training with Frank Lloyd Wright before starting his own career in California. Another Chicago hotel, the Stevens (now Chicago Hilton and Towers; pls. 86, 87) by Holabird and Roche, became internationally famous as the largest hotel in the world when it was built in 1927.

Thus, Burnham's ideas spread across the world in his buildings and city plans, and in the work of his followers and architectural supporters. But more specifically, his 1909 vision of Chicago shaped the appearance of the city for the boom decades that followed between the end of World War I and the Great Depression of the 1930s.

cultural buildings such as Orchestra Hall (fig. 21) of 1903, which his firm designed, as well as the Field Museum of Natural History, begun by Burnham but completed by his successor firm Graham, Anderson, Probst and White, after Burnham's death in 1912.

The Chicago Plan drawings were publicly unveiled and exhibited at the Art Institute on July 5, 1909, when the book was published. After the drawings were exhibited in Chicago, they were requested for city plan-

Cat. no. 206, detail

198. P. B. Wight. Perspective rendering of a competitive design for the Chicago Public Library, 1891. Ink on paper, 54 x 74. Gift of Peter B. Wight to The Art Institute of Chicago. (See plate 64.)

199. John Wellborn Root. Perspective rendering for a proposed Fine Arts Museum (The Art Institute of Chicago?) for the World's Columbian Exposition, Chicago, delineated by Paul Lautrup, c. 1890. Pencil and watercolor on paper, 55.5 x 115. Gift of John Wellborn Root, Jr., to The Art Institute of Chicago. (See plate 62.)

200. Peter J. Weber. Elevation study of the Partello Tower Company or Elevated Electric Railroad Tower (for the World's Columbian Exposition?), February 26, 1892. Pencil on tracing paper, approx. 53.5 x 42. Gift of Bertram A. Weber to The Art Institute of Chicago.

201. Peter J. Weber. Elevation of proposed design for entrance to World's Columbian Exposition fairgrounds on 64th Street, December 31, 1892. Ink on linen, 51 x 55.5. Gift of Bertram A. Weber to The Art Institute of Chicago. (See plate 67.)

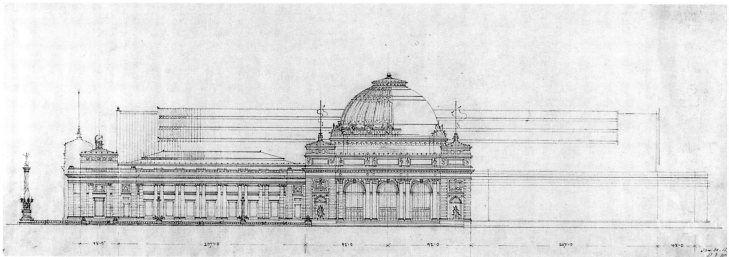

Cat. no. 207

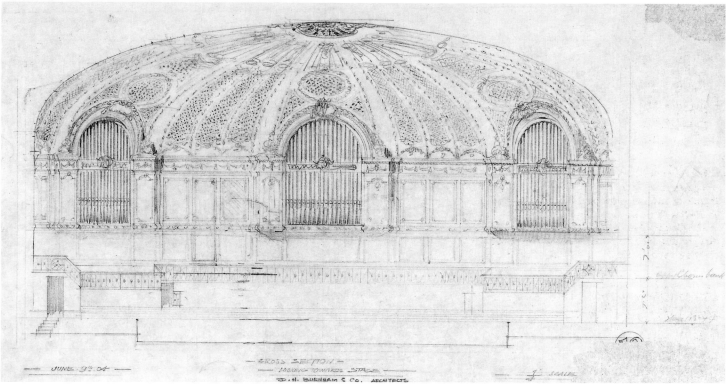

Cat. no. 217

202. Peter J. Weber. Elevation of proposed design for entrance to the World's Columbian Exposition fairgrounds on 60th Street, January 7, 1893. Ink on linen, 49 x 75.5. Gift of Bertram A. Weber to The Art Institute of Chicago. (See plate 68.)

203. Peter J. Weber. Perspective rendering of the Chocolat Menier Pavilion, World's Columbian Exposition, 1893 (demolished). Colored lithograph, 41.5 x 55. Gift of Bertram A. Weber to The Art Institute of Chicago. (See plate 63.)

204. Peter J. Weber. Sketch section of the Chocolat Menier Pavilion, March 8, 1893. Pencil and colored pencil on tracing paper, 41 x 48.5. Gift of Bertram A. Weber to The Art Institute of Chicago.

205. Peter J. Weber. Sketch elevation, section, and plan of the Chocolat Menier Pavilion, March 5, 1893. Ink, pencil, and wash on paper, 54 x 53.7. Gift of Bertram A. Weber to The Art Institute of Chicago.

206. Peter J. Weber for Charles B. Atwood, Architect. Elevation and partial plan of the exhibition pavilion for Messrs. Cluett Coon and Co., World's Columbian Exposition, January 3, 1893. Blueprint, 66 x 65.5. Gift of Bertram A. Weber to The Art Institute of Chicago.

207. Peter J. Weber. Elevation of a proposed exhibition hall for the lakefront (in Grant Park), Chicago, 1898. Ink and colored ink on linen, 37.5 x 85. Restricted Gift of the Architecture Society Fellows to The Art Institute of Chicago.

208. Peter J. Weber. Window from the Casino (demolished), Ravinia, Highland Park, Illinois, 1904. Lead and colored glass, 56.4 x 81. Gift of the Ravinia Festival to The Art Institute of Chicago.

209. William C. Whitney. Perspective rendering of the Minnesota Pavilion, World's Columbian Exposition, 1893 (demolished). Watercolor on paper, 36.4 x 44.5. Lent by the Northwest Architectural Archives, the University of Minnesota.

210. Lewis Edward Hickmott. Perspective view of the Court of Honor, World's Columbian Exposition, 1894. Oil on canvas, 130 x 203.5. Lent by the Chicago Historical Society. (See plate 60.)

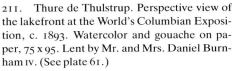

Cat. no. 223

Cat. no. 224

211.   Thure de Thulstrup. Perspective view of the lakefront at the World's Columbian Exposition, c. 1893. Watercolor and gouache on paper, 75 x 95. Lent by Mr. and Mrs. Daniel Burnham IV. (See plate 61.)

212.   Daniel H. Burnham. Perspective sketch for a South Shore park, c. 1896. Watercolor on paper, 16 x 25. Gift of Hubert Burnham and Daniel Burnham, Jr., to The Art Institute of Chicago.

213.   D. H. Burnham and Co. Perspective rendering of proposed addition to the 1897 Land Title and Trust Co. Building, 1400 Chestnut Street, Philadelphia, delineated by Hughson Hawley, 1900. Pencil and watercolor on paper, 132.7 x 77.1. The Art Institute of Chicago. (See plate 56.)

214.   D. H. Burnham and Co. Perspective rendering of the Flatiron Building, 23rd Street and Broadway, New York, drawn by Jules Guérin, 1902. Charcoal and ink wash on underpainted linen, 80 x 50.8. Restricted gift of the Thomas J. and Mary E. Eyerman Foundation to The Art Institute of Chicago. (See plate 54.)

215.   D. H. Burnham and Co. Block from the Railway Exchange Building, 224 South Michi-

Cat. no. 235

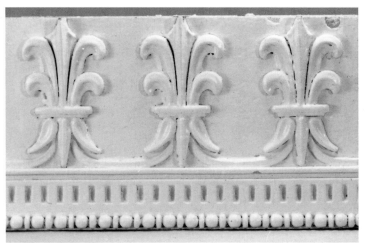

Cat. no. 226, detail

Cat. no. 226

gan Avenue, Chicago, 1903-04. White glazed terracotta, 23 x 49.5 x 23. Gift of the Santa Fe Southern Pacific Corporation to The Art Institute of Chicago.

216.   D. H. Burnham and Co. Perspective study of Orchestra Hall, 220 South Michigan Avenue, Chicago, c. 1904. Pencil on tracing paper, approx. 115 x 66. Restricted gift of the Frank E. and Seba B. Payne Foundation to The Art Institute of Chicago.

217.   D. H. Burnham and Co. Cross Section looking toward the stage of Orchestra Hall, June 9, 1904. Pencil and colored pencil on tracing paper, approx. 40.5 x 73.5. Restricted gift of the Frank E. and Seba B. Payne Foundation to The Art Institute of Chicago.

218.   D. H. Burnham and Co. Elevation study for the Cliff Dwellers Club penthouse atop Or-

chestra Hall, c. 1907. Pencil and colored pencil on tracing paper, approx. 50 x 92. Restricted gift of the Frank E. and Seba B. Payne Foundation to The Art Institute of Chicago.

219.   D. H. Burnham and Co. with Swales, Atkinson, and Burnet. Perspective view of Selfridge's Department Store, Oxford Street, London, delineated by Harold Oakley, c. 1906. Toned print, 63.5 x 104. Gift of Harry J. Scharres to The Art Institute of Chicago. (See Harris, fig. 15, p. 146.)

220.   D. H. Burnham and Co., later Graham, Burnham and Co. Perspective study of the proposed colonnade, Eaton's Department Store, Toronto, delineated by J.L.B., January 20, 1912. Pencil on tracing paper, 122 x 83. Department of Architecture Purchase, The Art Institute of Chicago. (See plate 55.)

221.   D. H. Burnham and Co., later Graham, Burnham and Co. Sketch elevation of the proposed Eaton's Department Store, February 14, 1912. Pencil and red pencil on tracing paper, 64.6 x 55.8. Restricted gift of the Benefactors of Architecture, The Art Institute of Chicago.

222.   D. H. Burnham and Co., later Graham, Burnham and Co., and re-labeled Graham, Anderson, Probst and White. Perspective rendering of the proposed Eaton's Department Store, 1912. Pencil on tracing paper, 64 x 97.5. Department of Architecture Purchase, The Art Institute of Chicago.

223.   D. H. Burnham and Co., later Graham, Burnham and Co. Perspective study of the interior atrium of the proposed Eaton's Department Store, view similar to Marshall Field's Department Store, Chicago, c. 1912. Pencil on

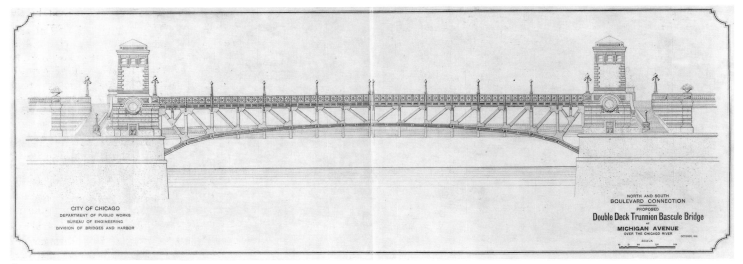

Cat. no. 237

Cat. no. 238

tracing paper, 65 x 45. Restricted gift of the Benefactors of Architecture, The Art Institute of Chicago.

224. D. H. Burnham and Co., later Graham, Burnham and Co. Two perspective studies of the interior atrium of the proposed Eaton's Department Store, similar to Parisian Department Store, c. 1912. Pencil on tracing paper, 87.5 x 57, and 87.5 x 60.5. Restricted gift of the Benefactors of Architecture, The Art Institute of Chicago. (See Harris, fig. 17, p. 147.)

225. D. H. Burnham and Co., later Graham, Burnham and Co. Two perspective renderings for the proposed facade treatments of the Con-

way Building, 111 West Washington Street, Chicago, delineated by C.B., c. 1912-14. Watercolor on paper, each 96 x 44. Lent by Rubloff Inc. (See plate 59.)

226. D. H. Burnham and Co., later Graham, Burnham and Co. Fragments from the lobby of the Conway Building, 1912-14. Glazed terracotta, each approx. 30 x 15 x 7. Gifts of Jack Train Associates and Pepper Construction Co. to The Art Institute of Chicago.

227. Jules Guérin for Daniel H. Burnham and Edward H. Bennett. View of Chicago from Jackson Park to Grant Park, 1907, plate 49 from the *Plan of Chicago,* 1909. Watercolor and pen-

cil on paper, 104 x 477. On permanent loan to The Art Institute of Chicago from the City of Chicago. (See plates 70, 71.)

228. Jules Guérin for Daniel H. Burnham and Edward H. Bennett. View of Chicago looking west, December 1907, plate 87 from the *Plan of Chicago,* 1909. Watercolor and pencil on paper, 145.5 x 233. Lent by Patrick Shaw. Paris and Chicago showing only. (See plate 78.)

229. Jules Guérin for Daniel H. Burnham and Edward H. Bennett. Rendering of the proposed boulevard to connect the north and south sides of the river, Chicago, c. 1908, plate 112 from the *Plan of Chicago,* 1909. Pencil, watercolor, and

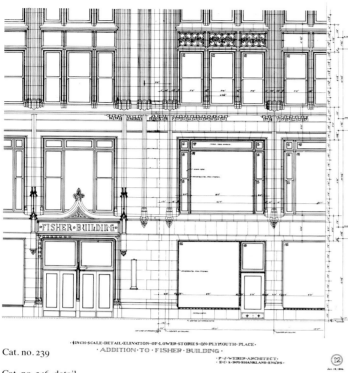

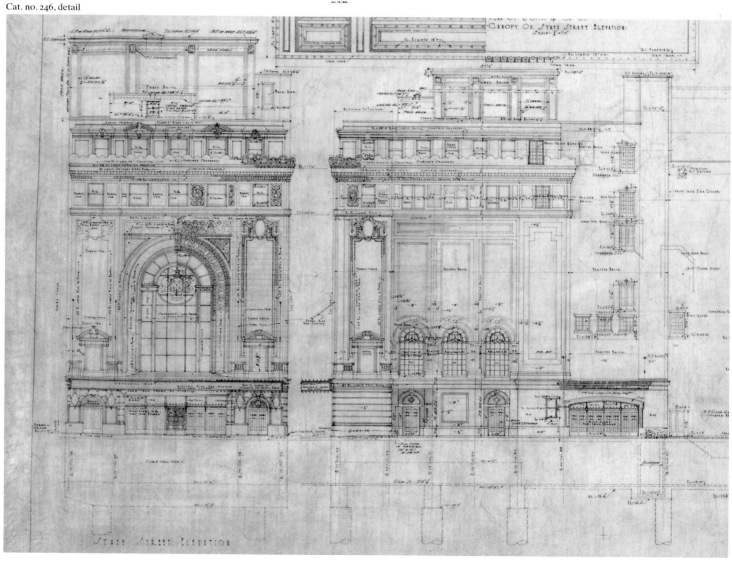

Cat. no. 239

Cat. no. 246, detail

tempera on paper, 185 x 145. Lent by the Chicago Historical Society. (See plate 77.)

230. Chris. U. Bagge for Daniel H. Burnham and Edward H. Bennett. View of Michigan Avenue looking towards the south, Chicago, c. 1908, plate 118 from the *Plan of Chicago,* 1909. Pencil, watercolor, and tempera on paper, 75 x 103. Lent by the Chicago Historical Society. (See plate 76.)

231. Jules Guérin for Daniel H. Burnham and Edward H. Bennett. View of the railway station scheme west of the river, Chicago, 1908, plate 122 from the *Plan of Chicago,* 1909. Pencil and watercolor on paper, 88 x 198. On permanent loan to The Art Institute of Chicago from the City of Chicago. (See Draper, fig. 4, p. 109.)

232. Jules Guérin for Daniel H. Burnham and Edward H. Bennett. View west of the proposed Civic Center Plaza, Chicago, 1908, plate 132 from the *Plan of Chicago,* 1909. Pencil and watercolor on paper, 76 x 105. On permanent loan to The Art Institute of Chicago from the City of Chicago. (See plate 73.)

233. Attributed to Fernand Janin for Daniel H. Burnham and Edward H. Bennett. Plan of

Cat. no. 250

the business center of Chicago, c. 1908, plate 129 from the *Plan of Chicago,* 1909. Pencil, ink, and wash on paper, 171 x 89.5. On permanent loan to The Art Institute of Chicago from the City of Chicago. (See plate 74.)

234. Jules Guérin for Daniel H. Burnham and Edward H. Bennett. Rendered elevation of the proposed Civic Center, Chicago, 1908. Ink, colored ink, watercolor, and pencil on paper, 76.8 x 58.5. Gift of Edward H. Bennett, Jr., to The Art Institute of Chicago. (See plate 69.)

235. Fernand Janin for Daniel H. Burnham and Edward H. Bennett. Elevation of the proposed Civic Center, Chicago, 1908, plate 131 from the *Plan of Chicago,* 1909. Ink and wash on paper, 103 x 305. On permanent loan to The Art Institute of Chicago from the City of Chicago. (See plate 75.)

236. Jules Guérin for Daniel H. Burnham and Edward H. Bennett. View of the proposed development of the City Center, Chicago, 1907, plate 137 from the *Plan of Chicago,* 1909. Tempera and pencil on toned paper, 84.7 x 122. On permanent loan to The Art Institute of Chicago from the City of Chicago. (See plate 72.)

237. Edward H. Bennett. Proposed double deck trunnion bascule bridge at Michigan Avenue, Chicago, October 1912. Ink on linen, 59 x 131.5. Lent by the City of Chicago, Department of Public Works, Bureau of Engineering.

238. Edward H. Bennett. Proposed shore development, Cedar Rapids, Iowa, c. 1916. Ink on paper, 74.5 x 112. Lent by the Cedar Rapids Art Museum, City of Cedar Rapids Collection.

239. Peter J. Weber. Three drawings for an addition to the Fisher Building (D. H. Burnham and Co., 1894-96), Dearborn at Van Buren streets, Chicago, January 18-26, 1906. Ink and

colored ink on linen, 106.5 x 77, 93 x 76.5, 116 x 76.5. Gift of Bertram A. Weber to The Art Institute of Chicago. (See plates 18, 19.)

240. Peter J. Weber. Perspective rendering of a skyscraper in the Chicago School style, 1910. Pencil, gouache, and watercolor on illustration board, 83.7 x 42.7. Gift of Bertram A. Weber to The Art Institute of Chicago. (See plate 81.)

241. Peter J. Weber. Perspective rendering of a skyscraper in the classical style, c. 1910-15. Ink and watercolor on paper, approx. 101 x 60. Gift of Bertram A. Weber to The Art Institute of Chicago. (See plate 82.)

242. Marshall and Fox. Perspective study of the Blackstone Hotel (1908) and Theater (1910) with Proposed Annex (c. 1911-15 unexecuted), Chicago, delineated by J.N.T. (J. N. Tilton, Jr.). Ink on paper, 37.2 x 36. Lent by the University of Texas at Austin, Architectural Drawings Collection. (See plate 84.)

243. Marshall and Fox. Rental plan for 1550 North State Parkway, Chicago, c. 1910-11. Ink on linen, 88.3 x 90.2. Lent by the University of Texas at Austin, Architectural Drawings Collection.

244. Marshall and Fox. North Avenue elevation of 1550 North State Parkway, delineated by P.N. and S.S.N., c. 1911. Ink on linen, 127 x 85. Lent by The University of Texas at Austin, Architectural Drawings Collection.

245. Peter J. Weber. Perspective rendering for 3400 North Sheridan Road, Chicago, initialled L. R., c. 1915-17. Pencil and gouache on illustration board, 77.5 x 58. Gift of Bertram A. Weber to The Art Institute of Chicago. (See plate 89.)

246. Rapp and Rapp. Elevation of the Capital Theater (later Chicago Theater), 175 North

State Street, Chicago, March 27, 1920, April 21, 1920, January 28, 1921. Ink on linen, 78 x 111. Lent by the Rapp and Rapp Collection.

247. Benjamin Marshall of Marshall and Fox. Perspective sketch of the bedroom for Warren Wright, 209 East Lake Shore Drive, Chicago, c. 1924. Pencil on paper, 28 x 35.5. Lent by the University of Texas at Austin, Architectural Drawings Collection.

248. Benjamin Marshall of Marshall and Fox. Two elevation studies for the bathrooms for Warren Wright, c. 1924. Pencil and colored pencil on paper, 40 x 42.5 and 43.5 x 59.5. Lent by the University of Texas at Austin, Architectural Drawings Collection.

249. Holabird and Roche. Perspective rendering of the lobby with proposed decoration, Palmer House, 17 East Monroe Street, Chicago, drawn by Mack, Jenny, and Tyler, decorators, 1925. Watercolor on illustration board, 68.7 x 55.7. Restricted gift of the Benefactors of Architecture, The Art Institute of Chicago. (See Westfall, "From Homes to Towers," fig. 16, p. 280.)

250. Holabird and Roche. Perspective rendering of the Empire Style Dining Room with proposed decoration, Palmer House, drawn by Mack, Jenny, and Tyler, decorators, 1925. Watercolor on illustration board, 57 x 80. Restricted gift of the Benefactors of Architecture, The Art Institute of Chicago.

251. Marshall and Fox. Perspective rendering of the Edgewater Beach Apartments, southeast corner of Bryn Mawr Avenue and Sheridan Road, Chicago, delineated by Charles Dornbusch, 1927. Pencil and colored pencil on paper, 61.5 x 45.7. Lent by the University of Texas at Austin, Architectural Drawings Collection. (See plate 85.)

VII. Metropolis on the Magnificent Mile: The International Competition for the Chicago Tribune Tower, 1922.

Although the term "Magnificent Mile" was created by the real estate developer Arthur Rubloff to promote his proposed development of North Michigan Avenue after the World War II, it is ultimately to Burnham's credit that Michigan Avenue was able to develop into the showcase street that it currently is. The 1920 opening of the Michigan Avenue Bridge and the widening of the avenue into a grand boulevard can be traced to the 1909 *Plan of Chicago*. Real estate development in the early twenties near the bridge included Alfred S. Alschuler's London Guarantee Building (fig. 22), the Wrigley Building by Graham, Anderson, Probst and White, and the Chicago Tribune tower that architects Howells and Hood built after winning a major international competition that drew architects from all over the world, including a number from Germany and Northern Europe. Comparison of American entries with European ones often reveals the latter group's theoretical projections about Chicago in relation to the Americans' practicality. The entries by Gropius, Loos, Rosen, and Saarinen, for instance, deal more with principles and theory of design than do those of the American competitors, who provided more conservatively stylish, yet buildable, designs, usually in the Gothic style. In fact, competitor Richard Yoshijiro Mine consciously emulated an American skyscraper prototype – the 1914 Woolworth Building in New York by Cass Gilbert – then the world's tallest and, hence, most visibly acceptable and desirable skyscraper.

Although limestone skyscrapers were built in the loop area of Chicago

Fig. 22 Alfred S. Alschuler, Entrance of the London Guarantee and Accident Building (now Stone Container Building), 360 North Michigan Avenue, 1923 (altered).

Fig. 23 Chicago's Near North Side at Night, c. 1930-35. Major lighted buildings are, left to right: the Palmolive Building by Holabird and Root, 1928-29 (left, background); LaSalle-Wacker Building by Holabird and Root in association with Rebori, Wentworth, Dewey and McCormick, 1929-30 (left, foreground); the Wrigley Building by Graham, Anderson, Probst and White, 1919-24; and the Chicago Tribune tower by Howells and Hood, 1922-25 (both center, background); the Jewelers Building by Giaver and Dinkelberg with Thielbar and Fugard, 1926 (right, middleground); and the Carbide and Carbon Building by Hubert Burnham and Daniel Burnham, Jr., 1928-29.

during the boom decade of the twenties, it is the white terracotta Wrigley Building and limestone London Guarantee and Chicago Tribune buildings that set the tone for other skyscrapers in this metropolis of mid-America during the 1920s (fig. 23), all part of a conscious effort to make Michigan Avenue even grander than Parisian boulevards. For instance, chewing gum magnate William Wrigley paid to adorn two of the Michigan Avenue bridge-houses with sculptures in an effort to make this "gateway as famous as the Place de la Concorde in Paris."

The active building boom of the 1920s essentially codified the position of Chicago as the cosmopolitan capital of the Midwest, due in good part to Daniel H. Burnham's previous groundwork within the city. With the onset of the Great Depression of the 1930s and World War II, very few buildings were added to the cityscape, even though some architectural interchanges continued with Europe in the 1933 Century of Progress Exposition and the migration of noted German architects who fled Nazi Germany in the late 1930s. But, for all intents and purposes, the city's image as a metropolis of mid-America continued through the late 1920s and 1930s, and the strength of that image cannot be diminished by the negative associations that Chicago has had regarding gangsters, speakeasies, and prohibition during this time period. The appearance of this metropolis, then, was essentially the same until after World War II when architects like Ludwig Mies van der Rohe, and the firms of Skidmore, Owings and Merrill, and C. F. Murphy Associates began to reshape the skyline into what we experience today.

Cat. no. 252, detail

Cat. no. 259

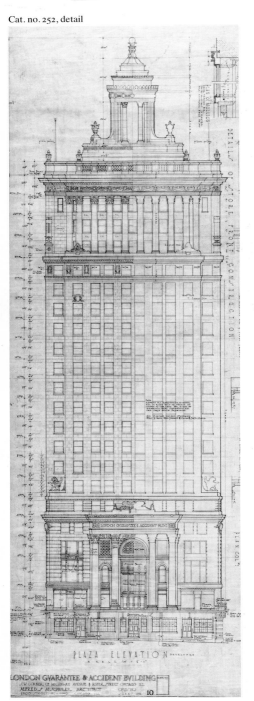

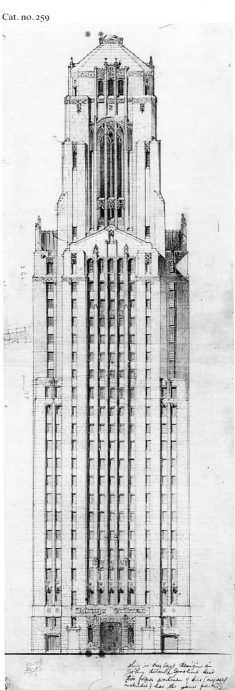

252. Alfred S. Alschuler. Elevation of the London Guarantee Building, 360 North Michigan Avenue, Chicago, 1922. Ink on linen, 132 x 75. Gift of Friedman, Alschuler, and Sincere to The Art Institute of Chicago.

253. Graham, Anderson, Probst, and White. Finial from the tower of the Wrigley Building, 410 North Michigan Avenue, Chicago, 1921, 1924 addition. Glazed terracotta, 85 x 110. Gift of the William Wrigley, Jr., Co. to The Art Institute of Chicago.

254. Chicago Tribune Competition book (1923) and models of selected entries constructed in 1987 by Richard Tickner for The Art Institute of Chicago.

255. Richard Yoshijiro Mine. Competitive entry for the Chicago Tribune Tower, Michigan Avenue elevation, 1922. Ink and wash on paper, 140.3 x 59.7. Gift of Richard Yoshijiro Mine to The Art Institute of Chicago. (See plate 92.)

256. Walter Gropius. Competitive entry for the Chicago Tribune Tower, Michigan Avenue elevation, 1922. Ink on paper, 170.2 x 91.5. Lent by Harvard University Art Museums (Busch-Reisinger Museum), gift of Walter Gropius. (See plate 93.)

257. R. Harold Zook. Competitive entry for the Chicago Tribune Tower, perspective view, 1922. Ink and wash on paper, 151 x 73.7. Lent by Robert H. Reinhold.

258. William Drummond. Competitive entry for the Chicago Tribune Tower, preliminary perspective study, 1922. Pencil, colored pencil, and watercolor on paper, 59.7 x 35.6. Lent by the Chicago Architecture Foundation. (See plate 90.)

259. Ralph Walker. Competitive entry for the Chicago Tribune Tower, study elevation, 1922. Pencil on tracing paper, 71.1 x 24.1. Lent by Haines Lundberg Waehler, successor firm to Vorhees, Gmelin and Walker and McKenzie, Vorhees and Gmelin.

260. Leroy Buffington. Competitive entry for the Chicago Tribune Tower, study elevation and section, 1922. Pencil on paper, 34.3 x 66. Lent by the Northwest Architectural Archives, University of Minnesota.

Cat. no. 257

Cat. no. 261

261. I. N. Phelps Stokes. Competitive entry for the Chicago Tribune Tower, perspective study, 1922. Ink and wash on paper, 69.2 x 36. Lent by the Avery Architecture and Fine Arts Library, Columbia University.

262. Anton S. Rosen. Competitive entry for the Chicago Tribune Tower, sketch elevation, 1922. Charcoal on paper, 77.7 x 39.6. Lent by the Kunstakademiets Bibliotek, Copenhagen.

263. Anton S. Rosen. Competitive entry for the Chicago Tribune Tower, study elevation of top stories, 1922. Ink and wash on paper, 31.8 x 35.2. Lent by the Kunstakademiets Bibliotek, Copenhagen.

264. Holabird and Roche. Competitive entry for the Chicago Tribune Tower, study elevation, 1922. Ink and wash on paper, 70.5 x 32.7. Lent by the Chicago Historical Society, gift of Holabird and Root. (See plate 91.)

265. Holabird and Roche. Competitive entry for the Chicago Tribune Tower, study elevation, 1922. Pencil, ink, and wash on paper, 70.5 x 30.5. Lent by the Chicago Historical Society, gift of Holabird and Root.

266. Eliel Saarinen. Competitive entry for the Chicago Tribune Tower, south elevation study, 1922. Pencil on tracing paper, approx. 79 x 26. Lent by the Museum of Finnish Architecture.

267. Raymond Hood of Howells and Hood. Competitive entry for the Chicago Tribune Tower, early facade study no. 19, Michigan Avenue elevation, 1922. Pencil and watercolor on illustration board, 61.5 x 33.5. Lent by the Raymond M. Hood Papers, Archives of American Art, Smithsonian Institution.

268. Raymond Hood of Howells and Hood. Competitive entry to the Chicago Tribune Tower, early perspective study no. 21, 1922. Pencil and watercolor on illustration board, 74 x 50.5. Lent by the Raymond M. Hood Papers, Archives of American Art, Smithsonian Institution.

Cat. no. 273   Cat. no. 263   Cat. no. 274

269. Raymond Hood of Howells and Hood. Competitive entry to the Chicago Tribune Tower, perspective study no. 35, 1922. Pencil and wash on illustration board, 69 x 41. Lent by the Raymond M. Hood Papers, Archives of American Art, Smithsonian Institution. (See plate 94.)

270. Raymond Hood of Howells and Hood. Competitive entry to the Chicago Tribune Tower, perspective study no. 32, 1922. Pencil and watercolor on illustration board, 50.4 x 51.5. Lent by the Raymond M. Hood Papers, Ar-

Cat. no. 270

chives of American Art, Smithsonian Institution.

271. Full scale plaster mockup of Gothic details for the Chicago Tribune Tower, 425 North Michigan Avenue, Chicago, c. 1922. Lent by the Chicago Tribune.

272. Model of proposed additions to the Tribune Tower, c. 1940. Lent by the Chicago Tribune.

273. Graham, Anderson, Probst, and White. Two preliminary studies for the National Life Insurance Tower, northwest corner of Erie

Street and Michigan Avenue, Chicago, c. 1921-23. Pencil and colored pencil on tracing paper, each approx. 70 x 45.5. Department of Architecture Purchase, The Art Institute of Chicago.

274. Graham, Anderson, Probst, and White. Three finished studies (Gothic, Italian, Classic) for the National Life Insurance Tower, c. 1921-23. Pencil on tracing paper, each approx. 73.5 x 51.5. Restricted gift of the Benefactors of Architecture, The Art Institute of Chicago.

275. Eliel Saarinen. Site plan and section of

the Chicago Lakefront Project, 1923. Ink, pencil, and blue pencil on tracing paper, approx. 48.9 x 145. Lent by the Museum of Finnish Architecture.

276. Eliel Saarinen. Perspective study of the Chicago Lakefront Project, 1923. Pencil on tracing paper, 52.7 x 39.8. Lent by the Cranbrook Academy of Art Museum. (See plate 95.)

277. Night view model of Chicago's business district in the late 1920s. Constructed in 1987 by Richard Tickner for The Art Institute of Chicago.

Photography Credits

Note. All photographs used as illustrations in the essays are in the collections of The Art Institute of Chicago, except those indicated below which were supplied by other institutions, agencies, or individual photographers. In the plates and catalogue sections, photographs of objects were supplied by lending institutions unless otherwise indicated below. Wherever possible, photographs have been credited to the original photographers, regardless of the source of the photograph.

Front cover   Howard N. Kaplan

Frontispiece   Chicago Aerial Survey Co.

ESSAYS

Zukowsky
1, 19. Chicago Aerial Survey Co.; 2. Historic American Buildings Survey; 3, 7-11. J. W. Taylor; 12. Richard Nickel; 13, 15. Courtesy of Commonwealth Edison; 14. R. Capes; 16. Ken Dequaine; 17. Courtesy of Historisches Archiv Fried. Krupp GmbH, Essen; 21. Kaufmann and Fabry.

Miller
1. Jex Bardwell, courtesy of the Chicago Historical Society; 2. Alexander Hesler, courtesy of the Chicago Historical Society; 3, 4, 6. Courtesy of the Chicago Historical Society.

Larson
1. Courtesy of the Chicago Historical Society; 9. Courtesy of the Newberry Library; 14. J. W. Taylor; 15, 20, 21. Courtesy of Gerald R. Larson.

Klotz
1, 6, 7, 17, 23. J. W. Taylor; 4. Barnum and Barnum; 5. Kaufmann and Fabry; 8, 10-12. Courtesy of Heinrich Klotz; 13, 19, 20, 22. Chicago Architectural Photographing Co., courtesy of David Phillips; 18. Courtesy of the Chicago Historical Society; 21. Richard Nickel; 24. Chicago Sun-Times.

Westfall
2. Alexander Hesler, courtesy of the Chicago Historical Society; 5, 7-9. John Gronkowski.

Geraniotis
1. Tom Cinoman; 2. Historic American Buildings Survey; 10, 20. J. W. Taylor.

Draper
2. Courtesy of the Map Section, Library of the University of Illinois at Chicago; 3. Detroit Publishing Co.; 7. Joan Draper; 13. J. W. Taylor; 18. Chicago Aerial Survey Co.

Loyrette
6, 9. J. W. Taylor; 7. R. A. Beck; 8. Grignon; 10, 13, 14. Chicago Architectural Photographing Co., courtesy of David Phillips; 15. Courtesy of the Montauk Co.

Harris
1, 7, 18, 19. J. W. Taylor; 3, 8, 9, 13, 14, 16. Postcards, courtesy of Neil Harris; 21, 25. Joseph A. Lundin; 22, 24. Fred G. Korth; 23. Chicago Architectural Photographing Co., courtesy of David Phillips; 26. Courtesy of Sears, Roebuck and Co.

Clausen
1. Courtesy of Chicago Historical Society; 4. J. W. Taylor; 5-7. Courtesy of Hasbrouck Peterson Associates; 9, 10, 12. John Gronkowski; 11. Philip Turner, for Historic American Buildings Survey; 14. Cervin Robinson, for Historic American Buildings Survey.

Schlereth
1. Harold Allen; 2-4, 14, 22, 23. J. W. Taylor; 10. Courtesy of the Procter and Gamble Company; 11. Thomas J. Schlereth; 19. Chicago Architectural Photographing Co., courtesy of David Phillips; 20. Courtesy of the Commission on Chicago Historical and Architectural Landmarks.

Harrington
1, 7, 9-10, 14, 18, 20. Courtesy of the Chicago Architecture Foundation; 2. Bob Thall, Commission on Chicago Historical and Architectural Landmarks, 1982; 3. Courtesy of I C Industries; 4. Plan adapted from the *Historic American Buildings Survey;* 8. Cervin Robinson, for Historic American Buildings Survey; 11. Plan adapted from Commission on Chicago Historical and Architectural Landmarks, *John J. Glessner House* (Chicago, 1984); 15-17, 19, 21. Kaufmann and Fabry, Courtesy of the Chicago Architecture Foundation.

Wilson
1, 2. Chicago Architectural Photographing Co., courtesy of David Phillips; 6, 7, 15. J. W. Taylor; 12. Courtesy of Northwestern University; 13. Architectural Drawings Collection, University of California, Santa Barbara; 18, 19. Courtesy of Alice Ryerson Hayes.

Weingarden
1, 17, 20, 21. Chicago Architectural Photographing Co., courtesy of David Phillips; 6. Historical Collections, Bentley Historical Library, University of Michigan; 8, 15. The Avery Architectural Library, Columbia University; 9. The Saint Louis Art Museum; 14. Courtesy of Crombie Taylor, FAIA.

Westfall
1, 10, 11, 15. J. W. Taylor; 9, 17-21, 25. Chicago Architectural Photographing Co., courtesy of David Phillips.

Chappell
1, 7, 14, 15. Courtesy of the William Wrigley Jr. Company; 2, 4, 8. Chicago Architectural Photographing Co., courtesy of David Phillips; 3. Kaufmann and Fabry, courtesy of the Chicago Historical Society; 9. Courtesy of the Royal Institute of British Architects; 12. Wurts Brothers; 14. Ron Gordon.

Van Zanten
1, 12, 13. Courtesy of the Australian Information Service; 14-20. Courtesy of Australian Archives, Australian Capital Territory Regional Office.

Tigerman
1. Aerial Photograph Co.; 2. Chicago Aerial Survey Co.

PLATES
11, 21, 39. Hedrich-Blessing; 12, 17. Bob Thall; 15, 16, Courtesy of the Montauk Co.; 25, 42, 86, 88, 96. Howard N. Kaplan; 28-30, 33, 35, 38, 78, 83, 90. Kathleen Culbert-Aguilar; 31, 32. Judith Bromley; 45. Geremy Butler; 51, 53. Chicago Architectural Photographing Co., courtesy of David Phillips; 52. Chester Brummel; 57. Courtesy of Continental Illinois National Bank and Trust; 58. Courtesy of Santa Fe Southern Pacific Corporation; 59. Courtesy of Rubloff Inc.; 65. J. W. Taylor; 66. Courtesy of Holabird and Root; 87. Courtesy of Chicago Hilton and Towers.

CATALOGUE
Figures
2, 7, 8, 10, 21. J. W. Taylor; 4. Ron Gordon; 5, 15, 16. Chicago Architectural Photographing Co., courtesy of David Phillips; 9, 14. Harold Allen, for the Historic American Buildings Survey; 12. Richard Nickel; 18-20. Detroit Publishing Co.

Exhibition checklist
152. Richard Mather; 189, 246. Kathleen Culbert-Aguilar; 217. Michael Tropea.

Selected Bibliography

Compiled by Stephen Sennott
with the assistance of Ines Dresel, Maya Moran,
Gabriella Scanu, and John Zukowsky.

The entries included in this bibliography frequently highlight the European relationship to Chicago architecture, and the annotations of earlier publications often reflect those international connections. In addition, a number of standard works on Chicago architecture and architects, mostly published in the last forty years, have been included. Many of the references listed here are to be found in the Burnham Library of Architecture at The Art Institute of Chicago, but they exist as well in other major research libraries. We encourage the reader to consult the bibliographies in the later sources for further information.

Part 1: Earlier Sources

Akademie der Künste zu Berlin. *Ausstellung neuer amerikanischer Baukunst.* Berlin, 1926.
With a foreword by Irving Pond and essays by Louis Sullivan and Thomas Tallmadge, this exhibition catalogue examines work by Sullivan and Bertram Goodhue, among other American architects. In fact, an entire gallery was given to display Sullivan's work.

"Die amerikanischen Thurmhäuser." *Deutsche Bauzeitung* 26 (Jan. 16, 1892), pp. 29-30.
American office buildings in New York, Boston, and Chicago are briefly analyzed with reference to eclecticism and the dominating influence of English Norman Romanesque architecture.

"Architekten-Verein zu Berlin." *Deutsche Bauzeitung* 29 (Mar. 13, 1895), p. 30.
Brief article reports on Karl Hinckeldeyn, who knew Louis Sullivan's lecture on polychromy in buildings, and who described work by Adler and Sullivan and Healy and Millet in Chicago.

Ashbee, Charles R. *American Sheaves and English Seed Corn.* London and New York, 1901.
A report written for the National Trust, sponsor of his American travels, that documents Ashbee's trip to major American cities, including Chicago where he lectured at the Art Institute about architectural preservation, modern architecture, the Pre-Raphaelite Brotherhood, and design in industry.

Ashbee, Charles R. Introduction to *Frank Lloyd Wright: Ausgeführte Bauten.* Berlin, 1911.
As a result of his long professional association that originated in Chicago, Frank Lloyd Wright invited Ashbee, whom he felt was sympathetic to his architecture and design theories, to comment upon his work at the time it was introduced to a European audience. The introduction was translated, in slightly altered form, in "Frank Lloyd Wright: A Study and an Appreciation," *Western Architect* 19 (Feb. 1913), pp. 17-19.

Ashbee, Charles R., "Frank Lloyd Wright: Chicago." In *Sonderheft der Architektur des XX. Jahrhunderts.* Vol. 2, ch. 8. Berlin, 1911.
After summarizing buildings by American architects Richardson and McKim, Mead and White, among others, Ashbee celebrates Chicago architect Wright as a new spirit in American architecture influenced by the design principles of the Arts and Crafts movement, German Secession, and European art nouveau.

"Aus dem technischen Vereinsleben Amerikas." *Deutsche Bauzeitung* 24 (Jan. 15, 1890), pp. 25-30.
This article notes the frequency of exchange between technical journals of Germany and America, the 1887 American Institute of Architecture meeting in Chicago, the activities of the Western Association of Architects in Chicago, and discusses the similarity of the A.I.A. to other German and European associations. Daniel Burnham is seen as an important spokesman for American architects.

Badovici, Jean. *Frank Lloyd Wright, Architecte Americain.* Paris, 1930.
A very useful collection of early photographs and drawings of buildings and projects from 1901 to 1923, including interior views, facades, and decorative details of the Imperial Hotel, Midway Gardens, Taliesin, Coonley House, and Robie House, among others. A brief biography of Wright assigns the architect the same importance in America that Berlage had for Holland or that Garnier and Perret had for France. Previously, Badovici had written articles about Wright in *L'Architecture Vivante* 2 (1924) and *Cahiers d'art* 1, 2 (1926).

Behne, Adolf. *Der moderne Zweckbau.* Munich, 1926.
Behne discusses the influence of Wright's ideas on Behrens, Gropius, Mendelsohn, and Mies van der Rohe in Germany; Oud, Wils, van t'Hoff, and Greve in Holland; Le Corbusier in Switzerland; and even several Czechoslovakian architects. Wright's 1908 article, "In the Cause of Architecture," is frequently quoted.

Behne, Adolf. *Neues Wohnen – Neues Bauen.* Leipzig, 1927.
In this text on modern domestic architecture, Behne considers Wright the most significant American architect, praising his designs for their lack of reference to past traditions.

Behrendt, Walter C. "Skyscrapers in Germany." *Journal of the American Institute of Architects* 21 (Sept. 1923), pp. 365-70.
The author discusses post-World War I erection of tall office buildings in Germany and England based on earlier American models. He argues that the skyscraper was accepted more easily by German architects than by English architects, since Germans imitated steel cage construction in engineering, though they introduced their own planning ideas.

Behrendt, Walter C. *Der Sieg des neuen Baustils.* Stuttgart, 1927.
In addition to a discussion of German and northern European industrial architecture of Taut, Oud, Dudok, Le Corbusier, Behrens, Mendelsohn, and others, Behrendt addresses the Chicago Tribune tower competition, contrasting the winning entry by Howells and Hood with the entry by Walter Gropius and Adolph Meyer. After discussing the work of Henry van de Velde, Behrendt discusses Wright's work as America's foremost architect in this new style. Wright's work is seen as influential in architecture of other northern European countries. Steel frame construction methods and Burnham and Root's Masonic Temple are illustrated in photographs.

Behrendt, Walter C. *Modern Building: Its Nature, Problems, and Forms.* New York, 1937.
Celebrating the "new spirit" of the International Style and the rise of modernism, Behrendt discusses engineers, art nouveau, and significant American architects such as Richardson, Sullivan, and Wright.

Berlage, Hendrik P. "Art and Community." *Western Architect* 18 (1912), pp. 85-89.
Berlage surveys eclecticism and its inherent lack of spiritual ideas that results from imitation. He champions "reality in construction" and ornamentation in modern architecture in Europe and America. He also authored "Foundations and Development of Architecture," *Western Architect* 18 (1912), pp. 96-99, 104-108, which discusses the influence of Viollet-le-Duc on modern architecture.

Berlage, Hendrik P. *Amerikanische Reisherinneringen.* Rotterdam, 1913.
Berlage's recollections of his journey to America in 1911 include discussion of Richardson's Romanesque style in Boston and Chicago, tall office buildings in New York, Sullivan's writings and buildings in Chicago, and Wright's architecture in the Midwest.

Bing, Samuel. *Artistic America, Tiffany Glass, and Art Nouveau.* Translated by Benita Eisler. Cambridge, Mass., 1970.
This volume puts together three of Bing's late 1890s and early 1900s essays that discuss art and architecture in America, Tiffany's glass, and art nouveau. The translation of *La Culture artistique en amerique* (1895) includes a section on American architecture, examining and praising the work of Richardson and Sullivan, among others. Sullivan's Auditorium Building and his Transportation Building for the World's Columbian Exposition are especially praised. It should be noted that Gabriel P. Weisberg, *Art Nouveau Bing: Paris Style 1900* (New York, 1986), properly corrects Bing's first name to Siegfried.

Birkmire, William H. *The Planning and Construction of American Theatres.* New York and London, 1906.
Considering plans, elevations, interior decoration, ornament, and relevant architectural ordinances, the author examines the complex theater and opera house program of buildings in American cities. Adler and Sullivan's Auditorium, built to surpass New York's Metropolitan Opera, is praised for its truss construction and hydraulic elevators. The elevators were based upon examples in Budapest, Vienna, and Halle.

Bouilhet, André. "L'Exposition de Chicago: Notes de voyage d'un orfèvre." *Revue des Arts Décoratifs* 14 (1893), pp. 65-79.
The author discusses architecture at the World's Columbian Exposition, praising in particular Adler and Sullivan's Transportation Building and Henry Ives Cobb's Fisheries Building, as well as Adler and Sullivan's Auditorium.

Edward H. Bennett

Daniel H. Burnham

Bragdon, Claude. "'Made in France' Architecture."
  Architectural Record 16 (Dec. 1904), pp. 561-68.
Remarking on the short time since Richardson's architecture dominated American building, Bragdon
examines the subsequent influence of Beaux-Arts
classical architecture. Bragdon cautions that this imitation of the classic tradition still might not train an
architect to design well for American needs and new
methods of construction. Louis Sullivan, on the other
hand, in Bragdon's estimate, stands for invention instead of imitation, and for democracy over aristocracy.

Bragdon, Claude. "Architecture in the United States:
  The Skyscraper." *Architectural Record* 26
  (Aug. 1909), pp. 84-96.
In the third part of a series on American architecture,
Bragdon examines the rapid development of the skyscraper in New York and Chicago and urges restrictive
legislation to prevent concentration in urban populations. He quotes selection of favorable skyscraper
descriptions from Paul Bourget's *Outre-Mer* (1895).

"Briefe von der Columbien Weltausstellung."
  Deutsche Bauzeitung 27 (June 28, 1893), pp. 313-
  14.
One of the several notices in the 1893 volume regarding the World's Columbian Exposition in Chicago,
this discusses Machinery Hall and examines its metal
frame construction.

Brinkmann, A. E. *Stadtbaukunst vom Mittelalter bis
  zur Neuzeit.* Wilpark-Potsdam, 1925.
In this survey, the author includes Daniel Burnham's
Chicago Plan, which was illustrated at the 1912
Düsseldorf exhibition, as well as the park system for
Boston and Chicago.

Burnham, Daniel H., and Edward H. Bennett. *Plan
  of Chicago.* Edited by Charles Moore. Chicago,
  1909.
This classic summation of Burnham's planning ideas
was prepared under the auspices of the Commerical
Club. Its lengthy descriptive essays discuss Chicago's
intended relation to European and American city
planning.

Calonne, Alphonse de. "The French Universal Ex-
  position of 1900." *Architectural Record* 5 (Jan.-
  Mar. 1896), pp. 217-26.
The author explains how the siting of the French ex-

position, commissioned in 1892 for completion in
1900, was modelled after the World's Columbian Exposition in Chicago in order to insure comparable
unity and grandeur.

Caparn, H. A. "The Riddle of the Tall Building: Has
  the Skyscraper a Place in American Architecture?"
  Craftsman 10 (Apr. 1906), pp. 477-88.
The author attacks skyscrapers as expressive of "tyranny and ruthlessness of modern business." He sees
most tall buildings as ugly and imitative of one another
with inconsistencies of vertical and horizontal elements. Yet he praises Sullivan's Garrick Theatre and
Schlesinger and Mayer Store, which he commends for
their honest cage-like expression of steel construction,
similar to the Eiffel Tower or the Crystal Palace.

Emerson, William, "The World's Fair Buildings,
  Chicago." *The Architectural Journal* 1, 3rd ser.
  (Nov. 1893-Oct. 1894), pp. 65-74.
Acting as a member of a jury for architecture on
behalf of the United Kingdom, the author describes
the ordered plan, site, and harmonious design of the
fair, praising McKim, Mead and White's Agriculture
Building, but faulting Adler and Sullivan's Transportation Building for its ornament and allegorical sculpture.

Freitag, Joseph K. *Architectural Engineering.* 2nd. ed.
  New York, 1907.
While the first edition of 1886 focused primarily on
Chicago's tall buildings, this second, revised edition
examines skyscrapers from New York and other East
Coast cities that rival those from Chicago.

Fries, Henri de. *Moderne Villen und Landhäuser.*
  Berlin, 1924.
Berlin architect de Fries illustrates contemporary
country houses and villas by young architects mostly
living in northern Europe and on the east and west
coasts of the United States. In the introductory essay,
however, he considers Wright the greatest living architect, and suggests that plans and elevations of several German and Dutch architects share characteristics with the work of Wright and the Greene brothers
from California.

German-American Biographical Publishing Company. *Chicago und sein Deutschtum.* Cleveland,
  1901-02.
The editors of the German-American Biographical

Publishing Company gathered hundreds of photographs and essays to trace the role of German-American citizens in the development of the city. A large
biographical section is accompanied by photographs
of related buildings and residences.

Gerson, Ernst. "Reise-Eindrücke in Nord Amerika."
  Stadtbau 24 (1929), pp. 293-300.
Having traveled to Detroit, Chicago, and New York,
Gerson highlights New York's Woolworth Building
and the skyscrapers along Michigan Avenue and the
Chicago River.

Gilbert, Paul, and Charles L. Bryson. *Chicago and Its
  Makers.* Chicago, 1929.
This standard work examines Chicago's history from
the earliest settlement to the planning of the 1933
Century of Progress Exposition. Hundreds of historic
photographs record every building type in Chicago up
to 1929. These accompany individual biographies of
important Chicago industrialists, philanthropists, and
commercial leaders, such as Harry G. Selfridge, the
Chicago merchandiser who moved to London to establish Selfridge's, Ltd. and hired Daniel H. Burnham
to design an important commercial building based on
Chicago's department stores.

Gmelin, Leopold. "American Architecture from a
  German Point of View." *The Forum* 27 (Mar. 1899-
  Aug. 1899), pp. 690-704.
Gmelin praises the originality of 1890s American architecture, citing Richard Morris Hunt's Administration Building at the World's Columbian Exposition.
Regarding Chicago itself, the author examines the
city's gridded street plan, renowned skyscrapers, un-
restricted height in building codes, elevators, iron and
steel construction, and expensive urban space. Gmelin published an earlier survey of this type in *Deutsche
Bauzeitung* 28 (1894), pp. 453-56, 532-34.

Graef, Paul. *Neubauten in Nordamerika.* Berlin,
  1897-1905.
With a foreword by Karl Hinckeldeyn, this large volume consists primarily of plans, photographs, and
brief descriptions of materials and costs for many residential and commercial buildings in Boston, Detroit,
and Chicago. Most of the buildings and architects are
from Chicago including work by Burnham and Root,
W. W. Boyington, Treat and Foltz, Holabird and
Roche, William Le Baron Jenney, and others.

Greber, Jacques. *L'Architecture aux Etats-Unis.*
  Paris, 1920.
The author surveys American architecture from colonial New England through skyscrapers in the early
1900s. Greber includes many examples from the area
such as Howard Van Doren Shaw's work in Lake
Forest, Ill., Burnham's Continental and Commercial
Bank Building, the Peoples Gas Company Building,
and his Union Stations in Chicago and Washington,
D.C. Edward H. Bennett's plan for Minneapolis is
compared to Burnham's city plan for Chicago,
Washington, D.C., and San Francisco, and to Greber's own plans for Philadelphia.

Hegemann, Werner. *Amerikanische Parkanlagen.*
  Berlin, 1911.
This volume of essays and illustrations was published
to accompany an exhibition that described and promoted American park planning in Boston, New York,
Washington, Philadelphia, and Chicago. Several park
plans for these cities by Frederick Law Olmsted are
illustrated, including plans for Jackson Park, Sherman
Park, Gage Park, and David Square, all in Chicago.

Hegemann, Werner. *Der Städtebau nach den Ergeb-
  nissen der Allgemeinen Städtebau-Ausstellung.* Berlin, 1913.
Published on the occasion of a 1912 Düsseldorf exhibi-

tion of town planning in Paris, Vienna, Budapest, Munich, Cologne, London, Stockholm, Chicago, and Boston, Hegemann's two-volume text examines Burnham's *Plan of Chicago* and several European cities' plans in relation to Berlin's city plan.

Hegemann, Werner. *Amerikanische Architektur und Stadtbaukunst.* Berlin, 1927.

A comprehensive volume that examines radial and centralized planning of several American cities including Burnham's plans for Cleveland, Chicago, and Manila, as well as Bennett's work for Minneapolis and Chicago. Hegemann also examines the Tribune tower competition, with 28 illustrations; office building projects by Graham, Anderson, Probst and White; various expositions in Chicago, St. Louis, and San Diego; and Wright's Martin House, Taliesin, Coonley House, and Larkin Building. Sullivan's Stock Exchange, Wainwright Building and Tomb, and Charnley House, Andrew Rebori's plans for the development of North Michigan Avenue, and Holabird and Roche's Grant Park Stadium are all discussed as well.

"Henry Richardson und seine Bedeutung für die amerikanische Architektur." *Deutsche Bauzeitung* 26 (Feb. 6, 1892), pp. 64-66.

This article illustrates Trinity Church in Boston and discusses several early 1880s buildings in Massachussetts. It also examines the Romanesque character of his buildings and his sparse use of ornament. This article testifies to German awareness of Richardson's work at the time of his, and his successor firm's, Chicago buildings.

Hermant, Jacques. "L'Architecture à l'Amerique et à la World's Fair." *Gazette des Beaux-Arts* (July-Dec. 1893), pp. 237-53, 416-25, 441-61.

Lengthy examination of the architecture at the World's Columbian Exposition that singles out for special praise Cobb's Fisheries Building and Sullivan's Transportation Building. (See above entry by André Bouilhet for similar observations).

Herzberg, A. "Die Ausstellung Deutscher Architektur- und Ingenieur-Werke auf der Columbischen Weltausstellung zu Chicago." *Deutsche Bauzeitung* 27 (Dec. 16, 1893), pp. 613-15.

This article discusses the German architecture and engineering exhibitions that were erected in Chicago, thus providing an opportunity for German and Chicago architects to meet.

Hilberseimer, Ludwig. *Großstadt-Architektur.* Stuttgart, 1927.

Hilberseimer emphasizes Chicago's significance to the development of residential, industrial, and commercial architecture in Europe. He examines, for instance, the influence of Wright's Lexington Terrace in Chicago upon the domestic architecture of Dutch architect J.J.P. Oud. The Surf Apartment Hotel's plan and the Holabird and Roche Palmer House are illustrated. Regarding commercial architecture, the facades of Richardson's Marshall Field Wholesale Store, Adler and Sullivan's Auditorium Theater, and the Carson Pirie Scott Store are examined in relation to Otto Wagner's Neumann Store in Vienna. Navy Pier's plan and its accessibility to vehicular traffic are praised. Root's famed Monadnock Building and Sullivan's Schiller Building are also discussed, as is the work of German émigrés Baumann and Huehl.

Hitchcock, Henry-Russell, and Philip Johnson. *Modern Architecture: International Exhibition.* New York, 1932.

With contrast and reference to the World's Columbian Exposition of 1893 and the Chicago Tribune tower competition of 1922, this illustrated exhibition catalogue, devoted to the International Style, includes essays and bibliographies on Wright, Gropius, Le Corbusier, Oud, Mies van der Rohe, Hood, Howe and Lescaze, Neutra, and the Bowman Brothers. Of Chicago architects, Wright is presented as a fundamental source for European modernists such as Oud, Mies, and Gropius. The Bowman Brothers of Chicago are included for the structural frankness of their steel construction.

Jessen, Peter. "Kunstleben und Kunstpflege in den Vereinigten Staaten." *Kunstgewerbeblatt* 27 (1915-16), pp. 221-28.

Having travelled to Boston, New York, Los Angeles, and Chicago, the author discusses applied arts of Tiffany and other reputable Arts and Crafts designers, designs of Whitney Warren, private presses, the Boston Arts and Crafts Society, and several buildings by Chicago architects. Burnham's Peoples Gas Company Building, a residence by Shaw, an auditorium interior by Dwight Perkins, and Wright's Coonley House are illustrated. Some, like Richard Schmidt's Garfield Park structures, reflect influence from the Arts and Crafts movement.

Jones, John H., and Fred Britten, eds. *A Half Century of Chicago Buildings.* Chicago, 1910.

A useful source that documents building laws and ordinances effective in Chicago in 1910. Chicago architects and authors, including Frost, Holabird, Per-

kins, Schmidt, and others, contribute articles on subjects such as railway terminals, theaters, reinforced concrete, libraries and museums, and real estate.

Kostanecki, Michal. "Rozwoj Nowoczesnej Architektury Amerykanskiej." *Architektura: Budownictwo* 2 (1932), pp. 33-48.

This rare Polish account of the rapid development of American architecture from the 1870s through the 1930s features Chicago in the work of Adler and Sullivan, Burnham and Root, Holabird and Roche, and Frank Lloyd Wright and discusses their buildings favorably in relation to New York architects. Events discussed include the World's Columbian Exposition of 1893 and the Chicago Tribune tower competition of 1922.

Kunz, Fritz. *Der Hotelbau von heute im In- und Ausland.* Stuttgart, 1930.

This book focuses on the technical aspects of hotels, mostly in Europe, but it features, in a pictorial section at the end, two new American hotels – the Stevens (now Chicago Hilton and Towers) by Holabird and Roche and the Arizona-Biltmore Hotel by Albert Chase McArthur (with Frank Lloyd Wright).

Mendelsohn, Erich. *Amerika: Bilderbuch eines Architekten.* Berlin, 1928.

Largely illustrations of Chicago and New York architecture, this volume serves to introduce a Euro-

Daniel H. Burnham and John Wellborn Root in their office in the Rookery

Irving K. Pond

pean audience to recent American architecture and includes early views of Michigan Avenue, buildings bounding the elevated train tracks, the Chicago Tribune tower under construction, grain elevators, Root's Monadnock Building, and Wright's Unity Temple and Heurtley House.

Mendelsohn, Erich. *Briefe eines Architekten*. Passau, 1961.
Published posthumously but relevant to his years in America, this volume of letters includes reference to Mendelsohn's trip to America in 1924. Recording his observations, he admired the Woolworth Building in New York and Wright's Larkin Building in Buffalo, noting Wright's disciplined ornament and monumental proportions. In Detroit, Mendelsohn met with Emil Lorch, an art historian who knew Sullivan and studied Wright's development, and Eliel Saarinen, who was working on various Chicago projects. At Taliesin in Wisconsin, he visited Wright, who learned of Mendelsohn through Richard Neutra. Mendelsohn and Barry Byrne visited Wright's Coonley House and Midway Gardens. Later, in 1929, Mendelsohn gave the opening speech for the Wright exhibition at the Berlin Academy of Arts.

Millet, Louis. "L'Architecture aux Etats-Unis et l'Influence Francais." *France-Amerique* (1912), pp. 240-44; (1913), pp. 288-91.
A designer of stained glass who graduated from the Ecole des Beaux-Arts and established his partnership with George Healy in Chicago, Millet here writes of the influence of French architectural education and the Ecole des Beaux-Arts on American architecture.

Monroe, Harriet. *John Wellborn Root. A Study of His Life and Work*. New York, 1896.
An important, early architectural biography of Root by his well-known sister-in-law shortly after his death in 1891 at a time when he was serving as Burnham's chief designer for the World's Columbian Exposition.

Moore, Charles. *Daniel H. Burnham: Architect, Planner of Cities*. 2 vols., 1921.
In this standard, two-volume biography and survey of

Burnham's career and architecture, Moore includes drawings and photographs related to Burnham's entire career. Burnham's role in skeleton construction and early skyscrapers, Richardson's influence, and the work of Burnham and Root prior to the 1893 Exposition are also considered. A chronological list served as the basis for one used in Thomas S. Hines, *Burnham of Chicago* (1974).

Neutra, Richard J. *Amerika: Die Stilbildung des neuen Bauens in den Vereinigten Staaten*. Vienna, 1930.
A well-illustrated volume in which Neutra examines building materials and types of construction in modern American architecture, including wood frame, skeletal steel cage and skyscraper building methods. He devotes chapters to Burnham, Sullivan and Root, Wright and Irving Gill, illustrating a 1923 Chicago office building, Taliesin, Midway Gardens, and the Glencoe Country Club by Wright; two 1916 plans for a quarter section by Wright and Drummond; 1915-16 inner-city parks and park buildings by Schmidt, Garden and Martin; Root's Monadnock Building; Holabird and Roche's 1915 Century Building; hotels by Marshall and Fox; a skyscraper project by Walter Ahlschlager; and William Drummond's River Forest Women's Club.

Neutra, Richard J. *Wie baut Amerika?* Stuttgart, 1927.
Construction, plans, and elevations of completed buildings are illustrated in chapters that discuss the building industry developments of construction of tall buildings, residential architecture, Chicago's Palmer House Hotel and hotel architecture, zoning laws and related setback design, and construction materials. Neutra discusses and illustrates several buildings from Chicago, including Sullivan's Carson Pirie Scott Store and especially the Palmer House Hotel under construction.

Nimmons, George C. "Skyscrapers in America." *Journal of the American Institute of Architects* 21 (Sept. 1923), pp. 370-72.
In response to a Sept. 1923 article in the same journal by Behrendt (see above), Nimmons argues that high land values motivated rectangular plans and defends the central court plan and the use of fireproof materials.

Orear, G. W. *Commercial and Architectural Chicago*. Chicago, 1887.
Photographic and engraved views by Chapin and Gulick record Chicago's commercial and architectural development in the decades previous to the fire. It records the fire, including a description of how the fire melted the metal elements of buildings. It suggests that architects have learned the benefits of brick over metal as a relatively more fireproof material.

Oud, Jacobus J. P. "Architectonische Beschouwing bij Bijlage VII." *De Stijl* 1, 4 (Feb. 1918), pp. 39-41.
Dutch architect Oud comments specifically on the Robie House and discusses its plan in terms of the house's purposes. Oud also compares the house with particular elements of modern painting of the Futurists and the Cubists.

Oud, Jacobus J. P. *Holländische Architektur*. Munich, 1926.
After discussing the development of modern Dutch architecture, Oud examines the influence of Wright upon European architecture. Although the illustrations are devoted exclusively to late 19th and early 20th-century architecture in Holland by Berlage, de Klerk, and others, Oud also illustrates Lonberg-Holm's unsubmitted entry for the 1922 Chicago Tribune tower competition.

Richard E. Schmidt

Pierce, Bessie Louise, and Joe L. Norris, eds. *As Others See Chicago: Impressions of Visitors, 1673-1933*. Chicago, 1933.
These selected letters, articles, and book chapters record the varied responses of visiting authors and immigrants from Europe and America, discussing subjects such as pre-fire construction, street planning and landscape, monotonous buildings, and picturesque villas. Scotch scientist William Ferguson commented in 1855 on the city's grid layout and buildings; F. B. Zincke wrote in 1867 about Chicago's buildings, including the Sherman House Hotel, the domed City Hall, Michigan Avenue residences, and Trinity Church; New York author Julian Ralph contributed articles on Chicago to *Harper's Magazine* in the early 1890s that referred to the city's tall buildings and the "Chicago method" of construction.

Pond, Irving K. *The Meaning of Architecture: An Essay in Constructive Criticism*. Boston, 1918.
This Chicago architect and educator prepared a series of essays on architectural principles dealing with the spirit of ancient Greek art as it was inherited during the Renaissance, as well as on the expressive and creative architecture of the Midwest. For Pond, the horizontality of this architecture recalls the spirit of the prairie and democracy.

Ponten, Josef. *Architektur die nicht gebaut wurde. Mit am Werke Heinz Rosemann und Hedwig Schmelz*. 2 vols. Stuttgart, 1925.
This work surveys a number of unexecuted projects from the Renaissance through the early 20th century, and ends with a section on "Cities of the Future" that features Griffin's Plan of Canberra and the Chicago Plan by Burnham and Bennett.

Purcell, William, and George G. Elmslie. "Purcell and Elmslie." *Western Architect* 21 (Jan. 1915), pp. 1-8.
The editors published this issue as a separate treatment of Prairie School architecture and the designs of Purcell and Elmslie. The architects' correspondence and writings from Berlage and others address the Arts and Crafts movement.

Louis H. Sullivan

Thomas E. Tallmadge

Rappold, Otto. *Der Bau der Wolkenkratzer.* Munich and Berlin, 1913.
This volume surveys the latest in skyscraper design in New York and then examines briefly the skyscraper's earlier development in Chicago. The remainder of this large volume addresses recent technical and construction developments of structures in New York, such as the Singer and Woolworth Buildings and Metropolitan Life Tower, and in Chicago examples such as Burnham's Butler Brothers Building and the La Salle Hotel by Holabird and Roche. The book contains useful technical drawings and construction photographs.

Rey, A. "Les Grands Magasins aux Etats-Unis." *L'Architecture* 34 (July 10, 1921), pp. 3-4.
Briefly hints at the design of American department stores and their relation to French design principles.

Saylor, Henry H. *Bungalows.* New York, 1911.
In addition to defining several bungalow types, their plans, materials, interiors, and mechanical systems, the author discusses the "Chicago School type" of bungalow, illustrating examples by Schmidt, Garden and Martin, and by Tallmadge and Watson based on the Indian bungalow precedent.

Schmidt, Richard E., and John Allan Hornsby. *The Modern Hospital.* Philadelphia and London, 1913.
This is a pioneering textbook on hospital design coauthored by a Bavarian-born Chicago architect whose firm, Schmidt, Garden and Martin, specialized in such work.

Schuyler, Montgomery. *American Architecture and Other Writings.* Edited by William H. Jordy and Ralph Coe. 2 vols. Cambridge, Mass., 1961.
In 1891, Schuyler published a book of seven essays, *American Architecture – Studies,* and this two-volume set is intended to show Schuyler's wide thinking about American architecture as represented in his writings from the 1870s to 1914. Schuyler's subjects that are relevant to Chicago architecture include Leopold Eidlitz, the Romanesque Revival, the evolution of the skyscraper, the tall buildings of Adler and Sullivan

and D. H. Burnham and Co., the Beaux-Arts response expressed in the World's Columbian Exposition, and the work of Sullivan and Wright prior to 1914. Of special note is his article "Glimpses of Western Architecture: Chicago," originally published in *Harper's Magazine* 83 (Aug. 1891), pp. 395-406; (Sept. 1891), pp. 540-70.

Simon, Andreas. *Chicago, die Gartenstadt: Unsere Parks, Boulevards, und Friedhöfe, in Wort und Bild.* Chicago, 1893.
Published the same year as the World's Columbian Exposition, this guidebook to Chicago surveys the city's structures in parks, cemeteries, and boulevards. Predictably, lengthy sections discuss German commerical activity in Chicago.

Starrett, Theodore. *Skyscraper-Building.* New York, 1907.
Brief informative essays by Starrett gathered from New York newspapers that discuss materials, cost, construction, and the architectural profession with regard to skyscrapers in New York and Chicago.

Starrett, Col. W. A. *Skyscrapers and the Men Who Build Them.* New York, 1928.
An author who attributes the first skyscraper to Chicago, architect Starrett examines planning, zoning laws, style, materials, and construction of skyscrapers from Jenney's Home Insurance Building to the Rapp Brothers' Paramount Building in New York from 1927. Chicago architects and builders include George Fuller, John Griffiths, Jenney, Burnham and Root, as well as subjects such as the Columbian Exposition, air rights, and the use of terracotta or stone in construction.

Sullivan, Louis. "The Chicago Tribune Competition." *Architectural Record* 53 (Feb. 1923), pp. 151-57.
Sullivan writes philosophically about "masters of ideas" and democratic ideals in contrast to more conservative notions, and he describes how these ideas were reflected in the first prize entry by Howells and Hood and the superior second prize entry by Eliel Saarinen.

Sullivan, Louis. *Kindergarten Chats and Other Writings.* Edited by Isabella Athey. New York, 1947.
This early compilation was published in the Documents of Modern Art series edited by Robert Motherwell for Wittenborn Art Books. Among other writings it includes Sullivan's famous essays on "Ornament in Architecture" (1892) and "The Tall Office Building Artistically Considered" (1896), as well as an extensive bibliography of his writings.

Tallmadge, Thomas E. "The Chicago School." *Architectural Review* 15 (Apr. 1908), pp. 69-74.
This Chicago architect was among the first to summarize and explain the works of the Chicago School, noting the many significant buildings and architects that had already distinguished the city's architecture. His later books *Architecture in Old Chicago* (Chicago, 1941) and *The Story of Architecture in America* (New York, 1927) are standard works in the historiography of Chicago's architecture.

Taut, Bruno. *Die neue Baukunst in Europa und Amerika.* Stuttgart, 1929. Translated as *Modern Architecture.* London, 1929.
Architect Taut, famous for the glass pavilion at the 1914 Werkbund Exhibition, examines plans and elevations for a variety of building types. In Chicago architecture, Taut singles out Wright's and Sullivan's tall office buildings for their clear construction, smooth fenestration, and distinct expression of structure and construction. Taut illustrates Root's Monadnock Building, Sullivan's Carson Pirie Scott Store, and Burnham's Peoples Gas Company Building. He

finds little to praise in the American skyscraper as it developed after the 1890s. He recognizes forms of European designers Olbrich, Mackintosh, Wagner, and Behrens in Wright's work. Taut ranks Wright with Wagner and Berlage as one of three highly inspirational architects.

Unwin, Raymond, and Paul Waterhouse. *Old Towns and New Needs. Also the Town Extension Plan.* Manchester, 1912.
In his lectures on old towns and the town extension plan, Unwin examines Düsseldorf, Cologne, and Berlin as sound examples of urban planning in reference to Manchester and the English cities and the nearby suburbs. Rapidly growing Chicago is contrasted to the planning of Cologne; Unwin faults Chicago's gridiron as simplistic and without reference to the environment. Nonetheless, he praises Chicago's new civic spirit that has begun to improve the urban setting with fine parks, preserved lakefront, and lengthy boulevards. Parks and playgrounds with fieldhouses are illustrated.

Van Brunt, Henry. *The Essays of Henry Van Brunt.* Edited by William A. Coles. Cambridge, Mass., 1969.
Coles selects twenty-two essays to represent the range of Van Brunt's ideas about architecture. Several essays relate closely to Chicago architecture: "Architecture of the West" (1889) addresses architectural transition in Western civilization and claims that Chicago stands for the most advanced ideas in architectural reform because of the city's lack of schools, precedents, and past traditions. Other relevant essays discuss John Wellborn Root and the World's Columbian Exposition. Many buildings by European architects are illustrated in conjunction with work in Chicago by Burnham and Root, Cobb and Frost, Holabird and Roche, and Adler and Sullivan.

Van Rensselaer, Mariana Griswold. *Henry Hobson Richardson and His Works.* Boston, 1888.
Early comprehensive study of Richardson's buildings and career illustrated with original line drawings.

From Chicago, Richardson's Marshall Field Wholesale Store and Glessner House are discussed.

"Die Vertretung der deutschen Architektur auf der Weltausstellung in Chicago 1893." *Deutsche Bauzeitung* 26 (June 29, 1892), p. 309.
A brief, illustrated article that summarizes the work of German architects and educators who helped to organize Germany's architectural exhibit at the World's Columbian Exposition.

Vogel, F. Rudolph. *Das amerikanische Haus.* Berlin, 1910.
Vogel examines the influential exchange of ideas in architecture between America and Europe, utilizing photographs and illustrations from American periodicals *American Architect* and *Architectural Record*. From Chicago, the residential architecture of Silsbee, Cobb, Pond, Sullivan, and Wright are discussed.

Von Holst, Herman. *Modern American Homes.* Chicago, 1912.
Chicago architect Von Holst gathers examples of expensive and inexpensive residential types of various materials designed in the fashionable styles including bungalows and country houses. Works by Chicago architects Walter Burley Griffin, Henry Holsman, E. E. Roberts, and others are illustrated in plan and interior and exterior views.

Von Holst, Herman. *Country and Suburban Houses of the Prairie School Period.* 1913. Reprint. Chicago, 1982.
Von Holst considers the design of the individual home in the context of a "back to nature" movement with photographs of plans and elevations of one- and two-story homes constructed in various materials and designed primarily by Chicago architects such as Tallmadge and Watson, Griffin, Roberts, Holsman, R. C. Spencer, and others.

Wattjes, J. G. *Moderne Architectuur.* Amsterdam, 1927.
Brief essays accompany this photographic survey of contemporary architecture by architects from northern Europe and the United States; among the buildings by Chicago architects included are works by Sullivan, Schmidt, Garden and Martin, and Wright dating between 1903 and the 1920s.

Wight, Peter B. "Additions to Chicago's Skyline: A Few Recent Skyscrapers." *Architectural Record* 28 (July 1910), pp. 15-24.
Wight, a Chicago architect and prolific architectural writer, summarizes contemporary competition for the tallest building in New York and Chicago and the desire of some critics to limit skyscraper height. Numerous important skyscrapers by Chicago architects are mentioned, including Holabird and Roche's new City Hall, La Salle Hotel, and McCormick Building; D. H. Burnham and Co.'s Peoples Gas Company Building; and Marshall and Fox's Steger Building.

Wijdeveld, Hendrik Theodore. *The Life Work of the American Architect Frank Lloyd Wright.* Santpoort, Holland, 1925.
As the famous *Ausgeführte Bauten und Entwürfe von Frank Lloyd Wright* of 1910 introduced Wright's work to Berlin and German architects, this monograph by the Dutch architect Wijdeveld formally introduced Wright's buildings to a widespread Dutch audience. The book is based, in part, on articles about Wright that Wijdeveld published in his journal *Wendigen* from the early 1920s.

Wohler, Gerhard. "Das Hochhaus im Wettbewerb der Chicago Tribune." *Deutsche Bauzeitung* 58 (1924), pp. 325 ff.
This important article discusses and illustrates com-

Arthur Woltersdorf

petition designs submitted by leading architects from twenty-three countries. From 263 entries, 135 were submitted by American architects. Germany submitted more than any other foreign country; it is suggested that this large production demonstrates German architects' involvement with American, particularly Chicago, architecture.

Woltersdorf, Arthur, ed. *Living Architecture.* Chicago, 1930.
A collection of essays by Chicago architects Schmidt, Zimmerman, Pond, Holabird, Woltersdorf, and others that examine tall buildings, college campus plans, opera houses in Europe and America, cinema theater architecture, hospitals, churches of Chicago, brick architecture, among other topics. With regard to European and Chicago architecture, for example, Chicago's Civic Opera House is compared with the Staatstheater in Stuttgart in plan. Other important Chicago buildings include the Shedd Aquarium, Palmolive Building, Eliel Saarinen's second-prize design for the Tribune tower, the University of Chicago's Chapel, and the famous group of tall buildings at Michigan Avenue and the Chicago River.

Wright, Frank Lloyd. *An Autobiography.* London and New York, 1932.
Although Wright in his early essay "The Art and Craft of the Machine" (1901) touched on Europe and the importance of William Morris, it was in his autobiography, in its many editions through the 1950s, that he expanded upon his early interest in Viollet-le-Duc, despite his dislike of Parisian culture and his love of German literature and music. The book is especially important for capturing the atmosphere of his early years in Chicago while he was working for Adler and Sullivan.

Yerbury, Francis R. *Modern Dutch Buildings.* New York, 1931.
This volume consists mostly of photographs of modern Dutch architecture by Baunders, Berlage, Dudok, Kramer, de Klerk, and others of the new movement, as well as an essay in which Wright, along with Baillie-

Scott, Voysey, and Mackintosh, is credited with strong influence in Dutch architecture and theory.

Part II: Later Sources

Andrew, David. *Louis Sullivan and the Polemics of Modern Architecture.* Urbana and Chicago, 1985.

Andrews, Wayne. *Architecture in Chicago and Mid-America.* New York, 1968.

Bach, Ira J., ed. *Chicago's Famous Buildings.* 3rd. ed. Chicago, 1980.

Block, Jean F. *Hyde Park Houses.* Chicago, 1978.

— *The Uses of Gothic: Planning and Building the Campus of the University of Chicago, 1892-1932.* Chicago, 1983.

Boris, Eileen. *Art and Labor: Ruskin, Morris, and the Craftsman Ideal in America.* Philadelphia, 1986.

Brooks, H. Allen. *Writings on Wright: Selected Comment on Frank Lloyd Wright.* Cambridge, Mass., 1981.

— *The Prairie School: Frank Lloyd Wright and His Midwest Contemporaries.* Toronto, 1972.

Bruegmann, Robert, Sarah Clark, Paul Florian, Douglas Stoher, and Cynthia Weese. *A Guide to 150 Years of Chicago Architecture.* Chicago, 1985.

Burg, David F. *Chicago's White City of 1893.* Lexington, Ky., 1976.

Chappell, Sally Kitt, and Ann Van Zanten. *Barry Byrne. John Lloyd Wright. Architecture and Design.* Chicago, 1982.

Charerbhak, Wichit. "Architectural Criticism as Reflected in Publications on Chicago Commercial Architecture in the 1880s and 1890s." Ph.D. diss., University of Michigan, 1978.

Ciucci, Giorgio, Francesco Dal Co, Mario Manieri-Elia, and Manfredo Tafuri. *The American City: From the Civil War to the New Deal.* Translated by Barbara Luigia La Penta. Cambridge, Mass., 1979.

Cohen, Stuart, and Stanley Tigerman. *Chicago Architects.* Chicago, 1976.

Condit, Carl W. *The Rise of the Skyscraper.* Chicago, 1952.

— *The Chicago School of Architecture: A History of Commercial and Public Building in the Chicago Area, 1875-1925.* Chicago, 1964.

— *Chicago, 1910-29: Buildings, Planning, and Urban Technology.* Chicago, 1974.

Connors, Joseph. *The Robie House of Frank Lloyd Wright.* Chicago, 1984.

Crawford, Alan. *C. R. Ashbee: Architect, Designer and Romantic Socialist.* New Haven, Conn., 1985.

Cummings, Kathleen R. *Architectural Records in Chicago.* Chicago, 1981.

Darling, Sharon. *Chicago Metalsmiths.* Chicago, 1977.

— *Chicago Ceramics and Glass: An Illustrated History from 1871-1933.* Chicago, 1979.

— *Chicago Furniture: Art, Craft, and Industry, 1833-1983,* Chicago and New York, 1984.

Duis, Perry. *Chicago: Creating New Traditions.* Chicago, 1976.

Draper, Joan E. *Edward H. Bennett: Architect and City Planner, 1874-1954.* Chicago, 1982.

Drury, John. *Old Chicago Houses.* Chicago, 1941.

Eaton, Leonard K. *Landscape Artist in America: The Life and Work of Jens Jensen.* Chicago and London, 1964.

Eaton, Leonard K. *American Architecture Come of Age: European Reaction to H. H. Richardson and Louis Sullivan.* Cambridge, Mass., 1972.

Gebhard, David. "C.F.A. Voysey — To and From America." *Journal of the Society of Architectural Historians* 30 (Dec. 1971), pp. 304-12.

Geraniotis, Roula. "German Architects in Nineteenth-Century Chicago." Ph.D. diss., University of Illinois, 1985.

Graf, Otto A., David Hanks, and Jennifer Toher. *Frank Lloyd Wright: Architectural Drawings and Decorative Art.* London, 1985.

Grube, Oswald, Peter C. Pran, and Franz Schulze. *One Hundred Years of Architecture in Chicago.* Rev. English ed. Translated by David Norris. Chicago, 1976.

Hanks, David A. *The Decorative Designs of Frank Lloyd Wright.* New York, 1979.

Hasbrouck, Wilbert R., ed. *Chicago School: Architectural Essays from 1900 to 1909.* Park Forest, Ill., 1967.

– "The Early Years of the Chicago Architectural Club." *Chicago Architectural Journal* 1 (1981), pp. 7-14.

Hines, Thomas S. *Burnham of Chicago: Architect and Planner.* New York, 1974.

Hitchcock, Henry-Russell, Jr. *In the Nature of Materials: The Buildings of Frank Lloyd Wright, 1887-1941.* New York, 1942.

– *Wright's Influence Abroad.* New York, 1940.

– "American Influence Abroad." In *The Rise of an American Architecture,* edited by Edgar Kaufmann, Jr. New York, 1970.

Hoffman, Donald. "Chicago Architecture: The Other Side." In *American Architecture: Innovation and Tradition,* edited by David DeLong, Helen Searing, and Robert A. M. Stern. New York, 1986.

– *The Architecture of John Wellborn Root.* Baltimore and London, 1973.

– *Frank Lloyd Wright's Robie House.* New York, 1984.

Johnson, Donald L. *The Architecture of Walter Burley Griffin.* South Melbourne, Australia, 1977.

Karlowicz, Titus M. "The Architecture of the World's Columbian Exposition." Ph.D. diss., Northwestern University, 1965.

Kaufmann, Edgar, Jr. *An American Architecture: Frank Lloyd Wright.* New York, 1955.

Kaufmann, Edgar, Jr., and Ben Raeburn, eds. *Frank Lloyd Wright: Writings and Buildings.* New York, 1960.

Kief-Niederwohrmeier, Heide. *Frank Lloyd Wright und Europa: Architekturelemente, Naturverhältnis, Publikationen, Einflüsse.* Stuttgart, 1983.

Koch, Robert. "American Influence Abroad, 1886 and Later." *Journal of the Society of Architectural Historians* 18 (May 1959), pp. 66-69.

Kuhn, Gerald W. "A History of the Financing of Commercial Structures in the Chicago Central Business District, 1868 to 1934." D.B.A. thesis, Indiana University, 1969.

Lambourne, Lionel. *Utopian Craftsmen: The Arts and Crafts Movement from the Cotswolds to Chicago.* Salt Lake City, Utah, 1980.

Landau, Sarah B. *P. B. Wight: Architect, Contractor, and Critic, 1838-1925.* Chicago, 1981.

Lewis, Dudley. "Evaluation of American Architecture by European Critics, 1875-1900." Ph.D. diss., University of Wisconsin, 1962.

– "European Profile of American Architecture." *Journal of the Society of Architectural Historians* 37 (1978), pp. 265-82.

Lewis, Julius. "Henry Ives Cobb and the Chicago School." Ph.D. diss., University of Chicago, 1954.

Manson, Grant. *Frank Lloyd Wright to 1910.* New York, 1958.

Mayer, Harold M., and Richard C. Wade. *Chicago: Growth of a Metropolis.* Chicago, 1969.

Meehan, Patrick J., ed. *The Master Architect. Conversations with Frank Lloyd Wright.* New York, 1984.

Menocal, Narciso. *Architecture as Nature: The Transcendentalist Idea of Louis Sullivan.* Madison, 1981.

Morrison, Hugh. *Louis Sullivan: Prophet of Modern Architecture.* New York, 1935.

Nederlandse Architektur 1880-1930: Americana. Amsterdam, 1975.

Ochsner, Jeffrey K. *H. H. Richardson: Complete Architectural Works.* Cambridge, Mass., 1982.

O'Gorman, James F. "The Marshall Field Wholesale Store: Materials Toward a Monograph." *Journal of the Society of Architectural Historians* 37 (Oct. 1978), pp. 175-94.

Peisch, Mark L. *The Chicago School of Architecture: Early Followers of Sullivan and Wright.* New York, 1964.

Pfeiffer, Bruce B., ed. *Frank Lloyd Wright: Letters to Architects.* Fresno, 1984.

Posener, Julius. *Anfänge des Funktionalismus, Von Arts and Crafts zum Deutschen Werkbund.* Berlin, 1964.

Prestiano, Robert V. "'The Inland Architect': A Study of the Contents, Influence, and Significance of Chicago's Major, Late Nineteenth Century Architectural Periodical." Ph.D. diss., Northwestern University, 1973.

Randall, Frank A. *History of the Development of Building Construction in Chicago.* Urbana, Ill. 1949.

Reinink, A.W. "American Influences on Late Nineteenth Century Architecture in the Netherlands." *Journal of the Society of Architectural Historians* 29 (1970), pp. 163-74.

Robertson, Cheryl, and Terence Marvel. *The Domestic Scene (1897-1927). George M. Niedecken, Interior Architect.* Milwaukee, 1981.

Rudd, William J., comp. *Historic American Buildings Survey: Chicago and Nearby Illinois Area.* Chicago, 1966.

Schlereth, Thomas J. "Solon Spencer Beman, 1853-1914: The Social History of a Midwest Architect." *Chicago Architectural Journal* 5 (1985), pp. 8-31.

Scully, Vincent. *Frank Lloyd Wright.* New York, 1960.

Smith, Norris K. *Frank Lloyd Wright: A Study in Architectural Content.* Englewood Cliffs, N.J., 1966.

Spencer, Brian A., and Victoria T. Hansen, eds. *The Prairie School Tradition.* Milwaukee, 1979.

Sprague, Paul. *The Drawings of Louis Henry Sullivan.* Princeton, 1979.

– "The Origin of Balloon Framing." *Journal of the Society of Architectural Historians* 40, 4 (Dec. 1981), pp. 311-19.

Storrer, William S. *The Architecture of Frank Lloyd Wright.* 2nd. ed. Cambridge, Mass., 1978.

Sweeney, Robert L. *Frank Lloyd Wright: An Annotated Bibliography.* Los Angeles, 1978.

Szarkowski, John. *The Idea of Louis Sullivan.* Minneapolis, 1956.

Takayama, Masami, ed. "The Chicago School of Architecture." *Process Architecture* 35 (1982).

Tigerman, Stanley, ed. *Chicago Tribune Tower Competition.* 2nd. rev. ed. New York, 1981.

Tolzmann, Rainer H. "Objective Architecture: American Influences in the Development of Modern German Architecture." Ph.D. diss., University of Michigan, 1975.

Tselos, Dimitri. "Frank Lloyd Wright and World Architecture." *Journal of the Society of Architectural Historians* 28 (Mar. 1969), pp. 58-72.

Turak, Theodore. *William Le Baron Jenney: A Pioneer of Modern Architecture.* Ann Arbor, Mich., 1986.

Frank Lloyd Wright

Twombly, Robert C. *Frank Lloyd Wright: His Life and His Architecture.* New York, 1979.

– *Louis Sullivan and His Life.* New York, 1986.

Van Leeuwen, Thomas A. P. "The Skyward Trend of Thought: Some Ideas on the History of the Methodology of the Skyscraper." In *American Architecture: Innovation and Tradition,* edited by David DeLong, Helen Searing, and Robert A. M. Stern. New York, 1985.

Van Zanten, David. *Walter Burley Griffin: Selected Designs.* Palos Park, Ill., 1970.

Weingarden, Lauren. "Louis H. Sullivan's Metaphysics of Architecture (1885-1901): Sources and Correspondences with Symbolist Art Theories." Ph.D. diss., University of Chicago, 1981.

Wille, Lois. *Forever Open Clear and Free.* Chicago, 1972.

de Wit, Wim, ed. *Louis Sullivan: The Function of Ornament.* New York, 1986.

Wright, Frank Lloyd. *An American Architecture.* New York, 1955.

Wright, Gwendolyn. *Moralism and the Moral Home: Domestic Architecture and Cultural Conflict in Chicago 1873-1913.* Chicago, 1980.

Zukowsky, John, Pauline Saliga, and Rebecca Rubin. *Chicago Architects Design: A Century of Architectural Drawings from The Art Institute of Chicago.* Chicago, 1982.

Zukowsky, John, David Van Zanten, and Carol Herselle Krinsky. *Chicago and New York: Architectural Interactions.* Chicago, 1984.

Zukowsky, John. "The Chicago Architectural Club, 1895-1940." *Chicago Architectural Journal* 2 (1982), pp. 170-74.

Zukowsky, John, Sally Chappell, and Robert Bruegmann. *The Plan of Chicago: 1909-1979.* Chicago, 1979.

Index

Numbers in **bold type** refer to pages with illustrations.